L'EUROPE

Le français est la langue officielle

Le français est une des langues officielles

DÉPARTEMENTS ET TERRITOIRES D'OUTRE-MER

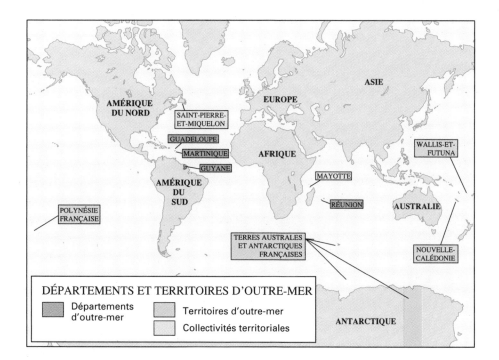

Départements d'outre-mer

Territoires d'outre-mer

Collectivités territoriales

À VOUS!

À VOUS!

The Global French Experience

AN INTRODUCTORY COURSE

Véronique Anover
California State University, San Marcos

Theresa A. Antes
University of Florida

Houghton Mifflin Company   Boston   New York

Publisher: Rolando Hernández

Senior Sponsoring Editor: Glenn A. Wilson

Executive Marketing Director: Eileen Bernadette Moran

Marketing Assistant: Lorreen Ruth Pelletier

Development Editors: Erin Kern, Florence Kilgo

Editorial Assistant: Erin Beasley

Project Editors: Harriet C. Dishman, Stacy Drew

Art and Design Manager: Gary Crespo

Cover Design Manager: Anne S. Katzeff

Senior Photo Editor: Jennifer Meyer Dare

Composition Buyer: Chuck Dutton

New Title Project Manager: James Lonergan

Cover Photo © The Copyright Group/SuperStock

Printed in the U.S.A.

Library of Congress Control Number: 2006924975

Instructor's Annotated Edition
ISBN-10: 0-618-40734-0
ISBN-13: 978-0-618-40734-7

For orders, use student text ISBNs
ISBN-10: 0-618-25981-3
ISBN-13: 978-0-618-25981-6

1 2 3 4 5 6 7 8 9-DOW-11 10 09 08 07

Contents

To the Instructor

To the Instructor

Overview

À vous! is a comprehensive introductory program for use in elementary French classes at the college level. It is designed to be flexible enough to allow for use across two or three semesters, and contains material of interest for all students, whether they are traditional or nontraditional, true or false beginners, residential or commuter. It incorporates the best aspects of various theories of second-language acquisition and focuses on all skills crucial to the learning and use of a foreign language: high-frequency vocabulary that is of interest to today's students; grammar explanations that are complete and comprehensible; a focus on all skills, both receptive and productive; task-based activities that simulate what students will do during their first travel- or study-abroad experiences; and high-interest culture topics that invite cross-cultural comparisons. We incorporate all areas of the French-speaking world, inviting students, through the use of authentic materials, to get to know the richness of the French language and the many diverse Francophone cultures. Finally, *À vous!* is unique in its approach, for it encourages students to view language learning as a total-body experience. While much of what occurs during language learning is cognitive, the emotions and the senses contribute in very important ways to one's understanding of and reaction to another language and culture; this program strives to provide activities that encourage students to bring all the senses into play.

The following are some of the many distinctive features of *À vous!*:

- ■ **A concerted effort to reach students where they are:** Thematic topics and vocabulary that are of interest to them; grammar explanations that assume little or no prior understanding of grammar, yet do not condescend; culture that is both authentic and of interest to today's college-age students; task-based activities that allow them to practice what they will do in the real world.

- ■ **A unique combined inductive and deductive approach, with a special focus on inductive activities:** In *À vous!*, students initially develop their comprehension. Only after they practice understanding meaning through an inductive approach to language acquisition, are they presented with formal, deductive explanations. Finally, they return to inductive activities that permit them to synthesize and demonstrate their new skills. Thus, students close the loop by showing how they function in the language after an inductive introduction, concrete deductive explanations and rules, and finally, application of their more fully developed skills to higher-level inductive activities.

- ■ **A process approach to *all* skills, including grammar:** Vocabulary and grammar are continuously recycled and integrated into a wide variety of activities; no topic is dealt with only once.

- ■ **A complete integration of *all* materials in the text, including the photos:** *Every* aspect of this program provides the instructor with explicit means of incorporating it into the daily lesson, including discussion questions and teaching tips for the photos.

■ **Extensive instructor annotations:** A wealth of annotations include ideas for a class website or newsletter, accommodations for varied learning styles, games, etc., in addition to the more traditional answers and suggestions for expanding an activity or providing additional linguistic or cultural details.

■ *Mise en pratique:* These special sections follow every four chapters, and provide additional activities for practicing grammar, vocabulary, culture, and the four skills.

Organization of *À vous!*

■ **Four units that allow for a progression from the inside out:** *À vous!* contains 16 chapters, which are subdivided into four units of four chapters each. The approach starts with self-expression and moves outward from the self to interactions between the self and society, following the characteristic progression in which a second language is acquired. These chronological units (**Je suis comme je suis, Ma vie d'aujourd'hui et d'hier, Ma place dans le monde,** and **Ma vie de demain**) focus on themes of interest to all students.

■ *Mise en pratique:* Each unit is followed by a **Mise en pratique,** an innovative section focusing on a particular region of the French-speaking world, and recycling the material from all four chapters, providing additional practice of grammar, vocabulary, culture, and the four skills. This section allows students to involve all the senses in learning French, asking them to discover a region through a series of Internet activities, to view its monuments and attractions, to taste (virtually and literally) the foods of the region, to analyze its culture, to listen to its music, and so on. A foray into the region in question, these sections can also serve as midterm and final exam review, as they practice all the skills that are traditionally tested.

■ **Topics and vocabulary that are of interest to today's students:** *À vous!* introduces the topics and vocabulary that students often request. Although it contains many of the topics traditionally found in first-year textbooks, *À vous!* goes beyond traditional texts, giving the students the means to talk about the topics that are of interest to them. When discussing sports, for example, we introduce extreme sports; when discussing health, we deal with issues of fitness; when dealing with technology and media, we introduce vocabulary that describes the devices that students have today: digital cameras, PDAs, MP3 players. This vocabulary is accompanied by illustrations whenever possible; students are thus encouraged to comprehend and learn the meaning of the word through visuals, rather than through translation from English. The expanded vocabulary that is found in each chapter is divided into **Vocabulaire essentiel** and **Expansion personnelle,** from which students are invited to choose vocabulary that is relevant to their lives and make it part of their active vocabulary, thus mirroring vocabulary acquisition in real life. The vocabulary activities practice all vocabulary, but they aim to develop productive knowledge of the **Vocabulaire essentiel** and receptive knowledge of the **Expansion personnelle.** The **Lexique** at the end of each chapter is subdivided as well, giving instructors the option of making students responsible for only the **Vocabulaire essentiel** or for all of the vocabulary presented in the chapter, including the **Expansion personnelle.** This latter option may well be of interest for honors classes or for classes with false beginners, who will be challenged by the new vocabulary, thus providing a unique level of interest for these learners.

■ **Inductive sections followed by deductive explanations:** The inductive sections in *À vous!* are uniquely and carefully designed in accordance with authentic language acquisition. Each chapter starts with a section labeled **Commençons!**, which includes a text or a dialogue. While these sections contain grammar that the students will focus on later in the chapter, these segments are initially presented solely as a means to introduce vocabulary. Students thus read the text for overall comprehension. Later they examine the vocabulary of the text in more detail. A combination of activities labeled **Vous avez bien compris?** and **À vous!** facilitate this progression in comprehension, and also supports the internalization of vocabulary from the **Vocabulaire essentiel** and the **Expansion personnelle** by means of communicative activities. It is only later that the grammar is explained and, at this time, students are invited to return to the text that they read earlier, to find examples of the grammar point that has been discussed, to give an explanation for why a particular form is used or what that form would look like in the negative, in another person, etc. These activities, labeled **Vérifiez votre compréhension,** allow students to verify that they have in fact understood the grammar explanation before proceeding to the skill-getting and skill-using activities that accompany it.

■ **Grammar explanations that reach today's learners:** In writing our grammar explanations, we had two main goals: to be complete and to be comprehensible. In assuming no prior knowledge of grammatical terminology on the part of the students, we explain first what it means to conjugate a verb, for example, and then demonstrate the conjugation of the verb in question. Grammar explanations address the students directly, treating them as the intelligent adults that they are; we strive to be complete without being overwhelming. As with all of the other skills addressed throughout *À vous!,* we take a process-oriented approach to grammar learning. A particular strength of our program is that grammar is continuously recycled. For example, each time a new verb is introduced, students are asked to produce it in all the tenses that they have previously studied. It is not assumed that they will automatically transfer their knowledge of how one negates or forms the imperfect of a given verb; they are reminded of the process and are asked to use it. In addition, when presenting grammar, we have kept the students' needs in mind and have organized our chapters and ordered the grammar presentations according to the functions that the students will need to carry out. Unlike textbooks that follow a traditional progression, we have occasionally stepped out of tradition, considering student needs instead. A close inspection of *À vous!* will reveal, for example, that we have chosen to present the conditional before the future: students already have the *near future,* and can accomplish almost any future-time task they need by using that tense; the conditional, however, is essential both for expressing politeness and for talking about hypothetical situations, and there is no other tense that can replace it. The reader may also notice that *À vous!* does not always follow a rigid chapter outline. While the format is generally similar (vocabulary followed by grammar followed by culture, and then communicative activities), there is not a preordained number of **leçons, étapes,** or even grammatical structures in each unit. Because we have grouped together the structures that felt logical for discussion of a particular theme, the number varies from chapter to chapter.

■ **A process-oriented approach to all aspects of language learning:** As with grammar, vocabulary is continuously recycled throughout *À vous!*. Vocabulary from previous chapters is brought in and linked to associated vocabulary in the chapter under study, because second-language learning is a cumulative process. Likewise, *À vous!* takes a process approach to reading, writing, listening, and speaking. It continually encourages students to think first about strategies for each of these skills and provides them with specific strategies as needed. It walks them through the notions of brainstorming and organizing, prompts them to read, write, speak, or listen, and, finally, to return to edit and evaluate.

■ **An emphasis on all the senses:** We realize that today's learners are different from those of even a decade ago and benefit from a multisensory approach to learning. Cognitive science has shown us that there is a wide variety of preferred learning styles; some students learn better aurally, others learn better visually, and still others are more kinesthetically inclined. We therefore invite students to incorporate all the modalities into the learning experience, and we aim to provide materials and activities that will work for all students as they move toward proficiency. It is our hope that a total-body experience, through which learners can draw on their own personal strengths and modes of processing, will encourage those who might otherwise be inclined to discontinue their language study, to pursue it beyond the first semester or first year.

■ **Instructor annotations provide a rich variety of teaching material:** In addition to providing answers, the annotations include ideas for creating a class website or newsletter, for expanding upon activities, for filling out grammatical explanations if desired, for supporting various learning styles, for handling issues of privacy in a classroom where a great deal of personal information is exchanged, etc. We know that the instructor's job is a challenging one, and have taken great care to incorporate the most successful of our own activities and strategies throughout the text and in the annotations.

À vous! and Current Theories of Second-Language Acquisition

À vous! does not adopt any one theory of second-language acquisition, but instead borrows concepts from several, incorporating the best of each. We provide ample authentic input, allowing students to deal with both grammar and vocabulary inductively, with a concentration on comprehension, before being asked to use the same structures for production. This same progression is in keeping with cognitive approaches to second language acquisition, allowing students to work with material first as memorized routines or patterns, to be analyzed and grammaticized later. Deductive grammar presentations aim to help them with this analysis, providing many skill-based activities to support their deducing and assimilating rules. At the same time, in accordance with the cognitivist belief that noticing is a key factor in acquisition, we provide abundant opportunities for noticing to take place. As indicated above, through the use of thought-provoking activities after each grammar presentation, we urge students to return to previously studied texts to notice the use of these same structures in the input. It is our hope that this strategy will foster comprehension of these contextualized constructions among students who might not otherwise make this connection.

From interactive/sociolinguistic theories of second-language acquisition, we borrow the notion that interaction is crucial to assimilation of a language.

Therefore, all sets of activities contain not only written practice but also extensive interpersonal work, at both the meaningful and communicative levels. This approach is applied to both grammar and vocabulary, allowing students to work together to build a complete language system, by providing each other with important feedback through communicative activities. *À vous!* combines an eclectic mix of second-language theories in order to appeal to a wide variety of teaching styles, as well as to meet the varied needs of first-year French students. We encourage instructors to use what works best for them and their students, adjusting their usage as needs change. We firmly believe that a language class should be built around a group of students, with the textbook serving as a tool, and we strive to provide you with just such a tool in *À vous!*

Instructor Components of the Program

Instructor's Annotated Edition

The Instructor's Annotated Edition (IAE) of *À vous!* provides annotations containing classroom tips, cultural information, ideas for additional activities, answers to Student Textbook activities, and the scripts for the In-Text Audio activities.

Online Teaching Center

The Online Teaching Center contains a wealth of instructor resources, including:
• Audioscripts for the In-Text Audio activities and the Student Activities Manual Audio Program
• Videoscript
• Student Activities Manual Answer Key
• Sample syllabi
• Lesson plans
• PowerPoint slides and overhead transparencies of art and grammar charts
• An integration guide that provides tips for incorporating the various technology-based components of *À vous!* into your course
  A complete Testing Program (in PDF format for printing as is, and in Word so instructors can modify the tests) and Testing Program Answer Key are available on an Instructor ClassPrep CD-ROM as an added security measure. The testing program audioscript as well as the Student Activities Manual Answer Key are provided on this CD-ROM as well.

Video (VHS/DVD)

The video that accompanies *À vous!* consists of four segments that incorporate vocabulary, structures, and cultural material from each of the four units of the book. It follows the daily lives of four college roommates, each from a different Francophone country or region (France, Belgium, Morocco, and Quebec). The focal point of each episode is the preparation of a recipe, which corresponds to those featured in the unit-ending **Mise en pratique** sections of the book, and, in the process, the roommates share their experiences with and insights into their respective cultures.

Testing Audio CD

This CD contains the recorded material corresponding to the listening portions of the Testing Program.

Course Management Powered by Quia

This electronic version of the Student Activities Manual includes automatic grading of discrete-answer exercises, and the capability for instructors to review and revise grading decisions, give feedback to students, and grade open-ended exercises individually. Instructors can also customize exercises, as well as create their own exercises and quizzes. Audio files for the lab program are also included.

Course Management Powered by BlackBoard and WebCT

Content specific to the *À vous!* program is offered in formats that are compatible with these popular course management systems. This allows instructors at institutions that use these tools the flexibility of using an in-house system to individualize their instruction without having to create basic content for the site; it also creates a secure, private forum that enriches the classroom experience.

Student Components of the Program

Student Textbook

The Student Textbook contains the information and activities that students need for in-class use. It is divided into sixteen core chapters, each containing vocabulary and grammar presentations and activities, listening practice, and cultural information and activities. Reading selections and writing practice are featured in alternating chapters. The back of the book contains valuable reference sections, including French-English and English-French glossaries, verb charts, and a vocabulary list of classroom-related terms.

Student Activities Manual

The Student Activities Manual (SAM) is intended as a way for students to get extra practice outside of class. It contains both workbook (written practice of the grammar and vocabulary presented in the Student Textbook) and lab manual (listening and pronunciation practice) components.

SAM Audio Program

The SAM Audio Program contains the pronunciation and listening practice that corresponds to the listening portions of the Student Activities Manual. The SAM Audio Program is meant for students to use outside of class, at home, in the dorm, or at the language lab.

e-SAM Powered by Quia

Instructors may choose to use the e-SAM, which is an electronic version of the printed Student Activities Manual. It allows students to complete the same practice as presented in the print version, but in a computerized format that provides immediate feedback for many exercises. The audio corresponding to the lab exercises is also included.

Online Study Center

This icon in the Student Text points to the Online Study Center for *À vous!* (accessed through the Product Information Center at **http://college.hmco.com/ pic/avous1e**). As shown below, a specific product will be indicated under this icon to direct students to it. The *À vous!* Online Study Center contains the following:

■ Web Search Activities are provided to further practice of chapter vocabulary and grammar structures and enhance students' cultural knowledge through exploration of authentic French-language websites.

■ Web Links connect students to a variety of French-language sites appropriate to the textbook's chapter themes and content, inviting students into authentic experiences of French-speaking cultures and language.

■ Flashcards help students learn chapter vocabulary.

Online Study Center
Flashcards

■ ACE Practice Tests are designed to help students practice chapter vocabulary and grammar and to assess their progress via immediate feedback.

Online Study Center
ACE

■ ACE Video Activities are designed to reinforce comprehension and provide extra practice.

■ Language Skills Practice denotes sections that provide a variety of activities on key structures and vocabulary from the book, from games to art-based exercises, and video and audio clips.

Online Study Center
Language Skills Practice

■ Downloadable .mp3 audio files of the In-Text Audio files, corresponding to the Student Textbook listening activities, allow students to review the activities or prepare them as homework.

BlackBoard and WebCT Basic

These course management systems provide content specific to the *À vous!* program, allowing instructors to individualize their instruction and creating a secure, private forum that enriches the classroom experience.

À VOUS!

The Global French Experience

AN INTRODUCTORY COURSE

Véronique Anover
California State University, San Marcos

Theresa A. Antes
University of Florida

Houghton Mifflin Company   Boston   New York

Publisher: Rolando Hernández

Senior Sponsoring Editor: Glenn A. Wilson

Executive Marketing Director: Eileen Bernadette Moran

Marketing Assistant: Lorreen Ruth Pelletier

Development Editors: Erin Kern, Florence Kilgo

Editorial Assistant: Erin Beasley

Project Editors: Harriet C. Dishman, Stacy Drew

Art and Design Manager: Gary Crespo

Cover Design Manager: Anne S. Katzeff

Senior Photo Editor: Jennifer Meyer Dare

Composition Buyer: Chuck Dutton

New Title Project Manager: James Lonergan

Cover Photo © The Copyright Group/SuperStock

Printed in the U.S.A.

Library of Congress Control Number: 2006924975

Instructor's Annotated Edition
ISBN-10: 0-618-40734-0
ISBN-13: 978-0-618-40734-7

For orders, use student text ISBNs
ISBN-10: 0-618-25981-3
ISBN-13: 978-0-618-25981-6

1 2 3 4 5 6 7 8 9-DOW-11 10 09 08 07

Table of Contents

Scope and Sequence

UNITÉ 1: Je suis comme je suis (xxiv)

	VOCABULARY	STRUCTURES	CULTURE
Chapitre 1: Qui es-tu?	Basic conversations (4) Introductions; making plans (15)	**Tu** vs. **vous** (7) The alphabet (9) Numbers 0–30 (17)	Greetings and goodbyes in Francophone countries (12) Universities in France (20)
Chapitre 2: Je suis…	Describing yourself and others (30, 38) Sports and leisure activities (47)	The verb **être** (33) Negation (34) The verb **avoir** (39) Adjective agreement (41) Regular **-er** verbs (49) Definite articles (50)	Portrait of some French and Francophone speakers (45) Is there a "typical" French person? (53)
Chapitre 3: Ma famille et mes amis	Daily activities; professions; pets (59) Family members (74) Days of the week and months of the year (79)	Regular and stem-changing **-er** verbs (61) Yes/no questions (63) Indefinite articles (65) Professions and indefinite articles (69) Possessive adjectives (77) **On** and **il y a** (81) Numbers 31–60 (83)	The French and their pets (71) Mother's Day in the Central African Republic (84)
Chapitre 4: Mon appartement	Describing an apartment or house (94) Stores (101) Prepositions (108) Household chores; the weather (117)	The near future; the verb **aller;** contractions with **à** (96) Numbers 61–1,000,000 (102) Regular **-ir** verbs (103) Prepositions and contractions with definite articles (111) Adjectives of color (113) The verb **faire** (120)	Housing in Francophone Europe (106) Winter in Quebec (123)

Mise en pratique, Unité 1: La Wallonie (128)

UNITÉ 2: Ma vie d'aujourd'hui et d'hier (134)

	VOCABULARY	STRUCTURES	CULTURE
Chapitre 5: Ma ville	Specialty shops (138) Clothing (148) Public transportation (160) Giving directions (168)	Regular **-re** verbs (141) Partitive articles and expressions of quantity (143) The verbs **mettre, porter,** and **essayer** (151) The pronouns **y** and **en** (154) The verbs **prendre, comprendre** and **apprendre** (162) Telling time (163) Giving commands (169)	**Brasseries** (158) French supermarkets (172)
Chapitre 6: Mes goûts gastronomiques	Expressions with **avoir;** eating at a restaurant (183) Foods (195) Table settings (203)	The verbs **vouloir** and **boire;** review of the partitive (184) Adverbs (187) The verbs **devoir** and **pouvoir** (200) The comparative (206) The superlative (209)	French bread and cheese (191) Eating in Africa (212)
Chapitre 7: Les infos qui m'entourent	The media (219, 228) Events in our lives (236)	**Passé composé** with **avoir** (221) Negative and interrogative of the **passé composé** (224) **Passé composé** with **être** (230) Interrogative pronoun **quel** (237) **Passé composé** with **y, en,** and adverbs (240) The verbs **lire, dire, écrire** (242)	French television (234) Newspapers and radio in Senegal (246)
Chapitre 8: Mes relations amoureuses et amicales	Daily routines (256) Romantic and friendly relationships (265) Cars and driving (272) Personal relationships (278)	Present tense of reflexive verbs (258) Reflexive verbs in the near future (261) Reciprocal verbs (267) Negations: **ne...plus, ne jamais, ne...rien, ne...personne** (268) **Passé composé** of reflexive and reciprocal verbs (274) The verbs **conduire** and **rouler;** the verbs **quitter, partir,** and **sortir** (279)	A Moroccan wedding (263) Interracial and intercultural marriage in France (270)

Mise en pratique, Unité 2: La Provence (286)

UNITÉ 3: Ma place dans le monde (292)

UNITÉ 4: Ma vie de demain (410)

	VOCABULARY	STRUCTURES	CULTURE
Chapitre 13: Ma vie branchée!	Modern technology (414) Extreme sports and other sports (423)	The verbs **connaître** and **savoir** (415) The future tense (425)	The Minitel (419) The Internet in Africa (430)
Chapitre 14: Je suis en forme!	Fitness and exercise (438) Sports and physical activities (449)	The present subjunctive (440) The subjunctive of irregular verbs (442) Subjunctive vs. infinitives (453) Disjunctive pronouns (455)	How the French attain well-being (446) The French and soccer (457)
Chapitre 15: Ma santé	Internal organs; medical remedies (463) Emotions; dieting (472)	The subjunctive with expressions of emotion and volition (466) The subjunctive with expressions of judgment and doubt (475)	Health care in France (469) The "**crise de foie**" (479)
Chapitre 16: Mes voyages et mes souvenirs	Travel by train and plane (491) Making hotel reservations; tourist activities (502)	Prepositions used with continents, countries, and cities (495) The verbs **se souvenir de** and **se rappeler de** (504) Relative pronouns **qui** and **que** (506) Relative pronouns **dont** and **où** (508)	The French and wine (499) The expression "**Je me souviens**" in Quebec (512)

Mise en pratique, Unité 4: Le Québec (518)

To the Student

We hope you will enjoy using and learning from *À vous!* In addition to your student textbook, the *À vous!* program offers a variety of components to help you get the most out of your Introductory French course. Whether you learn best from conversations and working with groups, from reading or writing, or from using multimedia such as audio, video, or online activities, *À vous!* can help you learn effectively and, hopefully, help you have fun in the process, too.

Following are the components available to you as part of the *À vous!* program.

Student Components

Student Textbook

The Student Textbook contains the information and activities that you will need for in-class use. It is divided into sixteen core chapters, each containing vocabulary and grammar presentations and activities, listening practice, and cultural information and activities. Reading selections and writing practice are featured in alternating chapters. The back of the book contains valuable reference sections, including French-English and English-French glossaries, verb charts, and a vocabulary list of classroom-related terms.

In-Text Audio

In your book, this icon refers you to the In-Text Audio, which is packaged with the Student Textbook and contains recordings of the **Commençons!/Continuons!** dialogues from each chapter, as well as the listening segments for the **À l'écoute!** exercises. Your instructor may play the audio during class time or assign you to do the listening activities outside of class.

Student Activities Manual

The Student Activities Manual is intended as a way for you to get extra practice outside of class. It contains both workbook (written practice of the grammar and vocabulary presented in the Student Textbook) and lab manual (listening and pronunciation practice) components.

SAM Audio Program

The SAM Audio Program contains the pronunciation and listening practice that corresponds to the listening portions of the Student Activities Manual. The SAM Audio Program is meant for you to use outside of class at the language lab.

e-SAM powered by Quia

Your instructor may choose to use the e-SAM, which is an electronic version of the printed Student Activities Manual. It allows you to complete the same practice as presented in the print version, but in a computerized format that provides immediate feedback for many exercises. The audio corresponding to the lab exercises is also included.

Online Study Center

Online Study Center

This icon points to the Online Study Center for *À vous!* (accessed through the Product Information Center at **http://college.hmco.com/pic/avous1e**). As shown below, a specific product will be indicated under this icon to direct you to it. The *À vous!* Online Study Center contains the following:

- ■ Web Search Activities are designed to give you further practice of chapter vocabulary and grammar structures and enhance your cultural knowledge through exploration of authentic French-language websites.

- ■ Web Links connect you to a variety of French-language sites appropriate to the textbook's chapter themes and content, inviting you into authentic experiences of French-speaking cultures and language.

- ■ Flashcards help you learn chapter vocabulary.

Online Study Center
Flashcards
Online Study Center
ACE

- ■ ACE Practice Tests are designed to help you practice chapter vocabulary and grammar and to assess your own progress via immediate feedback.

- ■ ACE Video Activities are designed to reinforce comprehension and provide extra practice.

Online Study Center
Language Skills Practice

- ■ Language Skills Practice denotes sections that provide a variety of activities on key structures and vocabulary from the book, from games to art-based exercises, and video and audio clips.

- ■ Downloadable .mp3 audio files of the In-Text Audio files, corresponding to the Student Textbook listening activities, allow you to review the activities or prepare them as homework.

BlackBoard and WebCT Basic

These course management systems provide content specific to the *À vous!* program, allowing your instructor to individualize his or her instruction and creating a secure, private forum that enriches the classroom experience.

Overview

An Overview of the Textbook's Main Features

À vous! contains 16 chapters, which are subdivided into four units of four chapters each. Each unit is followed by a unique section called **Mise en pratique,** which focuses on one particular region of the French-speaking world, and brings together the material from all four chapters.

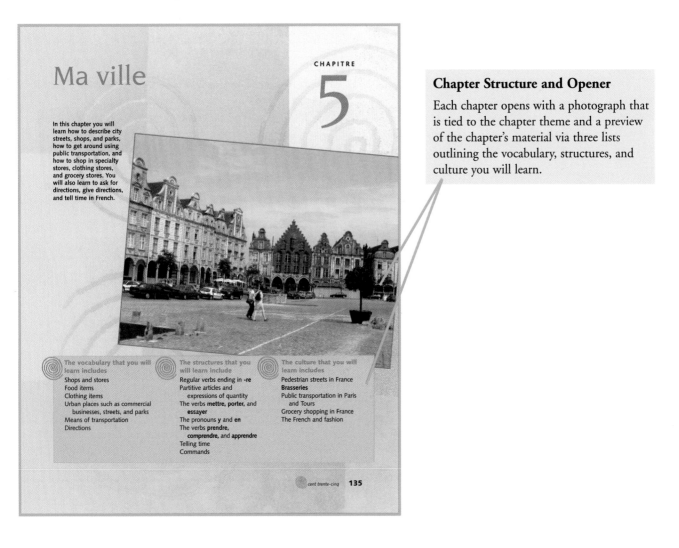

Chapter Structure and Opener

Each chapter opens with a photograph that is tied to the chapter theme and a preview of the chapter's material via three lists outlining the vocabulary, structures, and culture you will learn.

Commençons!

Each **Commençons!** begins with a text or dialogue whose sole purpose is to introduce you to vocabulary and have you focus on comprehension in very general terms.

Commençons!

On fait les courses

Après les cours à l'université, Aude et Jean-Jacques vont faire les courses. Leur réfrigérateur est vide[1]! Aude a la liste des provisions[2] et Jean-Jacques a le chariot à provisions[3].

Comme il est tard et ils sont fatigués après une longue journée à l'université, Aude et Jean-Jacques décident d'aller faire les courses dans une grande surface (c'est-à-dire un supermarché) au lieu d'aller[4] chez les petits commerçants du quartier.

Jean-Jacques et Aude vont au supermarché Carrefour.

Au rayon crémerie

AUDE: Bonjour, Monsieur. Je voudrais[5] un morceau de Gruyère et je vais prendre[6] aussi une tranche de Roquefort.
LE CRÉMIER: Très bien! Voilà vos fromages. Et avec ceci[7]?
AUDE: Je vais prendre aussi une douzaine d'œufs.

Au rayon boucherie

JEAN-JACQUES: Bonjour, Monsieur. Je voudrais un poulet fermier[8] et deux tranches de bœuf.
LE BOUCHER: J'ai un beau poulet d'un kilo 200 grammes pour vous et voilà vos deux tranches de bœuf. Et avec ceci?
JEAN-JACQUES: C'est tout, merci.

[1]*empty* [2]*shopping list* [3]*shopping cart* [4]*instead of going* [5]*I would like* [6]*to take / to buy* [7]*Anything else?* [8]*farm-raised chicken*

136 *cent trente-six* À vous!

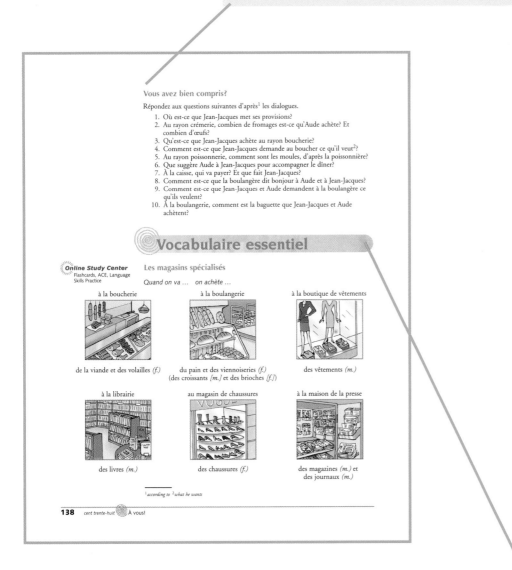

Vous avez bien compris?

Répondez aux questions suivantes d'après[1] les dialogues.

1. Où est-ce que Jean-Jacques met ses provisions?
2. Au rayon crémerie, combien de fromages est-ce qu'Aude achète? Et combien d'œufs?
3. Qu'est-ce que Jean-Jacques achète au rayon boucherie?
4. Comment est-ce que Jean-Jacques demande au boucher ce qu'il veut[2]?
5. Au rayon poissonnerie, comment sont les moules, d'après la poissonnière?
6. Que suggère Aude à Jean-Jacques pour accompagner le dîner?
7. À la caisse, qui va payer? Et que fait Jean-Jacques?
8. Comment est-ce que la boulangère dit bonjour à Aude et à Jean-Jacques?
9. Comment est-ce que Jean-Jacques et Aude demandent à la boulangère ce qu'ils veulent?
10. À la boulangerie, comment est la baguette que Jean-Jacques et Aude achètent?

Vocabulaire essentiel

Online Study Center
Flashcards, ACE, Language
Skills Practice

Les magasins spécialisés

Quand on va … on achète …

à la boucherie

de la viande et des volailles *(f.)*

à la boulangerie

du pain et des viennoiseries *(f.)*
(des croissants *[m.]* et des brioches *[f.]*)

à la boutique de vêtements

des vêtements *(m.)*

à la librairie

des livres *(m.)*

au magasin de chaussures

des chaussures *(f.)*

à la maison de la presse

des magazines *(m.)* et
des journaux *(m.)*

[1]*according to* [2]*what he wants*

138 *cent trente-huit* À vous!

Expansion personnelle

The **Expansion personnelle** vocabulary invites you to choose vocabulary that is relevant to your own life, and then incorporate it as part of your active vocabulary. In doing so, you acquire vocabulary for communicating in real-life situations.

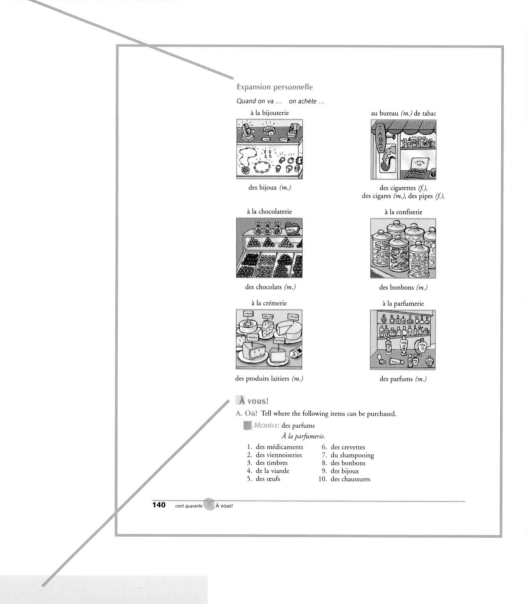

Expansion personnelle

Quand on va … on achète …

à la bijouterie

des bijoux *(m.)*

au bureau *(m.)* de tabac

des cigarettes *(f.)*,
des cigares *(m.)*, des pipes *(f.)*,

à la chocolaterie

des chocolats *(m.)*

à la confiserie

des bonbons *(m.)*

à la crémerie

des produits laitiers *(m.)*

à la parfumerie

des parfums *(m.)*

À vous!

A. Où? Tell where the following items can be purchased.

MODÈLE: des parfums
À la parfumerie.

1. des médicaments
2. des viennoiseries
3. des timbres
4. de la viande
5. des œufs
6. des crevettes
7. du shampooing
8. des bonbons
9. des bijoux
10. des chaussures

À vous!

Each **À vous!** section gives you the opportunity to put your comprehension to use, practicing the vocabulary you have learned, as well as incorporating the vocabulary you have chosen from the **Expansion personnelle.**

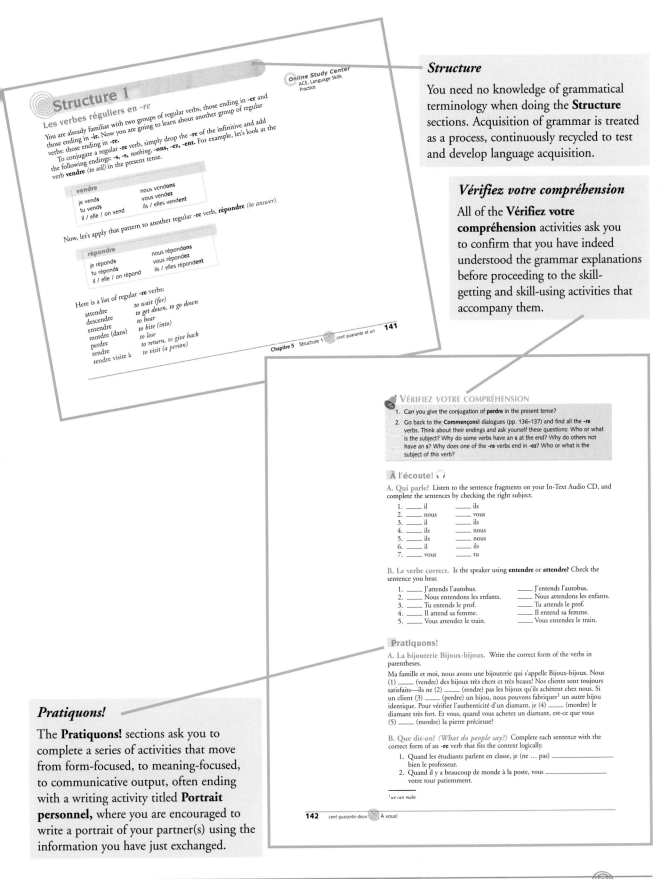

Structure 1

Les verbes réguliers en -re

You are already familiar with two groups of regular verbs, those ending in **-er** and those ending in **-ir**. Now you are going to learn about another group of regular verbs: those ending in **-re**.

To conjugate a regular **-re** verb, simply drop the **-re** of the infinitive and add the following endings: **-s, -s,** *nothing,* **-ons, -ez, -ent.** For example, let's look at the verb **vendre** *(to sell)* in the present tense.

vendre	
je vend**s**	nous vend**ons**
tu vend**s**	vous vend**ez**
il / elle / on vend	ils / elles vend**ent**

Now, let's apply that pattern to another regular **-re** verb, **répondre** *(to answer).*

répondre	
je répond**s**	nous répond**ons**
tu répond**s**	vous répond**ez**
il / elle / on répond	ils / elles répond**ent**

Here is a list of regular **-re** verbs:

attendre	to wait (for)
descendre	to get down, to go down
entendre	to hear
mordre (dans)	to bite (into)
perdre	to lose
rendre	to return, to give back
rendre visite à	to visit (a person)

Structure

You need no knowledge of grammatical terminology when doing the **Structure** sections. Acquisition of grammar is treated as a process, continuously recycled to test and develop language acquisition.

Vérifiez votre compréhension

All of the **Vérifiez votre compréhension** activities ask you to confirm that you have indeed understood the grammar explanations before proceeding to the skill-getting and skill-using activities that accompany them.

VÉRIFIEZ VOTRE COMPRÉHENSION

1. Can you give the conjugation of **perdre** in the present tense?
2. Go back to the **Commençons!** dialogues (pp. 136–137) and find all the **-re** verbs. Think about their endings and ask yourself these questions: Who or what is the subject? Why do some verbs have an **s** at the end? Why do others not have an **s**? Why does one of the **-re** verbs end in **-ez**? Who or what is the subject of this verb?

À l'écoute!

A. Qui parle? Listen to the sentence fragments on your In-Text Audio CD, and complete the sentences by checking the right subject.

1. ____ il   ____ ils
2. ____ nous   ____ vous
3. ____ il   ____ ils
4. ____ ils   ____ nous
5. ____ ils   ____ nous
6. ____ il   ____ ils
7. ____ vous   ____ tu

B. Le verbe correct. Is the speaker using **entendre** or **attendre?** Check the sentence you hear.

1. ____ J'attends l'autobus.   ____ J'entends l'autobus.
2. ____ Nous entendons les enfants. ____ Nous attendons les enfants.
3. ____ Tu entends le prof.   ____ Tu attends le prof.
4. ____ Il attend sa femme.   ____ Il entend sa femme.
5. ____ Vous attendez le train.   ____ Vous entendez le train.

Pratiquons!

A. La bijouterie Bijoux-bijoux. Write the correct form of the verbs in parentheses.

Ma famille et moi, nous avons une bijouterie qui s'appelle Bijoux-bijoux. Nous (1) ____ (vendre) des bijoux très chers et très beaux! Nos clients sont toujours satisfaits—ils ne (2) ____ (rendre) pas les bijoux qu'ils achètent chez nous. Si un client (3) ____ (perdre) un bijou, nous pouvons fabriquer[1] un autre bijou identique. Pour vérifier l'authenticité d'un diamant, je (4) ____ (mordre) le diamant très fort. Et vous, quand vous achetez un diamant, est-ce que vous (5) ____ (mordre) la pierre précieuse?

B. Que dit-on? *(What do people say?)* Complete each sentence with the correct form of an **-re** verb that fits the context logically.

1. Quand les étudiants parlent en classe, je (ne ... pas) ____ bien le professeur.
2. Quand il y a beaucoup de monde à la poste, vous ____ votre tour patiemment.

[1] *we can make*

Pratiquons!

The **Pratiquons!** sections ask you to complete a series of activities that move from form-focused, to meaning-focused, to communicative output, often ending with a writing activity titled **Portrait personnel,** where you are encouraged to write a portrait of your partner(s) using the information you have just exchanged.

Continuons!

À vous! presents its material in manageable sections throughout each chapter. Though the book does not follow a rigid chapter outline, the format is generally the same across chapters. While there is no preordained number of sections, there is a commitment to grouping the structures logically to support the discussion of each chapter's theme.

Continuons!

Partie I: Au magasin de vêtements

C'est samedi après-midi et Aude et Jean-Jacques vont faire les magasins[1] dans une rue piétonne, la rue Sainte-Catherine, à Bordeaux.

Aude et Jean-Jacques entrent dans Promod.

AUDE: Il fait beau aujourd'hui, n'est-ce pas, Jean-Jacques?
JEAN-JACQUES: Oui! L'été arrive!
AUDE: Je voudrais acheter un bikini, une robe[2] blanche et des sandales. Et toi?
JEAN-JACQUES: Moi, je voudrais des jeans et un tee-shirt.
AUDE: On va à Promod? Je suis sûre de trouver un mignon bikini.
JEAN-JACQUES: Je préfère un bikini sexy!
AUDE: Ne sois pas bête[3], Jean-Jacques!

LA VENDEUSE: Bonjour! Je peux vous aider?
AUDE: Oui, je cherche un bikini, taille 38.
JEAN-JACQUES (À AUDE): Un bikini sexy!
AUDE (À JEAN-JACQUES): Chut![4] Tu es pénible![5]
LA VENDEUSE: Pardon, Monsieur, je n'entends pas bien ce que vous dites[6].
JEAN-JACQUES (TOUT ROUGE): Euh, ce n'est rien d'important …
AUDE (À LA VENDEUSE): Est-ce que je peux essayer[7] ce bikini jaune et bleu, s'il vous plaît?
LA VENDEUSE: Oui, les cabines d'essayage[8] sont à droite[9].

Clothing and shoe sizes in France are different than in the United States.

Women's pants, dresses, blouses

USA	France
2	32
4	34
6	36
8	38
10	40
12	42
14	44

Men's shirts

USA	France
15	38
15½	39
16	40
16½	41
17	42

Women's shoes

USA	France
6	36
7	37,5
8	38,5
9	40
10	42

Men's shoes

USA	France
8	41
9	42,5
10	44
11	45
12	46

[1] to go shopping [2] dress [3] Don't be silly! [4] Shh! / Hush! [5] You're a pain! [6] what you're saying [7] Can I try on…? [8] dressing rooms [9] to the right

---

À vous de parler!

In groups of three to four, you are asked to engage in a task-based activity and then create a dialogue based on the theme of the chapter using the vocabulary and grammar you have learned.

À vous de parler!

A. Au supermarché. In groups of three, pretend that you are shopping at a supermarket. Two of you will be the customers and one of you the clerk at the different departments. First, make a list with the food items you need to buy. Then, create a dialogue between the customers and the clerk in the different food departments at the supermarket. (You may use the dialogues at the beginning of the chapter as models.) Make sure that the customers and the clerk greet each other each time.

[1] during

On fait les courses comme ça au supermarché en France[1]

When going to the supermarket, the first thing you do is get a shopping cart, right? Well, people do that in France too, but it gets a little tricky! All the shopping carts are tied together by a chain at the supermarket entrance. In order to get a cart, the customer must deposit a coin (50 cents of a euro) into a coin slot on the cart. This unties the chain and releases the cart. The customer can get the coin back by returning the cart and chaining it up again with the others.

Once inside, customers must weigh their fruits and vegetables before going to the cash register, as the cashier will not weigh them. There are digital scales located throughout the produce department. Each scale has buttons with pictures of each variety of fruit and vegetable available at the store. The customer presses the right button, and a self-adhesive price tag comes out of the scale.

Finally, after customers have paid at the cash register, they must bag their own purchases. And there are no paper bags, only plastic bags. In some supermarkets, customers are charged for each plastic bag they use!

Réfléchissons!

1. Why do you think that the French must deposit a coin in a shopping cart before they can use it? Is it the same in your country? Where do you take and leave the carts?
2. Do you think it is a good idea to weigh your own produce rather than having the cashier weigh it for you? Why or why not? Why do you think that it is done that way in France?
3. Do you like the fact that in the United States someone bags your purchases for you? How about the fact that you can have someone put your purchases in your car? What is customer service like in your country?

À vous de lire!

A. Stratégies. The reading passage in this section contains information about fashion—**la mode**—in France. Before reading the passage, skim it very quickly. Underline terms that are familiar to you from this chapter and that you believe will be important for understanding the text. Look in particular for terms that are frequently repeated—these are undoubtedly key terms in the text. Are there other words in the text that you have not yet seen but whose meaning you can guess because they are cognates? Remember that you don't need to understand every word in order to understand the gist of a text!

---

[1]The information in this section applies to both France and Francophone Europe.

Réfléchissons!

Here you are presented with a culture box describing different aspects of life in France and the Francophone world. Following the reading is a series of questions to help you spark a discussion with your partner. The questions also invite cross-cultural comparisons based on the theme of the chapter.

À vous de lire!

The reading sections continue with the process approach to learning, and are found in *odd-numbered chapters*. These sections present strategies such as skimming, scanning, and a focus on repetition and cognates, to name a few. You are then given pre-, during-, and post-reading activities to aid in your comprehension.

À vous d'écrire!

The process approach to learning is also applied in the writing sections. Found in *even-numbered chapters,* the writing sections contain pre-, during-, and post-activities, are thematically related to the chapter content, and are accompanied by strategies.

À vous d'écrire!

You are going to spend a year abroad (choose a city in France, Francophone Europe, Canada, or West Africa). You need to rent a fully furnished apartment for one year, and you are going to write an email in French to a real estate agent who can help you find an apartment.

A. Stratégies. Keep in mind the vocabulary and the expressions that you have just seen in this chapter and in previous chapters. Do not try to translate directly from your own language in order to express your ideas. Use the words that you already know. Pay attention to noun-adjective agreement, spelling, and sentence structure.

B. Organisons-nous! First, think about how you would start your message. Decide in which city you are going to be spending a year and in what type of neighborhood you would like to live (for example, near the university, or near a park, etc). Greet the real estate agent in your email and tell him/her the reason you are writing.

Next, consider the type of apartment that you would like to rent, and write a brief description in French. There is no need at this point to write complete sentences. Your description could be as short as "one bedroom with a balcony, two bathrooms, a big kitchen, and a living room."

Finally, make a list in French of questions that you would like to ask the real estate agent, such as how much the rent is for a one-bedroom apartment, what the neighborhood is like in which s/he is looking to find you an apartment, how many floors there are in the buildings, etc.

C. Pensons-y! Now that you have decided what type of apartment you are looking for, make a list of the furniture and appliances that you would like to have in each room, and where you would like them to be. Start with **Je voudrais ...** *(I would like . . .).*

Kitchen
Bedroom
Bathroom
Living room
Dining room
Additional rooms/features

Expressions utiles
Monsieur ... / Madame ...
Je me permets de vous
contacter parce que je ...
Bien cordialement.

D. Révisons! Exchange your draft with a classmate. Then check each other's drafts. Check the spelling of the words as well as the prepositions. Check the way s/he phrased his/her questions. Did s/he make agreements between adjectives and nouns? Does s/he have the correct articles with the nouns? Correct each other's work before you begin activity E.

E. Écrivons! Now that you have drafted the main ideas that you would like to include in your email, create a coherent paragraph. In order to make your email more personal, tell the real estate agent a little about yourself (your likes and dislikes) and why you are going abroad.

124 *cent vingt-quatre* À vous!

MISE EN PRATIQUE

Mise en pratique

The **Mise en pratique,** capstone sections following every unit, help you see how learning French is not only a cognitive endeavor but a total-body experience.

À vous de découvrir!

Online Study Center

Pour faire les activités ci-dessous, allez au *Online Study Center* et choisissez *Mise en pratique*. Vous y trouverez des sites Internet correspondants aux mots ou phrases en caractères gras dans chaque activité.

La Provence

Dans cette unité, nous vous proposons de découvrir la Provence. Pour votre visite virtuelle, travaillez avec un(e) ou deux camarade(s) de classe. À l'aide des sites Internet correspondants à chaque section, recherchez les thèmes suivants.

A. Informations générales. Allez au **Site Web de Houghton Mifflin** et cliquez sur **Mise en Pratique 2.** Vous allez voir plusieurs sites web pour Provence. Allez visiter un ou plusieurs de ces sites, et répondez aux questions suivantes.

1. Quelle région géographique est inclue dans la Provence?
2. Cochez (____✓____) ce qu'on peut y trouver:
   - ____ des villages
   - ____ des villes de taille moyenne
   - ____ des grandes villes
   - ____ la montagne
   - ____ la mer
   - ____ la campagne
3. Comment est-ce que vous décririez[1] la Provence? _____

À vous de découvrir! invites you to discover a region of the Francophone world, in this instance, Provence, through a variety of webquest activities. You will learn about the geography, history, and culture of the region.

À vous de déguster! features one dish from the region highlighted, asks you questions to acquaint you with regional specialties in general, and then presents you with a recipe featuring these ingredients.

À vous de déguster!

La gastronomie provençale

Nous vous proposons de goûter quelques spécialités de la gastronomie provençale, qui utilise surtout les produits agricoles régionaux. Avant de parler de plats spécifiques, testez vos connaissances sur les produits typiques de Provence. Faites l'activité A, et si vous ne savez pas les réponses, devinez!

A. Produits provençaux. Mettez un cercle autour de la réponse correcte.

1. C'est un fruit (ou un légume!) rouge qui pousse partout, et qui est un ingrédient important dans la cuisine provençale et italienne.
   - a. la cerise
   - b. la tomate
   - c. la fraise
2. C'est un fruit qu'on utilise pour faire une boisson alcoolique.
   - a. le raisin
   - b. la pomme
   - c. la framboise
3. C'est un fruit qui pousse dans la région méditerranéenne, et que l'on presse pour obtenir une huile très fine.
   - a. le raisin
   - b. l'olive
   - c. l'orange
4. C'est une plante avec une fleur violette. On l'utilise dans la préparation des crèmes médicinales, des parfums et des savons, mais aussi comme herbe dans la cuisine.
   - a. la tulipe
   - b. l'iris
   - c. la lavande

Unité 2 Mise en pratique deux cent quatre-vingt-sept **287**

Soupe de melon à la menthe: pour 4 personnes

1 gros melon à maturité
1 orange
10 cl. de porto (ou moscatel)
2 cuillères à soupe de sucre en poudre
10 cl. de crème fraîche
125 gr. de framboises
quelques tiges[2] de menthe fraîche

Presser le jus de l'orange. Ouvrir le melon, retirer[3] les graines et les fibres, puis prélever[4] la chair[5] avec une cuillère. Passer la pulpe au mixeur avec le jus d'orange, le porto et le sucre. Ajouter à cela la crème, et mixer pour obtenir une consistance veloutée. Verser[6] dans un saladier, et ajouter deux tiges de menthe lavées et séchées. Couvrir de film étirable et laissez-la se refroidir au réfrigérateur pendant 6 heures. Pour la servir, verser la soupe dans quatre jolies coupes à dessert, et décorez-la avec quelques framboises et une feuille de menthe.

À vous d'analyser presents a cultural or literary reading from the target Francophone region and asks you comprehension and interpretive questions as a way to help you better understand the culture of each area.

À vous d'analyser

Regardez les annonces publicitaires suivantes. Elles viennent toutes du festival de théâtre d'Avignon, où, chaque été, on peut voir plus de 660 pièces de théâtre différentes! Lisez rapidement les renseignements pour chaque pièce, et puis répondez aux questions qui suivent.

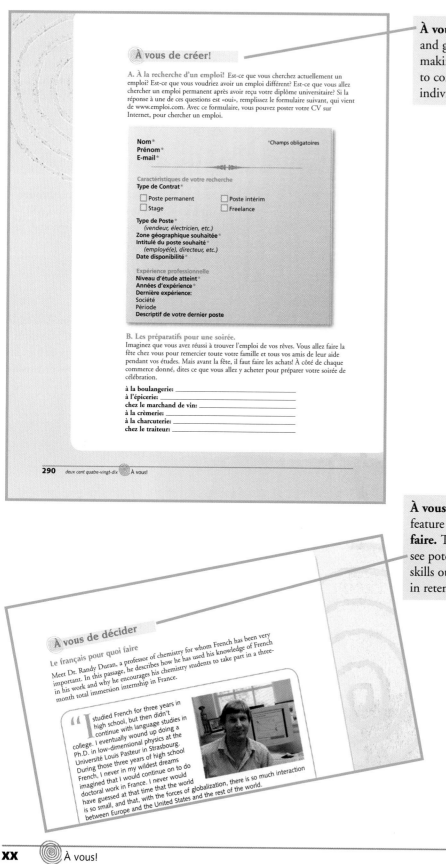

À vous de créer! recycles the vocabulary and grammar from the four chapters making up the unit, giving you a chance to combine points that were studied individually into a "big picture."

À vous de créer!

A. À la recherche d'un emploi! Est-ce que vous cherchez actuellement un emploi? Est-ce que vous voudriez avoir un emploi différent? Est-ce que vous allez chercher un emploi permanent après avoir reçu votre diplôme universitaire? Si la réponse à une de ces questions est «oui», remplissez le formulaire suivant, qui vient de www.emploi.com. Avec ce formulaire, vous pouvez poster votre CV sur Internet, pour chercher un emploi.

Nom*	*Champs obligatoires
Prénom*	
E-mail*	

Caractéristiques de votre recherche
Type de Contrat*

☐ Poste permanent ☐ Poste intérim
☐ Stage ☐ Freelance

Type de Poste*
(vendeur, électricien, etc.)
Zone géographique souhaitée*
Intitulé du poste souhaité*
(employé(e), directeur, etc.)
Date disponibilité*

Expérience professionnelle
Niveau d'étude atteint*
Années d'expérience*
Dernière expérience:
Société
Période
Descriptif de votre dernier poste

B. Les préparatifs pour une soirée.
Imaginez que vous avez réussi à trouver l'emploi de vos rêves. Vous allez faire la fête chez vous pour remercier toute votre famille et tous vos amis de leur aide pendant vos études. Mais avant la fête, il faut faire les achats! À côté de chaque commerce donné, dites ce que vous allez y acheter pour préparer votre soirée de célébration.

à la boulangerie: _____
à l'épicerie: _____
chez le marchand de vin: _____
à la crèmerie: _____
à la charcuterie: _____
chez le traiteur: _____

À vous décider ends this section with a feature entitled **Le Français pour quoi faire.** This feature is designed to help you see potential uses of your French language skills outside of the classroom, and thus aid in retention beyond the first-year course.

À vous de décider

Le français pour quoi faire

Meet Dr. Randy Duran, a professor of chemistry for whom French has been very important. In this passage, he describes how he has used his knowledge of French in his work and why he encourages his chemistry students to take part in a three-month total immersion internship in France.

"I studied French for three years in high school, but then didn't continue with language studies in college. I eventually wound up doing a Ph.D. in low-dimensional physics at the Université Louis Pasteur in Strasbourg. During those three years of high school French, I never in my wildest dreams imagined that I would continue on to do doctoral work in France. I never would have guessed at that time that the world is so small, and that, with the forces of globalization, there is so much interaction between Europe and the United States and the rest of the world.

Acknowledgments

As with any first edition of a language textbook, the first edition of *À vous!* represents years of idea sharing, writing, revising, and fine tuning. We are very grateful to everyone who has had a hand in this process, as the project would not have come to fruition without their participation.

In particular, we would like to thank the entire editorial staff at Houghton Mifflin. You are a group of committed professionals, and your guidance and support have been instrumental in the development of *À vous!* We are deeply indebted to Randy Welch and Beth Kramer for believing in our project and encouraging our ideas, and to freelance editor Nancy Geilen for her expert advice in the early stages of development. We had fun working with you, Nancy, and your continued support is much appreciated! We are also extremely grateful to Erin Kern, who took over our project at later stages, helping us to fine-tune the text and develop the ancillary materials. Erin, we sincerely appreciate your hard work, your gentle personality, and your professionalism. In addition, we would like to thank Rosemary Jaffe, Florence Kilgo, and freelancers Stacy Drew and Nancy Milner Kelly for working so smoothly and efficiently with us on the finishing touches of *À vous!* Our gratitude also goes to Eileen Bernadette Moran in marketing for her "tasty" ideas and her sincere excitement about our project, to Laurel Miller for her expertise in the development of the technology ancillaries, and finally, but not least, to Glenn Wilson, Van Strength, and Rolando Hernández for their strong support. We would also like to express our appreciation to those behind the scenes at Houghton Mifflin whose names are perhaps unknown to us (an entire army of support!) but who were involved nonetheless in the making of *À vous!*

We are also very indebted to the many colleagues across the country who served as reviewers, reading everything from the most preliminary to the most final chapters. *À vous!* would not be the book that it is today had it not been for your constructive criticism. We acknowledge:

Linda Quinn Allen, Iowa State University
Margaret Healy Beauvois, University of Tennessee
Tony C. Beld, University of New Orleans
Edith J. Benkov, San Diego State University
Tom Blair, City College of San Francisco
Lucille Boilard-Harkin, Pima Community College
Kimberlee Campbell, New York University
Robert R. Daniel, St. Joseph's University
James N. Davis, University of Arkansas
Maureen Gillespie Dawson, Notre Dame University
Margaret Dempster, Northwestern University
Peter Dola, University of North Carolina
Annie Duménil, University of South Carolina
Beatrice Dupuy, Louisiana State University
Alain-Philippe Durand, University of Rhode Island
Hilary Fisher, University of Oregon

Claude J. Fouillade, New Mexico State University
Sabine Gabaron, University of Michigan
Sarah Gendron, Marquette University
Susan Grayson, Occidental College
Janel Pettes Guikema, Grand Valley State University
Suzanne Hendrickson, Arizona State University
Jacqueline Klaassen, City College San Francisco
Marie Léticée, University of Central Florida
Roy Luna, Miami Dade College
Lara Finklea Mangiafico, Montgomery County Public Schools
Hedwige Meyer, University of Washington
James G. Mitchell, Florida State University
Christine Moisset, University of Pennsylvania
Markus Muller, California State University, Long Beach
Helene Neu, University of Michigan, Ann Arbor
David O'Connell, Georgia State University
David Pellow, North Carolina Central University
Marie-Noëlle Olivier, University of Nevada, Las Vegas
Wendy Pfeffer, University of Louisville
Viviane Ritzi-Marouf, Folsom Lake College
Kelly Jean Sax, Indiana University
Patricia Siegel, SUNY Brockport
Emese Soos, Tufts University
Rosalie Vermette, Indiana University–Purdue University
Lawrence Williams, University of North Texas
Wynne Wong, The Ohio State University

Last but not least, we are very thankful to our friends and to various shopkeepers who opened their homes and/or businesses to us for photos, and to our dear students, who are our constant source of inspiration. Thank you for your willingness to appear in *À vous!*, for providing us with photographs and ideas, and for pilot testing some of the activities; it is for you that we have written *À vous!* We offer this text, in your honor, to our future students, who we hope will embrace French with all their senses.

Véronique's acknowledgments
I would like to dedicate *À vous!* to a very special student, Ivy Kensinger, who after her extremely serious car accident, and having almost lost her lungs, uttered her first words in French. Her love for French is embodied in her. May you fully recover soon, Ivy.

I personally would like to thank my former Houghton Mifflin sales representative, Mary Ellen Bray, for her support and her friendship, as well as my dear French Graduate Teaching Associate Ms. Cindy Pinhal for her thorough revisions in the SAM. I am also thankful to Garrett Collins from Cal State San Marcos for sharing his beautiful photographs of France, some of which appear in the main text. A big thank you to my students who have shared with me their pictures from their trips to France and the Francophone world, and the ones who have willingly posed for some of the pictures included in *À vous!* Last but not least, I thank my two dear colleagues at Cal State San Marcos Dr. Silvia Rolle and Dr. Jill Pellettieri for their support and friendship.

I would like to express my gratitude to my co-author, Theresa Antes, for sharing her passion for teaching French with me, for her innovative ideas, her creative mind, and her endless energy. It is a true pleasure to work with you, Theresa.

Finalement, je voudrais remercier toute ma famille et mes amis en France, en Espagne et aux États-Unis pour leur appui et leur amour pendant ce long trajet qu'a duré *À vous!,* de sa conception à sa création. Particulièrement mes chers parents à qui je dois mon amour pour les langues et mes deux hommes—le petit et le grand—à qui je dois beaucoup de bonnes choses.

V.A.

Theresa's acknowledgments

I would like to thank my family, first and foremost, for their constant support through the writing process. My "projects" take me away from you all too often, and I thank you for understanding those times when I just need to work! I dedicate this book to my sister Judy, who has taught me the true meaning of courage and perseverance. Thanks, too, to those colleagues and mentors who have shared their best practices with me over the past twenty years. Many of those practices make their way into my classroom and have also found their way into this text.

Finally, an extreme debt of gratitude goes to my co-author, Véronique Anover, for never complaining when another project took me away from this one. It is an amazing thing to compare ideas with someone and realize that while the exact ideas may differ, the philosophy behind them is truly the same! The pleasure of this partnership has been all mine.

T.A.A.

UNITÉ

1

JE SUIS COMME JE SUIS

Qui es-tu?

In this chapter, you will learn basic greetings in French, as well as how to introduce yourself, how to ask how someone is, and how to give someone your phone number or address. You will also learn important differences between American and Francophone cultures, and the effects that they have on everyday language (for example, the way we greet peers versus people of a different age or social class).

The vocabulary that you will learn includes

Basic conversational
   expressions:
  Asking someone's name
  Saying hello and goodbye
  Asking how someone is
Making plans:
  Exchanging telephone
    numbers
  Asking if someone is free
  Talking about time of day

The structures that you will learn include

The alphabet
Tu vs. **vous**
Numbers 0–30

The culture that you will study includes

Greetings and goodbyes in
   various Francophone
   countries
The university system in
   France

Commençons!

Play the audio for students, or read the dialogues aloud for them as they look at the drawings. Have them concentrate on understanding the gist of each conversation, rather than understanding every word. After you have read each dialogue, have students explain what they think the people involved might be saying to one another. Highlight the fact that it is not important that they understand every word, but rather that they figure out from context what is going on. Use individual sentences as examples: point out the cognates in **"Je suis content de travailler avec vous ce semestre"** and ask students what they think M. Grandjean is saying.

1. Au début du semestre, en classe de philosophie 🎧

CAROLINE: Bonjour. Je m'appelle Caroline. Et toi? Comment tu t'appelles?
MATHIEU: Je m'appelle Mathieu. Et voici Bernadette.
CAROLINE: Salut, Bernadette. Comment vas-tu?
BERNADETTE: Bonjour, Caroline. Je vais bien, merci. Et toi, ça va?
CAROLINE: Oui, ça va.
MATHIEU: Voilà le professeur, Monsieur Grandjean.
BERNADETTE: Chhhut … la classe commence.

2. Le professeur se présente et fait l'appel

MONSIEUR GRANDJEAN: Bonjour. Je suis le professeur Grandjean. Je suis prof de philosophie, et je suis content de travailler avec vous ce semestre. Je vais faire l'appel; levez le doigt, s'il vous plaît. Caroline Aband?
CAROLINE: Présente.
MONSIEUR GRANDJEAN: Très bien. Bonjour, Mademoiselle. Claire Alexandre? Claire Alexandre? A-L-E-X-A-N-D-R-E? Alexandre, Claire? Non? O.K. Mathieu Beauclair?
MATHIEU: Présent, Monsieur.

Point out the expressions **faire l'appel** and **lever le doigt**. These are expressions that you can use from the start as part of your classroom management. Point out the cultural difference between raising one's hand (as is common in the U.S.) and raising one's index finger (as is common in France). Have students adopt the French gesture in class.

3. À la fin de la classe

> MATHIEU: Au revoir, Caroline. À demain.
> CAROLINE: Au revoir, Mathieu. Ciao, Bernadette. À plus!
> BERNADETTE: À bientôt!

4. Après la classe

> BERNADETTE: Bonjour, Professeur Grandjean. Comment allez-vous?
> MONSIEUR GRANDJEAN: Bien, merci. Et vous, Mademoiselle … euh … rappelez-moi[1] … Comment vous appelez-vous?
> BERNADETTE: Je suis Bernadette Toussaint. Je suis dans votre classe de philosophie.
> MONSIEUR GRANDJEAN: Ah, oui, Mademoiselle Toussaint. Excusez-moi! Voici ma collègue, le professeur Mansour.
> BERNADETTE: Enchantée, Madame!
> PROFESSEUR MANSOUR: Enchantée, Mademoiselle.

---

[1] *remind me*

Vous avez bien compris?

A. Give a one-sentence summary of what is happening in each of the preceding mini-dialogues.

B. Answer the following questions about the mini-dialogues. In some cases, more than one response is possible; list all that you find.
1. How can you say *hello* or *hi* to someone in French?
2. How do you ask someone what his/her name is? How do you respond to this question? Did you notice that the students use a different question than the professor uses? Why do you think this might be the case?
3. In the mini-dialogues, there are three ways to ask how someone is. Can you find them? What do you think the differences between them might be?
4. How do you say *please* in French?
5. How can you say *goodbye* in French? List all the expressions that you find in these dialogues. What do you think the differences are between these expressions?
6. How do you say *It's nice to meet you* in French?

C. Now let's go one step further! Try to answer the following questions in French.
1. Comment s'appellent les trois étudiants[1]? Ils s'appellent
   _____, _____ et _____.
2. Et le professeur? Il s'appelle _____.
3. Comment va Bernadette? Elle va _____.
4. Monsieur Grandjean est professeur de _____.
5. Il fait _____ au début de la classe.

Vocabulaire essentiel

Salutations

There are two ways to say hello in French:

Bonjour.	*Hello. (used with anyone)*
Salut.	*Hi. (used in informal situations, with close friends and peers)*

To say goodbye you can choose from many expressions:

Au revoir.	*Goodbye.*
À bientôt.	*See you soon.*
À demain.	*See you tomorrow.*
À plus. / À plus tard.	*See you later.*
À tout à l'heure.	*See you in a while.*
Ciao.	*See you.*
Salut.	*Bye.*

---
[1]*students*

Présentations

To introduce yourself, say:

Je m'appelle … (Bernard, Cristelle, etc.)	*My name is . . .*
Je suis …	*I am . . .*

To ask a peer his/her name, you can say:

Comment tu t'appelles? / Comment t'appelles-tu?[1]	*What is your name?*
Qui es-tu?	*Who are you?*
Tu es … ?	*Are you . . . ?*

To ask a nonpeer (e.g., a professor, a person older than you) his/her name, say:

Comment vous appelez-vous?	*What is your name?*
Qui êtes-vous?	*Who are you?*

As you approach someone you do not know, choose from the following expressions:

Excusez-moi.	*Excuse me.*
Pardonnez-moi.	*Pardon me.*
Pardon, Madame / Monsieur / Mademoiselle.	*Excuse me, ma'am / sir / young lady.*

Present these in small groups, and give students a chance to practice expressions in each category, so that they are not overwhelmed with seeing this amount of new information all at once. Use choral drills, question/exchange within one category, etc. before moving on to activities that combine the various expressions.

To greet a person whom you have just met:

Enchanté. *(if you're a man)* / Enchantée. *(if you're a woman)*	*It's nice to meet you.*

Questions sur l'état général

To ask a peer how s/he is and to answer that question, choose from:

Comment vas-tu?	*How are you?*
Je vais bien, et toi?	*I'm doing well, and you? I'm good, and you?*
Très bien, merci.	*Very good/well, thank you.*
Comment ça va?	*How is it going?*
Ça va bien.	*It's going well.*
Ça va pas mal.	*It's going all right.*
Ça peut aller.	*It could be better.*
Ça va?	*Is it going okay? Is everything okay?*
Ça va.	*It's going okay.*
Comme ci, comme ça.	*So-so.*

To ask a nonpeer how s/he is and to respond, you can say:

Comment allez-vous?	*How are you?*
Je vais bien, merci.	*I'm doing well, thank you.*
(Je vais) pas mal.	*Not bad.*

---

[1]Both expressions mean *What is your name?;* The first one is most common, however, the second one is used in more formal situations, such as writing.

À vous!

A. Petits dialogues. Indicate if the following conversations are logical or not.

1. —Salut, Nina.
   —Comme ci, comme ça.   _____ logique   _____ pas logique

2. —Comment tu t'appelles?
   —Très bien, merci.   _____ logique   _____ pas logique

3. —Bonjour, Céline!
   —Salut, Paul. Ça va?   _____ logique   _____ pas logique

4. —Comment allez-vous?
   —Merci.   _____ logique   _____ pas logique

5. —À bientôt!
   —À demain.   _____ logique   _____ pas logique

6. —Comment t'appelles-tu?
   —Je m'appelle Delphine.   _____ logique   _____ pas logique

7. —Comment ça va?
   —Ça peut aller.   _____ logique   _____ pas logique

8. —Excusez-moi, Madame.
   Vous êtes Catherine Deneuve?
   —Je vais bien, merci.   _____ logique   _____ pas logique

9. —Qui êtes-vous?
   —Je m'appelle Jean-Luc Picon.   _____ logique   _____ pas logique

10. —Je m'appelle Bruno.
    —Enchanté.   _____ logique   _____ pas logique

11. —Comment vas-tu?
    —À tout à l'heure.   _____ logique   _____ pas logique

B. Présentations. Complete the following dialogues in a logical manner. (There may be more than one logical expression; choose any that is logical in the context.)

1. —Bonjour, je _____ David.
   —Bonjour, David, _____?
   —Ça peut aller, merci.

2. —Je m'appelle Amed et toi, _____?
   —Je m'appelle Céline.

3. —Au revoir, Leïla!
   — _____, Patrick.

4. —Jean-Marc, c'est Brigitte.
   —Bonjour, Brigitte, _____!
   — _____, Jean-Marc!

5. —Excusez-moi, Mademoiselle, _____?
   —Je _____ Joséphine Laurent. Et vous, Monsieur?

6. —À demain, Marie-Claire!
   — _____, Marc!

Structure 1

Les pronoms *tu* et *vous*

There are two ways to say *you* in French: **tu** and **vous.** We use **tu** with a person we know very well, such as a parent, a sibling, a friend, or someone we consider a peer, for example, a classmate or a person of our own age. We use **vous** with a person we do not know and/or to whom we want to show respect, such as an older person, a clerk, a bank teller, a salesperson, etc. We also use **vous** with someone who is in a superior position, such as a boss, a police officer, a professor, or a doctor.

Finally, we use **vous** whenever addressing more than one person. We may know every person in that group extremely well (and would use **tu** with them as individuals), but when we address them as a group we use **vous.** Examples of such groups include our parents, our grandparents, and our friends. Use **vous** whenever addressing more than one person, whether you know those people well or not.

To summarize, **tu** is used to address one person in a familiar way; **vous** is used for one person formally or for any group of people.

Online Study Center
ACE, Language Skills Practice

VÉRIFIEZ VOTRE COMPRÉHENSION

Now go back to the *Commençons!* dialogues at the beginning of the chapter (pp. 2–3). Underline each use of **tu** and **vous,** and explain, for each one, why the speaker chose that pronoun. For each instance of **vous,** tell whether it is used to address one person formally or to address a group of people.

This section will recur throughout the text, as a way to foster consciousness raising among your students. Take a few moments to answer each question with them, always referring back to the section(s) indicated. Help students to realize that they have already seen and understood (at a global level) the structures that they will be studying in detail.

Pratiquons!

A. *Tu* **ou** *vous?* In the space provided in the bubbles on pages 7–9, indicate whether you would use **tu** or **vous** with the following persons.

1.   2.

Answer Key: 1. tu 2. vous 3. vous 4. tu 5. tu 6. vous 7. vous 8. vous 9. tu 10. vous

Point out that in most families, parents, children, grandchildren, and grandparents all use **tu** with one another. Contrast #4 with #8, however, where the young woman uses **vous** when addressing her parents as a couple.

3.

4.

5.

6.

7.

8.

9.

10.

B. Voilà Caroline! In each of the following sentences, Bernadette is speaking with Mathieu. Imagine that Caroline joins the conversation. Change the sentences to reflect the form that Bernadette would use if she were speaking with both Mathieu and Caroline. If no change is necessary, explain why not.

1. Comment t'appelles-tu?
2. Comment vas-tu?
3. Bonjour!
4. À bientôt!
5. Qui es-tu?
6. Comment ça va?
7. Au revoir!

Answer Key: 1. Comment vous appelez-vous? 2. Comment allez-vous? 3. *No change necessary—this expression is both singular and plural.* 4. *No change necessary—this expression is both singular and plural.* 5. Qui êtes-vous? 6. *No change necessary—this expression is both singular and plural.* 7. *No change necessary—this expression is both singular and plural.*

Structure 2

L'alphabet français

There are 26 characters in the French alphabet. Their approximate pronunciation is as follows. Listen to the In-Text Audio CD for the exact pronunciation.

A	*ah*	J	*jee*	S	*ess*
B	*bay*	K	*ka*	T	*tay*
C	*say*	L	*el*	U	*u*
D	*day*	M	*em*	V	*vay*
E	*euh*	N	*en*	W	*doo-bluh-vay*
F	*ef*	O	*o*	X	*eeks*
G	*jay*	P	*pay*	Y	*ee-grek*
H	*aash*	Q	*qu*	Z	*zed*
I	*ee*	R	*erh*		

Online Study Center
ACE, Language Skills Practice

Model the pronunciation of the alphabet and the diacritical marks for your students, then have them repeat once in a choral drill.

Speakers of French consider accents part of the spelling of a word. The major accents are as follows:

` accent grave
´ accent aigu
^ accent circonflexe
¨ tréma

These accents are read as follows when combined with a letter:

à *ah* accent grave
é *euh* accent aigu
ô *o* accent circonflexe
ë *euh* tréma

There is one final symbol in French used to show that the letter **c** should be pronounced as an **s** rather than a **k.** It is called a cedilla, or in French, a **cédille.**

ç *say* cédille

An apostrophe is indicated with the word **apostrophe** in French.

À l'écoute!

Transcript: 1. Mes initiales? C'est G.V. 2. Mes initiales? C'est E.M. 3. Mes initiales? C'est S.R. 4. Mes initiales? C'est H.T. 5. Mes initiales? C'est J.P. 6. Mes initiales? C'est R.B. 7. Mes initiales? C'est V.J. 8. Mes initiales? C'est X.L. 9. Mes initiales? C'est M.I. 10. Mes initiales? C'est Y.C.

For added practice, have students read each set of initials out loud. Then have them say their own initials or those of someone in the class. To make a game of it, send five students to the board. Have other students call out their initials for the students at the board to write. The student who writes the most correctly wins.

Listen to the following sentences, and indicate the initials that you hear.

MODÈLE: You hear: Mes initiales? C'est T.A.

You check: ✓ T.A.   _____ T.E.

1. _____ G.V.   _____ J.V.
2. _____ I.M.   _____ E.M.
3. _____ C.R.   _____ S.R.
4. _____ H.T.   _____ A.T.
5. _____ J.P.   _____ G.P.
6. _____ R.B.   _____ E.B.
7. _____ W.J.   _____ V.J.
8. _____ X.L.   _____ I.L.
9. _____ M.E.   _____ M.I.
10. _____ Y.C.   _____ I.C.

Pratiquons!

A. Qui êtes-vous? Comment ça s'épelle? *(How do you spell that?)*
Introduce yourself to your classmate. Spell out your name for her/him, so s/he can write it down.

MODÈLE: —*Je m'appelle Cathy Blume. Ça s'épelle C-A-T-H-Y B-L-U-M-E.*

—*Bonjour, Cathy. Je m'appelle Patrick Frèrebeau. Ça s'épelle P-A-T-R-I-C-K F-R-E accent grave-R-E-B-E-A-U.*

B. Le mot secret. Taking turns with a partner, select a word or expression from the following list. Spell it out for your partner, who must write it down without looking, and then pronounce it out loud. Continue, alternating words, until you have spelled them all out.

Present **nouveau mot** to students as a vocabulary phrase, so that they can signal to their partner the start of a new word in an expression.

Read the model for your students, to be sure that everyone understands the goal of the activity and to provide a model for pronunciation. As students become more proficient, have them read the models.

> MODÈLE: —*Le mot secret (L'expression secrète) s'épelle: J-E* nouveau mot *M-apostrophe-A-P-P-E-L-L-E.*
>
> —*Ah, c'est «je m'appelle».*
>
> —*Oui, c'est ça!*

1. bientôt
2. pardon
3. ça va mal
4. bonjour
5. excusez-moi

6. très bien
7. qui êtes-vous
8. à tout à l'heure
9. ça s'épelle

C. Des célébrités. Choose your favorite celebrity for each of the following categories. Spell the names out to your neighbor to see if s/he can guess who they are.

Photos such as these appear periodically in each chapter. Encourage students to read the caption and, whenever possible, to figure out what each question means without translating for them; then allow them to explain their answer in English, if necessary.

> MODÈLE: —*Mon acteur préféré s'appelle: J-A-M-I-E* nouveau mot *F-O-X-X*
>
> —*Il s'appelle Jamie Foxx?*
>
> —*Oui, c'est ça!*

1. acteur / actrice
2. auteur / poète
3. réalisateur *(movie director)*
4. présentateur de télévision *(news anchor)*
5. athlète
6. professeur
7. chanteur

À vous de parler!

A. Présentations. Greet five classmates, doing the following:

- Say hello, tell them your name, and ask them their name.
- Ask how they are; tell them how you are.
- Say goodbye. Use a variety of expressions.

Then greet your professor, and ask him/her how s/he is. *Pay attention to the expressions and pronouns you use for a peer versus those you use for your professor.*

> MODÈLE: —*Salut! Je m'appelle Philippe. Et toi, comment tu t'appelles?*
>
> —*Bonjour, Philippe. Je suis Robert. Comment ça va?*
>
> —*Ca va bien, merci! Au revoir, Robert.*
>
> —*Au revoir, Philippe!*

Les Baux de Provence.
Des étudiants en Provence. Pensez à trois questions logiques entre les étudiants.

Les Baux de Provence is a medieval village located in the south of France.

Le saviez-vous? (Did you know it?)

Petit lexique utile (Useful lexical terms)

s'embrasser = to kiss on the cheeks or the mouth

une bise, un bisou ou un baiser = a kiss on either the cheek or the mouth

un bisou sur la joue = a light kiss on the cheek

un baiser sur la bouche = a kiss on the mouth

Attention! Never say **baiser** without **un** before it when you want to say a kiss! **Baiser** by itself means to have intercourse in slang! Since we are talking about slang, do you know how the French say to give someone a French kiss? They say **rouler un patin**, literally, to spin the wheel of a roller skate! Finally, to say to shake hands in French, we say **se serrer la main** (literally, to squeeze each other's hand).

B. Conversations. Form groups of three or four, and introduce yourself to your classmates. Ask each classmate how to spell his/her name, and write it down. Continue the conversation.

MODÈLE: —*Bonjour, je m'appelle Karine Blondeau. Et toi?*

—*Je m'appelle Raïsa Haj.*

—*Raïsa Haj. Comment ça s'épelle?*

—*Raïsa: R-A-I tréma-S-A Haj: H-A-J. Et Karine, comment ça*
—*s'épelle?*

—*Karine: K-A-R-I-N-E Blondeau: B-L-O-N-D-E-A-U.*

—*Enchantée, Karine. Comment vas-tu?*

—*Je vais bien, merci. Et toi, ça va?*

—*Ça va pas mal, merci.*

Online Study Center
Web Search Activities

Les francophones se saluent comme ça

The use of personal space differs widely from one culture to another. In general, personal space is not as restricted in the Francophone cultures as it is in the United States. Body contact occurs much more often in the Francophone world. Nevertheless, there are differences in typical greetings throughout the Francophone world.

Les Tunisiens: In Tunisia, people greet each other differently depending on whether they come from the capital, Tunis, or from a small town or village. In Tunis, friends and family members kiss each other on both cheeks when saying hello and goodbye: men kiss both men and women, and women also kiss women and men. This is called **faire la bise** in French, and it is not at all romantic. In small towns and villages in Tunisia, greetings are essentially the same except that after kissing on both cheeks, Tunisians hug each other for a long time. If Tunisians have just been introduced to each other, they shake hands; this is true for both men and women.

Les Canadiens: In Canada, French Canadian friends hug each other like Americans do. In some families, relatives kiss each other on both cheeks. Men who are related tend to shake hands when greeting one another. When meeting for the first time, both men and women shake hands.

Les Belges, les Suisses et les Français: The way Belgian, Swiss, and French people greet each other

among friends and family members is very similar. In all three countries, men and women kiss each other on the cheeks. **La bise** is exchanged between women, between men and women, and occasionally between male family members. In general, however, men tend to shake hands when greeting one another.

The main distinction between greetings in Belgium, Switzerland, and France lies in the number of kisses exchanged. Belgians tend to give three kisses, Parisians two (but people in the South of France give up to five kisses!), and the Swiss two. They rarely hug, unless it is a romantic long hug followed or preceded by a kiss on the mouth!

When meeting for the first time, people in all three countries usually shake hands, but women will occasionally exchange **la bise**—this is especially true if a woman is introducing one close friend to another close friend and it is assumed that they will also share a friendship.

When leaving, people once again kiss one another on the cheeks. In fact, it is considered rude not to say goodbye to each person individually!

🗣 Réfléchissons

With a partner, discuss the following questions. When you have finished, share your responses with the whole class to see if you are all in agreement.

1. How do American friends and family members greet one another? Do you kiss and hug family members when greeting them? Do you do so in public, or only at home? What about among your friends? Are there differences depending on whether the person that you are greeting is a man or a woman?
2. How do you greet someone that you are meeting for the first time? Would you ever hug or kiss that person? Under what circumstances?
3. List all the differences that you can think of in typical greetings between Americans and between people in the Francophone groups listed in the reading.
4. Francophone speakers often have a different sense of personal space than Americans. When talking to each other they tend to stand quite close. How is the sense of personal space in your country? Are you uncomfortable when someone is too close to you? Why?

After hearing students' responses to these questions, discuss with them how important it is not to stereotype persons of other cultures. While it is tempting to make generalizations about other cultures, we must realize that they are simply that—generalizations—and do not necessarily apply to every member of the culture. Illustrate this point by explaining some French stereotypes about Americans (they all live in big houses; they're superficial; they smile all the time, etc.).

Continuons!

Au restaurant universitaire

SOPHIE:	Ah! Mathieu, Caroline et Bernadette—bonjour! Comment allez-vous?
MATHIEU, CAROLINE ET BERNADETTE:	Salut, Sophie, ça va bien, et toi?
SOPHIE:	Moi, ça va super bien! Je vous présente Nathalie et Éric.
BERNADETTE:	Bonjour, je suis Bernadette.
CAROLINE:	Et moi, c'est Caroline, et voilà Mathieu.
NATHALIE ET ÉRIC:	Bonjour, tout le monde![1]
SOPHIE:	Vous êtes libres ce week-end? Je fais une fête chez moi samedi.[2]
BERNADETTE:	Chouette! J'adore danser!
ÉRIC:	Moi aussi!
MATHIEU:	Dis, Sophie, quel est ton numéro de téléphone?
SOPHIE:	C'est le 05.18.30.26.12. À samedi!

---

[1] *Hello, everyone!* [2] *I am having a party at my place on Saturday.*

Vous avez bien compris?

A. Answer the following questions about the preceding dialogue. In some cases, more than one response is possible; list all that you find.

1. Based on the drawings, what body language accompanies greetings in French? How do women greet other women? And how do men greet one another?
2. How do we ask *Are you free (to do something)?*
3. How do we ask for a friend's telephone number?
4. How do we respond?
5. In previous dialogues we have seen different ways to say goodbye. What is another way used in this dialogue? What do you think this expression means?

B. Now let's go one step further! Fill in the blanks (in French!) according to the dialogue.

1. Une expression pour présenter des amis: _____
2. Sophie fait une _____ samedi.
3. Bernadette adore _____. Éric adore _____ aussi.
4. Le numéro de téléphone de Sophie c'est le _____.

Vocabulaire essentiel

Présentations

To present people to someone you call **tu:**

Je te présente _____ (et _____). (Et voilà _____.)
(Michel …), c'est _____.

To present people to someone you call **vous:**

Je vous présente _____ (et _____). (Et voilà _____.)
(Madame Leclair), c'est _____.

To introduce yourself:

Je m'appelle …
Je suis …
Moi, c'est …

Online Study Center
Flashcards, ACE, Language Skills Practice

Des projets

To ask if someone is free to do something:

For someone you call **tu:**	Tu es libre …?
For someone you call **vous:**	Vous êtes libre …?
For a group of people:	Vous êtes libre**s**?

To talk about time:

ce matin	*this morning*
ce soir	*this evening*
ce week-end	*this weekend*
aujourd'hui	*today*

To ask someone for his or her telephone number:

For a person you call **tu:**	Quel est ton numéro de téléphone?
For a person you call **vous:**	Quel est votre numéro de téléphone?
To answer:	C'est le …

À vous!

A. Que dit-on? *(What do we say?)* Consider the following situations, and indicate if the speaker would most likely use **je te présente** or **je vous présente** to make the introduction.

1. student introducing his girlfriend to his parents
2. student introducing her best friend to her roommate
3. student introducing three apartment-mates to her father
4. student introducing his father to his professor
5. you introducing your parents to the president of the university

B. Finissons la conversation! *(Let's finish the conversation!)* Complete the following dialogues in a logical way. Then, compare your responses with those of a partner.

1. CHRISTINE: Bonjour, Joël. Comment vas-tu?
   JOËL: _____, et toi?
   CHRISTINE: Je vais bien, merci. Joël, _____ Lucie.
   Lucie, c'est Joël.
   JOËL: Bonjour, Lucie.
   LUCIE: Enchantée, Joël.
   CHRISTINE: Vous _____ ce week-end? Allons *(Let's go)*
   au cinéma.
   JOËL ET LUCIE: Oui, bonne idée!

2. SIMON: Excusez-moi, Monsieur Leclair. _____
   Madame Amon.
   MONSIEUR LECLAIR: Bonjour, Madame.
   MADAME AMON: _____, Monsieur. _____?
   MONSIEUR LECLAIR: Je vais très bien, merci.

Tu es libre ce week-end? Ces personnes sont libres. Et toi?

This is a photo of Omaha Beach in Normandy. It was one of the D-Day beaches in World War II, but is now used for recreation once again.

Structure 3

Les chiffres de 0 à 30

Online Study Center
ACE, Language Skills
Practice

Here are the numbers in French from 0 to 30. Memorize the spelling and make sure that you take some time to practice the pronunciation.

0	zéro	10	dix	20	vingt
1	un	11	onze	21	vingt et un
2	deux	12	douze	22	vingt-deux
3	trois	13	treize	23	vingt-trois
4	quatre	14	quatorze	24	vingt-quatre
5	cinq	15	quinze	25	vingt-cinq
6	six	16	seize	26	vingt-six
7	sept	17	dix-sept	27	vingt-sept
8	huit	18	dix-huit	28	vingt-huit
9	neuf	19	dix-neuf	29	vingt-neuf
				30	trente

VÉRIFIEZ VOTRE COMPRÉHENSION

Much of language learning is paying attention to patterns that are repeated. What patterns can you find in the numbers 1–30 in French? In what ways are they similar to or different from the corresponding English numbers?

À l'écoute!

Listen to the following sentences, and indicate the number that is used in each one.

MODÈLE:

You hear:
—Mathieu, tu as combien de cousins?

—J'en ai sept.

("Matthew, how many cousins do you have?"
"I have seven [of them].")

You check: __✓__ 7 _____ 17

1. _____ 6 _____ 16
2. _____ 2 _____ 12
3. _____ 13 _____ 3
4. _____ 9 _____ 2
5. _____ 4 _____ 14
6. _____ 12 _____ 10
7. _____ 16 _____ 6
8. _____ 30 _____ 13

Transcript: 1. Bernadette, tu as combien de cousins? J'en ai six. 2. Caroline, tu as combien de cousins? J'en ai deux. 3. Robert, tu as combien de cousins? J'en ai trois. 4. Philippe, tu as combien de cousins? J'en ai neuf. 5. Sophie, tu as combien de cousins? J'en ai quatorze. 6. Éric, tu as combien de cousins? J'en ai douze. 7. Simon, tu as combien de cousins? J'en ai seize. 8. Nathalie, tu as combien de cousins? J'en ai treize.

For added practice, have students read both numbers in each item out loud, paying attention to how their meaning changes if they say "J'en ai *deux*" or "J'en ai *douze*." Then have them tell how many cousins they have. (If they have more than 30, have them consider only one side of the family.)

Choose the amounts for each check, making sure to include those numbers that routinely cause problems for students because of either pronunciation or orthography.

Pratiquons!

A. Ça coûte … *(That costs . . .)* Imagine that you are shopping, and you have decided to pay by check. Your instructor will give you a number. Fill out the checks in the spaces provided. Write down the numbers in letters *and* in numbers, the way you would on an American check.

MODÈLE: Your instructor says: *Ça coûte 23 euros.*

You write: **23** on the first line and **_vingt-trois_** on the second line.

1.

2.

3.

4.

5.

6.

7.

8.
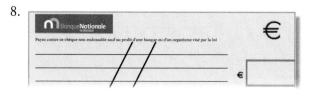

9.
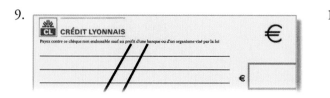

10.

B. C'est combien? *(How much is it?)* With a partner, take turns asking and telling how much the following items cost, using the prices that you see on the tags. Follow the model.

MODÈLE:

18 €

—*C'est combien?*
—*C'est dix-huit euros.*

1. **4 Francs Suisses**
2. **22 DIRHAMS**
3. **16 Dinars**
4. **9€**
5. **12 €**
6. **21 Francs Suisses**
7. **30€**
8. **17 DIRHAMS**
9. **25€**
10. **11 Dinars**

À vous de parler!

A. Contacts. Go around the class and introduce yourself to five classmates. Ask them how they are doing. Tell them how you are doing. Get their first names (**prénoms**) and their phone numbers and write them down in the spaces provided. If you do not know how to spell a name, ask your classmate to spell it out for you: **Comment ça s'épelle?** Say *goodbye, see you later, see you soon,* etc. Finally, read each telephone number out loud. The person whose phone number you just read will say «**Allô? Bonjour!**»

1. Prénom _____ Numéro de téléphone _____
2. Prénom _____ Numéro de téléphone _____
3. Prénom _____ Numéro de téléphone _____
4. Prénom _____ Numéro de téléphone _____
5. Prénom _____ Numéro de téléphone _____

B. Je te présente … Based on the information you gathered in activity A, introduce several of your classmates to other classmates and to your teacher.

- Use a variety of expressions to introduce one another.
- Use a French gesture when being introduced (i.e., shake hands, kiss, etc., as you feel is appropriate).

MODÈLE: —*Daniel, je te présente Robert.*
—*Bonjour, Robert. Enchanté.*
—*Enchanté. Voilà Suzanne.*
—*Bonjour, Suzanne.*
—*Enchantée!*

From this point on, start using French numbers to refer to pages in the textbook and Student Activities Manual (SAM). Avoid the temptation to translate into English: using only French will force students to make these numbers part of their active vocabulary. (If necessary, write the number on the board rather than translating.)

Because security and privacy are always an issue, for activities such as this, encourage students to change their phone numbers.

Dans un parc à Québec. Est-ce que ces femmes utilisent **tu** ou **vous?** Expliquez votre réponse.

C. Jeu de rôles *(Role-play).* In groups of three, create a role-play dialogue in which you each adopt a specific role (student[s], professor[s], colleague[s], etc.).

- Greet and introduce one another and have a basic conversation.
- Pay specific attention to the different forms of the expressions that you use, depending on whether you would call one another **tu** or **vous.**
- Try to use a variety of expressions, to make your dialogue as interesting as possible.

 MODÈLE: —*Professeur Micah, je suis Caroline Richard. Et voici Paul Trudeau.*

—*Bonjour!*

—*Bonjour, Professeur Micah. Comment allez-vous?*

—*Bien, merci. Et vous, comment allez-vous?*

—*Je vais très bien, merci. À demain, Monsieur—je suis dans votre classe!*

—*Très bien! À demain!*

Online Study Center
Web Search Activities

Les universités en France sont comme ça!

Universities in France resemble those in the United States in many ways, but differ substantially in other ways. Students in France who wish to study at the university level must pass **le bac** (the **baccalauréat** exam) in high school. A passing score on this exam gives them admission to any university of their choice; otherwise, admission is not allowed. In this way, admission is more restricted than in the U.S., where no national standards exist. (Individual universities in the U.S. determine their own admission policies, often based on SAT or ACT scores, but also have policies to admit students who have not taken such exams.) In France, not only is **le bac** required, but there are different exams based on the intended major of the student. There is a **bac-sciences,** for those who want to major in the natural sciences, and a **bac-lettres,** for those wanting to major in the humanities or social sciences, for example. The exam that a student takes determines which major(s) s/he will be allowed to pursue at the university level.

The French university system has undergone important changes in the last several years in order to make its degrees conform with those granted by other European universities. Under the new system, students from other European Union countries can study in France and obtain the equivalent of a diploma from their own country, and vice versa. In 2005 the French university system adopted the LMD reform. LMD stands for **Licence** (a three-year degree), **Master** (a five-year degree), and **Doctorat** (a six- to nine-year degree).

In France, the cost of a college education is much lower than in the United States for several reasons. First, all universities are controlled by the national government, and tuition is the same at all. Because France is a socialist republic, these fees are very low, consisting of only a small "per credit" fee for each course taken. There is no competition between private and public universities, and no fees other than those for the classes that the student is taking. Every student enrolled in a university gets health insurance.

Student life is also different in substantial ways in France. All universities have dormitories **(la cité universitaire,** or **la cité U)** and cafeterias **(la cafète, le restaurant universitaire,** or **le restau U),** but many students choose to attend the university that is closest to their home, and therefore continue to live at home with their families. Those who live in dormitories tend to stay there through the week, and then go home on the weekend. For these reasons, in addition to the fact that many of the universities are located in urban areas, campuses as we know them in the United States generally do not exist in France. Buildings are usually grouped in the same general area of town, but are intermixed with local businesses and residential areas. In this way, the university is not set apart from the town in which it is located, but is an integral part of it. Finally, intramural and club sports are popular at most universities, but there are no interuniversity sports—students are at the university to study, and sports have no prominence. Students find other reasons to come together—concerts, lectures, discussions at the local café—rather than gathering around a weekend football game!

With all these differences, how can we say that French universities are similar to their American counterparts? They offer courses in many disciplines, preparing students for professional careers of all sorts. They bring together students from many different ethnicities, social classes, nationalities, and backgrounds, both those with a family tradition of attending college and those who are the first generation in their family to earn a college degree. And perhaps most importantly, they provide a natural setting for conferences, concerts, poetry readings, debates, and the like, and in this way serve as a major cultural magnet for the town in which they are located, which often derives much of its identity from the college located there.

You may want to describe for students the French university degrees that were granted prior to the adoption of the LMD in 2005. The old degrees are being phased out, but most French universities still grant them, and they are still considered valid. Students may obtain **le DEUG (diplôme d'études universitaires générales)** (a two-year degree), **la Licence** (a three-year degree), **la Maîtrise** (a four-year degree) or **le DEA (diplôme d'études approfondies),** and **le DESS (diplôme d'enseignement secondaire supérieur).**

Réfléchissons

Answer the following questions based on the cultural reading.

1. What is your opinion of a national standardized exam that is mandatory for admission to college? Does this help to assure quality among the universities in the country, or does it limit access? Would you be in favor of such an exam in the U.S.?

2. What do you think of a national educational system that covers *all* educational levels, from preschool through college? Are there advantages that you can think of to not having private and public universities? What about disadvantages?

3. Are you surprised that there are no interuniversity sports in France (or in Europe, for that matter)? How would your university change if it had only club sports?

4. Imagine that you have decided to study abroad for a semester. What similarities do you think you would find between students in France and yourself? What differences?

**Online Study Center**
Language Skills Practice

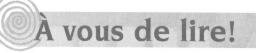
À vous de lire!

A. Stratégies. Before reading, you should determine what your purpose for reading is, as this will change the way that you read. There are many ways that we can read: we can skim a passage to determine if it meets our interests, we can scan it to see if it has particular information that we are looking for, or we can read it in depth for complete understanding. Before you start to read, look at the activities provided with the reading passage to see what your goal is. If you are supposed to skim for general comprehension or scan for specific information, but you try to read for complete understanding, you may experience a frustration that was not intended! Likewise, if you only scan an article but the questions require complete comprehension, you may be unable to answer them. Determine your purpose before reading, then read as necessary with that purpose in mind.

Answer Key: *Answers will vary.*

B. Avant de lire. The readings in this section come from the official web sites for several French universities. Before reading, answer the following questions, then move on to activity C.

1. Have you ever looked at the official web site for your university? If so, what type of information did you find on it? Check the items in the following list that were included on your university web site. (If you have not looked, try to guess what information might be included.)

_____ Types of courses offered	_____ Date of sessions
_____ Information about the town	_____ Student opinions
_____ Photos of students	_____ Photos of professors
_____ Degrees offered	_____ Student grades
_____ Links to area newspapers	_____ Samples of exams
_____ Dates of exams	_____ Sporting events

2. When and why do you read your university's web site? What kind of information are you generally looking for? Why would you consult *another* university's web site?
3. What do you think the target audience for university web sites is? Do the web sites serve more than one potential audience? In what ways?
4. Look at the ad for the Sorbonne. It lists four different sessions: **Session d'*automne*, session d'*hiver*, session de *printemps*,** and **session d'*été*.** What do you think the difference is between these sessions? (Hint: Let your knowledge of English guide you!)
5. In the Sorbonne ad, what other unfamiliar words can you figure out the meaning of, based on your knowledge of vocabulary from this chapter and of English?

C. Lisons! Read the following web sites in stages, answering the following questions. There will be many words that you have not yet seen; concentrate on figuring out what you can, using words that you saw in this chapter, words that ressemble English words (we call these "cognates"), and words that you can figure out from the context. The rest will take care of itself!

Answer Key: 1a. Types of courses offered, admission requirements, dates of sessions, international students; b. specializations of the university, international students, French students; c. specializations of the university, French students

1. First, *skim* each web site briefly to understand the general nature of its message. Check the item(s) that best represent(s) the information included, and the intended audience.

   a. La Sorbonne:

   Information included:
   _____ Types of courses offered
   _____ Information about Paris
   _____ Information about student housing
   _____ Admission requirements
   _____ Specializations of the university
   _____ Dates of sessions

   Intended audience:
   _____ Parents of students
   _____ International students
   _____ French students

   b. Université de Nantes:

   Information included:
   _____ Types of courses offered
   _____ Information about Nantes
   _____ Information about student housing
   _____ Admission requirements
   _____ Specializations of the university
   _____ Dates of sessions

   Intended audience:
   _____ Parents of students
   _____ International students
   _____ French students

   c. Université Montpellier 1:

   Information included:
   _____ Types of courses offered
   _____ Information about Montpellier
   _____ Information about student housing
   _____ Admission requirements
   _____ Specializations of the university
   _____ Dates of sessions

   Intended audience:
   _____ Parents of students
   _____ International students
   _____ French students

2. Now *scan* each web site for more specific information, answering the questions that follow.

2a. French civilization; grammar, phonetics, and French civilization; morning or afternoon throughout the year;
b. humanities and social sciences, science and technology, law, economics, health, technology;
c. students interested in humanities and social sciences, fine arts, communication, etc.; d. Montpellier 1; e. health (sciences)

a. What exactly would you study if you went to the Sorbonne to do the program presented on this web page? What courses would you take? When would those courses take place?

b. What type of specialization could you pursue at the Université de Nantes?

c. For whom would the Université de Montpellier *not* be a good choice (i.e., what majors are you not likely to find there, based on the specializations listed on this web page)?

d. If you wanted to study sports and sports medicine, which of these universities would be your best choice?

e. Both the Université de Nantes and the Université Montpellier 1 list **santé** as one of their areas of specialization. What do you think this term might mean, based on the information that follows it on the Université Montpellier 1 web site?

Cours de Civilisation Française de la Sorbonne

Les cours

Les Cours de Civilisation Française de la Sorbonne s'adressent aux étudiants étrangers[1]. Ils comprennent des «cours pratiques» de grammaire, de la phonétique en laboratoire et des conférences de civilisation française.

EXAMENS à la fin de chaque session:

* * * * * *

☞ CERTIFICATS—DIPLÔMES
Activités annexes: visites de musées, excursions.

☞ CONDITIONS D'ADMISSION
- 18 ans minimum
- Équivalence officielle du Baccalauréat français
- Visa de long séjour pour les pays hors Union européenne (faire une «demande de pré-inscription» par courrier).

☞ DATES ET HEURES DE COURS
Session d'automne
Dates: de septembre à décembre.
Inscriptions: début septembre.
Heures des cours:
Grammaire, phonétique: l'après-midi.
Conférences: 12h–13h.

Session d'hiver
Dates: d'octobre à janvier.
Inscriptions: fin septembre.
Heures des cours:
Grammaire, phonétique: matin ou après-midi au choix; + cours du soir.
Conférences: matin ou après-midi selon niveau.

Session de printemps
Dates: de février à mai.
Inscriptions: fin janvier.
Heures des cours:
Grammaire, phonétique: matin ou après-midi au choix; + cours du soir.
Conférences: matin ou après-midi selon niveau.

Session d'été
Dates: entre juin et septembre 4, 6, 8 ou 11 semaines.
Inscriptions: 1 semaine avant chaque session.
Grammaire, phonétique: le matin.
Conférences: l'après-midi.

☞ PROGRAMMES DÉTAILLÉS ET TARIFS SUR DEMANDE.

---

[1]*internationaux*

L'université de Nantes

Avec ses 32 000 étudiants, l'Université de Nantes est la 4e de France. Elle est composée de 6 ensembles: Lettres et sciences humaines, Sciences et techniques, Droit, Sciences économiques, Santé, Technologie.

Chaque ensemble se compose lui-même d'UFR (Unités de formation et de recherche). Vous en trouverez la liste complète sur la page d'accueil du site web.

L'université de Nantes accueille chaque année plus de 2750 étudiants étrangers venant de 110 pays du monde. Ouverte vers l'extérieur avec plus de 100 accords internationaux, elle a fait de l'internationalisation de la formation une de ses priorités.

Elle compte 73 équipes de recherche, dont beaucoup travaillent dans des secteurs de pointe, par exemple en recherche médicale (immunologie, traitement des cancers, nutrition), robotique, sciences des matériaux, sciences de la mer, sciences sociales.

Université Montpellier 1

Forte d'une longue tradition en matière médicale et juridique, l'Université Montpellier 1 a su préserver ses caractéristiques tout en s'ouvrant au monde du XXIème siècle. Université pluridisciplinaire, ce sont les UFR (Unités de formation et recherche) et Instituts regroupant une à plusieurs disciplines fondamentales qui organisent les enseignements autour de trois axes principaux:

Autour de l'axe droit, économie, gestion, et administration, se regroupent:
- l'UFR de Droit
- l'UFR d'Administration Économique et Sociale (AES)
- l'UFR de Sciences Économiques
- l'Institut Supérieur de l'Entreprise de Montpellier (ISEM)
- l'Institut de Préparation à l'Administration Générale (IPAG)

Autour de l'axe Santé, se regroupent:
- l'UFR de Médecine
- l'UFR d'Odontologie
- l'UFR de Sciences Pharmaceutiques et Biologiques

Autour de l'axe Sport, s'est développée jusqu'ici:
- l'UFR Sciences et Techniques des Activités Physiques et Sportives (STAPS)

Answer Key: *Answers will vary.*

D. Après la lecture. Answer the questions that follow, based on the information that you learned while reading.

1. Think back to the information that you predicted would appear on a university web site. Do these sites provide that information, in general? In what ways did they provide or not provide what you expected to find?

2. Based on your own interests, would one of these programs interest you more than others? Which one, and why?

3. How do these universities compare to American universities, based on what you read? In what ways are they different?

4. What parts of American university life are not represented on these web pages? Why do you think this is the case? (Is it because they are not part of French university life, or are they simply not mentioned on this page?)

5. What percentage of these sites would you say that you were able to read in French? Does this surprise you?

As students answer these questions, encourage them not to form judgments about French universities based on just one web page from each. Remind them that no web page contains all the information about an institution, but provides links to further sites that couldn't be presented here. Therefore, students might get a snapshot of a university, but will not get the entire picture unless they go further on their own. Encourage them to do so before judging the universities!

Lexique 🎧

Salutations *greetings and goodbyes*

À bientôt. *See you soon.*
À demain. *See you tomorrow.*
À plus. / À plus tard. *See you later.*
À tout à l'heure. *See you in a while.*

Au revoir. *Goodbye.*
Bonjour. *Hello.*
Ciao. *See you.*
Salut. *Hi. / Bye. (informal)*

The vocabulary in most chapters of this text is divided into **Vocabulaire essentiel** (i.e., vocabulary that all students are expected to learn and be able to use productively) and **Expansion personnelle** (terms that students often ask for, and that are not provided in many texts). Encourage students to choose the vocabulary that is relevant to them from the **Expansion personnelle** section, and to learn those words for productive use; the rest they should be able to recognize after completing the activities in the text and the SAM—even if they can't use them productively. All vocabulary in this chapter is considered **vocabulaire essentiel** as it is essential to basic communication in French.

Présentations *introductions*

Comment tu t'appelles? / Comment t'appelles-tu? *What is your name? (informal)*
Comment vous appelez-vous? *What is your name? (formal)*
Enchanté. / Enchantée. *It's nice to meet you. (masculine / feminine)*
Excusez-moi. *Excuse me.*
Je m'appelle … *My name is …*
Je suis … *I am …*

Moi, c'est … *Me, my name is … / Me, I am …*
Pardon, Madame / Monsieur / Mademoiselle. *Excuse me, ma'am / sir / young lady.*
Pardonnez-moi. *Pardon me.*
Qui es-tu? *Who are you? (informal)*
Qui êtes-vous? *Who are you? (formal)*
Tu es … ? *Are you … ?*

Je te présente … *This is … (informal) (literally: I present … to you.)*
Je vous présente … *This is … (formal) (literally: I present … to you.)*
(Madame Leclair), c'est … *(Mrs. Leclair), this is …*
et voilà … *and here is …*

Questions sur l'état général *questions about general state of being*

Ça va? *Is it going okay? Is everything okay?*
Ça va. *It's going okay.*
Comme ci, comme ça. *So-so.*
Comment ça va? *How is it going?*
Ça va bien. *It's going well.*

Ça va pas mal. *It's going all right.*
Ça peut aller. *It could be better.*
Comment allez-vous? *How are you?*
Je vais bien, merci. *I'm doing well, thank you.*
(Je vais) pas mal. *Not bad.*

Comment vas-tu? *How are you?*
Je vais bien, et toi? *I'm doing well, and you? / I'm good, and you?*
Très bien, merci. *Very good/well, thank you.*

Des projets *plans*

aujourd'hui *today*
ce matin *this morning*
ce soir *this evening*
ce week-end *this weekend*
Quel est ton numéro de téléphone? *What's your phone number? (informal)*

Quel est votre numéro de téléphone? *What's your phone number? (formal)*
C'est le … *It's …*
Tu es libre? *Are you free? (informal)*

Vous êtes libre? *Are you free? (formal, singular)*
Vous êtes libres? *Are you free? (plural)*

Je suis comme je suis

In this chapter you will learn how to describe yourself and others. You will also talk about your likes and dislikes.

The vocabulary that you will learn includes

Describing yourself and others
Talking about your personality
Talking about where you come from
More greetings
Formulating questions
Talking about leisure activities

The structures that you will learn include

The verbs **être** and **avoir**
Negation
Noun and adjective agreement
Regular **-er** verbs
Definite articles

The culture that you will study includes

A portrait of the French and Francophones

Commençons!

Je suis ...

In this chapter you will learn how to describe yourself and others and to talk about your hobbies and activities. First, meet the following people and Boulotte (the dog) as they describe themselves to you.

Alain
Je suis de Fort-de-France
    (Martinique).
Je suis grand.
Je suis sportif.
Je suis intelligent.
Je ne suis pas bavard.

Bébé Alex
Je suis de Bordeaux (France).
Je suis tout petit.
Je ne suis pas grand.
Je suis content.
Je suis gentil.
Je suis mignon!

Rhaimona
Je suis de Moorea (Tahiti).
Je suis petite.
Je suis sympathique.
Je suis mignonne.
Je suis intelligente.

Lucien
Je suis de Pointe-à-Pitre
    (Guadeloupe).
Je suis grand.
Je suis mince.
Je suis beau.
Je suis bavard.

Yolanda
Je suis de Montréal (Canada).
Je suis grande.
Je suis sportive.
Je suis contente.
Je suis bavarde et amusante.

Boulotte
Je suis de Toulouse
    (France).
Je suis fort.
Je suis méchant.
Je suis poilu.
Je suis courageux.

Vous avez bien compris?

Complete the following sentences based on the preceding descriptions. Since more than one response is possible in some cases, choose a logical one.

1. Yolanda: Je suis _____ et *(and)* je suis _____.
2. Lucien: Je suis _____.
3. Alex: Je suis _____ petit. Je ne suis pas _____.
4. Boulotte: Je suis _____.
5. Alain: Je suis _____. Je suis de _____.
6. Rhaimona: Je suis _____ et je _____ Moorea.

Now, Alain wants you to meet his friends, Anou and Gérard. He is describing them to you.

Anou
Elle est de Bruxelles (Belgique).
Elle est petite et mince.
Elle est élégante.
Elle est belle.
Elle n'est pas timide.

Gérard
Il est de Québec (Canada).
Il est grand.
Il est optimiste.
Il est bavard.
Il est gentil.

Online Study Center
Language Skills Practice

Answer Key. Possible answers:
1. grande / bavarde 2. beau
3. tout / grand 4. poilu 5. sportif / Fort-de-France 6. mignonne / suis de

In this activity, students have to go back to the descriptions to fill in the blanks. Since more than one response is possible, ask students to give you other adjectives that apply to each person. Students have been exposed to the differences in pronunciation between masculine and feminine adjectives, so make sure that they pronounce these adjectives correctly right away. Model the correct way by having them listen to the In-Text Audio CD.

Vous avez bien compris?

Vrai ou faux? *(True or false?)* Indicate whether the following statements about Anou and Gérard are **vrai** ou **faux.** Correct the sentences that are not true.

1. Gérard n'est pas bavard. ____ vrai ____ faux
2. Anou est grande. ____ vrai ____ faux
3. Anou n'est pas élégante. ____ vrai ____ faux
4. Gérard est pessimiste. ____ vrai ____ faux
5. Gérard est grand. ____ vrai ____ faux
6. Gérard n'est pas gentil. ____ vrai ____ faux
7. Anou est timide. ____ vrai ____ faux
8. Anou est belle. ____ vrai ____ faux

Make sure that students hear the differences between masculine and feminine adjectives and pronounce them correctly.

Answer Key: 1. faux: Il est bavard. 2. faux: Elle est petite. 3. faux: Elle est élégante. 4. faux: Il est optimiste. 5. vrai 6. faux: Il est gentil. 7. faux: Elle n'est pas timide. 8. vrai

Vocabulaire essentiel

Online Study Center
Flashcards, ACE, Language
Skills Practice

Les adjectifs descriptifs (1)

Following is a list of physical and emotional descriptors. Some of these words you are already familiar with from the descriptions in *Commençons!;* others will be new to you. Can you guess the meaning of the new words? Many of them are cognates, so they are very similar to their English equivalents. You will find translations next to the words that are not cognates. The following adjectives are the same in their masculine and feminine forms.

optimiste	riche	triste	*sad*
pessimiste	pauvre	timide	
super	sympathique	jeune	*young*
stupide	antipathique *unfriendly*	mince	*thin*

The following adjectives are spelled differently in their masculine and feminine forms.

To talk about a male	*To talk about a female*	

beau	belle	
laid	laide	*ugly*
mignon	mignonne	
grand	grande	
petit	petite	
(tout) petit	(toute) petite	
vieux	vieille	*old*
sportif	sportive	
élégant	élégante	
bavard	bavarde	*talkative*
content	contente	*happy*
gentil	gentille	*nice*
méchant	méchante	*mean*
intelligent	intelligente	
courageux	courageuse	
poilu	poilue	*hairy*
fort	forte	*strong*
amusant	amusante	
ennuyeux	ennuyeuse	*boring*
provocateur	provocatrice	
gros	grosse	*big*

À vous!

A. Comment sont-ils? *(What are they like?)* Choose from the list provided the adjectives that best characterize the following famous personalities.

1.  Tom Cruise. Il est … (timide / mince / petit / sympa / élégant / beau / amusant / fort / intelligent / laid / mignon / méchant).

2. Céline Dion. Elle est … (ennuyeuse / gentille / belle / intelligente / amusante / pauvre / mince / poilue / jeune).

3.  Larry King. Il est … (riche / amusant / bavard / beau / poilu / intelligent / petit / élégant / laid / ennuyeux / vieux).

4. Oprah Winfrey. Elle est … (mince / très riche / optimiste / belle / amusante / élégante / intelligente / bavarde / sympathique).

5. 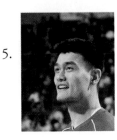 Yao Ming. Il est … (paresseux / gros / fort / laid / sportif / pauvre / grand / beau / mince / ennuyeux / amusant).

6. Michael Moore. Il est … (amusant / intelligent / provocateur / mince / courageux / élégant / beau / petit / optimiste).

7.  Julia Roberts. Elle est … (jolie / timide / sympathique / vieille / élégante / laide / mince / petite / ennuyeuse / jeune).

Now, compare the characteristics you gave to each one of the preceding celebrities with your classmates. Are you in agreement with your classmates?

B. Trouvez-les *(Find them).* First, look at the following drawings. Then, describe them to your classmate without following the numerical order in which they appear. Your classmate will tell you which drawing you are describing.

1.

2.

3.

4.

5.

6.

C. Et toi, tu es comment? *(And you, what are you like?)* Find out how your classmate views himself/herself. Your classmate will start his or her answers by saying **Je suis ...** *(I am . . .).*

MODÈLE: Tu es riche?
Non! Je suis pauvre! / Oui! Je suis très riche!

1. Tu es beau (belle)?
2. Tu es optimiste?
3. Tu es mince?
4. Tu es grand(e)?
5. Tu es méchant(e)?

6. Tu es intelligent(e)?
7. Tu es ennuyeux (ennuyeuse)?
8. Tu es intelligent(e)?
9. Tu es provocateur (provocatrice)?
10. Tu es content(e)?

Tell students that they should not answer just by saying **oui** or **non.** They need to find the opposite adjectives when appropriate, since they do not yet know how to negate a sentence in French. For example, for the first question, they could answer: **Oui, je suis beau** or **Non, je suis laid.** Remind students to use the feminine form of the adjective when the subject is a woman.

Now, share your partner's answers with the class to find out the following information.

1. Qui est le plus grand / la plus grande de la classe[1]? C'est[2] _____.
2. Qui est le plus mince / la plus mince de la classe? C'est _____.
3. Qui est le plus optimiste / la plus optimiste de la classe? C'est _____.
4. Qui est le plus content / la plus contente de la classe? C'est _____.

Structure 1

Le verbe *être* 🎧

As a follow-up to this activity you may want to ask students to give their opinion of celebrities. For example, you may ask the class: a. Qui est l'acteur de cinéma le plus beau? (If you use PowerPoint slides, have several photos of male actors. If not, bring in pictures from magazines.) b. Qui est la chanteuse la plus provocatrice? c. Qui est le réalisateur le plus riche? d. Qui est le philosophe / l'écrivain le plus pessimiste? e. Qui est le président le plus intelligent?

Online Study Center
ACE, Language Skills Practice

A verb, when you see it in the dictionary, is listed in its *infinitive* form. This is the form of the verb that is used when you do not want to specify a subject or a tense, for example, after another verb (*I want **to see** that movie*). In order to use most verbs, however, we need to conjugate them; that is, we need to put them in the appropriate form to agree with the subject we have chosen, and in the tense that we want to express (*I **want** vs. she **wants** vs. I **wanted**,* for example).

In French, we distinguish between irregular and regular verbs. First, you will learn the irregular verbs **être** and **avoir.** Irregular verbs do not follow any standard pattern of conjugation, and must be memorized individually. Regular verbs, on the other hand, are conjugated alike; therefore, once you learn how to conjugate one verb, you can apply the same pattern to other verbs that are like it. This makes it easy to use verbs that you have just learned, because you can predict what the forms will be.

To describe your personality and/or your physical features, use the verb **être** *(to be)*. For example: **je suis grand; je suis sympathique; je suis intelligente.**

Here is the conjugation of the verb **être.**

être	
je **suis**	*I am*
tu **es**	*you are*
il / elle / on **est**	*he / she / one is; we are*
nous **sommes**	*we are*
vous **êtes**	*you are*
ils / elles **sont**	*they (masc.) / they (fem.) are*

Subject pronouns in French (**je, tu, il, elle, on, nous, vous, ils, elles**) are indispensable in the sentence (unlike in Spanish, for example). You must always use them with verbs.

The pronoun **on** means *one* or *we.* For example:

On est content dans la classe de français.

One is happy in French class.
or
We are happy in French class.

_____
[1] *Who is the tallest in the class?* [2] *It is*

On is always conjugated in the third person singular, like he/she **(il/elle).**
The pronoun **ils** refers to a group of males, or a group composed of males and females. The pronoun **elles,** on the other hand, can be used only when you are talking about all females. Even when there is only one male in the group, **ils** is still used. For example:

> Catherine, Sylvie, Patricia et Roger sont français; ils sont sympathiques.
> *Catherine, Sylvie, Patricia, and Roger are French; they are friendly.*

To indicate what city you are from, use **être de: je suis de Paris, je suis de Québec, je suis de Genève.** Before a city that starts with an **h** or a vowel, use **être d': je suis d'Abidjan, je suis d'Angers.**

La négation: *ne ... pas / n' ... pas*

To negate a sentence, use **ne ... pas** around the main verb. With a verb that starts with an **h** or a vowel, use **n' ... pas.** Compare the affirmative mode versus the negative in the following sentences.

Affirmative	*Negative*
Je suis riche.	Je **ne** suis **pas** riche.
Tu es optimiste.	Tu **n'**es **pas** optimiste.
Elle est belle.	Elle **n'**est **pas** belle.
Nous sommes grands.	Nous **ne** sommes **pas** grands.
Vous êtes bavards.	Vous **n'**êtes **pas** bavards.
Ils sont gentils.	Ils **ne** sont **pas** gentils.

VÉRIFIEZ VOTRE COMPRÉHENSION

1. Go back to the **Commençons!** section and look at the affirmative sentences and the negative ones. Pay attention to the order of the words.

2. How would you negate what Gérard says?

À l'écoute!

Before doing this activity, you may want to remind students that when there are both feminine and masculine nouns in a group, even if there is only one masculine noun, the gender of that group is masculine.

Transcript: 1. Elle est contente. 2. Vous êtes sympathique. 3. Nous sommes heureux. 4. Tu es intelligent. 5. Ils sont amusants. 6. Elles sont bavardes. 7. Je suis grand. 8. Vous êtes petits. 9. Il est mince. 10. Nous sommes françaises.

A. Answer Key: 1. F 2. F&M 3. F&M 4. M 5. F&M 6. F 7. M 8. F&M 9. M 10. F

A. Féminin ou masculin? Listen to the following sentences, and indicate whether the subject of each one is feminine (F) or masculine (M), or if it could be either or could represent a mixed group (F&M). Check the correct answer.

MODÈLE: You hear: *Je suis gentille.*

You check: ✓ F ____ M ____ F&M

1. ____ F	____ M	____ F&M
2. ____ F	____ M	____ F&M
3. ____ F	____ M	____ F&M
4. ____ F	____ M	____ F&M
5. ____ F	____ M	____ F&M
6. ____ F	____ M	____ F&M
7. ____ F	____ M	____ F&M
8. ____ F	____ M	____ F&M
9. ____ F	____ M	____ F&M
10. ____ F	____ M	____ F&M

B. Singulier ou pluriel? Listen to the following sentences. If the sentence is about one person, check S for singular. If it is about more than one person, check P for plural. Check the question mark if you can't tell. Attention! Sometimes you cannot distinguish singular and plural phonetically.

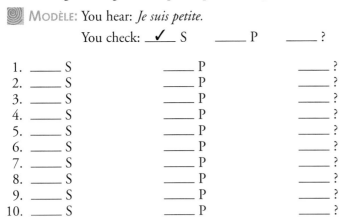 MODÈLE: You hear: *Je suis petite.*

You check: __✔__ S _____ P _____ ?

1. ____ S	____ P	____ ?
2. ____ S	____ P	____ ?
3. ____ S	____ P	____ ?
4. ____ S	____ P	____ ?
5. ____ S	____ P	____ ?
6. ____ S	____ P	____ ?
7. ____ S	____ P	____ ?
8. ____ S	____ P	____ ?
9. ____ S	____ P	____ ?
10. ____ S	____ P	____ ?

Before starting this activity, give examples of sentences in which number is not clear phonetically. Show students why the number can or cannot be heard in your examples. Examples: **Tu es pauvre** = S, **Vous êtes triste** = ?, etc.

Transcript: 1. Elle est belle. 2. Nous sommes sportives. 3. Ils sont beaux. 4. Il est intelligent. 5. Elles sont sympathiques. 6. On est bavard. 7. Vous êtes méchants. 8. Tu es canadienne. 9. Je suis jolie. 10. Tu es riche.

B. Answer Key: 1. S 2. P 3. P 4. S 5. P 6. ? 7. ? 8. S 9. S 10. S

Pratiquons!

A. Descriptions. Match the drawings with the sentences.

Answer Key: 1. d. 2. e. 3. f. 4. b. 5. c. 6. a.

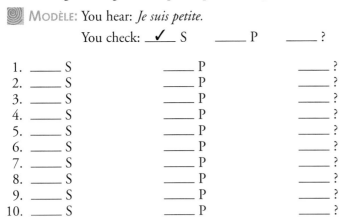 MODÈLE: *Il est gros.*

1.  2.

a. Ils sont tristes.
b. Elle est élégante.
c. Elles sont belles.
d. Il est mince.
e. Elle est toute petite.
f. Ils sont méchants.

3. 4. 5. 6.

B. Anou et sa famille *(Anou and her family).* Anou (whom you met at the beginning of the chapter) is talking about herself and her family. Fill in the blanks with the correct form of the verb **être.**

Bonjour! Je (1) _____ de Bruxelles. Mon mari[1], Jean, (2) _____ de Québec. Nous (3) _____ grands-parents. Alex (4) _____ notre petit-fils[2]. Patricia et Marine (5) _____ nos filles[3]. Elles (6) _____ très intelligentes et très belles! Patricia (7) _____ mariée. Et vous, vous (8) _____ mariés[4]?

C. Oui ou non. Say if the descriptions match the pictures or not. Correct the wrong descriptions. Follow the model.

MODÈLE:

Il est gentil.

You say: *Mais non! Il n'est pas gentil. Il est méchant!*

1. Il est mince.

2. Nous sommes timides.

3. Bernard et Marc sont pauvres.

4. Thomas est content.

5. Ils sont ennuyeux.

6. Sylvie et Corinne sont jeunes.

7. Monsieur Duros est gros.

---

[1] *husband* [2] *grandson* [3] *daughters* [4] *married*

Continuous!

Partie I: Des descriptions 🎧

Online Study Center
ACE, Language Skills
Practice

Now, some of the people you met previously are talking about their own physical features. They are describing themselves to you.

Bébé Alex
J'ai les cheveux châtains[1] et très courts.
J'ai les yeux bleus.
J'ai quatre dents[2].

Rhaimona
J'ai les cheveux noirs et lisses.
J'ai les yeux verts.
J'ai les cheveux longs.

Lucien
J'ai les yeux noirs.
J'ai les cheveux mi-longs et frisés.

Yolanda
J'ai les cheveux blonds et courts.
J'ai les yeux bleus.

Now, Lucien tells you what Anou and Gérard look like.

Anou
Elle a les cheveux blonds, courts et un peu[3] bouclés.
Elle a les yeux bleus.

Gérard
Il a les cheveux lisses et gris.
Il a les yeux noirs.

---

[1]The adjective **châtain** is always *masculine*. It is invariable in gender, i.e., it never adds an **-e.** However, it agrees in number with the noun: **les cheveux châtains.** [2]*teeth* [3]*a little bit*

Vous avez bien compris?

Qui est-ce? *(Who is it?)* Write the name of the person(s) who is (are) making the following statements about their physical appearance.

1. J'ai les cheveux très courts.   _____
2. J'ai les cheveux frisés.   _____
3. J'ai les cheveux mi-longs.   _____
4. J'ai les cheveux gris.   _____
5. J'ai les yeux verts.   _____
6. J'ai les yeux bleus.   _____

Vocabulaire essentiel

Online Study Center
Flashcards, ACE, Language
Skills Practice

Les adjectifs descriptifs (2)

Here are some adjectives for describing hair and eye color.

Les cheveux

bruns   noirs   roux

Les yeux

bleus   noirs

verts   marron[1]

---

[1]The adjective **marron** is always masculine. It is invariable, i.e., it never adds an **-e** or an **-s,** no matter the gender or number of the noun it is modifying.

À vous!

A. Cheveux et yeux. Look at the following people and decide which adjectives from the *Continuons!* and *Vocabulaire essentiel* sections fit them best.

MODÈLE:

Stéphane a …

Stéphane a les cheveux châtains et les yeux marron.

1. Alexandre a …

2.  Marie-Louise a …

3.  Laura a …

4.  Éric a …

Answer Key. Possible answers: 1. les cheveux châtains et les yeux marron 2. les cheveux bruns et les yeux noirs 3. les cheveux longs et les yeux marron 4. les cheveux blonds et les yeux marron

B. Devinez! *(Guess!)* Take turns describing one of your classmates to the class. The class will guess which student has been described.

MODÈLE: Il a les cheveux longs et blonds. Il a les yeux bleus. Il est très sympa et très beau!

You may have students use the vocabulary from the beginning of the chapter in addition to the vocabulary presented in this *Continuons!* section.

Structure 2

Le verbe *avoir*

When talking about possessions and parts of the body, use the verb **avoir** as you have seen in the *Continuons!* section: **j'ai les yeux bleus, j'ai les cheveux frisés.** Here is the conjugation of the verb **avoir.**

Online Study Center
ACE, Language Skills Practice

avoir		Negation
j'**ai**	*I have*	Je n'ai pas les
tu **as**	*you have*	cheveux lisses.
il / elle / on **a**	*he / she / one has*	
nous **avons**	*we have*	Nous n'avons pas
vous **avez**	*you have*	les yeux marron.
ils / elles **ont**	*they (masc.) / they (fem.) have*	

VÉRIFIEZ VOTRE COMPRÉHENSION

1. Go back to the **Continuons!** section (p. 37) and read the descriptions again.
2. How does Yolanda say *I have blue eyes?*
3. How does Lucien say about Anou that *she has short blond hair?*

Pratiquons!

Answer Key: 1. c. 2. d. 3. a. 4. f. 5. e. 6. b.

A. Qui a quoi? *(Who has what?)* Match each subject in the left column with an appropriate sentence completion in the right column. Make sure that the verb form agrees with the subject.

1. Frédéric
2. Les étudiants
3. Je (J')
4. Nous
5. Tu
6. Vous

a. ai les yeux marron.
b. avez les yeux noirs.
c. a les cheveux bouclés.
d. ont les cheveux roux.
e. as les cheveux très courts.
f. avons les yeux bleus.

Answer Key. Possible answers: 1. Laura n'a pas les cheveux frisés; elle a les cheveux lisses. Elle n'a pas les yeux bleus; elle a les yeux marron. 2. Alexandre n'a pas les cheveux longs; il a les cheveux courts. Il n'a pas les yeux noirs; il a les yeux marron. 3. Éric n'a pas les cheveux bruns; il a les cheveux blonds. Il n'a pas les yeux verts; il a les yeux marron. 4. Marie-Louise n'a pas les cheveux lisses; elle a les cheveux bouclés. Elle n'a pas les yeux bleus; elle a les yeux noirs.

B. Descriptions. Look at the following photos. For each one, first tell what kind of hair the person does *not* have, and then go on to describe the person's hair. Next, do the same thing for the person's eyes.

MODÈLE: Stéphane

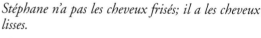

Stéphane n'a pas les cheveux frisés; il a les cheveux lisses.

Il n'a pas les yeux verts; il a les yeux marron.

1. Laura

2. Alexandre

3. Éric

4. Marie-Louise

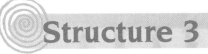

Structure 3

L'accord des adjectifs 🎧

Online Study Center
ACE, Language Skills
Practice

Look at the following descriptions:

Les yeux bleus et grands

Article[1]	Noun	Adjectives
Les	yeux *(m., pl.)*	bleus *(m., pl.)* et grands *(m., pl.)*

Patricia est intelligente et belle.

Subject	Adjectives
Patricia *(f., sing.)*	intelligente *(f., sing.)* et belle *(f., sing.)*

In French, articles and adjectives agree with the nouns they modify in gender (masculine / feminine) and in number (singular / plural). The feminine of regular adjectives is formed by adding an **e** to the masculine form, and the plural of both masculine and feminine adjectives is formed by adding an **s.** Look at the examples in the following chart.

Masculine singular	Feminine singular	Masculine plural	Feminine plural
grand	grande	grands	grandes
petit	petite	petits	petites
laid	laide	laids	laides
bavard	bavarde	bavards	bavardes
fort	forte	forts	fortes
vert	verte	verts	vertes

The following adjectives have a spelling change in the feminine form:

Masculine	Feminine
gentil	gentille
vieux	vieille
blanc	blanche
roux	rousse
beau	belle
courageux	courageuse
sportif	sportive
mignon	mignonne

This picture was taken in Marrakesh, Morocco.

C'est au Maroc *(Morocco)* ou en Côte d'Ivoire *(Ivory Coast)*?

[1]You will study the gender and number of the definite articles (**le, la, l', les**) later in this chapter.

Attention!

- Adjectives that end in **e (sympathique)** do not add an extra **e** for the feminine.
- Adjectives that end in **-eux (ennuyeux)** change **-eux** to **-euse** to form the feminine: **ennuyeuse.** Exception: **vieux** (masculine) → **vieille** (feminine).
- Adjectives that end in **-if (actif)** change **-if** to **-ive** in the feminine form: **active.**
- Adjectives that end in **-on (mignon)** double the final **-n** then add an **e** in the feminine: **mignonne.**
- Adjectives that end in **-eau** or **-au** form the plural by adding an **x** instead of an **s: beaux.**
- Adjectives that end in **-eux (ennuyeux)** do not add an **s** for the masculine plural: **ils sont ennuyeux** vs. **elles sont ennuyeuses.**
- When the adjectives **beau** and **vieux** are used before a masculine noun that starts with a vowel, they take the special forms **bel** and **vieil: un vieil homme, un bel homme**[1].

Ask students to do the *Vérifiez votre compréhension* at home. The next day of instruction, check students' answers. You may use this section as a warm-up activity.

VÉRIFIEZ VOTRE COMPRÉHENSION

1. Go back to the **Commençons!** section on p. 28 and find two adjectives that have the same form in the feminine and the masculine. Then find two adjectives that are spelled differently in the masculine and the feminine.

2. How would you write in French *she is generous, she is cute, they* **(ils)** *are boring,* and *they* **(ils)** *are old?*

Pratiquons!

Answer Key: 1. f. 2. b. 3. e. 4. c. 5. a. 6. d

A. Qui est-ce? *(Who is it?)* Look at the pictures and decide which person has the physical description listed. Write their names below their pictures.

1.
2.
3.

a. David a les cheveux longs et blonds.
b. Marianne a les cheveux tressés.
c. Renée et Andrée ont les cheveux lisses et les yeux bleus.
d. Folco a les poils noirs.
e. Pascal et Dominique ont les cheveux frisés.
f. Anne et Sophie ont les cheveux roux.

4.
5.
6.

---

[1]The **h** in French is silent; therefore, it is treated as if it were not there.

B. Descriptions.
Look at the pictures and describe the hair and eye color of each person. Use the appropriate form of the verb **avoir.**

MODÈLE: Elle

Elle a les cheveux lisses et les yeux noirs. Elle a les cheveux châtains.

1. Nous
2. Je
3. Elle
4. Il / Elle
5. Tu
6. Vous
7. Il

À l'écoute!

Online Study Center
ACE

Les verbes *être* et *avoir*
Distinguishing between the pronunciation of **être** and **avoir** can be difficult. It takes lots of practice listening not to confuse them.

Repeat the following sentences and phrases.

Tu es gentil.	Tu as les cheveux courts.
Tu es	Tu as
Il est grand.	Elle a les yeux noirs.
Il est	Elle a
Elles sont contentes.	Elles ont les cheveux bouclés.
Elles sont	Elles ont

Now, check the phrases that you hear.

1. _____ Tu es   _____ Tu as
2. _____ Ils ont   _____ Ils sont
3. _____ Elle a   _____ Elle est
4. _____ Il est   _____ Il a
5. _____ Elles sont   _____ Elles ont

À vous de parler!

A. Devinez! *(Guess!)* Describe a celebrity without saying his/her name. (Talk about height, personality, hair, and eyes.) Ask your classmates to guess who it is.

B. Cherchons … *(Let's look for . . .)* Find classmates who fit the following descriptions. Write their names next to the descriptions. Report back to the class on whom you found. Then talk a little bit about each student, mentioning his or her physical appearance and personality.

MODÈLE: You see: Une étudiante avec[1] les cheveux bruns et très courts.

You say: *Juliette a les cheveux bruns et très courts. Elle est sympathique et intelligente. Elle est très belle aussi!*

1. Une étudiante avec les cheveux blonds et longs.
2. Une étudiante avec les yeux verts.
3. Un étudiant avec les yeux bleus.
4. Une étudiante avec les cheveux roux.
5. Un étudiant ou une étudiante avec les cheveux bouclés.
6. Un étudiant bavard.
7. Une étudiante élégante.
8. Un étudiant et une étudiante amusants.
9. Une étudiante contente.
10. Un étudiant timide.

The *Portrait personnel* section is intended to serve as a free-writing activity (as opposed to the process writing activity that appears at the end of each even-numbered chapter). These sections appear periodically in all chapters, depending on the chapter themes. Space is allotted for students to write a short portrait of a person, with, at times, a comparison to themselves.

You may want to post these *Portraits personnels* on the Web (your class home page) and treat them as chats. At the end of the semester, students will have a class "portrait." You may ask students to turn in their writings once a week or to keep them all together and turn them in at the end of the semester, or you may use the information in these *Portraits* to start a discussion in class.

Portrait personnel

On a separate sheet of paper, write a short paragraph describing the classmate seated next to you. Talk about his or her physical features and personality. How do you compare with your classmate?

MODÈLES: Vivian a les cheveux noirs. J'ai les cheveux bruns.

or Ian est bavard. Je ne suis pas bavarde.

C'est en France ou aux États-Unis *(United States)*?
Beaubourg is in Paris in Le Centre Pompidou.

---

[1] *with*

Les Français et les francophones sont comme ça

Online Study Center
Web Search Activities

Vous allez connaître[1] de vrais[2] Français et francophones. Lisez[3] leurs descriptions physiques.

Elle est de Paris. Elle a les cheveux bruns, longs et lisses. Elle est très sympa. Elle a les yeux verts. Elle est petite et mince. Elle est jeune. Elle est étudiante à l'université.

Sandrine

Elle est de Tunis. Elle a les cheveux noirs, longs et lisses. Elle est grande et mince. Elle est amusante et sportive. Elle est mère de famille et femme au foyer[4]. Elle a trois enfants.

Rahma

Il est de Pointe-à-Pitre, Guadeloupe. Il est mince. Il est fort et sportif. Il est intelligent. Il est écrivain[5]. Il a les cheveux noirs et frisés. Il est mignon!

Alix

Il est canadien. Il a les cheveux gris. Il est gentil. Il est amusant. Il est beau! Il est acteur de théâtre.

Jean

Elle est de Genève (Suisse). Elle est femme d'affaires[6]. Elle a les cheveux longs. Elle est très intelligente. Elle a les yeux marron. Elle est jeune maman[7].

Ana

Réfléchissons

1. What are the Americans that you know like? Are they very different from the French/Francophone people that you just met? Explain your answer.
2. Do you have a stereotypical image of the French and Francophone people? When you think about a man/woman from France, what image comes to your mind? And a man/woman from Morocco or Tunisia? How about someone from the French Caribbean (Martinique, Guadeloupe)? Did the people you just met conform to the images you had in mind? How do you think that the French/Francophone people view Americans? What is the stereotypical image they may have? Why is it or is it not a good idea to stereotype?

Ask students if they can guess the meaning of the following idiomatic expressions about physical traits. Explain to them what idiomatic expressions are: expressions that cannot be translated literally or directly. Therefore, it can be very hard to guess what they mean. To say a man is very handsome: **Il est beau comme un dieu!** (He is as handsome as a god!) To say a woman is very beautiful: **Quel canon!** (What a cannon!) **Elle est belle comme un astre!** (She is as beautiful as a star!) To say someone is very strong: **Il (Elle) est fort(e) comme un taureau!** (He/She is as strong as a bull!) To say someone is very talkative: **Il (Elle) est bavard(e) comme une pie!** (He/She chatters like a magpie.) You may want to ask students what English idiomatic expressions they would use to say that someone is very beautiful, handsome, strong, or talkative.

---

[1] *You are going to meet* [2] *real* [3] *Read* [4] *housewife* [5] *writer* [6] *businesswoman* [7] *young mother*

Partie II: Mes préférences

In the preceding **Comme ça** section you met a few French and francophone people. Now they are going to tell you their likes and dislikes.

Bonjour, je m'appelle Rahma.
J'adore les bébés!
Je déteste le football américain!
Je préfère le cinéma.
Je préfère les films d'aventure et les
    films d'épouvante.

Bonjour. Je m'appelle Jean.
Je suis sportif et très actif.
J'aime le football américain.
J'aime les pièces de théâtre.
J'aime les films romantiques.

Salut! Je m'appelle Alix.
Je n'aime pas les films romantiques.
Je suis intelligent et sympathique.
J'aime le tennis, mais je n'aime pas
    le base-ball.
J'adore le rock.

Answer Key: 1. Alix 2. Rahma
3. Jean 4. Jean 5. Rahma
6. Jean 7. Alix

Vous avez bien compris?

Tell which people in the preceding **Continuons!** section have the following likes and dislikes.

1. Cette personne[1] *(f.)* n'aime pas le base-ball. _____

2. Cette personne adore les bébés. _____

3. Cette personne aime les films romantiques. _____

4. Cette personne aime les pièces de théâtre. _____

5. Cette personne n'aime pas le football américain. _____

6. Cette personne est sportive. _____

7. Cette personne aime beaucoup[2] le rock. _____

---

[1] *This person* [2] *a lot*

Vocabulaire essentiel

Online Study Center
Flashcards, ACE, Language
Skills Practice

Les sports et les passe-temps

le football/le foot

le football américain

le basket

le volley

le tennis

le rugby

l'athlétisme (*m.*[1])

la musculation

le yoga

le karaté

le base-ball

la natation

le judo

le golf

le surf

---

[1]This abbreviation indicates the gender (masculine or feminine) of a noun; see the explanation of definite articles
later in this chapter for more information.

Les films

les comédies *(f.)*, les comédies romantiques *(f.)*, les comédies musicales *(f.)*, les films d'aventure *(m.)*, les films d'épouvante *(m.)* / les thrillers *(m.)*, les films dramatiques *(m.)*, les films de science-fiction *(m.)*, les films policiers *(m.)*, les films de guerre *(m.) (war movies)*, les westerns *(m.)*, les films historiques *(m.)*

Le théâtre

Tell students that **théâtre** in French always refers to a live performance. **Le cinéma** is used for a movie theater.

les pièces (comiques, dramatiques) *(f.)*, l'opéra *(m.)*, les comédies musicales *(f.)*, le théâtre classique, le théâtre moderne, les pièces musicales *(f.)*

La musique

la musique classique, le rock, le jazz, le rap

À vous!

Answer Key: 1. *Notting Hill* / comédie romantique 2. *Troy* / film historique 3. *Silence of the Lambs* / film d'épouvante/ thriller 4. *2001: A Space Odyssey* / film de science-fiction 5. *Duplex* / comédie 6. *Saving Private Ryan* / film de guerre 7. *The Royal Tenenbaums* / comédie 8. *Van Helsing* / thriller/ film d'épouvante

A. Titres de films. Following is a list of movie titles. Guess the English title, and name the genre to which each belongs.

> MODÈLE: *L'Exorciste*
>
> *The Exorcist / film d'épouvante*

1. *Coup de foudre à Notting Hill*
2. *Troie*
3. *Le Silence des agneaux*
4. *2001: L'odyssée de l'espace*
5. *Duplex*
6. *Il faut sauver le soldat Ryan*
7. *La Famille Tenenbaum*
8. *Van Helsing*

B. Goûts personnels *(Personal tastes)*. Complete the following sentences, choosing appropriate words to describe yourself and others, as indicated.

1. J'aime _____, mais je n'aime pas _____.
2. J'adore _____. (les sports)
3. Je déteste _____. (les films)
4. Mon passe-temps préféré, c'est _____.
5. Mon meilleur ami[1] aime _____. (les sports)
6. Ma meilleure amie[2] aime _____. (les films)

C. Moi et mes goûts *(Me and my tastes)*. Using adjectives and pastimes that you learned in this chapter, describe yourself to the class.

> MODÈLE: J'aime les comédies et les films dramatiques, mais je n'aime pas le base-ball. J'adore le théâtre, et je déteste les films d'épouvante. Mon passe-temps préféré, c'est le yoga. Je suis sociable et amusant(e). Je ne suis pas très sportif/sportive.

---

[1] *My best male friend* [2] *My best female friend*

Structure 4

Les verbes en -er (Introduction)

The most common type of regular verb in French has an infinitive ending in **-er.** The infinitive is the form that corresponds to the *to* form in English *(to like, to prefer).* In order to conjugate a verb in French, you must first drop the infinitive ending, and then add the ending that corresponds to the subject you have chosen. The present indicative tense (the form used to indicate facts in the present) for **-er** verbs follows.

Online Study Center
ACE, Language Skills Practice

In this section, only a few **-er** verbs are introduced so that students are not overwhelmed with new material.

détester	
je détest**e**	nous détest**ons**
tu détest**es**	vous détest**ez**
il / elle / on détest**e**	ils / elles détest**ent**

préférer	
je préfère[1]	nous préfér**ons**
tu préfè**res**	vous préfér**ez**
il / elle / on préfère	ils / elles préfè**rent**

Memorize these forms—once you know them, you can use them for any regular **-er** verb. The negative of these verbs is formed in the same way as for **avoir** and **être: ne** is placed before the verb, and **pas** after it.

je n'aime pas   tu ne détestes pas   vous ne préférez pas

VÉRIFIEZ VOTRE COMPRÉHENSION

1. Go back to the **Continuons!** section (p. 46) and underline the verbs. With the exception of **m'appelle,** which has some slight irregularities, which verbs follow the pattern for regular **-er** verbs? What would their infinitives be?

2. Which non **-er** verb do you see? What is its infinitive?

Pratiquons!

A. Les films et les sports. Rewrite the following sentences, substituting the subject pronouns in parentheses. Pay special attention to the form of the verb.

1. Tu *adores* le karaté. (je / nous / elle)
2. Vous *aimez* les comédies musicales? (tu / il / nous)
3. Je *préfère* le rugby, mais j'*aime* aussi le lacrosse. (vous / ils / tu)
4. Tu *détestes* les films d'aventure? C'est bizarre! (vous / je / elles)
5. Il n'*aime* pas les films d'épouvante. (tu / nous / vous)
6. Elles *adorent* le yoga. (vous / on / tu)

Answer Key: 1. j'adore / nous adorons / elle adore 2. tu aimes / il aime / nous aimons 3. vous préférez; vous aimez / ils préfèrent; ils aiment / tu préfères; tu aimes 4. vous détestez / je déteste / elles détestent 5. tu n'aimes pas / nous n'aimons pas / vous n'aimez pas 6. vous adorez / on adore / tu adores

---

[1]Notice that there is an important spelling change that happens with the verb **préférer:** in the infinitive and the **nous** and **vous** forms, the second syllable has an **é: préférer, vous préférez.** The other forms, however, have an **è.** This is caused by phonetic changes that will be explained later. For now, however, remember that accents are considered crucial to the correct spelling of all words in French; using the wrong accent here means that you have not conjugated the verb correctly!

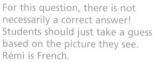

B. Moi aussi! *(Me too!)* Using the verbs and pastimes listed in activity A, tell a classmate if those pastimes correspond to your tastes. Ask your classmate about her or his tastes.

> MODÈLE: Moi aussi, j'adore le karaté, et toi *(and you)?*
>
> ou: Pas moi *(not me)*, je n'aime pas le karaté, et toi?

C. Et toi? Find classmates who have the following likes and dislikes. Write their names in the spaces provided. Report your findings to the class.

> MODÈLE: Un étudiant qui[1] aime le karaté.
>
> You ask: *Tu aimes le karaté, [Justin]?*
>
> You report: *Justin aime le karaté.*

1. Un étudiant qui aime le tennis. _____
2. Une étudiante qui adore les films de guerre. _____
3. Un étudiant qui aime l'opéra. _____
4. Un étudiant et une étudiante qui adorent le français. _____ et _____
5. Une étudiante qui adore le jazz. _____
6. Une étudiante qui déteste les comédies. _____
7. Un étudiant qui n'aime pas les films de science-fiction. _____
8. Un étudiant qui n'aime pas les films historiques. _____
9. Une étudiante qui adore le foot. _____
10. Un étudiant et une étudiante qui aiment la musique classique. _____ et _____

For this question, there is not necessarily a correct answer! Students should just take a guess based on the picture they see. Rémi is French.

Il s'appelle Rémi. Comment est-il physiquement? Il est français, canadien, belge ou suisse?

Structure 5

Online Study Center
ACE, Language Skills
Practice

Les articles définis 🎧

In the preceding exercise, you used a definite article to introduce each of the activities that you talked about. Whereas nouns in English can often appear alone *(I like football),* nouns in French must almost always be accompanied by an article **(J'aime *le* football).** When talking about likes and dislikes, the *definite article* is called for. This is the form that corresponds to the article *the* in English, but its uses are more varied in French. As in English, it is used to talk about specific items, but it is also used to talk about general categories, especially when describing oneself **(j'ai les yeux bleus)** and for talking about likes and dislikes.

You may have noticed in the preceding **Vocabulaire essentiel** section that the forms of the definite article are also more varied than in English. Unlike the English definite article, which has only one form, the French definite article appears in four separate forms.

Masculine singular	Feminine singular	Masculine and feminine plural
le l' *(before a vowel)*	la l' *(before a vowel)*	les

[1]*who*

These different forms exist because French nouns are marked for both number and gender, as are the articles that accompany them: **le livre** vs. **les livres.** However, you will *hear* the number or gender marking only on the article. To determine whether a speaker is talking about one book or many books, you must learn to listen to the article before the noun, instead of listening to the end of the noun.

Notice that both **le** and **la** become **l'** before a vowel sound. The only way to know if the following noun is masculine or feminine is to have memorized its gender:

l'athlétisme *(m.)*

Likewise the plural form of the article is the same for both genders, and thus provides no information concerning the gender of the noun:

les pièces dramatiques *(f.)*
les films de guerre *(m.)*

VÉRIFIEZ VOTRE COMPRÉHENSION

1. Go back to the **Continuons!** section (p. 46) and read the text one more time.

2. How does Jean say what he likes?

3. How does Alix say what he does not like? Can you tell if the noun in the sentence is feminine or masculine just from the article?

À l'écoute!

A. Singulier ou pluriel? Listen and check which noun you hear, the singular or the plural one. Remember that the only distinction between singular and plural is in the pronunciation of the definite article.

1. _____ la comédie   _____ les comédies
2. _____ le théâtre   _____ les théâtres
3. _____ la pièce   _____ les pièces
4. _____ le film d'aventure _____ les films d'aventure
5. _____ le match   _____ les matchs
6. _____ le sport   _____ les sports

Transcript: 1. les comédies 2. le théâtre 3. la pièce 4. les films d'aventure 5. les matchs 6. le sport

B. Masculin ou féminin? Listen to the sentences, and indicate whether each article that you hear is masculine or feminine. If the form of the article doesn't provide a clear indication of gender, check the question mark.

1. _____ masc.   _____ fem.   _____ ?
2. _____ masc.   _____ fem.   _____ ?
3. _____ masc.   _____ fem.   _____ ?
4. _____ masc.   _____ fem.   _____ ?
5. _____ masc.   _____ fem.   _____ ?

Transcript: 1. J'aime la natation. 2. Tu détestes le volley. 3. Je préfère les films romantiques. 4. Vous adorez le football? 5. Tu n'aimes pas l'aikido?

Pratiquons!

A. Préférences. Rahma is going to talk about her likes and dislikes as well as those of her friends. Complete the sentences with the appropriate definite articles. If the definite article is **l'** or **les,** indicate whether the noun is masculine or feminine.

J'aime (1) _____ base-ball, mais je n'aime pas (2) _____ football américain. Mes amis aiment assez¹ tous (3) _____ sports: (4) _____ tennis, (5) _____ golf, (6) _____ natation et (7) _____ musculation. Ils aiment beaucoup² (8) _____ comédies musicales et moi aussi. J'aime beaucoup (9) _____ musique, spécialement (10) _____ opéra et (11) _____ jazz. Mes amis détestent (12) _____ opéra. C'est dommage³!

B. Descriptions et préférences. Based on the descriptions given, complete the sentences in a logical way.

 MODÈLE: Marianne est grande. Elle préfère *le basket.*

1. Juliette est paresseuse. Elle n'aime pas _____.
2. Armelle est très intelligente. Elle adore _____.
3. Arnaud adore les sports individuels. Il aime surtout _____.
4. Thierry est très fort. Il aime _____.
5. Robert est un vieil homme. Il n'aime pas _____.
6. Nathalie est jeune. Elle adore _____.
7. Jean-Jacques préfère les sports d'équipe⁴. Il aime _____.

À vous de parler!

A. Un entretien (*An interview*). Interview a partner to find out what pastimes s/he enjoys. Share your favorite pastimes with him/her also.

1. Tu aimes les sports? Moi, j'aime _____, mais je n'aime pas _____.
2. Comme films, je préfère _____. Et toi?
3. Tu préfères l'opéra ou les pièces musicales?
4. Tu préfères le théâtre classique ou le théâtre moderne?
5. Je déteste _____. J'adore _____. Et toi?
6. Tu préfères Sting ou U2? Moi, j'aime _____.
7. Comme actrice, je préfère _____ parce qu'elle⁵ est _____. Et toi?
8. Comme acteur, je préfère _____ parce qu'il est _____. Et toi?

Do you and your partner have a lot in common? Tell the class what preferences you have in common as well as the ones you don't share.

B. Qui est-ce? *(Who is it?)* Create a description of someone in your class. Talk about what s/he looks like, what her/his personality is like, what s/he likes to do, etc. Your classmates will try to guess who you are talking about.

MODÈLE: Cette personne est grande et blonde. Elle aime le cinéma, mais elle n'aime pas les films d'épouvante. Elle préfère le rock et elle déteste la musique classique.

---

¹*quite* ²*a lot* ³*What a pity!* ⁴*team sports* ⁵*because she*

Les Français sont comme ça

How can we describe the typical French person? It is as hard to describe a typical French person as it is to describe a typical American. Throughout this chapter, you have seen the faces of many different speakers of French. While these speakers come from many countries throughout the world, the face of a "typical" French man or woman is no less diverse.

Currently, there are approximately 62 million inhabitants in France, of whom about 11 million live in the Paris metropolitan region. The other inhabitants live in smaller urban regions (such as Lyon and Toulouse) and in truly rural villages throughout the French mainland. The density of the French population thus ranges from a staggering 20,000 inhabitants per square kilometer in Paris to only 10 in the mountainous regions, resulting, as you can imagine, in vastly different lifestyles!

Continental France has witnessed waves of immigration for more than 150 years, first from European neighbors seeking work in France (especially Portuguese, Italians, Greeks, Armenians, Russians, and Spaniards), and then people from former colonies (Moroccans, Tunisians, Algerians, Senegalese, Vietnamese, etc.) who came seeking educational and work opportunities. The result of these various waves of immigration is that currently one of every four French inhabitants can claim to have foreign roots.[1] This again changes the "face" of France, making it increasingly more difficult to describe a typical French man or woman.

The arrival of immigrants from various parts of the world has also had a profound effect on French society. Although fifty years ago the country claimed to be overwhelmingly Catholic, the last several decades have seen an important growth in other religions, with Islam now representing the second religion of France, with an estimated 4–5 million followers.[2] At the same time, Buddhism, Judaism, and a number of other religions are represented on French soil and help to shape the French experience.

So what does the typical French person look like? S/he is tall *and* short, dark- *and* light-skinned, with blond, brunette, *and* black hair, and eyes of every possible color. S/he leads a city *or* a country life, and attends religious services regularly, occasionally, *or* not at all. In other words, s/he closely resembles her/his American cousins!

Réfléchissons

1. What does it mean to be French in the 21st century?
2. In what ways does the French experience parallel the American experience?

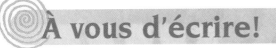

À vous d'écrire!

Now that you know some French, you have decided to enter into e-mail communication with a native French speaker. Your first step is to write to your new key-pal and introduce yourself to him/her. In this first note, you'll want to tell your key-pal who you are, where you're from, what you're like (both physically and

[1] Ministère des Affaires étrangères
[2] *Time Europe,* 12 Juin, 2000. Vol. 155, No. 23

generally), and what you like and don't like to do in your leisure time. Follow the steps below to write this first note.

A. Stratégies. One of the most important things to remember when writing in a foreign language is to use the language that you know how to use, rather than trying to express yourself as you would in your native language. While these sentences may seem very simplistic to start with, they will be much more comprehensible (and thus more successful) than sentences you attempt to create with words or grammar that you have not yet learned.

Additionally, remember that writing is a form of communication; when you write, you generally have a specific person or audience in mind, and this determines the style of language that you use and the degree of familiarity that is acceptable.

Consider your audience for this particular activity: To whom are you writing? For what purpose? What form of address would you use to ask this person about him/herself?

B. Organisons-nous! *(Let's get organized!)* What are the types of information that you want to include in your note to your key-pal? Make a quick outline of your self-description on a separate sheet of paper. (Think in general categories only for the moment, jotting a few words down in English.)

C. Pensons-y! *(Let's think about it!)* For each of the following categories, list some of the words in French that you would use to describe yourself. Don't write any sentences yet; simply list words and phrases that you might eventually incorporate into your note.

Apparence physique
Personnalité
Passe-temps *(hobbies)*

Elle s'appelle Laurie. Comment est-elle physiquement? Elle est française ou américaine?

For this question, there is not necessarily a correct answer! Students should just take a guess based on the picture they see. Laurie is American.

Now, using the words and phrases that you listed, start to write some complete sentences in French. How are these words incorporated into sentences in French? What verbs do they generally appear with, and how are these verbs conjugated? List some of these sentences.

D. Révisons. Look back over the sentences that you have just created.

- Are they phrased as a native speaker of French would phrase them? (Look back at the examples in the chapter if you are unsure.)
- Have you conjugated the verbs in your sentences according to the subject pronouns that you used?
- Have you made sure to use the correct form of the adjectives and articles in each sentence?

Make any corrections that you need to, and add any additional sentences that you feel are necessary to describe yourself.

E. Écrivons! Now that you have several sentences that you are happy with, organize them into a coherent paragraph. How would you introduce yourself to your key-pal in a way that includes all this material? Write your paragraph on your sheet of paper. You can begin with *Salut!* and end with *Amitiés, ...*

Lexique 🎧

Vocabulaire essentiel

Les adjectifs descriptifs *descriptive adjectives*

amusant / amusante *amusing, funny*
antipathique *unfriendly*
bavard / bavarde *talkative*
beau / belle *handsome / beautiful*
content / contente *happy*
courageux / courageuse *courageous, brave*
élégant / élégante *elegant*
ennuyeux / ennuyeuse *boring*
fort / forte *strong*
gentil / gentille *nice*
grand / grande *tall, big*

gros / grosse *big, fat*
intelligent / intelligente *intelligent*
jeune *young*
laid / laide *ugly*
méchant / méchante *mean*
mignon / mignonne *cute*
mince *thin*
optimiste *optimistic*
pauvre *poor*
pessimiste *pessimistic*
petit / petite *short, small*
poilu / poilue *hairy*

provocateur / provocatrice *provocative*
riche *rich*
sportif / sportive *athletic*
stupide *stupid*
super *super*
sympathique *friendly*
timide *timid, shy*
tout petit / toute petite *very little*
triste *sad*
vieux / vieille *old*

Les cheveux *hair*

blonds *blond*
bouclés *curly*
bruns *brown*
châtains *light brown*

courts *short*
frisés *very curly*
gris *gray*
lisses *straight*

longs *long*
mi-longs *shoulder-length*
noirs *dark*
roux *red*

Les yeux *eyes*

bleus *blue*
marron *brown*

noirs *dark*
verts *green*

Les sports et les passe-temps *sports and pastimes*

l'athlétisme *track and field*
le base-ball *baseball*
le basket *basketball*
le football/le foot *soccer*
le football américain *football*

le golf *golf*
le judo *judo*
le karaté *karate*
la musculation *weightlifting*
la natation *swimming*

le rugby *rugby*
le surf *surfing*
le tennis *tennis*
le volley *volleyball*
le yoga *yoga*

Les films *movies*

les comédies *(f.)* *comedies*
les comédies musicales *(f.)*
  musical comedies
les comédies romantiques *(f.)*
  romantic comedies
les films d'aventure *(m.)*
  adventure movies
les films d'épouvante *(m.)* *horror
  movies*

les films de guerre *(m.)* *war
  movies*
les films de science-fiction *(m.)*
  science-fiction movies
les films dramatiques *(m.)*
  dramas
les films historiques *(m.)*
  historical movies

les films policiers *(m.)* *detective
  films*
les thrillers *(m.)* *thrillers*
les westerns *(m.)* *westerns*

Le théâtre *theater*

les comédies musicales *(f.)*
  musical comedies
l'opéra *(m.)* *opera*
les pièces comiques *(f.)* *comic
  plays*

les pièces dramatiques *(f.)* *drama*
les pièces musicales *(f.)* *musical
  plays*

le théâtre classique *classic theater*
le théâtre moderne *modern
  theater*

La musique *music*

le jazz *jazz*
la musique classique *classical
  music*

le rap *rap*
le rock *rock*

Ma famille et mes amis

In this chapter, you will learn how to describe your family, how to talk about common activities using **-er** verbs, and how to ask and answer basic questions. You will learn the numbers from 30 to 69 and nouns for pets and common professions, and you will learn how to talk about where you and your family live and what you like to do.

 The vocabulary that you will learn includes

Daily activities such as hobbies and work
Family members and pets
The days of the week
The months of the year

The structures that you will learn include

Regular and irregular verbs ending in **-er**
Questions with **est-ce que** and **n'est-ce pas**
Indefinite articles
Possessive adjectives
On and **il y a**
Numbers 30–69

The culture that you will study includes

The French and their pets
Mother's Day in Central Africa

Commençons!

Qui êtes-vous? Où est-ce que vous habitez? Avec qui? Qu'est-ce que vous aimez faire le week-end? ○

Read through the text a first time for students, then ask them to guess the general meaning of each sentence. What is each person talking about here? Point out the number of cognates (**mots apparentés**) and their value when learning a foreign language. Ask students to identify some cognates that help them to figure out the meaning of a sentence even if they don't know all the words. Point out that some **mots non-apparentés** may look like cognates (e.g., **travailler** looks like *travel*), and

Je m'appelle Lucien.
Je suis étudiant à l'université de Bordeaux.
J'ai une fiancée. Elle s'appelle Pascale. Elle est belle et dynamique!
J'étudie beaucoup, mais je ne travaille pas.
Je n'ai pas beaucoup d'argent, donc, je ne mange jamais[1] au restaurant.
J'habite dans une cité universitaire. Ma chambre est petite, mais confortable.
Le soir, j'écoute de la musique. J'aime surtout le rock classique.

Je m'appelle Yolanda. Je suis mariée.
J'habite une maison à Montréal avec ma famille.
Le week-end, nous regardons la télé, ou nous jouons au Monopoly.
Nous ne voyageons pas souvent, mais de temps en temps nous aimons aller à Toronto.
Je suis femme d'affaires, et je travaille dans un bureau. Je parle français, anglais et espagnol.

that students should be careful of them. Ask students to figure out their meaning from the context. Then focus on the verbs that are repeated several times, and ask students to guess what each verb means.

Je suis médecin. Je m'appelle Roland Gaillard.
Je travaille dans un hôpital à Paris.
Normalement, je commence à 7 h du matin, et je termine à 18 h. C'est une journée très longue!
Je suis marié, mais je n'ai pas d'enfants.
Le week-end, ma femme et moi, nous jouons au tennis.
Nous voyageons souvent aussi—nous aimons visiter la Belgique et le Luxembourg, parce que nous avons de la famille là-bas.

Je m'appelle Claire. Je suis divorcée, avec deux enfants.
Je suis pilote chez Air France, donc je voyage souvent!
Mes enfants et moi, nous habitons à Grenoble.
Nous cherchons un nouvel appartement— notre appartement est trop petit.
Mes enfants aiment jouer au football, et ils aiment aussi regarder les sports à la télévision.
Le week-end, nous mangeons chez mes parents. Ils habitent à Grenoble aussi.
Nous avons un chien. Il s'appelle Marcel.

---

[1]ne … jamais-*never*

Vous avez bien compris?

Answer the following questions with a word or two. In some cases, more than one response may be correct.

1. Qui habite dans un appartement?
2. Qui n'est pas marié?
3. Qui aime regarder la télé?
4. Comment s'appelle la personne qui ne mange pas au restaurant?
5. Quelle est la profession de Roland? Et de Yolanda?
6. Où est-ce que Yolanda habite? Et Lucien?
7. Qu'est-ce que Claire cherche?
8. Quelle est la musique préférée de Lucien?
9. Quel est le sport préféré de Roland?

Mots utiles

qui = who
où = where
qu'est-ce que = what
quel(le) = which/what

Vocabulaire essentiel

Les activités, les professions, les animaux domestiques

Online Study Center
Flashcards, ACE, Language Skills Practice

Verbes apparentés

commencer
danser
préparer
regarder
téléphoner à
terminer
voyager

Verbes à réviser (to review)
adorer
aimer
détester
préférer

Verbes non apparentés

acheter *(to buy)*
appeler *(to call)*, s'appeler[1]
   (to be called, to be named)
chanter *(to sing)*
chercher *(to look for)*
écouter *(to listen)*
étudier *(to study)*
fumer *(to smoke)*
habiter *(to live)*
jouer à *(to play a sport)*
manger *(to eat)*
parler *(to speak)*
pratiquer *(to practice, to participate in)*
travailler *(to work)*
trouver *(to find)*

Read through the vocabulary for your students, acting out the meaning whenever you can. Then read the list a second time and have the class repeat.

Pour parler des professions

il / elle est étudiant(e)   homme / femme d'affaires
              professeur   secrétaire
              pilote   agent de police
              médecin   agent de voyage
              dentiste   ingénieur
              architecte

A picture file of photos cut out of magazines is very useful for introducing this kind of vocabulary. Sometimes you can find photos of actors playing roles in these professions. If you use PowerPoint, you can scan photos from magazines or download them from the Internet.

---

[1]This is known as a pronominal verb, because it uses an object pronoun in addition to the subject pronoun. These verbs will be introduced in a later chapter; you have, however, already seen several forms of this verb: **je m'appelle, tu t'appelles, vous vous appelez,** etc.

Pour parler de vos animaux

j'ai   un chien   un chat   un hamster   un lapin

un poisson rouge   un cochon d'Inde   un oiseau

À vous!

A. Activités. Recalling vocabulary that you learned in Chapters 1 and 2, tell which activities you associate with the following verbs.

MODÈLE: regarder

regarder une comédie musicale

1. écouter
2. regarder
3. jouer (au …)
4. pratiquer
5. étudier
6. parler

B. Les professions. Name some of the activities associated with the following professions.

MODÈLE: un pilote

voyager souvent, travailler le week-end, etc.

1. un homme d'affaires / une femme d'affaires
2. un étudiant
3. un médecin
4. un professeur
5. un agent de police
6. un agent de voyage

C. Les animaux domestiques. Determine the best pet for someone with the following living arrangements.

1. un petit appartement
2. une chambre[1] à l'université
3. une maison[2]
4. une maison et trois petits enfants
5. un appartement spacieux
6. un énorme jardin[3]

---

[1]*a room* [2]*a house* [3]*yard*

Structure 1

Les verbes en -er

Online Study Center
ACE, Language Skills
Practice

In Chapter 2, you learned several regular **-er** verbs. Remember that these verbs are conjugated by dropping the **-er** infinitive ending and adding an appropriate present tense ending, which varies according to the subject pronoun. Here is the conjugation of the verb **chanter,** *to sing.*

chanter	
je chant**e**	nous chant**ons**
tu chant**es**	vous chant**ez**
il / elle / on chant**e**	ils / elles chant**ent**

Review the pronunciation of these verbs, highlighting the identical sound of the 1st, 2nd, and 3rd person singular and the 3rd person plural, in particular.

These present tense verbs have several translations in English: **je chante** can mean *I sing, I am singing,* or *I do sing.* The context will help you determine which meaning the speaker intends.

Notice the **-er** verbs that are presented in the *Vocabulaire essentiel* on page 59. These verbs are all conjugated in the same way.[1]

Reminder: The negative of these verbs is formed in the same way as for **être** and **avoir: n(e) ... pas** is placed around the verb.

Il ne chante pas bien.
Je n'étudie pas le week-end.
Nous ne regardons pas souvent la télé.

- **Stem-changing verbs:** A few verbs in French have spelling variations. You saw the changes that affect the verb **préférer** in Chapter 2. Similar changes occur in the verbs **acheter** *(to buy)* and **appeler** *(to call).*

acheter	
j'achète	nous achetons
tu achètes	vous achetez
il / elle / on achète	ils / elles achètent

appeler	
j'appelle	nous appelons
tu appelles	vous appelez
il / elle / on appelle	ils / elles appellent

---

[1]The *nous* form of verbs that end in **-ger** and **-cer** is slightly different from that of other verbs:

nous chant**ons**   but: nous mang**eons**   nous voyag**eons**
je commen**ce**   vous commen**cez**   but: nous commen**çons**

This change is made for phonetic reasons, but it is very important to the spelling of these verbs!

Verbs conjugated like **acheter** and **appeler** are frequently referred to as *stem-changing verbs*. Notice that in both cases, the **nous** and **vous** forms keep the original form of the infinitive, and the four other forms have a different stem.

- **Combining two verbs:** Like English, French often combines two verbs to include the meaning of both in a single sentence. This is especially common with verbs that express likes and dislikes. When this happens, the first verb is always conjugated, and the second is always left in the infinitive.

J'**aime voyager** en Europe.	*I like to travel in Europe.*
Il **préfère manger** au restaurant.	*He prefers to eat in a restaurant.*
Nous **détestons travailler** le week-end!	*We hate to work on weekends!*
Vous **n'aimez pas regarder** la télévision?	*Don't you like to watch television?*

VÉRIFIEZ VOTRE COMPRÉHENSION

1. Return to the **Commençons!** section on page 58, where Yolanda, Lucien, Roland, and Claire introduce themselves. Which **-er** verbs do they use to talk about their activities? Underline them, and explain the subject pronoun and ending used with each.

2. Are there any stem-changing verbs used by these four people? Which ones? What stem is used?

3. Do you see any *verb + infinitive* combinations? What do these verbs express?

Pratiquons!

A. Des activités. Complete each sentence with the correct form of the given verb. Then repeat the sentence with each pronoun in parentheses.

1. *jouer:* Lucien _____ au football le week-end. (ils / vous / je)
2. *fumer:* Elle ne _____ pas. (tu / nous / on)
3. *voyager:* Ils _____ souvent à Paris. (je / vous / elle)
4. *adorer:* Philippe _____ travailler à la banque. (tu / on / elles)
5. *habiter:* Tu _____ sur le campus? (il / vous / ils / je)
6. *acheter:* Vous _____ souvent des cigarettes. (tu / elle / nous)
7. *commencer:* Nous _____ le Chapitre 3. (je / vous / les étudiants)

B. Mes préférences. Using the verbs **aimer, adorer, préférer,** and **détester,** create sentences to explain the likes and dislikes of the following people.

MODÈLE: Moi / manger au fast-food

Je déteste manger au fast-food. **ou** *J'adore manger au fast-food.*

1. Moi / préparer un examen
2. Mon professeur / parler anglais en classe
3. Mes parents / voyager
4. Moi / habiter sur le campus
5. Mon professeur / travailler à l'université
6. Moi / regarder un film d'épouvante
7. Mes parents / appeler ma famille au téléphone
8. Mes amis / fumer des cigarettes
9. Moi / danser la musique rave

Have students do activity A individually (as homework, if you wish), but then go over the answers with them to verify that they are ready to move on.

Answer Key: 1. Lucien joue / Ils jouent / Vous jouez / Je joue 2. Elle ne fume pas / tu ne fumes pas / Nous ne fumons pas / On ne fume pas 3. Ils voyagent / Je voyage / Vous voyagez / Elle voyage 4. Philippe adore / Tu adores / On adore / Elles adorent 5. Tu habites / Il habite / Vous habitez / Ils habitent / J'habite 6. Vous achetez / Tu achètes / Elle achète / Nous achetons 7. Nous commençons / Je commence / Vous commencez / Les étudiants commencent

Draw students' attention to the elision with **habiter** and the spelling changes with **acheter** and **commencer.**

Make sure that students produce meaningful sentences that truly express their likes and dislikes. Draw students' attention to the spelling changes with **préférer** and to cases of elision. If necessary, remind students that the second verb is always in the infinitive.

Answer Key. Possible answers: 1. Je déteste 2. Mon professeur n'aime pas 3. Mes parents aiment 4. Je préfère 5. Mon professeur aime 6. J'aime 7. Mes parents adorent 8. Mes amis détestent 9. J'adore

Structure 2

Les verbes en -er: l'interrogation avec des réponses affirmatives (*oui*) ou négatives (*non*)

Online Study Center
ACE, Language Skills
Practice

There are several simple ways to ask yes/no questions in French.

1. The simplest way is to use a *rising intonation* for your sentence to signal that you are not making a statement, but rather, asking a question. Listen to the In-Text Audio CD, and compare the following sentences.

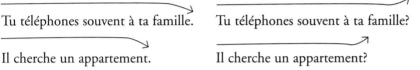

Tu téléphones souvent à ta famille. Tu téléphones souvent à ta famille?

Il cherche un appartement. Il cherche un appartement?

2. Another way to ask a yes/no question is to add **est-ce que** to the beginning of a sentence. This expression has no direct equivalent in English; it simply signals to a French speaker that what s/he is about to hear is a question.

   Est-ce que tu téléphones souvent à ta famille?
   Est-ce qu'il cherche un appartement?

   Notice that the **que** becomes **qu'** before a subject pronoun beginning with a vowel.

3. A third way to ask a simple yes/no question is to add **n'est-ce pas?** to the end of your statement. This is functionally equivalent to asking . . . *right?* at the end of a statement in English, and is therefore only used when you believe that you are correct!

   Tu téléphones souvent à ta famille, n'est-ce pas?
   Il cherche un appartement, n'est-ce pas?

4. In written language and more formal speech, you will also encounter *inversion* of the subject pronoun and the verb. This is yet another way to ask a yes/no question, and it is equivalent to, but generally considered more formal than, the forms you have seen above. You should learn to recognize this form, as you will often see it in written language or hear it in fixed expressions that have not changed over time.

   Téléphones-tu souvent à ta famille? = Tu téléphones souvent à ta famille?
   Parlez-vous souvent au téléphone? = Est-ce que vous parlez souvent au téléphone?

Model these and other examples for your students. Have them repeat in choral drill and/or individually.

Model the pronunciation of **est-ce que** and **n'est-ce pas** for students. Have them repeat in choral drill.

Inversion is presented for recognition purposes only, as it is used infrequently in spoken French. If you wish, you may present more information, for example: inversion does not usually occur with noun subjects, but only with pronoun subjects; a -t- is inserted **(Va-t-il au supermarché?)** between vowels, etc. This information will not be presented in *À vous!*

VÉRIFIEZ VOTRE COMPRÉHENSION

Go back to the **Commençons!** section at the beginning of this chapter (p. 58), and underline all the questions that you find. Explain how they are formed. Think back to the expressions that you learned in Chapters 1 and 2 as well. Which of those questions are formed with inversion? Which ones with **est-ce que?** Which ones with simple intonation?

À l'écoute!

Listen, and indicate whether each sentence you hear is a declarative statement or a question.

1. _____ statement   _____ question
2. _____ statement   _____ question
3. _____ statement   _____ question
4. _____ statement   _____ question
5. _____ statement   _____ question
6. _____ statement   _____ question
7. _____ statement   _____ question
8. _____ statement   _____ question
9. _____ statement   _____ question
10. _____ statement   _____ question

Pratiquons!

A. Des questions. You work for the campus newspaper, and you have been asked to interview students at your university for an article about student life. Use the verbs and activities listed to form questions to ask your interviewees.

Using intonation

1. chanter bien
2. étudier le week-end
3. parler chinois
4. écouter souvent de la musique classique
5. aimer voyager
6. ?

Using *est-ce que*

7. manger au restaurant
8. travailler
9. habiter un appartement
10. jouer au football / au tennis
11. préférer parler français ou anglais
12. ?

Using *n'est-ce pas*

13. étudier le français
14. regarder la télévision
15. terminer toujours tes devoirs[1]
16. ne ... pas / fumer
17. détester travailler le week-end
18. ?

---

[1]*always finish your homework*

B. Les interviews. Now ask a partner the questions that you created in activity A, noting his/her answers carefully. Share his/her answers with the class.

Portrait personnel

Write a short description of the person you interviewed in activity B, using the information that s/he gave you. You don't need to include all the information; simply use what you find the most interesting.

Have students include only first names (or have them adopt French first names) and then use these *Portrait personnel* activities as a basis for a class bulletin board, web site, or newsletter. "Publishing" their written work may motivate students to pay more attention to both form and meaning.

Structure 3

Les articles indéfinis

- **Indefinite articles in an affirmative sentence.** Like English, French has both definite and indefinite articles. As you saw in Chapter 2, the definite articles are used to talk about likes and dislikes (**J'aime *les* films d'aventure**), as well as to talk about specific nouns (***Le* professeur est amusant**).

  Indefinite articles are used to introduce an item that you have not previously talked about. They correspond roughly to *a, an,* or *some* in English. As you saw with the definite articles, there are different forms of the indefinite article, depending on the gender and number of the following noun.

Online Study Center
ACE, Language Skills Practice

Masculine singular	Feminine singular	Masculine/ feminine plural
un	une	des

Un is used for masculine nouns.

  un film
  un homme
  un animal

Une is used for feminine nouns.

  une comédie
  une femme
  une personne

Des is used for all plural nouns.

  des hommes
  des animaux
  des comédies
  des personnes

Reminder: Nouns in French very rarely appear without an article. Even in the plural, the article is stated in French, whereas in English it is often omitted.

J'ai **des** enfants.   *I have children.*
Je regarde **des** films d'aventure.   *I watch action movies.*

À l'écoute!

Transcript: 1. C'est un sport inté-ressant. 2. C'est une femme dynamique. 3. Ce sont des per-sonnes intelligentes. 4. C'est un film amusant. 5. Ce sont des jeux vidéo. 6. C'est une comédie musicale.

Listen to the sentences, and indicate whether each noun being described is masculine, feminine, or plural.

1. _____ masculine   _____ feminine   _____ plural
2. _____ masculine   _____ feminine   _____ plural
3. _____ masculine   _____ feminine   _____ plural
4. _____ masculine   _____ feminine   _____ plural
5. _____ masculine   _____ feminine   _____ plural
6. _____ masculine   _____ feminine   _____ plural

- **Indefinite articles in negative sentences.** When an indefinite article follows a verb in the negative, the article becomes simply **de.** This happens regardless of the noun's gender or number.

  J'ai **un** chien.   Je n'ai pas **de** chien.
  Nous avons **des** poissons rouges.   Nous n'avons pas **de** poissons rouges.

  This is equivalent to using *any* in English: *I don't have any dogs / any goldfish.*

  When the verb is **être,** however, the article does not change:

  C'est **un** film romantique? Non, ce n'est pas **un** film romantique, c'est **un** film dramatique.

  This is because when we use the verb **être** we are talking about a definition, and we want to keep the sense of *a/an: It's not a romantic film; it's a drama.*

  These rules do not apply to definite articles, which do not change in the negative:

  J'aime **le** football.   Je n'aime pas **le** football.

- **Using definite and indefinite articles.** As noted above, indefinite articles are usually used to introduce an object into a conversation for the first time. Once the object is known to your listener, a definite article is used.

  J'ai **un** chien. Il s'appelle Marcel. **Le** chien de mes parents s'appelle Renaud. **Les** chiens aiment jouer ensemble.

  The definite article is also used to talk about categories as a whole (these are often expressed in the singular in French, but in the plural in English), and to express likes and dislikes.

  Le chat est un animal domestique. *(Cats are pets.)*
  Suzanne aime **les** chats, mais elle déteste **les** chiens.
  Moi, je préfère **les** cochons d'Inde!

VÉRIFIEZ VOTRE COMPRÉHENSION

Return to the statements made by Lucien, Roland, Yolanda, and Claire in the **Commençons!** section, and underline the definite and indefinite articles. Justify their use.

Pratiquons!

A. Substitution. Look at the following drawings. There are two verbs associated with each drawing: **adorer** and **acheter.** Choose the definite or the indefinite article that goes with each verb and the noun pictured. Remember that with **adorer** you must use a definite article and with **acheter** an indefinite article. Follow the model.

 Modèle:

J'adore les DVD; j'achète un DVD.

Point out that in French, like English, you may sometimes use a plural noun in one instance, but a singular noun in another. For example, we say *I like DVDs* (always in the plural) but *I buy a DVD* or *I buy DVDs* (singular or plural), depending on the context. The same is generally true of French.

Answer Key: 1. les oiseaux; des oiseaux 2. les films; un film 3. les poissons rouges; un poisson rouge 4. les livres; des livres 5. les animaux domestiques; des animaux domestiques 6. la télévision; des téléviseurs

1.  J'adore …; j'achète …

2.  J'adore …; j'achète …

3.  J'adore …; j'achète …

4.  J'adore …; j'achète …

5.  J'adore …; j'achète …

6. 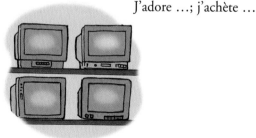 J'adore …; j'achète …

B. Une entrevue. With a classmate, ask and answer questions based on the cues. Vary the ways in which you form your questions. Record your partner's responses so you can report them to the entire class.

MODÈLE: avoir un chat

—*Est-ce que tu as un chat?*

—*Oui, j'ai un chat. / Non, je n'ai pas de chat.*

1. avoir un(e) fiancé(e)
2. regarder souvent des films d'épouvante
3. manger un sandwich en classe
4. fumer une pipe
5. préparer un examen important
6. avoir un animal domestique
7. écouter des concerts à la radio
8. chanter des opéras
9. ?

C. Portrait personnel. Write a brief description of your partner based on his/her answers to the questions in activity B and any others that you may have asked him/her. In addition, give your own answers to the questions.

MODÈLE: Matthieu a un chien, mais moi, je n'ai pas de chien. Je déteste les chiens! Je préfère les chats.

D. Préférences / Activités. Use the given verbs to tell the likes or dislikes of the person indicated. Then tell how often the person does the activity. If you like, you may use the adverbs **souvent, quelquefois,** or **rarement.**

MODÈLE: moi: aimer / regarder
film(s) d'aventure

*J'aime **les** films d'aventure. Je regarde souvent **un** film.*

1. moi: aimer / écouter
concert(s) de rock
2. nous: préférer / regarder
comédie(s)
3. mes parents: détester / ne … pas regarder
match(s) de football américain
4. moi: préférer / avoir
chien(s)
5. Philippe: détester / ne … pas avoir
chat(s)

Mots utiles. Adverbs in French are placed after the verb they describe. The following are adverbs of frequency.

souvent = often

quelquefois = sometimes

rarement = rarely

Structure 4

Les professions et les articles indéfinis

Some nouns have both a masculine and a feminine form, and the form you use depends on the gender of the person described. In such cases, both the article and the noun give us information concerning the person's sex.

un étudiant   **une** étudiant**e**
un avocat   **une** avocat**e**

Certain professions, however, were traditionally held only by men or only by women, and in France, the nouns for those professions retain their traditional gender, either masculine:

un médecin / **un** docteur
un professeur
un pilote

or feminine:

une secrétaire
une infirmière[1]

In other countries, particularly Canada, the language is evolving to allow both masculine and feminine forms of these nouns:

un / **une** pilote
un / **une** dentiste
un professeur / **une** professeure
un / **une** secrétaire

When describing one's profession, an article is generally *not* used.

Je suis étudiante.
Il est dentiste.
Elle est infirmière.
Ils sont professeurs.

If you add an adjective to these statements, however, an article is also added, and the pronouns **il(s)** and **elle(s)** change to **ce:**

Je suis **une** étudiante sérieuse.
C'est **un** dentiste amusant.
C'est **une** infirmière sympathique.
Ce sont **des** professeurs intéressants.

Online Study Center
ACE, Language Skills
Practice

Un pique-nique. Voici des amis qui font un pique-nique. Quelle est leur profession, d'après vous *(in your opinion)*? Imaginez ce qu'ils aiment faire le week-end. Quelles activités est-ce qu'ils préfèrent?

Point out the spelling of the feminine noun **professeure**. This form is not yet used in France, although **la prof** is.

Point out to students that with unmodified nouns of profession, the profession functions as a sort of adjective, and therefore no article is required. If the noun of profession is modified, however, the profession must function as a noun in order to permit another adjective, and therefore the article is added. Encourage your students to get used to using **c'est un, c'est une, ce sont des**—when the article is present, they should use **ce**.

VÉRIFIEZ VOTRE COMPRÉHENSION

Return to the statements made by Lucien, Roland, Yolanda, and Claire in the **Commençons!** section, and underline their professions. Do they use an indefinite article to describe what they do? Why or why not?

---

[1] *nurse*

Pratiquons!

A. Des professions. Give the profession of each person listed, choosing from the following options: **médecin, professeur, étudiant, pilote, architecte, infirmière, ingénieur, homme / femme d'affaires.**

> MODÈLE: Andy Taylor (Il habite à Mayberry.)
>
> *Il est agent de police.*

1. Gregory House
2. I. M. Pei
3. Florence Nightingale
4. Gustave Eiffel
5. Amelia Earhart
6. Donald Trump
7. vous

B. Des détails. Redo activity A, adding an adjective to each of your descriptions.

> MODÈLE: Andy Taylor
>
> *C'est un agent de police sympathique.*

À vous de parler!

A. Je me présente! Using Yolanda, Lucien, Roland, and Claire's self-descriptions in the ***Commençons!*** section as a model, briefly describe yourself. Who are you? What do you do? What do you like / dislike? Do you have any pets?

B. Un sondage *(A survey).* In groups of four or five, ask your classmates questions based on the following cues. Make sure that each classmate answers each question, so that you can establish percentages for the class as a whole when you have finished.

1. avoir un chien / un chat
2. préférer les chiens / les chats
3. regarder souvent des films / la télévision
4. préférer les films / la télévision
5. fumer
6. parler une autre langue (le français, l'espagnol, … ?)
7. étudier une autre langue
8. travailler
9. danser en boîte[1] le week-end

Have students take turns presenting themselves to the class. Encourage others to ask follow-up questions, and ask some questions yourself. This could be used as a warm-up listening activity over several days.

Figure the percentages for each of these questions with the class. Record the percentages and exchange them with another teacher to facilitate activity C, which you will do the following day. If you have access to pen pals or key pals, have your students ask these questions of their Francophone peers, and then do the comparisons.

---

[1] *at a nightclub*

C. Des comparaisons. Compare your class's responses to those of another class (your teacher will provide you with these). How does your class compare to the other class? With your classmates, establish several comparisons. Are you more alike, or more different from the other class? On which points do you differ?

> MODÈLE: Les étudiants dans l'autre classe préfèrent les chiens, mais nous préférons les chats …

Les Français aiment leurs chiens comme ça

Online Study Center
Web Search Activities

Do you have a pet? Do you consider it a part of your family? In France, dogs are very important to family life. Many families have a dog, even if they live in a small apartment. What's more, the dog is considered a member of the family and accompanies the family on outings to the park, to a café, or even to the corner bakery to buy bread. Dogs are permitted in the post office, in department stores, in supermarkets, and even on public transportation. On buses and in the subway, dogs sit on their owners' laps, and in restaurants they wait under the table. Most French people would consider it cruel to leave the dog at home while they went out to have fun!

While we often think of the poodle as the prototypical French dog, the truth is that the French love all varieties of dogs, even large dogs. German shepherds, for example, are a favorite, and are owned by people living in large houses as well as small Parisian apartments. In many of the large cities in France, there are so many dogs that the cities have hired people with the specific job of keeping the sidewalks clean. These employees ride small motorcycles with vacuums attached, and clean up after dogs. In the United States we say that dogs are man's best friend; in France it's true to say that "les Français sont les meilleurs amis des chiens!"

Réfléchissons

1. Do you have a dog? If so, what role does that dog play in your life? How do you think the American view of dogs compares to the French view? Would you be shocked to see a dog in a park? In a restaurant? In a supermarket? Why or why not?
2. The French take their dogs everywhere. In your opinion, are they going too far? How are dogs treated differently in your country? Do you object to seeing dogs in certain places? Where and why?
3. What would you say is the typical American pet for those who live in the city? In the suburbs? And in the country?
4. Is there a stereotypical American dog? If so, what is it? Compare your response to that of your classmates.

Continuons!

Point out that in France and in the French-speaking countries in Europe, families have an average of two children and a dog. It is very common for couples to live together unmarried until they have their first child. After their first child is born, they usually get married.

Claudine
Moi, je suis étudiante aussi. J'étudie la chimie pour être pharmacienne.

La famille de Claudine 🎧

Claudine Dupuis has brought her family photo album to show you. She is going to tell you a little bit about the members of her family.

Bonjour! Je m'appelle Claudine Dupuis et je suis de Genève. J'ai une grande famille: on est cinq, bon[1], six avec Filou! Commençons par mes parents. J'adore mes parents!

Valérie
Papa est ingénieur et maman est médecin.
Mon père et ma mère sont très intelligents.

Cyrille

Serge
Mon frère Serge est barman. Il n'étudie pas.

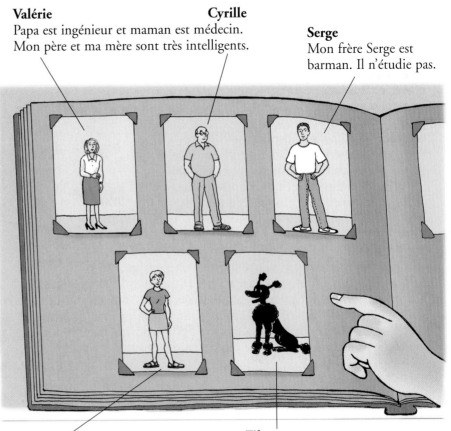

Delphine
Ma sœur jumelle Delphine est étudiante en mathématiques.

Filou
Mon chien Filou est très intelligent: il n'étudie pas et il ne travaille pas!

Now that you have met Claudine's immediate family—**la famille proche**—she is going to tell you about the rest of her family. She will start with the paternal side—**la famille paternelle.**

Ma famille paternelle est super!

---

[1] *well*

Marcel

Papi Marcel fume une pipe. Tous les matins[1], mon grand-père achète le journal et une baguette. C'est le papi parfait! Il parle de sa jeunesse[2] et il aime gâter[3] son petit-fils, Serge, et ses petites-filles.

Germaine

Mamie Germaine est une cuisinière[4] excellente. Il y a toujours[5] des desserts délicieux chez elle[6]. Sa mousse au chocolat est mon dessert préféré!

Charlotte et Thierry

Tonton Thierry est très amusant. Mon oncle travaille à la télévision pour la chaîne de musique M6. Il est directeur de publicité. Sa femme, tatie Charlotte, est moderne et jeune. Ma tante voyage souvent: elle est femme d'affaires. Mon oncle et ma tante ont une fille. Leur fille s'appelle Isabelle.

Isabelle

Ma cousine, Isabelle (on l'appelle[7] Zaza!) est très moderne aussi[8]. Elle est fille unique[9]. Elle étudie au lycée Jules Ferry.

Tell students the difference in usage between **tatie** and **tante**, **tonton** and **oncle**, **mamie** or **grand-maman** and **grand-mère**, **papi** or **grand-papa** and **grand-père**. When talking about a family member, particularly in a more formal situation, the standard nouns are used: **Mon grand-père habite à Paris.** When talking to a family member directly, or when talking about him/her in a less formal situation (to a friend, for example), the term of affection is used: **Papi Marcel arrive ce week-end.**

Finally, Claudine is going to show you the maternal side of her family—**la famille maternelle.**

Ma famille maternelle est originale! Il y a trois membres dans ma famille maternelle:

Angèle

Ma grand-mère est divorcée. Elle habite à Québec. Elle parle anglais parfaitement. Mamie est professeur de mathématiques à l'université Laval. Mamie préfère Delphine parce qu'elle étudie les mathématiques! Elle a une fille, Monique, mais elle n'a pas de fils.

Monique

Ma tante Monique est célibataire. Elle n'est pas mariée. Elle n'est pas fiancée. Elle a un petit ami[10]. Son petit ami, **Amed,** est journaliste. Amed parle arabe et français.

---

[1]*every morning* [2]*youth* [3]*to spoil* [4]*cook* [5]*always* [6]*at her place* [7]*we call her* [8]*also* [9]*an only child*
[10]*boyfriend*

Vous avez bien compris?

A. Identify the following members of Claudine's family.

1. Il est ingénieur: _____
2. Il fume la pipe: _____
3. Elle est divorcée: _____
4. Ils ont une fille unique: _____
5. Il parle arabe et français: _____
6. Il travaille à la télévision: _____
7. Elle prépare des desserts délicieux: _____
8. Elle étudie la chimie: _____
9. Il ne travaille pas et il n'étudie pas: _____
10. Elle est célibataire: _____

B. Complete the following sentences about Claudine's family.

1. Tatie Charlotte est *(profession)* _____.
2. Delphine est étudiante en _____.
3. Zaza est fille _____.
4. Delphine et Claudine sont *(twins)* _____.
5. Papi Marcel achète _____ et _____.
6. La mère de Claudine s'appelle _____.
7. Claudine a un frère: *(name)* _____.
8. La grand-mère maternelle de Claudine habite à _____.

Vocabulaire essentiel

La famille

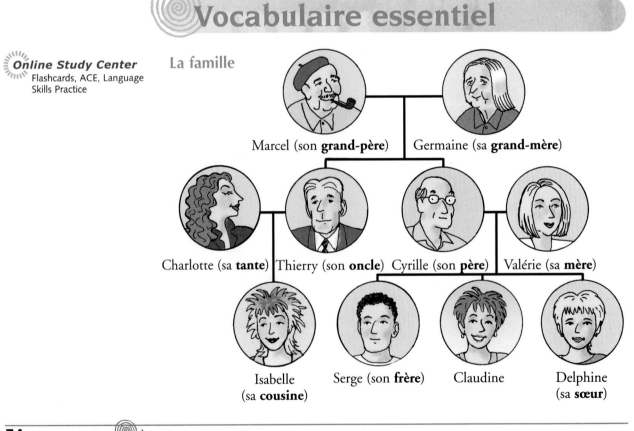

Marcel (son **grand-père**) — Germaine (sa **grand-mère**)

Charlotte (sa **tante**) Thierry (son **oncle**) Cyrille (son **père**) Valérie (sa **mère**)

Isabelle (sa **cousine**) — Serge (son **frère**) — Claudine — Delphine (sa **sœur**)

Autres membres de la famille proche *(Other close family members)*

le mari	*husband*
la femme	*wife*
les enfants *(m. / f.)*	*children*
la fille	*daughter*
le fils	*son*
le cousin / la cousine	
la nièce	
le neveu	

Membres de la famille par alliance *(Family members through marriage)*

le beau-père	*stepfather / father-in-law*
la belle-mère	*stepmother / mother-in-law*
le beau-frère	*brother-in-law*
la belle-sœur	*sister-in-law*
le petit ami / la petite amie	*boyfriend / girlfriend*

être … adopté(e)
     divorcé(e)
     fiancé(e)
     marié(e)
     séparé(e)
     célibataire   *single*

If you feel it is appropriate for your students, you might also introduce the terms **amant** *(male lover)*, **maîtresse** *(female lover)*, and **avoir une aventure** *(to have an affair)*.

Expansion personnelle

les frères jumeaux	*twin brothers*
les sœurs jumelles	*twin sisters*
le demi-frère	*half brother / stepbrother*
la demi-sœur	*half sister/ stepsister*

être … veuve *(f.)*   *widow*
     veuf *(m.)*   *widower*
     orphelin(e)   *orphan*
     amoureux / amoureuse   *in love (m. / f.)*

Un mariage. Quels âges (approximativement) ont cette femme et son mari? Quels membres de la famille sont toujours présents à un mariage?

À vous!

To continue this activity, have students write their own definitions, and then have their classmates guess the answer.

Answer Key: 1. père / beau-père 2. tante 3. cousines 4. frères 5. célibataire 6. orpheline 7. nièce 8. beau-frère / demi-frère 9. mariée

A. Liens parentaux. Complete the following definitions regarding family members.

1. Le mari de ma mère, c'est mon _____.
2. La femme de mon oncle, c'est ma _____.
3. Les filles de mes oncles, ce sont mes _____.
4. Les fils de mes parents, ce sont mes _____.
5. Une personne qui n'est pas mariée est _____.
6. Une personne qui n'a pas de parents est _____.
7. La fille de mon frère est ma _____.
8. Le fils de mon beau-père est mon _____.
9. J'ai un mari, je suis _____.

B. Ma famille. Choose the descriptions that best describe your family.

1. Ma famille paternelle / maternelle est (grande, petite, super, ennuyeuse, amusante, …).
2. Il y a (deux, trois, quatre, cinq … membres) dans ma famille.
3. J'ai (un[e], deux …) sœur(s) / frère(s) (je suis [fille / fils] unique).
4. Ma mère (travaille pour … / ne travaille pas, habite à …, parle espagnol / français …).
5. Mon père (travaille pour … / ne travaille pas, voyage souvent à … / ne voyage pas, fume / ne fume pas).
6. De toute ma famille, je préfère mon / ma (frère, sœur, père, mère, grand-père, grand-mère, ?).
7. Mon grand-père / Ma grand-mère (habite à, me gâte[1] / ne me gâte pas, ?).

C. Ta famille. Among your classmates, find students with the following family situations. Write the names of the students for each situation. Ask the follow-up questions in parentheses to get more details.

Before starting this activity you may want to ask the class to work together on phrasing their questions. For example, for #1, ask students how they would formulate the appropriate question (Tu es fils unique?). Do the same for each item.

Trouvez …

1. un étudiant ou[2] une étudiante qui est fils / fille unique (Tu aimes être fils / fille unique?)
2. un étudiant ou une étudiante qui est marié(e) (Depuis combien de temps[3]?)
3. un étudiant ou une étudiante qui a un enfant (Il / Elle s'appelle comment?)
4. un étudiant ou une étudiante qui a une mère femme d'affaires (Elle travaille où[4]?)
5. un étudiant ou une étudiante qui a un père ingénieur (Il travaille où?)
6. un étudiant ou une étudiante qui a plus de[5] quatre frères ou sœurs (Ils s'appellent comment?)
7. un étudiant ou une étudiante qui a un demi-frère ou une demi-sœur (Il / Elle est gentil / gentille?)

---

[1]*spoils me* [2]*or* [3]*For how long?* [4]*where* [5]*more than*

Portrait personnel

Now report your findings from activity C to the class! Be sure to include a variety of information about a number of your classmates.

 MODÈLE: *Rob n'est pas fils unique. Jen est mariée depuis deux ans[1]. …*

Structure 5

Les adjectifs possessifs

The possessive adjectives have the following forms in French:

Masculine singular	Feminine singular	Masculine and feminine plural
mon	ma	mes
ton	ta	tes
son	sa	ses
notre	notre	nos
votre	votre	vos
leur	leur	leurs

The possessive adjectives in French agree in gender and in number with the noun they precede, for example:

La sœur de mon père est jolie.	*My father's sister is pretty.*
Sa sœur est jolie.	*His sister is pretty.*

Sœur is feminine singular, and that is why the possessive adjective **sa** is also in the feminine singular. In English the possessive adjectives agree with the person who possesses: ***his** sister,* ***his** father,* ***his** daughter,* ***his** children;* in French, on the contrary, possessive adjectives agree with what is "possessed": *sa* **sœur**, *son* **père**, *sa* **fille**, *ses* **enfants. Sa fille,** therefore, can mean either *her daughter* or *his daughter.*

Attention! Before a feminine noun beginning with a vowel, **ma, ta,** and **sa** become **mon, ton,** and **son.**

Mon amie Juliette est pilote à Air France.
Ton étudiante Sylvie parle français parfaitement.

VÉRIFIEZ VOTRE COMPRÉHENSION

1. Go back to the illustration in the **Continuons!** section on page 72, in which Claudine is showing her family album. Identify the possessive adjectives, then say whether each one is masculine singular, feminine singular, or plural. For example: **Mon frère Serge est barman.** Why does Claudine use **mon** and not **ma?** With what noun does **mon** agree?

2. Do the same for the first illustration on page 73 (Claudine's paternal family). For example, ask yourself why it is **Leur fille s'appelle Isabelle** (talking about **oncle Thierry** and **tante Charlotte**).

---

[1]*for two years*

Have students either present this material orally or write a short paragraph for publication in the class newspaper or on the class web site. If you choose to have students present their information orally, you might use it for a direct follow-up to the activity, for a warm-up the next day, or both.

Online Study Center
ACE, Language Skills Practice

À l'écoute! 🎧

Listen to the sentences on your In-Text Audio CD, and indicate whether the possessive adjective you hear is singular or plural.

1. _____ singular   _____ plural
2. _____ singular   _____ plural
3. _____ singular   _____ plural
4. _____ singular   _____ plural
5. _____ singular   _____ plural
6. _____ singular   _____ plural
7. _____ singular   _____ plural
8. _____ singular   _____ plural
9. _____ singular   _____ plural
10. _____ singular   _____ plural

Pratiquons!

A. Des familles. Some French speakers are describing their families. Complete the sentences with the correct possessive adjectives.

Anne: «Il y a cinq membres dans (1) _____ famille: (2) _____ père, (3) _____ mère et (4) _____ deux sœurs. (5) _____ parents sont suisses. (6) _____ *(Our)* famille habite toute à Genève. Et (7) _____ *(your)* parents, où est-ce qu'ils habitent?»

Jean-Jacques et Marie-Do. Jean-Jacques: «(8) _____ *(Our)* familles sont très différentes. Les parents de Marie-Do sont divorcés. (9) _____ *(Her)* mère habite à Lyon et (10) _____ *(her)* père habite à Marseille. (11) _____ *(Their)* trois filles sont des triplées!»

Marie-Do: «La famille de Jean-Jacques est très unie *(united)*. (12) _____ *(His)* parents sont mariés depuis trente ans. Jean-Jacques est (13) _____ *(their)* fils unique. Il a de la chance[1] d'avoir une petite famille unie!»

👥**B. Vous vous souvenez?** *(Do you remember?)* With a classmate, try— without looking at the text!—to answer the following questions about Claudine's family. Use possessive adjectives in your answers. Then, go back to the text to check how good your memory was!

1. Comment est le grand-père paternel de Claudine? _____ grand-père est _____.

2. Comment est la grand-mère maternelle de Claudine? _____ grand-mère est _____.

3. Comment s'appellent l'oncle et la tante paternels de Claudine? _____ oncle paternel s'appelle _____ et sa tante paternelle s'appelle _____.

---

[1] *He is lucky*

4. Quel est le nom de la fille de l'oncle et de la tante paternels de Claudine?
   _____ fille s'appelle _____.
5. Qu'étudie la sœur jumelle de Claudine? _____ sœur étudie
   _____.

C. Vos amis. With a classmate, talk about your friends: your best friend, your childhood friends, your friends at the university. Talk about your enemies too! Don't forget to use a possessive adjective with each noun.

1. meilleur(e) ami(e) est (suggestions: sympa; marié[e]; célibataire; étudiant[e] à …), travaille à …
2. ami(e) d'enfance est (suggestions: blond[e]; grand[e]; gentil[le]; adopté[e]; étudiant[e] à …), habite à …
3. ami(e) d'enfance a (suggestions: une sœur; un frère; trois cousins; un chien; un enfant …)
4. ami(e)s à l'université sont (suggestions: intelligent[e]s; amusant[e]s; dans ma classe de …; bavard[e]s …)
5. ennemi(e) est (suggestions: méchant[e]; laid[e]; ennuyeux[-se]; stupide …)

Vocabulaire essentiel

Les jours de la semaine et les mois de l'année

Voici l'agenda électronique[1] de Cyrille Dupuis (le père de Claudine), ingénieur à Citroën.

OCTOBRE

lundi 3:
  rendez-vous avec Renault
mardi 4:
  chercher les enfants
mercredi 5:
  voyage à Nice
jeudi 6:
  téléphoner à Peugeot
vendredi 7:
  déjeuner avec le PDG de Ford
samedi 8:
  dîner avec les Dumoulin
dimanche 9:
  match de foot des enfants

[1]*electronic planner*

Practice the pronunciation of the months in choral drill before going on to *Claudine est curieuse.*

Voilà les mois de l'année en français. *(Here are the months in French.)*

janvier	avril	juillet	octobre
février	mai	août	novembre
mars	juin	septembre	décembre

DÉCEMBRE
NOVEMBRE
OCTOBRE
SEPTEMBRE
AOÛT
JUILLET
JUIN
MAI
AVRIL
MARS
FÉVRIER
JANVIER

lundi	mardi	mercredi	jeudi	vendredi	samedi	dimanche
1	2	3	4	5	6	7
8	9	10	11	12	13	14
15	16	17	18	19	20	21
22	23	24	25	26	27	28
29	30	31				

Stress the fact that **le jeudi, le vendredi,** etc., mean *every Thursday, every Friday,* etc. Therefore, when giving a particular date, **le** is not used in front of the day. **mercredi 5 janvier.** You may want to ask students to give you today's date and to tell you what they watch on TV on a particular day.

Claudine est curieuse! Regardez le calendrier et lisez les questions de Claudine.

Claudine wants to know when your birthday is:

CLAUDINE: Quelle est la date de ton anniversaire?
VOUS: Mon anniversaire c'est le 2 août, et toi?

Now she wants to know what today's date is:

CLAUDINE: Quelle est la date aujourd'hui?
VOUS: C'est le 30 septembre.

If she had wanted to know what day of the week it was, she would have asked:

CLAUDINE: C'est quel jour aujourd'hui?
VOUS: C'est mardi.

For the month, she would have said:

CLAUDINE: C'est quel mois aujourd'hui?
VOUS: C'est janvier.

Finally, Claudine asks you what you watch on TV *every* Thursday evening:

CLAUDINE: Qu'est-ce que tu regardes **le** jeudi soir à la télé?
VOUS: Je regarde *CSI* **le** jeudi soir.

À vous!

A. Que fait Cyrille Dupuis? *(What is Cyrille Dupuis doing?)* Look at Cyrille Dupuis's planner (page 79) and tell what he is doing on the following days.

mardi 4 octobre: Il _____.

mercredi 5 octobre: Il _____.

vendredi 7 octobre: Il _____.

samedi 8 octobre: Il _____.

B. Comment dit-on … ? *(How do you say . . . ?)* Which questions would you ask to obtain the following information?

1. Today's date: _____
2. What day today is: _____
3. Someone's birthday: _____
4. What TV program someone watches on a particular day of the week (the same day every week): _____
5. What month it is now: _____

C. Et après? *(And after?)* Complete the following sequence of months.

octobre, _____, décembre, _____,

_____, _____, avril, mai, _____,

_____, _____, septembre

Structure 6

Le pronom *on* et l'expression *il y a*

The subject pronoun **on** has two principal uses.

- To make a general statement.

On mange bien en France.	*One eats / **People** eat well in France.*
Comment dit-**on** *book* en français?	*How does **one** say* book *in French?*
On dit «livre».	***One** says "livre."*
Généralement, **on** ne travaille pas le dimanche.	*Generally, **one** does not work on Sundays.*

You have seen this use in previous chapters.

- **On** can also replace **nous** to mean *we*. This use is informal (used among friends or family).

Le samedi soir, mes amis et moi, **on** danse beaucoup.	*On Saturday evenings, my friends and I, **we** dance a lot.*
On n'aime pas les devoirs!	***We** do not like homework!*

The subject pronoun **on** is always conjugated in the third person singular (like **il** and **elle**), regardless of whether it means *one, people,* or *we*.

On est content avec nos amis.	***We** are happy with our friends.*
On ne fume pas en classe.	***One** does not smoke in class.*

The expression **il y a** is used to indicate existence. It is usually combined either with an indefinite quantity (introduced by an indefinite article: **un, une, des**) or with a fixed quantity (introduced by a specific number). **Il y a** means *there is* or *there are.*

- **Il y a** followed by an indefinite article:

  Il y a un chien dans la salle de classe.   ***There is*** *a dog in the classroom.*
  Il y a des étudiants sur le campus.   ***There are*** *students on campus.*

- **Il y a** followed by a number:

  Il y a 28 jours au mois de février.   ***There are*** *28 days in the month of February.*

Remind students that the indefinite article always changes to de in the negative: *j'ai un chien* → *je n'ai pas de chien.*

- To negate **il y a, n'** is placed before **y, pas** is placed after **a,** and the indefinite article is replaced by **de:**

  Il y a *un* chien dans la classe. → Il **n'**y a **pas** *de* chien dans la classe.
  Il y a *des* étudiants dans la classe. → Il **n'**y a **pas** *d'*étudiants dans la classe.

- When **il n'y a pas** is followed by a number, there is no need to add **de:**

  Il y a 30 jours au mois de novembre. → Il **n'**y a **pas** 30 jours au mois de février.

VÉRIFIEZ VOTRE COMPRÉHENSION

Go back to the **Continuons!** section on pages 72–73 where Claudine is talking about her family. Find sentences in which **on** and **il y a** are used, and think about their usage in each case. For example, in the first sentence, Claudine says **On est cinq dans ma famille.** Does **on** here mean *one, people,* or *we?*

Pratiquons!

A. Dans la classe de français. Are the following statements **vrai** (true) or **faux** (false)?

For listening practice, this activity can be done orally with books closed. Read the sentences to the class and have students respond with **vrai** or **faux**.

Answer Key: Answers may vary.

1. On chante en classe.   _____ vrai   _____ faux
2. On parle anglais en classe.   _____ vrai   _____ faux
3. On ne fume pas en classe.   _____ vrai   _____ faux
4. On mange en classe.   _____ vrai   _____ faux
5. On regarde la télévision en classe.   _____ vrai   _____ faux
6. On n'écoute pas le professeur en classe.   _____ vrai   _____ faux
7. Il y a trois professeurs dans la classe.   _____ vrai   _____ faux
8. Il y a vingt-deux étudiants dans la classe.   _____ vrai   _____ faux
9. Il n'y a pas de fenêtres[1] dans la salle de classe.   _____ vrai   _____ faux

---

[1] *windows*

82   *quatre-vingt-deux*   À vous!

B. Mes amis et moi, on ... Tell the class what you do with your friends on the following days. Start your sentences with **Mes amis et moi, on ...** .

Indicate to students that they have to use **on** in their sentences.

1. jeudi
2. vendredi
3. *(every)* samedi
4. dimanche

Structure 7

Les chiffres de 30 à 69

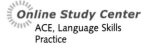**Online Study Center**
ACE, Language Skills Practice

The numbers 30–69 follow the same pattern as the numbers 20–29:

trente	quarante	cinquante	soixante
trente et un	quarante et un	cinquante et un	soixante et un
trente-deux	quarante-deux	cinquante-deux	soixante-deux
trente-trois	quarante-trois	cinquante-trois	soixante-trois
trente-quatre	quarante-quatre	cinquante-quatre	soixante-quatre
trente-cinq	quarante-cinq	cinquante-cinq	soixante-cinq
trente-six	quarante-six	cinquante-six	soixante-six
trente-sept	quarante-sept	cinquante-sept	soixante-sept
trente-huit	quarante-huit	cinquante-huit	soixante-huit
trente-neuf	quarante-neuf	cinquante-neuf	soixante-neuf

You may want to present the numbers using choral response to help students practice their pronunciation.

Pratiquons!

A. Combien de jours? Look at the calendar and say how many days there are in the following months.

1. 31 2. 31 3. 31 4. 30 5. 31
6. 30 7. 28

1. En janvier
2. En août
3. En mars
4. En juin
5. En juillet
6. En novembre
7. En février

B. Des chiffres exacts *(Exact numbers)*. Ask your classmates the following questions. Go around the class, if need be, to find the answers!

1. Combien d'étudiants est-ce qu'il y a dans la classe?
2. Combien d'étudiantes avec les cheveux frisés est-ce qu'il y a dans la classe?
3. Combien d'étudiants avec les yeux verts est-ce qu'il y a dans la classe?
4. Combien d'étudiants avec des lunettes est-ce qu'il y a dans la classe de français?
5. Combien de membres est-ce qu'il y a dans ta famille?
6. Est-ce qu'il y a des chiens et des chats dans ta famille? Combien?
7. Tu as combien de cousins et cousines?

C. Un examen d'arithmétique *(A math test).* Do the math! Use the appropriate French expressions, as in the models.

MODÈLES: 18 + 7   *Dix-huit **plus** sept **font** vingt-cinq.*

42 − 12   *Quarante-deux **moins** douze **font** trente.*

1. 32 + 26
2. 49 + 14
3. 28 + 33

4. 57 − 51
5. 64 − 30
6. 69 − 41

À vous de parler!

A. Des présentations. Bring in a picture of your family, and introduce your family to the class. Use Claudine's text on pages 72–73 as a reference if necessary.

Mots utiles: mon anniversaire de mariage; mon anniversaire; mes fiançailles[1]; la naissance[2] de mon fils / ma fille; mon voyage à …; la rupture avec mon petit ami / ma petite amie

B. Des dates importantes. Ask your classmates what the most important date in their lives is and how they celebrate it.

Questions: *Quelle est la date la plus importante de ta vie? Comment est-ce que tu célèbres cette date?*

En Centrafrique la fête des mères est comme ça

La République Centrafricaine est située entre le Soudan à l'est, le Tchad au nord, le Cameroun à l'ouest et la République démocratique du Congo au sud[3]. Les Centrafricains parlent sängö et français. La capitale est Bangui. La fête des mères en Centrafrique n'est pas une fête familiale. Les mères se réunissent entre elles et célèbrent cette fête ensemble dans un bar ou dans un restaurant. Les hommes ne sont pas invités et les enfants non plus[4].

[1]*engagement* [2]*birth* [3]Look at the map inside the cover of your textbook to locate **la République Centrafricaine.** [4]*neither*

Réfléchissons

1. How is Mother's Day celebrated in your country? What do you think of the way women from the Central African Republic celebrate Mother's Day? Do you think it is a good idea? Why?
2. Do you celebrate Mother's Day? How?
3. Should Mother's Day be celebrated at all? Do you believe that Mother's Day is purely a commercial holiday? Or do you think that mothers should be honored every day, not only on a special occasion one day a year?

Une borie. Voici deux photos d'une borie[1], une ancienne maison que l'on trouve en Provence (dans le sud de la France). Quelle est la relation probable entre ces trois femmes?

À vous de lire!

A. Stratégies. Look at the reading title on page 86 and try to guess which topics might be mentioned in the text. Ask yourself the following questions: What type of information can I expect to find in this text? What is the text going to talk about? What words or expressions pertaining to the family from the vocabulary in this chapter will I probably see in this text?

---

[1]**Bories** were built in the Middle Ages by shepherds living in the south of France. They all have the same unusual shape because they were built without mortar—gravity has held them together for nearly a thousand years! Many are still very safe; this one is used as an art studio by the oldest woman in the photos, Claude Astrachan, who is a well-known sculptor in France.

B. Avant de lire. Read the numbered, bold-faced category headers in the first paragraph, and define what each category (1–6) refers to, without reading the explanations that follow each one. Write your definitions / translations here.

1. _____
2. _____
3. _____
4. _____
5. _____
6. _____

The second paragraph mentions a **médaille d'honneur de la famille nombreuse.** To whom do you think such an award would be given? Why?

    Scan the fourth paragraph, and write a list of the family members that are mentioned. Next, search for key words that would explain their role. Finally, using the context in this paragraph, try to guess the meaning of *crèches* (or *garderies*) and *nounous.*

C. Lisons! Now read the passage more thoroughly, and then answer the questions that follow.

La famille française contemporaine

Il y a plusieurs[1] types de familles en France:

1) **La famille monoparentale.** Un seul parent élève[2] les enfants. En général c'est la mère qui s'occupe des enfants.

2) **Les unions libres.** Le couple n'est pas marié. La naissance[3] d'un enfant ne change pas la situation.

3) **La famille recomposée.** Existe après un divorce ou une séparation. Dans la famille il y a des demi-frères ou des demi-sœurs, une belle-mère ou un beau-père.

4) **Les couples mixtes.** Un des époux appartient à une autre race.

5) **Les couples modernes.** La femme travaille et le mari aussi. Les deux conjoints contribuent financièrement aux dépenses[4] familiales. En général, ces couples élèvent les enfants ensemble.

6) **Les couples traditionnels.** La femme ne travaille pas, elle reste au foyer et s'occupe des enfants.

    La natalité est en baisse en France: la moyenne[5] est de un ou deux enfants. En 1920 le gouvernement crée «la médaille d'honneur de la famille nombreuse» pour récompenser les familles avec quatre enfants ou plus[6] qui

---

[1]*several* [2]*raises* [3]*birth* [4]*expenses* [5]*average* [6]*or more*

élèvent «dignement» leurs enfants. La médaille de bronze est attribuée aux familles avec quatre ou cinq enfants; la médaille d'argent aux familles avec six ou sept enfants; et la médaille d'or aux familles avec huit enfants ou plus. Aujourd'hui, il est rare de trouver en France des familles avec plus de huit enfants, mais évidemment ça existe!

Les mariages diminuent aussi et les divorces augmentent. Dans les grandes villes les mariages terminent fréquemment en divorce: un mariage sur trois[1]. L'homme se marie en moyenne à 27 ans et la femme à 25 ans.

Quand les enfants sont petits (de un à trois ans), ce sont souvent les grands-parents qui s'occupent de leurs petits-enfants. Les grands-parents constituent un support important pour l'éducation des enfants. Pour les personnes qui n'ont pas leur famille (les grands-parents, par exemple) à proximité[2], les crèches (appelées aussi garderies) et les nounous sont une option possible. Les crèches et les nounous sont subventionnées par l'État et elles ne sont pas chères.

Les enfants adultes habitent à la maison avec leurs parents jusqu'à ce qu'ils[3] trouvent un travail stable et une indépendance financière ou jusqu'au jour de leur mariage. En moyenne, ils habitent à la maison jusqu'à l'âge de 25 ans.

D. Après la lecture. Answer the following questions about the reading.

1. Dans la famille monoparentale, qui est responsable des enfants le plus souvent?
2. Dans les couples modernes, qui s'occupe des enfants?
3. Est-ce que la natalité augmente en France? Combien d'enfants est-ce que les couples ont?
4. Quelle est la médaille d'honneur la plus honorifique?
5. Est-ce que les divorces diminuent? Où est-ce qu'il y a surtout des divorces?
6. Est-ce que le rôle des grands-parents est important? Pourquoi?
7. Quelles sont les deux possibilités pour la garde des enfants à l'extérieur des familles?
8. Quand est-ce que les enfants adultes deviennent complètement indépendants?

Quelle est votre opinion?

9. En France, le métissage (le mariage entre races différentes) est très commun. Est-ce qu'il y a beaucoup de couples mixtes aux États-Unis? Où est-ce qu'on trouve les mariages mixtes, en général?
10. Est-ce que les couples pratiquent les unions libres aux États-Unis? Les mariages diminuent-ils ou augmentent-ils?
11. Aux États-Unis, est-ce que le rôle de la famille proche est similaire à celui de la famille proche en France? Est-ce que les crèches sont chères? Et les nounous?
12. Quelle est votre opinion sur le fait que les enfants français adultes habitent avec leurs parents jusqu'à l'âge de 25 ans en moyenne? Est-ce similaire dans votre pays[4]? Habitez-vous chez vos parents? Pourquoi?

You may choose to have your students answer these questions in English or French (or a combination), to allow them to truly express themselves. You may want to ask students their opinions on receiving a **médaille** for being a good and responsible parent of a large family.

---

[1] *one out of three* [2] *near* [3] *until they* [4] *country*

Vocabulaire essentiel

Verbes et expressions verbales *verbs and verbal expressions*

acheter *to buy*
appeler *to call*
s'appeler *to be named*
chanter *to sing*
chercher *to look for*
commencer *to begin*
danser *to dance*
écouter *to listen to*

être ... adopté(e) *to be . . . adopted*
    célibataire   *single*
    divorcé(e)   *divorced*
    fiancé(e)   *engaged*
    marié(e)   *married*
    séparé(e)   *separated*
étudier *to study*
fumer *to smoke*
habiter *to live*
jouer à *to play a sport*

manger *to eat*
parler *to speak*
pratiquer *to practice,*
    to participate in
préparer *to prepare*
téléphoner à *to telephone*
terminer *to finish*
travailler *to work*
trouver *to find*
voyager *to travel*

La famille *the family*

Membres de la famille proche *close family members*

le cousin / la cousine *cousin*
    (masc. / fem.)
un(e) enfant *child*
la femme *wife*
la fille *daughter*
le fils *son*

le frère *brother*
la grand-mère *grandmother*
le grand-père *grandfather*
le mari *husband*
la mère *mother*
le neveu *nephew*

la nièce *niece*
l'oncle *(m.) uncle*
le père *father*
la sœur *sister*
la tante *aunt*

Membres de la famille par alliance *family members through marriage*

le beau-père *stepfather or father-in-law*
le beau-frère *brother-in-law*
la belle-mère *stepmother or mother-in-law*
la belle-sœur *sister-in-law*

le petit ami / la petite amie *boyfriend / girlfriend*

Les professions *professions*

un agent de police *police officer*
un agent de voyage *travel agent*
un architecte *architect*
un dentiste *dentist*
un étudiant / une étudiante *student*

un homme d'affaires / une femme
    d'affaires *businessman /*
    businesswoman
une infirmière *nurse*
un ingénieur *engineer*

un médecin *doctor*
un pilote *pilot*
un professeur *professor*
une secrétaire *secretary*

Les animaux domestiques *pets*

un chat *cat*
un chien *dog*
un cochon d'Inde *guinea pig*
un hamster *hamster*

un lapin *rabbit*
un oiseau *bird*
un poisson rouge *goldfish*

Les jours de la semaine *days of the week*

lundi *Monday*
mardi *Tuesday*
mercredi *Wednesday*
jeudi *Thursday*

vendredi *Friday*
samedi *Saturday*
dimanche *Sunday*

Les mois de l'année *months of the year*

janvier *January*
février *February*
mars *March*
avril *April*
mai *May*
juin *June*

juillet *July*
août *August*
septembre *September*
octobre *October*
novembre *November*
décembre *December*

Expansion personnelle

Verbes et expressions verbales *verbs and verbal expressions*

être ... amoureux *(m.)* / amoureuse *(f.) in love*
        orphelin(e) *orphan*
        veuf *(m.)* / veuve *(f.) widower / widow*
gâter *to spoil*

Noms *nouns*

un anniversaire *birthday*
un chiffre *number*
le demi-frère *half brother or stepbrother*
la demi-sœur *half sister or stepsister*
un(e) ennemi(e) *enemy*
les frères jumeaux *(m. pl.) twin brothers*
les sœurs jumelles *(f. pl.) twin sisters*

Mon appartement

In this chapter you will learn what sort of homes the French and other Francophones live in. You will get a look at apartment living in Geneva, Switzerland. You will also learn how to run errands and talk about the weather.

The vocabulary that you will learn includes

Describing an apartment or a house
Running errands
Talking about the weather
Renting an apartment or a house

The structures that you will learn include

The near future
The verb **aller (à)**
The numbers from 70 to 1,000,000
The pronoun **y (allons-y)**
Regular verbs ending in **-ir**
Prepositions and contractions with definite articles
Adjectives of color
The verb **faire**

The culture that you will study includes

Differences and similarities between housing in the United States and in France
Winter in Quebec

Commençons!

L'appartement d'Aurélie 🎧

Today, Aurélie Marquis is going to show you her apartment in Geneva, Switzerland. You should feel special given that the Swiss, like the French and the Belgians, usually do not show their homes—not even to their friends. Friends stay in the living room or in the dining area. Neither the hostess nor the host will offer a guided tour of the house!

Online Study Center
Language Skills Practice
You may want to expand this introduction by telling students that guests do not enter the kitchen even if it is to offer help.

Tell students that in Switzerland (as well as in France, Belgium, and Luxembourg), windows have external shutters, **les volets,** or rolling shutters, **les persiennes,** in more modern buildings. These shutters are functional—they are opened in the morning and closed at night. There are no inside blinds, but curtains, **des rideaux,** are common.

des volets *(m.)*

le portail

> Bienvenue chez moi[1]!
> Je m'appelle Aurélie Marquis et vous allez visiter[2] mon appartement à Genève en Suisse. Mon appartement a quatre pièces[3]. Mon immeuble[4] a cinq étages[5]. J'habite au troisième étage. J'habite toute seule: je n'ai pas de colocataire[6]. On y va[7]?

---

[1] *Welcome to my place!* [2] *are going to visit* [3] *rooms* [4] *building* [5] *floors* [6] *roommate*
[7] *Shall we go?*

l'ascenseur *(m.)*

les boîtes *(f.)* aux lettres

les escaliers *(m.)*

Voilà le portail de mon immeuble. Nous n'avons pas de concierge. Je suis locataire[1] et mon loyer[2] est assez cher: mille francs suisses par mois. C'est normal, j'habite à Genève, en Suisse!

Nous allons monter en ascenseur, d'accord? Les escaliers, c'est trop fatigant!

Nous allons entrer dans mon appartement par la cuisine. Ma cuisine est toute petite (c'est une kitchenette), mais elle est très pratique. Elle est bien équipée: il y a un micro-ondes, un four, un réfrigérateur, un évier, une cuisinière et une machine à laver.

---

[1]*tenant* [2]*rent*

Tell students that it is common in Europe to have rugs rather than wall-to-wall carpets. Floors are wooden, but tiled in the bathroom and kitchen.

Ensuite, vous allez voir[1] le salon et la salle à manger. J'aime mon salon parce qu'il est très lumineux[2]. J'ai deux grandes baies vitrées et un balcon qui donne sur la rue[3]. Mon sofa est très confortable. J'ai aussi un fauteuil[4]. Voilà ma chaîne stéréo (elle est super!) et mon téléviseur. Ma salle à manger est très simple: un tapis, une table et deux chaises.

Point out that in Francophone Europe, the toilet is in a separate room, **le cabinet de toilette** or **les toilettes.** Usually that room has a sink and a small window.

Finalement, vous allez voir la salle de bains. Il n'y a pas de fenêtre. Il y a une douche mais il n'y a pas de baignoire[5]. Il y a un lavabo et un miroir. Le cabinet de toilette est séparé.

Vous aimez mon appartement? Il est chouette[6], non?

Maintenant, nous allons aller dans ma chambre. Vous allez aimer ma chambre! Elle est petite mais elle a une grande fenêtre qui donne sur un parc public. J'ai un ordinateur et un bureau—j'adore surfer le Net, et vous? J'ai aussi un lit et un tapis de course. Le tapis de course c'est un cadeau de mon petit ami américain! Il est sympa, n'est-ce pas?

---

[1] *you are going to see* [2] *sunny* [3] *overlooking the street* [4] *armchair* [5] *bathtub* [6] *cool; nice*

Vous avez bien compris?

Read the following statements about Aurélie's apartment and check **vrai** or **faux**. Correct the false statements.

1. La chambre d'Aurélie a une petite fenêtre. _____ vrai _____ faux

2. Dans la cuisine d'Aurélie il n'y a pas de machine à laver. _____ vrai _____ faux

3. Aurélie a une baignoire dans la salle de bains. _____ vrai _____ faux

4. Le colocataire d'Aurélie est américain. _____ vrai _____ faux

5. Dans le salon Aurélie a un sofa et une baie vitrée. _____ vrai _____ faux

6. Dans la salle à manger il y a cinq chaises. _____ vrai _____ faux

7. Dans le salon il y a un tapis de course. _____ vrai _____ faux

8. Le cabinet de toilette n'est pas dans la salle de bains. _____ vrai _____ faux

9. L'appartement d'Aurélie est cher. _____ vrai _____ faux

Vocabulaire essentiel

Le logement et la maison

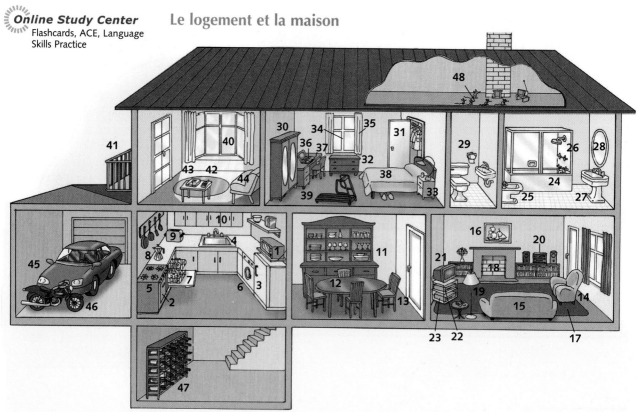

Dans la cuisine
1. un (four à) micro-ondes
2. un four
3. un réfrigérateur
4. un évier
5. une cuisinière
6. une machine à laver
7. un lave-vaisselle
8. une cafetière
9. un grille-pain
10. *les placards

Dans la salle à manger
11. un buffet
12. une table
13. une chaise

Dans le salon
14. un fauteuil
15. un canapé / un sofa
16. un tableau
17. un tapis

18. *une cheminée
19. une lampe
20. une chaîne stéréo
21. une télévision
22. un lecteur de DVD
23. un magnéto(scope)

Dans la salle de bains
24. une baignoire
25. *un bidet
26. une douche
27. un lavabo
28. un miroir
29. le WC / le cabinet de toilette / les toilettes *(f.)*

Dans la chambre
30. une armoire
31. un placard
32. une commode
33. une table de nuit
34. une fenêtre

35. les rideaux
36. un ordinateur
37. un bureau
38. un lit
39. *un tapis de course

Dans la salle de séjour
40. *une baie vitrée
41. *un balcon
42. un téléphone (sans fil)
43. un répondeur automatique
44. un futon

Dans le garage
45. une voiture
46. une moto

Dans la cave
47. le vin

Dans *le grenier
48. *des souris *(f.)*

Expansion personnelle

The vocabulary words that are marked with an asterisk (*) are for your
Expansion personnelle.

Remind students that the goal of the *Expansion personnelle* is to expand their vocabulary when doing an activity or when writing. Students are not responsible for learning this vocabulary section, unless you decide otherwise.

À vous!

A. Où se trouve ... ? *(Where is . . . ?)* Indicate in which rooms the following items can be found.

MODÈLE: une cafetière

Il y a une cafetière dans la cuisine.

1. une baignoire
2. une commode
3. un évier
4. un répondeur automatique
5. un lit
6. le vin
7. un fauteuil
8. un grille-pain
9. un tableau
10. un buffet

B. Où fais-tu … ? *(Where do you do . . . ?)* Indicate in which rooms you do the following things. Use complete sentences.

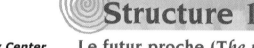 MODÈLE: manger

> *Je mange dans la cuisine ou dans la salle à manger.*

1. manger
2. regarder un film
3. écouter de la musique
4. parler au téléphone
5. travailler sur l'ordinateur
6. étudier
7. fumer
8. chanter
9. préparer le dîner

C. Ce que je possède *(What I own).* Tell a classmate what things you have in each of the following rooms. Then reverse roles. Who has the most things?

1. la cuisine
2. la chambre
3. le salon
4. la salle de bains

Structure 1

Online Study Center
ACE, Language Skills Practice

Le futur proche (*The near future*)

- When reading Aurélie's text, you probably noticed the appearance of a new verb and a new construction. For example, in the first paragraph Aurélie says: «**vous allez visiter**» *(you are going to visit)*. This new construction is called **le futur proche** *(the near future)*. It is used to convey an action that is likely to happen in the near future (in the next couple of minutes, or in a couple of hours, or in the next few days).

- The near future is formed with the verb **aller** *(to go)* plus the verb carrying the main action, which is left in the infinitive. For example, if you want to say, "we are going to eat at a restaurant," you use **aller** conjugated + **manger** in the infinitive (not conjugated).

Nous allons manger au restaurant.

- The conjugation of **aller** is irregular in all forms except for the first and second person plural (**nous** and **vous**).

aller	
je vais	nous **all**ons
tu vas	vous **allez**
il / elle / on va	ils vont

- To make a sentence in the near future negative, **ne** is placed before **aller** and **pas** after it.

Affirmative: Je vais commencer mes devoirs ce soir.
Negative: Je **ne** vais **pas** commencer mes devoirs ce soir.

- To ask a question in the near future, **est-ce que** is placed at the beginning of the sentence.

Est-ce que vous allez acheter le CD de Seal?

Aller + à

- The verb **aller** can also be used to talk about going to a specific place. When this is the case, it is followed by the preposition **à** *(to)*.

Je vais **à** la maison.
Tu vas **à** l'université.

- Before masculine singular nouns, the preposition **à** contracts with the definite article **le** to become **au.**

Chloé va **au** cinéma. **(à + le = au)**

- Before masculine plural nouns, the preposition **à** contracts with the definite article **les** to become **aux.**

Céline et David vont **aux** supermarchés chers[1]. **(à + les = aux)**

- There are two common expressions with **aller** that are used to invite someone to go somewhere: **Allons-y** *(Let's go)* and **On y va?** *(Shall we go?).*

 VÉRIFIEZ VOTRE COMPRÉHENSION

1. Go back to the **Commençons!** section on pages 91–93 and find where Aurélie uses the expression **allons-y** or **on y va.** Why does she use it? In what context?

2. Reread Aurélie's description of her apartment one more time to see the use of the near future (**aller** + infinitive) in context. Underline each of the near futures that you find.

Pratiquons!

A. Demain matin *(Tomorrow morning).* Lucien is going to tell you what he and his friend Alain are going to do tomorrow morning. Complete the paragraph with the correct form of the verb **aller.**

Answer Key: 1. vais 2. vais 3. va 4. allons 5. allons 6. allons 7. vont 8. vais 9. va

Demain, je (1) _____ manger le petit déjeuner sur le balcon. Je (2) _____ contempler les palmiers et la mer[2]. Mon copain Alain (3) _____ téléphoner à 10 heures. Alain et moi, nous (4) _____ aller au parc public faire du jogging. Ensuite, nous (5) _____ chercher le pain et nous (6) _____ acheter le journal. Les vendeurs de journaux (7) _____ commenter les derniers événements[3] politiques. Finalement, je (8) _____ rentrer chez moi et Alain (9) _____ aller chez lui[4].

---

[1] *expensive* [2] *sea* [3] *events* [4] *home*

B. Dans quelques années *(In a few years).* Tell what these celebrities are going to do, using the expressions provided. Answer in the affirmative or the negative.

> ◎ MODÈLE: John Travolta / être Président des États-Unis
>
> *Dans quelques années, John Travolta va être Président des États-Unis. / Dans quelques années, John Travolta ne va pas être Président des États-Unis.*

1. Nicole Kidman / gagner un autre Oscar
2. Madonna / avoir un quatrième enfant
3. Jodie Foster et John Travolta / habiter à la Maison-Blanche ensemble[1]
4. Brad Pitt / sortir avec[2] Anna Nicole Smith
5. Steven Spielberg / filmer *E.T. 2*
6. Larry King et Beyoncé / chanter ensemble sur un nouveau CD

C. Pas maintenant! Ask a classmate if s/he is going to do the following things. Your classmate is going to answer with a complete sentence, using **pas maintenant.** Follow the model.

> ◎ MODÈLE: écouter le prof
>
> —*Est-ce que tu vas écouter le prof?*
>
> —*Je ne vais pas écouter le prof maintenant!*

1. étudier la leçon de français
2. travailler sur l'ordinateur
3. regarder le DVD de *À vous!*
4. parler au prof
5. participer aux activités en classe
6. aller au laboratoire de langues
7. téléphoner au prof de français

D. Le livreur *(The delivery person).* A client has ordered some furniture and appliances to be delivered to his house. You are **le livreur** and are calling to update your client. Use the near future to say which item you are going to deliver **(livrer)** and when.

> ◎ MODÈLE:
>
> 15 minutes
>
> *Je vais livrer la table dans quinze minutes.*

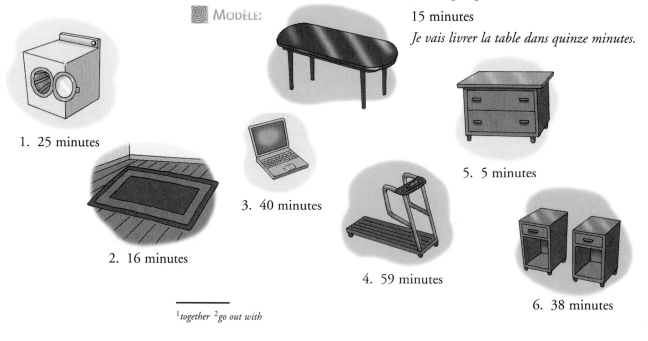

1. 25 minutes
2. 16 minutes
3. 40 minutes
4. 59 minutes
5. 5 minutes
6. 38 minutes

---

[1]*together* [2]*go out with*

Continuons!

Partie I: Le quartier d'Aurélie

Online Study Center
Language Skills Practice

Now that you have visited Aurélie's apartment, she is going to show you her neighborhood. She will tell you where she likes to shop and hang out.

Coucou[1]! C'est encore moi, Aurélie! Après la visite de mon appartement, nous allons visiter mon quartier. Dans mon quartier, il y a de tout[2]:

Voilà la boulangerie-pâtisserie où j'achète ma baguette et mes croissants tous les matins.

Près de la boulangerie il y a une boucherie-charcuterie et une poissonnerie.

---

[1] *Hey! Hi!* Also means *Peek-a-boo!* [2] *everything*

À droite de la boucherie-charcuterie il y a la poste.

À côté du parc public il y a une brasserie. La bière de la brasserie est excellente! Vous aimez la bière? Je vous invite[1] à boire[2] une bière, d'accord[3]?

À gauche[4] de la boucherie-charcuterie il y a une épicerie où on trouve[5] de tout! Au fond[6] de ma rue il y a un parc public pour les enfants et pour les adultes et une pharmacie.

Vous avez bien compris?

Do you know where the following items can be purchased? Match each item on the left with the appropriate store in the right-hand column.

1. _____ le saumon
2. _____ l'aspirine (f.)
3. _____ la bière
4. _____ les saucisses
5. _____ le pain
6. _____ les huîtres[7]
7. _____ les timbres[8]
8. _____ les fruits
9. _____ les conserves[9]
10. _____ les tartes

a. à la boulangerie-pâtisserie
b. à la poste
c. à l'épicerie
d. à la poissonnerie
e. à la pharmacie
f. à la brasserie
g. à la boucherie-charcuterie

---

[1] invite you [2] to drink [3] OK [4] On the left [5] find [6] At the end [7] oysters [8] stamps [9] canned goods

Vocabulaire essentiel

Les magasins (Stores)

Online Study Center
Flashcards, ACE, Language
Skills Practice

la boucherie-charcuterie	*butcher shop and deli*	la poissonnerie	*fish market*
la boulangerie-pâtisserie	*bakery-pastry shop*	la poste	*post office*
la brasserie	*brewery/pub*	le quartier	*neighborhood*
le parc public	*public park*	l'épicerie (f.)	*grocery store*
la pharmacie	*pharmacy*		

À vous!

A. Le quartier de Benoît. This is Benoît Laterre's neighborhood in Marseilles (France). Identify the businesses and places, and write down their names next to the appropriate numbers.

Answer Key: 1. un parc public
2. une pharmacie 3. une
boulangerie 4. une boucherie
5. une poissonnerie 6. une
brasserie

1. _____ 3. _____ 5. _____

2. _____ 4. _____ 6. _____

The street of the
fishing cat.

These are two street signs in Paris. In your country, are street signs ever located on the outside walls of buildings? Can you guess what the street name means in the photo to the left? Do any streets in your neighborhood have unusual names? What are they?

B. Où va Benoît? Indicate where Benoît goes to buy the following things.

 MODÈLE: Pour acheter du saumon, il va à la *poissonnerie*.

1. Pour acheter des croissants, il va à la _____.
2. Pour acheter de l'aspirine, il va à la _____.
3. Pour poster une lettre, il va à la _____.
4. Pour acheter du saucisson, il va à la _____.
5. Pour acheter des bananes, il va à l'_____.
6. Pour acheter du poisson[1], il va à la _____.

 # Structure 2

Les chiffres de 70 à 1 000 000

You already know how to form the numbers from 0 to 69. In this chapter you'll see the rules for forming the numbers from 70 to 1 million.

soixante-dix	quatre-vingts	quatre-vingt-dix
soixante et onze	quatre-vingt-un	quatre-vingt-onze
soixante-douze	quatre-vingt-deux	quatre-vingt-douze
…	…	…
soixante-dix-neuf	quatre-vingt-neuf	quatre-vingt-dix-neuf

100	cent	200 deux cents	1 000 mille
101	cent un	283 deux cent quatre-vingt-trois	2 000 deux mille
1 578	mille cinq cent soixante-dix-huit		1 000 000 un million

1 794 865 un million sept cent quatre-vingt-quatorze mille huit cent soixante-cinq

Attention!

- Notice that in standard French there is no word for *seventy* or *ninety.* The numbers from *seventy* to *seventy-nine* and from *ninety* to *ninety-nine* are formed by adding the teens to *sixty* and *eighty.*
- There is an **-s** on **cent** in **deux cents, trois cents, quatre cents,** etc., *but only* when **cent** is the last number in the sequence; for example, **cent** in the number **trois cent trois** (303) does not have an **-s.** There is also an **-s** in **quatre-vingts,** but no **-s** when another number is joined to **quatre-vingts,** for example, **quatre-vingt-deux. Mille,** on the other hand, never takes an **-s: deux mille, trois mille,** etc.
- **Cent, mille,** and **un million** plus another number have no hyphen: **cent soixante-deux; mille trois cent quarante-trois; un million trois cent mille cinq cent vingt-deux.**
- Notice that to say *one hundred* you simply say **cent** in French. Likewise, to say *one thousand* you simply say **mille.**

---

[1]*fish*

Pratiquons!

A. Au magasin. You are shopping with a friend. Look at the prices of the items you need to furnish your new apartment. Identify the items first, then say the price and finish by saying to your friend **"C'est trop cher!"**

MODÈLE: *Un téléphone sans fil,*
cent quatre-vingt-deux euros ...
C'est trop cher!

182 €

1. 63 €

2. 787 €

3. 1 298 €

4. 3 470 €

5. 98 €

6. 54 €

7. 321 €

B. C'est loin d'ici[1]? Aurélie and her friends are planning a short vacation. Following the model, read the number of kilometers between the following cities.

MODÈLE: Genève / Paris: 409

Genève est à quatre cent neuf kilomètres de Paris.

1. Genève / New York: 6 209
2. Genève / Londres: 755
3. Genève / Nice: 299
4. Genève / Lausanne: 65
5. Genève / Bern: 170
6. Genève / Buenos Aires: 11 080
7. Genève / Rome: 684

Structure 3

Les verbes réguliers en *-ir*

In Chapters 2 and 3 you learned about regular and stem-changing verbs ending in **-er.** Now you are going to learn about a second group of regular verbs ending in **-ir.** These verbs are conjugated by dropping the **-ir** ending and adding the following present tense endings: **-is, -is, -it, -issons, -issez, -issent.**

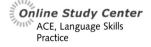
Online Study Center
ACE, Language Skills
Practice

---

[1] *Is it far from here?*

Have your students conjugate **réussir** and **choisir** to make sure that they keep the entire stem *(réuss- / chois-)* before adding the endings.

finir *(to finish)*	
je fin**is**	nous fin**issons**
tu fin**is**	vous fin**issez**
il / elle / on fin**it**	ils / elles fin**issent**

The following **-ir** verbs are also regular.

choisir *to choose*   **salir** *to dirty*
bâtir *to build*   **obéir à** *to obey*
punir *to punish*   **réussir à** *to succeed in, to pass (a test)*

- These verbs are negated in the same way as **-er** verbs.

  Je **ne** punis **pas** mon chien.
  Margot **ne** finit **pas** son examen de mathématiques.

- The verbs **réussir** and **obéir** are always used with the preposition **à.**

  Bébé Alex obéit à sa maman.
  Le chien obéit à son maître.
  Je réussis à mes examens.

Attention!

- When negating **réussir à** or **obéir à,** the preposition **à** stays outside the negation.

  Les enfants **n'**obéissent **pas** à leurs parents.

- Remember that the preposition **à** contracts with the articles **le** and **les** to form **au** and **aux.**

  Est-ce que les étudiants obéissent **aux** professeurs?
  J'obéis **au** prof de français!

Pratiquons!

Answer Key: 1. finissent
2. punit 3. bâtis
4. n'obéit pas 5. choisissez
6. salissons

A. Dans mon quartier. Tell what the following people in your neighborhood do. Complete the sentences with the correct form of the verb in parentheses.

1. Tous les matins, les enfants (finir) _____ les pâtisseries de la boulangerie-pâtisserie.
2. Mon voisin (punir) _____ son chat quand il est sur la table.
3. Tu (bâtir) _____ une nouvelle maison très moderne à côté de mon appartement.
4. Au parc, la petite fille (obéir) n'_____ pas à son père.
5. Vous (choisir) _____ un bon vin dans ma cave pour le dîner.
6. Mes amis et moi, nous (salir) _____ la cuisine quand on prépare le dîner.

B. Je suis choqué(e)! You just can't believe what your classmate is telling you. Compose a sentence based on the cue. Your partner will reply by repeating the sentence in the **tu** form and by saying, **"je suis choqué(e)!"**

Give students the correct form of the possessive adjectives they need to phrase their questions in #3 (tes amis; ton salon), #4 (ta petite sœur), and #5 (tes parents).

> MODÈLE: je / finir les activités dans le cahier
>
> —*Je finis les activités dans le cahier.*
>
> —*Tu finis les activités dans le cahier … je suis choqué(e)!*

1. je / finir les devoirs pour la classe de français
2. je / choisir des cours difficiles le semestre prochain[1]
3. mes amis / ne … pas / salir mon salon quand il y a une fête
4. ma petite sœur (mon petit frère) / obéir à mes parents toujours
5. mes parents / punir mes amis aussi

C. Oh, vraiment? *(Oh, really?)* Go back to activity B, **Je suis choqué(e)!,** and ask your classmate to tell you the truth about each statement. Reverse roles. Follow the model.

> MODÈLE: Toi: *Est-ce que tu finis vraiment les activités dans le cahier?*
> Ton/Ta partenaire: *Oui, je finis vraiment les activités dans le cahier. / Pas vraiment, je ne finis pas les activités dans le cahier.*

À vous de parler!

A. Votre maison/appartement. Your new in-laws are calling from abroad. They have not seen your new home yet. However, they are very curious and they want to know what your new house/apartment is like. Describe it to them and tell them what you have in each room, answering their questions in detail. Tell them also what your neighborhood is like.

Remind students to use only familiar vocabulary and to avoid literal translations and structures that they have not yet mastered.

Possible questions from the in-laws: What is your bedroom like? Do you have two beds or one bed? What is your kitchen like? Does it get dirty often? Do you have two bathrooms or one? etc. What is your . . . like?

> MODÈLE: —*Comment est votre chambre?*
>
> —*Notre chambre est …*

B. Le diseur (La diseuse) de bonne aventure *(The fortune-teller).* You are a famous fortune-teller. Two clients have come to you to find out what the future holds for them. Using the near future, make predictions based on your clients' questions.

Possible questions: Where am I going to live? Where am I going to work? Am I going to get married **(me marier)?** When? Am I going to have children? etc.

> MODÈLE: —*Est-ce que je vais terminer mes études?*
>
> —*Oui, vous allez terminer dans dix ans!*

---

[1]*next*

Les Européens habitent comme ça

En Europe francophone (c'est-à-dire en France, en Belgique, à Monaco, au Luxembourg et en Suisse), il est très commun d'habiter au centre-ville. Les Européens aiment bien leurs villes, et beaucoup de personnes préfèrent habiter dans un appartement en ville, plutôt que[1] d'habiter dans les banlieues[2]. Les vieux bâtiments sont surtout recherchés[3]; ce qui[4] est nouveau et moderne est beaucoup moins désirable. Les maisons au centre-ville sont assez rares; il y a surtout des appartements. Il n'est pas rare pour les familles qui habitent dans un appartement en ville d'avoir aussi une maison de vacances à la campagne[5]; comme ça ils peuvent quitter[6] la ville de temps en temps.

Dans les banlieues, c'est très différent. On trouve beaucoup de nouvelles maisons individuelles, et des immeubles modernes avec beaucoup d'appartements. Le problème, c'est qu'on n'a pas l'avantage d'habiter près[7] des magasins et des restaurants, et le trajet[8] pour aller au travail est plus long. Pour cette raison, les logements dans les banlieues sont moins chers[9] que les logements au centre-ville. C'est aussi dans les banlieues où l'on trouve les HLM—les habitations à loyer modéré[10]—pour les personnes qui ont besoin d'aide gouvernementale.

Réfléchissons

Compare housing in the United States and in Europe by answering the following questions.

1. What differences do you see between living downtown and living in the suburbs in the United States and in Europe? What are considered the advantages and disadvantages of each in the two cultures?
2. In the United States, where is subsidized housing generally located? And in Europe? What does this say about how these locations are perceived in the two cultures?
3. Can you think of any American towns where living downtown is as prized as it is in Europe? Why do you think this is the case?
4. Do you know many people with vacation homes? If not, what do the people you know do for vacation instead?

---

[1] *rather than* [2] *the suburbs* [3] *especially sought after* [4] *that which* [5] *in the country* [6] *can leave* [7] *near*
[8] *commute* [9] *less expensive* [10] *subsidized housing*

Partie II: Retournons à l'appartement d'Aurélie 🎧

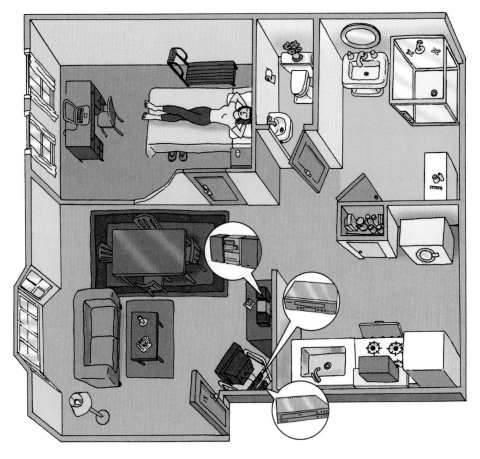

You may want to use a transparency of this graphic or PowerPoint slides as you read the text with students. Demonstrate the meaning of the prepositional phrases as you read.

Dans l'appartement d'Aurélie, il y a quatre pièces: une cuisine, un salon / une salle à manger, une chambre et une salle de bains. Il y a aussi un cabinet de toilette, bien sûr! Regardons ces pièces ensemble …

Dans la cuisine, il y a une cuisinière avec un four. La cuisinière est entre le réfrigérateur et l'évier. (Le réfrigérateur est à gauche de la cuisinière, et l'évier est à droite de la cuisinière.) Au-dessus de la cuisinière, il y a un four à micro-ondes. Dans le coin[1], il y a une machine à laver. La cuisine est jaune.

À côté de la cuisine, il y a un salon bleu. Dans cette pièce, il y a un sofa gris. Il n'y a pas de fauteuil. Devant le sofa il y a une table basse, et sous la table basse, il y a un tapis. À gauche du sofa, il y a une lampe. Dans le coin, il y a un téléviseur, avec un magnéto et un lecteur de DVD. Il y a aussi une chaîne stéréo. Derrière le sofa, il y a une baie vitrée, donc, c'est une pièce très lumineuse. À droite du sofa, il y a une table et quatre chaises. Il y a un grand tapis sous la table.

Derrière le salon, il y a une chambre. Aurélie aime bien sa chambre; elle est calme et accueillante[2]. Les murs sont verts et les rideaux sont crème[3]—c'est très joli! Dans sa chambre, elle a un grand lit. À côté du lit, il y a une table de nuit, et en face du lit, il y a un bureau. Sur le bureau, il y a un ordinateur. À droite du lit, il y a un tapis de course—Aurélie aime bien faire du sport.

Finalement, il y a la salle de bains. Elle est très petite, mais il y a l'essentiel—un lavabo et une douche. Au-dessus du lavabo, il y a un miroir. Le cabinet de toilette est à côté du lavabo. Dans le cabinet, il y a le WC et un lavabo.

---

[1] *corner* [2] *cozy* [3] When the noun **crème** is used as an adjective—as it is here—it is invariable.

Vous avez bien compris?

Describe Aurélie's apartment by completing the following statements with an appropriate word or expression. (Several answers may be logical—choose one.)

1. Il y a beaucoup de meubles dans le salon. À côté du sofa il y a _____ et devant le sofa il y a _____.
2. Dans la cuisine, il y a tout l'essentiel: un _____, un _____ et l'_____. Le micro-ondes est _____ de la cuisinière.
3. Aurélie aime bien les couleurs différentes: sa cuisine est _____, son salon est _____ et sa chambre est _____.
4. Pour se détendre[1] dans le salon, Aurélie a un _____, un _____ et une _____.

Vocabulaire essentiel

Les prépositions

à côté de	*beside, next to*	dans	*in*
à droite de	*to the right of*	derrière	*behind, in back of*
à gauche de	*to the left of*	devant	*in front of*
au-dessus de	*above, over*	entre	*between*
en face de	*in front of*	sous	*under*
près de	*close to*	sur	*on*
loin de	*far from*		

Les couleurs

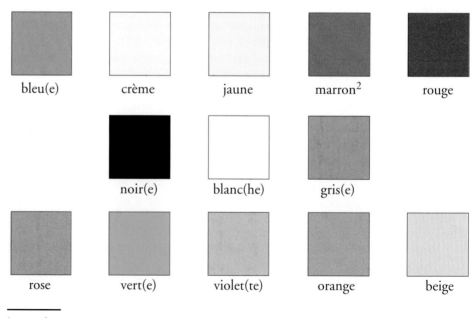

bleu(e)   crème   jaune   marron[2]   rouge

noir(e)   blanc(he)   gris(e)

rose   vert(e)   violet(te)   orange   beige

---

[1]*to relax* [2]Reminder: When talking about hair color, use **brun** for *brown*.

À vous!

A. Le studio de Lucien. Look at the floor plan of Lucien's studio, and say whether the following statements are **vrai** *(true)* or **faux** *(false)*. Correct the false statements.

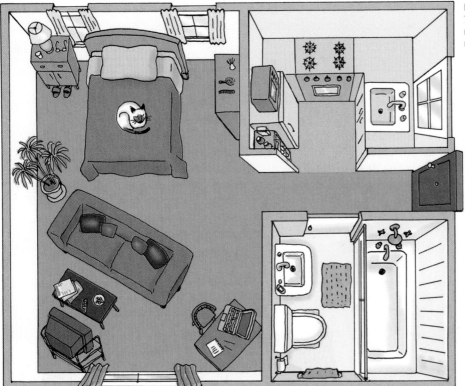

1. Dans l'appartement de Lucien, il y a deux lits. _____ vrai _____ faux

   _____

2. La table de nuit est à droite du lit. _____ vrai _____ faux

   _____

3. La commode est entre le lit et le coin-cuisine. _____ vrai _____ faux

   _____

4. Il n'y a pas de table dans la cuisine de Lucien. _____ vrai _____ faux

   _____

5. La table basse est derrière le sofa. _____ vrai _____ faux

   _____

6. Le bureau est à côté de la porte. _____ vrai _____ faux

   _____

7. Le téléviseur est dans le coin du salon. ____ vrai ____ faux

8. Le four à micro-ondes est sous le réfrigérateur. ____ vrai ____ faux

9. Sur le bureau de Lucien, il y a un ordinateur. ____ vrai ____ faux

10. Le lit est près du sofa. ____ vrai ____ faux

Have students use only the masculine when talking about colors in an abstract sense: **rouge, bleu, blanc.**

B. Quelles sont les couleurs? Which colors do you associate with the following? (There may be several possible answers in some cases.)

1. le drapeau[1] américain
2. votre université
3. la fête de saint Valentin
4. la fête de *Halloween*
5. Noël
6. les bébés
7. les voitures de sport
8. un arc-en-ciel[2]
9. Mardi Gras

How are the public restrooms in your country different from the one you see in this picture? How are they indicated? Are they indicated on a street sign?

Les toilettes publiques are not free in France (this picture was taken in Paris). They self-clean after the customer leaves. It is possible to use the restrooms at a business—a coffee shop, a restaurant, a department store, etc.—however, they are not free either. In department stores, in both men's and women's restrooms there is a female attendant who collects 1 euro and hands out toilet paper. In restaurants, **bistros**, and **brasseries**, one must order something in order to use the restroom.

[1]*flag* [2]*rainbow*

Structure 4

Les prépositions et les contractions

Online Study Center
ACE, Language Skills
Practice

- When describing where something is located in relation to something else, we use a preposition. A preposition in French may consist of one word or several. Compare the following French and English sentences.

Dans mon appartement, le sofa est **entre** deux tables.

*In my apartment, the sofa is **between** two tables.*

Sous le sofa, il y a un tapis.

***Under** the sofa, there is a rug.*

Devant le sofa, il y a un téléviseur.

***In front of** the sofa, there is a television.*

- Do not rely on English to tell you how many words the preposition should contain. As you can see from the preceding examples, the two languages are often quite different.

- You may have noticed in the **Vocabulaire essentiel** on page 108 that some of the French prepositions listed are followed by **de.** These words or expressions take **de** whenever they are followed by a noun.

Le fauteuil est **à gauche de** la table.

*The armchair is **to the left of** the table.*

You might want to indicate to your students that if the object of the preposition is not expressed, de is not used either: *Le fauteuil est à gauche.*

- One-word prepositions, on the other hand, never take **de.**

Le fauteuil est **devant** la lampe.

*The armchair is **in front of** the lamp.*

- Again, do not let English be your guide, as the languages often work quite differently in this regard! Memorize which phrases require **de** in French; this is the only way to know.

- When using **de,** you must pay attention to the definite article that follows it. The preposition **de** contracts with **le** and **les,** but not with **la** or **l',** to make the following forms.

Singular	Plural
du (= de + le)	des (= de + les)
de la	
de l'	

Le lit est **à côté <u>du</u>** téléviseur.

The bed is next to the television.

Le lit est **à côté <u>de la</u>** table.

The bed is next to the table.

Le lit est **à côté <u>de l'</u>**armoire.

The bed is next to the armoire.

Le lit est **à côté <u>des</u>** chaises.

The bed is next to the chairs.

Go back to the description of Aurélie's apartment in **Partie II** (p. 107), and underline all the prepositions that you find. Then answer the following questions.

1. What do these words and phrases mean in English?

2. Which prepositions take **de?** Why?

3. Has there been a contraction with the definite article? Why or why not?

4. Which prepositions do not take **de?**

Pratiquons!

A. Où sont-ils? Look at Lucien's apartment and answer the following questions. Some questions may have several possible answers.

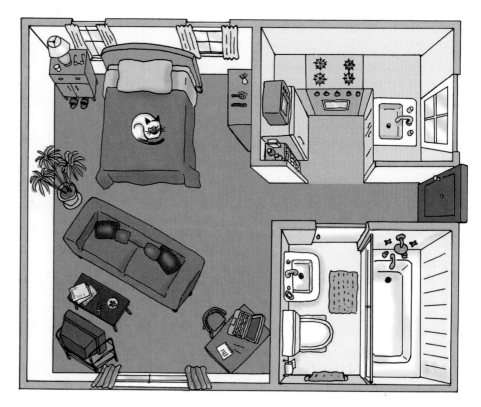

1. Combien de fenêtres est-ce qu'il y a dans l'appartement de Lucien?
2. Qu'est-ce qu'il y a dans la cuisine?
3. Est-ce que le four à micro-ondes est sur le réfrigérateur ou sous le réfrigérateur?
4. Où est l'ordinateur?

5. Où est le lit?
6. Est-ce que la table basse est devant le sofa ou derrière le sofa?
7. Où sont les placards?
8. Où est la porte[1]?
9. Où est le téléviseur?
10. Où est la commode?

B. Architectes. You are an architect, and you are talking to a client over the phone about a remodeling job. Ask your client the following questions so that you can draw a layout of his/her rooms, with furniture and appliances in place. Your client gives you precise details. Remember that you are talking on the phone and that your client cannot see your drawing! When you are finished, reverse roles. Did the drawings come close to your actual houses or apartments?

1. Est-ce que vous habitez dans une grande maison ou une petite maison? Où? Habitez-vous dans un appartement? Où? À quel étage?
2. Combien de pièces avez-vous?
3. Où sont les pièces? La cuisine? Le salon? La salle à manger? Le cabinet de toilette? etc.
4. Qu'est-ce qu'il y a dans chaque pièce? Où sont placés les meubles?
5. Est-ce que vous avez un bureau? Où est-il?
6. Qu'est-ce qu'il y a sur votre bureau? Est-ce que c'est en ordre ou en désordre?

Structure 5

Les adjectifs de couleur

Like all other French adjectives, adjectives describing color must agree in gender and number with the nouns they modify. Compare the forms of the adjective **vert** in the following sentences.

Mon salon est **vert**.	*My living room is green.*
Ma cuisine est **verte**.	*My kitchen is green.*
Mes rideaux sont **verts**.	*My curtains are green.*
Mes lampes sont **vertes**.	*My lamps are green.*

In French, adjectives for colors always come after the noun.

J'ai des lampes vertes et un sofa gris.

The rules for adjective agreement are the same as those that you learned in Chapter 2:

To form the feminine, add **-e** to the masculine form.

noir / noire; bleu / bleue

Tell students who live in a dorm to describe their parents' home instead of their room, so that students can use as much new vocabulary as possible.

Online Study Center
ACE, Language Skills Practice

Model the examples in this section, so that students can hear differences between masculine and feminine forms. Point out, too, that the **-s** in the plural is silent.

Remind students that they have already used certain adjectives of color when describing hair and eyes.

---

[1] *door*

To form the plural, add **-s.**

noirs / noires; bleus / bleues

Like all other adjectives, adjectives of color that already end in **-e** have the same form for the masculine and the feminine.

un sofa rouge / une chaise rouge

Likewise, adjectives ending in **-s** will not add another **-s** for the masculine plural, but will add **-es** for the feminine plural.

des sofas gris / des chaises grises

The adjective **blanc** has an irregular feminine form: **blanche.**

un réfrigérateur blanc / une cuisinière blanche

Note that **marron, crème,** and **orange** are invariable—their form never changes.

des sofas marron
des chaises orange
des murs crème

VÉRIFIEZ VOTRE COMPRÉHENSION

Return to the description of Aurélie's apartment in **Partie II** (p. 107). What adjectives of color do you find there? Why do these adjectives appear in the form that they are in?

Pratiquons!

A. Vos préférences. Imagine that you are about to move into a new apartment and are deciding on new furniture. State which color you prefer for the following items. Pay specific attention to the form of the adjective.

MODÈLE: Quelle couleur préférez-vous pour un fauteuil?

Je préfère un fauteuil bleu.

Quelle couleur préférez-vous ...

1. pour un sofa?
2. pour un tapis?
3. pour les chaises dans la salle à manger?
4. pour un réfrigérateur?
5. pour un couvre-lit[1]?
6. pour les murs[2] de votre salon?
7. pour les murs de votre chambre?
8. pour un fauteuil?
9. pour les rideaux?

---

[1]*bedspread* [2]*walls*

B. Chez moi, c'est ... *(At my house, it's . . .)* Interview a classmate to find out the color of various objects that s/he owns. Reverse roles. Do you like your partner's color taste?

1. De quelle couleur est ta chambre? Ton couvre-lit? Tes draps[1]?
2. Et les rideaux—de quelle couleur sont-ils?
3. De quelle couleur est ta maison / ton immeuble / ta résidence?
4. De quelle couleur est ton sofa? Et tes fauteuils?
5. As-tu une voiture? Elle est de quelle couleur? Et ta bicyclette?
6. De quelle couleur est ta salle de bains?

C. Les couleurs et les rêves *(Colors and dreams).* Colors can be symbolic in interpreting the meaning of your dreams. Try to remember your last dreams and the colors in them. Your partner is going to ask you some questions to help you remember. Then, together, look at each color and its symbolism. Can you give a better interpretation to your dreams? Reverse roles.

1. Est-ce que tes amis sont dans tes rêves? Ou tes ennemis? De quelles couleurs sont leurs vêtements[2]?
2. Est-ce que tes amis sont gentils ou méchants? Et tes ennemis? Y a-t-il des disputes entre vous?
3. Où est-ce que tu es dans tes rêves? À la maison? Dans le désert? Dans la forêt? Quelle est la couleur prédominante?
4. Est-ce que tes rêves ont lieu[3] le soir ou le jour?

Le symbolisme des couleurs

- Le bleu: c'est la couleur virginale, celle de Marie. Il représente la fidélité et la sérénité.
- Le vert: c'est la couleur de l'espérance et de la nature. Le vert symbolise une renaissance.
- Le rouge: c'est la couleur de la passion. Il symbolise le feu[4] dans la colère[5] et dans l'amour.
- Le jaune: c'est la couleur solaire. Il symbolise l'homme éclairé par la révélation divine. C'est aussi la couleur de la Foi[6]. Le jaune pâle représente aussi l'égoïsme[7] et la trahison[8].
- Le blanc: c'est la couleur de la Lune[9]. Il symbolise la pureté, la justice et la virginité. Le blanc associé avec la neige[10] symbolise l'infertilité.
- Le noir: c'est la couleur funèbre de Saturne. Il est associé avec la tristesse.

Portrait personnel

Do you know by now the apartment or house of one of your classmates? Choose a classmate whose house or apartment you remember and describe it. (You may use the drawings you made in activity B, **Architectes,** on page 113.) If you do not remember your partner's house or apartment, ask him/her some questions before beginning to write.

---

[1]*linens* [2]*clothes* [3]*take place* [4]*fire* [5]*anger* [6]*Faith* [7]*selfishness* [8]*betrayal* [9]*Moon* [10]*snow*

Partie III: Activités pendant le week-end

> Le week-end, Aurélie retourne à la maison de ses parents. Toute la famille est là, et tout le monde travaille. Il fait beau et pas trop chaud, donc son père, Michel, est dans le jardin. Il aime bien faire du jardinage. Sa sœur, Agnès, étend le linge et son frère, David, fait le repassage. David regarde la télé pendant qu'il travaille. Les jumelles[1], Léa et Andréa, font le clown devant David! La mère d'Aurélie, Cécile, est en train de peindre[2] la maison. Elle déteste faire du jardinage, mais elle adore faire du bricolage. Et Aurélie? Qu'est-ce qu'elle va faire? Elle va travailler à l'intérieur. Elle va passer l'aspirateur et elle va faire le ménage.

Vous avez bien compris?

Answer the following questions in French.

1. Qu'est-ce qu'Aurélie va faire aujourd'hui?
2. Que fait David pendant qu'il travaille?
3. Que font les jumelles?
4. Qui fait du jardinage?
5. Qui ne va certainement pas faire du jardinage? Pourquoi pas?
6. D'après vous[3], comment dit-on «faire le ménage» en anglais?

---

[1]*twins* [2]*is painting* [3]*In your opinion*

Travaux ménagers

Online Study Center
Flashcards, ACE, Language
Skills Practice

faire la cuisine

faire les courses *(f.)*

faire le linge / faire la lessive

faire le ménage

faire le repassage

faire la vaisselle

faire du bricolage

faire du jardinage

passer l'aspirateur *(m.)*

faire les devoirs *(m.)*

Expressions de temps

Quel temps fait-il?

Il fait beau.

Il fait chaud.

Il fait froid.

Il fait frais.

Il fait du vent.

Il fait du soleil.

Il neige.

Il pleut.

Les saisons

l'été *(m.)*

le printemps

l'hiver *(m.)*

l'automne *(m.)*

Expansion personnelle

Travaux ménagers

épousseter

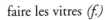

faire les vitres *(f.)*

étendre le linge

faire les valises *(f.)*

faire un gâteau

À vous!

A. Que faites-vous? For each of the following situations, tell which of the activities listed in the ***Vocabulaire essentiel*** is important to do or not to do.

> MODÈLE: avant l'arrivée de tes parents
>
> > *Avant l'arrivée de mes parents, il est important de…*
> > *faire le lit,*
> > *nettoyer[1] la salle de bains,*
> > *passer l'aspirateur.*

1. pour fêter[2] l'anniversaire d'un ami chez vous[3] (il est important de…)
2. avant d'aller en classe
3. pour nettoyer la maison
4. pour travailler à l'extérieur
5. pour aller en vacances

> Vocabulaire utile
> faire un voyage[4]

---

[1]*to clean* [2]*to celebrate* [3]*at your place* [4]*to take a trip*

 **B. Quel temps fait-il?** Tell the class what the weather is like in the city or town you come from for each of the following seasons. When you have finished, vote on whose hometown has the best weather (**le meilleur climat**).

1. Je suis de _____.
2. En hiver, il _____.
3. En été, il _____.
4. Au printemps, il _____.
5. En automne, il _____.
6. La saison que je préfère, c'est le _____ parce que _____.
7. La ville de _____ a le meilleur climat.

Structure 6

Online Study Center
ACE, Language Skills
Practice

Le verbe *faire*

The verb **faire** has an irregular conjugation.

faire	
je fais	nous fai**sons**
tu fais	vous fai**tes**
il / elle /on fait	ils / elles **font**

Point out the three different vowel sounds in the root of **faire**: [ə] in **faisons**, [ō] in **font**, and [ɛ] in the others.

Faire means *to do* or *to make*.

Je fais mes devoirs.   *I'm doing my homework. / I do my homework.*
Il fait un gâteau.   *He's making a cake. / He makes a cake.*

In addition, it is often used in idiomatic expressions, and therefore may be translated quite differently in English.

Nous faisons un voyage.   *We're taking a trip.*
Je fais la vaisselle.   *I'm washing / doing the dishes.*
Ils font du jardinage.   *They garden. / They do the gardening.*

Remind students that the present tense in French has three possible translations in English: **Je fais mes devoirs** = *I do my homework, I am doing my homework, I do do my homework* (emphatic). The context will help determine which one the speaker means.

Faire is also frequently used in expressions describing weather. In these expressions, the pronoun is always **il** and the verb is always conjugated in the third person singular.

Il fait beau.   *It's nice outside.*
Il fait du soleil.   *It's sunny.*

Two common weather expressions do not use **faire.** Instead, they use the verbs **neiger** *(to snow)* and **pleuvoir** *(to rain),* which have just one form in the present tense.

Il pleut.   *It's raining. / It rains.*
Il neige.   *It's snowing. / It snows.*

Reread the description of the weekend activities of Aurélie and her family on page 116. Then answer the following questions.

1. What idiomatic expressions contain **faire?** What do these expressions mean?

2. Are there any weather expressions with **faire?** If so, how is it conjugated, and why?

3. What other verbs are used? Are they regular or irregular verbs?

Pratiquons!

A. Que font ces personnes? Look at the drawings and tell what each person is doing. Then rewrite your sentences, substituting the subject pronouns in parentheses. Pay specific attention to the form of the verb.

Answer Key: 1. Il fait la vaisselle. (Je fais; Vous faites; On fait) 2. Ils font un voyage. (Tu fais; Nous faisons; Vous faites) 3. Elle fait du bricolage/de la peinture. (Elles font; Je fais; On fait) 4. Ils font du jardinage. (Vous faites; Nous faisons; Elle fait)

1.

Il … (Je / Vous / On)

2.

Ils … (Tu / Nous / Vous)

3.

Elle … (Elles / Je / On)

4.

Ils … (Vous / Nous / Elle)

B. Qui fait quoi chez vous? Ask your partner who does each of the following activities at his or her house. Then change roles.

MODÈLE: faire le repassage

—*Qui fait le repassage chez toi?*

—*Ma sœur fait le repassage chez moi.*

1. faire la vaisselle
2. faire la cuisine
3. passer l'aspirateur
4. faire la lessive
5. aimer faire du jardinage
6. faire le ménage
7. faire les devoirs

Answer Key. Possible answers:
1. Il fait froid. 2. Il fait très chaud et humide. 3. Il fait beau. 4. Il neige et il fait très froid. 5. Il pleut et il fait mauvais. 6. Il fait beau. 7. Il fait très chaud et il fait du soleil souvent. 8. *Answers will vary.*

C. Quel temps fait-il à … ? Ask and answer the following questions with a partner. There may be more than one appropriate answer; give as many as you can.

1. Quel temps fait-il à Chicago en décembre?
2. Quel temps fait-il à Houston en été?
3. Quel temps fait-il à Honolulu au printemps?
4. Quel temps fait-il à Québec en hiver?
5. Quel temps fait-il à Seattle en mars?
6. Quel temps fait-il à Atlanta en automne?
7. Quel temps fait-il à Dakar (au Sénégal) en juillet?
8. Quel temps fait-il dans ta ville en janvier?

Before beginning the activity, make sure students know how to formulate grammatically correct questions. Use the first item or two as models.

D. À la recherche d'un «oui»! Interview your classmates to find someone who does each of the following. Do not use the same classmate for more than one **oui** answer.

Trouvez une personne qui …

1. aime faire la vaisselle.
2. aime faire du jogging.
3. va faire le linge aujourd'hui.
4. finit toujours ses devoirs.
5. fait ses devoirs le samedi.
6. va faire des courses après la classe.
7. n'aime pas l'été.
8. adore l'hiver.
9. habite près de l'université.
10. travaille loin de l'université.

This activity can be done in groups of 3 or 4. If there are 4 students per group, 2 are the interior designers and the other 2 are the roommates. The floor plan can be drawn by the entire group or just by the roommates. If your classroom has a computer and a projector or if you can go to the computer lab, you may want to have your students look at the website www.paintcafe.com for ideas. This web site also has **le jeu des couleurs**, where students can find their optimum colors according to their personalities.

À vous de parler!

Vocabulaire utile
un décorateur / une décoratrice d'intérieur
le plan de la maison / de l'appartement
meubler[1]
décorer
peindre[2] les murs

A. Décorateur d'intérieur. You are an interior designer. Two roommates ask you to help them decorate their empty house. Look at their floor plan and decorate one room at a time. Decide with them on the furniture and appliances. Do not forget to talk about the colors of the walls and the furniture (sofas, curtains, rugs, etc.). Once you are done, show the newly designed house to the class. The class will vote on their favorite.

───────────────

[1]*to furnish* [2]*to paint*

B. L'agent immobilier. You and some classmates have decided to rent an apartment together in Paris. In groups of three or four, decide what kind of apartment you are going to rent (how many rooms, etc.). Explain to your real estate agent (your teacher) what your needs are; s/he will provide you with options. When you have chosen an apartment, discuss together how you will furnish it. Then, decide with your roommates who is going to do which housekeeping chores. When you have finished, explain your choices to the rest of the class. Each member of the group should speak at least once during this presentation.

> **Vocabulaire utile**
> louer un appartement /
>   une maison
> au premier étage /
>   au deuxième étage
> en banlieue
> au centre-ville
> une place de garage /
>   sans garage

Les Québécois s'amusent comme ça en hiver

Online Study Center
Web Search Activities

Au Québec, il fait très froid en hiver et il neige beaucoup. Malgré cela[1], les Québécois ne restent pas à l'intérieur pendant toute cette saison! Ils aiment beaucoup les sports d'hiver, et ils sortent[2] souvent pour faire du ski ou du patin à glace[3]. Pour célébrer cette belle saison, ils ont aussi un carnaval d'hiver chaque année. Le carnaval dure deux semaines en janvier et en février, et il y a beaucoup d'activités très variées pour toute la famille. Les activités les plus populaires sont les défilés[4], les promenades en traîneau à chien[5], les sculptures sur neige, les courses en canoë[6] et les courses d'attelages de chiens[7]. Il y a aussi une maison de glace et un grand bonhomme de neige[8]. Tout le monde sort pour s'amuser à l'extérieur—il fait froid, mais beau, et normalement il fait du soleil. Après, on retourne à la maison fatigué, mais de très bonne humeur. C'est vrai que l'hiver est dur au Québec, mais cela ne veut pas dire[9] que l'on ne peut pas[10] s'amuser!

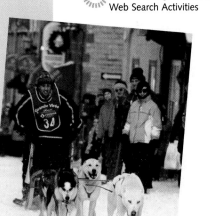

Réfléchissons

1. Why do you think the people of Quebec stage a winter carnival each year? What is its real purpose?
2. Do you live now, or have you ever lived, in a place where the climate is particularly severe? How do people adapt to it?
3. Can you think of any festivals that are similar to the Québécois winter carnival in purpose? What happens at these festivals? What do they celebrate? What would people from other climates think of these activities?
4. What is the main outdoor activity in the city where you live? When does it take place? What would people from other cultures think of this activity?

---

[1]*in spite of this* [2]*go out* [3]*ice skating* [4]*parades* [5]*dogsled* [6]*ice-canoe races (on snow-covered streets)*
[7]*dogsled races* [8]*snowman* [9]*does not mean* [10]*cannot*

À vous d'écrire!

You are going to spend a year abroad (choose a city in France, Francophone Europe, Canada, or West Africa). You need to rent a fully furnished apartment for one year, and you are going to write an email in French to a real estate agent who can help you find an apartment.

A. Stratégies. Keep in mind the vocabulary and the expressions that you have just seen in this chapter and in previous chapters. Do not try to translate directly from your own language in order to express your ideas. Use the words that you already know. Pay attention to noun-adjective agreement, spelling, and sentence structure.

B. Organisons-nous! First, think about how you would start your message. Decide in which city you are going to be spending a year and in what type of neighborhood you would like to live (for example, near the university, or near a park, etc). Greet the real estate agent in your email and tell him/her the reason you are writing.

Next, consider the type of apartment that you would like to rent, and write a brief description in French. There is no need at this point to write complete sentences. Your description could be as short as "one bedroom with a balcony, two bathrooms, a big kitchen, and a living room."

Finally, make a list in French of questions that you would like to ask the real estate agent, such as how much the rent is for a one-bedroom apartment, what the neighborhood is like in which s/he is looking to find you an apartment, how many floors there are in the buildings, etc.

C. Pensons-y! Now that you have decided what type of apartment you are looking for, make a list of the furniture and appliances that you would like to have in each room, and where you would like them to be. Start with **Je voudrais ...** *(I would like . . .).*

Kitchen
Bedroom
Bathroom
Living room
Dining room
Additional rooms/features

D. Révisons! Exchange your draft with a classmate. Then check each other's drafts. Check the spelling of the words as well as the prepositions. Check the way s/he phrased his/her questions. Did s/he make agreements between adjectives and nouns? Does s/he have the correct articles with the nouns? Correct each other's work before you begin activity E.

E. Écrivons! Now that you have drafted the main ideas that you would like to include in your email, create a coherent paragraph. In order to make your email more personal, tell the real estate agent a little about yourself (your likes and dislikes) and why you are going abroad.

> **Expressions utiles**
> Monsieur ... / Madame ...
> Je me permets de vous
>   contacter parce que je ...
> Bien cordialement,

Lexique ⌒

Vocabulaire essentiel

Le logement *housing*

un appartement *apartment*
un ascenseur *elevator*
une boîte aux lettres *mailbox*
un(e) colocataire *roommate*
un escalier *stairs*

un étage *floor*
un immeuble *apartment building*
un(e) locataire *tenant*
un loyer *rent*
une maison *house*

une pièce *room*
un portail *main entrance*
un volet *shutter*

La cuisine / La kitchenette *the kitchen / the kitchenette*

une cafetière *coffee maker*
une cuisinière *stove*
un évier *sink*
un four *oven*

un grille-pain *toaster*
un lave-vaisselle *dishwasher*
une machine à laver *washing machine*

un (four à) micro-ondes *microwave (oven)*
un réfrigérateur *refrigerator*

Le salon *the living room*

un canapé *couch*
une chaîne stéréo *stereo*
un fauteuil *armchair*
une lampe *lamp*

un lecteur de DVD *DVD player*
un magnéto(scope) *VCR*
un sofa *sofa*
un tableau *painting*

un tapis *rug*
une télévision /
  un téléviseur *television*

La salle à manger *the dining room*

un buffet *sideboard*
une chaise *chair*
une table *table*

La chambre *the bedroom*

une armoire *armoire*
un bureau *desk; office*
une commode *chest of drawers*

une fenêtre *window*
un lit *bed*
un ordinateur *computer*

un placard *closet*
les rideaux *(m.) curtains*
une table de nuit *nightstand*

La salle de bains *the bathroom*

une baignoire *bathtub*
une douche *shower*
un lavabo *sink*
un miroir *mirror*

le WC / le cabinet de toilette /
  les toilettes *(f. pl.) toilet,
  restroom*

La salle de séjour *the family room*

un futon *futon*
un répondeur automatique
    answering machine

un téléphone (sans fil) *(cordless)*
    phone

Le garage *the garage*

une moto *motorcycle*
une voiture *car*

La cave *the wine cellar*

le vin *wine*

Les magasins *stores*

la boucherie-charcuterie *butcher
    shop and deli*
la boulangerie-pâtisserie *bakery-
    pastry shop*

la brasserie *brewery/pub*
l'épicerie *(f.) grocery store*
le parc public *public park*
la pharmacie *pharmacy*

la poissonnerie *fish market*
la poste *post office*
le quartier *neighborhood*

Verbes *verbs*

aller *to go*
bâtir *to build*
choisir *to choose*

finir *to finish*
obéir (à) *to obey*
punir *to punish*

réussir (à) *to succeed (in)*
salir *to dirty*

Les prépositions *prepositions*

à côté de *beside, next to*
au-dessus de *above, over*
à droite de *to the right of*
à gauche de *to the left of*
dans *in*

derrière *behind, in back of*
devant *in front of*
en face de *in front of*
entre *between*
loin de *far (from)*

près de *close (to)*
sous *under*
sur *on*

Les couleurs *colors*

beige *beige*
blanc (blanche) *white*
bleu(e) *blue*
crème *cream*
gris(e) *gray*

jaune *yellow*
marron *chestnut brown*
noir(e) *black*
orange *orange*
rose *pink*

rouge *red*
vert(e) *green*
violet (violette) *purple*

Travaux ménagers *household chores*

faire du bricolage *to do repair work*
faire du jardinage *to do the gardening*
faire la cuisine *to cook*
faire la vaisselle *to do the dishes*

faire le linge / faire la lessive *to do the laundry*
faire le ménage *to do the housework*
faire le repassage *to do the ironing*
faire les courses *(f.) to run errands*

faire les devoirs *(m.) to do homework*
passer l'aspirateur *(m.) to vacuum*

Expressions de temps *weather expressions*

Il fait beau. *It's nice out.*
Il fait chaud. *It's warm.*
Il fait frais. *It's cool.*
Il fait froid. *It's cold.*

Il fait du soleil. *It's sunny.*
Il fait du vent. *It's windy.*
Il neige. *It's snowing.*

Il pleut. *It's raining.*
Quel temps fait-il? *What's the weather like?*

Les saisons *the seasons*

l'automne *(m.) autumn*
l'été *(m.) summer*

l'hiver *(m.) winter*
le printemps *spring*

Expansion personnelle

Le logement *housing*

une baie vitrée *bay window*
un balcon *balcony*
un bidet *bidet*
une cheminée *fireplace*

le grenier *attic*
les placards *(m.) kitchen cupboards*

des souris *(f.) mice*
un tapis de course *treadmill*

Travaux ménagers *household chores*

épousseter *to dust*
étendre le linge *to line-dry clothes*
faire les valises *(f.) to pack suitcases*

faire les vitres *(f.) to wash the windows*
faire un gâteau *to make a cake*

MISE EN PRATIQUE

À vous de découvrir!

Online Study Center

Pour faire les activités suivantes[1], allez au *Online Study Center* et choisissez **Mise en pratique.** Vous y trouverez des sites Internet correspondants aux mots ou phrases en caractères gras[2] dans chaque activité.

La Wallonie

Nous vous proposons de découvrir la Wallonie. Pour ceci vous allez «voyager» avec plusieurs camarades de classe. Mettez-vous en groupes de quatre pour faire une visite guidée des deux villes les plus importantes de la Wallonie. À l'aide des sites Internet correspondants à chaque section, vous allez rechercher les thèmes suivants.

A. La géographie. Explorez **la géographie de la Wallonie** et de la région wallonne. Où est située la Wallonie? Quelles en sont les régions et villes principales?

B. Découvrez Namur et Liège. Visitez **les villes de Namur et Liège** pour répondre aux questions suivantes.

1. Pourquoi est-ce que ces villes sont importantes?
2. Quels monuments et musées peut-on y trouver[3]?
3. À quels festivals est-ce qu'on peut aller et quand? Qu'est-ce qui vous intéresse[4] particulièrement?
4. Quels sont les châteaux à visiter dans la région de Wallonie?
5. Si vous voulez passer la nuit à Namur (ou à Liège), quelles sont ses possibilités de logement? Est-ce que c'est comme aux États-Unis? Pourquoi ou pourquoi pas?
6. Regardez les photos. Est-ce que ces villes ressemblent beaucoup aux villes américaines? Si oui, comment? Si non, pourquoi pas? Décrivez les villes typiques de la Wallonie.
7. Qu'est-ce que c'est que les Ardennes? Qu'est-ce qu'on peut y faire?

À vous de déguster[5]!

The *À vous de déguster* sections feature a typical fo[...] from the French or francophone region presented i[...] *À vous de découvrir* section. The communicative ac[...] ties in this section focus on comparing the featured regional food with a regional American product.

Spécialités gastronomiques belges

Connaissez-vous[6] la gastronomie belge? Nous vous proposons de savourer quelques spécialités gastronomiques belges. Mais d'abord[7], devinez quelles sont les spécialités les plus connues[8].

---

[1]*following* [2]*bold-faced* [3]*can one find there* [4]*What interests you* [5]*taste* [6]*Do you know* [7]*first* [8]*well known*

A. Spécialités belges. Pour trouver les spécialités belges, choisissez la réponse correcte:

1. Les Américains la mangent le matin au petit déjeuner avec du sirop.

   a. une tartine[1]   b. une gaufre[2]   c. une madeleine[3]

2. C'est une boisson[4] très populaire aux États-Unis et que les Américains boivent quand ils ont plus de 21 ans.

   a. la bière   b. la limonade   c. l'eau

3. C'est sucré et noir ou blanc. On peut utiliser ça pour faire des gâteaux et des mousses, des glaces et des boissons.

   a. le chocolat   b. le thé noir   c. le café

4. Généralement, on mange ça avec des hamburgers et du ketchup aux États-Unis.

   a. les légumes   b. les frites   c. les oignons

B. Les gaufres belges. Les Belges mangent leurs gaufres au petit déjeuner, au goûter[5] ou comme dessert. Au petit déjeuner, les gaufres sont servies nature[6], avec du sucre ou avec de la confiture[7]. Au goûter, les enfants aiment manger les gaufres avec de la crème chantilly[8] et des fruits. Comme dessert, on y met de la crème chantilly, de la glace ou du chocolat fondu[9]. Et vous, quand et comment mangez-vous vos gaufres?

Voici la recette[10] traditionnelle de la gaufre liégeoise. Elle est plus épaisse[11] que les gaufres américaines. Bon appétit!

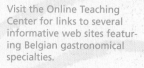

Gaufres liégeoises

250 grammes de sucre

200 grammes de beurre[12] fondu

500 grammes de farine[13]

20 grammes de levure[14]

100 + 100 millilitres de lait

3 jaunes d'œufs[15]

Une pincée de sel[16]

Mélanger la farine et la levure délayée[17] dans 100 millilitres de lait. Ajouter[18] le beurre, le sucre, les 3 jaunes d'œufs et les 100 millilitres de lait et bien mélanger. Dans le gaufrier[19] déposer 30 grammes de pâte à gaufre[20] jusqu'à ce que la gaufre soit bien dorée[21].

---

[1]*piece of toast with butter and jam* [2]*waffle* [3]*cookie that is usually lemon-flavored* [4]*drink* [5]*snacktime* [6]*without anything on top* [7]*jam* [8]*whipped cream* [9]*melted* [10]*recipe* [11]*thick* [12]*butter* [13]*flour* [14]*yeast* [15]*egg yolks* [16]*a pinch of salt* [17]*mixed* [18]*Add* [19]*waffle maker* [20]*waffle batter* [21]*until golden brown*

The *À vous d'analyser* sections feature a reading that is sociological (e.g., an advertisement), political (e.g., a newspaper article), or intellectual (e.g., a short story or poem) from a particular French or Francophone region. In the activities, students are asked to reflect on the reading and to make cultural comparisons.

À vous d'analyser

A. Voici un article paru dans le journal mensuel[1] de l'Université de Liège (l'ULg), *Le 15ème[2] jour du mois.* Lisez l'article une première fois et notez le sujet[3] principal.

Le Campus de Francorchamps

Un centre de compétence «automobile» ouvrira[4] ses portes en 2005

À Stavelot, en bordure du circuit de Spa-Francorchamps, se construit un Campus automobile, avec la collaboration de la faculté des Sciences appliquées de l'ULg. Cet outil permanent de formation et de valorisation des métiers techniques, qui ouvrira ses portes durant l'été 2005, est destiné à répondre à la hausse des besoins[5] dans l'industrie et la compétition automobiles. C'est le premier centre de compétence d'initiative interrégionale. Il représente un investissement de près de 8 millions d'euros provenant de la Région wallonne et de Fonds structurels européens (Interreg III Euregio).

Le Campus automobile, qui occupera une étendue d'un hectare, consistera en un bâtiment de 4 800 mètres carrés[6] comportant des stands de préparation avec accès direct au circuit pour des tests de véhicules. Outre[7] des salles informatisées, des locaux administratifs, il comprendra des ateliers[8] équipés pour l'usinage[9], la métrologie, les techniques de soudure[10], les systèmes électriques et électroniques, les travaux de carrosserie[11] ainsi que des bancs moteurs[12], des outillages spécialisés pour les matériels de pointe[13], les matériaux composites, le contrôle des carburants[14], etc. Une attention particulière sera portée aux énergies propres et aux problèmes d'environnement. L'objectif, avant tout social, est de former 500 demandeurs d'emplois[15] et 1 000 travailleurs en entreprise[16] entre 2005 et 2010.

B. Lisez l'article une seconde fois et répondez aux questions sur le texte en groupes de trois ou quatre étudiants.

1. Le centre mentionné dans cet article est une collaboration entre deux groupes. Quels sont ces deux groupes?
2. Est-ce qu'il existe un autre campus similaire?
3. Quelle est l'attention particulière de ce campus?
4. Quel est l'objectif[17] de ce campus qui va ouvrir ses portes en 2005?

C. Questions de réflexion. Avec votre groupe, répondez aux questions sur le sujet du texte.

1. Est-ce qu'il existe un centre similaire dans votre ville?
2. Si votre réponse est négative, est-ce que vous pensez qu'un centre de compétence automobile est nécessaire? Quel est le concurrent[18] le plus important des États-Unis en fabrication automobiles?

---

[1]*monthly* [2]*quinzième (fifteenth)* [3]*topic* [4]*will open* [5]*increase in the needs* [6]*square meters* [7]*Besides* [8]*workshops* [9]*manufacturing* [10]*welding* [11]*car body repair* [12]*engines* [13]*leading* [14]*fuel* [15]*job seekers* [16]*company workers* [17]*goal* [18]*competitor*

In France and in Francophone Europe, car races are quite popular. The most popular ones are the Paris-Dakar Rally and the **Vingt-Quatre Heures du Mans**.

3. Est-ce qu'il y a beaucoup de compétitions automobiles[1] dans votre ville (Formule 1, par exemple)? Est-ce que les compétitions automobiles sont populaires dans votre pays? Quelle est la compétition la plus connue?

 À vous de créer!

A. Je suis belge! Félicitations! Vous venez d'obtenir[2] la nationalité belge. Voici votre carte d'identité belge. Vous habitez à Bruxelles, la capitale européenne. Remplissez[3] votre carte d'identité avec les renseignements[4] qui vous sont demandés.

The *À vous de créer* sections practice grammar and vocabulary from the preceding unit of the text in contextualized and communicative activities related topically to the *Mise en pratique.*

Before they start working on these activities, students can take a virtual tour of Brussels by visiting www.ilotsacre.be, an excellent website that presents parts of Brussels with a live webcam, as well as an interactive map of the city.

Online Study Center

Votre photo

Nom: (nom de jeune fille[5] pour les femmes mariées)
_____ (Cherchez un nom de famille français ou francophone!)
Prénom(s): _____ (Changez aussi votre prénom.)
Sexe: M _____   F _____
Date de naissance: _____
(jour / mois / année)
Lieu de naissance: _____
(Ville de naissance)
État civil: Marié(e) _____ Divorcé(e) _____ Célibataire _____
Veuf (veuve) _____
Adresse: _____
(Si vous avez accès à l'Internet, cherchez une rue à Bruxelles. Dans la section **À vous de créer** de votre Online Study Center, vous trouverez un lien pour une carte interactive de Bruxelles.)
Couleur des yeux: _____
Couleur des cheveux: _____
Taille: _____ (en mètres et centimètres)
Profession: _____
Signature: _____

---

[1] car racing [2] you have just obtained [3] Fill out [4] information [5] maiden name

B. Vous cherchez un(e) colocataire[1]. Vous placez une annonce dans le journal pour trouver un(e) colocataire. Remplissez les tirets[2] avec les renseignements demandés.

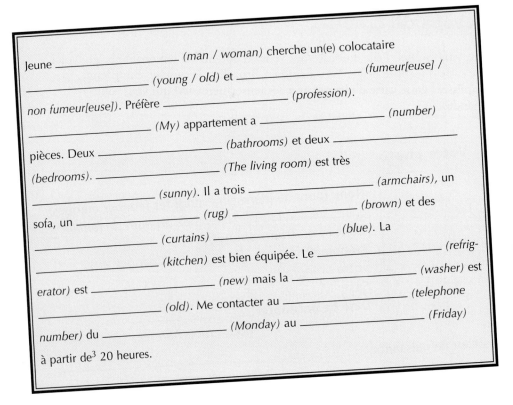

Jeune _____ (man / woman) cherche un(e) colocataire _____ (young / old) et _____ (fumeur[euse] / non fumeur[euse]). Préfère _____ (profession). _____ (My) appartement a _____ (number) pièces. Deux _____ (bathrooms) et deux _____ (bedrooms). _____ (The living room) est très _____ (sunny). Il a trois _____ (armchairs), un sofa, un _____ (rug) _____ (brown) et des _____ (curtains) _____ (blue). La _____ (kitchen) est bien équipée. Le _____ (refrigerator) est _____ (new) mais la _____ (washer) est _____ (old). Me contacter au _____ (telephone number) du _____ (Monday) au _____ (Friday) à partir de[3] 20 heures.

You may want to have students perform this conversation in front of the class.

C. Rencontres. Vous avez trouvé un(e) colocataire. Vous allez prendre un café (ou une bière!) à la Grand-Place à Bruxelles avec lui/elle. Posez-lui[4] des questions pour mieux le/la connaître[5].

1. *Questions sur sa famille:* Avez-vous une grande famille? D'où est votre famille?
2. *Questions sur son travail:* Où travaillez-vous? Aimez-vous votre travail? Travaillez-vous beaucoup?
3. *Questions sur ses goûts personnels:* Aimez-vous aller au cinéma? Quels films préférez-vous? Aimez-vous la musique? Quelle est votre musique préférée? Qu'est-ce que vous aimez faire comme sport?

---

[1]*roommate* [2]*Fill in the blanks* [3]*after* [4]*Ask him/her* [5]*to know him/her better*

À vous de décider: Le français pour quoi faire?

Follow-up: Ask students why they are taking French instead of another language. Ask them if they plan on continuing with French after they comply with the foreign language requirement. Why or why not?

Meet Brynn, a student of French and a college senior. She would like to share with you why she decided to study French and how she is using it daily. She will tell you as well how she is planning to use her French in the future, after she graduates. She hopes to convince you to continue studying French, so that you do not waste the time and effort that you have already invested in learning the language.

"I am studying French because I have always been fascinated with traveling. I have always wanted to travel, to have a broader view of the world, to learn in depth another culture and language, to be more educated and well-rounded. Why French? Because France is the country that fascinates me the most.

"I foresee using French for personal and professional benefit. I mentioned in my résumé that I studied abroad, and this turned out to be a very marketable asset. I have an advantage over other candidates that has opened doors for me in terms of business. A friend of the family who owns a company in the United States wants to offer me a job. His company is based in New York but has branches all over Europe. I would be asked to travel to France.

"At the present time I use my French more often than I thought. I am a bartender at a family restaurant and I have clients with whom I speak in French all the time. It is really cool to be able to hold a conversation with them! C'est super!"

MA VIE D'AUJOURD'HUI ET D'HIER

Ma ville

In this chapter you will learn how to describe city streets, shops, and parks, how to get around using public transportation, and how to shop in specialty stores, clothing stores, and grocery stores. You will also learn to ask for directions, give directions, and tell time in French.

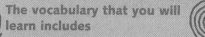
The vocabulary that you will learn includes

Shops and stores
Food items
Clothing items
Urban places such as commercial businesses, streets, and parks
Means of transportation
Directions

The structures that you will learn include

Regular verbs ending in **-re**
Partitive articles and expressions of quantity
The verbs **mettre, porter,** and **essayer**
The pronouns **y** and **en**
The verbs **prendre, comprendre,** and **apprendre**
Telling time
Commands

The culture that you will learn includes

Pedestrian streets in France
Brasseries
Public transportation in Paris and Tours
Grocery shopping in France
The French and fashion

Commençons!

On fait les courses 🎧

Après les cours à l'université, Aude et Jean-Jacques vont faire les courses. Leur réfrigérateur est vide[1]! Aude a la liste des provisions[2] et Jean-Jacques a le chariot à provisions[3].

Comme il est tard et ils sont fatigués après une longue journée à l'université, Aude et Jean-Jacques décident d'aller faire les courses dans une grande surface (c'est-à-dire un supermarché) au lieu d'aller[4] chez les petits commerçants du quartier.

Jean-Jacques et Aude vont au supermarché Carrefour.

Au rayon crémerie

AUDE:	Bonjour, Monsieur. Je voudrais[5] un morceau de Gruyère et je vais prendre[6] aussi une tranche de Roquefort.
LE CRÉMIER:	Très bien! Voilà vos fromages. Et avec ceci[7]?
AUDE:	Je vais prendre aussi une douzaine d'œufs.

Au rayon boucherie

JEAN-JACQUES:	Bonjour, Monsieur. Je voudrais un poulet fermier[8] et deux tranches de bœuf.
LE BOUCHER:	J'ai un beau poulet d'un kilo 200 grammes pour vous et voilà vos deux tranches de bœuf. Et avec ceci?
JEAN-JACQUES:	C'est tout, merci.

---

[1]*empty* [2]*shopping list* [3]*shopping cart* [4]*instead of going* [5]*I would like* [6]*to take / to buy* [7]*Anything else?* [8]*farm-raised chicken*

Au rayon poissonnerie

Il y a beaucoup de monde au rayon poissonnerie, alors Aude attend son tour[1] patiemment.

LA POISSONNIÈRE:	À qui le tour[2] maintenant?
AUDE RÉPOND RAPIDEMENT:	C'est à moi, Madame! Bonjour, Madame. Est-ce que vous vendez des moules?
LA POISSONNIÈRE:	Pardon, mais comme il y a beaucoup de monde, je n'entends[3] pas votre question.
AUDE RÉPÈTE SA QUESTION:	Est-ce que vous vendez des moules?
LA POISSONNIÈRE:	Ah! Mais oui! Et elles sont excellentes aujourd'hui.
AUDE:	Parfait! Alors, je voudrais un kilo de moules, s'il vous plaît. Et je voudrais aussi 500 grammes de crevettes.
LA POISSONNIÈRE:	Avec plaisir! Je vais choisir les plus grosses moules et les plus belles crevettes!
AUDE:	Merci, vous êtes très gentille! *(À Jean-Jacques:)* Jean-Jacques, ça te dit[4] une bouteille de vin rouge pour accompagner le dîner ce soir?
JEAN-JACQUES:	Ouais[5]! Quelle bonne idée!

À la caisse

AUDE:	Jean-Jacques, tu mets[6] les provisions dans le chariot? Moi, je vais payer la caissière, d'accord?
JEAN-JACQUES:	D'accord, ça marche[7]!

Jean-Jacques et Aude sortent[8] du supermarché. Ils vont acheter le pain. Pour le pain, ils préfèrent aller à la boulangerie.

Point out to students that at the cash register customers must place their purchases in bags or in their cart themselves. There is no one to do it for them.

À la boulangerie

JEAN-JACQUES ET AUDE:	Bonjour, Madame.
LA BOULANGÈRE:	Bonjour, Messieurs-Dames! Que désiriez-vous[9]?
JEAN-JACQUES:	Nous voudrions[10] une baguette, s'il vous plaît.
LA BOULANGÈRE:	La baguette, bien cuite[11] ou pas trop cuite[12]?
JEAN-JACQUES:	Bien cuite! C'est combien?
LA BOULANGÈRE:	Voilà votre baguette! C'est 1 euro.

---

[1] *waits her turn* [2] *Whose turn is it?* [3] *hear* [4] *What do you say about…?* [5] *Yeah!* [6] *put* [7] *That works (for me)!* [8] *leave* [9] *What would you like?* [10] *would like* [11] *well-baked* [12] *not baked too dark*

Vous avez bien compris?

Répondez aux questions suivantes d'après[1] les dialogues.

1. Où est-ce que Jean-Jacques met ses provisions?
2. Au rayon crémerie, combien de fromages est-ce qu'Aude achète? Et combien d'œufs?
3. Qu'est-ce que Jean-Jacques achète au rayon boucherie?
4. Comment est-ce que Jean-Jacques demande au boucher ce qu'il veut[2]?
5. Au rayon poissonnerie, comment sont les moules, d'après la poissonnière?
6. Que suggère Aude à Jean-Jacques pour accompagner le dîner?
7. À la caisse, qui va payer? Et que fait Jean-Jacques?
8. Comment est-ce que la boulangère dit bonjour à Aude et à Jean-Jacques?
9. Comment est-ce que Jean-Jacques et Aude demandent à la boulangère ce qu'ils veulent?
10. À la boulangerie, comment est la baguette que Jean-Jacques et Aude achètent?

Vocabulaire essentiel

Les magasins spécialisés

Quand on va …   on achète …

à la boucherie	à la boulangerie	à la boutique de vêtements
	 (top right)	

à la boucherie

de la viande et des volailles *(f.)*

à la boulangerie

du pain et des viennoiseries *(f.)*
(des croissants *[m.]* et des brioches *[f.]*)

à la boutique de vêtements

des vêtements *(m.)*

à la librairie

des livres *(m.)*

au magasin de chaussures

des chaussures *(f.)*

à la maison de la presse

des magazines *(m.)* et
des journaux *(m.)*

---

[1]*according to* [2]*what he wants*

à la papeterie

du papier, des enveloppes (f.)
et des cartes postales (f.)

à la pâtisserie

des pâtisseries (f.)

à la pharmacie

des médicaments (m.)

à la poissonnerie

du poisson et des fruits (m.)
de mer

à la poste

des timbres (m.)

au salon de coiffure

du shampooing (m.)

Faire les courses au supermarché *(to shop at the supermarket)*

les achats *(m.)*	*purchases*
le caissier / la caissière	*cashier*
le chariot à provisions	*shopping cart*
une grande surface	*supermarket*
la liste des provisions	*shopping list*
les petits commerçants *(m.)*	*small shops*
les provisions *(f.)*	*food supplies*
le rayon boucherie	*meat department*
le rayon crémerie	*dairy department*
le rayon poissonnerie	*seafood department*

Les produits alimentaires

une baguette	*loaf of French bread*
une baguette bien cuite	*well-baked loaf*
une baguette pas trop cuite	*not too dark loaf*
du bœuf *(m.)*	*beef*
des crevettes *(f.)*	*shrimp*
des moules *(f.)*	*mussels*
un poulet fermier	*farm-raised chicken*
du vin rouge *(m.)*	*red wine*

Expansion personnelle

Quand on va ... on achète ...

à la bijouterie

des bijoux *(m.)*

au bureau *(m.)* de tabac

des cigarettes *(f.)*,
des cigares *(m.)*, des pipes *(f.)*,

à la chocolaterie

des chocolats *(m.)*

à la confiserie

des bonbons *(m.)*

à la crémerie

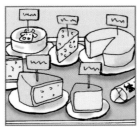

des produits laitiers *(m.)*

à la parfumerie

des parfums *(m.)*

À vous!

A. Où? Tell where the following items can be purchased.

◉ MODÈLE: des parfums

À la parfumerie.

1. des médicaments
2. des viennoiseries
3. des timbres
4. de la viande
5. des œufs
6. des crevettes
7. du shampooing
8. des bonbons
9. des bijoux
10. des chaussures

 **B. Le petit frère curieux!** You are about to leave the house to run some errands, but your little brother is very curious! He wants to know where you are going and what you are going to buy. With a classmate, play the role of the little brother and the older sibling.

MODÈLE: the bakery

—*Où vas-tu?*

—*Je vais à la boulangerie.*

—*Que vas-tu acheter?*

—*Je vais acheter du pain.*

1. the hairdresser
2. a newspaper shop
3. a stationery store
4. a clothing store
5. a pastry shop
6. a chocolate shop

Answer Key: 1. au salon de coiffure / du shampooing 2. à la maison de la presse / des journaux, des magazines 3. à la papeterie / des enveloppes, du papier, etc. 4. à la boutique de vêtements / des vêtements 5. à une pâtisserie / des pâtisseries 6. à une chocolaterie / des chocolats

Structure 1

Les verbes réguliers en *-re*

Online Study Center
ACE, Language Skills Practice

You are already familiar with two groups of regular verbs, those ending in **-er** and those ending in **-ir**. Now you are going to learn about another group of regular verbs: those ending in **-re**.

To conjugate a regular **-re** verb, simply drop the **-re** of the infinitive and add the following endings: **-s, -s,** *nothing,* **-ons, -ez, -ent.** For example, let's look at the verb **vendre** *(to sell)* in the present tense.

vendre	
je vend**s**	nous vend**ons**
tu vend**s**	vous vend**ez**
il / elle / on vend	ils / elles vend**ent**

Now, let's apply that pattern to another regular **-re** verb, **répondre** *(to answer).*

répondre	
je répond**s**	nous répond**ons**
tu répond**s**	vous répond**ez**
il / elle / on répond	ils / elles répond**ent**

Model pronunciation for students, then have them repeat. Point out that there is no difference in pronunciation between first-, second-, and third-person singular forms. Remind students that this is why subject pronouns are obligatory in French. Point out also that, unlike **-er** verbs, **-re** verbs differ in pronunciation in the third-person singular and third-person plural forms. Insist on this difference as students do the activities that follow, as it is crucial to comprehension.

Here is a list of regular **-re** verbs:

attendre	*to wait (for)*
descendre	*to get down, to go down*
entendre	*to hear*
mordre (dans)	*to bite (into)*
perdre	*to lose*
rendre	*to return, to give back*
rendre visite à	*to visit (a person)*

1. Can you give the conjugation of **perdre** in the present tense?

2. Go back to the **Commençons!** dialogues (pp. 136–137) and find all the **-re** verbs. Think about their endings and ask yourself these questions: Who or what is the subject? Why do some verbs have an **s** at the end? Why do others not have an **s**? Why does one of the **-re** verbs end in **-ez**? Who or what is the subject of this verb?

À l'écoute!

Transcript: 1. vend du shampooing 2. attendez votre tour 3. entendent les questions 4. descendent de la voiture 5. rendons les bijoux 6. perd ses livres 7. réponds aux questions

A. Qui parle? Listen to the sentence fragments on your In-Text Audio CD, and complete the sentences by checking the right subject.

1. _____ il   _____ ils
2. _____ nous   _____ vous
3. _____ il   _____ ils
4. _____ ils   _____ nous
5. _____ ils   _____ nous
6. _____ il   _____ ils
7. _____ vous   _____ tu

Have students translate the two sentences in #1. Point out that, without context, either is a logical translation. It is therefore very important to distinguish the pronunciation of these two verbs. Model the pronunciation of the infinitives, then have students do the activity. Go over the answers together, having students read the form they checked.

Transcript: 1. J'entends l'autobus. 2. Nous attendons les enfants. 3. Tu attends le prof. 4. Il entend sa femme. 5. Vous attendez le train.

B. Le verbe correct. Is the speaker using **entendre** or **attendre**? Check the sentence you hear.

1. _____ J'attends l'autobus.   _____ J'entends l'autobus.
2. _____ Nous entendons les enfants.   _____ Nous attendons les enfants.
3. _____ Tu entends le prof.   _____ Tu attends le prof.
4. _____ Il attend sa femme.   _____ Il entend sa femme.
5. _____ Vous attendez le train.   _____ Vous entendez le train.

Pratiquons!

Answer Key: 1. vendons 2. rendent 3. perd 4. mords 5. mordez

A. La bijouterie Bijoux-bijoux. Write the correct form of the verbs in parentheses.

Ma famille et moi, nous avons une bijouterie qui s'appelle Bijoux-bijoux. Nous (1) _____ (vendre) des bijoux très chers et très beaux! Nos clients sont toujours satisfaits—ils ne (2) _____ (rendre) pas les bijoux qu'ils achètent chez nous. Si un client (3) _____ (perdre) un bijou, nous pouvons fabriquer[1] un autre bijou identique. Pour vérifier l'authenticité d'un diamant, je (4) _____ (mordre) le diamant très fort. Et vous, quand vous achetez un diamant, est-ce que vous (5) _____ (mordre) la pierre précieuse?

Answer Key: 1. n'entends pas 2. attendez

B. Que dit-on? *(What do people say?)* Complete each sentence with the correct form of an **-re** verb that fits the context logically.

1. Quand les étudiants parlent en classe, je (ne … pas) _____ bien le professeur.
2. Quand il y a beaucoup de monde à la poste, vous _____ votre tour patiemment.

---

[1] *we can make*

3. Quand un étudiant finit son examen, il _____ l'examen au professeur.
4. Quand un chien est méchant, il _____ les enfants.
5. Quand c'est la Saint Valentin, les supermarchés _____ des chocolats et des cartes romantiques!

Answer Key: 3. rend 4. mord 5. vendent

C. Entretien. Interview a classmate and find out a little about his or her personality by asking the following questions. When you have finished, complete the *Portrait personnel* that follows.

Before beginning the activity, model the pronunciation of **patiement / impatiemment** (#4). Ask students to determine the meaning of these words, based on their context.

1. Est-ce que tu perds souvent tes clés[1]? Où? À la maison? À l'université? Dans un lieu public? Dans la voiture?
2. Toi et les autres étudiants dans ta classe, est-ce que vous répondez toujours aux questions du professeur de français? Pourquoi? Est-ce que ses questions sont faciles ou difficiles?
3. Est-ce que tu rends visite à tes parents? Souvent? Une fois par semaine? Une fois par mois? Une fois par semestre?
4. Est-ce que tu attends patiemment ou impatiemment ta meilleure amie / ton meilleur ami? Est-qu'il/elle est souvent en retard? Combien de temps[2] est-ce que tu attends ta meilleure amie / ton meilleur ami avant de partir[3]?

Portrait personnel

Write a brief paragraph about your classmate, using some of the adjectives that you learned in earlier chapters and justifying your description with some of the information that you learned in activity C.

MODÈLE: Karen est très désorganisée. Elle perd ses clés tous les jours …

Structure 2

L'article partitif et les expressions de quantité

Online Study Center
ACE, Language Skills Practice

- The partitive article is used in French to indicate *some* or *any*. In this chapter you have seen these articles used with food items, for example, **de la viande** *(some meat)*, **du pain** *(some bread)*, and **des crevettes** *(some shrimp)*. The partitive articles can be used in many other contexts, for example, **j'écoute de la musique** *(I listen to [some] music)* and **je regarde des films** *(I watch [some] movies)*.
- The partitive articles have the following forms.

Point out that *some* is not always expressed in English: **J'écoute de la musique** = *I listen to music / I listen to some music.*

du (masc. sing.)	du poisson	*some fish*
de la (fem. sing.)	de la viande	*some meat*
de l' (masc. or fem. sing. before a vowel)	de l'eau	*some water*
des (masc. and fem. plural)	des moules	*some mussels*

[1] *keys* [2] *How long* [3] *before leaving*

Chapitre 5 Structure 2 *cent quarante-trois* **143**

- In negative sentences, use **de** in the place of **du, de l', de la,** or **des.** Note that in negative sentences, the partitive article is often translated as *any*.

Je mange souvent **du** poulet.
I eat chicken often.

Je **ne** mange **pas** souvent *de* poulet.
I do not eat chicken often.

On vend **des** spaghettis.

On **ne** vend **pas** *de* spaghettis dans ce cafe.

We sell spaghetti.

We do not sell spaghetti at this café.

Vous achetez **de la** viande.
You buy (some) meat.

Vous **n'**achetez **pas** *de* viande.
You do not buy any meat.

Ils écoutent **de la** musique.
They listen to (some) music.

Ils **n'**écoutent **pas** *de* musique.
They do not listen to any music.

- The partitive articles indicate an undetermined quantity of something. They are used with uncountable nouns: **de la musique, de l'argent** *(some money),* **de l'intelligence** *(some intelligence),* **de la gentillesse** *(some kindness),* **des intérêts** *(some interest),* etc. In order to specify a quantity, an expression of quantity is used, followed by **de** and then the noun.

Je mange **une tranche** *de* fromage.
Je voudrais **un kilo** *de* chocolats.
Nous voudrions **une douzaine** *d'*œufs.

Point out that expressions of quantity, like negative verbs that take the partitive, are always followed by **de** or **d'**. This is similar to English usage: *a slice of cheese,* not *a slice of some cheese.*

- Following are some common expressions of quantity:

beaucoup de	*a lot of*	une tranche de	*a slice of*
un peu de	*a little (of)*	un morceau de	*a piece of*
assez de	*enough (of)*	une douzaine de	*a dozen (of)*
pas mal de	*quite a lot of*	un kilo de	*a kilo of*
moins de	*less (of)*	un litre de	*a liter of*
plus de	*more (of)*	un gramme de	*a gram of*
une bouteille de	*a bottle of*	un paquet de	*a pack of*
un sac de	*a bag of*	une boîte de	*a box of*

- These expressions do not change in negative sentences.

Catherine **n'**achète **pas** beaucoup *de* magazines.
Nous **ne** mangeons **pas** une tranche *de* pain.

- Do not use partitive articles with verbs that express likes or dislikes, such as **aimer, préférer, détester,** and **adorer.** Instead, use the definite articles, **le, la, l', les.**

Éric adore **le** chocolat.
Nathalie déteste **la** viande.
Roxanne n'aime pas **les** bonbons.

VÉRIFIEZ VOTRE COMPRÉHENSION

1. Go back to the **Commençons!** dialogues (pp. 136–137) between Aude, Jean-Jacques, and the clerks. Underline all the partitive articles as well as any expressions of quantity. Think about the meaning of each in its context.

2. Can you explain why Aude says, **un kilo de moules** rather than **un kilo des moules,** since **moules** is a plural noun?

Pratiquons!

A. Combien?
Identify the item and the quantity in each drawing. Then, tell where each item can be bought.

⊚ MODÈLE: *Un paquet de cigarettes. On achète un paquet de cigarettes au bureau de tabac.*

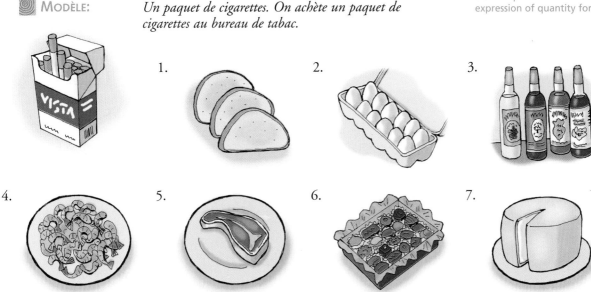

1.
2.
3.
4.
5.
6.
7.

While French speakers might also use the definite article in some of these sentences (e.g., #1: **On achète le pain** ...), have students concentrate on using either a partitive article or an expression of quantity for now.

B. Végétariens et carnivores!
Based on their lifestyles (vegetarian versus meat eaters), tell if the following people eat the food mentioned. Pay attention to differences in form between the affirmative and the negative.

⊚ MODÈLE: Sandrine est végétarienne. Mange-t-elle de la viande?

*Non, elle ne mange pas **de** viande.*

1. Olivia est végétarienne. Mange-t-elle du poisson?
2. Patrick est carnivore. Mange-t-il du poisson?
3. Mes parents sont carnivores. Mangent-ils des œufs?
4. Yves est végétarien. Mange-t-il du poulet?
5. Michel et Christine sont végétariens. Mangent-ils des viennoiseries?
6. Patricia est carnivore. Mange-t-elle du fromage?
7. Christian est végétarien. Mange-t-il du bœuf?

🗣️ C. Vos préférences.
Find out your classmate's personal and gastronomic tastes by asking her or him the following questions. Then, report your classmate's answers to the class.

1. Aimes-tu le vin rouge ou le vin blanc?
2. Préfères-tu le poisson ou la viande?
3. Est-ce que tu achètes des journaux souvent? Lesquels[1]?
4. Fumes-tu des cigarettes? Combien de cigarettes ou de paquets par jour?
5. Est-ce que tu achètes beaucoup de chaussures?
6. Est-ce que tu achètes plus de chaussures ou plus de vêtements?
7. Aimes-tu les livres? Quel est ton livre préféré?
8. Préfères-tu les livres ou les films? Quel est ton film préféré?

Answer Key: 1. Trois tranches de pain. On achète trois tranches de pain (On achète du pain) à la boulangerie. 2. Une douzaine d'œufs. On achète une douzaine d'œufs à la crémerie (au rayon crémerie). 3. Quatre bouteilles de vin. On achète quatre bouteilles de vin (on achète du vin) au supermarché (dans un supermarché / dans une grande surface). 4. Beaucoup de crevettes. On achète des crevettes à la poissonnerie. 5. Un morceau de viande. On achète de la viande à la boucherie. 6. Une boîte de chocolats. On achète une boîte de chocolats (on achète des chocolats) à la chocolaterie. 7. Un kilo de fromage. On achète un kilo de fromage (on achète du fromage) à la crémerie.

Answer Key: 1. Non, elle ne mange pas de poisson. 2. Oui, il mange du poisson. 3. Oui, ils mangent des œufs. 4. Non, il ne mange pas de poulet. 5. Oui, ils mangent des viennoiseries. 6. Oui, elle mange du fromage. 7. Non, il ne mange pas de bœuf.

---

[1] *Which ones?*

Continuons!

Online Study Center
Language Skills Practice

Mention to students that in France and in Francophone Europe it is very common to find pedestrian streets lined with shops. No cars are allowed, and shoppers can walk about freely. Shopping centers exist as well; however, shoppers tend to prefer pedestrian streets.

Clothing and shoe sizes in France are different than in the United States.

Women's pants, dresses, blouses

USA	France
2	32
4	34
6	36
8	38
10	40
12	42
14	44

Men's shirts

USA	France
15	38
15½	39
16	40
16½	41
17	42

Women's shoes

USA	France
6	36
7	37,5
8	38,5
9	40
10	42

Men's shoes

USA	France
8	41
9	42,5
10	44
11	45
12	46

Partie I: Au magasin de vêtements

C'est samedi après-midi et Aude et Jean-Jacques vont faire les magasins[1] dans une rue piétonne, la rue Sainte-Catherine, à Bordeaux.

Aude et Jean-Jacques entrent dans Promod.

AUDE:	Il fait beau aujourd'hui, n'est-ce pas, Jean-Jacques?
JEAN-JACQUES:	Oui! L'été arrive!
AUDE:	Je voudrais acheter un bikini, une robe[2] blanche et des sandales. Et toi?
JEAN-JACQUES:	Moi, je voudrais des jeans et un tee-shirt.
AUDE:	On va à Promod? Je suis sûre de trouver un mignon bikini.
JEAN-JACQUES:	Je préfère un bikini sexy!
AUDE:	Ne sois pas bête[3], Jean-Jacques!

LA VENDEUSE:	Bonjour! Je peux vous aider?
AUDE:	Oui, je cherche un bikini, taille 38.
JEAN-JACQUES (À AUDE):	Un bikini sexy!
AUDE (À JEAN-JACQUES):	Chut![4] Tu es pénible![5]
LA VENDEUSE:	Pardon, Monsieur, je n'entends pas bien ce que vous dites[6].
JEAN-JACQUES (TOUT ROUGE):	Euh, ce n'est rien d'important …
AUDE (À LA VENDEUSE):	Est-ce que je peux essayer[7] ce bikini jaune et bleu, s'il vous plaît?
LA VENDEUSE:	Oui, les cabines d'essayage[8] sont à droite[9].

---

[1] to go shopping [2] dress [3] Don't be silly! [4] Shh! / Hush! [5] You're a pain! [6] what you're saying [7] Can I try on…?
[8] dressing rooms [9] to the right

Dans la cabine d'essayage: Aude met[1] le bikini. Il est parfait pour elle.

LA VENDEUSE:	Le bikini vous va bien?[2]
AUDE:	Oui, merci. Il me va parfaitement! Je le prends.[3]

Aude et Jean-Jacques sortent[4] de Promod.

AUDE:	Où vas-tu acheter les jeans et le tee-shirt?
JEAN-JACQUES:	À Célio.
AUDE:	Encore? On y va toujours![5]
JEAN-JACQUES:	C'est normal. Il y a toujours des soldes[6] et leurs vêtements sont très bon marché.

Aude et Jean-Jacques sortent de Célio, les mains pleines[7].

AUDE:	J'aime beaucoup nos achats[8]!
JEAN-JACQUES:	Oui, moi aussi! Aude, est-ce que tu voudrais aller à la brasserie[9] Gambetta pour prendre une bière[10]?
AUDE:	Oh, oui! Je voudrais bien y aller!
JEAN-JACQUES:	Alors[11] allons-y!

Vous avez bien compris?

Tell if the following sentences are true (**vrai**) or false (**faux**) according to the preceding dialogues.

Answer Key: 1. vrai 2. faux 3. faux 4. faux 5. vrai 6. vrai 7. vrai 8. faux 9. vrai

1. Dans une rue piétonne il n'y a pas de voitures. _____ vrai _____ faux
2. Les Français préfèrent aller aux centres commerciaux. _____ vrai _____ faux
3. Il pleut. _____ vrai _____ faux
4. Aude voudrait une robe bleue. _____ vrai _____ faux
5. Aude choisit un mignon bikini à Promod. _____ vrai _____ faux
6. Jean-Jacques voudrait des jeans. _____ vrai _____ faux
7. À Célio les vêtements sont bon marché. _____ vrai _____ faux
8. Aude achète un chemisier à Promod. _____ vrai _____ faux
9. Après leurs achats, Aude et Jean-Jacques vont à la brasserie. _____ vrai _____ faux

---

[1]*puts on* [2]*Does the bikini fit you well?* [3]*I'll take it.* [4]*leave* [5]*We always go there!* [6]*sales* [7]*their hands full*
[8]*purchases* [9]*brewery* [10]*to have a beer* [11]*Then*

Vocabulaire essentiel

Les vêtements

un chemisier

une chemise

un tee-shirt

un sweat

une jupe

un tailleur

un costume

une cravate

une veste

un manteau

une écharpe

un imperméable

un pull(over)

un short

un pantalon

des chaussettes (f.)

des chaussures (f.)
de sport / des tennis

des bottes (f.)

un maillot de bain

un pyjama

Expansion personnelle

Quelques mots et expressions utiles quand on fait des courses

faire du lèche-vitrine — *to go window-shopping*
une rue piétonne — *pedestrian street*
des soldes *(m.)* — *sales*
les cabines *(f.)* d'essayage — *dressing rooms*
À qui le tour maintenant? — *Whose turn is it now?*
C'est mon tour. — *It's my turn.*
C'est combien? — *How much is it?*
C'est (trop) cher. — *It is (too) expensive.*
C'est bon marché. — *It is cheap.*
C'est soldé / en solde. — *It is on sale.*
Que désiriez-vous? — *What would you like?*
Et avec ceci? — *Anything else?*
C'est tout, merci. — *That's all, thank you.*

D'autres vêtements

un survêtement

un gilet

un caleçon

une culotte

un soutien-gorge

des bas *(m.)*

un foulard

une casquette

un chapeau

des lunettes *(f.)*

des lunettes *(f.)* de soleil

À vous!

A. Cherchez bien! For each item, find at least one student in the class who is wearing the following.

1. un pantalon marron
2. une casquette verte
3. des bottes noires
4. un pull rouge
5. des chaussures de sport Reebok
6. un foulard
7. un tee-shirt jaune
8. des chaussettes bleues

B. Les achats. With a classmate, play the role of a clerk **(le vendeur / la vendeuse)** and a customer **(le client / la cliente).** The clerk asks the client if s/he needs help and the client tells the clerk what s/he wants (the item pictured).

MODÈLE: LE VENDEUR / LA VENDEUSE: *Je peux vous aider?*

LE CLIENT / LA CLIENTE: *Oui, je voudrais une chemise.*

 1.  2.  3.  4.

 5.   6.  7.  8.

9. 10.

C. Que porte la famille de Claudine? *(What is Claudine's family wearing?)* Do you remember Claudine's family from Chapter 3? Look at the pictures and describe what each family member is wearing. Start your description with **Il/Elle porte ...** *(He/She is wearing . . .)* and include as many clothing items as you can identify.

1. Claudine
2. Valérie
3. Cyrille
4. Serge
5. Thierry
6. Charlotte
7. Isabelle
8. Angèle

To turn this activity into a game, have students do it without looking back at the vocabulary. (You may put them in pairs, if you like.) Award one point for each item of clothing correctly identified, with its article. The person or team with the most points wins.

Structure 3

Les verbes *mettre, porter* et *essayer*

Online Study Center
ACE, Language Skills
Practice

- In the *Continuons!* dialogues on pages 146–147, you saw the verbs **mettre** and **essayer** in context. **Mettre** means *to put on* and **essayer** means *to try on.* The third verb that you are going to learn now is **porter,** which means *to wear* or, in another context, *to bring (something to someone)*[1]. It is a regular **-er** verb:

porter	
je port**e**	nous port**ons**
tu port**es**	vous port**ez**
il / elle / on port**e**	ils / elles port**ent**

Les étudiants **portent** souvent des jeans.
Jeannette **porte** du vin à ses amis.

---

[1]When **porter** is used to mean *to bring,* it takes the preposition **à: Je porte son café à ma femme le matin.**

Point out that with the exception of the single **t** singular forms, **mettre** is conjugated like a regular **-re** verb. If you wish, you might have your students predict the conjugation of some verbs conjugated like **mettre**: **permettre, promettre, admettre,** etc. This reinforces the pattern and makes the verb seem less irregular.

If you feel your class is ready for it, explain that this spelling change occurs because of the phonetic context: when **y** occurs in the last syllable of the verb, it changes to **i** to avoid having the semiconsonant sound [j] at the end. When it is followed by another syllable, however, the glide is preferred, as it facilitates the pronunciation of the vowels on either side of it.

Remind students of the use of definite versus indefinite articles when going over these verbs: **Je porte** *le* **gâteau d'anniversaire** versus **Je porte** *un* **gâteau.**

- **Mettre** and **essayer** are irregular verbs. **Mettre** keeps the double **t** of the infinitive only in the plural forms.

mettre	
je mets	nous mettons
tu mets	vous mettez
il / elle / on met	ils / elles mettent

Le prof **met** toujours des vêtements de couleur noire.
Je **mets** un pyjama pour dormir.

- **Essayer** is conjugated like a regular **-er** verb, but the **y** of the infinitive changes to **i** in all but the **nous** and **vous** forms.

essayer	
j'essaie	nous essayons
tu essaies	vous essayez
il / elle / on essaie	ils / elles essaient

Thérèse **essaie** un mignon pantalon à Promod.
J'**essaie** des sandales au magasin de chaussures.

- When these verbs are used in the negative and are followed by an indefinite article or a partitive article, the article changes to **de.**

Mes parents ne portent pas **de** jeans.
(*Affirmative:* Mes parents portent **des** jeans.)

Je ne porte pas **de** vin à ton dîner.
(*Affirmative:* Je porte **du** vin à ton dîner.)

Ta sœur ne met pas **de** pull en hiver.
(*Affirmative:* Ta sœur met **un** pull en hiver.)

Je n'essaie pas **de** robe.
(*Affirmative:* J'essaie **une** robe.)

Attention! Remember that definite articles don't change in the negative.

Je n'essaie pas **la** robe rouge; j'essaie **la** robe bleue.

 VÉRIFIEZ VOTRE COMPRÉHENSION

1. Go back to the **Continuons!** text (pp. 146–147) and see how **mettre** and **essayer** are used in context. Look at the meaning and the structure of the sentences in which the two verbs appear. Explain the form of each one.

2. Try to explain why **essayer** is left in the infinitive form in the sentence **Est-ce que je peux essayer ce bikini?**

Pratiquons!

A. Histoire de sandales!
Complete the sentences with the correct form of the verb in parentheses.

Answer Key: 1. met 2. essaie 3. essaie 4. mettent 5. portent

Marine va au centre commercial aujourd'hui. Comme il fait chaud, elle (1) _____ (mettre) un short et un tee-shirt. Elle fait du lèche-vitrine. Elle regarde les magasins de chaussures parce qu'elle adore les chaussures! Elle découvre des sandales bon marché. Elle entre dans le magasin et elle (2) _____ (essayer) les sandales. Un autre cliente (3) _____ (essayer) les mêmes[1] sandales. Les sandales de Marine sont trop petites. Zut! Mais, les sandales de l'autre cliente sont trop grandes! Elles échangent leurs sandales et elles les[2] (4) _____ (mettre). Marine et l'autre cliente sortent[3] du magasin toutes contentes: elles (5) _____ (porter) leurs sandales!

B. Qu'est-ce que tu portes?
Tell what you wear on the following occasions. Use a complete sentence starting with **Je porte … .**

Answer Key. Possible answers: 1. Je porte un pantalon et un chemisier / une chemise. 2. Je porte un survêtement, un tee-shirt et des tennis. 3. Je porte un jean et un sweat. 4. Je porte une robe / un tailleur / un costume. 5. Je porte un jean et un chemisier / une chemise. 6. Je porte un short et un tee-shirt / un maillot de bain et des sandales. 7. Je porte une jupe / un pantalon et un chemisier / une chemise.

> **MODÈLE:** pour aller à la bibliothèque
>
> *Je porte un jean et un tee-shirt.*

1. pour aller dîner au restaurant avec ton (ta) petit(e) ami(e)
2. pour faire du jogging
3. pour aller au cinéma avec des amis
4. pour aller au mariage des amis
5. pour aller à l'université
6. pour aller à la plage[4]
7. pour aller danser

C. Normalement, oui ou non?
With a classmate, ask each other the following questions and answer with complete sentences. Who is more logical?

1. Est-ce que tu mets des chaussures de sport pour aller à un mariage?
2. Est-ce que les gens[5] mettent des sandales pour aller skier?
3. Portes-tu un imperméable pour aller nager?
4. Est-ce que les étudiants portent des casquettes en classe?
5. Est-ce que les hommes portent des soutien-gorges?
6. Essaies-tu les vêtements avant de les acheter[6]?
7. Est-ce que tu mets des bottes en été?
8. Est-ce que tu portes un survêtement pour faire de l'exercice?
9. Est-ce que tu mets des chaussettes avec des sandales?

Portrait personnel

Describe what you and your partner usually wear to class. Then, write what you each wear on weekends when you go out. Draw some comparisons between the two of you.

As a follow-up to this writing activity, you may want to ask students who they think is the best dressed in the class, the most elegant, or the most hip. You may also choose celebrities and ask students to describe what they wear and to vote on the celebrity who dresses the worst and the best. Provide the following expressions to help them: **le/la mieux habillé(e), le/la moins bien habillé(e), le/la plus élégant(e), le/la plus hip.**

> **Mots utiles**
> d'habitude
> le week-end
> pour venir en classe
> pour sortir
> pour aller au restaurant
> pour aller danser

---

[1] *the same* [2] *them* [3] *leave* [4] *beach* [5] *people* [6] *before buying them*

Structure 4

Online Study Center
ACE, Language Skills
Practice

Les pronoms *y* et *en*

Le pronom *y*

Pronouns are used to avoid repetition. They replace a noun that would otherwise be repeated too often. The pronoun **y** usually means *there,* and it replaces a prepositional phrase indicating a location, a place, or a destination. The phrase replaced by **y** is generally introduced by a preposition of location, such as **à** *(to),* **dans** *(in),* **en** *(in);* this preposition, along with the location, is replaced by **y.**

- The pronoun **y** is placed before a conjugated verb.

  Je vais **à la poste.** → J'**y** vais. *(I go there.)*
  Tu n'étudies pas **à la bibliothèque.** → Tu n'**y** étudies pas. *(You don't study there.)*
  Vous entrez **dans la maison.** → Vous **y** entrez. *(You enter there.)*
  Nous faisons nos courses **au centre commercial.** → Nous **y** faisons nos courses.
      (We shop there.)
  Je ne vais pas **à la pharmacie.** → Je n'**y** vais pas. *(I'm not going there.)*

- Remember that when there are two verbs in one sentence, the second verb stays in the infinitive form: **je vais manger.** If the pronoun **y** is used in such a sentence, it is placed before the infinitive, between the two verbs.

  Je vais voyager **à Bruxelles.** → Je vais **y** voyager. *(I am going to travel there.)*
  L'infirmière aime travailler **à l'hôpital.** → L'infirmière aime **y** travailler.
      (The nurse likes to work there.)
  Le pilote préfère piloter **dans un Airbus.** → Le pilote préfère **y** piloter.
      (The pilot prefers to pilot in one.)
  Le prof n'aime pas parler anglais **en classe.** → Le prof n'aime pas **y** parler
      anglais. *(The professor does not like to speak English there.)*

- In Chapter 4, you saw an expression with the pronoun **y** when you were visiting Aurélie Marquis's apartment in Geneva: **On y va?** Do you remember its meaning? It means *Shall we go?* When you were introduced to the verb **aller** in that same chapter, you saw another expression with the pronoun **y: Allons-y!** *(Let's go).* **Allons-y** is the logical answer to the question **On y va?**

  —On y va?   *Shall we go?*
  —Oui, allons-y!   *Yes, let's go!*

Assure students that they will learn how to use a pronoun to express *to think about someone* or *to answer someone* in a later chapter.

- The pronoun **y** is used with three verbs that do not indicate a place, a location, or a destination. These three verbs are: **penser à** *(to think about [someone or something]),* **répondre à,** and **croire à** *(to believe in [someone or something]).* With these verbs, the pronoun **y** is used to replace *something* in the sentence, but never *someone.* In these cases, the pronoun **y** means *it* or *them.*

  Je pense **à mes problèmes.** → J'**y** pense. *(I think about them.)*
  Vous répondez **à la question.** → Vous **y** répondez. *(You answer it.)*
  Il croit **au grand amour.** → Il **y** croit. *(He believes in it.)*
  Les étudiants vont penser **à l'examen.** → Les étudiants vont **y** penser.
      (The students are going to think about it.)

Le prof ne va pas répondre **aux questions** pendant l'examen. → Le prof ne va pas **y** répondre pendant l'examen. *(The professor is not going to answer them during the exam.)*

Le pronom *en*

The pronoun **en** is very similar to **y** in placement, but has a different function: **en** replaces a noun that is introduced by a quantity, and, if it is translated in English, generally means *of it/of them.* The quantity that introduces the noun may be represented by the partitive article, by a specific number, or by any other expression of quantity, such as the ones that you saw earlier in the chapter. Notice that the quantity itself is not replaced. Like **y, en** precedes the conjugated verb in the sentence:

Je mange **du fromage.** → J'**en** mange. *(I eat some [of it].)*
Il a **cinq livres.** → Il **en** a cinq. *(He has five [of them].)*
Je mange **beaucoup de fromage.** → J'**en** mange beaucoup. *(I eat a lot [of it].)*

If there is a verb + infinitive in the sentence, **en** precedes the infinitive:

Tu aimes manger **des escargots?** → Tu aimes **en** manger? *(Do you like to eat some [of them]?)*

When combined with the expression **il y a** *(there is/there are)*, **en** follows **y:**

Il y a **vingt-deux étudiants** en classe. → Il y **en** a vingt-deux. *(There are 22 of them.)*

VÉRIFIEZ VOTRE COMPRÉHENSION

1. Go back to the dialogues in **Continuons!** (pp. 146–147), and underline the pronoun **y** each time it appears. Think about what it is replacing and about its placement in the sentence. (Does it occur before the conjugated verb or before an infinitive? Why?)

2. Look at the use of the expression **Allons-y!** By saying that, how does Jean-Jacques strike you? Is he enthusiastic about going to the **brasserie** or not?

Pratiquons!

A. Rectifications. Answer the following questions according to the drawings and photos. Use the pronoun **y** in your answers.

Draw students' attention to the fact that the partitive changes to **de** in #2 and 4.

Answer Key: 1. Non, il n'y mange pas.

MODÈLE: Est-ce que Chloé rentre dans la salle de bains?

Non, Chloé n'y rentre pas. Elle rentre dans la cuisine.

1. Est-ce que Pierre mange au restaurant?

2. Est-ce que Jules et Georges regardent un film au cinéma?

3. Est-ce que Céline va acheter des vêtements à Promod?

4. Est-ce que les étudiants écoutent des CD au laboratoire?

5.  Est-ce que les professeurs finissent les corrections dans leurs bureaux?

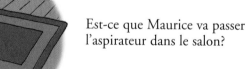

6. Est-ce que Paul achète du fromage à la crémerie?

7. Est-ce que Maurice va passer l'aspirateur dans le salon?

8. Est-ce que Aude et Jean-Jacques vont faire les magasins au centre commercial?

🗣️B. Ne répétez pas! Ask and answer the following questions. In your answers, replace the italicized phrase with the pronoun **y** in order to avoid repetition. Pay attention to the placement of the pronoun.

1. Tu vas *à la bibliothèque* souvent?
2. Tu aimes danser *en boîte?*
3. À quelle heure est-ce que tu arrives *en classe de français?*
4. Quand vas-tu *au cinéma?*
5. Est-ce que tu vas aller *à la maison* après le cours de français?
6. Est-ce qu'on vend des cigarettes *dans les magasins universitaires?*
7. Est-ce que tu prépares tes devoirs *dans ta chambre?*
8. Est-ce que tu manges *au restaurant* pendant[1] la semaine?

C. Qu'est-ce qu'il y a dans le placard? *(What's in the cupboard?)* You are helping Jean-Claude prepare his grocery list. He's asking questions and making a list while you check the cupboards. Answer his questions based on the indications below. Use the pronoun **en** in your response.

🌀 MODÈLE: Est-ce que j'ai *des oranges?* (oui)

Oui, tu *en* as.

1. Est-ce qu'il y a *des croissants* dans le placard? (oui)
2. J'ai besoin *d'une baguette?* (non)
3. Je vais acheter *du poulet?* (oui)
4. Est-ce que j'ai *des crevettes?* (non)
5. J'ai assez *de bonbons?* (non)
6. Il y a *une bouteille de vin?* (oui)
7. Est-ce que j'ai besoin *d'un paquet de cigarettes?* (non)

🗣️D. Vous êtes gourmand? With a partner, ask and answer the following questions, using the pronoun **en** in your response. When you have finished, tell if your partner is a **gourmand** or a **gourmet.**

1. Au supermarché, vous achetez beaucoup ou peu de pain?
2. Pour le petit déjeuner, vous manger un croissant ou trois croissants?
3. Vous préférez un verre de coca ou un litre de coca?
4. Vous mangez une tranche de fromage ou un paquet de fromage?
5. Le soir, vous mangez un morceau de bœuf ou un kilo de bœuf?
6. Le matin, vous aimez une tasse de café ou une carafe de café?
7. Pour le déjeuner, vous mangez un fruit ou beaucoup de fruits?
8. Avant d'aller au lit, vous mangez deux ou trois biscuits ou un paquet de biscuits?

À vous de parler!

🗣️A. Au supermarché. In groups of three, pretend that you are shopping at a supermarket. Two of you will be the customers and one of you the clerk at the different departments. First, make a list with the food items you need to buy. Then, create a dialogue between the customers and the clerk in the different food departments at the supermarket. (You may use the dialogues at the beginning of the chapter as models.) Make sure that the customers and the clerk greet each other each time.

---

[1]*during*

B. Au magasin de vêtements. You are going to go shopping at Promod (for women) and/or at Célio (for men). One of you plays the role of the clerk and the other two are the customers. Decide which clothing items you would like to purchase (color, size, price). In the store, the clerk greets the customers and asks if they need help. The customers tell the clerk what they need. Once they find what they want, the customers ask the clerk if they can try on the items. After they try them on, they decide if they are going to buy them.

Online Study Center
Web Search Activities

On fait comme ça dans une brasserie en Suisse[1]

The brasserie pictured here is located in Lausanne, Switzerland. A **brasserie** is the equivalent of a brewery. However, European **brasseries** are very different from American breweries. For instance, one may have a drink and/or a meal outside. There are usually tables and chairs placed on the sidewalk. Inside there is a bar and a restaurant. If you choose a seat outside, prices are going to be higher than inside, regardless of what you order. Normally, the Swiss like to sit outside—provided that the weather is nice—so that they can look at the people passing by. They like to talk about them too (the way they are dressed, the way they walk, their hairstyles, with whom they are walking, and so on). There are no refills, as there are in the United States, of any drink: sodas, coffee, or tea. And the drinks are served chilled, but without ice. Another difference is that, with the exception of beer, drinks come in one size only—the equivalent of the small size in the United States. At a **brasserie**, customers can choose between draft beer (**une pression** or **un demi[2]**), and bottled beer (**une bière[3]**). Beers can be **blondes, brunes, blanches, rouges, amères[4]**, or **fruitées[5]**. The legal drinking age in Switzerland and in Francophone Europe is 16. Smoking is allowed at 16 as well. However, the legal drinking and smoking age is not as strictly enforced as it is in the United States. Adolescents may drink a little wine at home on very special occasions (such as Christmas). Parents may add a few drops of wine to water for their children to taste.

Réfléchissons

1. In your country, are prices higher depending on where you sit in a microbrewery or a restaurant (inside, outside, at the bar)?
2. What custom described in this reading surprised you the most? Explain your answer.
3. What do you think about 16 as a legal drinking age? Do you think it is reasonable for an American 18-year-old to be able to vote but not to be able to drink legally? Explain your answer.

---

[1]The cultural differences described in the text also apply to France and to Francophone Europe.
[2]Both expressions mean *draft beer*, but of different sizes. [3]*beer* [4]*bitter* [5]*flavored with fruit*

Partie II: Une journée en ville 🎧

RER

la gare

le métro

transport métropolitain

le siège

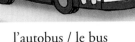

l'autobus / le bus

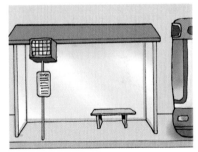

un arrêt de bus

Ce matin, Rafaël Richard, qui habite dans une banlieue[1] au sud-ouest de Paris, va faire des courses en ville. Pour arriver en ville, il va prendre le train, le métro et le bus. Rafaël va à la gare. Il n'a pas besoin d'acheter un billet, parce qu'il a une Carte Intégrale, qui est valable pour le RER, le métro et le bus. Il prend le train de 8 h 48 pour aller à Paris (le RER C, direction Versailles). Le train est bondé[2] parce que ce sont les heures de pointe[3]. Rafaël ne trouve pas de siège dans le train, donc, il reste debout. Il descend aux Invalides.

Ensuite, il prend le métro, direction Saint-Denis-Université. Il descend à Saint-Lazare et il commence ses courses. Rafaël va d'abord à sa pâtisserie préférée, et il achète un croissant qu'il mange tout de suite. Il continue ensuite avec ses autres

To help your students better understand this text, bring up the Internet on the screen in your classroom, and go to www.ratp.info/orienter/plans.php#. Click on the metro map and use it to guide students through this reading, following Rafaël's movements throughout the day.

---

[1]*suburb* [2]*full* [3]*rush hour*

courses: il va à la banque, au bureau de poste et à son grand magasin préféré, le Printemps. L'après-midi, il va chez le médecin et il passe ensuite à la pharmacie.

Pour rentrer à la maison, Rafaël prend le bus. Le bus est moins direct et plus lent, mais Rafaël n'est pas pressé[1]. Il lit les brochures qu'il a reçues[2] à la banque et chez le docteur, et il regarde les passants[3] par la fenêtre. Finalement, Rafaël prend le même train RER qu'il a pris[4] le matin. Il arrive chez lui à 6 h 30, après une journée très chargée à Paris.

Vous avez bien compris?

Answer the following questions about Rafaël's trip to the city.

1. Pourquoi est-ce que Rafaël va en ville?
2. Quels moyens de transport est-ce qu'il prend pour aller en ville? Et pour rentrer?
3. Pourquoi est-ce que Rafaël n'achète pas de billet de métro?
4. Quels sont les avantages du bus? Et les désavantages?

Vocabulaire essentiel

Les moyens de transport

un autobus / un bus
le métro
un train

Explain to students that an **autocar** makes trips between towns, often traveling on highways and major roads, while an **autobus** stays within a single city.

un autocar / un car

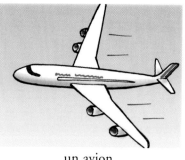

un avion

une voiture

un taxi

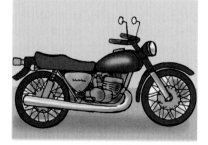

une motocyclette

une bicyclette / un vélo

---

[1]in a hurry [2]that he received [3]pedestrians [4]that he took

Pour faire les voyages

l'aéroport *(m.)*	*airport*
un vol	*flight*
la gare	*train station*
la gare routière	*bus station*
un trajet	*voyage, trip*
un arrêt de métro	*subway stop*
un arrêt de bus	*bus stop*
un billet	*ticket*

Les billets

aller-retour	*round-trip*
aller simple	*one-way*
une Carte Orange	*weekly or monthly pass*
une Carte Intégrale	*monthly or yearly pass*

À vous!

A. Comment y allez-vous? Tell how you travel to the following places. Vary your means of transportation whenever possible.

♿ MODÈLE: pour aller au supermarché

Je prends le bus. / Je prends ma voiture.

1. pour aller à la bibliothèque
2. pour descendre en ville
3. pour rendre visite à votre famille
4. pour aller en vacances
5. pour aller à la banque
6. pour sortir *(go out)* avec des amis le week-end
7. pour aller à la plage *(the beach)*

Now redo this activity, pretending that you live in Paris.

♿ MODÈLE: Pour aller au supermarché, je prends le métro.

B. Où allez-vous? Tell where you go to do the following things.

1. pour acheter une Carte Orange
2. pour prendre un vol
3. pour faire un trajet par autocar
4. pour faire un trajet par autobus
5. pour prendre le RER

Point out that most Parisians buy a Carte Orange, which gives them unlimited travel on the metro and buses. These cards can be purchased by the month or the week, and can include only the Paris metropolitan area or the suburbs (RER train lines), depending on the price. Parisians now also have the option of purchasing a Carte Intégrale, which includes some other tourist buses in Paris, and can be purchased for the month or the year.

Introduce the term **aller à pied** to give students an additional option.

Answer Key. Possible answers: 1. Je vais à pied. / Je prends ma bicyclette. 2. Je prends ma voiture. 3. Je prends ma voiture / le bus / un avion. 4. Je prends un avion. 5. Je prends ma voiture. 6. Je prends ma voiture / un taxi. 7. Je prends ma voiture / un bus.

Answer Key. Possible answers: 1. Je vais à pied. 2. Je prends le métro / le bus. 3. Je prends le bus / ma voiture. 4. Je prends le train. 5. Je vais à pied. 6. Je prends le métro / ma voiture / le bus. 7. Je prends le train / le bus / ma voiture.

Answer Key: 1. à une station de métro 2. à l'aéroport 3. à la gare routière 4. à un arrêt de bus 5. à un arrêt de métro / à la gare

Structure 5

Online Study Center
ACE, Language Skills
Practice

Les verbes *prendre, comprendre* et *apprendre*

- Earlier in this chapter, you learned how to conjugate regular **-re** verbs. Some verbs that end in **-re** are irregular, however, and must be memorized separately. **Prendre** *(to take)* is one of these verbs.

Model the pronunciation of the three stems, so that students can hear the different vowels in them. Point out that the vowel in the **je, tu,** and **il/elle** forms is the same, the vowel in the **nous** and **vous** forms is the same, and the **ils/elles** form has its own vowel sound.

prendre	
je prends	nous **prenons**
tu prends	vous **prenez**
il / elle / on prend	ils / elles **prennent**

Note that this verb has three different stems: one for the singular forms, one for the **nous** and **vous** forms, and one for the **ils/elles** form.

- **Comprendre** *(to understand)* and **apprendre** *(to learn)* are conjugated exactly like **prendre,** but with the prefix **com-** or **ap-.**

Je **comprends** l'espagnol.
Nous **apprenons** le calcul dans le cours de mathématiques.

VÉRIFIEZ VOTRE COMPRÉHENSION

1. Can you give the entire conjugation for **comprendre** and **apprendre?**

2. Look back at the explanation of the regular **-re** verbs in this chapter (p. 141). How are **prendre, apprendre,** and **comprendre** different from the regular **-re** verbs? For which persons, in particular, are there differences?

3. Look at the text describing Rafaël Richard's day in Paris (pp. 159–160). Find the forms of **prendre.** What would these forms be if Rafaël and Anne-Marie Richard went to town together (i.e., if the subject pronoun were **ils**)?

Transcript: 1. Ils comprennent bien le français. 2. Elle prend le bus tous les jours. 3. Elle apprend à chanter. 4. Elles prennent un vol à dix heures. 5. Il ne comprend pas le professeur.

À l'écoute! Listen to the sentences on your In-Text Audio CD, and check whether each sentence is about one person or several people.

	one person	several people
1.	_____	_____
2.	_____	_____
3.	_____	_____
4.	_____	_____
5.	_____	_____

Pratiquons!

A. Quel verbe? Quelle forme? Fill in the blanks with the correct form of the appropriate verb. Each verb can be used only once.

Answer Key: 1. vais 2. prends 3. aime 4. comprend 5. a 6. préfère 7. prennent 8. descendent 9. est 10. ai 11. apprends

avoir   prendre   aimer   comprendre   préférer   aller

Quand j(e) (1) _____ à Paris, j(e) (2) _____ toujours le métro. C'est rapide et confortable, et j(e) (3) _____ regarder les autres passagers. Mais ma mère déteste le métro! Elle n(e) (4) _____ pas le plan[1] et donc elle (5) _____ peur de se perdre[2]. Elle (6) _____ le bus.

apprendre   être   avoir   prendre   descendre

Pour partir[3] en vacances, mes parents (7) _____ normalement l'autocar. Ils peuvent[4] regarder par les fenêtres, et ils (8) _____ dans toutes les petites villes intéressantes. Pour moi, un voyage comme ça (9) _____ beaucoup trop lent[5] et ennuyeux! J(e) (10) _____ envie d'arriver vite à ma destination. J(e) (11) _____ à être plus patient; c'est nécessaire si je désire voyager avec mes parents!

B. Trouve-les! *(Find them!)* Go around the room to find students who fit the following criteria. Write down their names and report your findings to the class.

Before assigning this activity, model the first two or three questions with the students.

1. Trois étudiants qui comprennent une langue étrangère. Demandez à ces trois étudiants quelle langue ils comprennent.
2. Deux étudiants qui apprennent une autre langue en plus du français. Demandez à ces deux étudiants quelle langue ils apprennent.
3. Trois étudiants qui ne comprennent pas le professeur de français.
4. Un(e) étudiant(e) qui prend l'avion pour partir en vacances ou pour rentrer chez ses parents.
5. Deux étudiants qui prennent le bus quelquefois pour aller en ville.
6. Un étudiant qui ne prend jamais[6] de taxi.

Structure 6

L'heure

Online Study Center
ACE, Language Skills Practice

8 h 48   À huit heures quarante-huit du matin, Rafaël prend le train.

---

[1] *map* [2] *to get lost* [3] *leave* [4] *can* [5] *slow* [6] *never*

9 h 10   Il arrive à Paris à neuf heures dix.

9 h 30   À neuf heures et demie, il mange un croissant.

10 h 45   À onze heures moins le quart, il va à la banque.

12 h 20   Il prend le déjeuner à midi vingt.

1 h 55   À deux heures moins cinq de l'après-midi, il va au grand magasin.

6 h 15   À six heures et quart du soir, il reprend le train.

- To tell time in French, the hour comes first, and then the minutes. In English you can vary between saying that it is *four ten* (4:10) or *ten after four*, but in French, you have only one choice: **Il est quatre heures dix.**
- As you can see in the preceding example, numbers follow the hour directly. However, when you want to say that it is a quarter past or half past the hour, you use the conjunction **et: Il est cinq heures et quart. / Il est une heure et demie.**
- To indicate that the next hour is approaching (*five minutes to,* in English), the expression **moins** is used: **Il est sept heures moins cinq.**
- *Noon* is expressed by the word **midi,** and *midnight* by **minuit.** French speakers use the expression **douze heures** only when using the official time system (see the marginal note on p. 166). **Midi** and **minuit** are followed by the number of minutes, if necessary: **Il est midi dix. / Il est minuit et demi. / Il est minuit moins le quart.**
- Other expressions to indicate time of day are: **du matin** (*in the morning*), **de l'après-midi** (*in the afternoon*), and **du soir** (*in the evening / at night*). There is no other French equivalent for the English abbreviations A.M. and P.M.

Point out to students that there is no -s on **heure** in the expression **une heure.**

Point out to students that there is no -e on **demi** when used after the masculine expressions **midi** and **minuit,** but that there is an -e after the feminine **heure.**

VÉRIFIEZ VOTRE COMPRÉHENSION

1. How are *midnight* and *noon* expressed in French?

2. What does Monsieur Richard do at **onze heures moins le quart du matin?** And at **six heures et quart de l'après-midi?**

3. At what time does he go to the bank? When does he eat a croissant?

Explain to students that **midi** and **minuit** literally mean *midday* and *midnight*. This might help them to remember which is which. Point out, too, that there is no exact point at which the afternoon stops and the evening begins; thus, one person might say **six heures de l'après-midi,** while another will say **six heures du soir.**

Pratiquons!

A. La journée d'Anne-Marie Richard. You've seen Rafaël Richard's day. Now, say at what time his wife completes her activities.

MODÈLE: 8 h 30, aller au travail

À huit heures et demie du matin, Anne-Marie va au travail.

1. 9 h 10, parler avec le patron[1]
2. 10 h 40, aller à la poste
3. 11 h 15, retourner au bureau
4. entre 12 h et 1 h 30, prendre le déjeuner[2]
5. 2 h 30, assister à[3] une réunion
6. 2 h 45, prendre des notes
7. 4 h 20, téléphoner à un client
8. 5 h 50, faire une liste de choses à accomplir demain

#4: Point out that in France, most workers have an extended lunch hour, but that they then work later into the evening than in the U.S. The French work 35 hours a week and not 40.

Answer Key: 1. À neuf heures dix, elle parle avec le patron. 2. À dix heures quarante (À onze heures moins vingt) elle va à la poste. 3. À onze heures et quart, elle retourne au bureau. 4. Entre midi et une heure et demie, elle prend le déjeuner. 5. À deux heures et demie, elle assiste à une réunion. 6. À trois heures moins le quart, elle prend des notes. 7. À quatre heures vingt, elle téléphone à un client. 8. À six heures moins dix, elle fait une liste ...

---

[1] *boss* [2] *lunch* [3] *to attend*

B. À quelle heure est-ce que tu … ? Interview a partner to find out what time s/he does the following things.

◎ MODÈLE: arriver à l'université

À quelle heure est-ce que tu arrives à l'université?

1. prendre le petit déjeuner[1]
2. arriver à l'université
3. aller en classe de français
4. faire tes devoirs
5. rentrer chez toi
6. regarder ton programme préféré à la télé
7. aller au lit le soir

Portrait personnel

Write a description of your partner's day. When does s/he do each activity? How does this compare to your own day?

C. Quelle heure est-il? Restate the time, using the 24-hour clock.

◎ MODÈLE: 9 h 50 du soir

Il est vingt et une heures cinquante.

1. 6 h 30 du matin
2. 10 h 20 du soir
3. 1 h 15 de l'après-midi
4. 3 h 10 de l'après-midi
5. 7 h 08 du matin
6. 11 h 35 du soir

Answer Key: 1. Il est six heures trente. 2. Il est vingt-deux heures vingt. 3. Il est treize heures quinze. 4. Il est quinze heures dix. 5. Il est sept heures huit. 6. Il est vingt-trois heures trente-cinq.

Now, tell a classmate what you do at the above times.

◎ MODÈLE: À 6 h 30 je prends ma douche.

Point out that official time is so common in French-speaking countries that most digital clocks there give the time using the 24-hour clock.

In French-speaking countries, the 24-hour clock is used much more frequently than in the United States. We tend to think of this as "official" or "military" time, but other cultures use the 24-hour clock as a way of making clear whether an activity is scheduled for the morning or the afternoon. It is used for train and bus schedules, TV guides, movie and concert announcements, appointments, and class meetings. To convert from conventional time to official time, simply add 12 to the P.M. hours: 8:00 A.M. remains **huit heures,** but 8:00 P.M. becomes **vingt heures.** When using the 24-hour clock, the expressions **midi, minuit, quart,** and **demie** are not used, and minutes to the hour are not expressed: 4 h 55 is **quatre heures cinquante-cinq** (and not **cinq heures moins cinq,** as in conventional time).

---

[1] *breakfast*

Partie III: Un week-end à Tours

Rafaël et Anne-Marie Richard décident de passer le week-end à Tours, une jolie ville au sud-ouest de Paris. En sortant de la gare, ils ne savent pas où se trouve leur hôtel; ils demandent des renseignements[1] à un passant.

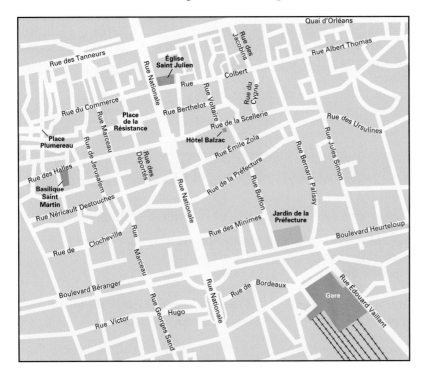

RAFAËL:	Excusez-moi, Monsieur. Pourriez-vous me dire[2] où se trouve l'hôtel Balzac, s'il vous plaît?
MONSIEUR:	Oui, Monsieur. C'est très simple. Vous êtes maintenant dans la rue Édouard Vaillant. Prenez cette rue jusqu'au boulevard Heurteloup. Tournez à gauche sur le boulevard, et continuez tout droit jusqu'à la Rue Buffon.
ANNE-MARIE:	… Boulevard Heurteloup … jusqu'à la rue Buffon.
MONSIEUR:	Oui. Il y a un jardin au coin du boulevard Heurteloup et de la rue Buffon. Au jardin, tournez à droite dans la rue Buffon, et continuez tout droit. Traversez la rue de la Préfecture et la rue Émile-Zola, et vous allez voir[3] l'Hôtel Balzac sur la gauche, au coin de la rue de la Scellerie. C'est à côté d'une épicerie, et en face d'une boulangerie.
RAFAËL:	Donc c'est à gauche, au coin de la rue Buffon et de la rue de la Scellerie.
MONSIEUR:	Oui, exactement.
RAFAËL:	Merci beaucoup, Monsieur.
MONSIEUR:	Je vous en prie.
ANNE-MARIE:	Et est-ce qu'il y a un bon restaurant dans les environs?
MONSIEUR:	Oui, la place de la Résistance, qui n'est pas très loin, il y a un très bon bistro. Ils ont de bons sandwichs et des omelettes.
ANNE-MARIE:	Merci bien, Monsieur.
MONSIEUR:	De rien, Madame. Bon séjour à Tours.
ANNE-MARIE:	Rafaël, marche vite! Je commence à avoir faim!

---

[1] *information / directions* [2] *Could you tell me…?* [3] *to see*

Vous avez bien compris?

Check whether the following statements are true or false, based on the preceding dialogue. If the statements are false, correct them.

1. Rafaël et Anne-Marie prennent le train pour aller à Tours. _____ vrai _____ faux
2. Rafaël donne des renseignements à un passant. _____ vrai _____ faux
3. Rafaël et Anne-Marie vont rester[1] avec des amis. _____ vrai _____ faux
4. L'Hôtel Balzac se trouve la place de la Résistance. _____ vrai _____ faux
5. La place de la Résistance est près de l'hôtel. _____ vrai _____ faux
6. Anne-Marie veut se dépêcher[2]. _____ vrai _____ faux

Vocabulaire essentiel

Pour demander des renseignements et donner des directions

Excusez-moi, Monsieur / Madame / Mademoiselle
Pardonnez-moi …
Pourriez-vous me dire …   *Could you tell me . . .*
Est-ce que vous savez …   *Do you know . . .*
Où se trouve (la gare / l'hôtel)?   *Where is (the train station / the hotel)?*
Je vous en prie. / De rien.   *You're welcome.*

Pour donner des directions

Prenez la rue … .   *Take . . . Street.*
Tournez à gauche.   *Turn left.*
Tournez à droite.   *Turn right.*
Continuez tout droit.   *Keep going straight.*
jusqu'à   *as far as*
Traversez …   *Cross . . .*
C'est à gauche.   *It's on the left.*
C'est à droite.   *It's on the right.*
C'est au coin.   *It's on the corner.*
C'est au centre.   *It's in the center.*
C'est à côté de …   *It's next to . . .*
C'est en face de …   *It's across from . . .*

N'oubliez pas![3]
When asking or giving directions, don't forget the words of common courtesy: **s'il vous plaît, merci,** and **de rien.**

À vous!

A. Des renseignements. Imagine that you are a resident of Tours. Give Rafaël and Anne-Marie directions to and from the following places.

1. de l'Hôtel Balzac à la place de la Résistance
2. de la place de la Résistance à la place Plumereau
3. de la place Plumereau à la basilique Saint-Martin
4. de la basilique Saint-Martin à l'église Saint-Julien

To correct the answers for this activity and the next, make a transparency of the map of Tours. Have one student read his/her directions, while another traces the route on the transparency with his/her finger. If the directions are wrong, or if the student tracing the route turns in the wrong direction, have the rest of the class make the correction.

Point out to students that streets are often named after famous French people, landmark buildings, or famous events (even famous dates), e.g., **la rue Émile-Zola, la place de la Résistance,** and **la rue de la Préfecture** on the map of Tours.

---

[1] *to stay* [2] *wants to hurry* [3] *Don't forget!*

B. Je suis perdu(e)! *(I'm lost!)* In pairs or in groups of three, create a dialogue similar to the one on page 167. Choose a starting point and a destination, and write a complete dialogue in which one person asks for directions and another gives them.

Structure 7

L'impératif

Online Study Center
ACE, Language Skills Practice

- The imperative mood is used to give commands. In French, as in English, it is formed by dropping the subject pronoun and using only the present tense form of the verb. Compare the following sentences.

Vous chantez.	*You sing. / You are singing.*
Chantez!	*Sing!*
Vous allez à la banque.	*You go / are going to the bank.*
Allez à la banque.	*Go to the bank.*
Vous ne parlez pas anglais en classe.	*You don't speak English in class.*
Ne parlez pas anglais en classe!	*Don't speak English in class!*

- When using the imperative in French, you must decide whether to use the **tu** or the **vous** form. (To review when to use **tu** and when to use **vous,** see Chapter 1.) To give a command, choose the **tu** or the **vous** form, then drop the subject pronoun. When writing, drop the final **-s** of the **tu** form of **-er** verbs and the verb **aller.**

Tourne à gauche.	*Turn left.*
Va jusqu'au coin.	*Go to the corner.*
Prends la rue Saint-Jacques.	*Take Saint Jacques Street.*
Ne descends pas la rue Zola.	*Don't go down Zola Street.*

- Commands by themselves can sound abrupt. You can soften them by adding **s'il te plaît** or **s'il vous plaît,** depending on whether you are using **tu** or **vous.**

Donnez-moi un kilo de tomates, s'il vous plaît.	*Give me a kilo of tomatoes, please.*
Écoute-moi, s'il te plaît.	*Listen to me, please.*

- French also has an imperative for the **nous** form. This is roughly equivalent to saying *let's . . .* in English, and it is used to make a suggestion rather than to give a command.

Allons au cinéma ce week-end.	*Let's go to the movies this weekend.*
Prenons un taxi.	*Let's take a taxi.*
N'allons pas en classe aujourd'hui!	*Let's not go to class today!*

- There are only a few irregular command forms in French; most use the present indicative of the verb. The verbs **être** and **avoir,** however, have irregular forms that must be memorized.

avoir:	**Aie** de la patience!	*Have patience!*
	N'**ayez** pas peur!	*Don't be afraid!*
	Ayons du courage.	*Let's be brave. (Let's have courage.)*
être:	Ne **sois** pas pénible!	*Don't be a pain!*
	Soyez patient!	*Be patient!*
	Soyons amis.	*Let's be friends.*

Take a moment to review in class a few of the commands that you use on a regular basis, so that students can check their answers in #4.

VÉRIFIEZ VOTRE COMPRÉHENSION

1. Go back to the dialogue between Rafaël, Anne-Marie, and the resident of Tours on page 167. What uses of the imperative can you find in the dialogue? Underline all the commands.

2. Are these commands formed with the **vous** form or the **tu** form of the verb? Why is that form used?

3. Are there any verbs in this passage that aren't in the imperative? Why does that happen?

4. What commands have you heard your instructor use in class? List as many as you can think of.

Pratiquons!

Answer Key: 1. Prenez beaucoup de photos. Ne perdez pas les passeports. Achetez des souvenirs. 2. Étudie beaucoup. Fais les activités orales au labo. Ne va pas au café-bar le soir avant. 3. Allons à la bibliothèque municipale. Chantons le karaoke. Faisons un petit voyage. 4. Vendez la maison. Allez en vacances. Soyez moins difficiles à plaire.

A. Toujours des solutions. Your family and friends tend to come to you to help them solve their problems. Give them logical commands, using the suggestions in parentheses or your own ideas. Choose the appropriate form of the verb **(tu, nous,** or **vous)** in the affirmative or the negative.

MODÈLE: Votre frère s'endort[1] souvent en classe. (prendre un cours tôt le matin / choisir un prof intéressant / être plus actif en classe / …)

C'est simple. Ne prends pas un cours tôt le matin. **ou** *Choisis des profs intéressants.* **ou** *Sois plus actif en classe.*

1. Vos amis vont bientôt voyager à Paris. (prendre beaucoup de photos / perdre les passeports / acheter des souvenirs / …)
2. Votre sœur va passer un examen très difficile en chimie. (étudier beaucoup / faire les activités orales au labo / aller au café-bar le soir avant / …)
3. Vous et vos amis cherchez une activité intéressante pour le week-end. (aller à la bibliothèque municipale / chanter le karaoke / faire un petit voyage / …)
4. Vos parents n'aiment pas leur maison. (vendre la maison / aller en vacances / être moins difficiles à plaire[2] / …)

---

[1]*falls asleep* [2]*to please*

B. Qu'est-ce qu'il faut faire pour … ? Give a classmate suggestions about what to do in the following situations. Use an appropriate imperative.

1. pour réussir dans le cours de français
2. pour s'amuser le week-end, sans quitter[1] le campus
3. pour voyager, sans payer trop
4. pour avoir de bonnes notes dans tous ses cours
5. pour avoir plus d'argent

À vous de parler!

A. Aller en vacances. In groups of three or four, create a role play in which you discuss plans for going on vacation. Make suggestions about where to go, when to leave and how long to stay, how to get there (what are the advantages of the various means of transportation that you could take?), and what to do once you get there. Use the verbs **prendre, apprendre,** and **comprendre** and the imperative as relevant. When you are finished, present your conversation to the class.

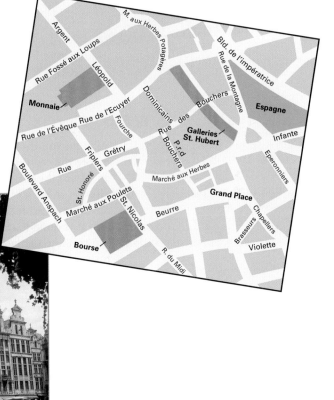

B. En ville! Imagine that it is the year 1850, and you and a friend are in downtown Brussels to do your market shopping. Based on the names of the streets, what types of markets/stores do you expect to find on each? What could you buy in each place? Map out how you will spend your day, discussing which streets you will visit and for what purpose. Incorporate the vocabulary that you have learned relating to stores and to giving directions.

---

[1]*leaving*

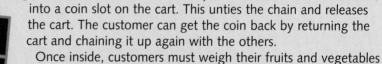
On fait les courses comme ça au supermarché en France[1]

When going to the supermarket, the first thing you do is get a shopping cart, right? Well, people do that in France too, but it gets a little tricky! All the shopping carts are tied together by a chain at the supermarket entrance. In order to get a cart, the customer must deposit a coin (50 cents of a euro) into a coin slot on the cart. This unties the chain and releases the cart. The customer can get the coin back by returning the cart and chaining it up again with the others.

Once inside, customers must weigh their fruits and vegetables before going to the cash register, as the cashier will not weigh them. There are digital scales located throughout the produce department. Each scale has buttons with pictures of each variety of fruit and vegetable available at the store. The customer presses the right button, and a self-adhesive price tag comes out of the scale.

Finally, after customers have paid at the cash register, they must bag their own purchases. And there are no paper bags, only plastic bags. In some supermarkets, customers are charged for each plastic bag they use!

The French use this system to avoid having to pick up scattered carts. Space is limited in the parking lots and on the streets.

The French weigh their own produce to save time at the cash register. Usually there are not as many cash registers available as there are in the U.S.

Réfléchissons

1. Why do you think that the French must deposit a coin in a shopping cart before they can use it? Is it the same in your country? Where do you take and leave the carts?
2. Do you think it is a good idea to weigh your own produce rather than having the cashier weigh it for you? Why or why not? Why do you think that it is done that way in France?
3. Do you like the fact that in the United States someone bags your purchases for you? How about the fact that you can have someone put your purchases in your car? What is customer service like in your country?

À vous de lire!

A. Stratégies. The reading passage in this section contains information about fashion—**la mode**—in France. Before reading the passage, skim it very quickly. Underline terms that are familiar to you from this chapter and that you believe will be important for understanding the text. Look in particular for terms that are frequently repeated—these are undoubtedly key terms in the text. Are there other words in the text that you have not yet seen but whose meaning you can guess because they are cognates? Remember that you don't need to understand every word in order to understand the gist of a text!

---

[1]The information in this section applies to both France and Francophone Europe.

B. Avant de lire. Look only at the title, the subtitles, and the tables. Can you predict what this reading is about? What type of information do you expect to find here? Compare your answers with those of a classmate to see if you have the same ideas about what you will find in this text.

Spend a few minutes in class looking at the titles, subtitles, and tables and answering these questions. Tables and charts are valuable tools in reading that students often overlook. Help students to establish, in advance, a framework for what they are about to read; research shows that this greatly facilitates the reading process.

C. Lisons! Read only the first two sections (**Définition** and **Enjeux**) of the text, and answer the questions that follow.

La mode

Définition

[...] La mode, c'est l'adhésion par le plus grand nombre à une façon aussi transitoire qu'impérieuse de se vêtir[1] ou de se comporter[2]. Cette façon peut être imposée par une personne célèbre (Madonna par exemple), par des couturiers[3] ou par des groupes (les motards, les Punks, etc.). En suivant[4] la mode, on était, il y a quelques décennies, «dans le vent», on est maintenant «branché[5]». [...]

Enjeux[6]

Les sexes s'habillaient pour se plaire[7]. [...] C'est l'homme qui a le premier rompu[8] le pacte social de séduction par l'habillement lorsqu'il a abandonné la couleur et l'originalité de la coupe[9]. D'où l'accusation contre l'Angleterre et son «*grey flannel suit*» qui s'est répandu dans tout l'Occident pour devenir l'uniforme de l'homme d'affaires contemporain.

[...] La femme a rompu l'ancien pacte d'une autre manière: en se dénudant le cou[10] et la naissance des seins[11] qui ont été pendant des siècles la partie du corps féminin la seule offerte à l'homme. L'érotisme contemporain a redécouvert la jambe[12] de la femme depuis la création de la fameuse minijupe, qui avait été précédée du maillot de bain découvrant bras[13] et jambes, quelques décennies auparavant, et transformé depuis en bikini. Les épaules[14], les seins et plus récemment le ventre[15] et le dos[16], chez les adolescentes du moins, se sont ensuite ajoutées à la liste des parties montrées.

La mode actuelle par rapport au temps passé semble avoir perdu[17] en esthétisme et en charme ce qu'elle a gagné[18] en confort et en simplification. L'uniformisation de la mode, le vêtement unisexe en particulier, n'apparaît-elle pas comme un appauvrissement[19] d'une des expressions humaines les plus visibles et les plus propices à la communication entre les hommes et les femmes?

1. Quelle est la définition de *la mode* donnée par le texte?
2. Comment s'appellent les personnes qui suivent la mode?
3. Selon le texte, comment est-ce que l'homme et la femme se sont séparés du «pacte social de séduction»?
4. Décrivez l'évolution de l'érotisme contemporain.
5. Comparez la mode actuelle avec la mode d'avant, selon le texte.
6. Comment est-ce que l'uniformisation de la mode cause un appauvrissement?

---

[1]*to dress* [2]*to behave* [3]*designers* [4]*By following* [5]*"hip"* [6]*stakes* [7]*to please each other* [8]*broken* [9]*the cut*
[10]*uncovering the neck* [11]*chest* [12]*leg* [13]*arms* [14]*shoulders* [15]*belly* [16]*back* [17]*to have lost* [18]*won* [19]*impoverishment*

- Now read the last two sections (**La haute couture** and **Une invention de Worth**), and answer the questions that follow.

La haute couture

Depuis le Grand Siècle de Louis XIV et sa cour fastueuse et extravagante, la France n'a cessé de lancer[1] la mode. Née à Paris, à la fin du XIXe siècle, la haute couture vint couronner[2] cette suprématie. C'est aujourd'hui encore une spécialité française, qui n'hésite pas à se nourrir de talents étrangers.

Une invention de Worth

Worth eut[3] l'idée de présenter ses créations à ses clientes—en premier lieu, la princesse de Metternich et l'impératrice Eugénie—en les faisant porter par des mannequins en chair et en os[4]. Le défilé de mode[5], inséparable aujourd'hui de l'idée même de collection, était né[6].

1. Où a commencé la haute couture et quand?
2. Est-ce que la haute couture est composée seulement de créateurs français? Expliquez votre réponse.
3. Comment a commencé le défilé de mode?

Finally, look at these charts and answer the questions that follow.

Consommation en valeur 2001 (par personne)

- Layette (0–1 ans): 577 euros
- Femme: 544 euros
- Homme: 368 euros
- Enfant (2–14 ans): 332 euros

Structure de la distribution (en parts de marché)

- Chaînes à 400 mètres carrés (m²): 22,4%
- Magasins indépendants: 19,6%
- Hypermarchés et supermarchés: 14,7%
- Grandes surfaces spécialisées: 12,2%
- Vente par correspondance: 8,4%
- Sport: 7%
- Grands magasins et magasins populaires: 6,7%
- Autres: 5,1%
- Marchés: 3,7%

---

[1]*launch* [2]*came to crown* [3]*had* [4]*live models* (literally: of flesh and bone) [5]*fashion show* [6]*was born*

Consommation de quelques produits

- Robes, jupes: 54 972 milliers de pièces
- Pantalons: 94 648 milliers de pièces
- Jeans: 53 632 milliers de pièces
- Pull-overs: 109 707 milliers de pièces
- Chemises et chemisiers: 65 243 milliers de pièces
- Layette: 87 116 milliers de pièces
- Sous-vêtements: 277 422 milliers de pièces
- Corseterie: 59 927 milliers de pièces
- Blousons, costumes, vestes et gilets: 43 751 milliers de pièces
- Manteaux, imperméables, anoraks, parkas: 37 780 milliers de pièces

1. D'après[1] le premier tableau, pour quels vêtements est-ce que les Français dépensent le plus d'argent? Et le moins?
2. D'après le deuxième tableau, où est la distribution la plus élevée? Et la moins élevée?
3. Finalement, regardez le troisième tableau. Quels sont les vêtements les plus achetés? Et les moins achetés?

D. Après la lecture

1. Compare what you learned from this text with your initial expectations (activity B, **Avant de lire**). How did your expectations help you to understand as you read? Were there any sections of the text that you didn't understand well? Bring these to the attention of your instructor.
2. Look at the charts again. Are you surprised by the figures? Why or why not? Compare the information in the charts with your own buying habits. On what do you spend the most? And the least? What article of clothing do you buy the most often? The least often?
3. Do you follow the fashion trends? Why or why not?
4. How did you react to the section entitled **Enjeux?** What is your opinion of unisex clothes?

You may wish to broaden the discussion by talking about the differences in clothing styles between France and the U.S. For example, in the U.S., comfort prevails over elegance. In New York City, it is common to see women walking on the street wearing an elegant suit with sneakers. This is rarely seen in Paris. You also may wish to discuss the writer Honoré de Balzac's statement "In her dress lies a woman's power."

Finally, you might further expand on the haute couture topic by talking about famous fashion designers, their designs, and their importance in the fashion industry and in the economy. Some of the most famous **créateurs** today are Balmain, Pierre Cardin, Carven, Chanel, Christian Dior, Louis Féraud, Givenchy, Lecoanet Henant, Christian Lacroix, Lapidus, Guy Laroche, Hanae Mori, Paco Rabanne, Nina Ricci, Yves Saint Laurent, Jean-Louis Scherrer, Torrente, Emanuel Ungaro. The most respected and admired haute couture designer of all time remains Coco Chanel.

---

[1] *According to*

Lexique

Vocabulaire essentiel

Faire les courses au supermarché *to shop at the supermarket*

les achats *(m.) purchases*
le caissier / la caissière *cashier*
le chariot à provisions *shopping cart*
une grande surface *supermarket*
la liste des provisions *shopping list*

les petits commerçants *(m.) small shops*
les provisions *(f.) food supplies*
le rayon boucherie *meat department*

le rayon crémerie *dairy department*
le rayon poissonnerie *seafood department*

Les produits alimentaires

une baguette *loaf of French bread*
une baguette bien cuite *well-baked loaf*

une baguette pas trop cuite *not too dark loaf*
du bœuf *(m.) beef*
des crevettes *(f.) shrimp*

des moules *(f.) mussels*
un poulet fermier *farm-raised chicken*
du vin rouge *(m.) red wine*

Les magasins spécialisés et leurs produits

une boucherie *butcher shop*
  de la viande *meat*
  des volailles *(f.) poultry*
une boulangerie *bakery*
  du pain *bread*
  des viennoiseries *(f.) pastries*
une boutique de vêtements *clothing store*
  des vêtements *(m.) clothing*
une brasserie *brewery*
  une bière *beer*
une librairie *bookstore*
  des livres *(m.) books*
un magasin de chaussures *shoe store*
  des chaussures *(f.) shoes*
la maison de la presse *magazine and newspaper store*
  des magazines *(m.) magazines*
  des journaux *(m.) newspapers*

une papeterie *stationery store*
  du papier *paper*
  des enveloppes *(f.) envelopes*
  des cartes postales *(f.) postcards*
une pâtisserie *pastry shop*
  des pâtisseries *(f.) pastries*
une pharmacie *pharmacy*
  des médicaments *(m.) medicine*
une poissonnerie *fish market*
  du poisson *fish*
  des fruits *(m.)* de mer *seafood*
la poste *post office*
  des timbres *(m.) stamps*
un salon de coiffure *hairdresser*
  du shampooing *shampoo*

Les expressions de quantité

assez de *enough (of)*
beaucoup de *a lot of*
une boîte de *a box of*
une bouteille de *a bottle (of)*
une douzaine de *a dozen (of)*
un gramme de *a gram of*

un kilo de *a kilo of*
un litre de *a liter of*
moins de *less (of)*
un morceau de *a piece of*
un paquet de *a pack of*
pas mal de *quite a lot of*

un peu de *a little*
plus de *more (of)*
un sac de *a bag of*
une tranche de *a slice of*

Faire les magasins *to go shopping*

bon marché *cheap, affordable*
les cabines (f.) d'essayage *dressing rooms*

une rue piétonne *pedestrian street*
des soldes (m.) *sales*

Les vêtements *clothing*

un bikini *two-piece bathing suit, bikini*
des bottes (f.) *boots*
des chaussettes (f.) *socks*
des chaussures (f.) de sport *sneakers*
une chemise *man's shirt*
un chemisier *woman's shirt*
un costume *man's suit*
une cravate *tie*

une écharpe *scarf*
un jean / des jeans *jeans*
une jupe *skirt*
un imperméable *raincoat*
un maillot de bain *one-piece bathing suit*
un manteau *coat*
un pantalon *pants*
un pull(over) *pullover, sweater*
un pyjama *pajamas*

une robe *dress*
des sandales (f.) *sandals*
un short *shorts*
un sweat *sweatshirt*
un tailleur *woman's suit*
un tee-shirt *tee-shirt*
des tennis (f.) *tennis shoes*
une veste *jacket*

Les moyens de transport *means of transportation*

un autocar / un car *motorcoach*
un autobus / un bus *city bus*
un avion *airplane*
une bicyclette / un vélo *bicycle*

un billet *ticket*
le métro *subway*
une motocyclette *motorcycle*
un taxi *taxi / cab*

un train *train*
une voiture *car*

Pour faire les voyages *to go on trips*

un aéroport *airport*
un arrêt de bus *bus stop*
un arrêt de métro *subway stop*

une gare *train station*
une gare routière *bus station*

un trajet *voyage, trip*
un vol *flight*

Les billets *tickets*

aller-retour *round trip*
aller simple *one-way*

une Carte Intégrale *monthly or yearly pass*

une Carte Orange *weekly or monthly pass*

Les verbes en -*re*

attendre *to wait*
descendre *to get down, to go down*

entendre *to hear*
mordre *to bite*
perdre *to lose*

rendre *to return, to give back*
répondre *to respond, to answer*
vendre *to sell*

Verbes utiles avec les vêtements

essayer *to try on*
mettre *to put on*
porter *to wear*

Verbes irréguliers en -*re*

apprendre *to learn*
comprendre *to understand*
prendre *to take*

Pour demander des renseignements *to ask directions*

Est-ce que vous savez …
   Do you know . . .
Excusez-moi … *Excuse me . . .*
Je vous en prie. / De rien. *You're welcome.*

Merci. *Thank you.*
Où se trouve (la gare / l'hôtel)? *Where is (the train station / the hotel)?*
Pardonnez-moi … *Pardon me . . .*

Pourriez-vous me dire …
   Could you tell me . . .
s'il vous plaît / s'il te plaît *please*

Pour donner des directions *to give directions*

Continuez tout droit. *Keep going straight.*
jusqu'à *as far as*
Prenez la rue … *Take . . . Street.*
Tournez à droite. *Turn right.*
Tournez à gauche. *Turn left.*
Traversez … *Cross . . .*

C'est … *It's . . .*
à côté de *next to*
à droite *on the right*
à gauche *on the left*
au coin *on the corner*
au centre *in the center*
en face de *across from*

Expansion personnelle

D'autres magasins spécialisés et leurs produits

une bijouterie *jewelry store*
    des bijoux *(m.) jewels*
un bureau de tabac *tobacco store*
    des cigarettes *(f.) cigarettes*
    des cigares *(m.) cigars*
    des pipes *(f.) pipes*
une chocolaterie *chocolate store*
    des chocolats *(m.) chocolates*
une confiserie *candy store*
    des bonbons *(m.) candy*
une crémerie *dairy*
    des produits laitiers *(m.) dairy products*
une parfumerie *perfume store*
    des parfums *(m.) perfumes*

D'autres vêtements

des bas *(m.) sheer stockings*
un caleçon *man's underwear*
une casquette *cap*
un chapeau *hat*
une culotte *woman's brief*

un foulard *scarf*
un gilet *cardigan sweater*
des lunettes *(f.) glasses*
des lunettes *(f.)* de
    soleil *sunglasses*

un soutien-gorge *bra*
un survêtement *jogging suit,*
    sweat suit

Quelques expressions utiles quand on fait les courses

À qui le tour maintenant? *Whose turn is it now?*
C'est bon marché. *It is cheap.*
C'est (trop) cher. *It is (too) expensive.*
C'est combien? *How much is it?*
C'est mon tour. *It is my turn.*

C'est tout, merci. *That is all, thank you.*
Et avec ceci? *Anything else?*
faire du lèche-vitrine *to go window-shopping*
Je peux vous aider? *Can I help you?*

Je voudrais … *I would like …*
Nous voudrions … *We would like …*
Que désiriez-vous? *What would you like?*
C'est soldé / en solde. *It is on sale.*

Mes goûts gastronomiques

Are you a gourmand or a gourmet? Do you like food in quantity, or do you prefer fine food for its quality? In this chapter, you will learn the French names of many of the foods that you eat, ways to express how you are feeling (for example, hungry, thirsty, or tired), and ways to express your desires, your capabilities, and your obligations.

The vocabulary that you will learn includes

Ordering at a restaurant
Paying at a restaurant
Expressing likes and dislikes
Expressions with **avoir**
Foods
Utensils used at the table

The structures that you will learn include

The verbs **vouloir, boire, devoir,** and **pouvoir**
Adverbs
Review of partitive articles (**de la, du, des**) and expressions of quantity
Comparatives and superlatives

The culture that you will learn includes

French table manners
Types of bread and cheese

Commençons!

Au bistro 🎧

Point out to students that the French tend to eat a larger meal at noon, and a small meal (soup, an omelet, a salad, or a sandwich) in the evening.

Online Study Center
Language Skills Practice

Le week-end, François et Chloé descendent en ville. Ils font des courses, et ensuite, ils vont au cinéma. En sortant du cinéma, ils font des projets pour le soir.

FRANÇOIS: Qu'est-ce que tu veux[1] faire maintenant, Chloé?

CHLOÉ: J'ai faim. Allons à ce petit bistro du coin pour prendre un sandwich.

FRANÇOIS: D'accord, mais moi, j'ai envie d'une omelette.

CHLOÉ: Comme tu veux—mais mangeons quelque chose!

Ils s'approchent du restaurant.

CHLOÉ: Regarde—il y a une table sur la terrasse.

FRANÇOIS: Oh, c'est bien. Comme ça, nous pouvons regarder les passants. Mais est-ce qu'on ne va pas avoir froid?

CHLOÉ: Mais non! Il fait beau ce soir. Allons-y!

Point out that in Francophone Europe, bistro customers typically seat themselves.

À la terrasse du bistro. Ils s'assoient[2].

FRANÇOIS: J'ai soif! Je vais prendre une bière.

CHLOÉ: Moi je ne peux pas! J'aurais trop sommeil après[3]! Je vais prendre une grande bouteille de Perrier.

FRANÇOIS: Fais comme tu veux! Moi, j'ai envie de boire une bonne bière!

Tell students that the French drink a lot of bottled water. Restaurants in France do not usually bring a glass of water unless it is requested; the client must then specify whether s/he wants tap water (**une carafe d'eau du robinet**) or bottled water (Évian, Perrier, etc.). Drinks are served cold but with no ice. There is a charge for the latter. Point out that Europeans in general drink less soda than Americans.

[1] *want* [2] *sit down* [3] *would get too sleepy afterward*

François et Chloé sont à leur table. Le serveur arrive.

SERVEUR: Bonjour, Messieurs-Dames. Est-ce que vous voudriez une boisson pour commencer?

CHLOÉ: Oui. Je voudrais un Perrier pour commencer, et après je voudrais aussi un sandwich au jambon-fromage, s'il vous plaît.

SERVEUR: Très bien. Et Monsieur?

FRANÇOIS: Je vais prendre une bière et une omelette, s'il vous plaît.

SERVEUR: Pour la bière, une pression[1] ou une bouteille?

FRANÇOIS: Une pression.

SERVEUR: D'accord.

Il s'en va[2] ... Il revient avec une bouteille d'eau et un verre de bière. François boit sa bière.

CHLOÉ: Tu bois vite[3], François!

FRANÇOIS: Oui, j'ai très soif. Et toi, tu ne bois pas?

CHLOÉ: Si, mais plus lentement[4]. Avec l'eau gazeuse, il faut[5] boire lentement!

Vous avez bien compris?

Answer the following questions by responding **vrai** or **faux.** If the sentence is false, correct it.

1. François et Chloé vont au cinéma après le bistro. _____ vrai _____ faux

2. Chloé veut manger un sandwich parce qu'elle a soif. _____ vrai _____ faux

3. François veut manger une omelette. _____ vrai _____ faux

4. François et Chloé s'assoient à la terrasse, mais ils ont froid. _____ vrai _____ faux

5. François veut regarder les passants. _____ vrai _____ faux

6. Comme boisson[6] , Chloé va prendre une bière. _____ vrai _____ faux

7. François va prendre une bouteille de bière. _____ vrai _____ faux

8. Chloé ne boit pas rapidement. _____ vrai _____ faux

---

[1]*draft beer* [2]*he leaves* [3]*fast* [4]*more slowly* [5]*it's necessary* [6]*a drink*

Vocabulaire essentiel

Expressions avec *avoir*

Il a faim.

Elle a soif.

Il a chaud.

Ils ont froid.

Elle a sommeil.

Ils ont de la chance.

Il a raison.

Il a tort.

Elle a envie d'une bague.

Son ami a besoin d'argent!

Ils ont peur du chien.

Elle a l'air intéressée mais il a l'air ennuyé.

Dans un bistro on mange ...

un sandwich
une pizza
des crêpes *(f.)*
une salade
une omelette
de la soupe
des frites *(f.)*

Dans un bistro on boit ...

un Coca
une limonade
un café (noir / crème / au lait)
un exprès
un thé (nature / au citron)
une bière / une pression
un vin (rouge / blanc / rosé)
de l'eau *(f.)* (plate / gazeuse)

Point out to students that the French typically drink **café au lait dans un bol** only for breakfast. This is a large cup of half coffee–half steamed milk. At other times of the day, those who don't like their coffee black drink a **café crème**, which is more coffee than cream. Have students note also that **limonade** is a false cognate: it is a carbonated lemon-lime soda, not lemonade.

Point out that **bistros** are cafés that typically serve a limited menu. They are a good place to go for a snack or a sandwich, but they generally do not serve complete meals.

À vous!

A. Comment se sentent-ils et que désirent-ils? Give an appropriate expres-sion with **avoir** to describe each situation. (Review the conjugation of the verb **avoir** in Chapter 2.) Sometimes more than one expression is logical—choose one. Don't forget to conjugate the verb appropriately for the subject pronoun.

1. Annie est dans le désert. Il fait 37 degrés[1]. Elle _____.
2. Jérome et Claire n'ont pas mangé[2] depuis midi. Il est maintenant 8 heures du soir. Ils _____.
3. Mes amis et moi désirons aller à la plage ce week-end, mais il n'y a pas de bus. Nous _____ d'une voiture.
4. Hélène se lève[3] à 6 heures du matin tous les jours. À 10 heures du soir, elle _____.
5. Roger pense que[4] deux plus deux font cinq. Il _____. Moi, je sais que deux plus deux font quatre. J(e) _____.
6. En hiver au Québec, il neige beaucoup. Il est nécessaire de porter un gros manteau, sinon[5] on _____.
7. Marc dort[6] de temps en temps en classe. Il _____ ennuyé. Pourtant[7], il réussit toujours aux examens. Il _____!
8. Souvent quand je fais mes devoirs, j(e) _____ d'un dictionnaire.
9. Quand je vois un gros chien qui a l'air méchant, j(e) _____.

**B. Qu'est-ce que tu vas prendre?** Working with a partner, imagine that you stop at a bistro in the following circumstances. Take turns reading the situa-tion and telling one another what you are going to order (**Je vais prendre ...**).

1. Il est 6 heures du soir. Vous avez un peu faim, mais vous allez manger à la maison avec votre famille dans une heure.
2. Il est 2 heures de l'après-midi. Vous êtes en classe. Vous avez soif.
3. Il est 5 heures du soir. Vous êtes à la maison, devant la télé. Vous avez soif, et un peu faim.
4. Il est 3 heures du matin. Vous êtes en boîte de nuit. Vous avez soif, mais vous n'avez pas faim.
5. Il est 10 heures du matin. Vous faites du tennis. Vous avez très soif.
6. Il est midi. Vous êtes sur le campus. Vous avez faim.

Structure 1

Les verbes *vouloir* et *boire*; révision du partitif

- The verb **vouloir** means *to want*. It is an irregular verb, with a stem change in the present indicative.

vouloir	
je veux	nous v**oul**ons
tu veux	vous v**oul**ez
il / elle / on veut	ils / elles veu**l**ent

---

[1]=98° Fahrenheit [2]*have not eaten* [3]*gets up* [4]*thinks that* [5]*or else* [6]*sleeps* [7]*However*

The verb **vouloir** is rarely used alone in French. It is generally followed by a noun:

Je veux **le nouveau CD** de Céline Dion.

or by another verb:

Je veux **aller** au cinéma ce soir.

- **Attention!** When **vouloir** is used with a noun, you must decide which type of article to use with that noun. If you can count the noun, use an indefinite article.

  Je veux **un** sandwich.
  Je veux **un** Coca. (You're going to drink the entire serving.)
  Je veux **une** salade. (You're in a restaurant where salads are sold in single-serve portions.)

  If you are using a noncount noun, or if you are going to eat or drink an unspecified amount, use a partitive article.

  Je veux **du** Coca. (The entire bottle is available; you're going to drink some of it.)
  Je veux **de la** salade. (You're at a salad bar; you'll take part of what's available.)
  Je veux **du** sucre dans mon café. (Sugar can't be counted; you're going to use some.)

  Finally, if you are talking about a specific item that everyone is already familiar with, use a definite article.

  Je veux / voudrais **le** plat du jour. (There is only one daily special—everyone knows what it is.)
  Je veux voir **le** film que Michelle a recommandé. (You're talking about a specific film here, the one Michelle recommended, rather than just any film.)

- **Reminder:** When requesting something in a store or ordering food in a restaurant, the *conditional* form of **vouloir** is often used, as a way of being more polite. You saw two of these forms in Chapter 5: **je voudrais** (*I would like*) / **nous voudrions** (*we would like*).

  Je voudrais un café crème, s'il vous plaît.

- The verb **boire** *(to drink)* is also an irregular verb with a stem change. By now you should see a pattern that you recognize.

boire	
je bois	nous b<u>uv</u>**ons**
tu bois	vous b<u>uv</u>**ez**
il / elle / on boit	ils / elles boiv**ent**

The verb **prendre** *(to take),* is often used in place of the verb **boire** in French.

Avec mon sandwich, je **bois** de l'eau / je **prends** de l'eau.

Point out two patterns with which the students should familiarize themselves concerning verb conjugations. The first is the -s, -s, -t / -x, -x, -t pattern: the **je** and **tu** forms end in -s or -x (je finis, je veux, tu bois), while the **il / elle / on** form ends in -t (il finit, il veut, on boit). The second pattern is found in stem-changing verbs in which the **nous** and **vous** forms are different from the others. Awareness of these two patterns may make the irregular verbs seem less arbitrary and therefore easier to remember.

Point out that **prendre** can substitute for either **manger** or **boire**, as it is a general term.

VÉRIFIEZ VOTRE COMPRÉHENSION

1. Go back to the conversation between François and Chloé (pp. 181–182) and the questions that follow, and underline each occurrence of the verbs **vouloir** and **boire**. How is the verb conjugated in each instance? What is the subject pronoun that accompanies it?

2. What is the object of **vouloir** in each case? (Is it a noun, or another verb?)

3. Can you give a rough translation for the expression **comme tu veux?** What would be an equivalent response in English?

4. In the preceding grammar explanation, we pointed out that you should see a pattern with which you are familiar. Can you explain what this pattern is?

À l'écoute!

Singulier ou pluriel? You will hear a series of sentences using the verbs **vouloir** and **boire.** Check whether each verb is singular or plural.

1. _____ singulier   _____ pluriel   4. _____ singulier   _____ pluriel
2. _____ singulier   _____ pluriel   5. _____ singulier   _____ pluriel
3. _____ singulier   _____ pluriel   6. _____ singulier   _____ pluriel

Pratiquons!

A. Qu'est-ce qu'ils veulent? You are talking about your desires with some friends. Complete the following sentences with the appropriate form of the verb **vouloir** in the present tense. Then substitute the pronouns in parentheses, and redo the sentence.

1. Je _____ une nouvelle voiture. (tu / nous / ils / elle)
2. Ma mère _____ faire un pique-nique ce week-end. (mes parents / vous / je)
3. Mon frère ne _____ pas faire ses devoirs! (les étudiants / je / nous)
4. Toi et moi, nous _____ souvent du chocolat! (toi et tes amis / toi / ma mère)
5. Et vous, qu'est-ce que vous _____?

B. Qu'est-ce qu'on boit? Create sentences with the appropriate form of the verbs **boire** or **prendre,** to tell what the following people drink on various occasions. Vary your responses in order to use both verbs. (If necessary, review the conjugation of the verb **prendre** in Chapter 5 before beginning.)

1. Mon frère / le week-end
2. Mes parents / avec les repas[1]
3. Moi / avant le cours de français
4. Le professeur / après le cours
5. Mes amis et moi / le vendredi soir
6. Les acteurs / la nuit des Oscars

---

[1]*meals*

Transcript: 1. Ils boivent souvent du Coca. 2. Elle veut du café. 3. Il ne boit jamais de thé. 4. Elles veulent manger au bistro. 5. Elles boivent un citron pressé avec le déjeuner. 6. Il ne veut pas de sandwich.

Answer Key: 1. pluriel 2. singulier 3. singulier 4. pluriel 5. pluriel 6. singulier

Remind students to make the appropriate changes to the possessive adjective in #3.

Answer Key: 1. Je veux / Tu veux / Nous voulons / Ils veulent / Elle veut 2. Elle veut / Ils veulent / Vous voulez / Je veux 3. Il ne veut pas / Ils ne veulent pas / Je ne veux pas / Nous ne voulons pas 4. Nous voulons / Vous voulez / Tu veux / Elle veut 5. Vous voulez

C. Et toi, qu'est-ce que tu bois? Ask a classmate questions to find out what s/he drinks with the following items. When you have finished, report your answers to the class.

⊚ MODÈLE: avec une crêpe

—*Qu'est-ce que tu bois avec une crêpe?*

—*Avec une crêpe, je bois de l'eau minérale.*

1. avec un sandwich
2. avec de la pizza
3. avec un croissant
4. avec une salade
5. avec une omelette
6. avec de la soupe
7. avec des frites

D. Une portion ou tout? *(All or part?)* Imagine that you are in the following situations. Tell what you want, using either a definite article, a partitive article, or an expression of quantity, as appropriate.

⊚ MODÈLE: Vous êtes avec des amis. Vous avez une grande bouteille de Coca.

Je voudrais du Coca. / Je veux boire du Coca. / Je vais prendre un verre de Coca.

1. Vous êtes seul(e)[1]. Vous avez une grande pizza.
2. Vous êtes en famille. Vous avez un gâteau au chocolat délicieux.
3. Vous êtes avec un ami. Vous avez tous les deux[2] un café.
4. Vous êtes nombreux. Vous avez une cafetière de café.
5. Vous êtes seul(e) dans un fast-food.
6. Vous êtes avec des amis à un dîner buffet.

Answer Key. Possible answers: 1. Je voudrais une tranche de pizza. 2. Je vais prendre deux morceaux de gâteau. 3. Je voudrais un croissant avec mon café. 4. Je vais prendre une tasse de café. 5. Je vais prendre des frites. 6. Je voudrais de la salade.

E. Au restaurant. The following sentences are often heard in French restaurants. Working with a partner, play the roles of a waiter/waitress and a customer. The customer answers the waiter/waitress's question, using the conditional form of the verb **vouloir (je voudrais, nous voudrions)** in order to be polite.

1. Bonjour, Monsieur. Est-ce que vous voudriez une boisson pour commencer?
2. Bonjour, Madame. Vous voulez manger quelque chose?
3. Bonsoir, Messieurs-Dames. Que voudriez-vous commander?
4. Bonsoir, Madame. Qu'est-ce que vous voudriez comme boisson?
5. Bonjour, Mesdames. Qu'est-ce que je peux vous servir[3]?
6. Bonjour, Mademoiselle. Qu'est-ce que je peux vous apporter[4]?

Structure 2

Les adverbes

Adverbs are generally used to tell *how* something is done, or *how often* something is done. They can modify a verb *(I cook **well** / I cook **often**)*, an adjective *(I am **very** tall)*, or another adverb *(I cook **very** well)*.

---

[1]*alone* [2]*each* [3]*what can I serve you* [4]*bring you*

- **Formation.** In French, there are two types of adverbs:

  1. Short forms that developed independently and are not based on an adjective.

très	*very*	trop	*too*
bien	*well*	peut-être	*maybe, possibly*
mal	*poorly, badly*	vite	*quickly*
beaucoup	*a lot*	souvent	*often*
assez	*enough*	parfois	*occasionally, sometimes*

  2. Long forms that are based on an adjective. These are similar to adverbs that end in *-ly* in English. To form an adverb from an adjective, we usually take the *feminine singular* form of the adjective and add **-ment**.

(lent) lente → lente**ment**	*(slow → slowly)*
(silencieux) silencieuse → silencieuse**ment**	*(silent → silently)*
(faux) fausse → fausse**ment**	*(false → falsely)*

     There are two exceptions to this rule, however.

     a. When the masculine form of the adjective ends in a vowel, **-ment** is added directly to the masculine form.

vrai → vrai**ment**	*(real → really; true → truly)*
absolu → absolu**ment**	*(absolute → absolutely)*

     b. When an adjective ends in **-ent** or **-ant** in the masculine, **-nt** is dropped and **-mment** is added:

prudent → prud**emment**	*(careful → carefully)*
intelligent → intellig**emment**	*(intelligent → intelligently)*
constant → const**amment**	*(constant → constantly)*

     Because adverbs do not modify nouns, they do not vary under any circumstances.

     > François boit **lentement.**
     > Chloé boit **lentement.**
     > François et Chloé boivent **lentement.**

- **Placement.** Unlike adverbs in English, adverbs in French come *after* the verb they modify rather than before it. This is true of all types of adverbs.

Je **vais souvent** au supermarché.	*I often go to the supermarket.*
Je **mange normalement** chez mes parents.	*I normally eat at my parents' house.*
Je **travaille vite.**	*I work quickly.*

  Adverbs that are used to modify an adjective or another adverb are placed directly before the word they modify, just as in English.

Elle est **très grande.**	*She is very tall.*
Je réponds **très vite.**	*I respond very quickly.*

VÉRIFIEZ VOTRE COMPRÉHENSION

1. Go back to the conversation between Chloé and François (pp. 181–182). Are there any adverbs in this dialogue? Which ones?

2. Explain how each adverb is formed (is it a simple form, or is it based on an adjective?). What does each adverb modify?

3. Can you explain why the adverbs are positioned where they are?

(margin note) Model the pronunciation of these adverbs for your students, pointing out that the endings **-emment** and **-amment** have the same pronunciation. Point out, too, that **lent** is an exception to this rule because it is monosyllabic; this adverb is formed from the feminine of the adjective: **lentement.**

Pratiquons!

A. Comment le font-ils? *(How do they do it?)* The following sentences give you an indication of their subjects' personalities. Use that adjective to form an adverb, and tell how those people do the activity indicated.

🌀 MODÈLE: François est très prudent. Il conduit[1] prudemment.

1. Chloé est *intelligente*. Elle étudie _____.
2. Ma mère est assez *silencieuse*. Elle fait la cuisine _____.
3. Les hommes politiques sont *ambitieux*. Ils travaillent _____.
4. Michel est un homme *désagréable*. Il parle _____.
5. Nous sommes *calmes*. Nous réagissons _____.
6. Ma sœur est *timide*. Elle parle _____ en classe.
7. Le prof n'est pas *méchant*. Il ne répond jamais[2] _____.
8. Christopher Reeve était[3] un homme *courageux*. Il a vécu sa vie[4] _____.
9. Béatrice est une femme très *polie*. Elle répond toujours _____.
10. Mon frère est très *patient*. Il attend _____ son bus le matin.

👥 B. Moi, je le fais comme ça. With a partner, take turns asking and answering the following questions. In your answers, use one of the adverbs provided (or another adverb of your choice). Notice that some questions ask *how;* others ask *when.* When you have finished, report your partner's responses to the class.

Suggested adverbs: bien, mal, souvent, toujours, vite, parfois, lentement, prudemment, sérieusement, rarement, constamment, poliment, patiemment ...

1. Comment est-ce que tu conduis?
2. Quand est-ce que tu regardes la télé?
3. Quand est-ce que tu parles au professeur de français?
4. Comment est-ce que tu réponds au professeur en classe?
5. Quand est-ce que tu vas au cinéma?
6. Comment est-ce que tu travailles?
7. Comment est-ce que tu chantes?
8. Quand est-ce que tu fais des courses?
9. Comment est-ce que tu danses?
10. Comment est-ce que tu étudies?

👥 C. C'est certain? Tell your partner with what degree of certainty you are going to do the following activities, using one of these adverbs: **certainement, absolument, évidemment, probablement, possiblement, peut-être.**

🌀 MODÈLE: Est-ce que tu vas recevoir ton diplôme ce semestre?

> *Je vais **certainement** recevoir mon diplôme ce semestre! / Je ne vais **probablement** pas recevoir mon diplôme ce semestre.*

1. Est-ce que tu vas à un concert ce week-end?
2. Est-ce que tu vas parler à tes parents ce soir?
3. Vas-tu faire tes devoirs cet après-midi?
4. Est-ce que tu vas dîner au restaurant bientôt?
5. Tu vas avoir des enfants un jour?
6. Est-ce que tu vas travailler le semestre prochain?
7. Est-ce que tu vas être professeur de français?

---

[1]*drives* [2]*never* [3]*was* [4]*lived his life*

Portrait personnel

Écrivez maintenant une description de votre partenaire, en disant ce que vous avez appris pendant votre conversation dans les activités B et C. Quel type de personne est-ce? Qu'est-ce qu'il/elle va absolument faire? Qu'est-ce qu'il/elle ne va probablement pas faire dans l'avenir? Utilisez des *adjectifs* et des *adverbes* dans votre description.

> MODÈLE: Paul est toujours pressé. Il conduit rapidement, et il va rarement au cinéma. Il ne va certainement pas aller au cinéma ce week-end.

À vous de parler!

A. Trouvez quelqu'un qui … Circulate around the room, and find someone who can answer **Oui** to one of the following questions. Ask him/her to provide you with details as indicated in parentheses. Once you have found a person who answers **Oui** to a question, you must move on to another person!

Trouvez quelqu'un qui …

1. a soif maintenant (Demandez-lui[1] ce qu'il/elle veut boire.)
2. fait normalement ses devoirs juste après la classe (Demandez-lui comment il/elle fait ses devoirs: seul[e]? en groupe? rapidement? etc.)
3. boit beaucoup de Coca (Demandez-lui quand est-ce qu'il/elle boit du Coca.)
4. veut étudier à la bibliothèque cet après-midi (Demandez-lui pourquoi.)
5. ne boit jamais[2] de café (Demandez-lui pourquoi.)
6. veut absolument voyager en France (Demandez-lui où et quand.)
7. ne fait jamais le ménage (Demandez-lui comment est sa maison/son appartement/sa chambre.)
8. a sommeil (Demandez-lui pourquoi.)
9. prend une salade tous les jours (Demandez-lui où.)
10. a envie de regarder un film français en classe demain (Demandez-lui lequel[3].)
11. parle couramment une autre langue (Demandez-lui laquelle[4] et pourquoi.)

After you have finished, choose three classmates who responded in the affirmative to any three questions and tell the class about them.

> MODÈLE: Rob ne fait jamais le ménage. Son appartement est terriblement sale[5]!

B. Scénarios. In groups of three or four, create a dialogue for one of the following situations. When you have finished, act out your dialogue for the rest of the class.

1. You and some friends have decided to go out this weekend. Talk about where you each want to go. What do you feel like doing? Why? If you decide to go to a restaurant, what will you eat and drink? If you are going somewhere else, what will you do? What will you do afterward?
2. Role-play the interaction between a waiter/waitress and some customers. Be sure to order both food and drinks.

[1]*Ask him/her* [2]*never* [3]*which one* [4]*which one (feminine)* [5]*dirty*

You may want to question the students further to make them provide more details. Example: Rob, pourquoi est-ce que tu ne fais jamais le ménage? Est-ce que tu fais la lessive? etc.

Point the students to the conversation between François and Chloé for a model for either of these conversations. Encourage students to be creative, but to use language that they already know for this activity.

En France, on mange le pain et le fromage comme ça

Bread and cheese are always present in French cuisine, and they are eaten together. They are the two most common food items that accompany almost every meal: **des tartines** for breakfast, and bread and cheese at lunch and dinner. The French continue the tradition of buying their bread every morning—or at the end of the day on their way home from work—at the **boulangerie.**

Bread is never cut at the table. When it comes to the table it has already been sliced and placed in a basket. Bread must be cut with a bread knife, **le couteau à pain,** and never torn apart with the hands. There are different types of bread that are frequently served at the table: **la baguette,** of course, but also **la boule campagnarde**[1], **la ficelle**[2], **la flûte,** or **la couronne**[3], depending on the occasion.

When cheese is brought to the table—at the end of a meal, right after the salad and before the dessert—it comes on a tray, **le plateau à fromage,** and there is a wide selection of varieties. Cheese that has already been cut into is normally served when eating among family. At the table, the cheese is cut with a special knife, **le couteau à fromage,** that comes with the tray. When the French help themselves to the cheese, they first cut it with **le couteau à fromage,** which has what looks like a fork at the end. Then, they pick up the piece of cheese with the end of **le couteau à fromage** before placing it on their plates without touching the cheese with their hands. Usually, the cheese tray circulates around the table only once. Therefore, if you are a cheese lover, make sure you help yourself generously! The French like cheese so much that it is very common for them to end a meal with cheese and to eat it as dessert!

Réfléchissons

1. Is cheese a big component of a meal in your country? When is it eaten? At the beginning of a meal, in the middle, or at the end, as in France?
2. How is cheese eaten in your country? Is it eaten only with bread, as in France?
3. What types of bread do you know? How often do you buy bread? Do you buy it every day, as the French do?
4. What French cheeses do you know? What is your favorite one?

You may wish to organize **une dégustation de fromages** with different **plateaux à fromage** in class. (Bring **un couteau à fromage** if you have one.) Have students volunteer to buy the most popular—and affordable—French cheeses and breads, such as **Brie, Camembert, Saint-André, Gruyère, Boursin, du fromage de chèvre** (tell students that it is made with goat's milk); **des baguettes, du pain complet** (whole-wheat bread), **des boules campagnardes,** or **des épis** (a baguette shaped into spikes, like an ear of wheat).

---

[1]**La boule campagnarde** is a round loaf of bread. [2]**La ficelle** and **la flûte** are very long and thin loaves of bread. **Ficelle** means *a string* and **flûte** *a flute,* like the musical instrument. [3]**La couronne** means literally *the crown.* It is round, with a hole in the middle.

Continuons!

Online Study Center
Language Skills Practice

Partie I: Chez le traiteur

Aujourd'hui, Chloé et François ne veulent pas cuisiner et ne veulent pas manger au restaurant, mais ils ont très faim! Alors, ils décident d'aller chez le traiteur[1] pour acheter leur dîner. Avez-vous faim et soif aussi? Voulez-vous accompagner Chloé et François?

Chloé et François regardent les plats offerts, et puis ils décident ce qu'ils veulent manger et boire. Voici ce qu'ils trouvent chez le traiteur aujourd'hui. Comme entrées et hors-d'œuvre[2] il y a:

du saumon fumé

des tomates provençales (f.)

de la soupe à l'oignon

du pâté de campagne

du foie gras

Chloé et François décident de prendre des tomates provençales. Et vous, qu'est-ce que vous allez prendre?

---

[1]Catering service. In France and Francophone Europe, it is possible to get meals already prepared from a catering service, or to have them delivered. [2]*appetizers*

Tell students what **foie gras** is if they do not know. Tell them that it is like pâté; however, the process of making **foie gras** is much longer and more complicated. **Foie gras** is made from the livers of geese that have undergone the process of **gavage. Gaver une oie** means to stuff the animal with very rich food for several months until the liver is engorged. Then, the liver is cooked and canned with a truffle that is found only in certain forests of France.

Ensuite, ils regardent les plats principaux[1]. Il y a beaucoup de choix très appétissants! Regardons:

du poulet rôti ou du porc rôti

des lasagnes *(f.)*

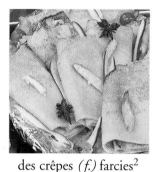

des crêpes *(f.)* farcies[2]

Tell students that **crêpes** can be made sweet or savory. They can be stuffed with chicken, shrimp, or mushrooms, just to name a few variations. They can also be served plain with powdered sugar sprinkled on top. This is an affordable dish that everyone loves to eat!

des boulettes *(f.)* de viande *(f.)*

une quiche ou une tarte salée

François voudrait bien manger du poulet, mais Chloé ne veut pas. Elle déclare qu'ils mangent trop de poulet! Après une longue discussion, ils décident de prendre des boulettes de viande. (Mais la prochaine fois, ils vont peut-être choisir des lasagnes!) Et vous, qu'est-ce que vous avez envie de manger?

Après ça, il faut choisir un légume. Regardons le choix qui leur est présenté:

des carottes râpées

des asperges à la mayonnaise

Qu'est-ce que vous pensez qu'ils vont choisir? Chloé adore les carottes râpées, alors c'est ce qu'ils choisissent. Est-ce que vous aimez les carottes?

---

[1]*main courses* [2]*stuffed*

Finalement, il faut choisir un dessert. C'est ce qu'il y a de plus difficile, parce que tout a l'air délicieux! Regardons avec eux:

un gâteau au chocolat

des glaces *(f.)* (au chocolat, à la vanille, à la fraise)

une crème brûlée

des tartelettes *(f.)* aux fruits

Qu'est-ce que vous allez choisir? François et Chloé n'ont pas pu se décider, donc ils ont pris des tartelettes et de la glace à la vanille!

Vous avez bien compris?

Tell if the following sentences are true **(vrai)** or false **(faux).** Correct the false statements.

1. Les tomates provençales sont une entrée. _____ vrai _____ faux
2. Les lasagnes sont des hors-d'œuvre. _____ vrai _____ faux
3. Les carottes râpées sont un légume. _____ vrai _____ faux
4. La glace est un dessert. _____ vrai _____ faux
5. Les boulettes de viande sont une entrée. _____ vrai _____ faux
6. La soupe à l'oignon est un plat principal. _____ vrai _____ faux
7. Les asperges sont un dessert. _____ vrai _____ faux
8. Le porc rôti est une entrée. _____ vrai _____ faux
9. Le saumon fumé est un plat principal. _____ vrai _____ faux
10. Le foie gras est un dessert. _____ vrai _____ faux

Vocabulaire essentiel

La nourriture

Here is some additional vocabulary related to food.

Les viandes *(f.)*

du bœuf

du veau

des côtelettes *(f.)*
d'agneau *(m.)*

Les poissons *(m.)*

du thon (grillé)

des truites *(f.)*

des sardines *(f.)*
à l'huile d'olive

Les fruits de mer *(m.)*

des crevettes *(f.)*

des huîtres
fraîches *(f.)*

une langouste

des moules *(f.)*

Les féculents *(m.)* (Starchy foods)

des pommes
de terre *(f.)*

des pâtes *(f.)*

du riz

Les légumes (m.)

des épinards *(m.)*

des haricots verts *(m.)*

des champignons *(m.)*

Les fruits (m.)

une poire

une banane

un abricot

une pomme

une orange

un citron

Les condiments (m.) et autres (Seasonings and others)

le sel

le poivre

le vinaigre

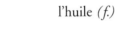
l'huile *(f.)*

le sucre

le lait

de la confiture de fraises

Les repas (m.) (Meals)

Pour ...	on prend ...
le petit déjeuner *(breakfast)*	des tartines *(f.)* avec du beurre et de la confiture des céréales *(f.)* avec du lait des croissants *(m.)*
le déjeuner *(lunch)*	une salade de la viande ou du poisson et des légumes *(m.)* un dessert
le goûter *(afternoon snack)*	un yaourt *(yogurt)* des biscuits *(m.) (cookies)* un fruit
le dîner *(dinner)*	de la soupe du jambon avec du fromage un fruit

Expansion personnelle

Les viandes et les volailles

du canard

du lapin aux pruneaux

du porc et des pommes au four

Les fruits de mer   *Les féculents*

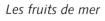

des coquilles Saint-Jacques *(f.)*

des haricots *(m.)*

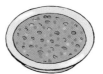

des lentilles *(f.)*

Les légumes

un chou-fleur

du céleri

un poivron rouge

Les fruits (m.)

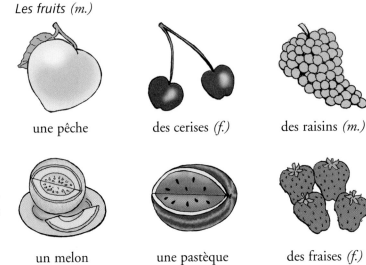

une pêche   des cerises (f.)   des raisins (m.)

un melon   une pastèque   des fraises (f.)

You may want to tell students that there is a word for *to snack:* **grignoter.** French kids **grignotent** frequently, especially **du chocolat, des biscuits et des bonbons!** And let's not forget **le Nutella,** a chocolate and hazelnut spread!

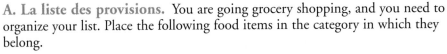 À vous!

A. La liste des provisions. You are going grocery shopping, and you need to organize your list. Place the following food items in the category in which they belong.

1. l'agneau   5. le poulet   9. le saumon
2. la pastèque   6. le chou-fleur   10. le sucre
3. les moules   7. une tarte   11. les haricots
4. le canard   8. l'eau gazeuse   12. les crevettes

Viandes et volailles	Poissons et fruits de mer	Féculents	Légumes

Fruits	Desserts	Condiments	Boissons

B. Définitions. Match the drawings in the left columns with the definitions in the right column.

a.   b.   c.

d.   e.   f.

g.   h.   i.

1. _____ C'est un fruit rond et jaune.

2. _____ C'est un légume que les lapins adorent.

3. _____ C'est blanc à l'extérieur et jaune à l'intérieur.

4. _____ C'est un liquide blanc.

5. _____ C'est froid et sucré.

6. _____ C'est le contraire du sucre.

7. _____ C'est une boisson alcoolisée.

8. _____ C'est délicieux avec du pain et du beurre.

9. _____ C'est un fruit de mer très cher.

C. Tes habitudes alimentaires. Ask a classmate the following questions about his or her eating habits. Then, your classmate will ask you the same questions. Report your findings to the class.

1. Qu'est-ce que tu prends d'habitude pour le petit déjeuner?
2. Combien de cafés est-ce que tu bois par jour?
3. Combien de bières est-ce que tu bois par semaine?
4. Est-ce que tu manges souvent des légumes? Quel légume est-ce que tu préfères?
5. Est-ce que tu grignotes[1] souvent? Qu'est-ce que tu grignotes? Des fruits? Des biscuits salés[2]? Du chocolat? Des biscuits?
6. Tu es gourmand(e)?[3] Quel est ton dessert préféré?
7. Est-ce que tu manges du canard ou du lapin quelquefois? Quelle viande est-ce que tu manges? Quelle viande est-ce que tu ne manges pas?
8. Tu aimes les fruits de mer? Lesquels?[4] Où est-ce que tu vas pour manger des fruits de mer?
9. Est-ce que tu voudrais goûter[5] du foie gras? Pourquoi?

Portrait personnel

Write a description of your partner's eating habits, based on his or her responses in activity C.

_____

[1] _snack_ [2] _crackers_ [3] _Do you have a sweet tooth?_ [4] _Which ones?_ [5] _to taste_

Structure 3

Online Study Center
ACE, Language Skills
Practice

Les verbes *devoir* et *pouvoir*

Earlier in this chapter you learned the conjugation of the verbs **boire** and **vouloir.** The conjugation of **devoir** *(to have to, must)* is similar to that of **boire,** and the conjugation of **pouvoir** *(to be able to, can)* is similar to that of **vouloir.**

Both **devoir** and **pouvoir** keep their stems in the **nous** and **vous** forms.

devoir	
je dois	nous devons
tu dois	vous devez
il / elle / on doit	ils / elles doivent

Attention! The verb **devoir** is normally followed by an infinitive.

On **doit** bien **manger** pour bien vivre.
Vous ne **devez** pas **boire** de bière si vous prenez votre voiture.
Je **dois acheter** du lait pour mon fils.

One must eat well to live well.
You must not drink beer if you take your car.
I have to buy milk for my son.

pouvoir	
je peux	nous pouvons
tu peux	vous pouvez
il / elle / on peut	ils / elles peuvent

Attention! Like **devoir,** the verb **pouvoir** is normally followed by an infinitive.

Vous **pouvez faire** un gâteau comme dessert?
Je ne **peux** pas **préparer** les fruits de mer.
Les étudiants **peuvent manger** beaucoup de pizza!

Can you make a cake for dessert?
I can't cook seafood.
Students can eat lots of pizza!

VÉRIFIEZ VOTRE COMPRÉHENSION

Go back to the **Structure 1** section (pp. 184–185) and look at the conjugations of the verbs **boire** and **vouloir.** Look for similarities and differences with the conjugations of **devoir** and **pouvoir.**

🎧 **À l'écoute!** You will hear a number of sentences that include the four verbs you have learned in this chapter: **vouloir, boire, devoir,** and **pouvoir.** Indicate whether each sentence is about one person or several people.

1. ＿＿＿ one person ＿＿＿ several people
2. ＿＿＿ one person ＿＿＿ several people
3. ＿＿＿ one person ＿＿＿ several people
4. ＿＿＿ one person ＿＿＿ several people
5. ＿＿＿ one person ＿＿＿ several people
6. ＿＿＿ one person ＿＿＿ several people
7. ＿＿＿ one person ＿＿＿ several people
8. ＿＿＿ one person ＿＿＿ several people

Transcript: 1. Ils veulent un sandwich. 2. Elle veut une glace. 3. Elles peuvent faire un gâteau. 4. Il doit acheter du pain. 5. Ils boivent trop de vin. 6. Il peut manger chez moi. 7. Ils doivent manger des légumes. 8. Elle boit de l'eau plate.

Answer Key: 1. several people 2. one person 3. several people 4. one person 5. several people 6. one person 7. several people 8. one person

Pratiquons!

A. Obligations et conséquences. For each sentence beginning in the left column, choose a logical completion from the right column. Write the correct form of the verbs in parentheses.

1. Si tu as soif, tu ...
2. Quand vous avez sommeil, vous ...
3. Ils sont végétariens: ils ne ...
4. Quand nous avons froid, nous ...
5. Je suis incapable de cuisiner, je ne ...
6. Quand Jules a faim, il ...

a. (devoir) mettre une veste.
b. (devoir) manger vite quelque chose.
c. (pouvoir) pas préparer des pâtes!
d. (devoir) boire.
e. (devoir) dormir[1].
f. (pouvoir) pas manger de viande.

Answer Key: 1. d. dois boire. 2. e. devez dormir. 3. f. peuvent pas manger de viande. 4. a. devons mettre une veste. 5. c. peux pas préparer des pâtes! 6. b. doit manger vite quelque chose.

B. Que doit-on faire? Answer the following questions, using the verb **devoir** in your answers.

1. Qu'est-ce qu'on doit faire pour avoir beaucoup d'argent?
2. Qu'est-ce que tu dois faire pour être heureux / heureuse?
3. Combien de fois par mois est-ce que tu dois faire le ménage?
4. Que doit-on faire pour avoir du succès avec les filles / les garçons?
5. Qu'est-ce que les Français doivent faire pour prendre un chariot au supermarché?
6. En Suisse, est-ce qu'on doit avoir 21 ans pour pouvoir boire?

Answer Key: 1–4. *Answers will vary.* 5. Ils doivent payer pour utiliser le chariot. Cet argent est remboursé quand ils ramènent le chariot à l'entrée du supermarché. 6. Non. En Suisse, on doit avoir 16 ans pour pouvoir boire.

C. Que peut-on faire? Answer the following questions, using the verb **pouvoir** in your answers.

1. Qu'est-ce que tu peux faire si tu ne comprends pas le prof de français?
2. Dans une brasserie, est-ce qu'on peut manger ou seulement[2] boire? Qu'est-ce qu'on peut boire dans une brasserie? Où peut-on boire et manger?
3. Est-ce que les Français peuvent voyager avec leurs chiens dans les autobus?
4. En France, est-ce qu'on peut acheter des médicaments au supermarché? Où peut-on acheter des médicaments?
5. En général, aux États-Unis, est-ce qu'on peut fumer dans les restaurants?

Answer Key: 1. *Answers will vary.* 2. On peut manger et boire. 3. Oui, ils peuvent voyager avec leurs chiens dans les autobus. 4. Non. On peut seulement acheter les médicaments dans une pharmacie. 5. Cela dépend de la ville et/ou de l'état. Il n'y a pas de règle nationale concernant où on peut fumer.

---

[1] *to sleep* [2] *only*

Online Study Center
Language Skills Practice

D. Entretien. With a partner, take turns asking and answering the questions.

1. Qu'est-ce que tu dois faire après la classe de français?
2. Qu'est-ce que tu voudrais faire dans la vie[1] mais tu ne peux pas pour le moment?
3. Peux-tu parler une autre langue? Laquelle?
4. Qu'est-ce que les étudiants doivent faire à votre université pour bien réussir dans leurs cours?
5. Est-ce que tu peux manger de tout[2]? Es-tu allergique à certains aliments[3]?
6. Où est-ce que tu dois aller demain matin?

Portrait personnel

Using the information that you learned from your partner in activity D, write a paragraph describing your partner and mentioning some of his or her *desires,* *capabilities,* and *responsibilities.*

Partie II: À table!

John rend visite à ses amis français Chloé et François dans leur appartement à Toulouse. John veut aider[4], alors il met la table[5] pour le déjeuner pendant que[6] Chloé finit de faire la cuisine.

JOHN: Chloé, pour la soupe, je mets les assiettes à soupe[7] ou je mets les bols?

CHLOÉ: Tu es marrant! Non, ne mets pas les bols pour la soupe. Les bols c'est pour le petit déjeuner. On y boit du café, du thé ou du chocolat chaud. N'oublie pas les cuillères à soupe et les serviettes[8] aussi!

JOHN: C'est vrai! Sur la table, j'ai les cuillères à café, mais pas les cuillères à soupe! J'ai une autre question, Chloé: les cuillères, elles vont à droite ou à gauche de l'assiette?

CHLOÉ: Ah! Ces Américains! Bon, la cuillère à soupe est à droite, à côté du couteau sur la serviette. Comme ça, tu vois[9]? Et la fourchette est à gauche.

JOHN: Je mets les verres à vin?

CHLOÉ: Oui, nous allons boire une bouteille de vin blanc d'Alsace avec le poisson.

JOHN: Chloé, le verre à eau est plus grand que[10] le verre à vin, n'est-ce pas?

CHLOÉ: Oui, c'est ça![11] Et la cuillère à café est plus petite que la cuillère à soupe!

JOHN: Ne te moque pas de moi[12], Chloé! Je sais que les cuillères à soupe sont les plus grandes[13]!

CHLOÉ: La table est super jolie. Merci, Johnny! À table![14]

JOHN: De rien, Chloé. Dis, ça sent[15] super bon!

---

[1]*life* [2]*everything* [3]*foods* [4]*to help* [5]*sets the table* [6]*while* [7]*Another way to say soup plate is* **une assiette creuse** (literally, *a hollow plate*). [8]*napkins* [9]*you see* [10]*bigger than* [11]*that's right* [12]*Don't make fun of me* [13]*biggest* [14]*Lunch (Dinner) is ready!* [15]*That smells* (**ça sent bon** = *it smells good;* **ça sent mauvais** = *that smells bad*)

Vous avez bien compris?

Complete the sentences, based on the preceding dialogue.

1. Pour manger de la soupe, on utilise une _____.
2. On sert[1] la soupe dans une _____.
3. On mange la viande avec une _____.
4. On coupe[2] la viande avec un _____.
5. On met le sucre dans le café avec la _____.
6. On boit le vin dans le _____.
7. On boit l'eau dans le _____.
8. On s'essuie la bouche[3] avec la _____.

Vocabulaire essentiel

À table!

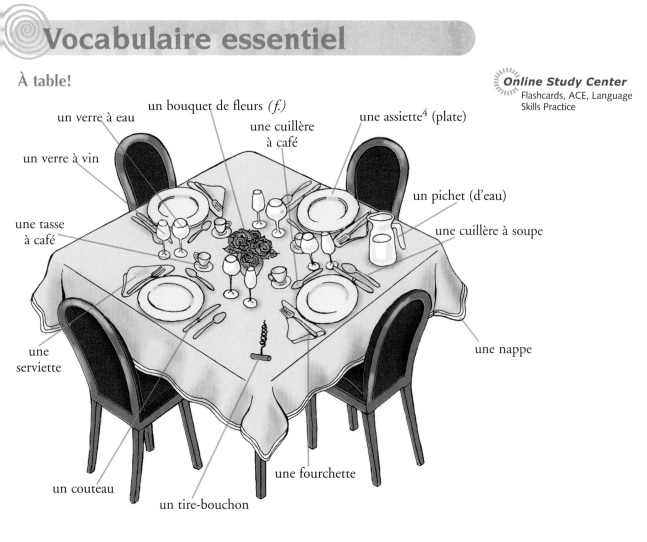

un verre à eau

un bouquet de fleurs (f.)

une cuillère
à café

une assiette[4] (plate)

un verre à vin

un pichet (d'eau)

une tasse
à café

une cuillère à soupe

une serviette

une nappe

un couteau

une fourchette

un tire-bouchon

---

[1]*serves* [2]*cuts* [3]*wipes one's mouth* [4]For a dessert plate, use **une assiette à dessert.**

Expansion personnelle

The following expressions are used to describe how food tastes or feels.

C'est bon[1]/ C'est exquis! /
C'est délicieux!

C'est mauvais[2]! / C'est dégueulasse! /
C'est dégoûtant!

C'est froid!

C'est chaud!

Ça brûle!

C'est épicé!

C'est sucré!

C'est salé!

C'est pourri!

---

[1]When something tastes good the French also say **miam!** which means *yummy!* [2]When something tastes bad the
French also say, **beurk!** which means *yuck!*

À vous!

A. Qu'est-ce que c'est? Choose the appropriate item on the right to complete the statement on the left.

1. On boit le café ou le thé au petit déjeuner dans
2. On met l'eau dans
3. Sous les couverts et la vaisselle[1] il y a
4. On boit le café au déjeuner ou au dîner dans
5. On ouvre une bouteille de vin avec
6. On mange de la viande dans

a. une assiette plate.
b. un tire-bouchon.
c. une tasse à café.
d. un pichet.
e. une nappe.
f. un bol.

B. Tu aimes? Tell your partner what you think of the following foods and beverages. After you have finished, decide who is harder to please when it comes to eating and drinking!

1. le sushi
2. le steak tartare
3. le poulet au curry
4. les escargots
5. le syrop de menthe[2]
6. les sorbets au citron
7. le foie gras
8. le lapin
9. la crème brûlée
10. la langue de bœuf[3]

C. Les bonnes manières à table. Find out how your partner eats. Ask him or her the following questions and then reverse roles.

1. Avec quoi est-ce que tu manges la pizza? Avec les mains[4] ou avec un couteau et une fourchette?
2. Dans quoi est-ce que tu manges la pizza? Dans des assiettes en papier ou dans le carton où est livrée la pizza[5]?
3. Comment est-ce que tu manges les frites? Avec les mains ou avec une fourchette?
4. D'habitude, est-ce que tu manges à table ou sur le fauteuil devant la télé?
5. Est-ce que tu mets une nappe sur la table? Quand est-ce que tu mets une nappe?
6. Est-ce que tu prends la fourchette avec la main droite ou avec la main gauche pour manger la viande?
7. Où est-ce que tu bois le vin? Dans un verrre à vin ou dans un verre à eau?

Once the students complete this activity, open a discussion about French table manners. For each question, ask students what they think the French do. Question #1: The French do not eat pizza with their hands. Generally, they use a knife and a fork. #2: The French do not eat pizza out of the box, nor do they eat from paper plates unless they are at a picnic. #3: The French do not eat fries with their hands either! Generally, they use a fork. And the majority do not eat their fries with ketchup. #4: The French like to eat at the table. They may have the TV on, but they do not eat on the couch. #5: The French usually have a tablecloth on the table when they eat (or a placemat—**un napperon / un set de table**). #6: The French cut their meat with the right hand and eat it with the left. They do not switch hands to cut and eat. The French eat with the right hand only when a knife is not needed for the dish. #7: The French do not drink wine from a water glass. They always use wine glasses! (This is a matter of taste as well as of good manners. The wine does not taste as good from a normal glass.)

---

[1]*cutlery and set of dishes* [2]*mint* [3]*beef tongue* [4]*hands* [5]*in the box in which the pizza is delivered*

Before introducing this structure, you may want to review the definition of adjectives and adverbs.

Online Study Center
ACE, Language Skills Practice

Structure 4

Le comparatif

The following expressions are used in French to compare two or more people, things, ideas, or actions.

Comparing adjectives	
plus + adjective + **que**	more (-er) . . . than
moins + adjective + **que**	less . . . than
aussi + adjective + **que**	as . . . as
the adjective **bon** (good) → **meilleur** + **que**	better than
the adjective **mauvais** (bad) → **pire** + **que**	worse than

Les voitures françaises sont **plus petites que** les voitures américaines.	*French cars are smaller than American cars.*
Les Français sont **moins sportifs que** les Américains.	*French people are less athletic than Americans.*
La glace à la vanille est **aussi bonne que** la glace au chocolat.	*Vanilla ice cream is as good as chocolate ice cream.*
Le fromage français est **meilleur que** le fromage américain.	*French cheese is better than American cheese.*

Notice from the preceding examples that the adjectives agree in gender and number with the first noun (i.e., the noun they modify).

Comparing adverbs	
plus + adverb + **que**	more . . . than
moins + adverb + **que**	less . . . than
aussi + adverb + **que**	as . . . as
the adverb **bien** → **mieux** + **que**	better than

Les trains américains roulent **plus lentement que** les trains français.	*American trains go more slowly than French trains.*
On communique par courrier **moins rapidement que** par e-mail[1].	*One communicates by regular mail less rapidly than by e-mail.*
En France, on voyage **aussi facilement** en train **qu'**en avion.	*In France, one travels as easily by train as by plane.*
Les joueurs de basket américains jouent bien au basket. Ils jouent **mieux** au basket **que** les joueurs de basket français.	*American basketball players play basketball well. They play basketball better than the French basketball players.*

---

[1]The word **courriel** is also used for *e-mail.*

Comparing nouns	
plus de + noun + **que**	*more . . . than*
moins de + noun + **que**	*less (fewer) . . . than*
autant de + noun + **que**	*as many . . . as / as much . . . as*

Les Français mangent **plus de fromage que** les Américains.
French people eat more cheese than Americans.

Les Français boivent **moins de Coca que** les Américains.
French people drink less Coke than Americans.

Les enfants français aiment **autant de dessins animés que** les enfants américains.
French kids like as many cartoons as American kids.

Attention! In all the preceding examples, quantities of nouns are being compared. That is why **de** is used in these expressions of comparison. They are similar to other expressions of quantity that you already know, such as **beaucoup de ... , trop de ... ,** etc. Notice that the comparison expression **autant de** + noun + **que** can mean *as many as* or *as much as,* depending on whether it is used with a count noun or a non-count noun.

Elle mange **autant de** pommes **que** moi.
She eats as many apples as I do.

Je mange **autant de** chocolat **que** ma sœur.
I eat as much chocolate as my sister.

- When comparing *verbs,* the expressions **plus que, moins que,** and **autant que** follow the verb immediately. These comparisons are used to show duration, frequency, or intensity.

Les Américains **conduisent plus que** les Français.
Americans drive more than the French.

Les Américains **marchent moins que** les Français.
Americans walk less than the French.

Le patron **travaille autant que** ses employés.
The boss works as much as his employees.

VÉRIFIEZ VOTRE COMPRÉHENSION

1. Go back to the **Partie II** dialogue on page 202 and look at the comparative expressions in context. What are Chloé and John comparing?

2. How would you say the opposite of each comparative expression?

Pratiquons!

A. Les comparaisons sont odieuses! First identify the part of speech of the words in boldface. Are they adjectives or adverbs? Then, make comparisons according to the cues in parentheses.

MODÈLE: **grande** → Ma chambre (*more . . . than*) ta chambre.

Ma chambre est plus grande que ta chambre.

1. **beau** → Mon chat est (*more . . . than*) ton chat.
2. **bien** → Ma voiture marche[1] (*better than*) ta voiture.

Answer Key: 1. plus beau que 2. mieux que 3. pires que 4. moins sale que 5. meilleur que 6. aussi cher que 7. pire que 8. plus jolis que

---
[1]*goes*

3. **mauvaises** → Tes notes[1] sont *(worse than)* mes notes.
4. **sale** → Ma maison est *(less . . . than)* ta maison.
5. **bon** → Mon dîner est *(better than)* ton dîner.
6. **cher** → Mon loyer est *(as . . . as)* ton loyer.
7. **mal** → Ta cuisine[2] est *(worse than)* ma cuisine.
8. **jolis** → Mes vêtements sont *(more . . . than)* tes vêtements.

B. Ah, bon? *(Oh, really?)* Tell if the first six statements about famous people are true or false. Correct the false statements. Give your personal opinion for numbers 7 and 8.

1. Tom Cruise est plus grand que Nicole Kidman.
2. Nicole Kidman a les cheveux moins frisés que Jennifer Aniston.
3. Le président des États-Unis gagne[3] autant d'argent que le président de Microsoft.
4. Steven Spielberg fait moins de films que Quentin Tarantino.
5. Barbara Walters est plus jeune que Katie Couric.
6. Oprah Winfrey est moins populaire que Rosie O'Donnell.
7. Martha Stewart cuisine mieux que Al Roker.
8. Jim Carrey est plus amusant que Mike Meyers.

C. Comparons nos opinions! With a classmate, compare the following items, using one of the cues in parentheses. Give your opinion, but be logical!

MODÈLE: Pour bien dormir, du café ou du lait chaud le soir? (meilleur / pire)

Le lait chaud est meilleur que le café pour bien dormir le soir.

1. Comme cadeau[4], une bouteille de champagne ou une bouteille de vin? (moins cher / plus cher / aussi cher)
2. Pour maigrir[5], une tarte ou des champignons? (moins gras[6] / plus gras / aussi gras)
3. Pour célébrer un anniversaire, une fête ou un dîner au restaurant? (plus amusant / moins amusant / aussi amusant)
4. Pour aller nager, un maillot de bain ou un bikini? (plus confortable / moins confortable / aussi confortable)
5. Comme hors d'œuvre, du foie gras ou des escargots? (meilleur / pire / aussi mauvais / aussi bon)
6. Comme viande, du lapin ou du poulet? (meilleur / pire / aussi mauvais / aussi bon)
7. Pour un rendez-vous amoureux, un dîner à la maison ou un film au cinéma? (plus romantique / moins romantique / aussi romantique)

Before doing activities B and C, have students tell if the comparative is used with an adjective, an adverb, or a noun in each item.

Answer Key: 1. faux / Nicole Kidman est plus grande que Tom Cruise. *or* Tom Cruise est plus petit que Nicole Kidman. 2. faux / Nicole Kidman a les cheveux plus frisés que Jennifer Aniston. 3. faux / Le président de Microsoft gagne plus d'argent que le président des États-Unis. 4. faux / Steven Spielberg fait plus de films que Quentin Tarantino. 5. faux / Barbara Walters est plus vieille que Katie Couric. 6. faux / Oprah Winfrey est plus populaire que Rosie O'Donnell. 7. *Student opinions will vary.* 8. *Student opinions will vary.*

---

[1]*grades* [2]*cooking* [3]*earns* [4]*As a gift* [5]*to lose weight* [6]*fattening*

Structure 5

Le superlatif

Online Study Center
ACE, Language Skills Practice

The **superlative** is used to express that someone or something is the best, the tallest, the worst, etc.

The superlative with adjectives	
le plus / la plus / les plus + adjective + **(de)**	*the most (the -est) . . . (of)*
le moins / la moins / les moins + adjective + **(de)**	*the least . . . (of)*
the adjective **bon** → **le meilleur /** **la meilleure / les meilleurs(es) + (de)**	*the best . . . (of)*
the adjective **mauvais** *(bad)* → **le plus mauvais / la plus mauvaise /** **les plus mauvais(es) + (de)**	*the worst . . . (of)*
or → **le pire / la pire / les pires + (de)**	*the worst . . . (of)*

Adjectives that normally precede the noun will do so in the superlative as well; those that follow the noun will also follow in the superlative.

Le français est **la plus belle** langue (**du** monde / **de la** planète)!

Je vais acheter la voiture **la moins chère** (**de** toutes).

Sharon Stone et Jodie Foster sont **les meilleures** actrices (**de** Hollywood).

Le Régent est **le plus mauvais** restaurant (**de** tous). OR: Le Régent est **le pire** restaurant (**de** tous).

French is the most beautiful language (in the world / on the planet)!

I'm going to buy the least expensive car (of all).

Sharon Stone and Jodie Foster are the best actresses (in Hollywood).

The Regent is the worst restaurant (of all).

Point out that in superlative expressions in which the adjective follows the noun, there is an article before the noun itself and another before the superlative.

Attention! Remember that a contraction is necessary with the definite article (**du, de la, de l', des**).

The superlative with adverbs	
le plus + adverb + **(de)**	*the most . . . (of)*
le moins + adverb + **(de)**	*the least . . . (of)*
the adverb **bien** → **le mieux + (de)**	*the best (of)*
the adverb **mal** → **le pire + (de)**	*the worst (of)*

Le prof parle **le plus rapidement** en français (**de** toute la classe).

Paul parle en classe **le moins souvent** (**des** étudiants).

Chloé cuisine **le mieux!**

John met la table **le pire!**

The professor speaks the most rapidly in French (of the entire class).

Paul speaks in class the least often (of the students).

Chloé cooks the best!

John sets the table the worst!

The superlative with nouns	
le plus de + noun + **(de)**	*the most . . . (of)*
le moins de + noun + **(de)**	*the least (the fewest) . . . (of)*

Ma sœur a **le plus de chaussures** (**de** toutes les femmes)—elle en a 250 paires!

My sister has the most shoes (of all the women)—she has 250 pairs!

En général, les étudiants ont **le moins d'argent** (**de la** population).

In general, students have the least money (of the general population).

VÉRIFIEZ VOTRE COMPRÉHENSION

Go back to the dialogue between Chloé and John (p. 202) and look at the superlative expressions. Ask yourself why the superlative is in the feminine form. What would the masculine form look like?

Before doing these activities, have students tell if the superlative is used with an adjective, a noun, or an adverb.

Pratiquons!

A. Ma vie est superlative! Et la tienne? *(My life is superlative! And yours?)* First, identify the part of speech of the words in boldface. Are they adjectives, adverbs, or nouns? Then, put them into the superlative form according to the cues in parentheses. Finally, answer the questions, using a superlative in your answer.

Answer Key: 1. le pire 2. le plus d'amis 3. la plus 4. la plus 5. le mieux 6. le moins de 7. le moins

1. Je cuisine **mal.** → De toute ma famille, je cuisine *(the worst)*. Et toi?
2. J'ai **des amis.** → J'ai *(the most)* amis. Et toi?
3. Ma voiture est **chère.** → Parmi mes amis, ma voiture est *(the most)* chère. Et toi?
4. Ma mère est **gentille.** → De tous les parents, ma mère est *(the most)* gentille. Et toi?
5. Je chante très **bien.** → Parmi mes amis, je chante *(the best)*. Et toi?
6. J'achète **des vêtements.** → J'achète *(the fewest)* vêtements de toute ma famille. Et toi?
7. Je travaille très **peu.** → Je travaille *(the least)* de tous mes amis. Et toi?

B. C'est vrai ou ce n'est pas vrai? Give your opinion about the following statements. Begin your response with **C'est vrai** if you agree with the statement or **Ce n'est pas vrai** if you disagree.

MODÈLE: Le champagne français est le moins cher.

Ce n'est pas vrai, le champagne français est le plus cher.

1. Anne Rice est la meilleure écrivaine de livres de vampires.
2. *Le Titanic* est le plus mauvais film de Hollywood.
3. San Diego est la plus grande ville des États-Unis.
4. La Floride est l'état le moins humide des États-Unis.
5. Sting chante le mieux de tous les chanteurs.
6. Calista Flockhart est l'actrice la plus grosse de Hollywood.
7. On mange le mieux à Toledo dans l'Ohio.
8. À Las Vegas, il neige le plus en hiver.

👥 **C. Vos goûts gastronomiques.** Ask a classmate the following questions to find out his or her gastronomical tastes. Then switch roles. Report your findings to the class.

1. Quel est le meilleur restaurant de ta ville?
2. Qui cuisine le mieux dans ta famille?
3. Dans quel restaurant peut-on trouver le menu le moins cher dans ton quartier?
4. Quel est le restaurant le plus romantique de ta ville?
5. Où peux-tu trouver les meilleures pâtisseries de la ville?
6. Est-ce que tu bois plus de bière que d'eau le week-end?
7. Est-ce que tu es le (la) plus gourmand(e) de tes amis?
8. Quelle est ta meilleure spécialité culinaire? Et ta pire spécialité?
9. Dans quel restaurant mange-t-on le pire?
10. Quel aliment aimes-tu le moins?

À vous de parler!

👥 **A. Bon appétit!** In groups of three or four, pretend that you are going to a **brasserie.** One of you is the waiter/waitress (**le serveur/la serveuse**) and the others are the clients. You arrive at the **brasserie** (find a name for it!) and you would like to sit outside. Order (**commander**) your food from the menu. You are very hungry and thirsty! Do not forget to leave the tip (**le pourboire**) after the meal. Also, as part of your conversation, talk about the pedestrians that pass by. Mention their looks and what they are wearing. And of course, **"bon appétit"!**

👥 **B. La concurrence universitaire.** You and your friends are discussing your university and its main rival. Discuss their students, faculty, libraries, campuses, etc., using comparative and superlative sentences.

⊚ MODÈLE: *Nous avons le plus beau campus.*

Oui, et en plus, nos étudiants travaillent plus sérieusement que leurs étudiants.

👥 **C. Jalousie!** For this activity, form groups of three. You and your friends are at a restaurant and you are talking about a common friend who seems to have it all: a wonderful house in a nice part of town, great culinary skills, a good-looking girlfriend/boyfriend, an expensive car, a perfect job, an expensive wardrobe, etc. You are all very jealous of this friend (find a name for him/her). In your conversation, compare the things this friend has with what you have, for example: his/her car is bigger and more expensive than your car; he/she is the best-looking; he/she can cook the best! End the conversation by either wanting to be like him (**lui**) or her (**elle**), or by not wanting to be like him/her, or find an ending of your own for your conversation.

If you wish, turn this activity into a competition. Have half of your students represent one university, and the other half its rival. Teams take turns giving a statement, and earn points for each grammatically correct sentence. For a greater challenge, specify each time whether the sentence must include an adjective, an adverb, or a noun and whether it must contain a comparative or a superlative.

On mange comme ça en Afrique

Online Study Center
Web Search Activities

Dans la plupart des pays africains, on n'utilise pas de couverts (des fourchettes, des couteaux, etc.) à table. Les Africains mangent avec la main droite. Dans les pays musulmans (tels que le Maroc ou l'Algérie), la main gauche ne peut pas toucher la nourriture; elle est réservée à l'hygiène personnelle exclusivement. Avant de mettre la nourriture sur la table, tout le monde se lave les mains dans une assiette creuse qui circule autour de la table et qui contient de l'eau savonneuse[1].

Quand on apporte la nourriture à table, tout le monde se sert sa portion d'un même récipient[2]. On utilise la main droite (ou on utilise du pain) pour prendre ce qui est dans l'assiette. (Le pain africain est plat—il ressemble plutôt à un *pita* qu'à une baguette.) Puisqu'on n'a pas d'assiette individuelle, il n'est pas mal vu de jeter les arêtes[3] de poisson par terre pendant qu'on mange. Dans quelques pays africains (le Cameroun, par exemple), les hommes mangent d'abord, les femmes après et les enfants en troisième lieu.

Les plats typiques dans beaucoup de pays africains incluent des lentilles, des arachides[4] et/ou un légume qui ressemble beaucoup à une pomme de terre douce. La viande de zèbre est très appréciée en Afrique, tout comme on apprécie le lapin ou le canard en France. En général, les Africains mangent tout ce qui leur est servi, sans laisser de restes[5]. Tout manger indique que les plats étaient très bons!

Réfléchissons

1. Dans votre pays, quels aliments est-ce qu'il est acceptable de manger avec les mains?
2. Pour quelles occasions ou pour quels aliments est-ce que tout le monde se sert sa portion d'un même récipient (ou plat) dans votre culture?
3. Est-ce que vous vous lavez les mains à table dans votre pays? Quand? Pour quels aliments?
4. Est-ce qu'il y a des choses que vous pouvez jeter par terre pendant que vous mangez? Lesquelles?

For #2, if students cannot think of an example, mention the fact that in the U.S., dipping vegetables in a communal dip is fairly common. For #3, the answer is yes, but generally *after* eating rather than before. (When seafood is served that requires peeling or using the hands, there are often finger bowls with water and lemon or cleansing wipes at each place setting.) For #4, you may want to remind students that in certain bars and restaurants, people throw peanut shells on the floor.

If you would like to expand on the topic of table manners, you may want to talk about France and Francophone Europe (for example, the fact that both hands have to be placed on the table at all times).

---

[1] *soapy* [2] *serving dish* [3] *bones* [4] *peanuts* [5] *leftovers*

À vous d'écrire!

Online Study Center
Language Skills Practice

Imagine that you have recently learned that your family will host an exchange student for a year. S/he will attend the same university as you, and will spend holidays with your family. In order to help the student prepare, you decide to write him/her a letter, in which you explain a little bit about your town and your university. You are going to tell him/her all the essentials, such as what s/he *is going to need* to bring from home for the year, what s/he will probably *want* to do and see in the area, what s/he *can* do on the weekends, what s/he *must* do to succeed in his/her classes, etc. You are going to tell the student where you live, where you go when you are *hungry or thirsty*, and where you study. You are going to fill him/her in on all the details, so that there will be no surprises upon his/her arrival!

A. Stratégies. Think about your audience. In Chapter 4, you wrote to a real estate agent; here, you are writing to a classmate. How will your language differ? What expressions might you use to begin and end your letter? With your intended audience in mind, think how you will organize the information in your letter before you begin to write.

B. Organisons-nous! Decide how many sections your letter will have. What are the main things that you want to tell your new classmate? Give each section a one- or two-word title (**ma famille, mon université, le week-end,** etc.), and decide on a logical order for all the sections. On a separate sheet of paper, list your sections in the order that they will appear. (You may use as many sections as you wish.)

C. Pensons-y! Now, for each section heading you listed, jot down some of your thoughts. If you listed **mon université** as a section, for example, what information are you going to include in that section? Write down some of the key vocabulary words that you will need, as well as some partial thoughts to get you started. Focus on the **avoir** expressions, the vocabulary and the new verbs that you learned in this chapter. Use language that you know to express yourself, rather than translating from English.

D. Écrivons! Write a first draft of your letter. Pay attention to content, making sure that you get all your ideas in and that you have expressed them coherently. Being coherent involves stating your ideas clearly, but also using correct vocabulary and grammar. When you have finished writing, ask yourself the following questions: Have I used the appropriate vocabulary words and spelled them correctly? Have I conjugated verbs as necessary? Do the nouns and adjectives agree? Make any changes necessary to your draft.

E. Révisons! Now that you have written a first draft of your letter, go back over it and look for ways in which you might improve it. Pay attention to organization and coherence, especially. Imagine that you are writing this letter for someone who does not know your family, your town, or your university. Will it make sense to him/her? What details must you provide to make the university scene comprehensible to someone who doesn't know it? Rewrite your letter on a clean sheet of paper, making corrections and additions as necessary. Turn it in when you have finished.

See the Online Teaching Center for ideas on using peer review as an additional step in the writing process. If you have time, have your students do a peer review of this letter, and then revise again.

Lexique

Vocabulaire essentiel

la carte *the menu*   chez le traiteur *at the caterer's*

Les entrées (f.) et les hors-d'œuvre (m.) *appetizers*

du foie gras *goose liver pâté*
du pâté de campagne *pâté*

du saumon fumé *smoked salmon*
de la soupe à l'oignon *onion soup*

des tomates provençales *(f.)*
   stuffed and baked tomatoes

Les plats principaux (m.) *main courses*

Les viandes (f.) et les volailles (f.) *meats and poultry*

du bœuf *beef*
des boulettes *(f.)* de viande
   meatballs

des côtelettes *(f.)* d'agneau *(m.)*
   lamb chops

du poulet ou du porc rôtis
   roasted chicken or pork
du veau *veal*

Les poissons (m.) *fish*

des sardines *(f.)* à l'huile d'olive
   sardines in olive oil
du thon (grillé) *(grilled) tuna*
des truites *(f.)* *trout*

Les fruits de mer (m.) *seafood*

des crevettes *(f.)* *shrimp*
des huîtres fraîches *(f.)* *raw oysters*

une langouste *lobster*
des moules *(f.)* *mussels*

Les légumes (m.) *vegetables*

des asperges *(f.)* (à la
   mayonnaise) *asparagus (with
   mayonnaise)*

des carottes (râpées) *(grated)*
   carrots
des champignons *(m.)* *mushrooms*

des épinards *(m.)* *spinach*
des haricots verts *green beans*

Les féculents (m.) *starchy foods*

des céréales *(f.)* *cereals*
des croissants *(m.)* *croissants*
des lasagnes *(f.)* *lasagna*

des pommes de terre *(f.)* *potatoes*
des pâtes *(f.)* *pasta*
du riz *rice*

des tartines *(f.)* (avec du beurre
   et de la confiture) *toasts (with
   butter and jam)*

Les fruits (m.) *fruits*

un abricot *apricot*
une banane *banana*

un citron *lemon*
une orange *orange*

une poire *pear*
une pomme *apple*

Les desserts (m.) *desserts*

des biscuits (m.) *cookies*
une crème brûlée *crème brulée*
un gâteau au chocolat (m.) *chocolate cake*

une glace au chocolat *chocolate ice cream*
une glace à la fraise *strawberry ice cream*

une glace à la vanille *vanilla ice cream*
des tartelettes (f.) aux fruits *mini-fruit tarts*
un yaourt *a yogurt*

Autres choses à manger *other things to eat*

une crêpe *crepe*
des frites (f.) *French fries*
une omelette *omelet*
une pizza

une quiche, une tarte salée *quiche*
une salade *salad*

un sandwich (au jambon-fromage) *(ham and cheese) sandwich*
de la soupe *soup*

Les condiments (m.) et autres *seasonings and others*

la confiture de fraises *strawberry jam*
l'huile (f.) *oil*

le lait *milk*
le poivre *pepper*
le sel *salt*

le sucre *sugar*
le vinaigre *vinegar*

Les repas (m.) *meals*

le déjeuner *lunch*
le dîner *dinner*

le goûter *afternoon snack*
le petit déjeuner *breakfast*

Les boissons (f.) *beverages*

une bière *beer*
une bouteille de bière *a beer bottle*
un café au lait *coffee with milk*
un café crème *coffee with cream*
un café noir *black coffee*
un Coca *Coke*

de l'eau gazeuse (f.) *carbonated water*
de l'eau plate (f.) *mineral water*
un exprès *expresso*
une limonade *carbonated lemon-lime soda*
une pression *draft beer*

un thé au citron *tea with lemon*
un thé nature *plain tea*
le vin (rouge / blanc / rosé) *wine (red / white / blush)*

À table! *lunch/dinner is ready!*

une assiette plate *plate*
une assiette à soupe *soup bowl*
un bol *bowl*
un bouquet de fleurs (f.) *bouquet of flowers*
un couteau *knife*

une cuillère à café *teaspoon*
une cuillère à soupe *tablespoon*
une fourchette *fork*
une nappe *tablecloth*
un pichet d'eau *pitcher of water*
une serviette *napkin*

une tasse à café *coffee cup*
un tire-bouchon *cork opener*
un verre à eau *water glass*
un verre à vin *wine glass*

Les expressions avec *avoir* avoir *expressions*

avoir l'air *to seem*
avoir besoin (de) *to need*
avoir de la chance *to be lucky*
avoir chaud *to be hot*

avoir envie (de) *to want / to feel like*
avoir faim *to be hungry*
avoir froid *to be cold*
avoir peur (de) *to be afraid*

avoir raison *to be right*
avoir soif *to be thirsty*
avoir sommeil *to be sleepy*
avoir tort *to be wrong*

Les adverbes *adverbs*

assez *enough*
beaucoup *a lot*
bien *well*
mal *poorly, badly*

parfois *occasionally, sometimes*
peut-être *maybe, possibly*
souvent *often*
très *very*

trop *too*
vite *quickly*

Expansion personnelle

Les viandes (f.) et les volailles (f.)

du canard *duck*
du lapin (aux pruneaux) *rabbit (with prunes)*

du porc et des pommes au four *pork with baked apples*

Les fruits (m.) de mer

des coquilles Saint-Jacques (f.) *scallops*

Les féculents (m.)

des haricots (m.) *red beans*
des lentilles (f.) *lentils*

Les légumes (m.)

du céleri *celery*
un chou-fleur *cauliflower*
un poivron rouge *red pepper*

Les fruits (m.)

des cerises (f.) *cherries*
des fraises (f.) *strawberries*

un melon *cantaloupe*
une pastèque *watermelon*

une pêche *peach*
des raisins (m.) *grapes*

Pour exprimer vos goûts *to express your tastes*

Ça brûle! *It burns!*
C'est bon. *It is good.*
C'est chaud. *It is hot.*
C'est dégoûtant! *It is disgusting!*
C'est dégueulasse! *It is disgusting!*

C'est délicieux! *It is delicious!*
C'est épicé! *It is spicy!*
C'est exquis! *It is exquisite!*
C'est froid! *It is cold!*
C'est mauvais! *It is bad!*

C'est pourri! *It is rotten!*
C'est salé! *It is salty!*
C'est sucré! *It is sweet!*

Les infos qui m'entourent

The topics in this chapter are television, radio, and print media such as magazines and newspapers. The Internet will be featured in Chapter 13: *Ma vie branchée*.

In this chapter you will learn about the different media that are popular in France and in the Francophone world. You will become familiar with French radio and television stations and with Canadian newspapers and magazines, and you will also read an article from a French magazine. You will also learn how to talk about things that happened in the past.

The vocabulary that you will learn includes

The media (radio, television, magazines, and newspapers)

Current events (crime, car accidents, and other newsworthy items)

The structures that you will learn include

The **passé composé** (past tense) with **avoir** and **être**

The **passé composé** in the negative and the interrogative

The interrogative pronoun **quel**

The **passé composé** with **y** and **en**

Placement of adverbs in the **passé composé**

The verbs **lire, dire,** and **écrire**

The culture that you will learn includes

Popular print media in Africa

French/Francophone television

French/Francophone radio stations

Commençons!

Online Study Center
Language Skills Practice

Les médias ◯

La radio

> *Christophe et Luc vont en voiture à l'université Le Mirail, à Toulouse.*
> CHRISTOPHE: Luc, ça te dit d'écouter un peu de musique?
> LUC: Ouais! Bonne idée! Je vais mettre NRJ[1], OK?
> CHRISTOPHE: D'accord! En plus, maintenant on passe[2] l'émission[3] *L'EuroHot 30* avec le hit parade pour le classement des tubes[4].
> LUC: C'est vrai! Super! J'aime bien Vincent, l'animateur de l'émission. Il est trop drôle!
> CHRISTOPHE: Oui, tu as raison, il est amusant. On a besoin de rigoler[5] avant notre cours de maths! Aujourd'hui, le prof rend les examens en classe ...

La télévision

> *Karim et Yasmina regardent la télévision dans leur salon à Marseille.*
> YASMINA: Karim, je ne veux pas regarder le foot encore! En plus, tu as regardé le match hier[6]. Peut-on changer de chaîne[7]?
> KARIM: Et quel programme est-ce que tu veux regarder? Des feuilletons[8] interminables?
> YASMINA: Eh bien non, Monsieur! Je voudrais regarder le journal télévisé sur TF1[9]. À la radio ce matin j'ai entendu que la grève[10] du RER est imminente. Si le RER va être en grève, je dois prendre ma voiture pour aller travailler.
> KARIM: D'accord, change de chaîne alors!
> YASMINA: Je ne peux pas, je n'ai pas la télécommande[11]! Comme tu es un zappeur et que tu n'arrêtes pas de zapper, la télécommande doit être dans ton fauteuil quelque part[12]!

Vous avez bien compris?

Choose the correct completion for each sentence.

1. NRJ est une _____.

   a. station de radio　　　　b. émission de radio

2. *L'EuroHot 30* avec Vincent est une émission _____.

   a. comique　　　　b. de musique

[1]This radio station is very popular among young people. The name sounds like **énergie.** [2]*is broadcasting* [3]*program* [4]*hit songs* [5]*to laugh* [6]*yesterday* [7]*channel* [8]*soap operas* [9]TF1 (Télévision Française 1) was one of the first French TV stations, along with **France 2, France 3,** and **France 5.** There are many other channels, although not as many as in the U.S. The most famous are: **Arte** (a somewhat intellectual network that broadcasts documentaries, political debates, programs on social issues, etc.); **Canal Jimmy** (a trendy cable TV network for a young audience); **Canal +** (a cable network that shows mostly movies); **M6** (a music/cartoon network for a very young audience); **TV5** (a channel that can be received in the U.S. via satellite). There is also **Pink TV** (a cable network for the gay community). [10]*strike* [11]*remote control* [12]*somewhere*

3. Vincent présente _____.

    a. les tubes   b. l'animateur

4. Yasmina veut regarder _____.

    a. des feuilletons   b. le journal télévisé

5. Yasmina veut changer de chaîne pour voir _____.

    a. le RER   b. la situation avec la grève

6. Karim _____ la télécommande.

    a. a   b. n'a pas

Vocabulaire essentiel

Les médias (1)

Online Study Center
Flashcards, ACE, Language
Skills Practice

À la télé on peut regarder ...

le journal télévisé (le JT)	*the television news*
un feuilleton romantique	*a soap opera*
la météo	*the weather*
une série (télévisée)	
un documentaire	
des talk-shows *(m.)*	
la télé-réalité	
des films *(m.)*	

On peut aussi ...

changer de chaîne	*to change channels*
faire du zapping	*to channel surf*

À la radio on peut écouter ...

les informations (les infos) *(f.)*	*the newscast*
les informations routières	*the traffic report*
une émission musicale	
une émission culturelle	
des tubes	*hit songs*

On peut aussi ...

changer de fréquence	*to change radio stations*

À la télé / Sur le petit écran   *On TV / On the small screen*

À la radio / Sur les ondes   *On the radio / On the airwaves*
on passe / on diffuse ...   *they broadcast . . .*

de la publicité (de la pub)	*advertisements*
un reportage	*a report*
des magazines *(m.)*	*exposés*
un match de foot en direct	*a live soccer game*
des divertissements *(m.)* / des jeux *(m.)*	*TV games*

des dessins animés *(m.)*   *cartoons*
une émission / un programme
des téléfilms *(m.)*
des sports *(m.)*
le hit parade

À la télé et à la radio ...

le présentateur (la présentatrice) présente   *the TV anchor presents*
l'animateur (animatrice) anime   *the DJ or the host announces or*
                                     hosts the show

À vous!

A. Programmes et émissions. Match each title of a TV or radio program with the category in which it belongs.

1. *La panthère rose*
2. *Les meilleurs tubes de l'été*
3. *Arts martiaux*
4. *L'actualité mondiale*
5. *Bob, le bricoleur*
6. *Will et Grace*
7. *Espèces en danger: les éléphants*
8. *Spécial Mozart*
9. *Qui veut gagner des millions?*
10. *Buffy contre les vampires*
11. *Zone interdite: drogue, anorexie, boulimie*

a. les sports
b. une série
c. des dessins animés
d. une émission musicale
e. un documentaire
f. le journal télévisé
g. un magazine
h. le hit parade
i. les divertissements

B. Tes préférences. Ask your classmate the following questions to find out about his or her favorite TV and radio programs. Then reverse roles. Report your findings to the class and compare the results with the entire class.

1. Est-ce que tu regardes des feuilletons? Quel est ton feuilleton préféré?
2. Regardes-tu les mêmes[1] feuilletons toutes les semaines? Lesquels[2] regardes-tu toujours?
3. Quand et où écoutes-tu la radio? Dans ta voiture le matin? Le soir à la maison, dans ta chambre?
4. Quelles émissions écoutes-tu à la radio? Le hit parade? Les infos? Les infos routières? Sur quelle fréquence?
5. Qui est ton animateur / ton animatrice préféré(e) à la radio?
6. Qui est ton présentateur / ta présentatrice préféré(e) à la télé?
7. Quels programmes est-ce que tu regardes le soir à la télé? Le JT? Des divertissements? Sur quelle(s) chaîne(s)?
8. Quelle est la chaîne télévisée que tu regardes le plus? Pourquoi?
9. Quelle est la chaîne télévisée que tu regardes le moins? Pourquoi?
10. Est-ce que tu zappes souvent? Es-tu un zappeur / une zappeuse? Qui a la télécommande chez toi?

---

[1]*same* [2]*Which ones*

Structure 1

Le passé composé avec le verbe *avoir*

Online Study Center
ACE, Language Skills
Practice

In previous chapters you learned two forms of the indicative mood: the present tense and the near future, as well as the imperative mood.

The present tense (**le présent**)

J'écoute le prof.   *I listen / am listening / do listen to the professor.*

Commands (**l'impératif**)

Écoute le prof!   *Listen to the professor!*

The near future (**le futur proche**)

Je vais écouter le prof.   *I am going to listen to the professor.*

Now you are going to learn a fourth form, the past tense, as expressed by the **passé composé.** This is the form that is used to talk about actions that were completed in the past. Just like the present tense, the **passé composé** has three possible translations in English.

J'ai écouté le prof.   *I listened to the professor. / I have listened to the professor. / I did listen to the professor.*

- The **passé composé** is formed by combining an auxiliary verb (also called a helping verb) with a past participle. For most verbs, the auxiliary verb is **avoir,** but for a few, **être** is used. For now, we'll concentrate on the **passé composé** with **avoir.**

  In the preceding example, **J'ai écouté le prof, ai** is the *auxiliary verb* **avoir** and **écouté** is the *past participle*. Here is the complete conjugation of the verb **écouter** in the **passé composé** with **avoir.**

écouter	
j'**ai** écouté	nous **avons** écouté
tu **as** écouté	vous **avez** écouté
il / elle / on **a** écouté	ils / elles **ont** écouté

- In English, regular past participles end in *-ed,* for example, *I haven't watch**ed** TV* or *I have work**ed** a lot.* In French, each group of verbs has a different ending for the past participle.

  1. For **-er** verbs, such as **manger, acheter, payer, parler, travailler,** etc., the past participle ends in **é.**

     J'ai **regardé** la télé.   *I watched / have watched TV.*
     Tu as **mangé** un sandwich.   *You ate / have eaten a sandwich.*

  2. For **-ir** verbs, such as **finir, réussir, choisir, obéir, bâtir,** etc., the past participle ends in **i.**

     Paul a **fini** ses devoirs.   *Paul finished / has finished his homework.*

     Nous avons **choisi** un bon repas. *We chose / have chosen a good meal.*

3. For regular **-re** verbs, such as **vendre, attendre, entendre, descendre, répondre, rendre,** the past participle ends in **u:**

J'ai **vendu** ma machine à laver.	*I sold / have sold my washing machine.*
Tu as **attendu** ton petit ami.	*You waited / have waited for your boyfriend.*

- Some past participles are irregular. You will need to memorize these past participles since they do not follow any particular rule.

être → été

J'ai **été** en Afrique en 1990.	*I was in Africa in 1990.*

avoir → eu

J'ai **eu** un zéro à l'examen de mathématiques.	*I got a zero on the math exam.*

faire → fait

Tu as **fait** tes courses à Carrefour.	*You did your grocery shopping at Carrefour.*

prendre → pris

comprendre → compris

apprendre → appris

Tu as **pris** le métro.	*You took the metro.*
Vous avez **compris** la leçon.	*You understood the lesson.*
Ils ont **appris** à nager.	*They learned how to swim.*

mettre → mis

J'ai **mis** ma robe blanche.	*I wore my white dress.*

vouloir → voulu

Le petit garçon a **voulu** manger une glace pour le dîner.	*The little boy wanted ice cream for dinner.*

pouvoir → pu

J'ai **pu** finir mes devoirs à temps.	*I was able to finish my homework on time.*

boire → bu

J'ai **bu** un Orangina.	*I drank an Orangina.*

VÉRIFIEZ VOTRE COMPRÉHENSION

Go back to the conversation between Karim and Yasmina on page 218. Identify the verbs that are in the **passé composé.** What are the infinitives of those verbs?

Pratiquons!

A. Une soirée à la maison. Do you remember Anou and Gérard from Chapter 2? Now you will see what they did last evening. Put the verbs in brackets in the **passé composé.**

Answer Key: 1. ont mangé 2. a préparé 3. a choisi 4. ont parlé 5. ont été 6. ont bu 7. ont pris 8. a débarrassé 9. a nettoyé 10. ont regardé

Hier, Gérard et Anou (1) _____ (manger) à la maison. Gérard (2) _____ (préparer) un poulet rôti. Anou (3) _____ (choisir) un vin rouge pour accompagner la viande. À table, ils (4) _____ (parler) de leurs prochaines vacances d'hiver dans les Alpes. Ce n'est pas la première fois qu'ils vont en Suisse. Ils y (5) _____ (être) deux fois déjà. Tout en parlant[1], Gérard et Anou (6) _____ (boire) toute la bouteille de vin! Ils (7) _____ (prendre) du café pour ne pas s'endormir[2].

Après le dîner, Anou (8) _____ (débarrasser[3]) la table et Gérard (9) _____ (nettoyer) la cuisine. Ensuite, ils (10) _____ (regarder) leur série préférée: *Les maîtresses de maison désespérées* avec Felicity Huffman.

Verify that students are choosing only verbs that are conjugated with **avoir** at this point.

Answer Key Ex. B: 1. Il a acheté du pain. 2. Il a attendu le bus. 3. Il a pris le bus. 4. Il a mis un tee-shirt. 5. Il a fait du jogging. 6. Il a été à un café. / Il a pris un café. 7. Il a préparé le dîner. 8. Il a dormi.

B. Qu'est-ce que Jérôme a fait hier? Look at the pictures and tell what Jérôme did yesterday.

1.

2.

3.

4.

5.

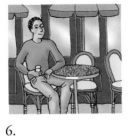

6.

7.

8.

---

[1] *While talking* [2] *in order not to fall asleep* [3] *to clear*

Structure 2

Online Study Center
ACE, Language Skills
Practice

La négation et les questions au passé composé

- When negating the **passé composé,** place **ne/n'** before the auxiliary verb and **pas** after the auxiliary verb.

  Fatou **n'**a **pas** regardé la télé hier. *Fatou did not watch TV yesterday.*
  Nous **n'**avons **pas** fini de faire le ménage. *We have not finished cleaning.*
  Mes amis **n'**ont **pas** voulu voir le film *My friends did not want to*
  Matrix Reloaded. *see Matrix Reloaded.*

- Question formation in the **passé composé** is the same as for the present tense.

  1. **Est-ce que** can be placed at the beginning of the sentence.

     Est-ce que tu as pris une aspirine? *Did you take an aspirin?*

  2. Intonation can be used for short yes/no questions.

     Tu as acheté une nouvelle voiture? *Did you buy a new car? / You bought a new car?*

  3. **N'est-ce pas?** can be placed at the end of the sentence.

     Vous avez parlé au prof, **n'est-ce pas?** *You talked to the professor, right?*

VÉRIFIEZ VOTRE COMPRÉHENSION

Go back to the dialogue on page 218 and change the sentences in the **passé composé** to the negative.

If you are teaching inversion, point out that it is the auxiliary verb that is inverted with the subject pronoun in the **passé composé.**

Pratiquons!

A. Non, non! Your classmate is trying to figure out what Franck did yesterday. Answer your classmate's questions in the negative, as in the model.

MODÈLE: acheter une voiture

—*Franck a acheté une voiture?*

—*Mais non! Hier, Franck n'a pas acheté de voiture!*

1. acheter des CD
2. prendre un avion
3. fumer dans la voiture
4. mettre ses chaussures de sport
5. acheter du vin
6. manger de la glace
7. être dans une boîte de nuit
8. danser

Answer Key: 1. Il a acheté des CD? / Mais non, il n'a pas acheté de CD. 2. Il a pris un avion? / Mais non, il n'a pas pris d'avion. 3. Il a fumé dans la voiture? / Mais non, il n'a pas fumé dans la voiture. 4. Il a mis ses chaussures de sport? / Mais non, il n'a pas mis ses chaussures de sport. 5. Il a nagé? / Mais non, il n'a pas nagé. 6. Il a mangé de la glace? / Mais non, il n'a pas mangé de glace. 7. Il a été dans une boîte de nuit? / Mais non, il n'a pas été dans une boîte de nuit. 8. Il a dansé? / Mais non, il n'a pas dansé.

🗣️ B. Et toi, qu'est-ce que tu as fait hier? Interview one of your classmates to find out what he or she did yesterday. Then reverse roles.

1. Est-ce que tu as pris ta voiture hier? As-tu écouté la radio dans ta voiture?
2. Est-ce que tu as mangé au restaurant? À la maison? Qu'est-ce que tu as mangé?
3. Est-ce que tu as regardé la télé hier soir ou hier après-midi? Quel programme as-tu regardé?
4. Est-ce que tu as travaillé hier? Où? Combien d'heures?
5. Est-ce que tu as fait du sport? Quel sport? Où?
6. Est-ce que tu as rendu visite à tes amis? Qu'est-ce que vous avez fait? Avez-vous parlé? Écouté de la musique? etc.
7. Est-ce que tu as appelé quelqu'un au téléphone? Qui?
8. Est-ce que tu as acheté quelque chose hier? Quoi?
9. Combien d'heures as-tu dormi? As-tu fait de beaux rêves[1] ou as-tu eu un cauchemar[2]?

Portrait personnel

Write a paragraph in which you describe the highlights of what your partner did yesterday. Compare your partner's activities with your own.

🌀 MODÈLE: Hier, Sam a fait du sport pendant trois heures. Elle a joué au tennis et au volley. Moi, j'ai regardé un film …

L'Opéra de Montréal. Préférez-vous voir les spectacles en direct, à la télé ou sur vidéo cassette ou DVD? Pourquoi?

---

[1]*nice dreams* [2]*nightmare*

Partie I: Chez le marchand de journaux 🎧

Do you like reading newspapers, weekly magazines, or fashion magazines?
The French and other Francophones get their daily news from the newspapers,
the TV, and/or the radio. In this section, you are going to see the different
newspapers and magazines that people read in France and in Quebec.

Vous êtes à Paris chez le marchand de journaux. Regardez comment le
vendeur range[1] les journaux et les magazines par catégories.

un magazine people

une revue de mode

un magazine hebdomadaire

un magazine hebdomadaire

un journal quotidien

[1] *arranges*

un journal quotidien

un guide des programmes télévisés

un magazine de santé

une revue critique de cinéma

une revue de cuisine

Aline habite à Québec. Samedi matin, elle est allée chez le marchand de journaux du coin. Elle a acheté un journal, *Le Soleil* du Québec, et une revue de mode, *Châtelaine*. Elle a payé 2 dollars canadiens pour le journal et 3,95 dollars pour la revue de mode. Ensuite, elle est entrée dans un café pour lire les journaux et boire un thé au lait. Elle n'a pas pu résister à un croissant encore tout chaud du four. Quel bon petit déjeuner, n'est-ce pas?

Vous avez bien compris?

#1: Even though the categories are indicated in French next to each cover, students are asked to guess the meaning of the categories in this activity.

1. Go back to the newsstand in Paris. Can you guess from the titles and the covers of the newspapers and magazines what types of periodicals these are? Can you place them into categories in English?
2. With a classmate, name an American newspaper or magazine that is equivalent to each of the following French publications.

   a. *L'Express*
   b. *Châtelaine*
   c. *Cahiers du Cinéma*
   d. *Le Monde*
   e. *Maxi Cuisine*
   f. *Top Santé*
   g. *Télé*

#1: Answer Key. Newspapers and magazines from France: Paris Match: entertainment magazine; Le Nouvel Observateur: weekly news magazine; Marie-Claire: fashion magazine; L'Express: weekly news magazine; Le Figaro: daily newspaper; Le Monde: daily newspaper; Télé-magazine: TV guide; Top Santé: health magazine; Maxi Cuisine: cooking magazine; Cahiers du cinéma: movie review

#2: Answer key. Possible answers: a. Time / Newsweek / US News and World Report b. Glamour / Redbook c. Preview d. New York Times / Washington Post e. Bon Appétit! f. Health g. TV Guide

Vocabulaire essentiel

Online Study Center
Flashcards, ACE, Language Skills Practice

Les médias (2)

Chez le marchand de journaux

un quotidien	*daily newspaper*
un hebdomadaire	*weekly magazine*
un mensuel	*monthly magazine*
un journal	*newspaper*
une revue de mode	*fashion magazine*
un magazine d'actualité	*news magazine*
un guide des programmes télévisés / un guide télé	*television guide*
la presse people	*entertainment magazines*
un magazine people	*entertainment magazine*
une revue de cuisine	*cooking magazine*
un magazine de santé	*health magazine*
une revue de sport	*sports magazine*

Les professionnels

un(e) journaliste
un(e) photographe
un(e) paparazzi

Les lecteurs

un lecteur / une lectrice	*reader*
un abonnement	*magazine/newspaper subscription*
un bulletin d'abonnement / un bon d'abonnement	*subscription form*
un(e) abonné(e)	*subscriber*

À vous!

A. Magazines et journaux. Give a French and an American title of a newspaper or magazine for each category listed.

1. une revue de mode mensuelle
2. un quotidien
3. une revue de cuisine
4. un magazine de santé
5. un magazine d'actualité hebdomadaire
6. un guide télé hebdomadaire
7. une revue critique de cinéma

B. Un abonnement. With a partner, fill out the following subscription forms for the French fashion magazine *Marie Claire* and for the French health magazine *Prima*.

MARIE CLAIRE ABONNEMENT
B 324 - 60732 Sainte-Geneviève Cedex
Téléphone: 08 25 12 02 18 *(0,15 € la min)*   Internet: http://abo.marieclaire.fr

Oui, je désire m'abonner pour 1 an (12 numéros) : 25 € (*) seulement au lieu de 30 €.

NOM...PRÉNOM...

ADRESSE ....

....

CODE POSTAL.............................VILLE ....

PAYS ....

❑ Ci-joint mon règlement par chèque à l'ordre de Marie Claire

❑ Je règle par carte bancaire   ❑ Amex   ❑ CB Visa

N° de carte ....Expire le...

Conformément à la loi «Informatique et Libertés», vous bénéficiez d'un droit d'accès et de rectification des données vous concernant. Sauf refus écrit de votre part auprès du Service Abonnement, ces informations pourront être utilisées par des tiers.

(*) Etranger envoi prioritaire: règlement par carte bancaire ou mandat international en €. Europe: 55 €. Etat-Unis, Canada: 63,50 €. Reste du monde: 85 €. DOM: 66,50 €. TOM: 119 €.   EP 43

Now, compare the prices of these two subscriptions with a subscription for an American fashion or health magazine. Which one is more expensive?

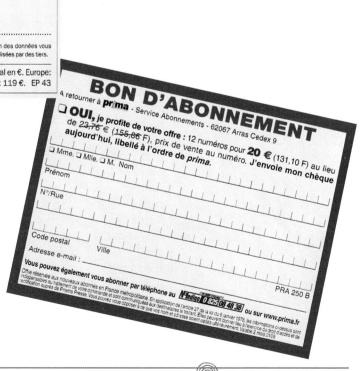

Online Study Center
ACE, Language Skills
Practice

Le passé composé avec le verbe *être*

- In *Structure 2* you learned the **passé composé** with the verb **avoir.**

  J'**ai mangé** une pomme.
  Tu **as compris** la leçon.
  Nous **avons été** en vacances à la plage.

  In French, not all verbs use the auxiliary verb **avoir** to form the **passé composé.** Some verbs form the **passé composé** with **être** as the auxiliary verb. To help you remember which verbs use **être,** look at the drawing **La maison d'être.** As you can see, most of the verbs in "The house of **être**" are verbs of motion.

Now, look at the past participles of the verbs in **La maison d'être.**

retourner	→	Pierrot est **retourné** à la maison.
aller	→	Un chien est **allé** faire une promenade.
rester	→	Le chat est **resté** sur le toit[1].
décéder	→	Quelqu'un[2] est **décédé.**
arriver	→	Pierrot est **arrivé** à la maison.
rentrer	→	Pierrot est **rentré** à la maison.
entrer	→	Pierrot est **entré** dans la maison.
monter	→	Luc est **monté** au premier étage.
passer	→	Un professeur est **passé** par la maison.
tomber	→	Un voleur[3] est **tombé** par la fenêtre.
sortir	→	Un voleur est **sorti** de la maison par la fenêtre.
partir	→	Un voleur est **parti** de la maison par la fenêtre.
descendre	→	Charles est **descendu** de la maison avec sa fiancée.
venir	→	Pierrot est **venu** à la maison.
revenir	→	Pierrot est **revenu** à la maison.
naître	→	Un petit bébé est **né.**
mourir	→	Quelqu'un est **mort.**

---

[1]*roof* [2]*Someone* [3]*thief*

- The past participles of verbs that are conjugated with **être** in the **passé composé** agree in number (singular or plural) and gender (masculine or feminine) with the subject of the sentence. (The past participles of verbs that use **avoir** in the **passé composé** do not agree with the subject.)

Samedi dernier, je suis allé(**e**) au cinéma.   *Last Saturday, I went to the movies.*
Samedi dernier tu es allé(**e**) au cinéma.
Samedi dernier, Bruno est allé au cinéma.
Samedi dernier, Élise est allé**e** au cinéma.

Samedi dernier, nous sommes allé(**e**)**s** au cinéma.
Samedi dernier, vous êtes allé(**e**)(**s**) au cinéma.
Samedi dernier, Anne et Éric sont allé**s** au cinéma.
Samedi dernier, Michelle et Julie sont allé**es** au cinéma.

- The negative of the **passé composé** with **être** is formed in the same way as the **passé composé** with **avoir.** The first part of the negative (**ne/n'**) is placed before **être** and the second part (**pas**) is placed after **être.**

Elle **n'**est **pas** partie avec son petit ami.
Nous **ne** sommes **pas** allés au restaurant.

- Interrogatives of the **passé composé** with **être** are formed in the same way as for the **passé composé** with **avoir.**

Using **est-ce que:** Est-ce que tu es rentré tard hier soir?
Using intonation: Tu es rentré tard hier soir?

VÉRIFIEZ VOTRE COMPRÉHENSION

1. Look at **La maison d'être** and think how you would say the following sentences in French:

   Pierrot went in the house. (*to go in* = **entrer dans**)
   Pierrot went upstairs (**en haut**).
   Pierrot fell down the stairs (**dans l'escalier**).
   Pierrot left.

2. Look at the following statements, paying particular attention to the endings of the past participles. What does each past participle agree with?

   Juliette est resté**e** en France deux ans.
   Éva et Sandra sont passé**es** chez moi à midi.
   Ils sont parti**s** en Martinique.
   Luc est arrivé**é** en classe en retard.

3. Go back to the paragraph where Aline bought a newspaper (p. 228). Why is there an **e** at the end of the past participle in the sentence **Aline est allée chez le marchand de journaux?** If Aline had gone to the newsstand with her brother, what would the past participle look like?

4. Are there any sentences in that paragraph in which the **passé composé** is conjugated with the verb **avoir?** Why are these verbs conjugated with **avoir?** Is there agreement of the past participle with the subject?

À l'écoute!

Transcript: 1. J'ai acheté un stylo. 2. Je mange une pomme. 3. J'ai compris la leçon. 4. J'ai fait une tarte. 5. Je choisis une robe rouge. 6. J'ai écouté la radio.

A. Présent ou passé composé? Indicate whether each sentence you hear is in the present or the **passé composé.**

1. _____ présent _____ passé composé
2. _____ présent _____ passé composé
3. _____ présent _____ passé composé
4. _____ présent _____ passé composé
5. _____ présent _____ passé composé
6. _____ présent _____ passé composé

Transcript: 1. Tu as payé. 2. Il est parti. 3. Ils sont allés. 4. Il a mis. 5. Ils ont trouvé. 6. Tu es sorti.

B. Être ou avoir? For each sentence you hear, indicate whether the auxiliary verb (the helping verb) is **être** or **avoir.**

1. _____ être _____ avoir   4. _____ être _____ avoir
2. _____ être _____ avoir   5. _____ être _____ avoir
3. _____ être _____ avoir   6. _____ être _____ avoir

Pratiquons!

Answer Key: 1. sont arrivées 2. est entrée 3. est tombée 4. est sortie 5. est allée 6. est venue 7. sont restées 8. sont montées 9. sont descendues 10. sont parties

A. Les enfants n'arrêtent jamais! Put the verbs in parentheses in the **passé composé.** Pay attention to the agreement of the past participle (Martine and Marine are twin girls!).

Martine et Marine sont des jumelles de 4 ans. Voici leur journée hier chez Papi et Mamie:

Martine et Marine (1) _____ (arriver) chez Papi et Mamie à dix heures. Martine (2) _____ (entrer) en courant[1] dans la maison et elle (3) _____ (tomber). Marine (4) _____ (sortir) dans le jardin en courant aussi et elle (5) _____ (aller) jouer directement dans le bac à sable[2]. Martine (6) _____ (venir) jouer avec Marine et elles (7) _____ (rester) un petit moment dans le bac à sable. Ensuite, Martine et Marine (8) _____ (monter) sur un arbre et elles (9) _____ (descendre) de l'arbre au moins[3] vingt fois! À treize heures, elles (10) _____ (partir) chez elles après un bon déjeuner et un matin mouvementé[4].

Answer Key: 1. a regardé 2. est retournée 3. a acheté 4. sont allés 5. a joué 6. a regardé 7. sont tombés 8. est restée

B. Qu'ont fait les célébrités? Look at how celebrities spend their free time. Decide first if the underlined present-tense verbs take **être** or **avoir** in the **passé composé.** Then, convert these sentences to the **passé composé.**

1. Vendredi soir, Leonardo DiCaprio regarde son feuilleton préféré à la télé.
2. La femme du président retourne au programme de Larry King.
3. Beyoncé achète une revue de mode à l'aéroport pour lire dans l'avion avant de partir en Europe.
4. Tous les acteurs de *Will et Grace* vont aux studios de Hollywood pour regarder en direct le dernier tournage[5] de la série *Everybody Loves Raymond*.
5. Le Docteur Phil joue avec ses chiens pour oublier ses problèmes.
6. Halle Berry regarde un documentaire très intéressant sur les chats.
7. Dans le film *Mission Impossible III*, Tom Cruise et Kerri Russell tombent d'une moto.
8. Dimanche matin, Penelope Cruz reste à la maison pour lire son journal tranquillement.

_____

[1]*running* [2]*sandbox* [3]*at least* [4]*busy* [5]*filming*

C. Entretien. Ask a classmate questions in the **passé composé,** based on the following cues. Then reverse roles.

1. Où / tu / aller / hier soir?
2. À quelle heure / tu / rentrer / à la maison hier après-midi?
3. À quelle heure / tu / arriver / à l'université?
4. Quand et où / tu / tomber?
5. Tes copains et toi / où / vous / sortir / le week-end dernier?
6. Comment / tu / venir / à l'université ce matin? À pied? En voiture? En autobus? En métro?
7. Tes parents et toi / quand et où / vous / partir / en vacances tous ensemble en famille?

Before beginning the activity, have students phrase the first couple of questions to make sure they are doing so correctly. If you are teaching inversion, ask them to vary between using **est-ce que** and inversion.

Portrait personnel

Write a short paragraph about what you did last weekend. Did you go to the movies? Did you watch a movie at home? Did you go out for dinner? Did you fix dinner at home for you and your friends? Did you go out shopping? Compare this to what your partner did, based on his/her responses in activity C.

À vous de parler!

A. À vous de jouer! Form groups of three or four students each. Each group describes a TV or radio show to the rest of the class. The other groups guess which show is being described. The groups who are guessing may ask questions of the presenters, but only questions that can be answered by **oui** or by **non!**

You could make this game an extra-credit activity: the group that guesses right the most is the one that wins an extra point for homework, for example.

B. En direct! Work with a partner. Pretend that one of you is a famous TV anchor. You are interviewing a famous figure—actor/actress, writer, researcher, singer, politician, etc. Your partner is the interviewee and you are the interviewer. The interviewer asks questions, mainly in the **passé composé.** For example, to an actor/actress: Did you go to the Oscars last year? Did you see lots of your friends there? Did you go with your husband? What did you wear? How did you arrive? Where did you stay? etc. Role-play your interview in front of the class.

Before conducting this activity, you may want to brainstorm with students for possible questions and answers using the **passé composé.** (Remind students that a journalist would use **vous** in his/her questions.) You may also want to bring several microphones (or make some with paper) to class to make the activity more realistic.

Key words:

l'année dernière	*last year*
la semaine dernière	*last week*
le mois dernier	*last month*
samedi dernier / lundi dernier	*last Saturday / Monday*
en décembre dernier	*last December*
hier matin / après-midi	*yesterday morning / afternoon*
hier soir	*last night*
avant-hier	*the day before yesterday*

Point out that the French pay an annual tax for having a TV.

La télévision en France est comme ça

Compared to American television, French television appears to offer a very limited selection, at least at first glance. As you saw earlier in the chapter, there are four broadcast networks in France: TF1, France 2, France 3, and France 5, which are available to anyone with an antenna (and good reception!), and which offer a variety of French, British, and American television shows. The latter are often dubbed into French. For those who have cable, several more stations are available. These include those previously mentioned (Canal +, Arte, M6, TV5, and Canal Jimmy), as well as LCI, an all-news network, and the Assemblée Nationale channel, which shows the proceedings of the French National Assembly.

To Americans accustomed to cable, and now digital cable, this seems like a very limited selection indeed! So how do the French deal with a limited number of choices? First, they tend to rely on their television less for entertainment than do Americans. The news comes on at 8:00 P.M., attesting to the fact that the French consider television primarily a source of information and use the prime-time hours for that purpose. Results of a recent survey concerning programming in France may surprise you: when asked what they would like to see more of on television, the number one response from the French was documentaries. This was followed by cultural programs and films, as second and third choices. Sports, sitcoms and series, and game shows were all at the very bottom of the list. (And in case you think that it was the older population that voted for these choices, you should know that 50% of the 24–34 age group proclaimed a need for more documentaries, while 57% of the 18–24 age group asked for more films!)

Second, movies (seen on the big screen) remain extremely popular in France. Movie theaters continue to give discounts to young people, students, large families, and retirees to allow them to attend often. Entertainment is thus moved outside of the home and shared with others. Finally, the French have started to do what many Americans have done to increase their viewing options at home: they purchase satellite dishes. Use of a satellite in France allows viewers to receive programs from all over Europe, shown in their original language. In this way, television can be not only entertainment, but also a learning experience!

Réfléchissons

1. How many television stations do you currently receive? How many of those do you watch on a regular basis? Would you willingly give up those that you don't watch? Why or why not?
2. What would you personally like to see more of on television? How does this compare to the French response?
3. Are you interested in being able to view programs from other countries in their original language? Why or why not?
4. What role do you think Americans in general assign to TV viewing?

Partie II: À la une[1]! 🎧

You are listening to the news on a French radio station, and you hear the following news clips. Read along while you listen to your In-Text Audio CD.

Aujourd'hui, c'est l'anniversaire de la mort de Marie Curie. Madame Curie est née en Pologne en 1867 et elle est partie à Paris alors qu'elle était[2] encore une jeune fille. Elle y a vécu[3] pendant le reste de sa vie, et y a rencontré son mari, Pierre Curie. Marie Curie a gagné deux prix Nobel dans sa vie. Elle a partagé le premier prix, en physique, avec son mari Pierre et le physicien Antoine Becquerel, pour leur recherche concernant les propriétés radioactives de l'uranium. Elle a gagné le deuxième prix en chimie, pour la découverte de deux autres éléments chimiques, le radium et le polonium. Marie Curie est morte en 1934.

Ce soir, à la Sorbonne, le physicien anglais Stephen Hawkins rendra[4] hommage à Marie Curie. La cérémonie est ouverte au public.

Un terrible accident a causé un immense embouteillage[5] pendant les heures de pointe ce matin à Paris. Les freins[6] d'un gros camion[7] chargé de journaux ont lâché[8] à un croisement très fréquenté. Il a heurté[9] deux voitures et ensuite une boulangerie, qui a pris feu[10] peu de temps après le choc. Les journaux dans le camion ont aussi brûlé[11], provoquant encore de petits incendies partout. Les pompiers[12] et le SAMU[13] sont arrivés; ils ont fermé la rue pendant plus de quatre heures. Les pompiers y sont toujours. Il y a trois personnes à l'hôpital, dont une grièvement blessée, mais, miraculeusement, il n'y a pas eu de morts dans cet accident.

Et finalement, un incident comique: Ce matin, à Toulouse, il y a eu un crime bizarre. En plein jour[14], un homme est entré dans un bureau de tabac et a demandé de l'argent et des cigarettes. Il a prétendu[15] avoir une bombe, et a menacé de la faire exploser si on ne lui donnait pas ce qu'il voulait[16]. Il a même montré un détonateur, ce qui a fait très peur aux employés. Il a de nouveau demandé de l'argent et des cigarettes: on lui en a donné. Mais les employés du bureau de tabac ont remarqué qu'en sortant il a utilisé le détonateur pour allumer une de ses cigarettes! La police a arrêté le voleur peu de temps après dans un parc. Quelle a été sa bombe? Une orange! Quel a été son détonateur? Un briquet[17]!

Vous avez bien compris?

Briefly answer the following questions. (A few words will suffice.)
1. En quelle année est-ce que Marie Curie est née?
2. Quand est-ce qu'elle est morte?
3. Quels prix est-ce que Marie Curie a gagnés?
4. Deux groupes différents sont allés aider à l'accident à Paris. Lesquels[18]?
5. Qui est mort dans l'accident?
6. Qu'est-ce qui a causé l'accident?
7. Qu'est-ce qui s'est passé[19] à Toulouse?
8. Qu'est-ce que le voleur a demandé?
9. Est-ce que le voleur avait vraiment une bombe?
10. Est-ce qu'il a réussi son vol[20]? Expliquez votre réponse.

Answer Key: 1. en 1867 2. en 1934 3. le prix Nobel de physique et le prix Nobel de chimie 4. les pompiers et le SAMU 5. Il n'y a pas eu de morts. 6. Les freins d'un camion ont lâché. 7. un crime bizarre 8. des cigarettes et de l'argent 9. Non (c'était une orange). 10. Non. La police l'a arrêté.

---

[1]*On the front page* [2]*while she was* [3]*lived* [4]*will pay* [5]*traffic jam* [6]*brakes* [7]*truck* [8]*failed* [9]*ran into* [10]*fire* [11]*burned* [12]*firefighters* [13]*le SAMU = le Service d'aide médicale d'urgence* [14]*In broad daylight* [15]*claimed* [16]*what he wanted* [17]*cigarette lighter* [18]*Which ones* [19]*What happened* [20]*theft*

Vocabulaire essentiel

Les événements de la vie

Événements positifs

jouer dans un groupe (musical)
jouer dans un orchestre
chanter dans une chorale
chanter dans un groupe (musical)
donner un concert
participer à un match (sportif)
gagner un match
participer à une manifestation *(a demonstration)*
participer à un défilé *(parade)*
publier
    un poème
    un livre
    un article
    une lettre à l'éditeur
donner une conférence
écouter une conférence

Événements négatifs

perdre un match (sportif)
avoir un accident
être victime d'un crime
être volé(e)   *to be robbed*
un vol   *a robbery*

Expansion personnelle

Événements positifs

gagner un prix
    le prix Nobel
    le prix Pulitzer (prix américain pour le journalisme)
    le prix Goncourt (prix littéraire français)
sauver la vie à quelqu'un

Événements négatifs

causer un accident
commettre un crime
être cambriolé(e)   *to be burglarized*
un cambriolage   *a burglary (a break-in)*

À vous!

A. Peut-être ou peut-être pas. Tell how certain it is that you will accomplish each of the following things in your lifetime. Use adverbs such as **certainement, probablement, peut-être, probablement pas, certainement pas,** etc. in your response.

MODÈLE: publier une lettre à l'éditeur dans le journal de votre ville

> *Je vais probablement publier une lettre à l'éditeur dans le journal de ma ville un jour. / Je ne vais probablement jamais publier une lettre à l'éditeur dans le journal de ma ville.*

1. donner un concert de musique classique
2. participer à une manifestation
3. avoir un accident
4. participer à un match sportif
5. jouer dans un groupe (de rock)
6. écouter une conférence
7. commettre un crime
8. publier un poème ou un article
9. sauver la vie à quelqu'un
10. chanter dans une chorale

Answers will vary widely. To correct, you might have students categorize their answers together, telling you what they are certain they will or will not do, etc.

To expand, choose some celebrities and have students make predictions about them. For example: Josh Groban va certainement donner un concert, mais il ne va probablement pas commettre de crime.

B. Qu'est-ce qu'ils ont fait? Tell what the following people did last night. Choose any logical activity, and use the **passé composé.**

> **MODÈLE:** Grant Hill, joueur de basket américain
>
> *Il a participé à un match sportif. / Son équipe[1] a gagné un match.*

1. Yo Yo Ma, celliste
2. John Grisham, auteur
3. Stephen Hawkins, physicien
4. Kelly Clarkson, chanteuse
5. Mary Jo Pierce, joueuse de tennis
6. Jimmy Hoffa, Jr., chef de syndicat[2]
7. Les membres de Coldplay
8. Oscar de la Hoya, boxeur
9. Votre professeur de français

Answer Key. Possible answers: 1. Il a donné un concert. 2. Il a publié un livre. 3. Il a donné / écouté une conférence. 4. Elle a chanté / a donné un concert. 5. Elle a participé à un match de tennis. 6. Il a participé à une manifestation. 7. Ils ont donné un concert. 8. Il a gagné / perdu un match. 9. *Answers will vary.*

Structure 4

Le pronom interrogatif *quel*

Online Study Center
ACE, Language Skills Practice

The truck driver whose accident you read about in the *Continuons!* section (p. 235) is reporting his accident to the police. Look carefully at the forms of the pronoun **quel.**

🎧 *Au commissariat de police*

LE POLICIER: Monsieur, **quel** est votre nom?
LE CAMIONNEUR: Christian Sounage.
LE POLICIER: **Quelle** est votre adresse?
LE CAMIONNEUR: 36, rue Pasteur. 75000 Paris.
LE POLICIER: **Quelle** est votre assurance?
LE CAMIONNEUR: C'est le Groupe Azur.

As a cultural note, tell the students that in small towns and cities the police station is called a **gendarmerie** and the police officers **gendarmes.**

---

[1] *team* [2] *union leader*

LE POLICIER: **Quels** sont les dégâts[1] causés par l'accident?
LE CAMIONNEUR: J'ai heurté deux voitures et, après, une boulangerie. La boulangerie a pris feu.
LE POLICIER: **Quelles** sont vos pertes[2] matérielles?
LE CAMIONNEUR: J'ai perdu toute ma cargaison de journaux.

- After reading this dialogue, can you tell what the four different forms of the pronoun **quel** are, and why the forms vary?

    If you said that each of these forms corresponds in gender and number with the noun it refers to, you guessed right! For example, in the second and third questions, **quelle** is in the feminine singular form because it agrees with **adresse** *(f.s.)* and **assurance** *(f.s.)*.

- The pronoun **quel** can be followed by the verb **être** or by the noun its question refers to.

Quel + *noun* + *verb*   Quel + *être* + *noun*

Quelle voiture a causé l'accident?   Quelle est ta voiture préférée?
Quel article as-tu publié?   Quels sont les articles les plus intéressants?

- In questions in the **passé composé** using **quel,** the past participle agrees in number and gender with the noun that **quel** modifies if the noun is the direct object of the verb. Look at the following examples.

Quelle musique as-tu écouté**e**?
Quels programmes est-ce que tu as regardé**s**?
Quelles robes avez-vous acheté**es**?

Pratiquons!

A. Déclaration de vol. Your roommate stole some of your belongings and disappeared. You are reporting the robbery to a police officer (your partner). Complete the sentences with the correct form of the pronoun **quel** and with other missing words when necessary (be logical!). When you are finished, present your dialogue to the class.

VOUS: Bonjour, Monsieur le policier. Je voudrais déclarer un vol.
LE POLICIER: (1) _____ vol voulez-vous déclarer?
VOUS: Le vol de mon appartement par ma (mon) camarade de chambre.
LE POLICIER: (2) _____ est votre adresse *(f.)*?
VOUS: C'est (3) _____.
LE POLICIER: (4) _____ est le nom de votre camarade de chambre?
VOUS: Elle (Il) s'appelle (5) _____.
LE POLICIER: (6) _____ est sa profession?
VOUS: Elle (Il) est (7) _____.
LE POLICIER: (8) _____ voiture conduit-elle (il)?
VOUS: Elle (Il) conduit une (9) _____.
LE POLICIER: (10) _____ est la couleur de sa voiture?
VOUS: Elle est (11) _____.
LE POLICIER: (12) _____ est la couleur de ses cheveux?

You may want to reassure students by telling them that they are not responsible for knowing the gender of nouns that they have not seen before, such as **assurance, dégâts,** and **pertes,** which appear in the dialogue for demonstration purposes only. The gender will be provided next to nouns that students are seeing for the first time.

Answer Key (Answers will vary for #3, 5, 7, 9, 11, 13, 15, 17, 19):
1. Quel 2. Quelle 4. Quel 6. Quelle 8. Quelle 10. Quelle 12. Quelle 14. Quelle 16. Quels 18. Quels

_____
[1] *damage* [2] *losses*

VOUS: Ils sont (13) _____.

LE POLICIER: (14) _____ est la couleur de ses yeux?

VOUS: Ils sont (15) _____.

LE POLICIER: (16) _____ objets personnels *(m.)* est-ce qu'elle (il) a volés?

VOUS: (17) _____. *(List some personal items.)*

LE POLICIER: (18) _____ meubles est-ce qu'elle (il) a emportés[1]?

VOUS: (19) _____.

LE POLICIER: Merci de votre déclaration. Nous vous appellerons dès que[2] nous trouverons votre camarade de chambre.

B. Correcteur d'erreurs.

Pierce Brosnan, who just finished filming his last James Bond movie, was interviewed for a popular magazine. The journalist who wrote the interview made some grammatical mistakes. You are in charge of proofreading the article and correcting his mistakes, which are underlined. Write your corrections in the spaces provided. Pay particular attention to past participle agreements in questions in the **passé composé** with **quel**.

LE JOURNALISTE: Bonjour, Monsieur Brosnan. Quelle (1) _____ est le titre du dernier James Bond que vous avez tourné?

PB: Je ne peux pas vous le dire! C'est un secret!

LE JOURNALISTE: Quelles actrices avez-vous rencontré (2) _____ dans le film?

PB: Karen Mulder et Sharon Stone.

LE JOURNALISTE: Quel (3) _____ sont leurs rôles?

PB: Karen Mulder a un rôle de séductrice et Sharon Stone a le rôle de la méchante femme calculatrice qui veut éliminer James Bond.

LE JOURNALISTE: Quelle (4) _____ est le groupe musical qui a composé la bande sonore[3]?

PB: Paul McCartney a composé toute la musique du film.

LE JOURNALISTE: Quelles voitures avez-vous conduit (5) _____?

PB: Pour mon dernier James Bond j'ai conduit des Mercedes.

LE JOURNALISTE: Quelle (6) _____ sont vos projets *(m.)* maintenant que vous avez terminé le tournage de votre dernier James Bond?

PB: Je vais passer tout mon temps libre avec ma famille.

Portrait personnel

Write a short paragraph about an unpleasant incident that happened to you. You may use the following questions as a springboard: Did anyone ever break into your house or apartment? Or, have you ever been robbed? Your purse taken? Your wallet? Your car? Did you see the thief? What did the thief do? What did you do? What did they steal from your house? Have you had a car accident? What happened? What did you hit? What hit you? What did you do?

Refer students to the events recounted on p. 235 as a model. If students have experienced neither of these events themselves, ask them to write about someone who has, or make up a story. Publish these accounts in a class newspaper.

[1] *did s/he take* [2] *as soon as* [3] *sound track*

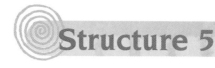

Structure 5

Le passé composé avec les pronoms *y* et *en* et avec les adverbes

• When the pronouns **y** and **en** accompany a verb in the **passé composé,** they follow the same rule as when they accompany a verb in the present: the pronoun is placed *before* the conjugated verb. In the case of the **passé composé,** the conjugated verb is the auxiliary verb (**avoir** or **être**).

Nous sommes allés **à Paris.**	*We went to Paris.*
Nous **y** sommes allés.	*We went there.*
J'ai mangé **à ce restaurant** hier.	*I ate at that restaurant yesterday.*
J'**y** ai mangé hier.	*I ate there yesterday.*
J'ai mangé **de la pizza.**	*I ate some pizza.*
J'**en** ai mangé.	*I ate some (of it).*
Ma mère a bu **du vin.**	*My mother drank some wine.*
Ma mère **en** a bu.	*My mother drank some (of it).*

If the sentence is in the negative, **ne** precedes the pronoun, and **pas** follows the conjugated verb.

Je n'ai pas mangé **dans ce restaurant.**	*I didn't eat in that restaurant.*
Je n'**y** ai pas mangé.	*I didn't eat there.*
Mon père n'a pas mangé **de salade.**	*My father didn't eat any salad.*
Mon père n'**en** a pas mangé.	*My father didn't eat any (of it).*

• When an adverb accompanies the **passé composé,** its placement will vary depending on the type of adverb that it is.

  Short adverbs (those that are not based on an adjective) generally come immediately after the conjugated verb (i.e., the auxiliary).

Elle a **bien** compris la conférence.	*She understood the lecture well.*
Nous sommes **vite** descendus en ville.	*We went downtown quickly.*
J'ai **trop** mangé hier soir!	*I ate too much last night!*

If the verb is in the negative, the adverb comes after **pas.**

Je n'ai pas **bien** compris la conférence.	*I didn't understand the lecture well.*

Long adverbs (those that are formed from an adjective), in contrast, normally come after the past participle.

Elle a parlé **constamment** ce soir.	*She talked constantly tonight.*
Nous avons conduit **rapidement** sur l'autoroute.	*We drove fast on the highway.*
Mon père était avec moi; je n'ai pas conduit **rapidement!**	*My father was with me; I didn't drive fast!*

VÉRIFIEZ VOTRE COMPRÉHENSION

1. Go back to the radio news clips (p. 235). Do any of the verbs appear with the pronoun **y** or **en?** Which ones? What does the pronoun stand for in each case?

2. Can you put those sentences in the negative? What would they look like?

3. Are there any adverbs? Underline them.

4. Where are they placed in relation to the verb? Can you explain why?

Pratiquons!

A. Logique / pas logique. Answer the following questions in the affirmative or the negative, based on what you feel is a logical response. Use a pronoun (**y** or **en**) to replace the italicized noun in the question. If you give a negative response, follow it with a logical alternative.

> MODÈLE: Annie et Jean-Pierre sont allés *à la librairie* pour regarder un film?
>
> *Mais non, ils n'y sont pas allés! Il sont allés au cinéma.*

1. Annie et Jean-Pierre sont allés *au supermarché* pour acheter du riz?
2. Ils sont allés *au supermarché* pour acheter du pain?
3. Ils ont mangé *du fromage* après le dîner?
4. Annie et Jean-Pierre ont voyagé *à Bruxelles* pour pratiquer leur anglais?
5. Ils ont bu *de la bière* avec le petit déjeuner?
6. Ils ont pris *des photos* pendant les vacances?
7. Ils ont voyagé *à Paris* pour voir la tour Eiffel?

B. Tu y es allé(e)? Tu en as mangé? Take turns asking and answering the following questions in the affirmative or the negative, replacing the noun in each question with **y** or **en.**

> MODÈLE: Tu as voyagé en France?
>
> *Oui, j'y ai voyagé. / Non, je n'y ai pas voyagé.*

1. Tu as mangé des cuisses de grenouille?
2. Tu es allé(e) au cinéma cette semaine?
3. Tu as voyagé au Canada?
4. Tu as bu du vin français?
5. Tu as pris de la pizza hier soir?
6. Tu es allé(e) en classe hier?
7. Tu as mangé des céréales ce matin?
8. Tu as voyagé à New York récemment?

Online Study Center
ACE, Language Skills Practice

C. Comment est-ce que tu l'as fait? Use adverbs to tell how you did each of the following activities yesterday. Be sure to put the verb in the **passé composé.** Suggested adverbs: **beaucoup, peu, trop, bien, vite, souvent, constamment, rarement, rapidement, soigneusement** *(carefully)*, **intelligemment, tristement, joyeusement, tranquillement.**

MODÈLE: manger

J'ai trop mangé hier. / J'ai mangé rapidement hier.

1. étudier
2. aller en classe
3. dormir
4. parler au téléphone
5. faire mes devoirs
6. regarder la télé
7. manger
8. écouter la radio

Structure 6

Les verbes *lire, dire* et *écrire*

There are three irregular verbs in French that are frequently used when talking about the media, and which have similar conjugations. These are the verbs **lire** *(to read),* **dire** *(to say),* and **écrire** *(to write).* Their conjugations in the present indicative are in the following chart, along with their past participles. From now on, when we introduce a new verb, we will give the past participle as well as the present tense. Unless otherwise indicated, the auxiliary verb is always **avoir.**

Notice the similarities between these three verbs, but also the very irregular **vous** form of the verb **dire.**

lire		dire		écrire	
je lis	nous lisons	je dis	nous disons	j'écris	nous écrivons
tu lis	vous lisez	tu dis	vous dites	tu écris	vous écrivez
il lit	ils lisent	il dit	ils disent	il écrit	ils écrivent
Past participle: lu		dit		écrit	

Note how these verbs are used in context:

Le matin, je **lis** toujours le journal avant d'aller au travail. Normalement, mon père ne **lit** pas le journal le matin; il préfère **lire** le soir, pendant qu'il regarde la télé.

Quand j'arrive au travail, je **lis** mon e-mail, et j'y réponds. Je parle moins fréquemment au téléphone maintenant; j'**écris** des e-mails à mes collègues dans le monde entier[1]. Nous **disons** que cela cause moins d'interruption que le téléphone. Notre patron[2] **dit** que c'est gratuit!

Ma mère **dit** que je passe trop de temps à l'ordinateur. C'est peut-être vrai! Hier soir, j'**ai lu** un journal français sur Internet, et ensuite j'**ai écrit** un e-mail à un ami au Texas. En tout, j'ai passé trois heures devant l'ordinateur. Que le temps passe vite! Finalement, ma mère **a dit** qu'elle avait besoin[3] de l'ordinateur. Elle y a passé deux heures!

---

[1]*the whole world / all over the world* [2]*boss* [3]*needed*

Vérifiez votre compréhension

1. In the last chapter, we talked about certain patterns that occur in irregular verbs. Do you see any familiar patterns here?

2. We asked you to notice that the **vous** form of **dire** is very irregular. What exactly is irregular about it? Can you think of any other verbs with a similar ending?

3. Most of the verbs in the examples in **Structure 6** are in the affirmative. What would the negative of each verb be? (Pay attention to whether the verb is in the present or the **passé composé**!)

Point out that both être (vous êtes) and faire (vous faites) have similar endings. These are the only other verbs in French that do not end in -ez in the second person plural of the present indicative.

À l'écoute!

A. Combien de personnes font cette activité? You will hear various activities described on your In-Text Audio CD. Indicate whether each activity is done by one person or by more than one person.

1. _____ une personne   _____ plus d'une personne
2. _____ une personne   _____ plus d'une personne
3. _____ une personne   _____ plus d'une personne
4. _____ une personne   _____ plus d'une personne
5. _____ une personne   _____ plus d'une personne
6. _____ une personne   _____ plus d'une personne

Transcript: 1. Il écrit à sa mère. 2. Elles disent que ce film est très bon. 3. Ils lisent un roman en classe. 4. On dit que cette pièce est terrible! 5. Elle lit souvent de la poésie. 6. Ils écrivent beaucoup de compositions.

B. C'est quand? For each sentence you hear, indicate whether the activity mentioned took place in the past, or is taking place in the present.

1. _____ passé   _____ présent   4. _____ passé   _____ présent
2. _____ passé   _____ présent   5. _____ passé   _____ présent
3. _____ passé   _____ présent   6. _____ passé   _____ présent

Transcript: 1. Je dis bonjour à la femme. 2. Nous lisons un hebdomadaire en classe. 3. Elle a lu un magazine dans le train. 4. Il écrit à sa mère le samedi. 5. J'ai dit bonjour à Monsieur Leclerc. 6. Vous avez écrit une lettre à l'éditeur?

Pratiquons!

A. Qu'est-ce qu'ils lisent? Tell what different people read by choosing from the options.

un roman	un manuel d'informatique	des revues
des compositions	des magazines	des poèmes
un journal hebdomadaire	des billets doux[1]	

1. Annette et Marie-Claire suivent un cours de poésie. Elles ...
2. Mon frère travaille chez IBM. Il ...
3. Ma fiancée et moi, nous habitons dans deux villes différentes. Nous ...
4. Je préfère lire des articles scientifiques. Je ...
5. Claude habite une petite ville. Elle ...
6. Vous et vos amis, vous aimez les photographies de mannequins[2] et les articles de mode. Vous ...
7. Pour te reposer[3] le soir, tu ...
8. Le/La pauvre prof! Le week-end, il/elle ...

Answer Key. Possible answers: 1. Elles lisent des poèmes. 2. Il lit un manuel d'informatique. 3. Nous lisons des billets doux. 4. Je lis des revues (scientifiques). 5. Elle lit un journal hebdomadaire. 6. Vous lisez des magazines. 7. Tu lis un roman. 8. Il/Elle lit des compositions.

---

[1]*love letters* [2]*models* [3]*relax*

B. Qui fait quoi?

For each of the following items, tell who among your family and friends does each activity. Use a complete sentence in your response.

MODÈLE: lire le journal le matin

> *Ma mère lit le journal le matin. / Mes amis lisent le journal le matin.*

1. dire que les films de Disney sont amusants
2. lire un quotidien
3. lire un hebdomadaire
4. écrire souvent des e-mails
5. lire un journal français
6. écrire des poèmes
7. dire «Allô» quand il / elle répond au téléphone
8. écrire des cartes postales pendant les vacances

C. Avantages / désavantages.

Complete the following paragraph with the appropriate form of the logical verb. Each verb will be used only once.

vouloir	écrire
dire	prendre
préférer	boire
lire	pouvoir

Le matin, je me lève[1], et je (1) _____ le journal pendant que je (2) _____ mon café. Mon mari (3) _____ une douche et ensuite il (4) _____ des courriels à sa famille au Canada. Ses parents (5) _____ que l'e-mail est mieux que le courrier parce que c'est plus rapide, et que c'est mieux que le téléphone parce que c'est gratuit! Nous (6) _____ aussi envoyer des photos par courriel, ce qui est super génial. Mais moi, je (7) _____ entendre la voix[2] de mes proches[3] de temps en temps. J'aime l'e-mail, mais je (8) _____ le téléphone!

D. Mais non, il l'a déjà fait!

A friend asks you if someone is currently doing an activity. Tell your friend that the person already did the activity, at the time indicated.

MODÈLE: Est-ce que Jean-Pierre écrit une composition? (hier soir)

> *Mais non, il a écrit la composition hier soir.*

1. Est-ce que les étudiants lisent un poème en classe? (hier)
2. Est-ce que Martine écrit à sa mère? (ce matin)
3. Nous lisons le Chapitre 6? (la semaine dernière)
4. On dit bonjour à Madame Ferrier? (déjà[4])
5. Vous écrivez une lettre à l'éditeur? (hier matin)
6. On lit *Le Petit Prince* ce semestre? (le semestre passé)

---

[1]*get up* [2]*voice* [3]*loved ones* [4]*already*

À vous de parler!

A. Sondage. In groups of three or four, ask and answer questions 1–8. When you have finished, answer questions 9 and 10 as a group.

In preparation for activity B in this section, take a few moments to tally each group's answers to the last two questions on the board.

1. Combien de fois par semaine est-ce que tu lis le journal? Quels journaux et magazines lis-tu? Est-ce que ce sont des quotidiens ou des hebdomadaires?
2. À quels magazines et revues es-tu abonné(e)?
3. Qu'est-ce que tu écoutes à la radio? De la musique? Des infos? Est-ce que tu écoutes la radio tous les jours?
4. Est-ce que tu regardes le journal télévisé le soir? Si oui, combien de fois par semaine? Si non, pourquoi pas?
5. Est-ce que tu parles souvent des actualités avec tes amis? Avec ta famille?
6. Est-ce que tu aimes discuter de la politique avec tes amis? De quoi parlez-vous?
7. Quand quelque chose de très important se passe dans le monde, où est-ce que tu te tournes pour t'informer[1]?
8. Est-ce que les journalistes sont honnêtes, à ton avis? Est-ce qu'ils font bien leur travail? Pourquoi penses-tu cela?
9. Dans votre groupe, en général, quels médias est-ce qu'on préfère pour s'informer? Pourquoi?
10. Comme groupe, est-ce que vous faites plutôt confiance à la presse ou à vos amis pour obtenir des informations importantes? Pourquoi?

B. La réponse des Français. Now read the following survey results. A group of 1,000 French people were asked questions similar to the ones you answered in activity A. Keeping the same groups you had in activity A, compare your responses in A with the responses in this survey, and answer the following questions.

1. De quels moyens est-ce que les Français se servent en particulier pour s'informer? Est-ce que la réponse est différente de celle de votre classe, ou la même?
2. Est-ce que les Français font plus confiance, moins confiance, ou égale confiance à la presse que votre classe?
3. Est-ce que vous voyez plus de similarités ou plus de différences entre les opinions des Français et les opinions de votre classe?

QUESTION 1 : Les journalistes vous paraissent-ils dans l'ensemble ... ?

	Oui	Non	Pas d'opinion
Exprimer des opinions diverses	62%	35%	3%
Décrire honnêtement la réalité des faits	41%	57%	2%
Faire de moins en moins bien leur travail	38%	59%	3%
Être en contact avec la même réalité que vous	38%	60%	2%

---

[1]*to get information*

QUESTION 2: Personnellement, pour vous informer de ce qui se passe dans la société, diriez-vous que pour chacun des acteurs ou éléments suivants, les sources d'information suivantes jouent un rôle très important, assez important, peu important ou pas important du tout?

	Très important	Assez important	Peu important	Pas du tout important
Les amis, la famille	50%	31%	15%	4%
La télévision	37%	39%	17%	7%
La radio	32%	42%	19%	7%
Les journaux quotidiens	26%	45%	17%	11%
L'évolution de la vie matérielle	28%	41%	20%	9%
Les magazines (hebdomadaires et mensuels)	10%	40%	34%	16%
Les collègues	14%	32%	26%	15%
Les partis politiques	15%	28%	30%	25%

Online Study Center
Web Search Activities

La presse est comme ça au Sénégal

The former French colony of Senegal, independent since 1960, enjoys a freedom of the press and a democratic government that are virtually unrivaled in the rest of Africa. According to many, this is no coincidence, as "newspapers and radio played a major role in the democratization process."[1] While many other former colonies still struggle to establish or maintain peaceful governance, Senegal is heralded as a "model of democracy in action in Africa, thanks in large measure to the active role of a free press."[2] With one government-controlled and four independent daily newspapers (all printed in French), and many FM radio stations, there is wide dissemination of information throughout the country. This information network was extensively praised in the peaceful transition of power after the presidential elections of 2000, when a new president, Abdoulaye Wade, replaced Abdou Diouf, who had governed for nineteen years. Whereas other developing countries often turned to a coup d'état to overthrow a leader, Senegal enjoyed peace, thanks in large part to the fact that its citizens were kept informed throughout the election process.

The Senegalese culture is still largely oral; therefore, FM radio has flourished there, and broadcasts can be heard in both French (the official language) and Wolof (the largest home language). While television has been slow to claim the African continent, due in large part to lack of resources, cell phones have not, and they contribute to the distribution of information on radio and in newspapers. In fact, during the 2000 elections it was reported that "urban

---

[1]Idriss Fall, Senegalese journalist with Voice of America: "Senegal's News Media: Engines of Democracy" (www.freedomforum.org/templates) [2]*Ibid.*

Senegalese were walking around with a radio glued to one ear and a mobile phone glued to the other. . . . The stations sent reporters to hundreds of individual voting bureaux and within minutes of the local returning officer announcing the result, the reporters got on their cellphones and broadcast it."[1]

This model of a free press is proliferating throughout Africa, where government-controlled media are increasingly being replaced by independent newspapers and radio stations and, in some cases, even privatized television. Freedom of the press, and especially dissemination of information by radio, is being hailed the "most powerful instrument for nation-building in Africa."[2]

Réfléchissons!

In groups of three or four, answer the following questions.

1. What does freedom of the press mean for you personally? Is it a freedom that you think about often, or that you sometimes take for granted? In what circumstances, if any, do you think specifically about freedom of the press?
2. What influence do you think the American government has on what is published or announced in the media? Would you be interested in reading a government-controlled newspaper, or listening to a government-controlled radio station? Why or why not?
3. What do you think freedom of the press means in the daily lives of people in Senegal or in other African countries?
4. How could such freedom of the press help in nation-building?

À vous de lire!

Online Study Center
Language Skills Practice

A. Stratégies. One way we can facilitate the reading process is to think about the topic before we begin to read. This often helps us to predict what we will find in the text and to fill in gaps when we encounter words or grammar constructions that are unfamiliar to us. The article that you are about to read, "*J'ai rendez-vous avec ma télé*," comes from the magazine *Marie Claire*[3]. Before you start reading this article, think about the information that you might find in it. Look at the title of the article: What does it suggest to you? What do you think this article is about?

Now, think about the programs that you like to watch on TV and why. Do you watch sports because you play sports or because you wish you could play a sport? Do you watch soap operas to turn your brain off? to forget about your problems? Do you watch *National Geographic* because you enjoy being an armchair traveler? Why do you watch TV in general? Do you leave your TV on just for background noise? If so, why?

---

[1]Mark Doyle: "Senegal: Where democracy was the winner" (http://news.bbc.co.uk/l/low/world/africa/686001)
[2]Akin Fatoyinbo, Senior Communication Specialist, The World Bank: "The Evolution of Mass Media in Africa" (www.adeanet.org/newsletter/Vol11No2) [3]This French magazine was the first of its genre to publish articles by French feminists in 1968, to talk about the contraceptive pill, maternity and work, and other subjects that aimed to liberate women. It is one of the most popular magazines among French women today.

B. Avant de lire

1. Look at the subtitles in the article. How many women are sharing their views? What are they talking about? Do they all have the same social status? Will their testimonies be the same?
2. Finally, look at the titles of the TV programs that appear in the article. Try to guess the types of programs they are. Share your thoughts with the class.
3. With a partner, explain the following quotations from the article.
   - "Dis-moi ce que tu regardes et je te dirai qui tu es."
   - "Les femmes préfèrent les émissions qui leur donnent leur ration d'émotions fortes."
   - "... aide-ménagère dans une maison de retraite."
   - "... être l'esclave de l'actualité."

Now, compare your explanations with a classmate's.

C. Lisons!

Before you start reading the following article, remember that you do not have to understand *everything*. After every few paragraphs, you will be asked to answer some questions. Read the paragraphs a second time before answering the questions. Once you have finished with the questions, continue with your reading.

J'ai rendez-vous avec ma télé

Fan de Star Academy, folle de Bachelor ou fidèle de TF1 ... nous avons demandé à quatre femmes très différentes de commenter leurs émissions préférées. Dis-moi ce que tu regardes, et je te dirai qui tu es ...

Certaines femmes adorent les magazines et les débats de société sérieux sur la chaîne Arte. Mais les études sont formelles: les femmes préfèrent les émissions qui leur donnent leur ration d'émotions fortes. «Pourquoi le public féminin aime-t-il les émissions faites pour une audience de masse? Parce qu'on y voit d'autres femmes s'exprimer. On peut donc fugitivement s'identifier à elles», explique la sociologue Divina Frau-Meigs. Un bénéfice ambigu pour les femmes ... car, «tout en donnant (en apparence) la parole aux femmes, ces émissions les font régresser. En effet, à la télé, les femmes apparaissent souvent dans des sphères privées, de l'intime, de la confidence. Il n'y a pas de traduction politique de leurs problèmes qui, pourtant, ont souvent une dimension collective.» Bref, la télé que les femmes aiment ... les dépolitise. Mais, la télé fait aussi l'union entre des publics séparés. Nous avons demandé à quatre femmes de nous parler de leurs émissions préférées.

Questions

1. Quelles sont les raisons que la psychologue Divina Frau-Meigs donne à propos des préférences télévisées de l'audience féminine?
2. Quelle est l'influence de la télé sur les femmes qui aiment cette télé? Pourquoi?
3. Qu'est-ce que la télé arrive à unir?

Here is a description of the programs that are listed in the article:

Les feux de l'amour: Soap opera.

Star Academy: TV game, similar to *Star Search* or *American Idol;* the main purpose is to discover an unknown young artist.

À la recherche de la nouvelle star: TV game. Same as above.

Pop Stars: TV game. Same as above.

C'est mon choix: TV magazine. Men and women talk about the personal choices they made in their lives.

Les soirées Thema: TV magazine. A current theme (political, social, economical) is treated in depth by experts in the field.

Ripostes (Replies): TV magazine; gives answers to current events, also treated in depth by a panel of experts.

C dans l'air (It's in the air): TV magazine; similar to above.

Arrêt sur image (Focus on the image): TV magazine; similar to above.

If you wish, you may break this reading up over several days, each day reading the response of only one woman and answering the questions that follow.

MAMYA, aide-ménagère dans une maison de retraite.
Ses émissions préférées:

- *Les feux de l'amour* (TF1)

  «Même si je suis très éloignée[1] de ces riches Américaines, les histoires de famille, je connais[2], sourit[3] Mamya. Quand mon père est mort, j'avais 10 ans. À 18 ans, je n'ai pas pu hériter. Comme mon père est décédé avant son père, nous les enfants n'avons eu droit à rien[4].»

- *Nass M'lah City* (TV Algérie)

  Cette série parle de la vie des gens du bled[5], une saga qui fait pleurer de rire les familles d'origine algérienne[6]. «Quand je regarde un épisode, j'ai l'impression d'être là-bas[7].»

Questions

4. Qu'est-ce qui arrivé à Mamya quand son père est décédé?
5. Dites les raisons pour lesquelles[8] elle aime regarder les programmes qui sont nommés dans le texte.

NELLY, étudiante en BTS d'informatique. Ses émissions préférées:

- *Star Academy* (TF1), *À la recherche de la nouvelle star* et
  Pop Stars (M6)

Nelly sait[9] que la gloire des «pop stars» est ephémère et que c'est choquant qu'un jeune anonyme se transforme en artiste en trois mois et qu'il vende beaucoup plus de disques que des chanteurs confirmés. Elle sait aussi que ces chansons sont commerciales, superficielles et remixées. «Et alors ... ?[10] Ces stars auront vécu[11] une expérience inoubliable[12]. D'ailleurs[13], qui, à mon âge ne veut pas être à leur place?» C'est décidé, Nelly va se présenter pour participer à la prochaine saison de la *Star Academy!*

Questions

6. Quel genre de programmes est-ce que Nelly aime? Sont-ils tous du même style?
7. Est-ce que Nelly connaît[14] les aspects négatifs de la vie d'une «pop star»? Expliquez votre réponse.
8. Pourquoi est-ce que Nelly croit[15] que c'est très bien d'être une «pop star»?
9. Qu'est-ce que Nelly a décidé?

JACQUIE, ex-employée RER. Son émission préférée:

- *C'est mon choix* (France 3)

  Les titres des émissions de *C'est mon choix* sont toujours très polémiques: «Je vis[16] avec ma femme et mon ex», «La nuit, j'ai une double vie», «J'ai deux mamans» ... Rapidement, Jacquie est devenue une adepte de cette émission: «Ce programme me permet de me forger une opinion, d'abandonner mes idées préconçues. Et quels progrès en matière de mœurs[17]! Les sujets qui m'ont le plus intéressée sont: celui[18] où les femmes élèvent seules un enfant et celui des femmes qui sont PDG[19]. Aujourd'hui, nous les femmes, avons des choix!»

---

[1]*far away* [2]*I know (all about them)* [3]*smiles* [4]*the right to anything* [5]*slang for "the boonies"* [6]*that makes Algerian families laugh until they cry* [7]*over there* [8]*for which* [9]*knows* [10]*So what?* [11]*will have lived* [12]*unforgettable* [13]*Moreover* [14]*knows* [15]*believes* [16]*live* [17]*social customs* [18]*the one* [19]*CEO (président-directeur général)*

Questions

10. Où est-ce que Jacquie travaillait[1]?
11. Pourquoi est-ce que Jacquie aime regarder *C'est mon choix?* Comment est-ce que ce programme lui a permis d'avoir sa propre opinion?
12. Quels sont les programmes que Jacquie aime le plus?

CHRIS, professeure[2]-documentaliste au collège Blaise-Pascal en Seine-et-Marne. Ses émissions préférées:

* *Les soirées Thema* (Arte)

  «Il y a des sujets sur *Thema* qui sont fantastiques, dit Chris. Comme celui sur l'Afghanistan. J'aime quand la télé prend le temps de creuser[3] un sujet profondément, sans être esclave de l'actualité. Quand je vois comment certains thèmes sont bâclés[4] dans les journaux télévisés, je me dis que ce n'est pas avec ça que le public va comprendre comment tourne le monde.»

* *Ripostes, C dans l'air* et *Arrêt sur image* (France 5)

  «*Ripostes* propose des débats comme "Les médias nous informent-ils ou nous manipulent-ils?" Bonnes questions! C'est tout le contraire de ces pseudo-débats sur les autres chaînes.»

  Chris travaille avec le Centre de liaison de l'enseignement et des moyens d'information, afin d'éduquer les étudiants aux médias. Son objectif est d'amener[5] les lycéens[6] à s'interroger[7]: des émissions comme *C'est mon choix, Ça se discute* ou *Toute la ville en parle* favorisent-elles de vrais débats ou sont-elles avant tout des divertissements?

Questions

13. En quoi est-ce que les programmes que Chris aime regarder sont différents des journaux télévisés?
14. Pourquoi est-ce qu'elle aime regarder *Ripostes?*
15. Décrivez le travail que Chris fait avec les étudiants. Quelle est la question principale qu'elle voudrait que ses étudiants se posent[8] sur certains programmes télévisés?

D. Après la lecture

These analytical questions are in English so that students will not feel frustrated trying to express their thoughts. You may decide to conduct discussions in French or to select some of the less analytical questions and ask them in French.

1. Do you agree with the sentence in the first paragraph: **«Dis-moi ce que tu regardes et je te dirai qui tu es»**? Explain why or why not.
2. Do women in America watch programs "high in emotional content"? If so, do they watch these programs for the same reasons mentioned by the French women and the psychologist in this article?
3. From the titles of the programs and the descriptions of them, do you think that French TV is any different from American TV? For example, what is the TV news in America like? Sensationalistic? Realistic? Does it cover a subject in depth?
4. Is there a TV network (like **Arte** in France) that covers topics in depth, with experts invited to give their opinions? Which one? Do you watch it? Explain why.
5. When you watch TV, do you think that you are being manipulated, with "pseudo-debates," for example? Explain your answer.

---

[1]*used to work* [2] Notice the spelling of **professeure** for a female professor. More and more the French use a feminine form for professions that were traditionally held by men, rather than using the wordy **une femme professeur.** [3]*dig into* [4]*botched* [5]*to lead* [6]*high school students* [7]**s' interroger:** *ask themselves* [8]**se posent:** *ask themselves*

Lexique ♫

Vocabulaire essentiel

À la radio on peut écouter …

une émission culturelle *cultural program*
une émission musicale *music program*
les informations (les infos) *(f.) newscast*

les informations routières *(f.) traffic report*
un talk-show *talk show*
des tubes *(m.) hit songs*

On peut aussi …

changer de fréquence *change the station*

À la télé on peut regarder …

un documentaire *documentary*
un feuilleton romantique *soap opera*
un film *movie*

le journal télévisé (le JT) *television news*
la météo *weather report*
une série (télévisée) *TV series*
la télé-réalité *reality show*

On peut aussi …

changer de chaîne *(f.) to change the channel*
faire du zapping *to channel surf*

À la télé et à la radio …

l'animateur / l'animatrice anime
the DJ or the host announces / hosts the show

le présentateur / la présentatrice présente
the TV anchor presents

À la télé / Sur le petit écran *on TV / on the small screen*
À la radio / Sur les ondes *on the radio / on the airwaves*
on passe / on diffuse … *they broadcast . . .*

un dessin animé *cartoon*
des divertissements *(m.)* / des jeux *(m.) TV games*
une émission *program*
le hit parade *top music hits*

un magazine *exposé*
un match de foot en direct *live soccer game*
un programme *program*
de la publicité *advertisements*

un reportage *report*
les sports *(m.) sports*
un téléfilm *TV movie*

Chez le marchand de journaux *at the newsstand*

un guide des programmes télévisés *television guide*
un guide télé *TV guide*
un hebdomadaire *weekly magazine*
un journal *newspaper*

un magazine d'actualité *news magazine*
un magazine de santé *health magazine*
un mensuel *monthly magazine*
la presse people *entertainment magazines*

un quotidien *daily newspaper*
un magazine people *entertainment magazine*
une revue critique de cinéma *movie review magazine*

une revue de cuisine *cooking magazine*

une revue de mode *fashion magazine*

une revue de sport *sports magazine*

Les professionnels

un(e) journaliste *journalist*

un(e) paparazzi *paparazzi*

un(e) photographe *photographer*

Les lecteurs

un(e) abonné(e) *subscriber*
un abonnement *magazine/ newspaper subscription*

un bon d'abonnement / un bulletin d'abonnement *subscription form*

un lecteur / une lectrice *reader*

Les événements de la vie

Événements positifs

chanter dans une chorale *to sing in a choir*
chanter dans un groupe *to sing in a band*
dire *to say*
donner un concert *to perform a concert*
donner une conférence *to present a paper*
écouter une conférence *to listen to a lecture*

écrire *to write*
gagner un match *to win a match*
jouer dans un groupe *to play in a band*
jouer dans un orchestre *to play in an orchestra*
lire *to read*
participer à un défilé *to march / participate in a parade*
participer à une manifestation *to take part in a demonstration*

participer à un match (sportif) *to play in a (sports) match / game*
publier *to publish*
  un article *article*
  une lettre à l'éditeur *letter to the editor*
  un livre *book*
  un poème *poem*

Événements négatifs

avoir un accident *to have an accident*
être victime d'un crime *to be a victim of a crime*

être volé(e) *to be robbed*
perdre un match (sportif) *to lose a (sports) match / game*
un vol *robbery*

Expansion personnelle

Les événements de la vie

Événements positifs

gagner un prix *to win a prize*
  le prix Goncourt *Goncourt Prize*
  le prix Nobel *Nobel Prize*
  le prix Pulitzer *Pulitzer Prize*
sauver la vie à quelqu'un *to save someone's life*

Événements négatifs

un cambriolage *burglary (break-in)*
causer un accident *to cause an accident*
commettre un crime *to commit a crime*
être cambriolé(e) *to be burglarized*

Mes relations amoureuses et amicales

There are things we do every day, such as waking up, getting dressed, and brushing our teeth. In this chapter, you will learn the pronominal verbs that are used to express our daily routine, negative expressions used to tell what we no longer do, haven't yet done, or never do, and vocabulary to talk about our relationships with others.

The vocabulary that you will learn includes

Reflexive and reciprocal verbs for expressing emotions
Reflexive and reciprocal verbs for talking about daily routine
Expressions related to marriage and divorce

The structures that you will learn include

Reflexive and reciprocal verbs in the present, **futur proche**, and **passé composé**
Negations: **ne ... plus, ne ... jamais, ne ... rien, ne ... personne**
The verbs **conduire, rouler, partir, sortir,** and **quitter** in the present and **passé composé**

The culture that you will learn includes

Interracial and intercultural marriage
Example of a French/Francophone wedding

Commençons!

Ma routine 🎧

Voici un test de personnalité. Lisez les questions et choisissez la réponse qui décrit le mieux votre personnalité. Ainsi[1], vous saurez[2] si vous êtes une personne stressée ou cool. Essayez de deviner[3] le vocabulaire que vous ne connaissez pas à l'aide des dessins[4] ou selon le contexte.

Psycho-test: êtes-vous une personne stressée ou cool?

1. À six heures du matin, **vous vous réveillez ...**
   a. _____ de bonne humeur, toujours content(e)
   b. _____ de mauvaise humeur, toujours fâché(e)

2. Généralement, le matin, **vous vous levez ...**
   a. _____ lentement
   b. _____ rapidement

3. D'habitude, le matin, **vous vous lavez ...**
   a. _____ tranquillement et minutieusement
   b. _____ toujours vite, vite, vite!

4. En général, **vous vous habillez ...**
   a. _____ confortablement: la commodité en premier
   b. _____ coquettement et inconfortablement: l'esthétique prime

5. **Vous vous maquillez** (les femmes) ... / **Vous vous rasez** (les hommes) ...
   a. _____ tous les jours sans exception
   b. _____ seulement le week-end

6. Normalement, au travail / à l'université **vous vous sentez ...**
   a. _____ bien
   b. _____ mal

7. **Vous vous rongez les ongles ...**
   a. _____ souvent: ça vous détend et ça vous relaxe quand vous êtes énervé(e) ou préoccupé(e)
   b. _____ jamais: vous n'êtes pas souvent nerveux(euse)

---

[1] *That way* [2] *you will know* [3] *Try to guess* [4] *drawings*

8. Quand vous êtes en voiture, **vous vous énervez ...**
   a. _____ facilement
   b. _____ difficilement

9. Le soir, généralement, **vous vous couchez ...**
   a. _____ tôt, avant 22 heures
   b. _____ tard, après 23 heures

10. Le soir, **vous vous endormez ...**
    a. _____ tout de suite et sans difficulté
    b. _____ avec difficulté

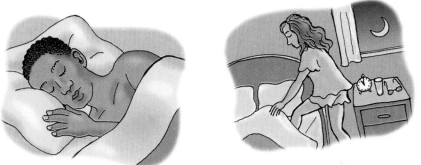

Résultat: Comptez combien de **a** et de **b** vous avez. Si vous avez plus de réponses **a** que de réponses **b,** vous êtes une personne stressée. Nous recommendons un bon massage. Si vous avez plus de réponses **b,** vous êtes une personne cool. Bravo! Continuez!

Vous avez bien compris?

Indicate whether the following statements and situations are **logique** or **pas logique.**

1. Quand vous buvez beaucoup, beaucoup de bières, vous vous sentez mal: vous avez une migraine et vous voulez vomir. _____ logique _____ pas logique
2. Vous vous lavez dans le garage. _____ logique _____ pas logique
3. Vous vous rasez les ongles. _____ logique _____ pas logique
4. En classe, vous vous levez quand vous voulez. _____ logique _____ pas logique
5. Vous vous habillez dans la chambre ou la salle de bains. _____ logique _____ pas logique
6. Vous vous maquillez les cheveux. _____ logique _____ pas logique

La routine

The following reflexive verbs are listed in the infinitive form.

se brosser les dents

se calmer

se démaquiller

se déshabiller

s'épiler

s'habiller

se laver les cheveux

se maquiller

se peigner les cheveux

se presser / se dépêcher

se promener

se reposer

se sécher les cheveux

Reminder: you saw several other reflexive verbs in the personality test. Go back to that test if you are unsure of their meaning.

se coucher	se lever	se ronger les ongles
s'endormir	se réveiller	se sentir bien / mal
s'énerver	se raser	

Since English translations are not provided for these reflexive verbs, give your students the translations of the first three verbs *(to brush one's teeth; to calm oneself down; to remove one's makeup)* so that the students get a general idea of how these verbs are different from others they have seen so far.

À vous!

A. Qu'est-ce qu'il/elle fait? Match the drawings with the statements.

1.

2.

3.

4.

5.

6.

7.

8.

9.

_____ a. Il/Elle se sèche les cheveux.

_____ b. Il/Elle se rase.

_____ c. Il/Elle se lave.

_____ d. Il/Elle se réveille.

_____ e. Il/Elle se déshabille.

_____ f. Il/Elle se ronge les ongles.

_____ g. Il/Elle s'habille.

_____ h. Il/Elle se couche.

_____ i. Il/Elle se brosse les dents.

B. La routine du prof. Ask your instructor what applies to him/her, using the choices in parentheses. Then, put the sentences in logical order to create a paragraph about your instructor's daily routine.

MODÈLE: Vous vous rongez les ongles (devant un film d'épouvante / de science-fiction).

Est-ce que vous vous rongez les ongles devant un film d'épouvante ou un film de science-fiction?

1. Vous vous couchez (tard / tôt).
2. Vous vous pressez pour aller à l'université (très souvent / pas souvent).
3. Vous vous habillez (dans la salle de bains / dans la chambre).
4. Vous vous endormez (facilement / difficilement).
5. Vous vous réveillez (de bonne humeur / de mauvaise humeur).
6. Vous vous brossez les dents (deux fois par jour / trois fois par jour).
7. Vous vous séchez les cheveux (toujours / jamais).
8. Vous vous lavez (dans la douche / dans la baignoire).
9. Vous vous levez (tout de suite / avec difficulté).

Structure 1

Online Study Center
ACE, Language Skills Practice

Les verbes réfléchis au présent

There are several types of pronominal verbs (verbs that are accompanied by a pronoun) in French. All are conjugated in the same way, but they have slightly different meanings. In this chapter you will learn *reflexive* (**réfléchis**) and *reciprocal* (**réciproques**) verbs. Reflexive verbs are used to indicate that the subject does something by itself and to itself. For example, in the morning, you dress (you dress yourself). *To dress (oneself)* is a reflexive action and it uses a reflexive verb. In English, you may omit the reflexive pronoun *oneself* and just say: *I dress in the morning.* However, in French, you may not omit the reflexive pronoun in a sentence that conveys the meaning of doing something to oneself. A reflexive action must always have a reflexive pronoun with the verb. Look at the following conjugation of **se raser** in the present tense. The reflexive pronouns are in boldface. These pronouns accompany all reflexive verbs.

You may want to have students repeat the paradigm after you, concentrating on the pronunciation of the subject pronouns combined with the reflexive pronouns, since this is a new feature for the students.

se raser	*to shave (oneself)*
je **me** rase	*I shave (myself)*
tu **te** rases	*you shave (yourself)*
il / elle / on **se** rase	*he / she / one shaves (himself / herself / oneself)*
nous **nous** rasons	*we shave (ourselves)*
vous **vous** rasez	*you shave (yourself / yourselves)*
ils / elles **se** rasent	*they shave (themselves)*

Before a vowel, **me, te,** and **se** become **m', t',** and **s'.**

Je **m'**énerve facilement.

- In order to remember which verbs are reflexive in French, you need to memorize the reflexive verbs introduced in the preceding vocabulary sections.
- The following reflexive verbs have spelling changes in the present tense.

se lever and **se promener:** Add an **accent grave** except in the **nous** and **vous** forms. (You saw the same spelling change with **acheter,** Chapter 3.)

se lever	se promener
je me lève	je me promène
tu te lèves	tu te promènes
il / elle / on se lève	il / elle / on se promène
nous nous levons	nous nous promenons
vous vous levez	vous vous promenez
ils / elles se lèvent	ils / elles se promènent

se sentir and **s'endormir**[1]**:** The stems change except in the *plural* forms.

se sentir	s'endormir
je me **sens** bien	je m'en**dors**
tu te **sens** bien	tu t'en**dors**
il / elle / on se **sent** bien	il / elle / on s'en**dort**
nous nous sentons bien	nous nous endormons
vous vous sentez bien	vous vous endormez
ils / elles se sentent bien	ils / elles s'endorment

Model the difference in pronunciation between the plural forms and the singular forms of these two verbs. Have students repeat.

se sécher: The **accent aigu** changes into an **accent grave** except in the **nous** and **vous** forms. (This is the same spelling change as for **préférer,** Chapter 3.)

se sécher	
je me sèche	nous nous séchons
tu te sèches	vous vous séchez
il / elle / on se sèche	ils / elles se sèchent

se ronger: As with all verbs that end in **-ger** (such as **manger** or **voyager,** which you learned in Chapter 3), the **e** is retained in the **nous** form: Nous nous rongeons les ongles.

- To negate reflexive verbs, place **ne** before the reflexive pronoun and **pas** after the verb.[2]

Tu **ne** te maquilles **pas.**
Nous **ne** nous réveillons **pas** tôt le samedi.

---

[1]**S'endormir** *(to fall asleep)* is based on the verb **dormir** *(to sleep),* and the two are conjugated in the same way. Can you give the forms of **dormir**? [2]To ask a *question using inversion,* place the reflexive pronoun first and invert the order of verb and subject: **Te** ronges-**tu** les ongles quand tu regardes un film d'épouvante? **Vous** endormez-**vous** rapidement après une longue journée?

You may want to provide students with more examples of reflexive and nonreflexive sentences. For example: Je baigne mon chien. / Mon chien se baigne au lac. Nous nous lavons les cheveux. / Nous lavons les cheveux de nos petits frères. etc.

- **Attention!** A reflexive verb may be turned into a nonreflexive one, depending on the action the speaker wishes to convey. Look at the following examples.

Aurélie **s'**habille.   *Aurélie is getting dressed.*
Aurélie habille le bébé.   *Aurélie is dressing the baby.*

In the first sentence, Aurélie is dressing herself. Therefore, in French it is necessary to use a reflexive pronoun with the verb (**s'habiller**) to indicate that meaning. In the second sentence, Aurélie is dressing someone else: the baby. The verb in this sentence (**habiller**) is not reflexive. Hence, it does not need a reflexive pronoun.

VÉRIFIEZ VOTRE COMPRÉHENSION

1. Go back to the personality test at the beginning of the chapter (pp. 254–255). Why are all the reflexive verbs conjugated in the second person plural form (**vous**)? Whom do they refer to? (Who is **vous?**)

2. Why are they all reflexive? What are they meant to indicate?

À l'écoute!

Transcript: 1. Il se sent très fatigué aujourd'hui. 2. Elle s'endort toujours avec son chat dans le lit. 3. Ils se sentent contents avec toi. 4. Elles se sentent en sécurité. 5. Il s'endort très tard. 6. Elles s'endorment en classe de français! 7. Elle se sent mal en bateau. 8. Ils s'endorment devant la télé.

Answer Key: 1. singulier 2. singulier 3. pluriel 4. pluriel 5. singulier 6. pluriel 7. singulier 8. pluriel

Pluriel ou singulier? You will hear a number of sentences that include the verbs **s'endormir** and **se sentir.** Indicate whether the verb is singular or plural.

1. _____ singulier   _____ pluriel   5. _____ singulier   _____ pluriel
2. _____ singulier   _____ pluriel   6. _____ singulier   _____ pluriel
3. _____ singulier   _____ pluriel   7. _____ singulier   _____ pluriel
4. _____ singulier   _____ pluriel   8. _____ singulier   _____ pluriel

Pratiquons!

Answer Key: 1. se lève 2. ne se lève pas 3. se lave 4. ne se sèche pas 5. se réveillent 6. se dépêche 7. se sent 8. se promène 9. s'endort

A. La routine d'Annette. Here is a typical day for Annette Fourcher and her family. Complete the sentences with the correct form of the verb in parentheses.

Annette Fourcher (1) _____ (se lever) toujours très tôt le matin, mais son mari (2) _____ (ne ... pas se lever) tôt. Annette fait du jogging et après elle (3) _____ (se laver).
Elle (4) _____ (ne ... pas se sécher) les cheveux parce que ses deux enfants (5) _____ (se réveiller) et ils appellent: «Maman, maman!»
Annette (6) _____ (se dépêcher) et va dire bonjour à ses enfants.
Elle (7) _____ (se sentir) contente avec sa famille réunie le matin. Après le petit déjeuner, Annette (8) _____ (se promener) avec ses enfants. L'après-midi elle travaille beaucoup et le soir, elle (9) _____ (s'endormir) très vite.

B. Questions indiscrètes. Ask a classmate the following indiscreet questions, then reverse roles. Report your findings to the rest of the class.

1. Est-ce que tu t'endors souvent en classe? Dans quelle classe est-ce que tu t'endors le plus souvent?
2. Te ronges-tu les ongles? Pourquoi? Quand?
3. Est-ce que tu te brosses les dents tous les jours? Combien de fois par jour?
4. À qui penses-tu[1] quand tu t'endors?

---

[1] *think about*

5. Est-ce que tu te sens bien dans la classe de français? Pourquoi oui ou pourquoi non?

6. T'énerves-tu avec tes profs? Avec qui est-ce que tu t'énerves le plus? Et le moins?

C. Ma journée typique. Tell a classmate what your typical day is like, then reverse roles. Compare your notes with the class to find out who has the best and the worst routines (e.g., who wakes up the latest, who gets up the earliest, etc.).

Portrait personnel

For your class website or journal, write a **portrait personnel** in which you compare and contrast your partner and yourself, based on the information that you learned in activities B and C.

> MODÈLE: Sam ne se ronge jamais les ongles, mais moi, je suis nerveux (nerveuse). Je me ronge toujours les ongles, surtout pendant un examen!

Structure 2

Les verbes réfléchis au futur proche

Online Study Center
ACE, Language Skills
Practice

You remember that to form a sentence in the **futur proche** you used the verb **aller** followed by an infinitive: **je vais manger.** With reflexive verbs, the reflexive pronoun agrees with the subject and the reflexive verb remains in the infinitive.

Je vais **me** coucher.	I am going to go to bed.
Tu vas **te** raser.	You are going to shave.
Martine va **s'**habiller.	Martine is going to get dressed.
Nous allons **nous** promener.	We are going to go for a walk.
Vous allez **vous** lever.	You are going to get up.
Les étudiants vont **se** dépêcher.	The students are going to hurry.

- To negate reflexive verbs in the **futur proche,** the negative words go around the conjugated verb—**aller** in this case—as usual.

Je **ne** vais **pas** me sécher les cheveux.
Vous **n'**allez **pas** vous presser.

VÉRIFIEZ VOTRE COMPRÉHENSION

1. Go back to the personality test at the beginning of the chapter (pp. 254–255). Look at the reflexive verbs in boldface. They are all conjugated in the **vous** form. How would you phrase question #1 in the **je** and the **tu** forms? How would you phrase question #2 in the **on** form? How about question #3 in the **nous** form? Finally, phrase question #4 in the **ils** form.

2. Try to negate question #5 in the personality test.

3. How would you phrase question #9 in the **futur proche?**

À l'écoute! 🎧

Transcript: 7. Paul se lève.
8. Nous ne nous lavons pas.
9. Vous vous lavez. 10. Tu vas te
lever. 11. Nous allons nous lever.
12. Je me lave.

Answer Key: 7. se lever 8. se
laver 9. se laver 10. se lever
11. se lever 12. se laver

A. Se lever ou se laver? Distinguishing between the verbs **se lever** and **se laver** can sometimes be difficult. Listen to and repeat the following sentences.

1. Je me lève. · Je me lave.
2. Il va se lever. · Il va se laver.
3. Nous n'allons pas nous laver. · Nous n'allons pas nous lever.
4. Vous voulez vous laver. · Vous voulez vous lever.
5. Tu te lèves. · Tu te laves.
6. Ils ne se lavent pas. · Ils ne se lèvent pas.

Now, check the verb that you hear.

7. _____ se lever _____ se laver   10. _____ se lever _____ se laver
8. _____ se lever _____ se laver   11. _____ se lever _____ se laver
9. _____ se lever _____ se laver   12. _____ se lever _____ se laver

Pratiquons!

Answer Key: 1. vais me réveiller
2. va s'énerver 3. vont se
presser 4. allons nous ronger les
ongles 5. allez vous habiller
confortablement 6. vas te
coucher tard 7. allons nous
endormir

A. Parlons de demain. Complete the sentences in a logical manner to tell what the following people on campus are going to do tomorrow. Choose the most appropriate verb for each situation.

se ronger les ongles   s'endormir   se presser
se réveiller   s'énerver   s'habiller confortablement
se coucher tard

1. Moi, je _____ de mauvaise humeur demain matin parce que je suis toujours fatigué(e).
2. La présidente _____ à cause des problèmes qu'elle ne peut pas résoudre: le parking, par exemple!
3. Les profs _____ pour arriver à l'heure.
4. Mes camarades de classe et moi, nous _____ parce que l'examen de français va être très difficile et nous sommes angoissés!
5. Toi et tes amis, vous _____ pour aller en boîte après les cours.
6. Tu _____ après avoir dansé avec tes amis.
7. Nous _____ tout de suite à la fin d'une longue journée!

👥 B. Pendant les vacances. Ask a classmate if she is going to do the following things while on vacation.

🌀 MODÈLE: se lever tôt / À quelle heure?

> *Est-ce que tu vas te lever tôt pendant les vacances? À quelle heure tu vas te lever?*

1. se lever tard / À quelle heure?
2. se coucher tôt / Pourquoi?
3. s'énerver / Quand?
4. se promener / Où?
5. s'habiller élégamment / Pour quelle occasion?
6. se baigner[1] à la plage[2] / piscine / Combien de fois par jour?
7. se presser / Pourquoi?
8. se reposer / Comment?

---

[1]*to go swimming* [2]*beach*

Portrait personnel

Based on your partner's answers in activity B, write a paragraph describing what s/he is or is not going to do on his/her next vacation. Compare this with the descriptions of other classmates, and vote on who is going to have the most interesting vacation.

On se marie comme ça au Maroc

Au Maroc, généralement les jeunes couples se marient par amour. Cependant, il y a encore des mariages arrangés. La famille de la mariée donne une dot[1] et la famille du marié contribue à payer les besoins ménagers, comme par exemple les meubles.

Les préparatifs avant le mariage sont assez traditionnels. Quelques jours avant le grand jour, la mariée est décorée à l'henné[2] par les «hennayats». Les hennayats tracent sur le corps de la femme des symboles de protection et de fécondité. Les décorations à l'henné représentent aussi la séduction, l'érotisme et la passion. Le jour du mariage, les cheveux de la mariée sont coiffés par une femme heureuse qui a un mari fidèle. Premièrement, cette femme met de l'henné dans les cheveux de la future épouse. Ensuite, elle place les cheveux dans un anneau d'argent[3] comme symbole de pureté. Après, une hennayat casse un œuf sur sa tête en signe de fécondité. Finalement, elle met dans la coiffure de la mariée deux dattes avec du miel[4].

Pendant la cérémonie, la mariée change sept fois de robe. Les deux époux sont placés sur deux plateaux que l'on tourne sept fois aussi. Dans un mariage marocain il y a toujours la présence des «neggafates», des femmes qui font respecter les traditions qui forment partie du patrimoine national.

Online Study Center
Web Search Activities

#1. In France as in the U.S., the tradition is for the bride to wear something old, something new, something borrowed, and something blue. As in the U.S., the bride throws her bouquet to the single women who are invited to the wedding; the one who gets the bouquet will get married next! **Les témoins** *(witnesses)* are the equivalent in France of the groomsmen and the bridesmaids. However, **les témoins** are not dressed alike and they do not stand beside the bride and groom during the ceremony. They sign the wedding certificate as witnesses of the ceremony. **Les demoiselles d'honneur** are the flower girls. The bride's father walks his daughter to the altar, and the groom's mother walks her son. **Les témoins** do not usher the guests, who sit wherever they want. Only the bride dresses in white. (Some brides prefer to wear a beige gown, a shorter dress, a suit, etc.) #3. In the U.S. the equivalent of the **neggafates** would be the wedding planner and the wedding consultants. They help to prepare and to orchestrate the weddings.

Réfléchissons

1. Quelles traditions conservez-vous? Comment est la tradition pour les mariages dans votre culture? Que fait le marié? Et la mariée? Que font les invités?
2. Le pouvoir de séduction reste très important chez la femme marocaine avec la décoration du corps à l'henné. Est-ce que ce symbolisme de séduction existe dans votre culture? Comment «se décorent» les mariées?
3. Dans votre pays, y a-t-il l'équivalent de «neggafates» pendant les mariages? Y a-t-il des femmes qui aident les mariés pendant la cérémonie religieuse? Comment s'appellent-elles?
4. Vous avez vu que les traditions sont très respectées dans les mariages marocains. D'après vous, est-ce une bonne idée de conserver les traditions? Pourquoi?

---

[1] *dowry* [2] **L'henné** is the henna plant. Dying agents, usually yellow or red, are extracted from it. Both women and men decorate their bodies with henna. The markings look like tattoos but are not permanent. Women also dye their hair with henna. [3] *silver ring* [4] *dates with honey*

Continuons!

Online Study Center
Language Skills Practice

Partie I: Une histoire d'amour

Everyone has a very best friend or a special person in his or her life. In this section, you will use pronominal verbs to express emotions and actions common in human relationships, such as *to love each other, to hate each other,* or *to talk to each other*. These verbs are called reciprocal verbs.

In Chapter 2, you met Anou (from Belgium) and Jean (from Canada). Listen to their love story (**une histoire d'amour**) on your In-Text Audio CD.

Anou et Jean sont mariés depuis 40 ans. Ils ont deux filles et deux petits-fils, Alexandre et Maximilien.

Ils s'aiment beaucoup.

Ils ne se disputent jamais.

Anou et Jean s'amusent beaucoup ensemble[1]: ils aiment se parler, se promener et s'embrasser.

Ils se rencontrent tous les jours à midi pour déjeuner en tête à tête au restaurant. Ils se téléphonent du travail au moins[2] une fois par jour pour se dire des mots tendres. C'est le grand amour!

L'histoire d'une rupture[3]

In Chapter 2 you also met Gérard and Yolanda. Listen to their story on your In-Text Audio CD.

Gérard et Yolanda se disputent souvent. Ils sont mariés depuis 50 ans.

Ils s'ennuient ensemble.

Ils se fâchent constamment. Ils ne s'embrassent jamais et ils ne se regardent jamais avec amour. Ils ne s'aiment plus[4]: ils se détestent et ils vont se séparer. Voilà l'histoire d'une rupture ... C'est dommage!

---

[1]*together* [2]*at least* [3]*breakup* [4]You will learn the negations **ne ... jamais** *(never)* and **ne ... plus** *(no longer / no more)* in the next **Structure** section.

Vous avez bien compris?

Based on the two stories in **Continuons!,** choose **vrai** or **faux** for the following statements. Correct the sentences that are wrong.

1. Anou et Jean ont trois filles. _____ vrai _____ faux
2. Anou et Jean ne s'aiment pas. _____ vrai _____ faux
3. Anou et Jean s'embrassent. _____ vrai _____ faux
4. Anou et Jean se disputent. _____ vrai _____ faux
5. Anou et Jean se téléphonent souvent. _____ vrai _____ faux
6. Gérard et Yolanda s'amusent ensemble. _____ vrai _____ faux
7. Gérard et Yolanda se disputent souvent. _____ vrai _____ faux
8. Gérard et Yolanda s'aiment beaucoup. _____ vrai _____ faux

Answer Key: 1. faux: Ils ont deux filles. 2. faux: Ils s'aiment. 3. vrai 4. faux: Ils ne se disputent pas. 5. vrai 6. faux: Ils s'ennuient. 7. vrai 8. faux: Ils se détestent.

Vocabulaire essentiel

Online Study Center
Flashcards, ACE, Language Skills Practice

Les relations amoureuses et amicales

aimer quelqu'un à la folie	to love someone madly	être fidèle à quelqu'un	to be faithful to someone
s'aimer	to love one another	le coup de foudre	love at first sight
l'amour *(m.)*	love	les amoureux	lovers
s'amuser	to have fun	s'entendre bien	to get along well
avoir une déception amoureuse	to have one's heart broken	s'entendre mal	not to get along
se détester	to hate one another	se fâcher	to get mad
se disputer	to argue with each other	se fiancer	to get engaged
divorcer	to get a divorce	se marier (avec)	to get married
s'embrasser	to kiss one another	se quitter	to leave each other
s'ennuyer	to be bored	se regarder	to look at one another
être amoureux (amoureuse) de quelqu'un	to be in love with someone	se réconcilier (avec)	to reconcile
		tromper quelqu'un	to cheat on someone

Expansion personnelle

Voici quelques expressions supplémentaires pour approfondir votre vocabulaire sur les relations amoureuses et amicales.

revenir ensemble	to get back together
se séparer	to be apart / to separate
se donner un baiser	to kiss (generally on the lips)
se faire la bise	to kiss (generally on the cheeks)
se raconter tout	to tell each other everything
tomber amoureux (amoureuse) de quelqu'un	to fall in love with someone

À vous!

A. L'histoire d'Adèle et de Pierre. Complete the paragraph with the correct form of one of the following verbs.

s'embrasser   se regarder
se parler   tomber amoureux
se fiancer   se promener
s'entendre

Adèle et Pierre sont en classe de français ensemble. Immédiatement, ils (1) _____ et c'est le coup de foudre et ils (2) _____. En classe, ils ne peuvent pas (3) _____, mais ils s'écrivent des lettres d'amour. Après la classe de français, Adèle et Pierre (4) _____ sur le campus la main dans la main[1]. De temps en temps, quand ils sont seuls et dans l'intimité, ils (5) _____. Ils ne se disputent pas souvent: ils (6) _____ très bien.

Un jour, en classe, Pierre demande au professeur de français comment on dit *Would you like to be my wife?* Le prof répond: «Voudrais-tu être ma femme?» Pierre et Adèle (7) _____ devant toute la classe et tous les étudiants sont invités au mariage!

B. Une rupture. Sylvie and Didier are about to break up. A friend asks you how their relationship is going. Answer your friend's questions.

1. Est-ce que Sylvie et Didier s'entendent bien?
2. Est-ce qu'ils vont se marier finalement?
3. Est-ce qu'ils s'amusent ensemble?
4. Est-ce qu'ils se racontent tout comme avant[2]?
5. Est-ce qu'ils se disputent souvent?
6. Est-ce qu'ils vont se réconcilier?
7. Alors[3], ils ne vont pas revenir ensemble?
8. Oh, là, là ... Alors, ils ne s'aiment pas du tout[4]?

C. Tes amis et tes amours. Ask a classmate the following questions regarding his or her friendships and relationships. Then reverse roles.

1. Es-tu amoureux (amoureuse)? C'est le coup de foudre? Tu crois au[5] coup de foudre?
2. Tu tombes amoureux (amoureuse) facilement?
3. Que fais-tu quand tu as une déception[6] amoureuse?
4. Dans ta famille, avec qui est-ce que tu t'entends très bien? Et très mal?
5. À qui est-ce que tu racontes tout?
6. Avec qui est-ce que tu t'amuses beaucoup?
7. Avec qui est-ce que tu t'ennuies le plus?
8. Es-tu fidèle à tes amis? Comment? Donne un exemple.

---

[1]*hand in hand* [2]*like before* [3]*Then* [4]*at all* [5]*believe in* [6]*disappointment*

Structure 3

Les verbes réciproques

Online Study Center
ACE, Language Skills
Practice

In **Structure 1** you saw one type of pronominal verb: the reflexive verb, used for actions that people do to themselves. Now you are going to learn about *reciprocal verbs*. They are called reciprocal because they describe a reciprocal action between two or more people. For example, when you say something like *We love each other*, you are indicating that the love between you and the other person goes both ways; hence, it is reciprocal. In French, reciprocal verbs are conjugated like reflexive verbs. Indeed, the sentence *We love each other* is **Nous nous aimons** in French. In this context, the pronoun **nous** does not mean *ourselves* but *each other*.

Point out to students that not all verbs listed in the *Vocabulaire essentiel* and in the *Expansion personnelle* sections are reciprocal. Identify together some of the nonreciprocal ones (**revenir ensemble, tromper quelqu'un, être amoureux[euse] de quelqu'un**) and discuss why they are not reciprocal. This is important, as students may tend to use all verbs in the reflexive/reciprocal form.

- Reciprocal verbs are usually used in the plural forms. Otherwise, they would not be reciprocal.

Nous nous parlons. (indicates a reciprocal action)	*We speak to each other.*
Je me parle. (indicates a reflexive action)	*I speak to myself.*

- Because it can have a plural meaning *(they, people, we)*, the subject pronoun **on** can also be reciprocal.

  On se parle souvent.   *We talk to each other often.*

VÉRIFIEZ VOTRE COMPRÉHENSION

1. Go back to the two stories in the **Continuons!** section (p. 264) and find all the reciprocal verbs. Think about the way they are conjugated and their meanings.

2. Look for reciprocal verbs that are not conjugated in the two stories. Why are they left in the infinitive form?

Pratiquons!

A. Petits potins! *(Little pieces of gossip!)* **Histoires d'amour et de ruptures.** One of your friends is a true gossip. S/he is now telling you some gossip about some of the characters from this chapter. Complete the following seven sentences with the verbs provided.

revenir	se marier	se donner des baisers
se disputer	se rencontrer	tromper
se quitter	tomber amoureux(euse)	divorcer

1. Anou et Jean sont toujours mariés, mais ces derniers temps[1], ils _____ beaucoup: ils se fâchent constamment. Vont-ils divorcer?

2. Yolanda _____ Gérard avec Jean. Yolanda et Gérard _____ donc: ils ne sont plus mariés.

3. Annette Fourcher et son ex-mari vont _____ une deuxième fois. Ils se sont fiancés à Paris.

Answer Key: 1. se disputent 2. trompe / divorcent 3. se marier 4. se rencontrent / se quittent 5. se donner des baisers 6. revenir 7. tombe amoureuse

[1]*lately*

4. Quand Adèle et Pierre _____ dans un restaurant à Cannes, c'est le coup de foudre. Depuis leur marriage, ils ne _____ pas une minute: ils sont inséparables.

5. Mais récemment, Didier a surpris Sylvie et Pierre en pleine démonstration affective sur la plage: les amoureux aiment _____ sur le sable[1]. Didier n'est pas content!

6. Yolanda et Gérard vont _____ ensemble! Incroyable, non?!

7. Mais récemment, Yolanda _____ d'un homme plus jeune qu'elle: le beau et sexy Didier! C'est le grand amour!

B. Ça ne va pas bien! Things are not going well in your relationship with your significant other. Using the cues provided, tell your mate why you think that your relationship is not harmonious. **Attention!** Not all verbs in the activity are reciprocal!

MODÈLE: se parler mal

Nous nous parlons mal.

1. ne ... pas s'embrasser sur la bouche / se faire seulement la bise
2. s'entendre mal / se disputer tout le temps[2]
3. se quitter tôt le soir
4. ne ... pas se raconter tout / ne ... pas se parler beaucoup
5. ne ... pas être fidèles
6. ne ... pas être amoureux comme avant

C. Réactions. As your partner repeats the arguments about your deteriorating relationship (from activity B), react to each one.

MODÈLE: se parler mal

—*Nous nous parlons mal.*
—*C'est normal, dernièrement[3] tu es très méchant(e).*

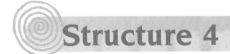

Structure 4

D'autres négations

In French as in English, there are several negations, such as *not, not anymore* or *no longer, nothing,* and *no one.* In French these negations are placed in the sentence like **ne ... pas.** Remember that with reciprocal and reflexive verbs, the reflexive pronoun is included between the negative words along with the verb.

* **ne ... plus** *(not anymore, no longer)*

Susie et Jean-Claude **ne** sont **plus** ensemble. Ils **ne** s'aiment **plus.**

Je **ne** bois **plus** de bière.

Susie and Jean-Claude are no longer together. They don't love each other anymore.

I no longer drink beer.

_____
[1]*sand* [2]*all the time* [3]*lately*

- **ne ... jamais** *(never)*

Vous **ne** vous disputez **jamais.**	*You never argue.*
Elle **ne** tombe **jamais** amoureuse.	*She never falls in love.*

- **ne ... rien** *(nothing, not . . . anything)*

Tu **ne** fais **rien** dans la maison.	*You do nothing in the house.*
Nous **n'**achetons **rien.**	*We're not buying anything.*

- **ne ... personne** *(anyone, no one)*

Je **ne** vois **personne.**	*I don't see anyone.*

Attention! When **ne ... personne** is used as the subject of the sentence, **personne** takes the place of the subject pronoun, and it is followed by **ne** + the verb. As in English, the verb is conjugated in the third person singular.

Personne ne parle en classe.	*No one speaks in class.*
Personne ne veut faire le ménage.	*No one wants to clean the house.*

VÉRIFIEZ VOTRE COMPRÉHENSION

1. Go back to the stories about Anou and Jean and Yolanda and Gérard on page 264 and find the negations other than **ne ... pas.** Observe how they are used in context.

2. How would you say in French that Gérard and Yolanda never look at each other? And that Anou and Jean no longer call each other on the phone?

Pratiquons!

A. Tu es très déprimé! David's best friend tells him why he thinks David is depressed. Complete the sentences with appropriate negations other than **ne ... pas.**

Je crois que tu es déprimé, David. Premièrement, tu (1) _____ veux _____ sortir avec les copains: tu restes toujours à la maison. Quand tu es à la maison, tu (2) _____ fais _____: tu es sur ton fauteuil à zapper. Deuxièmement, tu (3) _____ réponds _____ au téléphone quand on t'appelle. Alors, tu comprends maintenant pourquoi (4) _____ _____ t'appelle au téléphone. Troisièmement, tu as arrêté[1] de faire du sport. Pourquoi est-ce que tu (5) _____ joues _____ au tennis avec moi le samedi matin? Franchement, tu dois voir un docteur bientôt.

B. Ta nouvelle vie. Tell a classmate about changes that you have made in your lifestyle over the years. Mention five things that you no longer do and five things that you never do. Ask your partner some questions, too—s/he may answer in the affirmative or in the negative.

> MODÈLE: *Je ne fume plus et je ne mange jamais de viande. Et toi, est-ce que tu manges toujours beaucoup de fruits?*

---

[1]*stopped*

À vous de parler!

You may want to direct students back to the **psycho-test** at the beginning of the chapter. You may also bring a real French **psycho-test** to class for students to use as inspiration, or merely to see what it looks like.

**A. Un psycho-test.** You are a contributor to the French fashion magazine *Elle*. You and a colleague (your partner) are making up a personality test for the next issue. When you have finished the test, hand it out to other colleagues (your group members) to see if it works before it gets published. Share the results of the personality test with the rest of the class.

Idées pour le psycho-test

Êtes-vous heureux (heureuse) de votre vie?
Êtes-vous fidèle en amour? En amitié?
Avez-vous une vie équilibrée?
Êtes-vous une personne organisée ou désorganisée?

B. Devinez les célébrités. Tell the class a love story about a famous couple, or describe the routine of a famous person. Your classmates must guess who these people are.

Online Study Center
Web Search Activities

Les couples mixtes sont comme ça en France

En général, les Français se marient avec des personnes qui habitent à 100 kilomètres autour de[1] leur domicile. Mais, ce n'est pas le cas pour tous les Français. Il y a 10% de mariages qui sont mixtes et ce pourcentage augmente toujours. Les couples mixtes peuvent être formés par deux nationalités différentes ou par deux ethnies différentes. Les couples de mixité ethnique rencontrent plus de problèmes liés au racisme que les couples qui ont deux nationalités mais une même couleur de peau[2]. On appelle les enfants nés de couples mixtes ethniques des métis. Plus particulièrement, les enfants nés d'un couple blanc-noir sont des mulâtres. Souvent, les enfants mulâtres souffrent de leurs différences: ils ne sont considérés ni blancs en France, ni noirs en Afrique. Ils sont «caféolait[3]».

Si l'intégration sociale est parfois difficile, l'intégration familiale est encore plus compliquée: par exemple, les Français «blancs» ne voient pas bien que leur fils ou leur fille épouse un Maghrébin, un Martiniquais ou un Africain et vice versa.

Mais tout n'est pas négatif! Les couples mixtes symbolisent une alliance entre deux univers. Ils sont unis par un amour qui est plus grand et plus fort que tout: religion, langue, culture, etc. Ces couples incarnent le grand amour! De plus, la famille mixte est biculturelle et bi-identitaire. Finalement, ces couples mixtes ont une mentalité très ouverte: ils sont tolérants et respectueux des cultures différentes. Chacun dans le couple pratique des choses de la culture de l'autre et ils se sentent bien adaptés dans les deux cultures.

---

[1]*around* [2]*skin* [3]**Caféolait (café au lait)** means literally *coffee with milk*. Depending on how this expression is used, it could be offensive.

Réfléchissons

1. Dans votre pays, y a-t-il beaucoup de couples mixtes? Souffrent-ils de racisme aussi? Ont-ils des problèmes d'intégration?
2. Pensez-vous que les enfants métis ou «caféolait» ont des problèmes d'identité? Pourquoi?
3. Pensez-vous que l'amour qui unit les couples mixtes est plus pur et plus fort que l'amour qui existe dans les couples non-mixtes? Pourquoi?

Partie II: À un carrefour animé 🎧

Online Study Center
Language Skills Practice

L'AGENT DE POLICE: Monsieur, est-ce que vous vous êtes blessé dans l'accident?

MONSIEUR: Juste un peu. Je me suis coupé la main en sortant de la voiture, mais ce n'est pas grave.

L'AGENT: O.K. Expliquez-moi donc exactement ce qui s'est passé.

MONSIEUR: Bon. J'arrivais[1] au carrefour. J'avais la priorité[2], donc j'ai continué à rouler. Je n'ai pas regardé la route pendant une seconde, et *boum!* je me suis heurté contre la voiture de cette dame[3]. Elle ne s'est pas arrêtée pour me laisser la priorité. Et c'est clairement indiqué—elle a un stop en plus! Elle n'a même pas freiné.

L'AGENT: Je vois, calmez-vous, Monsieur. Vous avez dit que vous n'avez pas fait attention à la route pendant une seconde. Pourquoi? Est-ce qu'il y avait quelque chose d'intéressant ailleurs[4]?

MONSIEUR: Eh oui, euh non—pas exactement.

L'AGENT: Expliquez-vous, s'il vous plaît.

MONSIEUR: D'accord. J'ai dû quitter la maison ce matin sans me raser, mais je ne voulais pas arriver au travail comme ça. Ça ne fait pas très professionnel, vous savez. Alors, je me suis rasé dans la voiture—mais seulement quand il n'y avait[5] pas d'autres voitures, ou quand j'avais la priorité. Je suis très prudent, vous comprenez! C'est cette dame qui a causé cet accident!

UN AUTRE AGENT
DE POLICE: Madame, est-ce que vous vous êtes blessée?

MADAME: Non, pas du tout. Heureusement que j'avais mis[6] ma ceinture de sécurité!

L'AGENT: Oui, heureusement. Expliquez-moi exactement ce qui s'est passé.

MADAME: Je ne sais pas exactement. Ça s'est passé très vite. Je roulais[7] à la vitesse[8] indiquée, j'ai regardé dans le rétroviseur un instant, et *boum!* je me suis cognée contre la voiture de ce monsieur. Il ne s'est pas arrêté. Il devait[9] s'arrêter! Il y a un stop!

L'AGENT: Et pourquoi est-ce que vous avez regardé dans le rétroviseur? Il y avait quelqu'un derrière vous?

MADAME: Euh ... non, il n'y avait personne.

L'AGENT: Et alors?

MADAME: O.K., je confesse. J'étais[10] un peu pressée ce matin. J'ai quitté la maison sans me maquiller, et donc je me suis maquillée dans la voiture. J'étais en train[11] de me mettre le rouge à lèvres quand ce monsieur a causé l'accident!

---

[1]*I was arriving* [2]*I had the right of way.* **La priorité à droite** is part of the French road code. It stipulates that the driver coming from the right has the right of way, and all others must yield to that driver, even if they do not have a stop sign. This law does not apply, however, when there are posted four-way stop signs. In those cases, all drivers must stop. [3]*lady* [4]*elsewhere* [5]*there weren't* [6]*I had put on* [7]*I was driving* [8]*speed* [9]*He was supposed* [10]*I was* [11]*I was in the process of*

Vous avez bien compris?

Answer the following questions by checking the appropriate response.

	Monsieur	Madame	les deux
1. Qui s'est blessé dans l'accident?	_____	_____	_____
2. Qui était en retard ce matin?	_____	_____	_____
3. Qui ne regardait pas la rue au moment de l'accident?	_____	_____	_____
4. Qui veut avoir l'air professionnel?	_____	_____	_____
5. Qui s'est maquillé dans la voiture?	_____	_____	_____
6. Qui s'est rasé dans la voiture?	_____	_____	_____
7. Qui a un stop?	_____	_____	_____
8. D'après vous, qui a causé l'accident?	_____	_____	_____

Vocabulaire essentiel

La voiture

le rétroviseur

le volant

la ceinture de sécurité

les freins *(m.)*   l'accélérateur *(m.)*

les pneus *(m.)*

Pour conduire

appuyer sur l'accélérateur / accélérer
freiner / mettre les freins
s'arrêter
rouler vite / lentement

conduire prudemment / imprudemment
faire le plein *(to fill up)*
démarrer *(to start the engine)*

Expansion personnelle

Dans la voiture

les sièges *(m.)* arrière

les sièges *(m.)* avant

le pare-brise

les vitesses *(f.)*

les essuie-glaces *(m.)*

Pour conduire

mettre les essuie-glaces
laisser la priorité (à droite)

avoir un pneu crevé *(to have a flat tire)*
mettre de l'air dans les pneus / gonfler les pneus

À vous!

A. Un accident. The police are trying to establish the order of events in the accident described in ***Continuons!*** Recreate the chronology by numbering the following events. The first one has been numbered for you.

Answer Key: 2, 7, 1, 8, 3, 6, 4, 5

_____ Elle a décidé de se maquiller.

_____ Monsieur et Madame se sont disputés.

__1__ Madame a quitté sa maison en retard, donc elle s'est dépêchée.

_____ Elle a téléphoné à la police.

_____ Elle a pris[1] son rouge à lèvres de son sac.

_____ Monsieur et Madame se sont regardés.

_____ Elle s'est maquillée.

_____ La voiture de Madame s'est cognée contre la voiture de Monsieur.

B. En voiture. Tell what you do in each of the following situations when you are driving, using the verb in parentheses.

> **MODÈLE:** quand il pleut (mettre)
>
> *Quand il pleut, je mets les essuie-glaces.*

1. pour vous arrêter (mettre)
2. pour aller plus vite (appuyer sur)
3. quand vous avez un pneu crevé (gonfler)
4. pour tourner dans une rue (tourner)
5. pour voir s'il y a quelqu'un derrière vous (regarder dans)
6. quand vous n'avez pas d'essence[2] (faire)
7. quand il fait mauvais (conduire [je conduis])

Remind students that the second person pronoun **vous** of the cue must be replaced by a first person pronoun (**je, me, moi,** etc.) in their response.

Answer Key: 1. je mets les freins 2. j'appuie sur l'accélérateur 3. je gonfle le pneu 4. je tourne le volant 5. je regarde dans le rétroviseur 6. je fais le plein 7. je conduis prudemment

C. C'est normal? Tell if the first activity is logical or not when one is performing the second activity.

> **MODÈLE:** s'endormir / voyager dans un avion
>
> *Il est normal de s'endormir quand on voyage dans un avion.*

1. lire un magazine / voyager en train
2. se laver les cheveux / se doucher
3. se brosser les dents / conduire une voiture (on conduit)
4. regarder par la fenêtre / voyager en bus
5. se mettre du rouge à lèvres / se maquiller
6. s'endormir / être en classe
7. s'arrêter / avoir la priorité
8. se dépêcher / être en retard
9. s'habiller / aller travailler
10. manger / se brosser les dents
11. se coucher / aller danser

To help students structure their responses, consider putting the following on the board:

Il est normal de … quand on …
Il n'est pas normal de … quand on …

Answer Key: 1. normal / voyage 2. normal / se douche 3. pas normal / conduit 4. normal / voyage 5. normal / se maquille 6. pas normal / est 7. pas normal / a 8. normal / est 9. normal / va 10. pas normal / se brosse 11. pas normal / va

---

[1]*take out* [2]*gas*

Structure 5

Online Study Center
ACE, Language Skills
Practice

Les verbes pronominaux au passé composé

As you learned in this chapter, pronominal verbs are those verbs that require an object pronoun in addition to the subject pronoun. These pronouns show that the action of the verb is reflected back on the subject **(verbes réfléchis),** as in **je me rase,** or that the action occurs reciprocally between two subjects **(verbes réciproques),** for example, **nous nous téléphonons.**

In the **passé composé,** *all* pronominal verbs are conjugated with the verb **être.** Look at this conjugation of the verb **se laver** in the **passé composé.** Notice that both the object pronoun and the auxiliary verb change forms to agree with the subject pronoun. Notice too, that as with other verbs conjugated with **être,** the past participle agrees in gender and number with the subject pronoun.

se laver	
je **me suis** lavé(e)	nous **nous sommes** lavé(e)s
tu **t'es** lavé(e)	vous **vous êtes** lavé(e)(s)
il **s'est** lavé / on **s'est** lavé	ils **se sont** lavés
elle **s'est** lavée	elles **se sont** lavées

All other pronominal verbs are conjugated the same way in the **passé composé,** whether they have a reflexive or reciprocal meaning. There are two exceptions to the agreement rule, however:

- If the verb is followed by a noun that is its direct object, there is no agreement.

  Marie **s'est coupé** la main.
  Nous **nous sommes brossé** les dents.

Remind students of the verbs they have learned that require an *indirect* object: **parler à, téléphoner à, dire à, écrire à.** The past participles of these verbs do not agree when the verbs are used pronominally in the **passé composé.**

- If the reflexive pronoun is the indirect object of the verb, rather than the direct object, there is no agreement. Contrast the following:

  Elles **se sont regardées.** (On regarde *quelqu'un.* **Se** is a direct object[1]. There is agreement in this instance.)
  But: Ils **se sont téléphoné.** (On téléphone *à* quelqu'un. **Se** is an indirect object. There is no agreement here.)
  Nous **nous sommes écrit.** (On écrit *à* quelqu'un.)
  Elles **se sont parlé.** (On parle *à* quelqu'un.)

Negation. To negate pronominal verbs in the **passé composé,** place **ne** before the reflexive pronoun, and **pas, jamais, plus,** or **rien** after the auxiliary verb.

Je **ne** me suis **pas** lavé les cheveux ce matin.
Cet homme et moi, nous **ne** nous sommes **jamais** parlé.
Nous **ne** nous sommes **rien** dit.

---

[1]Reminder: A direct object is an object that follows the verb directly, without needing a preposition to introduce it. An indirect object, by contrast, always requires a preposition between the verb and the noun. Be aware that these can be different in English and French, for example, in English: *I listen **to** the radio,* but in French **J'écoute la radio.** A pronoun will have the same grammatical features as the noun it replaces.

Interrogation. The interrogative form is created in the same way as with other verbs.

- By simple intonation: Tu t'es reposé ce week-end?
- By adding **est-ce que** to the beginning of the sentence: **Est-ce que** tu t'es reposé ce week-end?[1]

VÉRIFIEZ VOTRE COMPRÉHENSION

Go back to the dialogues between the police officers and the accident victims (p. 271), and answer the following questions.

1. Which pronominal verbs are used in the **passé composé?** Underline them.

2. Look at the forms of each of the following: the reflexive pronouns, the auxiliary verbs, and the past participles. Can you explain why each has the form it does?

3. Are any of these verbs used in the negative or the interrogative? How is each formed?

4. Look in particular at the *first* question that each police officer asks each accident victim. Is this question exactly the same? If not, explain why not.

Answer Key: 1. Abdou s'est douché. 2. Clémentine s'est lavé les cheveux (no agreement because there is an object after the pronominal verb). 3. Ils se sont téléphoné (no agreement because **se** is an indirect object). 4. Il s'est rasé. 5. Il s'est habillé. 6. Elle s'est dépêchée. 7. Ils se sont mariés. 8. Ils se sont embrassés!

Pratiquons!

A. Une journée bien occupée. Abdou and Clémentine have both had a very busy day. Based on the following eight drawings, use pronominal verbs and the **passé composé** to tell what they did. Pay particular attention to the form of the past participle of each verb.

MODÈLE: Clémentine s'est levée très tôt!

1.　　　　　　　　2.　　　　　　　　3.　　　　　　　　4.

---

[1]You can also form a question by inversion. To do this, invert the subject pronoun and the verb (the reflexive pronoun stays in its usual position, before the verb): T'es-tu reposé ce week-end?

5.   6.   7.   8.

B. Quelle bagarre! *(What a fight!)* Complete the following paragraph with the appropriate verb in the **passé composé.** Pay attention to both the pronoun and the past participle. Camille is speaking.

se fâcher	se lever	se disputer	se laver
se dépêcher	ne ... pas se parler	se recoucher	

Hier, je (1) _____ avec mes camarades de chambre. Quelle bagarre! Cyrille (2) _____ très tôt, et il a réveillé toute la maison avec sa musique. Quand je lui ai demandé de faire moins de bruit, il (3) _____. Anaïs lui a dit qu'il n'était pas respectueux, et ensuite ils (4) _____ aussi! Je (5) _____, mais avec tout ce bruit, je n'ai pas pu me rendormir. Pendant le reste de la journée, j'étais de très mauvaise humeur!

Je (6) _____ une heure plus tard, et j'ai pris une douche. Anaïs (7) _____ juste après moi, et il n'y avait plus d'eau chaude! Pour cette raison, elle (8) _____ dans la douche. Elle était furieuse! Nous (9) _____ pendant tout le reste de la journée. Aujourd'hui, ça va mieux, mais ce n'est pas facile d'habiter avec deux camarades de chambre!

C. Hier / aujourd'hui. With a partner, take turns asking and answering questions based on the following cues, in order to compare and contrast what you did yesterday and what you are going to do today. Use the **passé composé** in the first response, and the **futur proche** in the second.

    MODÈLE: à quelle heure / se coucher

        —À quelle heure est-ce que tu t'es couché(e) hier?

        —Je me suis couché(e) à 11 heures.

        —Et à quelle heure est-ce que tu vas te coucher ce soir?

        —Je vais me coucher à 2 heures du matin!

  1. combien de fois / se brosser les dents
  2. (vous et vos amis) combien de fois / se téléphoner
  3. à quelle heure / se lever
  4. où / se reposer
  5. (vous et vos camarades de chambre) combien de fois / se disputer
  6. (vous et vos amis) où / se rencontrer

D. Hier, j'ai / je suis / je me suis … With a partner, take turns asking and answering the following questions about your activities yesterday. (Note that not all verbs are pronominal!) When you have finished, report your partner's activities to the class.

1. À quelle heure est-ce que tu t'es levé(e) hier?
2. Est-ce que tu t'es brossé les dents avant ou après le petit déjeuner?
3. Es-tu allé(e) au campus? Si oui, à quelle heure? Si non, pourquoi pas?
4. Combien de temps est-ce que tu as passé à faire les devoirs?
5. Est-ce que tu as eu un examen? Si oui, dans quel cours?
6. Qu'est-ce que tu as fait le soir?
7. As-tu dîné chez toi, ou es-tu allé(e) au restaurant?
8. À quelle heure est-ce que tu t'es couché(e)?
9. Est-ce que tu t'es endormi(e) tout de suite?

Portrait personnel

Based on your partner's answers in activities C and D, write a short paragraph in which you describe what s/he did yesterday. Compare that with what s/he is going to do tomorrow. As a class, decide who had the busiest day yesterday, and who will be busiest tomorrow.

Partie III: Abdou et Clémentine se parlent ◯

Online Study Center
Language Skills Practice

ABDOU:	Allez, ma chérie. Il faut partir maintenant si on veut arriver à l'opéra à l'heure.
CLÉMENTINE:	D'accord. Je suis presque prête. Je vais me dépêcher un peu. Mais est-ce qu'on ne pourrait pas prendre la voiture au lieu de[1] prendre le métro?
ABDOU:	Oh, Clémentine! Tu sais que je n'aime pas conduire à Paris! On y roule comme des fous[2]! J'ai peur d'avoir un accident.
CLÉMENTINE:	Mais tu conduis bien, toi.
ABDOU:	Oui, mais le problème ce n'est pas moi, ce sont les autres. En plus, si on prend la voiture, on doit la garer[3]. Avec le métro, c'est facile— on sort du métro, et on entre directement à l'opéra.
CLÉMENTINE:	D'accord, chéri, tu m'as convaincue. Je suis finalement prête. Allons-y!
ABDOU:	Oh mon amour, que tu es belle ce soir! Restons plutôt à la maison!

---

[1] *instead of* [2] *crazy people* [3] *park it*

Vocabulaire essentiel

Online Study Center
Flashcards, ACE,
Language Skills Practice

Pour parler de sa vie personnelle

Si on est marié(e):	mon mari / mon époux
	ma femme / mon épouse
Si on va se marier:	mon fiancé / ma fiancée
Si on vit[1] avec quelqu'un:	mon compagnon / ma compagne
Si on sort avec quelqu'un:	mon petit ami / ma petite amie
	mon ami(e)[2]
Pour parler d'un grand amour:	mon grand amour
	l'homme / la femme de ma vie

Expansion personnelle

Pour parler directement à la personne qu'on aime[3]

Pour les adultes

mon amour
mon chou (chou)[4]
mon doudou *(my sweetie)*
mon petit chou
mon chéri / ma chérie *(my darling)*

Pour les enfants

ma puce / mon puçon[5]
mon petit chaton[6]
mon tout petit *(my little one)*
mon petit lapin

Remind students that the possessive adjective agrees with the noun being modified, not the person being talked about. Thus, you might use **mon chou** for either a man or a woman.

Remind students that when speaking about someone else, rather than themselves, they must change the possessive adjective: Mon frère et sa femme habitent à Lille. / Et ton compagnon, est-ce qu'il vient ce soir aussi?

À vous!

A. Les couples. Using the words presented in the *Vocabulaire essentiel,* give synonyms for the following situations:

1. La femme de ton frère: c'est son _____.
2. La personne qui cohabite avec ton ami(e): c'est son / sa _____.
3. Le grand amour de ta vie: c'est le / la _____.
4. Une personne avec qui tu sors: c'est ton / ta _____.
5. Le mari de quelqu'un: c'est son _____.

Answer Key: 1. épouse 2. son compagnon / sa compagne 3. l'homme / la femme de ma vie 4. ton petit ami / ta petite amie 5. époux / mari

B. Des mots doux! Give a pet name (**des mots tendres, des mots doux**) for the following people.

1. ton (ta) fiancé(e)
2. ton (ta) petit(e) ami(e)
3. ton enfant
4. ton époux / épouse

Answer Key. Possible answers: 1. mon chéri / ma chérie / mon amour 2. mon chou-chou 3. ma puce / mon puçon / mon petit chaton 4. mon amour / mon doudou

---

[1]*is living* [2]Note that when you speak of someone as **mon ami(e),** the expression is generally understood in a romantic sense. To indicate that you are only friends, use the expression **un(e) de mes ami(e)s** or **un copain / une copine.** [3]Some of these pet names may seem a bit strange to you at first. Think, though, of the pet names that are used in English. What do you call the people you love? What do they call you? (The authors note a variety of names, ranging from *pumpkin* to *peaches* to *cupcake.* Maybe the French **chou** isn't so strange after all!) [4]*literally, cabbage* [5]*literally, flea* [6]*literally, kitten*

Structure 6

Les verbes *conduire* et *rouler*; les verbes *quitter*, *sortir* et *partir*

Online Study Center
ACE, Language Skills
Practice

As in English, French has several words with quite similar meanings but different uses. In this section, you will learn five such verbs.

The verbs **conduire** and **rouler** are both used in connection with driving a vehicle, but their usage differs.

Rouler is a regular **-er** verb that is used when you want to say, for example, *I ride a bike* (**Je roule à bicyclette**) or *I drive fast* (**Je roule vite**). For French speakers, it evokes the actual turning of the wheels, and is therefore used when you can conjure up that mental image. In the **passé composé,** it is conjugated with the verb **avoir.**

Hier, j'**ai roulé** à bicyclette pour aller en ville.

Conduire is a verb that is used when talking about driving a motorized vehicle, such as a car, bus, or truck. For French speakers, it evokes the notion of a **conducteur,** that is, the person responsible for steering or guiding the vehicle. Thus, while the French say **Je roule vite,** they tend to say **Je conduis prudemment.** The difference lies in the speed at which the wheels turn and the carefulness with which one guides the car. **Conduire** is an irregular verb, with the following conjugation.

conduire	
je conduis	nous conduisons
tu conduis	vous conduisez
il / elle / on conduit	ils / elles conduisent
passé composé: (avoir) conduit	

Model the pronunciation of the verb **conduire** in sentences, for example: **Je conduis rapidement. Tu conduis sur l'autoroute. Elle conduit sa voiture rouge.** ... Have students repeat after you.

Quitter, sortir, and **partir** all mean *to leave,* but their usage is very different. **Quitter** is a regular **-er** verb that can only be used to mean *to leave someplace or someone.* It must *always* be followed by a direct object. You must tell who or what you are leaving, otherwise the sentence is ungrammatical in French.

Je **quitte ma maison** à 7 h 30 du matin.
Elle **quitte sa mère** pour retourner au travail.

In the **passé composé, quitter** is conjugated with **avoir.**

Il **a quitté sa femme.**
Nous **avons quitté le restaurant** à 9 h.

Sortir means *to leave* in the sense of *to go out* or *to go out of* and generally implies that you will eventually be returning. It can also be used to mean *to go out with someone socially* or *to date.*

Je sors **avec** mes amis.
Nous sortons **de** la boulangerie.

Partir also means *to leave,* but does not imply that you will return. You can leave for work, leave on vacation, or leave for good.

Elle **part** au travail à 6 heures du matin.
Mes parents **partent** en voyage.

Sortir and **partir** are both irregular verbs, with very similar conjugations.

sortir		partir	
je **sors**	nous **sortons**	je **pars**	nous **partons**
tu **sors**	vous **sortez**	tu **pars**	vous **partez**
il / elle / on **sort**	ils / elles **sortent**	il / elle / on **part**	ils / elles **partent**
passé composé: (être) sorti		**passé composé:** (être) parti	

VÉRIFIEZ VOTRE COMPRÉHENSION

1. What patterns do you see in the present tense conjugation of **conduire, partir,** and **sortir?**

2. Look back at the dialogue between Abdou and Clémentine (p. 277). Which of the verbs **conduire, rouler, quitter, partir,** and **sortir** do they use? Can you explain the choice of each, given the context?

3. Can you give the entire conjugation of **conduire, partir,** and **sortir** in the **passé composé?**

À l'écoute! Listen to the following statements, then indicate whether each refers to one person or to several people.

	une personne	plusieurs personnes
1.	_____	_____
2.	_____	_____
3.	_____	_____
4.	_____	_____
5.	_____	_____
6.	_____	_____

Pratiquons!

A. La conduite de Simone. Simone is describing her daily commute to campus. Complete the following paragraph with the correct form of **rouler** or **conduire** in the present tense.

Je (1) _____ ma voiture pour aller au campus. Normalement, je (2) _____ vite, mais quand il y a beaucoup de circulation, je (3) _____ plus prudemment, bien sûr! Le problème, c'est que beaucoup d'autres étudiants (4) _____ pour aller au campus aussi, et il n'y a jamais assez de parking! Dans les parkings, on (5) _____ assez lentement, et s'il y a beaucoup de monde, on risque d'être en retard pour les cours. Pour cette raison, beaucoup de mes amis prennent le bus, ou (6) _____ à vélo. Et vous, est-ce que vous (7) _____ à l'université, ou est-ce que vous y allez à pied ou à vélo?

B. *Sortir, partir* **ou** *quitter?* Simone continues describing her day. Complete the paragraph with the correct form of **sortir, partir,** or **quitter** in the present tense.

Le lundi matin, je (1) _____ ma maison à 8 h 30. J'ai un cours à 9 h, alors je me dépêche. J'arrive à l'université vers 8 h 55, je (2) _____ de ma voiture et je vais vite à mon cours. Mon cours est au troisième étage, donc je prends l'ascenseur. Très souvent, mon prof y est aussi. Nous (3) _____ de l'ascenseur, et nous allons ensemble en classe. Nous (4) _____ la classe à 10 h 30, et je rencontre mes amis pour prendre un café. Mes amis (5) _____ avant moi, parce qu'ils ont un autre cours. Je reste encore quelques minutes, et puis je (6) _____ pour la bibliothèque, où je travaille jusqu'à 1 h. Mon amie Paule fait aussi des recherches à la bibliothèque, mais elle (7) _____ souvent parce qu'elle fume, et elle ne peut pas fumer dans la bibliothèque! Après avoir fini mes recherches, je (8) _____ chez moi. J'y arrive vers 3 h 30.

C. Échange. Ask a partner the following questions. When you've finished, report your findings to the rest of the class.

1. À quelle heure est-ce que tu as quitté ta maison / ta chambre aujourd'hui?
2. As-tu conduit à l'université? Si non, comment es-tu venu(e)?
3. En général, est-ce que tu roules vite ou lentement?
4. Est-ce que tu as jamais eu une contravention[1]?
5. Est-ce que tu es sorti(e) hier soir? Si oui, avec qui? Où es-tu allé(e)? Si non, qu'est-ce que tu as fait?
6. Quand tu pars en vacances, comment est-ce que tu y vas? (Est-ce que tu conduis? Est-ce que tu prends le bus ou l'avion?)
7. Quand est-ce que tu es parti(e) en vacances la dernière fois? Où es-tu allé(e)?
8. À quelle heure vas-tu quitter le campus aujourd'hui?
9. Est-ce que tu as quitté ta petite amie / ton petit ami récemment? Pourquoi?

Comment est la voiture Smart? Pourquoi est-elle si[2] petite? Est-ce qu'elle peut transporter des passagers? Comment la trouvez-vous (confortable, dangereuse, pratique, marrante, etc.)?

[1]*ticket* [2]*so*

À vous de parler!

A. Préparons une sortie! You and your friends are planning a weekend getaway. In groups of three or four, create a dialogue in which you talk about where you are going to go, how you are going to get there, what time you are going to leave, and what you are going to do each day while you're there. Incorporate as many pronominal verbs as you can, along with the verbs **sortir, partir, quitter, conduire,** and **rouler,** in the **futur proche.**

B. Oui, chéri(e)! With a partner, imagine a conversation between a couple who have been married for a long time or between two friends who have known each other for a long time. Talk about what you did the first time you went out, and compare that to what you do now on a typical Friday or Saturday evening. Incorporate as many verbs from this chapter as you can, along with some **mots tendres** for one another.

À vous d'écrire!

Online Study Center
Language Skills Practice

A. Stratégies. Writing often involves incorporating other language skills beyond grammar and vocabulary. Think of an occasion when you were inspired by something that you read or heard. Did the *topic* encourage you to express similar feelings? Did the *style* provide you with a model that you could emulate? Did the author's choice of vocabulary make you think about his or her perspective on the topic? Why did this writing or speech inspire you?

The song *"Ne me quitte pas"* by Jacques Brel (a Belgian singer and songwriter who was famous in the 1960s) is one of the most beautiful love songs written in French. You may want to print out the lyrics and discuss how the singer expresses his love and his sorrow. A link to the lyrics can be found on the Instructor Companion Website for *À vous!*. You will also find there another love song that is more contemporary: *"Le toi du moi"* by Carla Bruni.

B. Organisons-nous! Read the following excerpt from a love letter that was written by Napoléon to Joséphine. Note how the writer expresses his love for his wife. Note, too, the simplicity of the text. The language of this excerpt is not out of your reach. In fact, you could produce such a letter at the end of one semester of study! Read the text, then answer the questions that follow.

Lettre de Napoléon Bonaparte à Joséphine

Je vais me coucher, ma petite Joséphine, le cœur plein de ton adorable image, et navré[1] de rester tant de temps loin de toi; mais j'espère que, dans quelques jours, je serai[2] plus heureux et que je pourrai[3] à mon aise[4] te donner des preuves de l'amour ardent que tu m'as inspiré. Tu ne m'écris plus; tu ne penses plus à ton bon ami, cruelle femme! Ne sais-tu pas que sans toi, sans ton cœur, sans ton amour, il n'est[5] pour ton mari ni bonheur, ni vie. Bon Dieu! ...

---

[1]*extrêmement triste* [2]*vais être* [3]*vais pouvoir* [4]*avec satisfaction* [5]*il n'y a*

C. Pensons-y!

1. What makes the text "work"? What language has the author chosen to express his love?
2. Are there terms of endearment in the text? If so, which ones? If not, how does the author express his love without such terms?
3. If you were going to express your love for someone (a lover, a parent, a friend, etc.), which words and expressions would you use to do so?
4. Choose one person whom you love (romantically or otherwise), and list some of the ways that you know to express your love for that person in French. What will you write: A song? A poem? A letter? Something else? Will you address the person directly, or talk *about* him or her? Will you use any terms of endearment? If so, which ones? If not, how will you communicate your feelings?

Voici un couple de jeunes mariés près de l'église. Sont-ils déjà[1] mariés? Que fait la mariée? Qu'est-ce que les invités lancent aux mariés? Du riz? Qu'est-ce qu'on lance aux mariés aux États-Unis?

D. Écrivons!

Using the model in activity B or another model with which you are familiar, write a paragraph in which you express your love for someone. This may be in the form of a letter, a song, a poem, or a narrative. Be careful to use expressions and structures with which you are already familiar. Consider your audience carefully!

E. Révisons!

Review your text, answering the following questions:

How can you make the content clearer?
How can you make your message clearer?
How can you simplify rather than complicate your structures?

Look again at Napoléon's letter and note again its simplicity. Is your text equally simple, yet equally effective? If not, what changes would you propose? Rewrite your text, and then share it with the person for whom or about whom you have written it!

---

[1] *already*

Lexique ⌂

Vocabulaire essentiel

La routine

se brosser les dents *to brush one's teeth*
se calmer *to calm oneself down*
se coucher *to go to bed*
se démaquiller *to remove one's makeup*
se dépêcher *to hurry*
se déshabiller *to remove one's clothes*
s'endormir *to fall asleep*

s'énerver *to get nervous*
s'épiler *to use an epilator—women*
s'habiller *to get dressed*
se laver *to wash*
se lever *to get up*
se maquiller *to put makeup on*
se peigner les cheveux *to comb one's hair*
se presser *to hurry*

se promener *to go for a walk*
se raser *to shave*
se reposer *to rest*
se réveiller *to wake up*
se ronger les ongles *to bite one's nails*
se sécher les cheveux *to dry one's hair*
se sentir bien / mal *to feel well / bad*

Les relations amoureuses et amicales

Les noms

l'amour *(m.) love*   les amoureux *lovebirds / lovers*   le coup de foudre *love at first sight*

Les verbes

aimer quelqu'un à la folie *to love someone madly*
s'aimer *to love each other*
s'amuser *to have fun*
avoir une déception amoureuse *to have one's heart broken*
se détester *to hate each other*
se dire *to tell each other*
se disputer *to argue with each other*
divorcer *to get a divorce*
s'embrasser *to kiss each other*

s'ennuyer *to be bored*
s'entendre bien *to get along well*
s'entendre mal *to not get along well*
être amoureux(euse) de quelqu'un *to be in love with someone*
être fidèle à quelqu'un *to be faithful to someone*
se fâcher *to get mad*
se fiancer *to get engaged*
se marier (avec) *to get married*
partir *to leave (for an undetermined period of time)*

quitter *to leave (someone or something)*
se quitter *to leave each other*
se réconcilier (avec) *to reconcile*
se rencontrer *to meet each other*
se regarder *to look at each other*
sortir *to go out, to get out of, to leave (for a short time)*
se téléphoner *to call each other*
tromper quelqu'un *to cheat on someone*

Dans la voiture

l'accélérateur *(m.) gas pedal*
la ceinture de sécurité *seat belt*

les freins *(m.) brakes*
les pneus *(m.) tires*

le rétroviseur *rear-view mirror*
le volant *steering wheel*

Pour conduire

appuyer sur l'accélérateur / accélérer *to push on the accelerator, to accelerate*
s'arrêter *to stop*

conduire (prudemment / imprudemment) *to drive (carefully, carelessly)*
démarrer *to start the engine*
faire le plein *to fill up*

freiner / mettre les freins *to brake, to put on the brakes*
rouler (vite / lentement) *to drive (quickly / slowly)*

Pour parler de sa vie personnelle

mon compagnon / ma compagne *my partner*
ma femme / mon épouse *my wife / my spouse (fem.)*
mon / ma fiancé(e) *my fiancé(e)*

mon grand amour / l'homme/la femme de ma vie *my soulmate / my true love*
mon mari / mon époux *my husband / my spouse (masc.)*

mon petit ami / mon ami *my boyfriend*
ma petite amie / mon amie *my girlfriend*

Expansion personnelle

Expressions supplémentaires sur les relations amoureuses et amicales

se donner un baiser *to kiss (generally on the lips)*
se faire la bise *to kiss (generally on the cheeks)*

se raconter tout *to tell each other everything*
revenir ensemble *to get back together*

se séparer *to be apart / to separate*
tomber amoureux / amoureuse de quelqu'un *to fall in love with someone*

Dans la voiture

les essuie-glaces *(m.) windshield wipers*
le pare-brise *windshield*

les sièges *(m.)* (avant / arrière) *seats (front / back)*

les vitesses *(f.) gears*

Pour conduire

avoir un pneu crevé *to have a flat tire*
laisser la priorité (à droite) *to have the right of way (to the right)*

mettre les essuie-glaces *to start the windshield wipers*

mettre de l'air dans les pneus / gonfler les pneus *to put air in the tires*

Pour parler à la personne qu'on aime

Pour les adultes

mon amour *my love*
mon / ma chéri(e) *my darling*

mon chou (chou) *my cabbage*
mon doudou *my sweetie*

mon petit chou *my little cabbage*

Pour les enfants

mon petit chaton *my kitten*
mon petit lapin *my little rabbit*

ma puce / mon puçon *my flea*
mon tout petit *my little one*

MISE EN PRATIQUE

À vous de découvrir!

Pour faire les activités ci-dessous, allez au *Online Study Center* et choisissez *Mise en pratique.* Vous y trouverez des sites Internet correspondants aux mots ou phrases en caractères gras dans chaque activité.

La Provence

Dans cette unité, nous vous proposons de découvrir la Provence. Pour votre visite virtuelle, travaillez avec un(e) ou deux camarade(s) de classe. À l'aide des sites Internet correspondants à chaque section, recherchez les thèmes suivants.

A. Informations générales. Allez au **Site Web de Houghton Mifflin** et cliquez sur **Mise en Pratique 2.** Vous allez voir plusieurs sites web pour Provence. Allez visiter un ou plusieurs de ces sites, et répondez aux questions suivantes.

1. Quelle région géographique est inclue dans la Provence?
2. Cochez (____✓____) ce qu'on peut y trouver:
   _____ des villages   _____ la montagne
   _____ des villes de taille moyenne   _____ la mer
   _____ des grandes villes   _____ la campagne
3. Comment est-ce que vous décririez[1] la Provence?
   _____

Allez visiter la ville de **Nice.**

1. Quelle est la population de cette ville?
2. Imaginez que vous êtes là le week-end. Qu'est-ce que vous pouvez y faire?
   Activités à l'extérieur: _____
   Musées: _____
   Autres: _____
   Parmi ces activités, lesquelles vous intéressent le plus, personnellement?
   _____

Ensuite, allez visiter le village de **Barcelonnette** (dans les **Alpes de Haute Provence**).

1. Où se trouve ce village? Quelle en est la population?
2. Cette région a une abondance d'activités (sportives et artistiques). Faites une liste de cinq activités que vous trouvez intéressantes. Est-ce que vous voudriez essayer une de ces activités? Laquelle? Laquelle est-ce que vous n'oseriez pas[2] essayer?
   _____
   _____

#2 Possible answers: hikes, paragliding, hang-gliding, ultralight planes, downhill skiing, cross-country skiing, snow-shoeing, snowmobiling, dogsledding, craft workshops (faience-type earthenware, pottery, enamel, sculpture)

---

[1] *would you describe* [2] *wouldn't dare*

Finalement, allez visiter **Avignon.**

1. Où se trouve cette ville? Comment est-ce que vous pouvez y arriver?
2. Quelle en est la population?
3. Pourquoi est-ce que cette ville est célèbre? (Mentionnez au moins 3 choses.)
   _____   _____   _____
4. Qu'est-ce que vous voudriez visiter là-bas? Pourquoi?

Avignon is especially famous for the Palais des Papes (Pope's Palace), the Pont d'Avignon, and its annual theater festival. It also has several very good museums.

B. Produits régionaux.

1. D'après les sites que vous avez visités et les photos que vous avez vues, faites une liste des produits régionaux de Provence.

   Les fruits et les légumes produits en Provence:

   _____   _____
   _____   _____

   Les autres produits de Provence:

   _____   _____
   _____   _____

2. Devinez le climat de la Provence, en regardant cette liste de produits.
3. Est-ce que la région où vous habitez produit aussi quelques-uns de ces fruits ou légumes? Lesquels?
4. Lesquels de ces fruits et légumes est-ce que vous mangez souvent? Lesquels est-ce que vous ne mangez jamais? Pourquoi?

À vous de déguster!

La gastronomie provençale

Nous vous proposons de goûter quelques spécialités de la gastronomie provençale, qui utilise surtout les produits agricoles régionaux. Avant de parler de plats spécifiques, testez vos connaissances sur les produits typiques de Provence. Faites l'activité A, et si vous ne savez pas les réponses, devinez!

Answer Key: 1. b 2. a 3. b 4. c 5. a 6. b

A. Produits provençaux. Mettez un cercle autour de la réponse correcte.

1. C'est un fruit (ou un légume!) rouge qui pousse partout, et qui est un ingrédient important dans la cuisine provençale et italienne.

   a. la cerise   b. la tomate   c. la fraise

2. C'est un fruit qu'on utilise pour faire une boisson alcoolique.

   a. le raisin   b. la pomme   c. la framboise

3. C'est un fruit qui pousse dans la région méditerranéenne, et que l'on presse pour obtenir une huile très fine.

   a. le raisin   b. l'olive   c. l'orange

4. C'est une plante avec une fleur violette. On l'utilise dans la préparation des crèmes médicinales, des parfums et des savons, mais aussi comme herbe dans la cuisine.

   a. la tulipe   b. l'iris   c. la lavande

5. C'est une grande plante avec une fleur jaune énorme, que Van Gogh aimait peindre. Les oiseaux aiment beaucoup manger ses graines, et les hommes aussi!

    a. le tournesol   b. le dahlia   c. la jonquille[1]

6. C'est un fromage qui est fait dans la région, et qui doit son nom à un animal qui donne le lait qu'on utilise pour faire ce fromage. (Cet animal dit «bah ... bah»!)

    a. le brie   b. le chèvre   c. le camembert

Online Study Center
Language Skills Practice

B. La soupe de melon à la menthe.

Est-ce que vous aimez la soupe? En mangez-vous souvent? Très souvent, quand on pense à la soupe, on pense à un plat chaud; mais la soupe peut aussi être froide. En Provence, on mange beaucoup de soupe aux fruits, comme hors-d'œuvre ou même comme dessert. Les soupes froides sont surtout très populaires en été—quand il fait très chaud, c'est un plat froid et léger. La recette suivante est pour une soupe de melon. Est-ce que vous aimeriez l'essayer? Si oui, préparez-la à la maison. Elle est facile à préparer, bonne pour la santé et délicieuse!

Soupe de melon à la menthe: pour 4 personnes

1 gros melon à maturité
1 orange
10 cl. de porto (ou moscatel)
2 cuillères à soupe de sucre en poudre
10 cl. de crème fraîche
125 gr. de framboises
quelques tiges[2] de menthe fraîche

Presser le jus de l'orange. Ouvrir le melon, retirer[3] les graines et les fibres, puis prélever[4] la chair[5] avec une cuillère. Passer la pulpe au mixeur avec le jus d'orange, le porto et le sucre. Ajouter à cela la crème, et mixer pour obtenir une consistance veloutée. Verser[6] dans un saladier, et ajouter deux tiges de menthe lavées et séchées. Couvrir de film étirable et laissez-la se refroidir au réfrigérateur pendant 6 heures. Pour la servir, verser la soupe dans quatre jolies coupes à dessert, et décorez-la avec quelques framboises et une feuille de menthe.

À vous d'analyser

Regardez les annonces publicitaires suivantes. Elles viennent toutes du festival de théâtre d'Avignon, où, chaque été, on peut voir plus de 660 pièces de théâtre différentes! Lisez rapidement les renseignements pour chaque pièce, et puis répondez aux questions qui suivent.

---

[1] *daffodil* [2] *sprigs* [3] *remove* [4] *scoop out* [5] *flesh* [6] *Pour*

A. Réponses guidées.

1. Quelle pièce est basée sur une histoire vraie?
2. Vous êtes père ou mère de famille. À quelles pièces pouvez-vous amener les enfants?
3. Vous êtes avec un groupe d'amis, et vous cherchez quelque chose à faire le samedi après-midi. Quelle(s) pièce(s) pouvez-vous choisir?
4. Vous aimez surtout les comédies. Qu'est-ce que vous allez choisir?
5. Vos parents sont en ville, et ils aiment la musique et la danse. Qu'est-ce que vous allez choisir?
6. En général, qu'est-ce qu'il faut faire pour réserver vos places?
7. À votre avis, est-ce que ces pièces sont chères? Pourquoi mentionne-t-on des prix différents dans les publicités?
8. Et vous, personnellement, quelle pièce vous intéresse le plus? Pourquoi? Quelle pièce ne vous intéresse pas du tout? Pourquoi?
9. Allez-vous souvent au théâtre? Est-ce que vous voudriez être à Avignon en été pour voir le festival?

B. Jeu de rôles. Vous avez décidé d'aller voir une pièce de théâtre avec vos amis, mais vous avez des goûts très différents. Décidez quelle pièce vous allez voir, qui va faire les réservations, où vous allez vous rencontrer, ce que vous allez faire avant ou après la pièce (dîner? discothèque?), etc. Préparez le dialogue entre vous, et présentez-le devant la classe.

À vous de créer!

A. À la recherche d'un emploi! Est-ce que vous cherchez actuellement un emploi? Est-ce que vous voudriez avoir un emploi différent? Est-ce que vous allez chercher un emploi permanent après avoir reçu votre diplôme universitaire? Si la réponse à une de ces questions est «oui», remplissez le formulaire suivant, qui vient de www.emploi.com. Avec ce formulaire, vous pouvez poster votre CV sur Internet, pour chercher un emploi.

Nom*   *Champs obligatoires
Prénom*
E-mail*

Caractéristiques de votre recherche
Type de Contrat*

☐ Poste permanent   ☐ Poste intérim
☐ Stage   ☐ Freelance

Type de Poste*
    (vendeur, électricien, etc.)
Zone géographique souhaitée*
Intitulé du poste souhaité*
    (employé(e), directeur, etc.)
Date disponibilité*

Expérience professionnelle
Niveau d'étude atteint*
Années d'expérience*
Dernière expérience:
Société
Période
Descriptif de votre dernier poste

B. Les préparatifs pour une soirée.
Imaginez que vous avez réussi à trouver l'emploi de vos rêves. Vous allez faire la fête chez vous pour remercier toute votre famille et tous vos amis de leur aide pendant vos études. Mais avant la fête, il faut faire les achats! À côté de chaque commerce donné, dites ce que vous allez y acheter pour préparer votre soirée de célébration.

à la boulangerie: _____
à l'épicerie: _____
chez le marchand de vin: _____
à la crèmerie: _____
à la charcuterie: _____
chez le traiteur: _____

À vous de décider

Le français pour quoi faire

Meet Dr. Randy Duran, a professor of chemistry for whom French has been very important. In this passage, he describes how he has used his knowledge of French in his work and why he encourages his chemistry students to take part in a three-month total immersion internship in France.

"I studied French for three years in high school, but then didn't continue with language studies in college. I eventually wound up doing a Ph.D. in low-dimensional physics at the Université Louis Pasteur in Strasbourg. During those three years of high school French, I never in my wildest dreams imagined that I would continue on to do doctoral work in France. I never would have guessed at that time that the world  is so small, and that, with the forces of globalization, there is so much interaction between Europe and the United States and the rest of the world.

"Knowing French has been extremely valuable. There are a lot of discoveries that are made in science in other countries, and the scientific terminology comes from those countries in which the discovery is first made. Beyond that, knowledge of the language is extremely beneficial in interacting with international and multinational companies. When I got my degree, I had offers from companies all over Europe, because of my knowledge of the language. There are not a lot of Americans who go to a high level in both science and a foreign language, and that combination opens up many opportunities.

"In the internship program that I direct, we take the absolute highest level students that we can find from around the country, and these students are paid by the National Science Foundation, the CNRS, and the French Ministry of Research, and cosponsored by the University of Florida and a number of French universities to spend three months abroad in a total immersion situation in a world-class research laboratory. It's a very valuable work experience for them, and many of the students have continued on to great things, including one Rhodes scholar and a number of Goldwater scholars and other fellowship winners.

"We provide this experience because we feel that being able to read articles in scientific fields is certainly useful, but being able to interact with others in your field, to communicate verbally, is crucial. In today's world we are forced to communicate to be successful. Being able to understand others, and to make yourself understood, will open more doors than any other skill!"

3

MA PLACE DANS LE MONDE

LES TRÉS OR DU TEMPS

FO 423/1 et FO 413/2
Montres dame en or et 18 carats
ec et sans brillants, respectivement
ent Suisse à quartz et verre Saphir

Quand j'étais adolescent(e) ...

Do you have fond memories of your childhood? Do you like to tell others about where you lived, what you did as a child, what your best friends were like? Were you well behaved, or mischievous? In this chapter, you'll have a chance to look back (fondly, we hope!) on those bygone days, and to describe your life and actions to others.

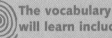

The vocabulary that you will learn includes

School life, including elementary, middle, and high school
Concerns of adolescents
Child-rearing

The grammar that you will learn includes

Formation and uses of the **imparfait**
Pronouns **y** and **en** with the **imparfait**
Interrogative pronouns, and forming questions using the **imparfait**

The culture that you will learn includes

What life is like for teenagers in France
Problems faced by adolescents in various Francophone countries

Commençons!

Une enfance heureuse 🎧

Sandrine, une prof de français qui habite maintenant aux États-Unis, se rappelle son adolescence en Belgique.

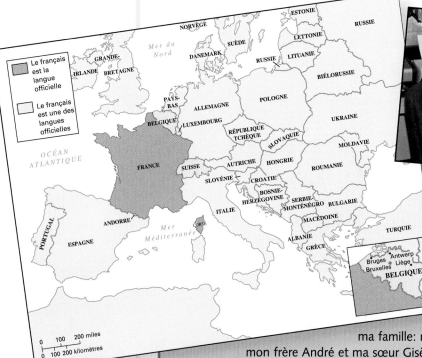

«Bonjour. Je m'appelle Sandrine. Je suis belge. J'habite maintenant aux États-Unis, mais quand j'étais petite, j'habitais avec ma famille à Bruxelles. (C'est la capitale de la Belgique.)

Nous étions cinq dans ma famille: mon père et ma mère, bien sûr, mon frère André et ma sœur Gisèle. Nous avions aussi un chien; il s'appelait Alphonse. Il était toujours très méchant! C'était une enfance très heureuse. Mon frère, ma sœur et moi, nous allions tous à la même école. Nous étions en pension, et donc nous ne retournions chez nous que pendant les grandes vacances. Nous étions dans des classes différentes, mais nous mangions à la cantine à midi et le soir, donc nous nous retrouvions souvent.

Pendant la récréation, j'aimais jouer avec mes amis, mais comme ma sœur était plus timide, elle voulait toujours rester près de moi pendant la récré. Quelquefois, c'était gênant, mais comme c'était ma petite sœur, je ne disais rien. Nous jouions bien ensemble. Mon frère préférait jouer avec ses amis—il ne voulait pas participer aux jeux des filles!

Le week-end, nous allions à la patinoire, au cinéma, à la bibliothèque et, quand nous étions plus grands, en boîtes de nuit. Quelquefois, nous passions la nuit chez des copains qui n'étaient pas en pension, et nous allions à des boums. C'était très amusant! Pendant les grandes vacances, nous retournions chez nos parents et nous voyagions tous ensemble. Nous avons visité la Grande-Bretagne, l'Allemagne, le Portugal et l'Italie.

Maintenant, je retourne assez rarement en Belgique; je suis mariée à un Américain et je travaille à Chicago. Mais j'ai de très bons souvenirs de mon enfance!»

Vous avez bien compris?

Répondez aux questions suivantes, selon le texte.

1. Sandrine a combien de frères et de sœurs?
2. Les enfants, où restaient-ils pendant la semaine, quand ils allaient à l'école?
3. Où mangeaient-ils?
4. Avec qui est-ce que Sandrine jouait pendant la récré? Et son frère? Pourquoi?
5. En général, pendant les grandes vacances, est-ce qu'ils restaient à l'école?
6. Qu'est-ce qu'ils ont fait de différent avec leurs parents?

Et vous?

7. Où est-ce que vous mangiez à midi quand vous étiez à l'école? (Je mangeais ...)
8. Avec qui jouiez-vous pendant la récré? (Je jouais ...)
9. Avez-vous voyagé à l'étranger avec vos parents? Où?

Beginning with this chapter, all direction lines are in French. Make sure that students know what to do before beginning each activity.

Since students have not yet learned the imperfect, allow them to answer in a word or two where possible. If students want to explain their responses (in #5, for example), allow them to pull sentences directly from the dialogue, then provide the correct form for them: #5: **Nous retournions chez nos parents → Ils retournaient chez leurs parents.** Do not insist on correct imperfect forms yet, as the goal here is only to check comprehension.

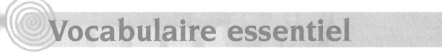

Vocabulaire essentiel

À l'école

Online Study Center
Flashcards, ACE,
Language Skills Practice

Les enfants de 5 à 10 ans vont à **l'école primaire.**

À l'âge de 11 ou 12 ans, on va au **collège.**

Les enfants de cet âge s'appellent **des élèves.**

Pour s'amuser entre les classes, les élèves vont à **la récréation / la récré.**

Quand on est adolescent, on étudie au **lycée.**

Les étudiants de cet âge s'appellent des **lycéens / lycéennes.**

Remind students of the contractions of the prepositions **à** and **de** and the definite articles. Point out examples in these sentences. Help students to determine the gender of the nouns involved, when possible. (Point out that **élève** can be masculine or feminine.)

À l'école, on mange à la **cantine.**

Si on passe les nuits à l'école pendant la semaine, on dort au **dortoir.**

Ces étudiants s'appellent **des pensionnaires;** ils sont **en pension.**

Pour s'amuser

Point out that in Francophone Europe it is not unusual for even elementary school students to be **pensionnaires;** boarding schools are more common in Europe than in the U.S., starting at an early age. Current estimates are that approximately 5% of all French high school students are **pensionnaires.**

On fait du sport au **gymnase** ou au **stade.**

En hiver, on peut s'amuser aussi à la **patinoire.**

Les lycéens et les étudiants d'université s'amusent quelquefois dans **une boîte de nuit** ou dans **une discothèque.**

Ils peuvent aussi assister à **une boum.**

These are words that students will use frequently, or that often cause confusion (**bibliothèque** vs. **librairie,** for example). Take a moment to review them, to point out the difference between **instituteur** or **maître/maîtresse** (an elementary school teacher) and **professeur** (a high school or college-level teacher), and to remind students of the various **matières** that they learned in previous chapters (**la biologie, les maths, le français,** etc.).

À revoir

la bibliothèque	un cours	une table
la librairie	une classe	la salle de classe
l'instituteur / l'institutrice	un bureau	les matières (f.)
un professeur /	un tableau	
une femme professeur		

À vous!

A. Identifications. Regardez les dessins suivants, et identifiez tout le vocabulaire que vous pouvez.

Encourage students to incorporate vocabulary from other chapters.

> 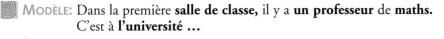 MODÈLE: Dans la première **salle de classe,** il y a **un professeur** de **maths.**
> C'est à **l'université** …

1.

2.

3.

4.

Answer Key: 1. une université / un professeur / des étudiants / les maths / des bureaux / un tableau / (un amphithéâtre / de la craie / des livres / des stylos) 2. un collège (ou un lycée) / une institutrice ou une maîtresse / des élèves / une table / la chimie / (un laboratoire / des cahiers) 3. une école primaire / un instituteur ou un maître / des élèves / des tables / un tableau / (des crayons / des crayons de couleur / du papier / des livres / l'alphabet / les numéros de 1 à 10) 4. un lycée (ou une université) / le gymnase / le stade / des professeurs (ou des entraîneurs) / la gymnastique / l'athlétisme / le football / le basket / le volley, etc.

B. Vrai ou faux? Indiquez si les phrases suivantes sont vraies ou fausses. Si elles sont fausses, corrigez-les!

Answer Key: 1. faux: … chaque élève a un pupitre. 2. vrai 3. vrai 4. faux: Quand on a six ans, on a un instituteur ou une institutrice (ou une maîtresse ou un maître). 5. faux: Les étudiants suivent des cours à l'université. / Les élèves suivent des cours au collège ou à l'école primaire. 6. vrai 7. faux: Les étudiants de 12 à 15 ans vont au collège; ce n'est pas du tout l'équivalent de l'université. 8. faux: On a des cours dans les salles de classe. / On dort dans les chambres.

1. Dans la salle de classe typique, chaque élève a un bureau. _____ vrai _____ faux
2. On écrit au tableau. _____ vrai _____ faux
3. On étudie normalement à la bibliothèque. _____ vrai _____ faux
4. Quand on a 6 ans, on a un professeur. _____ vrai _____ faux
5. Les élèves suivent des cours à l'université. _____ vrai _____ faux
6. Le week-end, pour s'amuser, les étudiants peuvent aller à une boum. _____ vrai _____ faux
7. Les étudiants de 18 à 22 ans vont au collège; c'est l'équivalent de l'université. _____ vrai _____ faux
8. On a des cours dans les chambres. _____ vrai _____ faux

C. Mon enfance. Terminez les dix phrases suivantes pour donner des détails sur votre enfance. Quand vous avez fini, comparez vos réponses avec les réponses de votre partenaire et décidez si vous avez eu des enfances similaires ou différentes. Expliquez vos comparaisons à la classe.

1. À l'école primaire, mon instituteur/institutrice préféré(e) s'appelait _____.

2. Ma matière préférée, c'était _____.

3. Dans une classe typique, il y avait _____ élèves. (Donnez un chiffre.)
4. À midi, je mangeais _____. (Où?)
5. *J'étais / Je n'étais pas* pensionnaire. (Choisissez la bonne réponse.)
6. À la récré, je jouais avec _____.
7. Nous jouions (à) _____.
8. Au collège, *il y avait une récré / il n'y avait plus de récré.* (Choisissez la bonne réponse.)
9. Au lycée, j'étais très fort(e) en _____, et nul(le) en _____!
10. J'étudiais normalement _____ _____. (Où et quand?)

Structure 1

Online Study Center
ACE, Language Skills
Practice

L'imparfait

In Chapter 7, you learned how to talk about completed past actions using the **passé composé.** In this chapter, you will learn another past tense, the **imparfait,** or imperfect, which is used to give descriptions, to talk about ongoing (but not completed) actions, and to talk about habitual actions in the past. In Chapter 10, you will have a chance to focus on the distinction between the **passé composé** and the **imparfait** more fully; for now, we will concentrate on the formation and uses of the **imparfait.**

Formation of the *imparfait.* The imperfect is the most regular tense in the French language. To form it, we start with the **nous** form of the verb in the present indicative, drop the **-ons** ending, and add the imperfect endings. These are the same for all verbs. The only irregular verb in the **imparfait** is **être.** Look at the following conjugations of **parler, finir, avoir,** and **être,** and listen to them on your In-Text Audio CD.

Review the pronunciation of these verbs with your students. Point out that all three singular forms and the third-person plural form all sound alike, and the importance of listening for the subject pronoun. Point out, too, the differences between the present and the imperfect.

parler		finir	
(nous parl~~ons~~)		(nous finiss~~ons~~)	
je parl**ais**	nous parl**ions**	je finiss**ais**	nous finiss**ions**
tu parl**ais**	vous parl**iez**	tu finiss**ais**	vous finiss**iez**
il parl**ait**	ils parl**aient**	elle finiss**ait**	elles finiss**aient**

avoir		être	
(nous av~~ons~~)		(nous ~~sommes~~)	
j'av**ais**	nous av**ions**	j'**étais**	nous ét**ions**
tu av**ais**	vous av**iez**	tu **étais**	vous ét**iez**
il av**ait**	ils av**aient**	elle **était**	elles ét**aient**

To negate a verb in the **imparfait,** follow the same rules as for the present: place **n(e)** before the verb and **pas / jamais / plus,** etc. after it.

> Adrianne **n'**avait **pas** de frères.
> Suzanne **ne** voulait **jamais** aller au cinéma avec nous.
> Il **n'**y avait **personne** dans la rue.
> Alain **ne** mangeait[1] **rien** au petit déjeuner.

Uses of the *imparfait*. The main difference between the **passé composé** and the **imparfait** is one of perspective. With the **passé composé,** we are focused on the fact that an event occurred at a specific point in time, and is now over. In other words, we are focused on the *completion* of that event. With the **imparfait,** we are more interested in the *process:* something was going on, or happened on repeated occasions, and the important point is the *duration,* rather than the completion, of that activity. The **imparfait** is therefore used for the following reasons:

- To give a description in the past:

  > Elle **portait** une jupe rouge.
  > Il **faisait** très beau.

- To talk about time, age, feelings, etc., when the duration is more important than the act:

  > Il **était** midi.   Paul **voulait** aller au cinéma.   J'**avais** 5 ans.

- To talk about habitually repeated actions in the past:

  > Le week-end, nous **faisions** toujours la grasse matinée.

- To talk about ongoing actions without a stated end:

  > Je **lisais** le journal pendant que mon mari **cuisinait.**

  This ongoing action is often interrupted by a verb in the **passé composé:**

  > Je **lisais** le journal quand le téléphone a sonné.

VÉRIFIEZ VOTRE COMPRÉHENSION

1. Look back at Sandrine's description of her childhood (p. 294). Which verbs are in the **imparfait?** What is the infinitive of each of these verbs?

2. For each of the verbs that you identified as being in the **imparfait,** tell what its usage is: Is Sandrine giving descriptions, talking about habitual actions, or talking about ongoing actions?

3. How is **être** irregular in the **imparfait?** What, exactly, is irregular about it?

À l'écoute! 🎧

Écoutez les phrases suivantes, et dites si le verbe est au présent ou à l'imparfait.

1. ____ présent	____ imparfait	5. ____ présent	____ imparfait
2. ____ présent	____ imparfait	6. ____ présent	____ imparfait
3. ____ présent	____ imparfait	7. ____ présent	____ imparfait
4. ____ présent	____ imparfait	8. ____ présent	____ imparfait

This activity is included because some students at this level still tend to pronounce the silent -e at the end of -er verbs in the present tense as [e]. Asking them to distinguish helps them to understand why the correct pronunciation of these verb forms is so important—they now hear a meaningful difference. At the same time, distinguishing between -ons / -ions and -ez / -iez also presents difficulties for many students. You may want to do this activity orally in class, and even expand on it with other sentences.

Audioscript: 1. J'étudiais beaucoup pour préparer les examens. 2. Nous choisissons des cours intéressants. 3. À midi, nous faisons des courses. 4. J'étudie tous les soirs à la bibliothèque. 5. Nous choisissons normalement des restaurants bon marché. 6. Nous faisions nos devoirs ensemble au lycée. 7. Il chantait dans une chorale. 8. Elle chante quand elle écoute la radio.

---

[1]Note that verbs ending in **-ger** add an **e** before the ending to all but the **nous** and **vous** forms (**je mangeais; nous mangions**). Verbs ending in **-cer** change the **c** to **ç** before the ending in all but the **nous** and **vous** forms (**je commençais; nous commencions**).

Pratiquons!

A. Ma vie au lycée. Complétez le paragraphe suivant avec le verbe logique à l'*imparfait*.

passer	avoir	manger
appeler	être (x2)	aller

Quand j(e) (1) _____ lycéen, j(e) (2) _____ trois «meilleurs» amis. Nous (3) _____ toujours le week-end ensemble; nous (4) _____ souvent à la discothèque ou (5) _____ au café. Nous (6) _____ vraiment inséparables! On (7) _____ mes copains et moi les «Quatre Mousquetaires»!

ne … pas faire	ne … pas aimer	préférer	finir
penser	ne … pas étudier	être	réussir

Malheureusement, ma mère (8) _____ beaucoup mon ami Olivier. Elle (9) _____ qu'il (10) _____ assez. Et c'est vrai—Olivier (11) _____ souvent ses devoirs! Il (12) _____ aller en boîtes de nuit qu'aller à la bibliothèque. Mes autres amis, par contre, (13) _____ toujours leurs devoirs et (14) _____ bien à leurs cours. En général, c(e) (15) _____ un bon groupe, et nous sommes toujours de bons amis.

B. Dans ma famille, c'était … qui faisait ça! Posez les questions suivantes à un(e) camarade de classe. Dites qui faisait les choses suivantes quand vous étiez petit(e).

1. Quand tu étais petit(e), qui faisait la vaisselle?
2. Qui cuisinait? Qu'est-ce qu'il/elle préparait normalement?
3. Qui se levait le plus tôt le matin? Pourquoi?
4. Qui se couchait le plus tard le soir? Pourquoi?
5. Qui faisait les courses? Où allait-il/elle?
6. Qui lisait le journal tous les jours? Qui ne lisait jamais le journal?
7. Qui choisissait les programmes que vous regardiez à la télévision?
8. Qui travaillait le plus dur? Expliquez votre réponse.
9. Qui parlait le plus souvent au téléphone?
10. Qui s'habillait de la façon la plus extravagante?
11. Qui s'amusait le plus?

Portrait personnel

Maintenant, écrivez un paragraphe à l'*imparfait,* où vous décrivez l'enfance de votre partenaire. Dites qui faisait quoi dans sa maison, et ensuite comparez-le à votre famille pendant votre enfance.

MODÈLE: Chez Jamie, son père faisait toujours la cuisine, mais chez moi, c'était ma mère qui cuisinait. La spécialité de son père, c'était le poulet et les pommes de terre …

C. J'étais comme ça à ce moment-là! Conjuguez les verbes donnés et puis terminez les phrases pour expliquer comment vous étiez au lycée. Ajoutez des adjectifs, des noms, des verbes, etc., pour compléter la phrase.

 MODÈLE: Je / être …

Au lycée, j'étais timide mais très studieux (studieuse).

1. Au lycée, je / aimer …
2. Je / ne … pas du tout aimer …
3. Pendant le week-end, mes amis et moi, nous / aller …
4. Nous / faire …
5. Je / manger …
6. Je / ne … pas manger …
7. Mon/Ma prof préféré(e) / enseigner …
8. Il/Elle / être …
9. Mes parents / détester …

As students give you their sentences, write the conjugated verb form on the board so that all may check their spelling. This is important, as many of the forms of the imperfect sound alike, and confusion often results. Have more than one student answer each question to show the variety of responses that are possible.

D. Voleur! Voleur! Regardez le dessin suivant pendant quelques minutes. Ensuite, imaginez que vous répondez aux questions d'un agent de police concernant un vol récent. Vous êtes une des personnes qui font la queue[1]—choisissez votre personnage, et répondez aux questions selon le point de vue de cette personne.

BANQUE CENTRALE

M. Frèrebeau   Mme Paul   Mlle Bouchard   M. Carros

1. Comment vous appelez-vous?
2. Combien de personnes faisaient la queue devant vous?
3. Qu'est-ce que vous regardiez pendant que vous attendiez?
4. La femme en tête de queue: est-ce qu'elle était grande ou petite?
5. Elle avait les cheveux blonds ou bruns?
6. Qu'est-ce qu'elle portait?
7. Est-ce qu'elle avait l'air nerveuse?
8. Est-ce qu'elle avait quelque chose dans les mains?
9. Saviez-vous qu'elle commettait un crime?
10. Aviez-vous peur?

Have students imagine the most likely response of each character, and compare their responses. Would they all say the same thing? To make the activity more realistic, have students close their books and respond to the questions orally once they've had time to consider them. Put the drawing on a transparency so that the other students in the class can check the accuracy of each "witness" as s/he responds.

---

[1]*is waiting in line*

À vous de parler!

To prepare for this activity, tell your students to bring in a photo of an important event in their lives. If you have a technologically adept class, you could have them scan their photos and send them to you by e-mail or bring them on a CD a couple of days in advance so that they can be displayed to the whole class electronically.

A. Un événement important. À l'aide d'une photo, racontez un événement important de votre vie à votre classe, en répondant aux questions suivantes.

1. C'était en quelle saison?
2. Quel âge aviez-vous?
3. Qui était présent?
4. Que portiez-vous?
5. Quelle heure était-il?
6. Comment vous sentiez-vous?
7. Où est-ce que vous étiez?
8. Est-ce que vous mangiez ou buviez quelque chose? Quoi?

Une occasion spéciale. Cette jeune fille assiste à une occasion spéciale. À votre avis, qu'est-ce que c'est? À quelles fêtes est-ce que vous avez assisté quand vous étiez adolescent(e)?

B. Le semestre passé. Avec deux autres partenaires, comparez le semestre passé avec ce semestre. Répondez aux questions suivantes, et puis faites un résumé de vos vies pendant le semestre passé (à *l'imparfait*) et ce semestre (au *présent*).

Le semestre passé

1. À quelle heure est-ce que vous vous leviez, normalement?
2. Vous étiez toujours au lycée, ou vous étiez déjà à l'université?
3. Où preniez-vous le déjeuner?
4. Vos cours étaient plus difficiles ou plus faciles, en général? Pourquoi?
5. Qu'est-ce que vous faisiez pour vous amuser?
6. Vous alliez souvent à des boums? en boîtes?
7. Vous parliez souvent à vos parents?
8. Vous dormiez beaucoup? Pourquoi ou pourquoi pas?

Ce semestre

1. À quelle heure est-ce que vous vous levez, en général?
2. Où est-ce que vous habitez?
3. Vous mangez normalement chez vous, au restaurant ou au resto-U?
4. Quel est votre cours le plus difficile?
5. Le week-end, qu'est-ce que vous aimez faire? Et le soir?
6. Vous allez souvent à des discothèques?
7. Combien de fois par semaine est-ce que vous parlez à vos parents?
8. À quelle heure est-ce que vous vous couchez?

Portrait personnel

Maintenant, écrivez un paragraphe pour votre site web ou journal de classe, où vous comparez vos semestres avec ceux de vos partenaires.

MODÈLE: Le semestre passé, nous étions tous les trois fatigués. Nous suivions beaucoup de cours, et nous nous couchions tard. Mais ce semestre c'est différent. Lucie a seulement trois cours, et Jérome et moi, quatre. En plus, nos cours sont plus faciles …

C. Jeu de rôles. Imaginez que vous êtes journaliste, et que votre partenaire est une célébrité que vous interviewez. Posez des questions concernant l'enfance de cette personne, par exemple: Où habitiez-vous? Quel était votre cours préféré au lycée? Comment s'appelait votre premier (première) petit(e) ami(e)?, etc. Votre partenaire va imaginer les réponses. Quand vous avez fini, jouez ce jeu de rôles pour la classe.

Give students some time to work out this interview, then have them role-play it for the class, or "publish" it in a class entertainment newspaper. To save time, you may choose to do this activity in groups of three (a celebrity couple, or a panel of journalists).

Les ados français sont comme ça

L'adolescence est une période difficile pour les parents et pour les enfants. C'est une période de transition et de grands changements avant l'arrivée de l'âge adulte. Élever un ado est donc compliqué. Selon les parents, les ados français de 12 à 18 ans sont difficiles à élever parce qu'ils ne respectent pas l'autorité parentale. (20% des ados refusent d'écouter et d'obéir les ordres qu'ils reçoivent à la maison et à l'école.) Selon les experts (les thérapeutes, les pédopsychologues et pédopsychiatres), l'autorité parentale est de plus en plus invisible et inexistante, car[1] la tendance des parents modernes c'est de vouloir être d'abord le copain des enfants et non une figure autoritaire. Depuis 1970, l'autorité et la discipline parentale ont beaucoup diminué. Les parents disent oui à tous les caprices et aux désirs de leurs enfants adolescents. Cependant, les experts disent que la discipline doit commencer dès[2] la petite enfance (de 12 mois à 4 ans). Si cette discipline n'a jamais existé, c'est impossible de l'imposer à l'adolescence. «L'enfant-roi»[3] devient alors «despote»[4].

L'ado français veut posséder ce que les copains possèdent: des CD, des vêtements de marque, des jeux vidéos, des téléphones portables ou des scooters. Les ados veulent être «branchés»[5] et font comme leurs copains pour être mieux acceptés par eux[6]. D'ailleurs, les jeunes qui fument des cigarettes «tirent leur première taffe»[7] vers 12 ou 13 ans. Quarante-sept pour cent d'adolescents (filles et garçons) de 18 à 19 ans sont des fumeurs. En France, il n'y a pas de limite d'âge pour acheter des cigarettes, ni pour acheter de l'alcool.

Online Study Center
Web Search Activities

---

[1] *because* [2] *as early as* [3] *"child-king"* [4] These terms come from the article *"Pourquoi ils font la loi"* (*Why they rule*) by Claire Chartier, published in *L'Express* (May 23, 2002). [5] **Être branché** means literally *to be plugged in.* It is slang for *to be "in."* [6] *them* [7] *take their first drag*

Les ados français ont leurs premières expériences sexuelles vers 17 ans. Par contre[1], dès 11 ans ils sont déjà bien informés sur les rapports sexuels grâce à[2] l'école, les parents et les magazines et les radios pour jeunes.

La majorité des ados entre 16 et 19 ans aiment faire du shopping, regarder la télé, aller au cinéma, «papoter» ou «tchatcher»[3], boire un pot[4], aller en boîte, «draguer»[5], faire un tour en scooter ou faire du sport.

Quelques chiffres intéressants sur les ados

- En 2001, 84% des adolescents disaient s'entendre «plutôt bien» avec leurs parents.
- Approximativement la moitié des jeunes de 17 ans ont fumé du hashish.
- 98% des adolescents qui fument des joints fument aussi du tabac et boivent de l'alcool.
- 16% des garçons de 19 ans fument régulièrement des joints.
- 62% des jeunes entre 13 et 19 ans ont des portables.
- L'argent de poche est de 29,28 euros à 17 ans.
- 58% des jeunes entre 13 et 19 ans possèdent un poste de télévision dans leur chambre.

Have students use an Internet currency converter to convert 29.28 euros into U.S. dollars. Then have them decide whether the amount is more or less than what American adolescents have in spending money.

Réfléchissons

1. Est-ce que les ados aux États-Unis passent aussi par une période difficile avec leurs parents et avec eux-mêmes[6]? Pourquoi? Que font les ados? Et les parents?
2. Comment sont les parents d'adolescents dans votre pays[7]? Sont-ils plus stricts que les parents en France, selon vous? Justifiez votre réponse.
3. Est-ce que les adolescents français sont très différents des ados américains? Aiment-ils faire les mêmes choses? Peuvent-ils les faire légalement? Achètent-ils les mêmes choses aussi? Donnez des exemples.
4. Beaucoup d'ados pensent qu'«on est ce qu'on a»[8]? Êtes-vous d'accord?
5. Regardez à nouveau les pourcentages à la fin du texte. En groupes de trois ou quatre, trouvez des données[9] similaires pour les adolescents dans votre pays. En classe, discutez de vos données et comparez vos pourcentages avec ceux du texte. Sont-ils très différents? Sur quels points?

For #5, direct students to search engines (such as Google) to carry out their research.

La fête de la musique. Quel type de musique font-ils? Quelle sorte de musique est-ce que vous préférez? Avez-vous un chanteur / une chanteuse favori(te)?

---

[1]*However* [2]*thanks to* [3]slang words for *yack* [4]*have a drink* [5]*flirt* [6]*themselves* [7]*country* [8]Quote taken from *Les Adolescents,* a study published by Michel Fize, a French sociologist. [9]*data*

Continuons!

Partie I: Un forum de discussion[1] dans un site imaginaire: www.monadolescence.com 🎧

Online Study Center
Language Skills Practice

@ chat pièce

◀ Arrière   ▶ Avant   ✖ Arrêt

adresse: @ http://www.monadolescence.com   ▶ aller

Mon adolescence

| Tous les forums de discussion | 3 Messages : la démo. 1–3 |

Sujet

Message recherché:
Que faisiez-vous pendant votre adolescence? Étiez-vous un démon ou étiez-vous un ange? Si vous avez des anecdotes amusantes ou effrayantes, on vous attend sur le forum de discussion!   (Soumettre)

De: **David (Bruxelles)**
Date: 13/9/06   Réponse ✉

Message d'origine de la discussion:
Quand j'avais 16 ans, j'étais la terreur de mon lycée! J'adorais embêter[2] les filles et je me disputais toujours avec les garçons. Comme j'étais assez grand et fort, je gagnais souvent aux bagarres[3]. Je fumais toujours des cigarettes en cachette[4] à la récréation. J'en fumais deux ou trois à toute vitesse! J'allais aux toilettes, j'ouvrais les fenêtres et je bloquais la porte d'entrée avec une chaise. Personne ne pouvait rentrer dans les toilettes pendant que j'y fumais!

De: **Luc (Strasbourg)**
Date: 13/9/06   Réponse ✉

Salut David,
Elle n'est pas mal ton histoire! Mon histoire est terrible. C'est la première fois que je la raconte[5] ... Quand j'habitais à Lyon et j'étais un ado, mes amis et moi nous conduisions sur la Rocade[6] en sens inverse quand nous sortions de boîte le samedi soir. Le danger nous faisait monter l'adrénaline! Heureusement qu'à 4 heures du matin il n'y avait personne sur la route et nous n'avons jamais eu d'accidents. Maintenant, j'ai 30 ans et je ne me sens pas fier[7] du tout quand je pense à cet épisode de ma jeunesse.

De: **Armelle (Monaco)**
Date: 13/9/06   Réponse ✉

Luc,
Le petit jeu que toi et tes amis faisiez pour vous amuser était vraiment atroce. Quand j'étais adolescente je n'obéissais pas à toutes les règles, mais je ne mettais pas la vie d'autres personnes en danger. Par exemple, quand j'avais 15 ans, je passais tous les étés à la plage chez mon grand-père. J'aimais beaucoup danser, mais quand je sortais, je devais être chez moi à 9 heures du soir au plus tard[8]. Et les boîtes ouvraient à 10 heures. Alors, je me couchais vers 11 heures et je faisais le mur[9] une heure après quand toute ma famille dormait. Je rentrais chez moi à 5 heures du matin exténuée mais contente. Bien sûr, le matin, je ne pouvais pas faire la grasse matinée et je me levais à 9 heures comme tout le monde! J'avais 15 ans ... ! Je pouvais faire des excès!

● zone d'internet

---

[1] *chat room*   [2] *annoy*   [3] *fights*   [4] *in secret / in hiding*   [5] *tell*   [6] *a bypass highway*   [7] *proud*   [8] *at the latest*   [9] *sneaked out*

Vous avez bien compris?

Après avoir lu le forum de discussion, dites si les affirmations sont vraies ou fausses. Rectifiez oralement les affirmations qui sont fausses.

1. David aimait jouer avec les filles. _____ vrai _____ faux
2. Armelle condamne ce que faisait Luc adolescent. _____ vrai _____ faux
3. Luc est gêné de dire son histoire. _____ vrai _____ faux
4. Luc mettait seulement sa vie en danger. _____ vrai _____ faux
5. Armelle partait en boîte à 11 heures. _____ vrai _____ faux
6. Luc conduisait avec ses amis pour aller en boîte. _____ vrai _____ faux
7. Personne ne pouvait utiliser les toilettes pendant la récréation quand David y était. _____ vrai _____ faux
8. Armelle faisait la grasse matinée. _____ vrai _____ faux

Vocabulaire essentiel

Les ados

Vous êtes dans un lycée. À l'entrée il y a une brochure sur les problèmes de l'adolescence. Lisez la brochure.

L'adolescence:

une période difficile de changements

• **Les ados . . .**
veulent **affirmer leur individualité**
veulent **affirmer leur personnalité**
sont **à la recherche de leur identité**
sont **complexés par leur look**
ont des **difficultés** (*f.*) à **s'accepter**
veulent **être à la mode**
ont des **troubles** (*m.*) **alimentaires** (l'anorexie par exemple)
ont des **troubles familiaux**

• **Souvent les ados pour se rebeller vont . . .**
avoir des relations sexuelles précoces
faire le mur
faire une fugue[1]
faire l'école buissonnière[2]
fumer des cigarettes
se droguer
se soûler[3]

• **Les problèmes les plus fréquents sont:**
l'alcoolisme
la délinquance
l'échec[4] **scolaire**
la toxicomanie
le tabagisme

Pour plus de renseignements sur les problèmes des adolescents, contactez le ministère de la Jeunesse de votre localité.

---

[1]*run away* [2]*skip school* [3]*get drunk* [4]*failure*

À vous!

A. Définitions. Relisez la brochure précédente et trouvez la définition correcte pour chaque mot et expression.

Answer Key: 1. h 2. d 3. f 4. a 5. g 6. c 7. b 8. e

1. Quand une personne boit trop de vin ou de bière.
2. Quand un jeune s'échappe de sa maison et ne revient plus.
3. Quand une personne ne s'aime pas.
4. Quand un adolescent n'a pas de bons résultats à l'école.
5. Quand un adolescent ne mange pas normalement.
6. Quand un jeune vole dans un magasin.
7. Quand un jeune s'achète les dernières nouveautés.
8. Quand un jeune ne va pas à l'école régulièrement.

a. l'échec scolaire
b. être à la mode
c. la délinquance juvénile
d. faire une fugue
e. faire l'école buissonnière
f. avoir des difficultés à s'accepter
g. avoir des troubles alimentaires
h. se soûler

B. La meilleure attitude. Identifiez les problèmes de ces adolescents d'après les dessins. Écrivez les problèmes de chacun(e)[1] sous les dessins.

1.

_____

2.

_____

3.

_____

4.

_____

5.

_____

Answer Key. Possible answers: 1. Le garçon est complexé par son look. / Il a des difficultés à s'accepter. 2. Il a des troubles familiaux. 3. La jeune fille fume des cigarettes. 4. La jeune fille fait le mur. 5. L'adolescent affirme son individualité / sa personnalité.

[1] _each one_

  **C. Votre adolescence.** Posez les questions suivantes à huit camarades de classe: quatre femmes et quatre hommes. Ensuite, dites à la classe qui a eu une adolescence plus difficile: les femmes ou les hommes. Comparez vos réponses et tirez-en une conclusion.

Quand tu étais adolescent(e) …

1. Est-ce que tu étais complexé(e) par ton look? Pourquoi? Qu'est-ce que tu aimais ou n'aimais pas de toi?
2. Est-ce que tu avais des troubles familiaux? Qu'est-ce qui se passait? T'entendais-tu mal avec tes parents? Avec tes frères et sœurs?
3. Est-ce que tu voulais affirmer ta personnalité? Comment? Étais-tu rebelle?
4. Que faisais-tu pour te rebeller?
5. Voulais-tu être à la mode? Comment est-ce que tu t'habillais?
6. Avais-tu de bonnes notes[1] à l'école?
7. Faisais-tu souvent l'école buissonnière?

Structure 2

Online Study Center
ACE, Language Skills Practice

This structure section reviews the pronouns **y** and **en** as well as shows the placement of these pronouns when they are used in the **imparfait**. Before starting this structure, remind students or ask students to summarize the uses of **y** (means *there;* replaces a location) and of **en** (means *some of it, some of them;* replaces a quantity).

Les pronoms *y* et *en* avec l'imparfait

In Chapters 4 and 5 you were introduced to the pronouns **y** and **en** in the present tense and in the near future. Now you will see how these two pronouns function similarly in the **imparfait.**

As in the present tense, **y** and **en** are placed before the conjugated verb in the **imparfait.**

> Quand j'avais 10 ans, j'allais à la plage tous les étés.
> Quand j'avais 10 ans, j'**y** allais tous les étés.

Négation:	Quand j'avais 10 ans, je n'**y** allais pas tous les étés.
Interrogation:	Est-ce que tu **y** allais tous les étés?
	Y allais-tu tous les étés?

> Quand j'étais adolescent, je fumais des cigarettes.
> Quand j'étais adolescent, j'**en** fumais.

Négation:	Quand j'étais adolescent, je n'**en** fumais pas.
Interrogation:	Est-ce que tu **en** fumais beaucoup?
	En fumais-tu beaucoup?

Attention! If the location or the quantity being replaced is the object of another *infinitive,* the pronoun precedes the infinitive rather than the conjugated verb, just as in the present tense or the near future.

> Josiane voulait manger à la cantine.
> Josiane voulait **y** manger.

Négation:	Josiane ne voulait pas **y** manger.
Interrogation:	Est-ce qu'elle voulait **y** manger?
	Voulait-elle **y** manger?

---

[1] *good grades*

Les enfants aimaient boire du jus d'orange.
Les enfants aimaient **en** boire.

Négation: Les enfants n'aimaient pas **en** boire.
Interrogation: Est-ce que les enfants aimaient **en** boire?
Aimaient-ils **en** boire?

Vérifiez votre compréhension

1. Read David's chat room message once again (p. 305). Find the pronouns **y** and **en** in his message. What words are they replacing?

2. Rewrite the sentences that you have found, putting them in the negative.

Pratiquons!

A. Y ou *en*? Lisez la conversation entre deux adolescents et choisissez le pronom correct ainsi que[1] l'espace le plus approprié pour chaque pronom.

GILLES: L'année dernière, je te voyais toujours au café le Grain Noir.
(1) Tu _____ allais _____ toujours avec Béatrice. Comment va-t-elle?
FRANÇOIS: Elle va bien, je crois.
GILLES: Qu'est-ce que vous preniez? Du café?
FRANÇOIS: (2) Non, nous n(e) _____ prenions _____ pas. Béatrice prenait du thé et moi, du Coca.
GILLES: (3) Béatrice _____ prenait _____ toujours?
FRANÇOIS: Oui. Mais pourquoi toutes ces questions?
GILLES: Parce que je voudrais inviter Béatrice au Grain Noir et je voudrais savoir ce qu'elle aime.
FRANÇOIS: (4) Tu _____ voudrais _____ inviter Béatrice? Bonne chance! Elle sort avec Paul maintenant!

B. Quand tu étais plus jeune. Posez les questions suivantes à votre camarade de classe sur son adolescence. Utilisez les pronoms **y** et **en** dans vos réponses. Ensuite, changez de rôle.

1. Quand tu étais adolescent(e), est-ce que tu allais au lycée tous les jours de la semaine?
2. Est-ce que tu restais à la maison le samedi soir? Qu'est-ce que tu faisais?
3. Est-ce que tu aimais regarder des comédies à la télé? Qu'est-ce que tu regardais?
4. Est-ce que tu avais beaucoup d'amis?
5. Est-ce que vous faisiez des folies[2], tes amis et toi? Comme quoi?
6. Est-ce que vous sortiez souvent au bowling? Où est-ce que vous sortiez d'habitude?
7. Quand tu rentrais du lycée, est-ce que tes parents étaient à la maison? Qu'est-ce que vous faisiez ensemble?
8. Est-ce que tu pratiquais un sport? Lequel[3]?

---

[1] *as well as* [2] *crazy things* [3] *Which one*

Partie II: Un enfant sage 🎧

Alexandre, un petit garçon de quatre ans, pose des questions à sa mère.

ALEXANDRE: Maman, quand j'avais deux ans, est-ce que tu **jouais avec** moi?

MAMAN: Mais oui! Bien sûr! Nous jouions à la balle et aussi avec ton train.

ALEXANDRE: Pourquoi à la balle, Maman?

MAMAN: Parce que tu adorais **donner des coups de pied** dans un ballon. Comme tous les petits garçons!

ALEXANDRE: Est-ce que je **faisais des bêtises**[1]?

MAMAN: Mmm … oui, de temps en temps!

ALEXANDRE: Pourquoi est-ce que je faisais des bêtises?

MAMAN: Tu faisais des bêtises quand tu t'ennuyais à la maison. À la crèche jamais. Tu étais toujours **sage**[2] à la crèche! Un petit ange!

ALEXANDRE: Est-ce que tu me **donnais la fessée**[3] quand j'étais **vilain?**

MAMAN: Jamais! Je te **punissais**[4], mais la fessée jamais!

ALEXANDRE: Comment est-ce que tu me punissais?

MAMAN: Je te **mettais au coin**[5] pendant quelques minutes.

ALEXANDRE: Et qu'est-ce que je faisais au coin?

MAMAN: **Tu pleurais!**

ALEXANDRE: Beaucoup?

MAMAN: Oh, là là oui! Beaucoup! Mais après quelques minutes, je ne pouvais plus résister et je te **faisais un gros bisou** pour te **consoler.** Comme ça!

In France, it is still common for parents to spank a child, **(donner une fessée / une baffe)** although the current tendency is to talk to the child first to make him/her understand what s/he did wrong.

---

[1]The expression in the infinitive is **faire des bêtises.** [2]*well-behaved* [3]The expression in the infinitive is **donner la fessée à quelqu'un (à un enfant).** [4]The infinitive of this verb is **punir. Punir** is conjugated like **finir. Une punition** is *a punishment.* [5]The expression **mettre au coin** means literally to place someone—a child—in a corner or to ask a child to stand in a corner. **Aller au coin** means *to go stand in the corner.*

Vous avez bien compris?

Choisissez la réponse correcte pour compléter chaque phrase basée sur le dialogue entre Alexandre et sa mère.

1. Alexandre allait au coin parce qu'il _____
   a. pleurait.
   b. faisait des bêtises.
   c. jouait avec le train.

2. _____ Alexandre était sage.
   a. À la crèche
   b. À la maison
   c. Au coin

3. Alexandre recevait _____
   a. une fessée.
   b. un baiser.
   c. un ange.

4. Alexandre pleurait _____
   a. à la crèche.
   b. quand il était vilain.
   c. au coin.

5. La maman d'Alexandre _____
   a. faisait des bêtises.
   b. consolait son fils.
   c. résistait.

Vocabulaire essentiel

L'enfance

L'enfance (de la naissance à l'adolescence)

Avant l'arrivée d'un enfant, une mère va …

You may want to add **allaiter un bébé** *(to breast-feed a baby)* or **donner le biberon à un bébé** *(to bottle-feed a baby)*. In Francophone Europe and France the recommended breast-feeding time is 3 to 6 months, like in the United States. However, the actual breast-feeding times vary from country to country. The actual breast-feeding time in France tends to be the lowest—compared to the rest of the European countries.

attendre un(e) enfant / être enceinte / avoir une grossesse

accoucher
(un accouchement)

Après la naissance du bébé les parents vont …

élever un(e) enfant bien élevé(e)	*to raise a well-behaved child*
élever un(e) enfant mal élevé(e)	*to raise a badly behaved child*
gâter un(e) enfant	*to spoil a child*
avoir un(e) enfant gâté(e) pourri(e)	*to have a spoiled rotten child*

Un bébé ou un enfant va …

faire des caprices *(m.)*

crier

pleurer

mordre[1]

être un ange

être un démon

désobéir

faire des câlins *(m.)*

faire la sieste

se faire mal

---

[1]The verb **mordre** is conjugated like **attendre.**

À vous!

A. Une journée typique du petit Louis. Quand le petit Louis avait 3 ans, ses journées étaient assez similaires et typiques. Regardez les dessins et décrivez une de ses journées. **Attention!** Mettez les verbes à l'imparfait. Commencez par «Quand le petit Louis avait trois ans …»

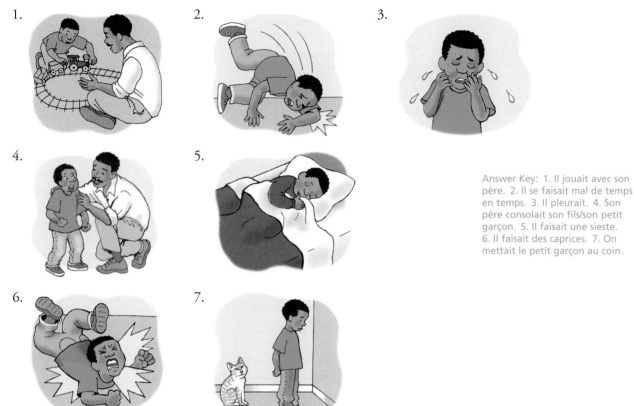

1.

2.

3.

4.

5.

Answer Key: 1. Il jouait avec son père. 2. Il se faisait mal de temps en temps. 3. Il pleurait. 4. Son père consolait son fils/son petit garçon. 5. Il faisait une sieste. 6. Il faisait des caprices. 7. On mettait le petit garçon au coin.

6.

7.

B. Votre journée typique. Interviewez un(e) camarade de classe pour savoir comment était une journée typique quand il/elle avait quatre ou cinq ans. Ensuite changez de rôles. Comparez vos réponses et dites à la classe qui de vous deux était le plus sage.

1. Qui t'élevait: ta mère, ton père ou les deux? Qui était le plus strict et te disciplinait le plus: ta mère ou ton père?
2. Comment est-ce qu'on te disciplinait?
3. Est-ce que tu pleurais beaucoup? Pourquoi?
4. Quand tu faisais des caprices, qu'est-ce que tu faisais? Tu donnais des coups de pied à tout le monde?
5. Où est-ce que tu faisais des caprices? Dans des lieux publics devant tout le monde comme le supermarché?
6. Quel genre[1] de bêtises est-ce que tu faisais?
7. Étais-tu gâté(e) pourri(e)? Qui te gâtait le plus dans ta famille? Comment est-ce qu'on te gâtait?
8. En général, étais-tu sage ou étais-tu un petit démon? Pourquoi?

---
[1] *What type*

Portrait personnel

Écrivez un paragraphe où vous décrivez l'enfance de votre partenaire. Comment était-il/elle comme enfant? Est-ce qu'il/elle était un enfant typique ou non? Expliquez votre réponse.

> MODÈLE: Karine était une enfant très sage. Elle ne faisait presque jamais de bêtises, sauf quand elle était très fatiguée …

Structure 3

Online Study Center
ACE, Language Skills Practice

This **Structure** section introduces some interrogative pronouns and serves as a review of the interrogative pronouns that have been covered so far. It also reinforces question formation in the **imparfait**.

Les pronoms interrogatifs et les questions à l'imparfait

As you saw in previous chapters, there are several options for formulating questions.

> Tu jouais avec ton frère quand tu étais petit?
> Est-ce que tu jouais avec ton frère quand tu étais petit?
> Jouais-tu avec ton frère quand tu étais petit?

With most of the *interrogative pronouns* (*who? what? when?* etc.), speakers do not use simple intonation, as they do for yes/no questions. The most common way to form a question using an interrogative pronoun is to use **est-ce que,** although inversion can also be used in more formal situations.

Point out to students that, when **qui** is the subject of the sentence, the third-person singular of the verb is used: Qui faisait des caprices? However, the form **qui est-ce que** is used when a direct object is needed: Qui est-ce que tu aimais le mieux?

If you have chosen to teach inversion actively, remind students that with pronominal verbs, inversion is still made between the verb and the subject pronoun. The reflexive pronoun is placed before the verb: Quand / à quelle heure nous couchions-nous, maman?; Pourquoi te rongeais-tu les ongles? Also remind students that when the subject is a noun, rather than a pronoun, this subject must appear before the verb and is replaced by a subject pronoun in the inverted form: Julien était-il un enfant sage? Speakers may, of course, always use **est-ce que** with a noun subject: Est-ce que Julien était un enfant sage?

- **quand** *(when)*
  Quand est-ce que tu allais à la crèche? Tous les jours?
  Quand allais-tu à la crèche? Tous les jours?

- **comment** *(how)*
  Comment est-ce que tu jouais? Avec tes trains? À la balle?
  Comment jouais-tu? Avec tes trains? À la balle?

- **où** *(where)*
  Où est-ce que vous faisiez des caprices le plus souvent?
  Où faisiez-vous des caprices le plus souvent?

- **pourquoi** *(why)* **/** (**parce que** *[because]*)
  Pourquoi est-ce que tu ne faisais pas la sieste?
  Pourquoi ne faisais-tu pas la sieste?
  Parce que je n'avais jamais sommeil!

- **combien de** *(how many)* + noun
  Combien de sœurs est-ce qu'elles avaient?
  Combien de sœurs avaient-elles?

- **qui** *(who, object of the sentence)*
  Qui est-ce que tu aimais le mieux?
  Qui aimais-tu le mieux?

- **que** *(what)*
  Qu'est-ce que tu regardais à la télé?
  Que regardais-tu à la télé?

The only interrogative pronoun that functions differently is **qui** *(who)* when it is the subject of the sentence. In this case, **qui** is followed directly by the verb; there is no inversion or **est-ce que.**

* **qui** *(who,* as a subject) + verb
  Qui te punissait?
  Qui désobéissait à ses maîtresses?
  Qui ne voulait pas aller au coin?

VÉRIFIEZ VOTRE COMPRÉHENSION

Go back to the dialogue between Alexandre and his mother (p. 310). Find the questions that have interrogative pronouns in them. Rephrase each question that you find with **est-ce que,** using inversion.

À l'écoute!

Écoutez les phrases, et dites si on pose une question à propos d'une personne ou d'une chose.

1. _____ une personne   _____ une chose
2. _____ une personne   _____ une chose
3. _____ une personne   _____ une chose
4. _____ une personne   _____ une chose
5. _____ une personne   _____ une chose
6. _____ une personne   _____ une chose

Audioscript: 1. Qui est-ce que tu as vu au cinéma? 2. Qu'est-ce que nous allons faire ce soir? 3. Qu'est-ce que vous avez choisi comme profession? 4. Qui est allé en France cet été? 5. Qui avez-vous rencontré en ville le week-end passé? 6. Qu'avons-nous choisi?

Pratiquons!

A. Questions pour un champion. Vos amis et vous regardez le jeu télévisé *Questions pour un champion.* D'abord, complétez les questions avec les pronoms interrogatifs appropriés. Ensuite, essayez de répondre aux questions.

1. _____ est l'homme le plus riche du monde?
   C'est _____.

2. _____ ça veut dire *hasta la vista* en espagnol?
   _____.

3. Le pape Benoît XVI, _____ habite-t-il?
   _____.

4. _____ est-ce que la Première Guerre mondiale a commencé?
   _____.

5. _____ d'habitants y a-t-il en France?
   _____.

6. _____ va-t-on pour visiter le Machu Picchu?
   _____.

Answer Key: 1. Qui / Bill Gates 2. Qu'est-ce que / À la prochaine 3. où / Au Vatican (à Rome) 4. Quand / En 1914 5. Combien / À peu près 60 millions 6. Où / Au Pérou

Before beginning, read the responses with your students. Have them pay attention to the tense of the verb in each, and to be sure to use the same tense in their questions. Remind students that a journalist would use **vous** in formulating his/her questions.

Answer Key. Possible answers: 1. Où habitiez-vous quand vous étiez petite? 2. Comment est-ce que vous parliez japonais? 3. Où alliez-vous à l'école? 4. Pourquoi est-ce que votre famille était au Japon? 5. Combien de livres est-ce que vous écrivez par an? 6. Comment s'appelle votre dernier livre? 7. Qu'est-ce que vous écrivez? / Quel type de livre est-ce que vous écrivez?

B. Un(e) journaliste. Vous êtes journaliste et vous préparez des questions pour l'écrivaine belge Amélie Nothomb[1]. Formulez vos questions en vous basant sur les réponses suivantes.

1. _____?

   Amélie: Quand j'étais petite, j'habitais au Japon.

2. _____?

   Amélie: Je parlais japonais parfaitement. Maintenant, je ne le parle plus aussi bien.

3. _____?

   Amélie: J'allais à l'école à Tokyo. J'étudiais au Lycée Français de Tokyo.

4. _____?

   Amélie: Ma famille était au Japon parce que mon père travaillait à l'ambassade de Belgique à Tokyo.

5. _____?

   Amélie: J'écris un livre par an.

6. _____?

   Amélie: Mon dernier livre s'appelle *Acide sulfurique.*

7. _____?

   Amélie: J'écris surtout des romans avec des components autobiographiques chargés d'humour!

À vous de parler!

A. Chez le psy[2]. Vous êtes un(e) psychologue spécialisé(e) dans les troubles familiaux chez les adolescents. Vous recevez dans votre cabinet[3] deux parents qui ont des problèmes avec leurs enfants adolescents. En groupe de trois, jouez le rôle des parents et le rôle du/de la psychologue. Les parents racontent les difficultés avec leur fille/fils et le/la psychologue donne des solutions ou des conseils[4] aux parents. Ensuite, les psychologues se réunissent (devant la classe) pour parler des cas les plus compliqués et des solutions proposées.

Ex. B: Students may interview mothers and fathers of class members; however, we recommend that students seek parents from outside the classroom. Hence, this activity must be assigned ahead of time. Allow students a week to conduct their surveys. Before students start working on this activity, do a little brainstorming session to come up with questions for their surveys. For example, students may want to ask first how many small children the parents have. Then, they would need to know if the child is a boy or a girl. Do both parents work? Is the child in day care, or with a nanny? Are they strict parents? How do they discipline their small children? How do the children obey? Do they throw tantrums? How often? Why? Etc.

B. Enquêtes *(Surveys).* Individuellement d'abord, cherchez trois parents de petits enfants (de 2 à 6 ans) et faites une enquête pour savoir quels enfants sont les plus difficiles à élever: les petites filles ou les petits garçons. Faites votre enquête et tirez-en vos conclusions. En groupe de trois, comparez vos conclusions et discutez-les avec la classe. Qui sont les plus dociles et les plus sages, les filles ou les garçons? Pourquoi? Y a-t-il de grandes différences entre petites filles et petits garçons? Pourquoi?

---

[1]The writer Amélie Nothomb is very popular in France and in Francophone Europe. She is originally from Belgium, although she lives in Paris. Nothomb's novels are very witty and original. [2]Slang term for **pyschiatre,** equivalent to *shrink* in English [3]*office* [4]*advice*

Les problèmes des adolescents sont comme ça …

Au Canada: la grossesse et les adolescentes

Dans la région de Québec le taux[1] de grossesses chez les adolescentes a tendance à diminuer. De nos jours, sur 1000 adolescentes entre 15 et 19 ans, 42,7 tombent enceinte et 21,5 ont recours à l'intervention volontaire de grossesse (l'avortement) ou IVG. Dans la région de Montréal, 7 adolescentes sur 10 choisissent l'IVG. Alors que 55% des adolescentes qui ont des relations sexuelles prennent la pilule contraceptive, 51% avouent[2] ne pas avoir utilisé de méthode contraceptive lors de la première relation sexuelle.

Grâce à une éducation sexuelle plus ouverte (à la maison et à l'école) et à un meilleur accès aux différentes méthodes contraceptives, le taux de grossesses diminue (surtout au Québec), mais il continue à être un problème important. Les adolescentes qui sont le plus affectées sont celles qui viennent de milieux défavorisés (au seuil de la pauvreté), ou de familles abusives ou décomposées (par exemple, lorsqu'il y a un divorce ou des violences familiales). Les adolescentes se sentent isolées, en manque de support et cherchent de l'affectivité ailleurs que[3] dans leurs familles. Souvent les pères adolescents eux aussi sont absents parce qu'ils ne peuvent pas affronter leur paternité précoce.

En France: la délinquance juvénile

En France, la délinquance juvénile atteint surtout les jeunes qui vivent dans les cités. Les cités ont été construites pour les familles défavorisées qui ont besoin de subventions de l'État: familles d'immigrés et familles pauvres. Les cités sont placées dans les banlieues des grandes villes. Les jeunes des cités se sentent mal intégrés dans la société ou même rejetés par la société. L'intégration, la marginalisation et l'inadaptation sont quelques facteurs pour la délinquance juvénile. L'échec scolaire, une éducation trop stricte ou pas assez stricte amènent[4] aussi les jeunes à commettre des délits[5]. En France, 5% des jeunes commettent 50% des délits.

Dans son système judiciaire, la France a des tribunaux spéciaux pour mineurs. Les mineurs (moins de 18 ans) ne sont pas jugés comme des adultes et leurs peines[6] sont moins strictes. Par exemple, sur 82 000 sanctions prononcées en 2000, seulement 9,3% ont été pour la prison ferme, c'est-à-dire sans liberté surveillée et sans possibilité de sortie jusqu'à la fin de la peine.

En Afrique: le sida[7]

En Afrique, le problème du sida est très grave: il affecte 1 million et demi d'enfants et d'adolescents, et ce chiffre est en progression. Même les adolescents qui ne sont pas infectés par le virus du sida souffrent fortement de répercussions directes. Par exemple, en matière d'éducation, le sida fait que les enfants et adolescents perdent leurs professeurs touchés par le virus. Dans les familles qui sont touchées par le virus, les filles sont obligées d'abandonner l'école pour s'occuper des membres qui restent. En plus, le

---

[1]rate [2]admit to [3]elsewhere than [4]bring [5]misdemeanors [6]penalties [7]AIDS

nombre d'adolescents et d'enfants orphelins qui ont vu leurs parents mourir du sida augmente chaque année. En 2020 on prédit qu'un quart[1] des enfants et des adolescents vont avoir un de leurs parents infecté par le sida.

Dans les familles affectées par le sida, le seuil de pauvreté augmente (beaucoup de malades du sida ne peuvent pas travailler). Ces familles sont isolées et rejetées par la société qui en a peur. Les jeunes dans ces familles qui ont leurs propres problèmes liés à l'adolescence (construction d'une identité, se faire accepter par les autres, etc.) en souffrent doublement.

Les adolescents qui sont touchés par la maladie reçoivent peu de soins et peu de traitements et ont du mal[2] à s'imaginer un bon futur.

Réfléchissons

1. Est-ce que le problème de grossesses chez les adolescentes est un problème aussi dans votre pays? Pourquoi? Par manque d'information? Par manque de communication entre parents et enfants?
2. Pensez-vous que la grossesse chez les ados peut être évitée[3], ou au moins[4] diminuée? Comment? Quelles solutions proposez-vous?
3. Vous avez vu les facteurs qui contribuent à la délinquance juvénile en France. Est-ce que dans votre pays la délinquance juvénile est causée par les mêmes facteurs?
4. Comment est le système judiciaire pour mineurs dans votre pays? Est-ce que les mineurs sont jugés comme les adultes? Êtes-vous d'accord avec les peines que reçoivent les mineurs? Pourquoi?
5. Comment est la situation du sida dans votre pays? Est-ce que le virus augmente ou est-il à la baisse[5]? Qui est le plus affecté dans votre pays par le virus?
6. Est-ce qu'il existe une solution pour essayer d'éliminer le virus du sida? Comment peut-on combattre le virus?
7. Est-ce que vous êtes souvent concerné(e) ou préoccupé(e) par les sujets traités chez les adolescents dans les trois textes? Lequel[6] vous préoccupe le plus? Pourquoi?

Online Study Center
Language Skills Practice

À vous de lire!

A. Stratégies. Guessing meaning from context. The following is an extract from a literary text, *La Gloire de mon père*, by Marcel Pagnol. Since this is an authentic document, it probably contains words that you have never seen before. Rather than turning immediately to a dictionary for help, consider the context in which the word appears.

- Look at the structure of the sentence. What part of speech is the word? (Is it a noun? An adjective? A verb?) When trying to figure out what a word means, we must not neglect its grammatical role; for example, knowing that **heureux** means *happy* and that **-ment** is a typical adverb ending in French can help us to

---

[1] *one quarter* [2] *have a hard time* [3] *avoided* [4] *at least* [5] *declining* [6] *Which one*

deduce that **heureusement** means *happily* or *fortunately*. Paying attention only to the meaning of **heureux** may not have led us to the same conclusion. Always work on the text from two angles: meaning and context.

- Try to confirm the meaning that you have attributed to unknown words. Can you verify your hypothesis somehow? In other words, does the word make sense with the meaning that you have attributed to it? Does it fit in the grammatical context as well?
- Continue reading without interruption whenever possible. Consult a dictionary only when you cannot make an educated guess at the meaning of the unknown word.

B. Avant de lire. Lisez le paragraphe suivant, et répondez aux questions.

- **Un peu de contexte.** Le narrateur de ce texte, Marcel, est un homme qui raconte son enfance. Il était le fils aîné de Joseph (un professeur) et d'Augustine (une couturière[1]). Dans ce texte, il avait presque six ans. C'était un garçon très intelligent, qui savait lire avant même d'aller à l'école. Il nous parle de ses journées à l'école et au parc.

- **Imaginons la scène.**
  1. Si le texte vient du point de vue d'un petit garçon, de quoi va-t-on probablement parler? Qu'est-ce que les garçons aiment faire? Imaginez ses activités typiques à l'école et au parc.
  2. Selon la description donnée, est-ce que vous pensez que Marcel va être un petit ange ou un petit démon? Expliquez votre réponse.
  3. Est-ce que les enfants très intelligents sont différents des autres enfants? Est-ce qu'ils posent quelquefois des problèmes à leurs maîtresses/maîtres? Expliquez votre réponse.
  4. Est-ce que vous aviez un(e) ami(e) très intelligent(e) dans le passé? Comment était-il/elle? Décrivez ses activités à l'école.

Discuss these questions briefly with students before having them read the passage. Ask them to search for verification of their hypotheses while reading.

- **Un peu de vocabulaire.** Lisez vite le texte une première fois. Essayez de déterminer le sens de chaque mot ou expression signalée, sans consulter un dictionnaire.

Le portrait de Mlle Guimard
  1. Paragraphe 2: «... pendant qu'elle parlait, son nez **remuait**»
  2. Paragraphe 2: «... elle avait de gros yeux **bombés**»
  3. Paragraphe 3: «... elle disait que je chantais **faux**»

Au parc
  4. Paragraphe 5: «... <elle> me conduisait ensuite, au moyen d'un tramway, jusqu'en ces **lieux** enchantés.» (Tuyau[2]: Regardez aussi le paragraphe 4.)
  5. Paragraphe 6: «On y trouvait ... des **étangs** où naviguaient des **flotilles de canards.**»

Have students read silently in class, concentrating on the words in boldface. Do not give them time to consult a dictionary; ask them instead to work from context. If they cannot explain the meaning of a word in French, have them try to act it out, rather than translating into English. Students may find this activity easier to do in pairs.

---

[1]*seamstress* [2]*Hint*

6. Paragraphe 7: «… un certain nombre de gens qui apprenaient à gouverner des bicyclettes: le regard fixe, les mâchoires serrées, ils **échappaient** soudain au professeur, traversaient l'allée, disparaissaient dans un fourré, et reparaissaient, leur machine **autour du cou.**»
7. Paragraphes 8–9: «… j'allais **vaquer** aux travaux de mon âge. … Ma principale occupation était de lancer du pain aux canards.»
8. Paragraphe 10: «Lorsque ma tante ne me regardait pas, tout en leur disant, d'une voix suave, des paroles de tendresse, je leur lançais aussi des **pierres,** avec la ferme intention d'en **tuer** un.»

You may wish to make several students (or pairs of students) "experts" responsible for a specific paragraph. For example, assign paragraph 2 to one/several pair(s) of students. Have them read it, answer the question, and then act it out for the others. If students finish early, they can move on and become "experts" of other paragraphs. Acting out the scenes in class forces students to concentrate on understanding the gist of the paragraph rather than every word, and brings the text to life. It is an excellent way to monitor general comprehension.

C. Lisons! Lisez le texte une deuxième fois, en vous concentrant sur les paragraphes suivants. Répondez aux questions, et suivez les indications indiquées.

Paragraphe 1: Approximativement quel âge avaient les élèves dans la classe de Mlle Guimard?
_____ 6 ans   _____ 11 ans   _____ 16 ans

Paragraphe 2: Selon Marcel, Mlle Guimard était:
_____ grande   _____ petite   _____ belle   _____ laide
Imitez-la!

Paragraphe 3: Dans la classe, Marcel:
_____ apprenait ses lettres   _____ était ignoré
Imitez ses actions en classe!

Paragraphe 4: Pendant les leçons de chant, Marcel:
_____ chantait bien   _____ ne chantait pas du tout
Les autres:
_____ chantaient fort   _____ restaient muets
Imitez-le!

Paragraphe 7: Au parc, Marcel aimait regarder les gens à bicyclette parce qu(e):
_____ ils roulaient bien.
_____ ils ne savaient pas rouler et ils avaient souvent des accidents.
Dessinez la scène!

Paragraphe 10: Marcel jetait _____ aux canards.
_____ du pain _____ des pierres _____ les deux
Imitez-le!

Souvenirs d'enfance

1 J'approchais de mes six ans, et j'allais à l'école dans la classe enfantine que dirigeait Mlle Guimard.
2 Mlle Guimard était très grande, avec une jolie petite moustache brune, et quand elle parlait, son nez remuait: pourtant je la trouvais laide, parce qu'elle était jaune comme un Chinois, et qu'elle avait de gros yeux bombés.
3 Elle apprenait patiemment leurs lettres à mes petits camarades, mais elle ne s'occupait pas de moi, parce que je lisais couramment, ce qu'elle considérait comme une inconvenance préméditée de la part de mon père. En revanche, pendant les leçons de chant, elle disait, devant toute la classe, que je chantais faux, et qu'il valait mieux me taire, ce que je faisais volontiers.

4 Pendant que la marmaille[1] s'époumonait[2] à suivre sa baguette, je restais muet, paisible, souriant; les yeux fermés, je me racontais des histoires, et je me promenais au bord de l'étang du parc Borély, qui est une sorte de parc de Saint-Cloud, au bout du Prado de Marseille.

5 Le jeudi et le dimanche, ma tante Rose, qui était la sœur aînée de ma mère, et qui était aussi jolie qu'elle, venait déjeuner à la maison, et me conduisait ensuite, au moyen d'un tramway, jusqu'en ces lieux enchantés.

6 On y trouvait des allées ombragées par d'antiques platanes, des bosquets sauvages, des pelouses qui vous invitaient à vous rouler dans l'herbe, des gardiens pour vous le défendre, et des étangs où naviguaient des flotilles de canards.

7 On y trouvait aussi, à cette époque, un certain nombre de gens qui apprenaient à gouverner des bicyclettes: le regard fixe, les mâchoires serrées, ils échappaient soudain au professeur, traversaient l'allée, disparaissaient dans un fourré, et reparaissaient, leur machine autour du cou. Ce spectacle ne manquait pas d'intérêt, et j'en riais aux larmes. Mais ma tante ne me laissait pas longtemps dans cette zone dangereuse: elle m'entraînait—la tête tournée en arrière—vers un coin tranquille, au bord de l'étang.

8 Nous nous installions sur un banc, toujours le même, devant un massif de lauriers, entre deux platanes; elle sortait un tricot de son sac, et j'allais vaquer aux travaux de mon âge.

9 Ma principale occupation était de lancer du pain aux canards. Ces stupides animaux me connaissaient bien. Dès que je montrais un croûton, leur flotille venait vers moi, à force de palmes, et je commençais ma distribution.

10 Lorsque ma tante ne me regardait pas, tout en leur disant, d'une voix suave, des paroles de tendresse, je leur lançais aussi des pierres, avec la ferme intention d'en tuer un. Cet espoir, toujours déçu, faisait le charme de ces sorties, et dans le grinçant tramway du Prado, j'avais des frémissements d'impatience.

D. Après la lecture. Relisez le texte une dernière fois, plus lentement, et répondez aux questions suivantes.

1. Est-ce que Marcel aime Mlle Guimard? Est-ce qu'il la respecte? Expliquez votre réponse, en donnant des exemples du texte.
2. Qu'est-ce qu'il fait en classe la majorité du temps? Pourquoi?
3. Avez-vous l'impression que Mlle Guimard est une bonne maîtresse? Expliquez votre réponse.
4. Pourquoi aime-t-il aller au parc avec sa tante? Qu'est-ce qu'il fait au parc?
5. Est-ce que sa tante est consciente de tout ce qu'il fait? Expliquez votre réponse.
6. Selon vous, est-ce que le narrateur est un enfant typique? Pourquoi ou pourquoi pas?
7. Avez-vous connu des enfants comme Marcel? Est-ce que vous étiez comme lui? Racontez un épisode de votre vie personnelle pour illustrer votre réponse.

Have students debate the responses to #1, 3, and/or 6. Suggested follow-up: *La Gloire de mon père* is readily available on DVD. Show students the film segment of this extract, then have them write their own memoirs of their childhood, focusing on description and repeated action—i.e., the **imparfait**.

---

[1]*gang of brats* [2]*shouted themselves hoarse*

Lexique 🎧

Vocabulaire essentiel

À l'école

la cantine *cafeteria*
le collège *middle school / junior high school*
le dortoir *dormitory*
l'école primaire *elementary school*

un(e) élève *student (elementary and middle school)*
le lycée *high school*
un(e) lycéen(ne) *high school student*

être en pension *to be in boarding school*
un(e) pensionnaire *boarding school student*

Pour s'amuser

une boîte de nuit *nightclub*
une boum *party*
une discothèque *discotheque*
le gymnase *gymnasium*

la patinoire *skating rink*
la récréation / la récré *recess*
le stade *stadium*

Vocabulaire à revoir

la bibliothèque
un bureau
une classe
un cours
l'instituteur / l'institutrice

la librairie
les matières (f.)
un professeur / une femme professeur
la salle de classe

une table
un tableau

Les ados *adolescents*

affirmer sa personnalité *to assert one's own personality*
affirmer son individualité (f.) *to assert one's own individuality*
avoir des difficultés (f.) à s'accepter *to have difficulties accepting oneself*
avoir des relations sexuelles précoces *to have early sexual relations*
avoir des troubles (m.) alimentaires *to have eating disorders*

avoir des troubles familiaux *to have family problems*
être à la mode *to be hip, fashionable*
être à la recherche de son identité (f.) *to seek one's own identity*
être complexé(e) par son look *to have a complex about one's appearance*
faire l'école buissonnière *to skip school*
faire une fugue *to run away*

faire le mur *to sneak out*
fumer des cigarettes *to smoke cigarettes*
se droguer *to use drugs*
se soûler *to get drunk*
se rebeller *to rebel*

Les problèmes les plus fréquents

l'alcoolisme *(m.)* *alcoholism*
la délinquance *juvenile crime*
l'échec *(m.)* scolaire *failure in school*

le tabagisme *smoking addiction*
la toxicomanie *drug addiction*

L'enfance (de la naissance à l'adolescence) *childhood years (from birth to adolescence)*

accoucher (un accouchement) *to give birth (the labor)*
attendre un(e) enfant / être enceinte / avoir une grossesse *to be pregnant*
avoir un(e) enfant gâté(e) pourri(e) *to have a spoiled rotten child*

consoler *to comfort*
donner la fessée (à) *to spank*
élever un(e) enfant bien élevé(e) *to raise a well-brought-up child*
élever un(e) enfant mal élevé(e) *to raise a badly behaved child*
gâter un(e) enfant *to spoil a child*

mettre au coin *to place a child on time out*
punir *to punish*

Un bébé ou un enfant va …

crier *to scream*
désobéir *to disobey*
donner des coups *(m.)* de pied *to kick*
être un ange *to be an angel*
être un démon *to be a devil*

être sage *to be well behaved*
être vilain *to behave badly; to be naughty*
faire des câlins *(m.)* *to cuddle*
faire des caprices *(m.)* *to throw a tantrum*

se faire mal *to hurt oneself*
faire la sieste *to take a nap*
jouer (avec) *to play (with)*
mordre *to bite*
pleurer *to cry*

Mon boulot

If you would like to work in France or in a Francophone country one day, you will find the content of this chapter useful. You will learn work-related vocabulary words and expressions; you will learn how to read a help-wanted advertisement and how to go on a job interview; and finally, you will learn about the working conditions in France and in the Francophone world as well as about women in the workplace.

De dimension internationale, notre société en forte croissance, commercialisant en France des services et équipements de télécommunication, souhaite renforcer son équipe marketing et pour cela recherche un(e)

Responsable
Communication Marketing Direct

Chargé(e) de définir et mettre en place les campagnes de communication vers ses clients et prospects, il ou elle :
• définit les objectifs découlant de la stratégie marketing de la société (acquisition et fidélisation),
• propose les techniques et moyens les plus efficaces,
• prépare les programmes d'actions,
• met en œuvre ces actions, contrôle et évalue les résultats.

Vous êtes un spécialiste du marketing direct (3 ans d'expérience) idéalement dans le domaine des services, créatif, bon rédacteur et proche du terrain.

SAFETY-KLEEN FRANCE, Société de Services auprès des garage et industries mécaniques, leader sur le marché du recyclage des solvants industriels, recherche pour son secteur SUD Parisien, un

Responsable de Centre de Services

A 30-35 ans, vous avez un fort potentiel commercial allié expérience affirmée du Service et de l'Animation des Hommes.

Vous serez responsable d'une équipe performante de commerciaux, dans un système de vente original.

Travailleur, volontaire et leader, vous serez en pleine progression sur un marché...

Après une formation...

VOUS AVEZ LA BOSSE DU COMMERCE

Rejoignez une société de prestation de services en informatique spécialisée dans le détachement de personnel (Analystes, Analystes-Programmeurs, Chefs de Projets, etc.), intervenant dans les environnements mini et grands systèmes IBM, VAX, UNIX. Afin de conforter notre développement, nous recherchons

1 INGENIEUR COMMERCIAL (H/F)   (réf. INC)

Pour ce poste il faut remplir les conditions suivantes :
• Avoir entre 26/35 ans et être de formation supérieure. • Posséder une expérience réussie de la fonction commerciale. • Dynamique, souple et très relationnel, vous êtes d'un tempérament de chasseur et d'éleveur. • Responsable et autonome vous devrez faire vos preuves très rapidement.

L'apport d'une clientèle grand compte serait très apprécié. Forte rémunération prévue sur la base d'un fixe et d'un pourcentage. Poste basé à Paris. Formation assurée.
Des déplacements sont à prévoir sur toute la France.

Écrire avec photo à SITINFO - 9, rue de Rocroy - 75010 PARIS.

Annuaire téléphonique code 11 SITINFO   SITINFO

ENTER DANS L'UNIVERS DU LUXE PAR LA GRANDE PORTE !

Notre société n'est hissée au tout premier rang de la distribution de produits "haut de gamme".

vendeurs en magasin

GSA

LOCARCHIVES

Nous sommes une société de services, 100 personnes - 1500 clients, spécialisée dans la gestion et le stockage d'archives. Avec plus de 30 % du marché et un développement de 20 % par an, notre image s'est imposée comme critère de professionnalisme. Notre expansion et l'élargissement de notre gamme de services nous conduisent à renforcer notre équipe commerciale en intégrant un

INGENIEUR COMMERCIAL (H/F)

Fort de votre expérience de la vente de solutions et de services, votre action commerciale couvrira l'étude des besoins, l'établissement des propositions commerciales et la conclusion des ventes auprès des responsables d'entreprises ou chefs des achats ou des services généraux chez nos clients situés à Paris ou en R.P.

De formation supérieure (Bac + 3), vous avez au moins 30 ans, une bonne capacité d'autonomie sur le terrain, le goût des chiffres pour l'établissement de devis personnalisés, la volonté de convaincre. La connaissance du marché bancaire serait un atout. Nos bureaux sont proches du périphérique Nord (St Denis Porte de Paris).

Adressez CV, lettre manuscrite, photo sous référence ICLOC à Florence DESPRAS, LOCARCHIVES, 60 rue de l'Arcade, 75008 PARIS.

YAMAHA MUSIQUE FRANCE recrute

attaché commercial H/F
Pour région Sud-Ouest

Venez rejoindre notre équipe...

8 COMMERCIAUX

Expérience commerciale et connaissances des produits instruments à vent souhaitées.

Envoyez-nous votre dossier - BP 70 77312 MARNE LA VALLEE Cedex 2.

• Salaire fixe + Primes +%   • Formation assurée
• Clientèle fournie (FRANCE)   • Excellente présentation
• Mobilité géographique (FRANCE)   • Charisme et crédibilité

Se présenter Hôtel PRIMAVERA 147 Ter rue d'Alésia 75014 Paris Mº Pernety ou Alésia, vendredi 23 Septembre à 9h30 à ou 11h30.

SOCIETE LEADER RENFORCE SON EQUIPE DE VENTE

VOTRE REUSSITE NOUS INTERESSE

"Le talent ne s'invente pas, il se construit"

Vous souhaitez débuter une carrière commerciale au sein d'un groupe performant. L'esprit d'équipe vous anime et l'ambition vous caractérise.

NOUS VOUS PROPOSONS :
- d'intégrer une Ecole de Vente reconnue,
- un plan de carrière commerciale,
- un salaire de 110 KF évolutif,
- un fixe + commissions + primes.

Merci d'adresser CV + photo + LM à Mr P. NAVARRO Le Marsola - 12, rue Jean Mermoz 93180 NOISY LE GRAND.

Commençons!

Une petite annonce 🎧

Vous rappelez-vous d'Alain? Vous l'avez rencontré au Chapitre 2. Alain habite à Fort-de-France en Martinique. Alain a un cabinet[1] d'architecte et il cherche un stagiaire[2] pour l'été. Voici l'**annonce** qu'il a mise dans le journal et sur le Web:

Cabinet d'architecte cherche stagiaire moins de 28 ans, bonnes connaissances d'anglais et d'informatique[3] de préférence le logiciel[4] ArchiCAD pour collaboration dans un bureau de +/−[5] 10 personnes à Fort-de-France. Projets publics et privés. Envoyer CV[6] à M. Alain Oncins 120 Rue des Alizés, Fort-de-France 97233 ou appeler le 5-98-04-32-55 pour plus de renseignements[7].

Abdourahma Stans est étudiant en architecture à *University of California*. Il est africain, du Sénégal. Il cherche un stage[8] pour l'été à l'étranger et hier il a trouvé la petite annonce d'Alain sur le Web. Quand il a lu l'annonce, Abdourahma était très content parce qu'il possédait toutes les qualifications que l'annonce demandait. Il a décidé d'appeler, mais c'est le répondeur automatique[9] qui a répondu.

«Bonjour! Vous êtes bien chez le cabinet d'architecte Oncins au 5-98-04-32-55. Nous ne pouvons pas répondre à votre appel en ce moment. Veuillez laisser[10] un message après le bip sonore. Merci!»

Après avoir écouté le répondeur, Abdourahma a laissé le message suivant: «Bonjour! Je m'appelle Abdourahma Stans. Je vous appelle de San Diego aux États-Unis. Je me permets de vous contacter à la suite de votre annonce parue sur le site web Outremer.com le 3 février 2007. Je suis très intéressé par votre poste. Vous pouvez me contacter au 1-619-555-31-32. Je vous ai aussi envoyé par courriel mon CV et mes qualifications. Merci!»

---

[1] *office* [2] *trainee* [3] *computing* [4] *software* [5] *plus ou moins* (more or less) [6] *curriculum vitae (résumé)*
[7] *information* [8] *internship* [9] *answering machine* [10] *Please leave*

Vous avez bien compris?

Mettez les définitions suivantes avec les mots appropriés.

1. _____ un(e) stagiaire
2. _____ un répondeur
3. _____ un CV
4. _____ un cabinet
5. _____ une annonce
6. _____ un poste
7. _____ un logiciel

a. un bureau
b. un job, un emploi
c. une personne qui perfectionne ses études de façon pratique
d. un programme d'informatique
e. une liste des qualifications
f. la machine qui remplace l'homme au téléphone
g. la description d'un poste

Vocabulaire essentiel

Le travail (1)

avoir un emploi / un poste / un job / un travail / un boulot[1] …	*to have a job*
avoir une formation …	*to have an education / training*
littéraire	
scientifique	
avoir un stage	*to have an internship*
à plein temps / à temps complet	*full-time*
à temps partiel / à mi-temps	*part-time*
un(e) candidat(e) / un(e) postulant(e) …	
cherche du travail	
passe / a un entretien	*has a job interview*
est embauché(e)	*is hired*
un(e) employé(e) …	
est licencié(e) / est mis(e) à la porte	*is fired*
fait la grève	*is on strike*
un(e) salarié(e) a / reçoit …	*a salaried employee gets*
un bon salaire / un mauvais salaire	
travailler / bosser[2] dans …	*to work in*
une boîte[3]	*a company*
une compagnie privée / publique / multinationale	
une société	
une entreprise privée / publique	

---

[1]**Un boulot** is slang. [2]**Bosser** is slang. [3]**Une boîte** is a slang word. It means *a box;* it is used in French to mean any workplace.

Expansion personnelle

un(e) candidat(e) / un(e) postulant(e) …
   est demandeur(euse) d'emploi — *is a job applicant*
   postule pour un poste — *applies for a position*
un(e) employé(e) qui ne travaille plus …
   est chômeur (chômeuse) — *is an unemployed person*
   est retraité(e)
   touche[1] le chômage / la retraite — *gets unemployment compensation / a pension*

À vous!

A. Recommandations. Votre ami(e) veut obtenir un entretien dans une compagnie très prestigieuse. Avec un(e) partenaire, faites une liste où vous indiquez les démarches[2] à suivre. Pour le faire, combinez les mots et expressions dans la colonne de gauche avec les phrases dans la colonne de droite.

Answer Key: 1. c 2. b or d 3. b or d 4. e 5. i 6. f, g, h, or j 7. f, g, h, or j 8. f, g, h, or j 9. f, g, h, or j 10. a

1. D'abord …
2. Ensuite …
3. Et puis …
4. Quelques jours avant l'entretien …
5. Le jour de l'entretien …
6. Quand tu passes l'entretien …
7. Pendant l'entretien …
8. Pendant l'entretien …
9. Pendant l'entretien …
10. Quelques jours après l'entretien …

a. tu es embauché(e)!
b. tu postules pour le poste.
c. tu cherches une annonce intéressante.
d. tu envoies ton CV quand tu réponds à l'annonce.
e. tu vas t'acheter un tailleur/costume élégant et discret.
f. tu poses des questions sur l'entreprise pour obtenir plus d'informations.
g. tu n'arrives pas en retard.
h. tu regardes ton interlocuteur dans les yeux.
i. tu es poli(e) et courtois(e).
j. tu réponds aux questions calmement et brièvement.

B. À l'ANPE (l'Agence nationale pour l'emploi). Vous êtes demandeur/ demandeuse d'emploi et vous allez à l'ANPE pour compléter un formulaire. Soyez logique!

Answer Key. Possible answers: Formation: littéraire / scientifique; Connaissances de: anglais, informatique, etc.; Vous cherchez un poste à mi-temps / à plein temps; Dans une enterprise privée / publique; Vous êtes au chômage depuis (date); Vous pouvez passer un entretien du (date) au (date); Courriel: (adresse électronique)

Nom: _____ Prénom: _____
Date: _____
Formation: _____
Connaissances de _____
Vous cherchez un poste _____ à plein temps _____ à mi-temps
   dans une entreprise _____.
Vous êtes au chômage depuis[3] _____
Vous pouvez passer l'entretien du _____
   au _____.
Désirez-vous recevoir des annonces électroniques? Oui _____ Non _____
Courriel: _____

---

[1]*receives* [2]*steps* [3]*since*

💬C. **Au travail!** Posez les questions suivantes à un(e) camarade de classe sur ses expériences dans le monde du travail.

1. Où travailles-tu? (Si tu n'as pas de travail, est-ce que tu veux obtenir un job? Où?)
2. As-tu un travail à mi-temps ou à temps complet? Combien d'heures par semaine est-ce que tu travailles? (Si tu ne travailles pas, dis-moi ce que tu préfères: un travail à plein temps ou à mi-temps? Pourquoi?)
3. Est-ce que tu reçois un bon salaire ou un mauvais salaire?
4. Quand tu passes un entretien, comment es-tu? Détendu(e) et calme, ou nerveux (nerveuse) et stressé(e)?
5. Comment t'habilles-tu quand tu passes un entretien?
6. As-tu jamais[1] été licencié(e)? Pourquoi?
7. Est-ce que c'est une bonne idée de faire la grève pour obtenir ce que l'on veut[2]?

Structure 1

Le passé composé et l'imparfait

When narrating in the past or speaking about the past, the **passé composé** and the **imparfait** each have a particular and distinctive usage.

Passé composé	**Imparfait**
An event that happened once	*Repeated events in the past or habitual actions*
Hier, j'ai passé un entretien. *Yesterday I had a job interview.*	Le mois dernier, je passais des entretiens toutes les semaines. *Last month I was having interviews every week.*
Pour une fois, je suis arrivée à l'heure à l'entretien! *For once, I arrived on time at the job interview!*	Avant, j'arrivais toujours à l'heure à mes entretiens. Maintenant, jamais! *Before, I always used to[3] arrive on time at my job interviews. Now, never!*
Completed actions or events (sometimes a time expression or a specific time is indicated)	*Ongoing actions or events, or events that happened over an extended period of time*
Hier, j'ai travaillé sans arrêt de 8 heures à 20 heures. *Yesterday, I worked nonstop from 8:00 A.M. to 8:00 P.M.*	Je travaillais avant ton arrivée. *I was working[4] before your arrival.*

---

[1]*Have you ever* [2]*what one wants* [3]In order to convey a habitual event or action, English speakers usually use the expression *used to* or *would:* for example, *I used to play tennis every Thursday* or *I would play tennis every Thursday* (**Je jouais au tennis le jeudi**). [4]Usually, the events or actions that are ongoing or in-progress are translated in English with the *-ing* ending. For example, *I was studying* (**j'étudiais**), *he was sleeping* (**il dormait**), *we were dancing* (**nous dansions**).

Series of actions or events that make the story line progress or add important information to the story[1]	*Descriptions and background information that set up a story; descriptions about age, physical state of being, and emotional state of mind*
Quand j'ai passé l'entretien, j'ai répondu aux questions calmement, j'ai regardé mon interlocuteur dans les yeux, j'ai posé des questions pertinentes et je suis parti avec un bon sentiment.	Le jour de mon entretien, il faisait beau, le soleil brillait et les oiseaux chantaient. C'était un bon signe! Je me sentais bien et j'étais de bonne humeur. Je portais un nouveau costume et j'étais très chic!
When I had the job interview, I answered all the questions calmly, I looked my interviewer in the eye, I asked pertinent questions, and and I left with a good feeling.	*On the day of my job interview, the weather was nice, the sun was shining, and the birds were singing. It was a good sign! I was feeling well, and I was in a good mood. I was wearing a new suit, and I was very chic!*

Interruption of an action or event	*Ongoing action that gets interrupted*
Le téléphone a sonné …	quand je répondais aux questions.
The telephone rang …	*when I was answering the questions.*
Je suis tombé de la chaise …	pendant que je passais mon entretien.
I fell out of my chair …	*while I was having my interview.*

Vérifiez votre compréhension

1. Relisez le texte où on présente Abdourahma Stans. Trouvez toutes les phrases au *passé composé*. Expliquez pourquoi les verbes sont au passé composé: Est-ce une action terminée? Est-ce une série d'actions qui font avancer la narration?

2. Dans ce même paragraphe trouvez les phrases à l'*imparfait* et expliquez l'usage de l'imparfait: Est-ce une description physique? Des émotions? Une action qui n'est pas complètement terminée?

À l'écoute!

A. Qu'entendez-vous? Écoutez les phrases suivantes et indiquez si elles sont au *passé composé* ou à l'*imparfait*.

1. _____ passé composé   _____ imparfait
2. _____ passé composé   _____ imparfait
3. _____ passé composé   _____ imparfait
4. _____ passé composé   _____ imparfait
5. _____ passé composé   _____ imparfait
6. _____ passé composé   _____ imparfait
7. _____ passé composé   _____ imparfait
8. _____ passé composé   _____ imparfait

You may want to have the students repeat each of these sentences. You may also want to make up your own sentences and add them to the activity.

Audioscript: 1. Pauline mangeait un sandwich. 2. Pauline a mangé un sandwich. 3. J'ai chanté une chanson. 4. J'ai acheté un CD. 5. Je parlais français. 6. J'ai parlé français. 7. J'ai fini mon travail. 8. Je travaillais beaucoup.

---

[1]These actions or events that make the story line progress often answer the question, "What happened (next)?"

Pratiquons!

A. Un entretien embarrassant. Coralie a passé un entretien chez Peugeot hier matin. Complétez le texte suivant en mettant les verbes entre parenthèses au *passé composé* ou à l'*imparfait* selon le cas.

Hier matin, Coralie (1) _____ (sortir) de chez elle à 7 heures pour arriver à son entretien avec la compagnie Peugeot à 9 heures. Elle (2) _____ (porter) un tailleur noir avec un chemisier blanc. Comme elle (3) _____ (être) très nerveuse et qu'elle ne (4) _____ (vouloir) pas être en retard, elle (5) _____ (décider) de prendre un taxi au lieu de prendre l'autobus. Coralie (6) _____ (arriver) à 7 h 30 à Peugeot. Très tôt! Comme elle (7) _____ (devoir) trouver quelque chose à faire pour tuer un peu de temps—elle (8) _____ (avoir) plus d'une heure avant son entretien!—elle (9) _____ (aller) dans un café. Elle (10) _____ (se mettre) au bar à côté d'un monsieur qui (11) _____ (lire) le journal tranquillement. Comme Coralie (12) _____ (se sentir) assez nerveuse, elle (13) _____ (commander) une bière pensant[1] se calmer un peu avec les effets de l'alcool. Quand le monsieur (14) _____ (entendre) Coralie, il (15) _____ (regarder) la jeune femme et il (16) _____ (commencer) à parler avec elle. Il lui (17) _____ (demander) si elle (18) _____ (travailler) dans le coin et si son travail (19) _____ (être) très stressant. Coralie (20) _____ (répondre) que non, qu'elle (21) _____ (chercher) du travail et qu'elle (22) _____ (avoir) un entretien avec Peugeot dans une heure et demie. Le monsieur (23) _____ (ne … rien dire) et Coralie (24) _____ (sentir) qu'il (25) _____ (examiner) sa bière de façon peu discrète. Le monsieur (26) _____ (dire) au revoir et il (27) _____ (partir).

Coralie (28) _____ (boire) sa bière et à 8:45 elle (29) _____ (arriver) à son entretien. Devinez qui elle (30) _____ (voir) assis[2] en face d'elle au bureau? Le monsieur du café! Coralie (31) _____ (être) très embarrassée. Qui boit une bière à 7 h 30 du matin? À coup sûr[3] le monsieur (32) _____ (penser) qu'elle (33) _____ (être) alcoolique!

B. Un patron un peu bizarre *(A slightly weird boss).* Lisez l'histoire du patron de Lisa et expliquez pourquoi les verbes sont au *passé composé* ou à l'*imparfait* (action habituelle, action isolée et inhabituelle, action terminée, action en progression, période indéterminée, description physique, description mentale ou description des émotions).

1. À son dernier poste, Lisa **avait** un patron qui **était** un peu bizarre.

   avait _____

   était _____

---

[1]*thinking* [2]*seated* [3]*For sure*

Answer Key: 1. est sortie 2. portait 3. était 4. voulait 5. a décidé 6. est arrivée 7. devait 8. avait 9. est allée 10. s'est mise 11. lisait 12. se sentait 13. a commandé 14. a entendu 15. a regardé 16. a commencé 17. a demandé 18. travaillait 19. était 20. a répondu 21. cherchait 22. avait 23. n'a rien dit 24. a senti 25. examinait 26. a dit 27. est parti 28. a bu 29. est arrivée 30. a vu 31. était 32. pensait / a pensé 33. était

Answer Key: 1. *avait*: dénote une période indéterminée; *était*: action habituelle, description mentale et émotionnelle

2. Le patron **arrivait** toujours en retard et il **entrait** dans le bureau sans jamais dire «Bonjour!»

arrivait _____

entrait _____

3. Un jour il **est arrivé** à l'heure et il **ne portait pas** son costume habituel. Il **avait** des jeans et des sandales.

est arrivé _____

ne portait pas _____

avait _____

4. En plus, il **a apporté** des croissants pour tout le monde et il **souriait** allègrement.

a apporté _____

souriait _____

5. Tous les employés le **regardaient** hallucinés!

regardaient _____

6. Mais, que **s'est-il passé?** Pourquoi le patron **a-t-il acheté** des croissants pour tout le monde ce matin?

s'est-il passé _____

a-t-il acheté _____

7. Le patron **a dit** à ses employés: «J'**ai gagné** au lotto et aujourd'hui c'est mon dernier jour au travail! Au revoir!»

a dit _____

ai gagné _____

C. Interruptions.

Hier, au boulot, Nicole a été interrompue constamment. Elle n'a pas pu terminer son travail. La pauvre! Complétez les phrases avec les verbes au *passé composé* ou à l'*imparfait* selon le cas.

1. Nicole écrivait sur l'ordinateur quand une collègue _____ (venir) lui poser une question.
2. La photocopieuse ne marchait pas, alors Nicole _____ (retourner) à son bureau.
3. Le téléphone a sonné pendant que Nicole _____ (parler) à son patron.
4. La chaise de Nicole _____ (tomber) en même temps que Nicole se levait.
5. Juste au moment où Nicole _____ (partir), le facteur[1] est arrivé.

D. Le monde du travail.

Posez les questions suivantes (pp. 331–332) à un(e) camarade de classe sur ses expériences dans le monde du travail.

1. À quel âge as-tu travaillé pour la première fois?
2. Que faisais-tu dans ton premier travail? Quelles étaient tes responsabilités?
3. As-tu eu un patron ou une patronne bizarre? Pourquoi était-il ou était-elle bizarre?
4. Quel travail as-tu détesté le plus? Pourquoi?
5. Quel poste as-tu préféré le plus? Pourquoi?

---

[1]*mail carrier*

Maintenant, cherchez le/la camarade qui …

1. a eu le plus mauvais travail de la classe.
2. a eu le/la meilleur(e) patron(ne) de la classe.
3. a commencé à travailler au plus bas âge.
4. à son premier travail avait le poste le plus difficile et avec le plus de responsabilités.
5. a eu le meilleur job de la classe.

Finalement, votre professeur va vous demander de donner vos réponses avec des détails. Par exemple, «Peter a eu le plus mauvais travail de la classe parce qu'il devait se lever tous les jours à 4 heures du matin pour distribuer des journaux.»

Portrait personnel

En fonction des renseignements que vous avez reçus dans l'activité D, *Le monde du travail,* écrivez un petit paragraphe sur le travail d'un(e) de vos camarades.

À vous de parler!

Direct students to activity C in the *À vous!* section for ideas as well as to review the pertinent vocabulary.

A. Le jour de l'entretien. En groupes de quatre ou cinq personnes, divisez-vous pour jouer le rôle du patron (de la patronne) et des employé(e)s qui écrivent une petite annonce pour un poste et le rôle du demandeur d'emploi et son époux (épouse). Pendant que le patron/la patronne et les employé(e)s écrivent la petite annonce, le/la candidat(e) raconte à sa femme (à son mari) ce qu'il/elle doit faire pour préparer un entretien (s'acheter un costume, préparer son CV, etc.). Ensuite, le/la candidat(e) va répondre à l'annonce au téléphone, et obtient un rendez-vous pour un entretien. Terminez l'activité par l'entretien. Jouez le rôle du patron (de la patronne), des employé(e)s, et du/de la candidat(e) qui passe l'entretien et de l'époux (de l'épouse). L'entretien peut très bien se passer ou très mal!

Remind students that their dialogue will have verbs in the **passé composé** and in the **imparfait** as they will need to talk about the activities that they completed at this job (past actions) and they will have to give a description of the job, the boss, the employees, and/or the company.

B. Parlons boulot. Vous êtes à une soirée chez des amis et vous parlez de choses et d'autres. En groupes de deux ou trois, composez un dialogue où vous racontez votre dernière expérience quand vous travailliez dans une super boîte (ou dans une boîte horrible). Vos camarades de classe dans votre groupe vous posent des questions pour en savoir plus.

Petite annonce. C'est pour quel poste? Quelles sont les qualifications demandées?

On travaille comme ça dans le monde francophone

Est-ce que vous avez un travail? Si oui, quelles sont vos conditions de travail? (Si non, pensez au travail d'un de vos parents.) Est-ce que vous êtes bien payé(e)? Combien d'heures par semaine est-ce que vous travaillez? Avez-vous droit à des congés payés? La réponse à ces questions dépend probablement de l'entreprise pour laquelle vous travaillez et de l'État où vous vivez, parce qu'aux États-Unis, il n'y a pas beaucoup de réglementations fédérales concernant le travail. Le gouvernement américain fixe le salaire minimum à 5,15 dollars de l'heure depuis 1997 (mais c'est plus élevé dans quelques états), avec des exceptions pour les étudiants, les travailleurs handicapés et les travailleurs recevant des pourboires. Le gouvernement laisse le choix à chaque compagnie de déterminer le nombre d'heures par semaine que leurs employés vont travailler, et de décider si c'est la compagnie qui va payer les vacances et d'autres avantages. La question des assurances est encore plus compliquée: les grandes compagnies sont obligées d'en fournir à leurs employés à plein temps, mais pas les petites, et aucune compagnie n'est obligée d'en fournir pour les employés à mi-temps.

Dans le monde francophone, c'est tout à fait différent. Pour avoir un aperçu plus large, nous avons choisi quatre pays francophones assez différents: la France, le Canada, la Tunisie et la Belgique. Nous allons maintenant revoir un peu ces questions du monde du travail. Les réponses vont quelquefois vous surprendre!

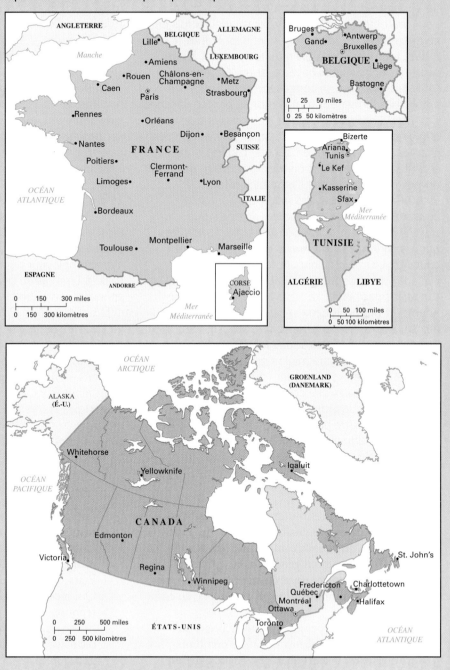

En France, le Salaire Minimum Interprofessionnel de Croissance (le SMIC) est calculé par mois et en 2005 il est en moyenne[1] de 1.200 euros par mois. Les jeunes sans expérience ou en stage de formation ou d'apprentissage et certains travailleurs handicapés reçoivent un salaire différent. Les serveurs et serveuses gagnent le SMIC, parce qu'ils ne reçoivent pas beaucoup de pourboires. La semaine de travail est de 35 heures en France, et on reçoit une bonification[2] pour toute heure supplémentaire, et quelquefois un compensateur[3] en plus. Tout salarié en France (c'est-à-dire, tout employé à plein temps), a droit à cinq semaines de vacances payées par an. En général, toute la France est en congé au mois d'août—les entreprises ferment et tout le monde part en vacances s'amuser! Les Français ne se posent pas la question d'avoir ou de ne pas avoir d'assurance médicale: les charges médicales sont en général couvertes par la sécurité sociale, et donc on n'est pas obligé de choisir un poste en fonction de l'assurance offerte.

Au Canada, les charges médicales sont aussi couvertes par la sécurité sociale, donc chaque travailleur (à plein temps ou à mi-temps), aussi bien que les chômeurs, les retraités et les jeunes sont couverts. Le salaire minimum (en avril 2005) au Canada varie par province, entre 5,90 et 8,00 dollars canadiens par heure. La semaine de travail est de 40 heures, et on reçoit deux semaines de congés payés par an, et une troisième semaine après cinq ans avec le même employeur (c'est une loi nationale).

En Tunisie, le salaire minimum varie selon si on est travailleur «interprofessionnel» ou «agricole», et selon le nombre d'heures que l'on travaille par semaine (il y a un salaire minimum pour une semaine de 40 heures, et un autre pour une semaine de 48 heures). Le Salaire Minimum Interprofessionnel Garanti (le SMIG) est calculé par mois et il est de 218 dinars (ou 173 dollars par mois en 2005) pour une semaine de 48 heures. Pour une semaine de 40 heures, le SMIG est de 181 dinars (ou l'équivalent de 151 dollars en 2005). Le Salaire Minimum Agricole (le SMAG) est normalement plus bas: 7 dinars par jour (ou 5,66 dollars en 2005). En Tunisie, on reçoit un jour de congé payé par mois (donc 12 jours par an); mais les jeunes travailleurs reçoivent plus de jours de congé: les travailleurs de moins de 18 ans ont droit à deux jours par mois (donc 24 jours par an), et les travailleurs de 18 à 20 ans reçoivent 1,5 jours par mois (ou 18 jours par an)! Les charges médicales sont assurées par le gouvernement.

En Belgique, on travaille 36 heures 40 minutes par semaine. Le salaire minimum est fixé par le gouvernement, mais varie par âge et selon le poste (les postes demandant plus de formation sont mieux payés). Un détail qui est assez intéressant, c'est que les jeunes travailleurs (de 18 à 21 ans) reçoivent un salaire plus élevé que les travailleurs plus âgés (de 21 ans et plus). Le salaire minimum en 2004 est de 1.317,50 euros. En Belgique, tous les salariés reçoivent quatre semaines de vacances payées, et une prime[4] de fin d'année en plus. Si on travaille chez le même employeur depuis six mois, cette prime est égale à un mois de salaire! En plus des vacances annuelles, on a droit à des congés payés pour différentes raisons. Par exemple, on peut demander un jour de congé payé à l'occasion de son mariage! Après cinq ans de travail chez le même employeur, on reçoit aussi un «congé d'ancienneté»: un jour après cinq ans, deux jours après dix ans, etc. Évidemment, ceci s'ajoute aux vacances annuelles. Comme dans la plupart des autres pays francophones, les charges médicales sont prises en charge par le gouvernement belge, et donc tout citoyen est couvert, même s'il ne travaille pas.[5]

Réfléchissons

1. Comparez les salaires minimums dans ces pays francophones avec le salaire minimum des États-Unis. Est-ce qu'ils sont comparables? Est-ce que les Américains sont en général mieux payés que les salariés dans d'autres pays? (Justifiez votre réponse en pensant au nombre d'heures travaillées, au coût de la vie, etc.)

2. Qu'est-ce que vous pensez du système belge, qui verse aux jeunes travailleurs un salaire minimum plus élevé qu'aux travailleurs plus âgés? Est-ce que c'est justifiable? Pourquoi pensez-vous que le gouvernement belge a créé ce salaire minimum variable?

3. Comparez la situation des salariés américains aux salariés francophones: Est-ce que la situation aux États-Unis est meilleure que la leur? Pourquoi? Qui reçoit les meilleurs avantages? Expliquez votre réponse.

4. Est-ce que vous voudriez travailler dans un de ces pays? Si oui, lequel et pourquoi? Si non, pourquoi pas?

---

[1]*average* [2]*bonus* [3]*time off* [4]*bonus* [5]Les renseignements sur les conditions du travail ont été tirés du Code du Travail national pour chacun des pays.

Continuons!

Un petit commerce 🎧

Emmanuelle Binoche est propriétaire d'une chocolaterie. Elle nous parle de son commerce et de son travail.

Online Study Center
Language Skills Practice

«Je suis chef d'entreprise. C'est une petite entreprise, mais le travail est quand même énorme. En général, je travaille 45 heures par semaine à la chocolaterie, et encore 10 heures par semaine chez moi, devant l'ordinateur. Au début, j'avais une associée, mais elle a dû déménager—son mari a eu des problèmes de santé, et ils voulaient être plus près d'un grand centre médical. Donc, maintenant je suis la seule à m'occuper de la chocolaterie: l'achat des produits, la préparation des chocolats, le service aux clients, la vente, la supervision des employés et la comptabilité. Je vais à la banque chaque soir, et je gère[1] les comptes bancaires à la fin de chaque semaine.

«J'emploie six à dix employés selon la saison. (À Noël, à la Saint-Valentin et à Pâques nous avons besoin de plus d'effectifs[2].) Trois de mes employés sont des chocolatiers confiseurs[3]: ils assurent la fabrication des chocolats faits à la main. Ce sont de vrais artistes! Évidemment, ils travaillent à plein temps, et ils reçoivent de très bons salaires. L'année dernière, je voulais embaucher un quatrième chocolatier confiseur, mais je n'ai pas pu—c'est un travail très spécifique, et il n'y a pas beaucoup de personnes dans cette région qui ont ce talent.

«Mes employés travaillent 35 heures par semaine, et ils ont cinq semaines de congés payés par an—c'est la loi en France! Je travaille beaucoup mais je prends au moins deux semaines de vacances par an. Je ferme la boutique, et je pars me reposer! Même la patronne a besoin de congé de temps en temps! Vous ne croyez pas?»

Vous avez bien compris?

Répondez aux phrases suivantes, selon le texte.

1. Quel est le poste d'Emmanuelle? Décrivez son travail.
2. Combien de personnes travaillent pour elle? Pourquoi y a-t-il quelquefois plus ou moins d'employés?
3. Est-ce que les chocolatiers confiseurs gagnent le SMIC? Expliquez votre réponse.
4. Quels avantages est-ce que ces personnes reçoivent?
5. Et Emmanuelle, reçoit-elle des avantages? De quelle sorte?

Answer Key: 1. Emmanuelle est chef d'entreprise; elle s'occupe de tout dans sa chocolaterie: l'achat des produits, la préparation des chocolats, le service aux clients, la vente, la supervision des employés et la comptabilité. Elle est aussi gérante. 2. Elle travaille seule à la direction, mais selon la saison (Noël, Pâques, etc.) elle emploie de six à dix employés. 3. Non, ils ne reçoivent pas le SMIC parce qu'ils sont chocolatiers confiseurs, c'est-à-dire des spécialistes dans la fabrication des chocolats. 4. Les employés travaillent 35 heures et ils ont 5 semaines de congés. 5. Elle aussi, elle prend des congés: 2 semaines par an.

---

[1]manage [2]employés [3]des artisans spécialisés dans la fabrication des chocolats

Vocabulaire essentiel

Online Study Center
Flashcards, ACE,
Language Skills Practice

Le travail (2)

le PDG (président directeur général)	*CEO*
le chef d'entreprise	*company head*
le gérant	*manager*
la gestion	*management*
recevoir le SMIC / être smicard(e)	*earn the minimum wage / be a minimum wage earner*
un commerce	*a business*
un horaire	*schedule*
la supervision	
la fabrication / la préparation	*production*
la vente	*sales*
l'achat (*m.*)	*purchase*
la clientèle / un(e) client(e)	*clientele / client*
la comptabilité	*accounting*
les avantages (*m.*) (sociaux/médicaux)	*(social/medical) benefits*
les congés payés (*m.*)	*paid holidays*
l'assurance médicale (*f.*)	*medical insurance*

À vous!

Answer Key: 1. d 2. a 3. h 4. g
5. b 6. e 7. c 8. f

A. Définitions. Pour chaque mot donné à gauche, trouvez la bonne définition à droite.

1. le congé
2. un smicard
3. une assurance
4. le chef d'entreprise
5. un employé
6. la clientèle
7. l'achat
8. un horaire

a. une personne qui gagne le salaire minimum
b. une personne qui travaille à plein temps, et pendant une période stable
c. le processus d'acheter les matériels nécessaires pour la fabrication d'un produit
d. une période pendant laquelle on ne travaille pas, mais pour laquelle on est payé
e. les personnes qui achètent un produit ou un service
f. un emploi du temps, qui spécifie les jours et les heures que l'on va travailler
g. la personne qui dirige une entreprise
h. un contrat qui paie les charges médicales

B. Donald Trump. Décrivez le travail de Donald Trump à un copain français qui ne le connaît pas[1]. Répondez aux questions suivantes pour faire la description de son travail.

1. Où est-ce qu'il travaille?
2. Décrivez son poste.

---

[1] *does not know him*

3. Quelles sont ses responsabilités?
4. Combien d'heures par semaine croyez-vous[1] qu'il travaille? trente-cinq heures, comme les Français?
5. Quels avantages croyez-vous qu'il reçoive?
6. Est-ce que Donald Trump est sévère avec ses employés?
7. Voudriez-vous travailler pour Donald Trump? Pourquoi?

C. Comparaisons. Mettez-vous en groupes de trois ou de quatre, et comparez vos jobs: qui travaille le plus; qui travaille le moins; qui est mieux payé; qui est payé le pire; qui aime son travail; qui s'épanouit[2] dans son travail; etc. Ensuite, commencez une discussion avec toute la classe sur vos emplois et sur les conditions de votre travail. Est-ce que les étudiants dans la classe sont satisfaits de leurs emplois ou non? Qu'est-ce qui détermine si on est satisfait de son travail?

Structure 2

Le passé composé et l'imparfait pour exprimer la subjectivité

Online Study Center
ACE, Language Skills Practice

As you saw earlier in this chapter, the uses of the **passé composé** are quite different from those of the **imparfait.** These differences are summarized on pages 328–329.

There are contexts, however, in which either tense may be correct, and your choice depends entirely on what you want to say. Compare the following examples:

Hier, il **a plu.**
Yesterday, it rained.

Hier, il **pleuvait,** donc j'ai pris un taxi au travail.
Yesterday, it was raining, so I took a taxi to work.

Il **a eu** ses 18 ans le jour même de l'accident.
He turned 18 the very day of his accident.

Il **avait** 18 ans le jour de l'accident.
He was 18 the day of his accident (and the days before and after, too).

Jeudi dernier, j'**ai eu** très mal à la tête.
Last Thursday I had a terrible headache.

Jeudi dernier, j'**avais** très mal à la tête, et j'ai manqué tous mes cours.
Last Thursday I had a terrible headache and missed all my classes.

If you are focusing on the action as being over and done with, you choose the **passé composé,** as in the sentences on the left. If, however, you are focusing on the action as ongoing, or if you are giving background description that includes another action, you use the **imparfait,** as in the sentences on the right.

---

[1]*do you think* [2]*is fulfilled*

Answer Key: 1. Il travaille à New York. 2. Il est homme d'affaires et il est le patron dans une série télévisée qui s'appelle *The Apprentice.* 3. Donald Trump est le PDG de toutes ses affaires: il embauche, il licencie, il prépare des stagiaires, il achète et vend des bâtiments, etc. 4. Il est difficile de dire exactement combien d'heures par semaine il travaille, mais c'est sûr qu'il travaille plus de 35 heures! Au moins 45 heures. *The Apprentice* prend certainement beaucoup de temps. 5. Comme il est plus que millionnaire, il peut se payer lui-même tous les avantages et tout le salaire qu'il désire! Il est probablement aussi très bien rémunéré dans son rôle comme patron sur *The Apprentice.* 6. Il a la réputation d'être sévère mais juste. Il est surtout très exigeant. 7. *Answers will vary.*

Time permitting, go over these sentences individually with the students, and ask them to justify the use of the **passé composé** or the **imparfait** in each, contrasting #1 with #3, #2 with #5, #4 with #6, etc.

Audioscript: 1. Hier, elle portait une robe bleue. 2. Il a fait très beau ce week-end. 3. J'ai porté une robe bleue pour le mariage de ma sœur. 4. Au lycée, j'ai joué dans l'équipe de football. 5. Nous voulions aller au parc ce week-end parce qu'il faisait très beau. 6. Ma sœur jouait bien de la clarinette au lycée.

À l'écoute! ◯

Écoutez les phrases suivantes, et dites si le verbe est au passé composé ou à l'imparfait.

1. _____ passé composé _____ imparfait
2. _____ passé composé _____ imparfait
3. _____ passé composé _____ imparfait
4. _____ passé composé _____ imparfait
5. _____ passé composé _____ imparfait
6. _____ passé composé _____ imparfait

Answer Key: 1. imparfait 2. passé composé 3. passé composé 4. passé composé 5. imparfait 6. imparfait

Certains verbes au passé composé et à l'imparfait

As translated into English, some verbs may mean entirely different things in the **passé composé** and the **imparfait.** These differences in meaning come back to the general distinction between these two tenses: the **passé composé** refers to completed actions, the **imparfait** to ongoing situations. Compare the following sentences:

vouloir

Hier, j'**ai voulu** aller au cinéma. J'ai téléphoné à mon amie Carole et nous avons vu *L'Auberge espagnole.*
Yesterday I wanted to go to the movies . . . (and I did). (action accomplished)

Hier, je **voulais** aller au cinéma, mais j'avais trop de travail à faire.
Yesterday, I wanted to go to the movies . . . (but I didn't). (description, no action)

pouvoir

Elle **a pu** trouver un très bon poste comme représentante d'assurances.
She succeeded in finding a very good job . . . (she was able, she did) (action accomplished)

Elle **pouvait** faire ses devoirs, mais elle était trop fatiguée.
She was capable of doing her homework . . . (but she didn't). (description, no action)

devoir

Il **a dû** aller à la bibliothèque.
He had to go to the library (and he went). (action accomplished)

Il **devait** aller à la bibliothèque, mais il a décidé d'aller au cinéma.
He was supposed to go to the library, but he decided to go to the movies. (obligation, no action)

◉ VÉRIFIEZ VOTRE COMPRÉHENSION

1. Retournez à la description de la chocolaterie d'Emmanuelle Binoche (p. 335). Soulignez tous les verbes au passé composé et à l'imparfait. Pouvez-vous justifier le temps qu'elle emploie dans chaque phrase?

2. Indiquez quel verbe et quel temps vous utiliseriez[1] pour communiquer les idées à la page suivante (ne traduisez pas la phrase).

---
[1] *would use*

> Yesterday, *it snowed.*
> I didn't go to class yesterday because *I had* a sore throat.
> *Marie was 19* when she got married.
> *They were supposed* to travel together this summer.
> *My parents wanted* four children, but *they had* just three.
> *I was able* to answer all the questions on the last exam and got a good grade!

Pratiquons!

A. Un week-end en famille. Jean-Jacques parle de son week-end chez ses grands-parents. Complétez ses phrases, en insérant la forme correcte (au passé composé ou à l'imparfait) du verbe entre parenthèses. Faites bien attention au contexte.

Le week-end dernier, j(e) (1) _____ (devoir) rendre visite à mes grands-parents. Ils n'habitent pas trop loin de chez moi, donc j(e) (2) _____ (pouvoir) conduire jusqu'à chez eux. J(e) (3) _____ (partir) tôt le matin, et j(e) (4) _____ (arriver) vers midi. Ma grand-mère (5) _____ (être) très contente de me voir! Il (6) _____ (pleuvoir) pendant tout le week-end, donc nous sommes restés à l'intérieur la plupart du temps. Nous (7) _____ (regarder) de vieilles photos de famille quand un de mes oncles (8) _____ (téléphoner). Il (9) _____ (être) bien surpris de m'entendre au téléphone. Je (10) _____ (s'amuser bien) avec mes grands-parents. C'est bizarre—je pense toujours que je vais m'ennuyer, mais finalement je m'amuse beaucoup quand je suis avec eux!

B. Obligations / désirs / possibilités. Maintenant, parlez du week-end dernier, en répondant aux questions suivantes. Faites bien attention à la distinction de sens entre le passé composé et l'imparfait dans vos réponses.

1. Qu'est-ce que vous deviez faire le week-end dernier? Qu'est-ce que vous vouliez faire?
2. Mentionnez une chose que vous avez absolument dû faire.
3. Avez-vous pu vous amuser un peu le week-end dernier? Comment?
4. Est-ce que vous pouviez aller au cinéma? Est-ce que vous y êtes allé?
5. Est-ce que vous avez pu faire les devoirs de français, ou avez-vous eu des difficultés? Expliquez votre réponse.

C. La Belle au Bois Dormant *(Sleeping Beauty).* Complétez le conte[1] suivant avec la forme correcte du verbe entre parenthèses. Choisissez entre le passé composé et l'imparfait pour chaque verbe.

Il était une fois un roi et une reine. Ils (1) _____ (être) très heureux, mais ils (2) _____ (ne ... pas avoir) d'enfants. Chaque nuit, avant de se coucher, la reine (3) _____ (prier[2]) pour avoir un enfant. Un jour, une grenouille est apparue[3] et (4) _____ (dire) à la reine: «Vos prières ont été entendues. Vous tomberez[4] enceinte.» Peu de temps après, la reine (5) _____ (tomber) enceinte, et elle (6) _____ (accoucher) d'une petite fille. La fille (7) _____ (être) extrêmement belle, et ses parents l'adoraient.

---

[1] *tale* [2] *to pray* [3] *appeared* [4] *will become*

Un mois après sa naissance, ils (8) _____ (décider) de donner une fête, et ils (9) _____ (inviter) tous les habitants et toutes les fées[1] du royaume. Mais malheureusement, ils (10) _____ (oublier) une vieille fée méchante qui (11) _____ (ne … pas habiter) avec les autres.

Le jour de la fête, tout allait bien. Il (12) _____ (faire) beau, le soleil (13) _____ (briller), et tout le monde (14) _____ (s'amuser). Finalement, les invités (15) _____ (présenter) leurs cadeaux au bébé. Les fées lui ont offert des cadeaux magnifiques: la beauté, la sagesse, l'innocence, etc. À ce moment-là, la vieille fée méchante (16) _____ (déclarer) que la jeune fille tomberait raide morte[2] à l'âge de quinze ans, à cause d'une piqûre de fuseau[3]. Une gentille fée qui n'avait pas encore offert son cadeau à la princesse (17) _____ (essayer) de l'aider: elle (18) _____ (changer) le sort[4] que lui avait jeté la méchante fée, en disant que la princesse ne mourrait pas[5], mais qu'elle tomberait dans un sommeil profond[6].

Évidemment, le roi et la reine (19) _____ (avoir) très peur. Le roi (20) _____ (demander) que tous les fuseaux du royaume soient détruits. Ils ont tous été détruits et pendant 15 ans, la princesse (21) _____ (grandir) entourée d'amour. C(e) (22) _____ (être) une jolie jeune fille sage, qui (23) _____ (donner) beaucoup de bonheur[7] à ses parents.

Mais un jour quand elle (24) _____ (avoir) 15 ans, elle (25) _____ (rencontrer) une vieille dame qui filait[8]. La princesse (26) _____ (être) une jeune fille curieuse; elle (27) _____ (demander) d'essayer, et elle (28) _____ (se piquer) avec le fuseau. Tout de suite, elle (29) _____ (tomber) dans un sommeil profond. Le roi (30) _____ (demander) à toutes les fées du royaume de venir à son aide, mais personne n(e) (31) _____ (pouvoir) la réveiller. Finalement, ils (32) _____ (mettre) la princesse sur un lit au milieu de la forêt, dans l'espoir[9] que quelqu'un viendrait[10] la réveiller.

Dans le royaume d'à côté, il y (33) _____ (avoir) un prince, qui (34) _____ (aimer) chasser[11]. Un jour, il (35) _____ (passer) par la forêt quand il (36) _____ (tomber) sur la belle princesse. Il (37) _____ (ne … pas pouvoir) s'empêcher[12] d'approcher; la princesse (38) _____ (être) la femme la plus belle qu'il avait jamais vue[13]! Pris[14] par sa beauté, il (39) _____ (décider) de l'embrasser. La princesse (40) _____ (se réveiller) tout de suite après!

Vous savez certainement le reste de l'histoire: ils (41) _____ (tomber) amoureux et (42) _____ (se marier). Peu de temps après, ils (43) _____ (avoir) un enfant. Il va sans dire que le roi et la reine (44) _____ (être) très heureux!

---

[1] *fairies* [2] *would fall down dead* [3] *needle prick* [4] *spell* [5] *wouldn't die* [6] *deep sleep* [7] *happiness* [8] *was weaving* [9] *hope* [10] *would come* [11] *to hunt* [12] *keep himself* [13] *had ever seen* [14] *Taken*

Portrait personnel

D'abord[1], demandez à un(e) camarade de classe comment a été sa dernière journée au travail: Qu'est-ce qu'il/elle a dû faire? Combien d'heures de travail est-ce qu'il/elle a dû travailler? À quelle heure a-t-il/elle commencé à travailler? etc. Ensuite[2], écrivez la journée de travail de votre camarade.

À vous de parler!

🗣A. Conversation. Posez les questions suivantes à un(e) camarade de classe. Ensuite, comparez vos réponses, et dites si vous avez eu des expériences plutôt semblables ou différentes.

1. Quand tu étais petit(e), est-ce que tu pouvais faire de la bicyclette? À quel âge as-tu appris à en faire?
2. Comment est-ce que tu allais à l'école? (À pied? À vélo? En bus?)
3. Où est-ce que tu es allé(e) pendant les vacances les plus mémorables de ta jeunesse?
4. Quand tu étais au lycée, est-ce que tu travaillais après l'école? Où? Pendant combien d'heures par semaine?

   • Si oui, est-ce que c'est parce que tu *devais* travailler, ou parce que tu *voulais* travailler?
   • Si non, qu'est-ce que tu faisais pour avoir de l'argent?

5. Pendant ta première semaine à l'université, qui as-tu rencontré? Comment? (Est-ce que vous aviez des amis en commun? Est-ce que vous étiez dans le même cours?)
6. Qu'est-ce que tu as dû faire hier soir? Est-ce que tu étais content(e) de le faire? Pourquoi ou pourquoi pas? Est-ce que tu dois faire la même chose ce soir?

🗣B. Jeu de rôles: Entrevue. Imaginez que vous postulez pour un des postes à la page 342. Avec un(e) partenaire, choisissez le poste qui vous intéresse le plus pour en parler à la classe tout en considérant les questions suivantes. Ensuite jouez les rôles du/de la patron(n)e et du/de la candidat(e).

• Si vous êtes le/la candidat(e), décidez comment vous allez vous présenter. Pensez aux questions suivantes, avant de vous présenter.

   Quelle est votre expérience? (Quel poste est-ce que vous avez déjà eu?)
   Qu'est-ce que vous avez dû faire dans ce poste?
   Qu'est-ce que vous avez appris dans un autre poste, qui vous serait utile[3] dans ce poste?
   Quelles autres qualifications avez-vous?
   Pourquoi voulez-vous travailler pour cette compagnie?

• Si vous êtes le/la patron(ne), pensez à la description de ce poste et à ce que vous voulez savoir, avant d'interviewer le/la candidat(e).

   Quelles sont les responsabilités de ce poste? Est-ce que cette personne a la formation / l'expérience nécessaire?
   Quels avantages allez-vous donner au/à la candidat(e)?
   Pourquoi est-ce que cette personne veut travailler chez vous?

Maintenant, jouez les rôles de ces deux personnes. À la fin, présentez votre dialogue à la classe.

---

[1] *First* [2] *Next* [3] *would help you*

Arrière ▶ Avant ✕ Arrêt

adresse: @ http://www.emploi-compagnie.com ▶ aller

Histoire

Recherche

RESPONSABLE INFORMATIQUE AU SEIN D'UN MUSÉE PARISIEN
Descriptif de poste
Important musée recherche un(e) RESPONSABLE INFORMATIQUE.
Vous allez avoir la responsabilité:
• de 60 PC (DELL)
• de 2 serveurs GNU/LINUX et 1 serveur NOVEL
• de la maintenance
• des relations avec les partenaires extérieurs
Rémunération   50K euros selon profil[1]
Compétences et expérience
Bac; License en sciences et informatique;
2 ans d'expérience dans le secteur professionnel.
Vous êtes dynamique et travailleur.

[Soumettre]

ASSISTANT(E) DENTAIRE / CONSEILLER(E) DE CLIENTELE
Descriptif de poste
Société de distribution de produits dentaires et laboratoire de prothèses
recherche un(e) assistant(e) dentaire / conseiller (conseillère) de clientèle pour
réceptionner les appels des clients afin de renseigner et vendre des produits
dentaires.
Rémunération   31K euros
Compétences et expérience
Bac; vous disposez d'une expérience impérative dans
le secteur médical (de préférence dans le secteur dentaire).
Vous êtes dynamique, motivé(e) avec une excellente expression verbale.

[Soumettre]

TÉLÉ-ENQUÊTEUR BILINGUE / MULTILINGUE
Descriptif de poste
Le poste de télé-enquêteur consiste à appeler des particuliers pour leur
demander leur opinion au sujet d'un produit ou d'un service. Nous recherchons
pour cette mission des personnes bilingues (langue maternelle). Les langues
concernées sont les suivantes : suédois, danois, allemand, anglais, flamand,
espagnol, tchèque, hébreu, portugais, grec, libanais, turc, italien, néerlandais,
marocain, russe.
Formation recherchée
Bac au minimum. Vous êtes bilingue / multilingue, avec une excellente
expression orale. Vous aimez le contact avec le public.
Rémunération   15 à 24K euros selon les heures travaillées

[Soumettre]

● zone d'internet

To do this activity, combine pairs into groups, and then sort students into **candidats** and **patrons.** This will guarantee that you have at least two of each in each group.

👥 **C. Après l'entrevue …** Avec un(e) nouveau (nouvelle) partenaire, parlez de votre entretien de l'activité B.

• Si vous avez été le/la candidat(e), trouvez un(e) autre candidat(e), et partagez vos expériences. Est-ce que vous allez être embauché(e)? Pourquoi ou pourquoi pas? Qu'est-ce que vous pensez de votre entretien?
• Si vous avez été le/la patron(ne), trouvez un(e) autre patron(ne), et parlez des candidats. Est-ce que vous allez embaucher cette personne? Pourquoi ou pourquoi pas? Quelles impressions avez-vous des candidats, en général? (Ils sont bien formés? Ils ont l'expérience nécessaire?)

---

[1] *according to experience*

D. Le poste de mes rêves. Décrivez votre poste idéal, en utilisant le vocabulaire du chapitre.

MODÈLE: Dans le poste de mes rêves, Oprah Winfrey est ma patronne. Je gagne 300,000 dollars par an, et je travaille à Chicago. Je fais les interviews de toutes les célébrités, et je choisis les livres pour son «club». J'ai huit semaines de congés payés par an—je dois voyager beaucoup dans ce poste, et c'est fatigant! J'ai un horaire très flexible—je peux fixer mes propres heures de travail. Je ne travaille pas plus de 30 heures par semaine.

Ensuite, comparez vos réponses avec trois ou quatre camarades. Qui a les rêves les plus réalistes? Les plus imaginatifs? Les plus impossibles? Expliquez vos réponses.

La condition sociale des femmes françaises et francophones est comme ça

Online Study Center
Web Search Activities

La condition des femmes dans le monde a beaucoup changé à partir de la révolution sexuelle des années 60. Déjà à partir de la Deuxième Guerre mondiale, les femmes ont fait partie de la main-d'œuvre[1] aux États-Unis, mais ce n'est qu'avec la révolution sexuelle qu'elles ont obtenu les mêmes conditions de travail, les mêmes salaires et les mêmes avantages que les hommes. Quelle est, vraiment, la condition des femmes dans le monde francophone? Est-ce que les femmes sont considérées comme égales aux hommes? Nous avons tendance quelquefois à croire que la situation des femmes aux États-Unis est bien meilleure que celle d'autres pays, mais est-ce que c'est toujours vrai? Faisons le parcours de quelques pays francophones pour faire la comparaison …

En Tunisie, par exemple, les femmes représentaient seulement 25% de la main-d'œuvre en 1997–98, mais elles représentaient 43% des étudiants à l'université. Actuellement, les femmes représentent 33% des fonctionnaires, 25% des avocats dans le pays entier, et 60% des juges dans la capitale (Tunis). Ceci suggère que leur condition s'améliore[2]. La loi exige un salaire égal pour les hommes et les femmes, et pour les mères de famille, le congé maternité est remboursé à 100%.[3] Le taux d'analphabétisme[4] des femmes tunisiennes reste toujours très élevé dans les régions rurales (27% des filles comparé à 7% des garçons), cependant il a été réduit considérablement dans les centres urbains (5,5% des filles, comparé à 2,2% des garçons). (La question aux États-Unis est très complexe: le gouvernement prétend[5] qu'il n'y a presque pas d'analphabétisme, mais d'autres groupes affirment qu'il y a beaucoup de personnes qui sont illettrées[6].)

En France, le taux d'analphabétisme est aussi très bas, et en général les femmes sont plus éduquées que les hommes: 81,2% des filles ont eu le bac en 1998, comparé à 76,5% des garçons. Au niveau universitaire, 56,4% des étudiants en premier cycle (l'équivalent du BA aux États-Unis) sont des femmes; elles forment 58% des étudiants de deuxième cycle (le MA aux

---

[1] *had entered the workforce* [2] *is improving* [3] Aux États-Unis, il n'y a aucune loi fédérale concernant le congé de maternité. En général c'est une décision laissée à l'employeur—il peut le payer ou non. [4] *illiteracy rate* [5] *claims* [6] *illiterate*

États-Unis). Malgré leurs études, il y a plus de femmes au chômage en France que d'hommes: le taux de chômage est de 11,9% pour les femmes, comparé à 8,5% pour les hommes. Quatre-vingts pour cent des femmes âgées de 25 à 49 ans travaillent actuellement, mais le taux est plus élevé pour les femmes célibataires ou sans enfants que pour les mères de famille: seulement 51% des femmes avec plus de deux enfants mineurs travaillent. En plus, les femmes réalisent plus souvent que les hommes des emplois à mi-temps—quelquefois par choix, d'autres fois par nécessité.

Ceci étant dit, les femmes françaises ont des droits que les femmes américaines n'ont pas: elles reçoivent un congé maternité, payé à 100%, de 16 semaines minimum.[1] (Si c'est leur troisième enfant, elles ont droit à 26 semaines, et si elles ont des jumeaux, à 34 semaines.) Elles ont aussi droit à des séances gratuites de préparation à l'accouchement, et elles restent plus longtemps à l'hôpital après la naissance du bébé. En plus, quand elles retournent au travail, les jeunes mères (de moins de 21 ans) reçoivent des jours de congé additionnels: 2 jours par an par enfant mineur.

Dans d'autres pays francophones développés, la situation est assez semblable: le congé maternité dure 15 semaines **(en Belgique)** jusqu'à un maximum de 52 semaines **au Canada.** Les frais sont remboursés totalement ou partiellement selon les pays. Même les pays francophones africains, où le pourcentage de femmes qui travaille reste assez bas, ont accordé, par législation fédérale, un congé maternité payé à toutes les femmes salariées (14 semaines, payées à 100%, **en Algérie, en Côte d'Ivoire, au Bénin, au Mali** et **au Sénégal,** par exemple).

Est-ce que la condition des femmes est vraiment meilleure aux États-Unis que dans d'autres pays? C'est une question difficile—il y a beaucoup de choses qui comptent pour déterminer ce qu'on appelle la «condition». Le rôle des femmes est déterminé par plusieurs facteurs: la tradition, la culture, la loi, etc., mais si le rôle des femmes dans ces pays est différent de celui des femmes aux États-Unis, leur condition n'est pas nécessairement pire. Il faut toujours s'informer avant de juger, n'est-ce pas?!

Réfléchissons

1. Quand vous pensez aux conditions de travail pour les hommes ou les femmes, à quoi pensez-vous? Quelle est votre définition de «condition»?
2. Que pensez-vous de la condition des femmes aux États-Unis et dans le monde? Est-ce que les femmes américaines sont privilégiées par rapport aux autres femmes dans le monde? Expliquez votre réponse.
3. Que pensez-vous des conditions de travail des employés aux États-Unis (hommes et femmes, employés minoritaires, employés âgés, etc.)? Est-ce que les conditions sont les mêmes pour tout le monde? Est-ce qu'elles devraient être les mêmes?

To broaden the discussion regarding women's social conditions, you may want to talk about **mai 68,** a crucial month and year for French women, who, thanks to feminist activists, obtained important rights such as legalized abortion, reimbursed contraceptives, salary equity, etc.

---

[1]La norme aux États-Unis est de 6 à 12 semaines.

À vous d'écrire!

A. Stratégies. Dans l'activité B vous allez répondre à une petite annonce. En général, quand vous répondez à une petite annonce, vous devez utiliser un langage et un ton formel et des formules de politesse spécifiques.

- Tout d'abord, quel sujet allez-vous utiliser? La deuxième personne du singulier (tu) ou la deuxième du pluriel (vous)?
- Lorsque vous commencez votre lettre, commencez par «Monsieur» (si c'est un homme) ou «Madame» (si c'est une femme) suivi d'une virgule[1]. Si vous savez le titre de la personne à qui vous écrivez, ajoutez son titre après «Monsieur» ou «Madame», par exemple, «Monsieur le Directeur» ou «Madame la Directrice».
- Donnez la raison pour laquelle vous envoyez cette lettre. Voici quelques formules utiles:

  «Je me permets de m'adresser à vous à la suite de la petite annonce parue dans *(nom du journal)*; je me permets de vous contacter après avoir lu la petite annonce dans ...; en réponse à votre offre d'emploi parue dans ... je vous envoie ma lettre de candidature; en réponse à votre annonce, parue dans ... je voudrais poser ma candidature au poste de ...»

- Ensuite, vous allez décrire vos qualifications. Voici quelques exemples:

  «Je pense être la personne la plus qualifiée pour le poste de ... *(nom du poste que vous avez choisi)* pour les raisons suivantes ... *(écrivez vos expériences professionnelles ainsi que votre formation et votre personnalité)*. Je pense que mon éducation, ainsi que mon expérience dans ... *(si le poste auquel vous postulez est dans l'hôtellerie, par exemple, écrivez le nom du/des restaurant(s) où vous avez travaillé et décrivez brièvement vos responsabilités)* me qualifient pour cet emploi.»

- Après, vous allez indiquer les documents que vous envoyez avec cette lettre: CV, lettres de recommandation, etc. Utilisez une de ces formules:

  «Vous trouverez ci-joint[2] mon curriculum vitae ainsi que trois lettres de recommandation.»

  «Vous trouverez ci-joint mon curriculum vitae et je peux me procurer des lettres de recommandation si vous le désirez.»

- Avant de terminer, démontrez votre intérêt et votre disponibilité:

  «Je me tiens à votre entière disposition pour une entrevue.»

  «Je suis entièrement à votre disposition pour un entretien.»

- Finalement, vous allez terminer votre lettre poliment. Voici quelques formules de politesse:

  «En l'attente d'une réponse favorable, je vous prie d'agréer[3], Monsieur, l'expression de mes salutations les plus distinguées.»

  «Dans l'espoir[4] d'une réponse favorable, je vous prie de recevoir, Monsieur, mes meilleures salutations.»

  «En l'attente de votre réponse, veuillez agréer, Monsieur, l'expression de mes salutations les plus empressées[5].»

You may want to ask students to give you some English expressions that are common in business letters in order to compare them with the ones used in French.

---

[1]*comma* [2]*enclosed* [3]*accept* [4]*hope* [5]*devoted*

Le restaurant français
Bon Appétit à Manhattan
cherche personnel qualifié pour trois postes:

1) **Chef Cuisinier**—spécialisé(e) en nouvelle cuisine, ayant trois ans d'expérience minimum et une formation dans l'hôtellerie.

2) **Gérant(e)**—une expérience de 5 ans minimum dans la gérance d'un grand restaurant est indispensable ainsi qu'une[1] formation dans l'hôtellerie.

3) **Serveur/serveuse**—formation hôtelière et expérience dans un restaurant de luxe indispensable.

Envoyez lettre de candidature et CV avant le 11 décembre à Mr. Jacques Lafaim au 1235 Fifth Avenue, NY, NY 10011.

B. Organisons-nous! D'abord, lisez la petite annonce. La petite annonce offre trois postes différents. Super! Vous découvrez que vous êtes parfaitement qualifié(e) pour l'un des postes! Décidez quel est le poste que vous voulez solliciter et pour lequel[2] vous êtes le/la mieux qualifié(e). Pensez d'abord à la description que vous allez faire pour prouver que vous êtes le/la meilleur(e) candidat(e) pour le poste. Ensuite, pensez aux postes que vous avez eus. Comment étaient ces postes? Aussi, pensez à votre personnalité: Êtes-vous un leader? Aimez-vous travailler la nuit? Aimez-vous travailler au service clientèle, face aux clients, ou préférez-vous rester bien tranquillement derrière votre ordinateur toute la journée?

C. Pensons-y! Voilà, vous venez de trouver le poste idéal que vous recherchiez depuis des mois et des mois! Premièrement, faites une liste des jobs que vous avez eus dans le domaine que vous avez choisi. Votre petit paragraphe doit contenir les renseignements suivants:

«J'ai travaillé comme … *(poste)*, dans le restaurant … *(nom du restaurant)* à … *(nom de la ville)* pendant … *(nombre d'années)*. J'étais chargé(e) de … *(responsabilités)*; je faisais / je m'occupais de … *(activités)*.»

Chef: _____

_____

_____

_____

_____

Gérant(e): _____

_____

_____

_____

_____

Serveur(euse): _____

_____

_____

_____

_____

[1] *as well as* [2] *for which*

Deuxièmement, faites une liste avec vos goûts personnels qui reflètent votre personnalité. Pensez aux caractéristiques suivantes: «J'aime travailler … (en équipe, seul, avec les clients, etc.). Je travaille mieux … (sous pression, le soir, le matin, etc.). Je suis une personne … (calme, stressé[e], organisé[e], artistique, créatrice, aimable, sympathique, etc.). J'adore … (travailler en collaboration, le matin tôt, tard le soir, etc.).»

Ma personnalité et mes goûts: _____

_____

_____

_____

_____

Finalement, pensez à la formation que vous avez reçue: Où avez-vous étudié? (Dans une école hôtelière? Dans une école d'arts culinaires? Avez-vous un diplôme en comptabilité, etc.)

🗣 **D. Révisons!** Avec un(e) camarade de classe, révisez ce que chacun(e) de vous[1] a écrit. Est-ce que les qualifications et les caractéristiques personnelles que vous avez décrites sont les nécessaires et les meilleures pour le poste que vous avez choisi? Pouvez-vous en ajouter[2] d'autres? Aidez votre camarade à trouver d'autres descriptions professionnelles et personnelles si besoin est[3]. N'hésitez pas à corriger les petites erreurs si vous en voyez!

E. Écrivons! Maintenant, vous allez écrire votre lettre répondant à l'annonce que vous avez lue. Utilisez les expressions dans l'activité A, *Stratégies,* pour formuler votre réponse. N'oubliez pas votre signature à la fin!

You may want to tell students that in France, in order to work at a restaurant, the employees must have obtained a degree from an **école hôtelière** that has prepared them to be specialized waiters: head waiter (**maître d'hôtel**) or wine waiter (**sommelier**); all great chefs have obtained a degree from an **école culinaire** that has trained them to be excellent cooks. One of the best **écoles hôtelières** is in Geneva. Every major French city has wonderful **écoles culinaires**, the best being in Paris, of course, and Lyon and Bordeaux.

Voici le petit commerce de Bouali Sambou au Sénégal, en Afrique. Il est le propriétaire. A-t-il des employés? Comment est son commerce (petit, grand, etc.)? Quels produits vend-il? Est-ce qu'il a des avantages (un salaire, une commission, etc.)? Y a-t-il des instruments technologiques dans son stand?

Voici un stand typique dans un marché africain. Les stands sont formés par des pans de tissus de chaque côté qui divisent chaque stand. Dans son commerce, Bouali vend des statuettes africaines, des vêtements africains, des tams-tams (petits tambours), des tableaux et des tapis. Son petit commerce est très modeste et il n'a probablement pas d'employés (peut-être que quelqu'un dans sa famille l'aide de temps en temps). Il ne reçoit sûrement aucun bénéfice puisqu'il est à son compte et il doit probablement travailler tous les jours. Le seul instrument technologique est le téléphone mobile qu'il est en train d'utiliser.

_____

[1]*each one of you* [2]*add* [3]*if need be*

Lexique ◯

Vocabulaire essentiel

Le travail

avoir un emploi / un job / un
   travail / un boulot (slang) / un
   poste *to have a job / position*
avoir une formation ...
   littéraire *to specialize in the
     humanities*
   scientifique *to specialize in
     the sciences*
avoir un stage *to have an
   internship*
   à mi-temps / à temps partiel
     part-time
   à plein temps / à temps
     complet *full-time*

un(e) candidat(e) / un(e)
   postulant(e) ... *a job
   candidate . . .*
   cherche du travail *looks for
     a job*
   est embauché(e) *is hired*
   passe / a un entretien *has an
     interview*
un(e) employé(e) ...
   est licencié(e) / mis(e) à la
     porte *is fired / kicked out*
   fait la grève *is on strike*
un(e) salarié(e) a / reçoit ... *an
   employee has / receives . . .*

un bon / mauvais salaire *a
   good / bad salary*
travailler / bosser (slang) dans
   ... *to work in . . .*
   une boîte *a company (slang)*
   une compagnie privée /
     publique / multinationale
     *a private / public /
     international company*
   une entreprise privée /
     publique *a private / public
     company*
   une société *a corporation*

Le monde du travail

l'achat (m.) *purchase*
l'assurance médicale (f.) *medical
   insurance*
les avantages (m.) (sociaux/medicaux)
   (social/medical) benefits
le chef d'entreprise *head of a
   company*
la clientèle / un(e)
   client(e) *clientele / client*

un commerce *a business*
la comptabilité *accounting*
les congés payés (m.) *paid
   holidays*
la fabrication *production*
le gérant *manager*
la gestion *management*
un horaire *schedule*
le patron / la patronne *boss*

le PDG (président directeur
   général) *CEO*
recevoir le SMIC / être
   smicard(e) *to earn the
   minimum wage / to be a
   minimum-wage earner*
la supervision *supervision*
la vente *sales*

Expansion personnelle

Le travail

un(e) candidat(e) / un(e)
   postulant(e) ...
   est demandeur(euse)
     d'emploi *is a job
     applicant*
   postule pour un poste *applies
     for a position*

un(e) employé(e) qui ne travaille
   plus ...
   est chômeur (chômeuse) *is
     an unemployed person*
   est retraité(e) *is a retired
     person*

touche le chômage / la
   retraite *receives
   unemployment / a pension*

Mes achats

Where do you live? Where do you shop? Do you spend your money liberally or do you carefully draw up a budget each month and stick to it? In this chapter, you'll learn how to describe your shopping and banking habits, and will have a chance to compare them to those of your classmates and to people in Francophone countries.

 The vocabulary that you will learn includes

Some businesses and their products and services
Banking
Your budget and your personal finances

 The structures that you will learn include

Direct object pronouns
Past participle agreement
Indirect object pronouns
Use of two pronouns in a sentence

The culture that you will learn includes

The euro, and the difficulties involved in the transition from francs to euros in France
What shopping is like in Burkina Faso

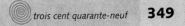

Commençons!

Chez les petits commerçants

Vous souvenez-vous d'Aurélie Marquis? C'est une jeune femme suisse—vous l'avez rencontrée au Chapitre 4. Ce soir, elle va donner une soirée, et elle a invité tous ses amis. Donc, ce matin, elle doit faire les courses—elle ne les a pas faites plus tôt, parce qu'elle veut des produits très frais. Elle ne va pas au supermarché—le supermarché, c'est pour les articles en papier, les boîtes de conserve, les légumes surgelés, les céréales, etc. Elle va chez les petits commerçants, pour acheter le plus frais possible!

D'abord, Aurélie passe à l'épicerie. Elle dit bonjour à l'épicier, Monsieur Dufruy (elle connaît tous les petits commerçants de son quartier par leurs noms!), et elle choisit quatre grosses tomates, des carottes, des concombres, des haricots verts, des fraises et du chocolat noir. Elle les achète, elle dit au revoir à Monsieur Dufruy et elle continue ses courses.

Ensuite, Aurélie s'arrête à la boucherie. Elle a besoin de huit côte de veau pour ce soir. Le boucher, Monsieur Lavache, recommande de steaks très tendres, et elle en achète huit. Elle regarde aussi le biftek, mais elle décide de servir du veau, comme prévu[1].

La boulangerie-pâtisserie est juste à côté, et elle y entre pour acheter des baguettes (bien sûr!) et un gâteau. Les gâteaux ont tous l'air délicieux—c'est difficile d'en choisir un! Elle les regarde longtemps, mais finalement elle choisit une belle tarte. Elle l'achète, et elle dit au revoir à Madame Levure, la boulangère.

Aurélie range ses achats dans sa cuisine, et elle sort faire une course de plus. Elle va chez le traiteur pour acheter des pommes de terre au gratin, qu'elle peut réchauffer[2] au four avant la soirée. Les courses finies, elle rentre à son appartement pour préparer le repas!

Après cela, elle passe à la crémerie-fromagerie pour acheter de la crème fraîche et du fromage mozzarella.

---

[1]*planned* [2]*warm up*

Vous avez bien compris?

Répondez aux questions suivantes, selon le texte.

1. Pourquoi est-ce qu'Aurélie ne va pas au supermarché pour faire ses courses?
2. Quel est le nom qu'on utilise pour parler de façon générale de tous les magasins qu'elle visite?
3. Où va-t-elle au début? Et à la fin? Qu'est-ce qu'elle achète dans ces deux endroits?
4. Qu'est-ce qu'on peut acheter dans une boulangerie? Et dans une pâtisserie? Et dans une crémerie?
5. Pouvez-vous deviner[1] comment on appelle un homme qui travaille dans une épicerie? Et une femme? Un homme qui travaille dans une boulangerie? Et une femme? Un homme qui travaille dans une boucherie? Et une femme?
6. Qu'en pensez-vous? Qu'est-ce qu'Aurélie va servir comme plat principal ce soir? Et comme légumes? Et comme dessert?

Vocabulaire essentiel

Les commerces et leurs produits

Online Study Center
Flashcards, ACE, Language Skills Practice

1. le (bureau de) tabac
2. le/la marchand(e) de tabac
3. les cigarettes *(f.)*
4. les pipes *(f.)*
5. le cigare
6. les tickets *(m.)* de bus / les carnets *(m.)* de bus

Point out to students that often businesses selling similar products are grouped together. Thus, one often finds a **boulangerie** sharing space with a **pâtisserie**; however, this does not preclude them from existing alone.

Point out the main differences between a **boucherie**, which specializes in butchered meats (beef, veal, and sometimes horse), and a **charcuterie**, which handles processed meats (ham, sausage, and salami, but also chicken and rabbit).

Time permitting, explain the cultural role of the **tabac** in France: it is here that one buys tobacco products, but also all sorts of newspapers, magazines, and even stamps, phone cards, and bus tickets. Often, the **tabac** is coupled with a **café**, and plays a central role in the daily life of French people. A **kiosque**, on the other hand, sells newspapers and magazines, but does not serve as a meeting place and therefore plays a less important role.

7. la charcuterie
8. le charcutier / la charcutière
9. les saucisses *(f.)*
10. le jambon
11. le saucisson
12. le poulet

---

[1] *Can you guess*

13. l'épicerie *(f.)*
14. l'épicier *(m.)* /
    l'épicière *(f.)*
15. des fruits *(m.)*
16. des légumes *(m.)*
17. des pâtes *(m.)*
18. du riz
19. des boîtes *(f.)*
    de conserve

20. le fleuriste
21. le/la fleuriste
22. les fleurs *(f.)*
23. les bouquets *(m.)*
24. les plantes *(f.)*

25. le kiosque (à journaux)
26. les journaux *(m.)*
27. les magazines *(m.)*
28. les chewing-gums *(m.)*
29. le/la marchand(e)
    de journaux

30. le/la marchand(e) de vin

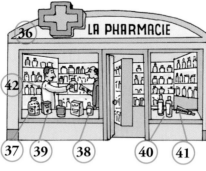

31. la parfumerie
32. le parfum
33. l'eau *(f.)* de toilette
34. le maquillage
35. le parfumeur /
    la parfumeuse

36. la pharmacie
37. l'aspirine *(f.)*
38. le sirop pour la toux[1]
39. les dragées *(f.)* pour la gorge[2]
40. le shampooing
41. le dentifrice
42. le/la pharmacien(ne)

43. la teinturerie
44. le lavage à sec[3]
45. le repassage[4]
46. le teinturier / la teinturière

---

[1]*cough* [2]*throat* [3]*dry cleaning* [4]*ironing*

Les petits commerces que vous avez visités au Chapitre 5:

la boucherie	la librairie
la boulangerie / pâtisserie	la papeterie
la chocolaterie	la poissonnerie
la crémerie / fromagerie	le traiteur

À vous!

A. Où va-t-on? Indiquez où on va pour acheter les produits suivants.

◉ MODÈLE: du pain

Pour acheter du pain, on va à la boulangerie.

1. du riz	6. du lait
2. des tulipes	7. du bifteck
3. des cigarettes	8. du poulet
4. un journal	9. du saumon
5. des éclairs au chocolat	10. des enveloppes

If you wish, you may have students redo the activity using **chez** and the name of the merchant: MODÈLE: 1. Pour acheter du pain, on va *chez le boulanger.*

Answer Key: 1. ... à l'épicerie 2. ... au fleuriste 3. ... au (bureau de) tabac 4. ... au kiosque à journaux 5. ... à la pâtisserie 6. ... à l'épicerie 7. ... à la boucherie 8. ... à la charcuterie 9. ... à la poissonnerie 10. ... à la papeterie

B. Au secours! *(Help!)* Tous les petits commerçants du quartier reçoivent leurs marchandises dans le même camion. Mais aujourd'hui, tout a été mélangé en cours de route[1]. Aidez les commerçants à déterminer qui devrait recevoir quels produits.

◉ MODÈLE: Voici trois cartons d'oranges.

C'est pour l'épicier.

1. Voici cinq flacons[2] d'eau de toilette.
2. Voici dix douzaines d'œufs.
3. Voici quarante bouteilles de vin rouge.
4. Voici un paquet de journaux.
5. Voici cinq douzaines de roses.
6. Voici trois grandes boîtes de cacao.
7. Voici quatre jambons.
8. Voici trente paquets de papier à lettres.

Answer Key: 1. C'est pour le/la parfumeur(euse). 2. C'est pour l'épicier(ère) (ou le/la pâtissier[ère], le/la boulanger [ère]). 3. C'est pour le/la marchand(e) de vin. 4. C'est pour le/la marchand(e) de tabac ou le/la marchand(e) de journaux. 5. C'est pour le/la fleuriste. 6. C'est pour le/la chocolatier(ère) (ou le/la pâtissier[ère]). 7. C'est pour le/la charcutier(ère). 8. C'est pour le/la marchand(e) de papier.

C. Dans votre quartier. Qu'est-ce qu'il y a dans votre quartier? Posez les questions suivantes à un(e) partenaire. Répondez-y en pensant à votre ville et, si possible, à votre quartier.

1. Dans votre quartier, est-ce qu'il y a une bonne boulangerie? Si oui, comment s'appelle-t-elle? Combien de fois par semaine ou par mois est-ce que vous y allez? Si non, où est-ce que vous achetez votre pain?
2. Est-ce que vous avez une petite épicerie préférée? Qu'est-ce que vous y achetez? Et qu'est-ce que vous achetez au supermarché?
3. Dans votre quartier, est-ce qu'il y a un café-tabac? Si non, où est-ce que vous allez pour acheter des journaux et des magazines? Et pour boire un verre avec des amis?
4. Est-ce qu'il y a une pharmacie dans votre quartier? Qu'est-ce que vous pouvez y acheter? Est-ce que vous connaissez votre pharmacien?
5. Où allez-vous pour acheter de la viande? Et pour acheter du poulet, du porc, des saucisses, etc.? Est-ce que vous avez une boucherie ou une charcuterie préférée, ou faites-vous vos courses plutôt[3] au supermarché?
6. À votre avis, quels sont les avantages d'acheter tous les produits dans un supermarché? Et d'acheter chez plusieurs commerçants différents? Préférez-vous le système français ou américain?

Mention the importance of the **quartier** in France. While people may live in a very large city (Paris, for example), they tend to limit many of their daily activities to their **quartier,** and are very loyal to neighborhood merchants. Many French people, for example, will always buy their bread from the same **boulangerie,** have an afternoon drink at the same **café,** etc.

---

[1]*in transit* [2]*bottles* [3]*instead*

Portrait personnel

Après avoir fait l'activité C, écrivez un paragraphe où vous décrivez le quartier de votre partenaire. Est-ce que vous habitez dans le même quartier? Si oui, êtes-vous d'accord avec les opinions de votre partenaire? Dites pourquoi ou pourquoi pas. Si non, comparez votre quartier avec celui de votre partenaire.

Structure 1

Online Study Center
ACE, Language Skills Practice

Les compléments d'objet direct

Direct object pronouns are used to replace a direct object noun[1] in a sentence. The direct object pronouns in French are as follows:

me	nous
te	vous
le, la	les

Notice that there is only one form for each of these pronouns, except in the third person singular, where the pronouns agree in gender with the noun that they replace.

Je regarde **le film.**	Je **le** regarde.
Je regarde **la télévision.**	Je **la** regarde.
Je regarde **les photos.**	Je **les** regarde.

These pronouns follow the same rules of placement as the other pronouns that you already know (**y** and **en**): in the present indicative, the **passé composé,** and the **imparfait** they are placed *immediately before* the verb.

Je choisis **les meilleurs fruits.**	Je **les** choisis.
Tu as mangé **le sandwich.**	Tu **l'**as mangé.
Il ne finissait jamais **ses devoirs.**	Il ne **les** finissait jamais.
Elle n'a pas compris **son prof.**	Elle ne **l'**a pas compris.

In negated sentences, the direct object pronouns are placed in between the negation (**ne ... pas**) along with the verb.

Je ne regarde pas **la télé** le samedi soir.	Je *ne* **la** regarde *pas* le samedi soir.
Samia n'aime pas **le vin blanc.**	Samia *ne* **l'**aime *pas.*

Point out that these rules concerning placement are exactly the same as for **y** and **en**, which students have seen in previous chapters. Pointing out similarities helps them to see that language generally follows consistent patterns, and is not as arbitrary as students sometimes think.

When there is more than one verb in the sentence, however, these pronouns precede the verb of which they are the object. This is the case not only in the *near future* (**aller** + infinitive) but also with other verbs that are followed by an infinitive (**aimer, vouloir, pouvoir,** etc.).

Je vais manger **la pomme.** (Manger quoi? La pomme.)	Je vais **la** manger.
Il aime préparer **le dîner.** (Préparer quoi? Le dîner.)	Il aime **le** préparer.
Nous voulons choisir **le film** ce soir.	Nous voulons **le** choisir.
Ils ne peuvent pas entendre **la radio.**	Ils ne peuvent pas **l'**entendre.

---

[1]Reminder: Direct objects are nouns that receive the action of the verb directly, with no preposition in between: **Je regarde** *la télévision.* Indirect objects require a preposition between the verb and the object: **Je téléphone** *à* **mes amis.** Direct objects answer the question *whom?* or *what?*; indirect objects answer the question *to whom? / for whom?* or *to what? / for what?*

In negative sentences with more than one verb, the negation is placed around the conjugated verb, and the pronouns come *before* the infinitive verb.

Mes parents ne vont pas prendre **l'avion.** Mes parents *ne* vont *pas* **le** prendre.

Alexandre ne veut pas manger **ses légumes.** Alexandre *ne* veut *pas* **les** manger.

Notice that the pronouns **me, te, le,** and **la** all drop their vowels before a word beginning with a vowel or a mute **h.**

Il ne **me** comprend pas.	BUT:	Il ne **m'**a pas compris.
Je **te** regarde.	BUT:	Je **t'**ai regardé.
Elle **le** mange.	BUT:	Elle **l'**a mangé.

In French, it is important to distinguish between direct object nouns, which are replaced by **le, la,** or **les,** and partitive expressions, which are replaced by **en.** Compare the following expressions:

J'aime **la pizza.**	Je **l'**aime.
Je mange **de la pizza** chaque jour.	J'**en** mange chaque jour.
J'ai acheté deux tranches **de pizza.**	J'**en** ai acheté deux tranches.
J'ai mangé **la pizza** tout de suite!	Je **l'**ai mangée[1] tout de suite!

🎉 Vérifiez votre compréhension

There are a few direct object pronouns in **Commençons!** (p. 350). Can you find them? What nouns do they replace?

À l'écoute! 🎧

Écoutez les phrases suivantes, et indiquez le nom que le complément d'objet direct représente.

🌀 Modèle: Vous entendez: Je les lis souvent.

Vous indiquez: _____ le journal ✓ les magazines.

1. _____ le film   _____ les films
2. _____ le chocolat   _____ les oranges
3. _____ le riz   _____ la soupe
4. _____ les actualités   _____ le téléfilm
5. _____ le fruit   _____ les fruits
6. _____ la pomme   _____ les pommes

Pratiquons!

A. Une femme difficile. Marc a décidé de préparer le dîner pour Anaïs, sa fiancée. Le seul problème, c'est qu'Anaïs est difficile à plaire! En regardant les dessins, dites ce qu'Anaïs pense de chaque idée. Utilisez un verbe tel que **aimer, adorer, détester, préférer,** et un complément d'objet direct dans votre réponse.

🌀 Modèle: Les tomates? ☺

Elle les aime.

1. Le chocolat? ☺ ☺
2. Le riz? ☺

Time permitting, this activity could be personalized and extended. Have students respond to each food item according to their own tastes, and list additional food items.

Answer Key: Possible answers: 1. Elle l'adore. 2. Elle l'aime.

---

[1]The addition of this feminine **-e** will be explained in *Structure 3.*

3. Elle ne les aime pas beaucoup. Elle préfère le riz. 4. Elle ne l'aime pas. 5. Elle le déteste. 6. Elle les aime. 7. Elle ne les aime pas beaucoup, mais elle ne les déteste pas non plus. 8. Elle ne l'aime pas beaucoup. 9. Elle les aime. 10. Elle ne les aime pas.

3. Les pommes de terre? ☺
4. La viande? ☹
5. Le fromage? ☹ ☹
6. Les pâtes? ☺
7. Les fruits et les légumes? ☺
8. Le broccoli? ☹
9. Les spaghetti? ☺
10. Les pommes frites? ☹

Qu'est-ce que vous suggérez que Marc prépare?

B. Les courses. C'est décidé—Marc sait ce qu'il va préparer. Il fait maintenant ses provisions. Récrivez les phrases suivantes en remplaçant le nom en italique par **le, la, les** ou **en,** selon le cas.

 MODÈLE: Il voit *la sauce tomate en conserve.*
Il la voit.

Answer Key: 1. Il les admire. 2. Il décide de la préparer lui-même. 3. Il en achète dix. 4. Il les pèse. 5. Il le sent. 6. Il en choisit deux. 7. Il les examine. 8. Il décide d'en servir. 9. Il n'en achète pas. 10. Il les paie. 11. Il rentre à la maison pour le préparer. 12. Il l'a oublié.

1. Ensuite, il admire *les tomates.* Elles sont belles et très rouges.
2. Il décide de préparer *la sauce* lui-même.
3. Il achète dix *grosses tomates.*
4. Il pèse[1] *les tomates.*
5. Puis, il sent *l'ail*[2].
6. Il choisit deux *gousses*[3].
7. Il examine *les pâtes.*
8. Il décide de servir *des spaghetti.*
9. Il n'achète pas *de fromage.*
10. Il paie *tous ses achats.*
11. Il rentre à la maison pour préparer *le dîner.*
12. Il a oublié *le chocolat.* Il va certainement retourner à l'épicerie!

**C. Réponses courtes.** Avec un(e) partenaire, répondez aux questions suivantes. Utilisez un complément d'objet direct dans votre réponse.

1. En général, est-ce que tu comprends le prof de français?
2. Quand et où est-ce que tu fais tes devoirs?
3. Est-ce que tu écoutes la radio pendant que tu travailles?
4. Regardes-tu la télé le soir?
5. Est-ce que tu vois[4] souvent tes parents?
6. Tu vas les voir cette semaine?
7. Est-ce que tes amis te comprennent?
8. Et toi, est-ce que tu me comprends?

Structure 2

Online Study Center
ACE, Language Skills Practice

Les compléments d'objet direct avec l'impératif

In the imperative, the placement of the direct object pronoun depends on whether the imperative is affirmative or negative. In a negative command, the pronoun comes before the conjugated verb, as usual.

Ne mange pas **mon chocolat!**   Ne **le** mange pas!
Ne brûlez pas **la soupe!**   Ne **la** brûlez pas!
                                          Ne **te** lève pas!
                                          Ne **vous** énervez pas!

---

[1] *weighs* [2] *garlic (m.)* [3] *cloves (of garlic)* [4] *voir = to see* (**tu vois**)

In an affirmative command, however, the pronoun is placed *after* the verb, and is connected to it by a hyphen. Note that **me** and **te** become **moi** and **toi** when placed after the verb.

Passez **le pain** par ici, s'il vous plaît.   Passez-**le** par ici, s'il vous plaît.
Mange **tes légumes!**   Mange-**les!**
    Lève-**toi,** s'il te plaît.

Pratiquons!

A. À la maison. Madame Aubry donne des ordres à ses enfants. Remplacez le nom en italique avec un complément d'objet direct.

    MODÈLE: Françoise et Patrice, mettez *la table,* s'il vous plaît.

        Mettez-la, s'il vous plaît.

1. Patrice, nettoie *ta chambre,* s'il te plaît.
2. Françoise, éteins[1] *la télé* et vient m'aider.
3. Jean-Marc, range *tes livres.*
4. Patrice, ne jette pas *ces papiers,* ils sont importants!
5. Françoise, aide *ton frère,* s'il te plaît.
6. Jean-Marc, ne provoque pas *le chien.*
7. Voilà, mes enfants, vous avez bien travaillé! Prenez *ces bonbons,* et allez jouer!

B. Situations hypothétiques. Imaginez que vous êtes dans les situations suivantes. Donnez un impératif logique, avec les verbes suggérés. Remplacez les noms avec des compléments d'objet direct.

    MODÈLE: Vous parlez avec vos camarades de classe à propos d'un examen. (se préparer / étudier les leçons / ne … pas se reposer)

        Préparons-nous bien!
        Étudions-les!
        Ne nous reposons pas maintenant!

1. Vous arrivez à la scène d'un accident. Vous parlez avec une femme blessée. (se calmer / ne … pas se lever)
2. Votre meilleur ami vient de rompre avec sa petite amie. (ne … pas s'énerver / ne … pas jeter ses billets doux / se rassurer)
3. Votre prof n'est pas très organisé(e) aujourd'hui! (ne … pas oublier ses livres / ne … pas perdre ses clés / se reposer ce week-end!)
4. Vous et vos amis voulez faire quelque chose ce week-end, mais vous ne savez[2] pas quoi. (se rencontrer au café / regarder le nouveau film au cinéma)

Structure 3

L'accord du participe passé

In Chapter 7, you learned that the **passé composé** is formed with an auxiliary verb, either **avoir** or **être.** You also learned that the past participle of verbs conjugated with **être** agrees with the subject, but that, in general, there is no agreement when the auxiliary used is **avoir.** This is true with one exception: in verbs conjugated

---

[1]*turn off* [2]*know; from the verb* **savoir:** *to know*

with **avoir,** there is agreement with a *preceding direct object.* This occurs in French when a noun is replaced by a direct object pronoun: the pronoun comes before the verb, and for that reason, the past participle agrees in gender and in number with the pronoun. Compare the following sentences:

J'ai **vu** les films.	BUT:	Je **les** ai vu**s**.
Elle a **compris** la question.	BUT:	Elle **l'**a compris**e**.
Ils ont **mangé** toutes les pommes.	BUT:	Ils **les** ont toutes mang**ées**.
Il a **fait** ses provisions.	BUT:	Il **les** a fait**es**.

Often this agreement has no effect on the pronunciation of the past participle, but it does show up in the written form. Listen as your teacher reads the preceding examples, to see which past participles have noticeably different oral forms.

Pratiquons!

This is the sidebar

To verify that students are making correct past participle agreements, have them write out this activity, or spell the forms for you to put on the board for all to see. Stress those cases where you can actually hear the agreement (#2, 3, 6), but point out that such cases are rare in French.

Answer Key: 1. Oui, maman, je t'ai écoutée. 2. ... je l'ai mise. 3. ... je l'ai éteinte. 4. ... je les ai fermées. 5. ... je les ai mangés. 6. ... je l'ai faite. 7. ... je les ai arrosées. 8. ... je l'ai lavée. 9. ... je l'ai appelé. 10. ... je l'ai promené.

A. Oui, maman! Maman veut savoir si vous avez fait tout ce qu'elle vous a demandé de faire. Répondez à ses questions, en employant un complément d'objet direct.

MODÈLE: Tu as fait tes devoirs?

Oui, maman, je les ai faits!

1. Tu m'as écoutée?
2. Tu as mis la table?
3. Tu as éteint[1] la télévision?
4. Tu as fermé les fenêtres?
5. Tu as mangé tes légumes?
6. Tu as fait la vaisselle?
7. Tu as arrosé[2] les plantes?
8. As-tu lavé la voiture?
9. As-tu appelé ton père?
10. As-tu promené le chien?

B. Je l'ai déjà fait / lu. Votre partenaire va vous poser des questions. Répondez honnêtement, selon votre situation personnelle.

MODÈLE: As-tu lu le journal aujourd'hui?

Oui, je l'ai (déjà) lu. / Non, je ne l'ai pas (encore) lu.

1. As-tu regardé les actualités *(f.)* à la télévision hier soir?
2. Tu as lu le dernier livre de Maya Angelou?
3. As-tu lu les poèmes *(m.)* de Charles Baudelaire?
4. Est-ce que tu as étudié la leçon pour demain?
5. Tu as regardé la vidéo pour ce chapitre?
6. Est-ce que tu as compris la section concernant les pronoms?

Answer Key: 1. Je (ne) les ai (pas) regardées. 2. Je (ne) l'ai (pas) lu. 3. Je (ne) les ai (pas) lus. 4. Je (ne) l'ai (pas encore) étudiée. 5. Je (ne) l'ai (pas encore) regardée. 6. Je (ne) l'ai (pas) comprise.

À vous de parler!

Add other categories as you see fit.

A. Une grande fête. Vous préparez une grande fête avec des amis. Créez un dialogue où vous décidez ce que vous allez servir à votre fête, et qui va être responsable de chaque chose. Qui va faire les provisions, et où va-t-il/elle pour les acheter? À la fin, présentez votre dialogue à la classe. Quand vous avez tous terminé, votez sur les catégories suivantes:

a. le menu le plus intéressant
b. la fête la plus gaie
c. le groupe qui a travaillé le plus et le groupe qui a travaillé le moins pour préparer la soirée

---

[1] *éteindre = to turn off* [2] *watered*

B. Les provisions. Maintenant, imaginez que vous faites les provisions pour la fête que vous préparez dans l'activité A. Avec un(e) partenaire, jouez le rôle d'un(e) marchand(e) et d'un(e) client(e). Entrez chez chaque petit(e) commerçant(e) que vous avez mentionné(e), et achetez tout ce dont vous avez besoin. N'oubliez pas de dire «Bonjour» et «Au revoir» au marchand (à la marchande)—c'est considéré impoli de ne pas le faire en France!

Before doing this activity, have students brainstorm some phrases that are useful for shopping. If they can't remember, refer them back to Chapter 5, where they learned a number of phrases normally exchanged between merchants and shoppers.

Online Study Center
Web Search Activities

On paie comme ça en France

Si vous avez voyagé en France il y a quelques années, vous avez payé tous vos achats en francs. En janvier 2003, cependant, 12 pays membres de l'Union européenne ont adopté une monnaie commune, appelée l'*euro*. On peut aller faire des courses dans presque toute l'Europe maintenant sans devoir changer de monnaie. C'est un grand avantage pour les voyageurs. Mais que pensent les Français de l'euro? Comment la transition de franc en euro s'est-elle passée?

Les sondages récents montrent que 88% des habitants en France pensent que le passage à l'euro s'est «plutôt bien passé».[1] Ils sont, pour la plupart, contents de cette nouvelle monnaie, mais ils avouent ne pas pouvoir distinguer les différentes pièces de monnaie (4 sur 5 avouent avoir des problèmes dans un sondage!)[2], et plusieurs disent qu'ils ont toujours des difficultés de conversion. Le plus grand problème pour la majorité des Français, c'est qu'ils ne savent pas automatiquement combien quelque chose devrait[3] coûter en euros. Ils ont grandi avec les francs, et ils ont bien assimilé ce système monétaire. Estimer combien quelque chose va coûter en euros est donc très difficile. Ils sont obligés de penser au prix en francs d'abord, et puis de convertir ce prix en euros. Le gouvernement a essayé d'aider un peu avec ce problème au début. Les marchands étaient obligés d'afficher les prix en francs et en euros pendant la première année. Il y avait aussi des sessions informatives pour éduquer le public. Mais maintenant que l'euro est bien intégré en France, on n'affiche pas toujours les prix en francs, et il n'y a plus de sessions pour éduquer le public. Néanmoins[4], beaucoup de gens disent qu'ils pensent toujours en francs. Quand ils voient un prix en euros, ils le convertissent mentalement en francs, pour décider si c'est bon marché ou trop cher.

Êtes-vous curieux de connaître les prix des produits alimentaires en France actuellement? Voici des exemples de prix, en euros, pour les produits que l'on achète le plus souvent[5]:

Les prix de produits alimentaires comme points de repère

50 centimes d'euro

- 1 litre de lait
- 2 kiwis
- 1 salade
- 1 paquet de biscuits petits beurres
- 1 paquet de chips de 100 g

---

[1]"Euro: un passage réussi selon une majorité de Français." *Fenêtre sur Europe*, 7 janvier 2002.
[2]Centre de Recherche et d'Information Nutritionnelles (CERIN) [3]*should* [4]*Nevertheless* [5]CERIN

70/80 centimes d'euro

- 2 petites boîtes de sauce tomate à la viande (1/8)
- 1 boîte de thon de 200 g
- 1 boîte de haricots verts
- 1 pâte brisée[1]
- 1 yaourt à boire

- 1 paquet de corn flakes
- 200 g de pâté de foie
- 1 sachet d'emmental râpé[2]
- 1 kg de semoule[3]
- 500 g de spaghetti

1 euro

- 1 kg de carottes
- 1 kg de pommes de terre
- 1 botte de radis
- 1 kg d'oignons blancs
- 1 litre de lait frais
- 1 pot de pâte à tartiner à la noisette[4]

- 1 boîte de lait concentré sucré
- 250 g de beurre
- 6 œufs
- 4 mousses au chocolat
- 1 paquet de purée en flocons[5]
- 8 yaourts nature

2 euros

- 1 kg de poireaux[6]
- 1 l d'huile de marque[7]
- 1 paquet de café moulu sans marque[8]

- 5 barres Mars
- 5 paquets de M & M
- 1 camembert

Le gouvernement français estime que c'est en faisant ces petits achats de tous les jours que le public va assimiler le nouveau système monétaire. Éventuellement, les Français vont réussir à utiliser ce système sans problème pour des acquisitions plus chères (des téléviseurs, des automobiles, des maisons, etc.). Mais jusqu'à ce moment-là, les Français vont continuer à convertir du système qu'ils comprennent le mieux—c'est-à-dire, les francs.

Réfléchissons

1. Quels sont les avantages que vous voyez dans une monnaie unique pour plusieurs pays? Et les désavantages?
2. Que diriez-vous[9] si on voulait adopter une monnaie commune pour les États-Unis, le Canada et le Mexique? Est-ce une bonne idée? Pourquoi ou pourquoi pas? (Je dirais que …)
3. Cherchez le taux de change[10] entre l'euro et le dollar américain. Combien d'euros est-ce qu'il y a dans un dollar? Regardez maintenant les listes précédentes, et comparez les prix en France aux prix aux États-Unis. Est-ce que les choses mentionnées sont plus ou moins chères, ou est-ce que les prix sont à peu près comparables? Expliquez votre réponse.

---

[1] *pie crust* [2] **Emmental** is a kind of cheese from Switzerland; **râpé** means shredded. [3] *semolina* [4] *hazelnut spread* [5] *instant mashed potatoes* [6] *leeks* [7] *brand name* [8] *without a brand name* [9] *would you say* [10] *exchange rate*

Continuons!

À la Banque Nationale de Paris (BNP) 🎧

Vous allez entrer à la BNP. Regardez les transactions que font les clients.

Online Study Center
Language Skills Practice

1. le guichet de caisse / à la caisse
2. le cassier / la caissière
3. Madame Richot dépose de l'argent à la banque.
4. le guichet automatique
5. Monsieur Povre retire de l'argent avec sa Carte Bleue.
6. le banquier / la banquière
7. Monsieur et Madame Jeuneau ouvrent un compte en banque.
8. La banquière leur donne une Carte Bleue et un carnet de chèques.
9. La banquière leur dit que les nouveaux clients ont accès à un coffre-fort.

Tell students that this Carte Bleue (CB) was issued by the Crédit Agricole (CA) and not by the BNP. Ask students to find the expiration date.

Au bureau d'échange

Monsieur Voyageur veut **échanger** des dollars en euros. Il demande à l'employé quel est **le taux de change.** Monsieur Voyageur a besoin de **monnaie** pour le taxi. L'employé lui donne **des pièces de monnaie et des billets** qu'il prend de la caisse.

Vous avez bien compris?

Vrai ou faux? Indiquez si les affirmations suivantes sont vraies ou fausses. Rectifiez les fausses affirmations.

1. Monsieur et Madame Jeuneau déposent de l'argent à la banque.
   _____ vrai _____ faux
2. Monsieur Povre retire de l'argent au guichet automatique.
   _____ vrai _____ faux
3. Madame Richot ouvre un compte en banque. _____ vrai _____ faux
4. La Carte Bleue s'utilise pour retirer de l'argent. _____ vrai _____ faux
5. La banquière s'occupe de Monsieur et Madame Jeuneau.
   _____ vrai _____ faux
6. La banquière donne à Monsieur Voyageur un carnet de chèques.
   _____ vrai _____ faux
7. Monsieur Voyageur veut des pièces de monnaie et des billets.
   _____ vrai _____ faux
8. Monsieur Voyageur voudrait aussi un coffre-fort. _____ vrai _____ faux

Vocabulaire essentiel

Les services bancaires

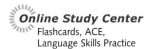
un compte en banque	*bank account*
un compte courant	*checking account*
un compte épargne	*savings account*
un chéquier / un carnet de chèques	*checkbook*
remplir un chèque	*to write a check*
toucher un chèque	*to cash a check*
une carte de crédit	*credit card*
le mot de passe	*password*
fermer un compte	*to close an account*

Les finances personnelles

Refer students to the footnote for some common slang expressions having to do with personal finances.

une dette	*a debt*
avoir des dettes	*to have debts*
avoir des investissements *(m.)*	*to have investments*
être endetté(e)	*to be in debt*
être riche	*to be rich*
être pauvre[1]	*to be poor*
économiser / épargner	*to save*
dépenser	*to spend*
gaspiller	*to waste*
être économe	*to be thrifty*
être dépensier (dépensière)	*to be a spendthrift*

Expansion personnelle

un chèque de voyage	*traveler's check*
un chèque sans provisions	*a check with no funds*
un relevé de compte	*bank statement*
un coffre-fort	*safe*

Les opérations et transactions à la banque

faire un emprunt / demander un prêt	*to ask for a loan*
emprunter de l'argent à quelqu'un	*to borrow money from someone*
prêter de l'argent à quelqu'un	*to lend money to someone*
rembourser quelqu'un ou quelque chose	*to pay back someone or something*
faire un emprunt hypothécaire / demander un prêt hypothécaire	*to ask for a mortgage loan*
demander une bourse	*to ask for a scholarship*
placer / investir de l'argent	*to invest money*

---

[1]In an informal setting, the following slang expressions are used: **Je suis fauché(e) et je n'ai pas un rond** (literally, *I'm broke and I don't have a penny*). (This phrase reflects the fact that coins are round.) By opposition, **avoir des ronds** means *to be loaded!*

À vous!

A. Premier jour au travail. Vous venez d'embaucher[1] un nouvel employé à la banque. C'est son premier jour et vous lui montrez les lieux de travail[2]. Identifiez les objets et les gens que vous voyez dans le dessin.

1. _____
2. _____
3. _____
4. _____
5. _____
6. _____
7. _____
8. _____
9. _____

**B. À la banque.** Vous êtes à Bordeaux depuis un mois. Votre meilleur(e) ami(e) arrive des États-Unis pour passer six mois avec vous. Il/Elle vous demande de l'aider à ouvrir un compte à la Banque d'Aquitaine. Répondez à ses questions avec précision.

1. Est-ce que les employés de la Banque d'Aquitaine parlent anglais? (Non, …)
2. Bon, alors je dois parler français! Où est-ce que je vais quand j'arrive à la banque avec mes dollars?
3. Où est-ce que je vais pour ouvrir un compte?
4. Quel compte me recommandes-tu d'ouvrir pour les dépenses de tous les jours?
5. Où est-ce que je vais pour toucher un chèque?
6. Avec quoi est-ce que je retire mon argent?
7. Comment est-ce que je fais pour remplir un chèque?

---

[1] *have just hired* [2] *workplace*

#2: Point out to students that in many large cities they can go to currency exchanges on the street; these generally charge more for making the exchange than banks, however.

#7: Show students how to write a check in French. Ask students what they think **Au porteur** means, where the date goes, where the amount in numbers and in letters must be written, where the space is for the signature. Then have them write the check on page 364 for the amount they wish.

C. Et tes finances? Comment sont vos camarades de classe avec leurs finances? En groupes de deux, posez-vous les questions suivantes à tour de rôle pour en savoir plus! Êtes-vous surpris(e) des résultats? Pourquoi?

1. Est-ce que tu paies tes achats en espèces ou avec la carte de crédit?
2. Combien de cartes de crédit as-tu? Est-ce que tu les utilises toutes?
3. As-tu beaucoup de dettes? Quand tu reçois le relevé des cartes de crédit[1], est-ce que tu paies le montant[2] dans sa totalité?
4. Tu prêtes de l'argent à tes amis? Est-ce qu'ils te rendent l'argent?
5. Tu empruntes de l'argent à tes amis? À tes parents? Quand?
6. Est-ce que tu as fait des emprunts à la banque? Pourquoi?
7. Es-tu dépensier (dépensière) ou économe?
8. Dans quel magasin est-ce que tu dépenses le plus? Qu'est-ce que tu y achètes?
9. Comment fais-tu des économies?

Structure 4

Les compléments d'objet indirect

Online Study Center
ACE, Language Skills
Practice

Earlier in this chapter you learned to use direct object pronouns. In this section you are going to learn the indirect object pronouns. In French, indirect objects are introduced by the preposition **à (au, aux, à la, à l')** followed by a noun referring to a person or persons.

Je réponds **au professeur.**
Elle emprunte de l'argent **à ses amis.**
Je ne prête jamais mon argent **à mon frère.**

The words in boldface are the indirect objects. They all refer to people. The following chart shows the indirect object pronouns that can be used to replace indirect object nouns. This is usually done in order to avoid repetition.

Masculine or feminine singular	Masculine or feminine plural
me *to me*	**nous** *to us*
te *to you*	**vous** *to you*
lui *to him / to her*	**leur** *to them*

---

[1] *credit card statement* [2] *amount*

Often, students get confused between invariable **leur** (indirect object) and variable **leur(s)** (possessive adjective). Point out the difference between the two: invariable **leur** replaces an indirect object introduced by à and means *to them*: **Je leur ai dit** *(I told them)*. Variable **leur(s)** is a possessive adjective and means *their*: **Ils aiment leur voiture. / Elles lisent leurs livres.** It may also be necessary at this point to remind students of the use of the possessive adjective **ses**.

Notice that the first and second person pronouns (**me**, **te**, **nous**, **vous**) are the same for both direct and indirect objects. The third person pronouns are different, however. The indirect object pronouns for the third person are **lui** in the singular and **leur** in the plural.

The placement of the indirect object pronouns in the sentence is the same as for other pronouns: before the conjugated verb.

Je réponds **au professeur.**	→	Je **lui** réponds.
Elle emprunte de l'argent **à ses parents.**	→	Elle **leur** emprunte de l'argent.
Je ne prête jamais mon argent **à mon frère.**	→	Je ne **lui** prête jamais mon argent.
(parler à)	→	Ta mère **te** parle tous les jours.

In the **passé composé,** the indirect object pronouns are placed before the auxiliary verb.

J'ai demandé un prêt hypothécaire **à la banquière.**	→	Je **lui** ai demandé un prêt hypothécaire.
Ma mère n'a pas donné ses économies **à ses enfants.**	→	Ma mère ne **leur** a pas donné ses économies.

When there is a *verb plus an infinitive* in the sentence, the indirect object pronouns follow the same rule as for other pronouns: they are placed before the infinitive (the nonconjugated verb).

Nous allons demander un carnet de chèques **au banquier.**	→	Nous allons **lui** demander un carnet de chèques.
Tu ne vas pas rendre la voiture **à tes parents.**	→	Tu ne vas pas **leur** rendre la voiture.
(envoyer à)	→	Ils vont **nous** envoyer la facture.

In negative commands, the indirect object pronouns are placed before the verb.

N'emprunte pas la carte de crédit **à tes parents.**	→	Ne **leur** emprunte pas la carte de crédit.
Ne **me** donne pas l'argent.		
Ne **me** téléphone pas.		

But in affirmative commands, they are attached to the verb with a hyphen.

Prête de l'argent **à ta sœur!**	→	Prête-**lui** de l'argent!
Répondez **aux profs.**	→	Répondez-**leur.**

As with the direct object pronouns, **me** and **te** change into **moi** and **toi** in affirmative commands.

(donner à)	→	Donne-**moi** l'argent!
(téléphoner à)	→	Téléphonez-**moi!**
(se brosser les dents)	→	Brosse-**toi** les dents!

Attention! Remember that the preposition **à** is also used to introduce a place or a location. In this case, it is not an indirect object, and the pronoun that is used is **y.** Compare these examples:

Je vais **à la banque.** (location: **y**)   → J'**y** vais.
Je parle **à mon banquier.**   → Je **lui** parle.
   (**à** + person: indirect object)
Nous retirons de l'argent **au guichet**   → Nous **y** retirons de l'argent.
   automatique. (location: **y**)
Nous posons des questions **aux caissières.** → Nous **leur** posons des questions.
   (**à** + persons: indirect object)

VÉRIFIEZ VOTRE COMPRÉHENSION

1. Look at the text at the beginning of the **Continuons!** section (pp. 361–362), and underline the indirect object pronouns. Identify to whom **lui** and **leur** refer in each sentence where they appear. Is **lui** the employee or the client? Does **leur** replace the clients or the bankers?

2. This ad says: «Offrez-lui une peau d'allure saine. Les nouveaux produits Neutrogena men.» Does the pronoun **lui** in the ad mean *her* or *him*? Why is there a hyphen before the pronoun?

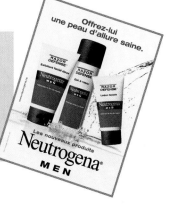

Pratiquons!

A. Le banquier blond! Voici une conversation entre deux amies, Sylvie et Caroline. Complétez les phrases avec les pronoms **lui** et **leur** qui manquent[1].

Answer Key: 1. lui 2. lui 3. lui 4. leur 5. lui 6. lui 7. leur 8. leur 9. lui

SYLVIE: Dis donc, Caroline, tu dis bonjour au banquier blond quand tu vas à la banque? Il est mignon, non?

CAROLINE: Non, je ne (1) _____ dis pas bonjour. Il n'est pas sympa avec moi et il n'est pas mignon du tout.

SYLVIE: Ah bon? Eh bien moi, je (2) _____ dis toujours bonjour et je (3) _____ demande toujours de m'aider. Je le trouve très mignon!

CAROLINE: Eh bien, moi non! Je fais mes opérations bancaires toute seule. Au fait[2], Sylvie, puisqu'on parle d'argent, finalement, tu as emprunté de l'argent à tes parents pour partir en voyage cet été avec les copains?

SYLVIE: Non. Franchement, je n'ai pas osé[3] (4) _____ emprunter de l'argent. Mon père vient de passer toutes ses économies à mon oncle qui est fauché après son divorce. Tu comprends, son ex-femme (5) _____ a vidé[4] tous ses comptes en banque avant de le quitter.

CAROLINE: Quoi? Son ex (6) _____ a enlevé tout son argent? Le pauvre … Et toi, alors? Comment vas-tu faire ce voyage? Tu l'as dit aux copains?

SYLVIE: Non, je ne (7) _____ ai pas encore dit. Je vais (8) _____ dire plus tard.

CAROLINE: J'ai une idée! Tu peux demander de l'argent à ton banquier blond qui est si mignon!

SYLVIE: Tu es folle! Je (9) _____ demande de m'aider avec mes finances, pas avec ma vie privée! Merci pour ton idée!

---

[1]*that are missing* [2]*By the way* [3]*didn't dare* [4]*emptied*

B. Que dit-on? Votre meilleur(e) ami(e) des États-Unis qui est à Bordeaux chez vous et que vous avez déjà aidé(e) (vous rappelez-vous dans la section *À Vous!,* activité C?) voudrait savoir ce qu'on dit en français dans les situations suivantes. Répondez à votre ami(e) avec des pronoms d'objet indirect.

MODÈLE: Que dit-on à la boulangère quand on veut du pain croustillant[1]?

On lui dit: «Bonjour, Madame, je voudrais une baguette bien cuite.»

1. Que dit-on au caissier quand on va au guichet à la banque?
2. Que dit-on aux serveurs quand on a fini de manger au restaurant?
3. Que dit-on à quelqu'un quand on lui a marché sur le pied[2]?
4. Que demande-t-on aux vendeuses quand on veut savoir si le tee-shirt qu'on a choisi est sa taille?
5. Que dit-on à l'employé à la gare qui vend les billets de train quand on veut partir en voyage un week-end?
6. Que dit-on au poissonnier quand on veut préparer une bouillabaisse?

Selon vous, qu'est-ce qu'on peut acheter dans cette galerie? Est-ce cher ou bon marché? Où est-ce que vous aimez acheter vos vêtements?

C. Obéissez-moi! Vous faites du baby-sitting pour deux enfants de quatre et six ans, Lulu et Juju. Vous leur donnez des ordres pour qu'ils arrêtent[3] de se disputer. En groupe de trois, écrivez les ordres selon les indications données. Utilisez les *pronoms d'objet indirect* dans vos ordres et soyez logiques!

MODÈLE: Juju prend le camion[4] de Lulu. (donner)

Donne-lui son camion!

1. Juju donne un coup de pied à Lulu. (ne ... pas donner)
2. Lulu coupe[5] les cheveux à Juju. (ne ... pas couper)
3. Juju veut sa voiture bleue, mais c'est Lulu qui a la voiture. (rendre)
4. Lulu et Juju vous mentent[6]. (dire la vérité)
5. Juju jette la soupe à la figure[7] de Lulu. (ne ... pas jeter)

---

[1]*crusty* [2]*stepped on his/her foot* [3]*stop* [4]*truck* [5]*is cutting* [6]*are lying* [7]*face*

6. Juju ne veut pas demander pardon à Lulu. (demander)
7. Juju demande enfin pardon à Lulu mais maintenant, Lulu ne veut pas faire la bise à Juju. (faire la bise)
8. Enfin dans leurs lits, Lulu décide de faire des chatouilles[1] à Juju. (ne … pas faire des chatouilles)

Maintenant que vous avez fait vos phrases, jouez les rôles du/de Juju, Lulu et du/de la baby-sitter.

À l'écoute! 🎧

Écoutez les phrases suivantes, et indiquez si le pronom dans chacune remplace un objet direct ou un objet indirect.

Audioscript: 1. Elle lui a parlé. 2. Ils t'ont téléphoné? 3. Nous les avons vus. 4. Tu leur as donné le cadeau? 5. Ma mère m'adore! 6. Vous lui avez dit bonjour. 7. Il vous a répondu. 8. Elles la regardent tous les soirs.

🌀 MODÈLE: Vous entendez: Je l'ai envoyé à ma sœur.

Vous indiquez: ✓ objet direct _____ objet indirect

1. _____ objet direct   _____ objet indirect
2. _____ objet direct   _____ objet indirect
3. _____ objet direct   _____ objet indirect
4. _____ objet direct   _____ objet indirect
5. _____ objet direct   _____ objet indirect
6. _____ objet direct   _____ objet indirect
7. _____ objet direct   _____ objet indirect
8. _____ objet direct   _____ objet indirect

🌀 Structure 5

L'ordre des pronoms dans la phrase

Online Study Center
ACE, Language Skills Practice

To avoid repetition in a conversation or a written text, it is normal to use pronouns. In fact, it is common to use two object pronouns in the same sentence: a direct object pronoun and an indirect object pronoun. This construction also happens in English, for example:

*I gave **the money to Brian**.* → *I gave **it to him**.*
*She writes **the letters to me**.* → *She writes **them to me**.*

The following chart shows the order of the pronouns in the present indicative, the **passé composé,** the **imparfait,** and the *negative* imperative.

subject	(ne)	me te nous vous	le la les	lui leur	verb	(pas)

Il **me** donne **la lettre**.   → Il **me la** donne.
Nous **vous** avons dit **les réponses**. → Nous **vous les** avons dit**es**.
Elle envoyait **le courriel à son ami**. → Elle **le lui** envoyait.
Ne **me** dis pas **la vérité**—je ne   → Ne **me la** dis pas—je ne
veux pas savoir!   veux pas savoir!

---

[1]*tickle*

In the *affirmative* imperative, however, the order is different.

verb	le la les	moi toi lui nous vous leur

Dis **la vérité à votre mère!** → Dis-**la-lui!**
Passez-**moi les pommes de terre.** → Passez-**les-moi.**

Pratiquons!

A. C'est barbant! *(That's so boring!)* Odile n'arrête pas de parler et quand elle parle elle est barbante car elle répète toujours la même histoire avec les mêmes personnes et les mêmes choses. Pour rendre son histoire moins barbante, récrivez-la en utilisant les *pronoms directs* et *indirects* qui conviennent en remplaçant les mots en italique. Odile parle à son ami Frédéric.

«Frédéric, je vais te raconter ma journée d'hier. Je vais te raconter (1) *ma journée* parce que ça a été une journée incroyable! D'abord, j'ai téléphoné à ma sœur. J'ai téléphoné (2) *à ma sœur* parce que c'était son anniversaire. J'aime téléphoner (3) *à ma sœur* parce qu'on rigole toujours ensemble. Elle me raconte les bêtises de son chat Minoulefou. Pendant qu'elle me raconte (4) *les bêtises de Minoulefou*, j'écoute (5) *ma sœur* attentivement. À la fin, nous éclatons de rire toutes les deux, tellement Minoulefou est marrant. Nous nous entendons très bien, ma sœur et moi. J'aime beaucoup (6) *ma sœur*. Ensuite, je suis allée à la banque pour consulter le banquier afin d'obtenir une bourse. J'ai parlé (7) *au banquier* et ensuite j'ai décidé de ne pas demander une bourse. Les intérêts sont trop élevés. Je ne veux pas rembourser (8) / *la bourse* / *à la banque* / toute ma vie. Figure-toi[1] que quand j'étais sur le point de partir, un voleur est entré dans la banque et il a demandé à la caissière tout l'argent de la caisse. Il a demandé (9) / *l'argent* / *à la caissière* / en criant. La caissière a donné (10) / *l'argent* / *au voleur* / et il est parti tout content.»

B. Tes amis et toi. En groupe de deux, posez-vous les questions suivantes à tour de rôle pour en savoir plus sur vos activités. Utilisez des pronoms directs et indirects dans vos réponses. (Attention! Parfois, vous pouvez avoir plusieurs pronoms dans une même réponse.)

1. Est-ce que tu prêtes tes vêtements à tes copains de temps en temps?
2. Tu invites souvent tes amis chez toi? Que faites-vous?
3. Est-ce que tu dis toujours la vérité à tes amis? Pourquoi?
4. Est-ce que tu vois tes amis souvent? Combien de fois par semaine?
5. Est-ce que tu parles au téléphone avec tes amis tous les jours? Pendant longtemps?
6. Est-ce que tu fais la bise à tes amies pour dire bonjour? Comment est-ce que tu dis bonjour à tes amies?

---

[1] *Imagine*

7. Est-ce que tu racontes tes problèmes à tes amis? Est-ce que vous vous aidez, tes amis et toi? Comment est-ce que vous vous aidez?
8. Est-ce que tu comprends tes amis? Y a t-il un(e) ami(e) que tu ne comprends pas? Pourquoi?

Portrait personnel

Après avoir répondu aux questions, décidez si votre camarade est …

a. un(e) ami(e) généreux (généreuse) ou radin(e)
b. un(e) bon(ne) ami(e) ou un(e) mauvais(e) ami(e)
c. un(e) ami(e) fiable ou non fiable
d. un(e) ami(e) désirable ou indésirable

Écrivez un paragraphe pour expliquer vos pensées!

Petit Dépanneur (Montréal). Ce type de magasin se trouve partout au Québec. D'après le nom, pouvez-vous deviner ce qu'ils vendent? (Tuyau: **dépanner =** *to help out of a jam*)

À vous de parler!

A. L'argent et les femmes et les hommes. Vous êtes journaliste pour la chaîne de télévision France 2. Vous préparez un programme sur les dépenses et les économies des hommes et des femmes afin de savoir en quoi les hommes et les femmes dépensent et économisent le plus. En groupes de trois, préparez des questions en relation avec le sujet. Ensuite, posez vos questions à vos camarades de classe. Quand vous aurez assez de réponses, tirez-en votre conclusion. Finalement, chaque groupe va présenter ses conclusions à la classe comme si vous étiez à la télé en train de faire un programme d'actualités. Est-ce que tous les groupes sont arrivés aux mêmes conclusions? Et vous, pensez-vous que les femmes sont plus dépensières que les hommes ou vice versa? En quoi? Commencez un débat.

Questions possibles

Demandez si la personne a un compte épargne.
Demandez si la personne a une ou plusieurs[1] cartes de crédit.
Demandez comment la personne règle (paie) ses achats. (En espèces[2], par chèque, etc.)
Demandez combien de fois par semaine la personne va faire ses courses au supermarché. Demandez combien d'argent la personne dépense en moyenne toutes les semaines.
Demandez quels sont les achats qui coûtent le plus et le moins. (Suggérez des produits et des services: des produits de beauté, le coiffeur, des vêtements, etc.)

For this activity, students may ask questions of classmates outside of the French class. You may want to help students to prepare their questions. We suggest that you expand the topic beyond the list of suggested questions. Remind students to use direct and indirect object pronouns as often as they can in their presentations. As a follow-up to this activity, you may want to have students search the Internet for information about French men and women and their finances. On what do French men and women spend more money? Less money? Make some comparisons with American men and women.

[1]*several* [2]*In cash*

For this activity, refer students to the beginning of the *Continuons!* section (pp. 361–362) and have them use the text as a model for their dialogues.

B. À la banque. Vous venez de gagner un million d'euros au Loto. Vous avez pris rendez-vous avec deux banquiers pour leur demander de vous aider à ouvrir un compte en banque et à placer votre argent. Les banquiers sont extrêmement aimables avec vous et ils vous traitent très bien: ils vous offrent tous les services que la banque possède parce que vous êtes un(e) client(e) très spécial(e)! En groupes de trois, jouez le rôle du (de la) client(e) et des deux banquiers: un banquier aide le/la client(e) à ouvrir des comptes et l'autre à placer l'argent dans de bons investissements.

Online Study Center
Web Search Activities

On fait les courses comme ça au Burkina Faso

Vous n'avez peut-être pas trouvé trop de différences entre faire les courses en France et faire les courses aux États-Unis. On a le choix entre les supermarchés et les petits commerçants dans les deux pays, et les produits ne diffèrent pas trop. Mais si vous alliez en Afrique, qu'est-ce que vous y trouveriez[1]? Nous avons posé cette question à Abdou, notre ami du Burkina Faso. Voici sa réponse:

«Au Burkina Faso, on a le même choix entre les supermarchés et les petits commerçants, mais seulement dans les grandes villes. Dans les villages, il n'y a pas de supermarchés parce que très souvent il n'y a pas d'électricité. Les supermarchés ont besoin de réfrigération, et ceci n'est pas possible s'il n'y a pas d'électricité! Donc, les personnes qui habitent dans les villages achètent leur nourriture chez les petits commerçants et, surtout, au marché en plein air. Pour le lait et la viande, il faut tout acheter frais, parce qu'on n'a pas de réfrigérateur à la maison non plus. Donc, on n'achète que[2] ce qu'on va manger ou boire pendant la journée. La cuisine au Burkina Faso incorpore beaucoup de fruits et de légumes pour cette raison aussi.

Dans les grandes villes il y a des supermarchés, mais beaucoup de personnes n'y vont pas. Les supermarchés sont surtout fréquentés par les intellectuels et les riches; la plupart de la population achète sa nourriture au marché, comme dans les villages. Mais les maisons dans les villes sont plus modernes, donc on peut acheter pour plusieurs jours à la fois—ce qu'on ne mange pas, on peut le mettre dans le réfrigérateur!

Les marchés sont très animés— c'est un lieu de rencontre[3] pour tout le village ou la ville. On peut tout y acheter—des vêtements, de la nourriture, même des animaux! On y va pour faire les courses,

---

[1] *would you find* [2] *buys only* [3] *meeting place*

bien sûr, mais on y va aussi pour se parler, s'amuser, se voir. C'est probablement pour cette raison que même les habitants des villes préfèrent le marché au supermarché.

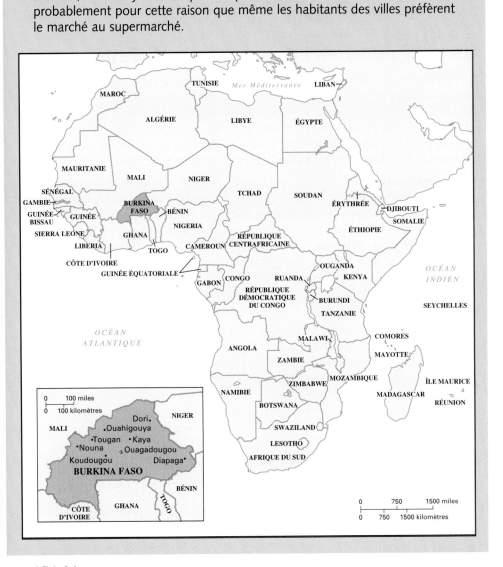

Réfléchissons

1. Est-ce que vous êtes surpris(e) de savoir qu'il y a des villages en Afrique qui n'ont pas d'électricité? Est-ce que vous aimeriez vivre dans un de ces villages? Pourquoi ou pourquoi pas? (J'aimerais … / Je n'aimerais pas …)

2. Comparez votre vie à la vie d'un habitant du Burkina Faso. (Pensez à ceux qui habitent dans une ville et puis à ceux qui habitent dans un village.) Combien de fois par semaine est-ce que vous faites les courses? Qu'est-ce que vous achetez? Si vous ne mangez pas tout ce que vous avez acheté, qu'est-ce que vous faites avec les restes?

3. Est-ce qu'il y a un équivalent du marché en plein air (du point de vue social *et* commercial) aux États-Unis? Expliquez votre réponse.

À vous de lire!

Un plan personnel de dépenses et d'épargne

A. Stratégies. Le sujet du texte que vous allez lire porte sur les finances personnelles: les dépenses et les économies. Ce texte a été sorti d'un site web canadien dédié aux femmes (mais dont les suggestions sont aussi très valables pour les hommes!). Les phrases suivantes sont tirées du texte. Trouvez la bonne définition pour chaque phrase. Ceci vous permettra de vous familiariser avec certains mots et d'en réviser d'autres avant de commencer la lecture.

1. votre budget
2. gérer la situation financière
3. mettre de l'argent de côté chaque mois
4. réduire les dépenses
5. consigner vos dépenses
6. tirer le meilleur parti de vos épargnes

a. diminuer la consommation
b. bien placer les économies
c. économiser de l'argent
d. plan pour les finances
e. noter les dépenses
f. administrer les finances

B. Avant de lire. Avant de lire, pensez à vos finances personnelles. Posez-vous les questions suivantes.

1. Avez-vous un budget? Le respectez-vous?
2. Dépensez-vous tout votre argent tous les mois?
3. Est-ce que votre salaire est plus élevé que vos dépenses, ou est-ce le contraire?
4. Payez-vous vos dettes ou est-ce qu'elles s'accumulent?
5. Avez-vous un compte épargne?
6. Est-ce que vos finances vous préoccupent?
7. Comment remédiez-vous vos problèmes financiers?

Si vous croyez que vous ne gérez pas bien vos finances, que vous êtes toujours endettés et que votre salaire ne suffit pas à payer vos factures, alors, le texte que vous allez lire va sûrement vous donner de bons conseils.

C. Lisons! Lisez la première partie du texte et répondez aux questions suivantes basées sur la lecture.

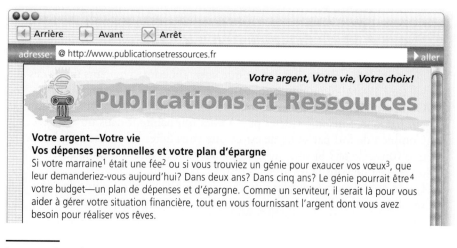

¹*godmother* ²*fairy* ³*to grant your wishes* ⁴*could be*

Les principaux éléments à inclure dans votre budget sont les suivants:
1. Vos objectifs financiers—à court terme et à long terme
2. La totalité de vos sources de revenu
3. La totalité de vos dépenses

QUELQUES CONSEILS POUR UTILISER CE PLAN

1. **Prenez le temps d'établir vos objectifs d'épargne,** qu'il s'agisse d'économiser pour faire un voyage, acheter une voiture ou un ordinateur ou poursuivre des études supérieures. Calculez ensuite combien vous devrez mettre de côté chaque mois au cours d'une période donnée pour atteindre ces objectifs.

2. **Réfléchissez bien à toutes vos dépenses mensuelles.** Il est évident que si vous habitez seule, vos dépenses seront différentes et plus élevées que si vous logez[1] encore chez vos parents. Indépendamment de votre situation, vous devez inscrire toutes vos dépenses.

3. **Comparez le total de vos dépenses et de vos économies à votre revenu global.** Si le premier total est inférieur, parfait! Mais s'il est supérieur, il faudra[2] modifier certains éléments, ce qui signifie trouver un moyen de réduire vos dépenses.

4. **Consignez[3] tout ce que vous dépensez pendant un mois au minimum.** Dépensez-vous réellement ce que vous aviez prévu dans votre budget? En consignant vos dépenses, vous serez en mesure de rajuster votre budget, de constater rapidement où va votre argent, de trouver des catégories de dépenses oubliées dans votre plan et de déterminer où vous pouvez réduire vos dépenses.

5. **Rendez-vous dans votre banque, votre caisse populaire ou votre société de fiducie[4] ou consultez leur site web pour obtenir de plus amples renseignements.** Demandez-leur quel type de compte vous conviendrait, comment elles peuvent vous aider à atteindre vos objectifs et comment vous pouvez gérer vos dettes tout en tirant le meilleur parti de vos épargnes.

> Aujourd'hui, tout le monde rêve d'indépendance et de savoir bien gérer son argent —avoir une «culture financière» est plus important pour les femmes que jamais. Avoir une culture financière signifie être capable de gagner sa vie, suivre l'évolution de son compte en banque, se servir du crédit judicieusement et mettre de l'argent de côté pour d'éventuels besoins à venir.

Questions

1. Que symbolise le génie? Pourquoi?
2. Pourquoi est-ce que le budget est comparé à un serviteur?
3. Comment peut-on réussir ses objectifs d'épargne?
4. Que faut-il faire si nos dépenses sont supérieures à notre revenu et à nos économies?
5. Pourquoi faut-il consigner nos dépenses?
6. D'après le texte, comment est-ce qu'une banque peut nous aider avec nos finances?

---

[1] *habitez* [2] *it will be necessary* [3] *Record* [4] *de placement*

Maintenant, lisez le reste du texte et répondez aux questions.

Pourquoi est-il si important d'avoir une culture financière?

- AUTONOMIE. L'autonomie financière signifie pouvoir prendre ses propres décisions, être indépendante et décider de sa propre vie—sans être obligée de s'entendre dire quoi faire ou comment mener sa vie par sa famille, son partenaire ou toute autre personne.
- POUVOIR. Le pouvoir de faire ses propres choix, de vivre selon ses propres règles et de créer ses propres occasions (près d'un tiers des sociétés au Canada sont aujourd'hui dirigées par des femmes).
- ÉGALITÉ. «L'égalité sociale des femmes passe par[1] leur égalité financière», déclare Valerie Hussey, co-propriétaire de Kids Can Press, une maison d'édition qui connaît un immense succès. «Il ne s'agit pas de gagner une fortune, mais bien de gagner son propre argent.»
- CHOIX. Qu'il s'agisse de décider de se marier, de voyager ou de déménager à l'autre bout du pays, de créer sa propre société ou de quitter son emploi, être indépendante financièrement signifie avoir un plus grand choix d'options.

zone d'internet

Questions

7. Qu'est-ce qu'on obtient si on a une «culture financière»? (Nommez les quatre points.)
8. Que peut-on faire quand on est autonome?
9. Quels avantages donne le pouvoir?
10. Ces suggestions ont été faites pour les femmes. Est-ce que vous les trouvez valables pour les hommes aussi? Pourquoi, ou pourquoi pas?

D. Après la lecture. Après avoir lu le texte, réfléchissez aux questions suivantes afin de commencer un débat avec vos camarades. Pour chaque question, formez des groupes de trois ou quatre étudiants qui répondront affirmativement et négativement.

1. En général, pensez-vous qu'aux États-Unis il y a une «culture financière»? Oui? Non? Pourquoi?
2. Croyez-vous qu'il est plus important pour les femmes que pour les hommes de bien gérer leur argent? Pourquoi, ou pourquoi pas?
3. Êtes-vous d'accord avec la phrase de Valerie Hussey: «L'égalité sociale des femmes passe par leur égalité financière»? Pourquoi, ou pourquoi pas?
4. Est-ce que l'égalité financière entre hommes et femmes existe? Élaborez votre réponse.

[1] *is achieved through*

Lexique 🎧

Vocabulaire essentiel

Les commerces et leurs produits

la charcuterie *delicatessen, (pork) butcher shop*
le charcutier / la charcutière *pork butcher*
le jambon *ham*
le poulet *chicken*
les saucisses *(f.)* *sausage*
le saucisson *salami*

l'épicerie *(f.)* *grocery store*
les boîtes *(f.)* de conserve *canned goods*
l'épicier / l'épicière *grocer*
les fruits *(m.)* *fruit*
les légumes *(m.)* *vegetables*
les pâtes *(m.)* *pasta*
le riz *rice*

le fleuriste *florist's shop*
les bouquets *(m.)* *bouquets*
le/la fleuriste *florist*
les fleurs *(f.)* *flowers*
les plantes *(f.)* *plants*

le kiosque (à journaux) *newsstand*
les chewing-gums *(m.)* *chewing gum*
les journaux *(m.)* *newspapers*
les magazines *(m.)* *magazines*
le/la marchand(e) de journaux *news vendor*

la parfumerie *perfume store*
l'eau *(f.)* de toilette *eau de toilette*
le maquillage *make-up*
le parfum *perfume*
le parfumeur / la parfumeuse *perfumer*

la pharmacie *pharmacy*
l'aspirine *(f.)* *aspirin*
le dentifrice *toothpaste*
les dragées *(f.)* pour la gorge *throat lozenges*
le/la pharmacien(ne) *pharmacist*
le shampooing *shampoo*
le sirop pour la toux *cough syrup*

le tabac *tobacco store*
le cigare *cigar*
les cigarettes *(f.)* *cigarettes*
les pipes *(f.)* *pipes*
le/la marchand(e) de tabac *tobacconist*
les tickets *(m.)* de bus *bus tickets*
les carnets *(m.)* *groups of tickets*

la teinturerie *dry cleaner's*
le lavage à sec *dry cleaning*
le repassage *ironing*
le teinturier / la teinturière *dry cleaner*

Les commerces à réviser

la boucherie *(beef) butcher shop*
la boulangerie / pâtisserie *bread bakery / pastry shop*
la chocolaterie *chocolate shop*
la crémerie / fromagerie *dairy / cheese store*
la librairie *bookstore*
le/la marchand(e) de vin *wine seller*
la papeterie *stationery store*
la poissonnerie *fish market*
le traiteur *caterer*

À la banque

le banquier / la banquière *personal banker*
des billets *bills*
le bureau d'échange *currency exchange office*
la caisse *teller window, cash drawer*

le caissier / la caissière *bank teller*
déposer de l'argent *to make a deposit*
échanger de l'argent *to exchange money*
le guichet automatique *ATM*
le guichet de caisse *teller window*

la monnaie *change, coins*
ouvrir un compte *to open an account*
des pièces *(f.)* de monnaie *coins*
retirer de l'argent *to withdraw money*
le taux de change *exchange rate*

Les services bancaires

une carte de crédit *credit card*
un chéquier / un carnet de chèques *checkbook*
un compte courant *checking account*
un compte en banque *bank account*

un compte épargne *savings account*
fermer un compte *to close an account*
le mot de passe *password*

remplir un chèque *to write a check*
toucher un chèque *to cash a check*

Les finances personnelles

avoir des dettes *to have debts*
avoir des investissements *to have investments*
dépenser *to spend*
une dette *a debt*

économiser *to save*
être dépensier (dépensière) *to be a spendthrift*
être économe *to be thrifty*
être endetté(e) *to be in debt*

être pauvre *to be poor*
être riche *to be rich*
épargner *to save*
gaspiller *to waste*

Expansion personnelle

un chèque sans provisions *a check with no funds*
un chèque de voyage *traveler's check*

un coffre-fort *a safe*
le relevé de compte *bank statement*

Les opérations et transactions à la banque

demander une bourse *to ask for a scholarship*
demander un prêt / faire un emprunt *to ask for a loan*
demander un prêt hypothécaire *to ask for a mortgage loan*

emprunter de l'argent à quelqu'un *to borrow money from someone*
faire un emprunt hypothécaire *to ask for a mortgage loan*
investir / placer de l'argent *to invest money*

prêter de l'argent à quelqu'un *to lend money to someone*
rembourser quelqu'un ou quelque chose *to pay back someone or something*

Mes rêves

If you could have your ideal life, what would it be? Soon you will be able to answer this question in French! In this chapter you will learn how to talk about your wishes and your dreams.

 The vocabulary that you will learn includes

Body parts and body image
Expressions of emotion
Ideal situations and your
　ideal self

 The structures that you will learn include

The use of indefinite and
　definite articles with parts
　of the body
The present conditional tense

The culture that you will learn includes

The French and their body
　image
French advertisements

trois cent soixante-dix-neuf **379**

Comment se protéger à la plage

Si vous allez vous exposer au soleil, il faut se protéger. Quand vous allez à la plage, utilisez une crème solaire avec un indice de protection 15, minimum, et si vous allez nager, utilisez une crème qui résiste à l'eau. Remettez de la crème toutes les deux heures, plus souvent si vous faites du sport ou si vous nagez. Évitez de rester longtemps au soleil entre onze heures du matin et deux heures de l'après-midi—c'est pendant cette période que le soleil est le plus fort.

Appliquez généreusement de la crème. Mettez-en vingt minutes avant l'exposition au soleil, pour lui donner le temps de bien pénétrer. Commencez par les jambes et les bras, et demandez à quelqu'un d'autre de vous en mettre sur le dos. N'oubliez pas de vous en mettre sur les pieds, et d'en remettre souvent si vous marchez dans l'eau. Mettez-vous-en généreusement sur le visage aussi, et n'oubliez surtout pas le nez et les oreilles—ce sont deux parties du visage qui brûlent facilement.

Il est important de mettre de la crème protectrice même si vous n'allez pas rester longtemps dehors—vous pouvez attraper un coup de soleil en quelques minutes quand le soleil est au zénith. N'oubliez pas de faire attention aux enfants aussi. Les dernières recherches médicales suggèrent qu'un seul coup de soleil sévère attrapé pendant l'enfance peut provoquer un cancer de peau plus tard.

Vous avez bien compris?

Répondez aux questions suivantes, selon le texte.

1. Quand est-ce qu'on doit mettre de la crème solaire?
2. Quand a-t-on besoin d'une crème qui résiste à l'eau?
3. Sur quelles parties du corps est-ce qu'on devrait commencer l'application de la crème solaire, et quand?
4. À quelles parties du corps est-ce qu'il faut surtout faire attention? Pourquoi?
5. Pourquoi faut-il faire attention aux enfants?
6. Et vous, est-ce que vous mettez de la crème solaire avant d'être exposé(e) au soleil? Pourquoi ou pourquoi pas?
7. Est-ce que vous avez déjà attrapé un coup de soleil sévère?

Vocabulaire essentiel

Les sens et les parties externes du corps

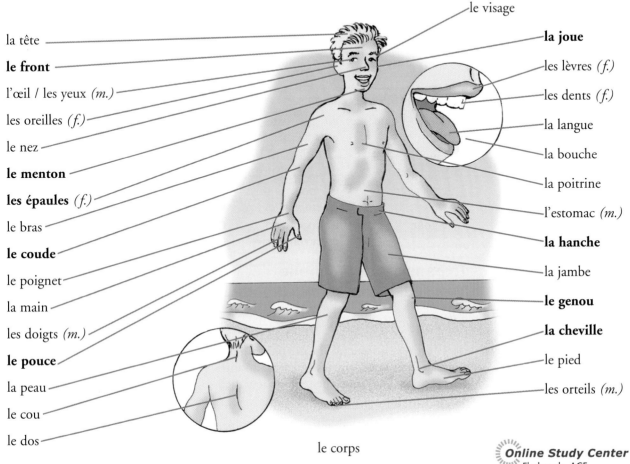

la tête

le front

l'œil / les yeux *(m.)*

les oreilles *(f.)*

le nez

le menton

les épaules *(f.)*

le bras

le coude

le poignet

la main

les doigts *(m.)*

le pouce

la peau

le cou

le dos

le visage

la joue

les lèvres *(f.)*

les dents *(f.)*

la langue

la bouche

la poitrine

l'estomac *(m.)*

la hanche

la jambe

le genou

la cheville

le pied

les orteils *(m.)*

le corps

À la découverte du français par tous nos sens[1]!

la vue   **l'odorat**   **le toucher**

---

[1] *Discovering French through all our senses!*

l'ouïe   le goût

Expressions relatives aux sens

la vue / l'ouïe	C'est splendide!	C'est atroce!
	C'est superbe!	C'est hideux!
l'odorat	Ça sent le parfum!	Ça sent mauvais!
	Ça sent les fleurs!	Ça pue!
le toucher	C'est mou!	C'est dur!
	C'est fin!	C'est épais!
le goût	C'est succulent!	C'est dégoûtant!
	C'est savoureux!	C'est répugnant!

Expansion personnelle

The words in bold letters in the body parts drawing are part of the *Expansion personnelle*.

À vous!

A. C'est quelle partie du corps? Indiquez la partie du corps qu'on utilise normalement pour faire les activités suivantes. (Quelquefois plus d'une réponse est possible. Choisissez une réponse logique.)

MODÈLE: chanter

Pour chanter, on utilise la bouche.

1. écouter de la musique
2. faire du jogging
3. regarder un film
4. jouer aux cartes
5. porter un sac à dos
6. rouler à bicyclette
7. manger
8. nager
9. sentir un parfum
10. faire une bise

B. C'est quoi sa spécialisation? Les personnes suivantes sont médecins spécialistes. Dites quelle partie du corps ils soignent[1].

MODÈLE: Paul Leclerc est dentiste.

Il soigne les dents.

1. Marie Saint-Cloud est ophtalmologue.
2. Jean-Luc Ferali est podologue.
3. Rashid Salim est kinésithérapeute[2].

---

[1] *treat* [2] *physical therapist*

To present these expressions, you may want to bring in pictures or slides of beautiful things and ugly things, tasty and not so tasty food, etc., and model the pronunciation before students use these expressions.

Some of these expressions can be used for all the senses, not only for the ones indicated on the list. For example, **c'est répugnant!** can be used to express something that tastes bad or that smells bad. Other expressions commonly used in familiar settings are: C'est moche! C'est affreux! C'est dégueu(lasse)! C'est exécrable! C'est extra(ordinaire)!

Answer Key: 1. les oreilles 2. les jambes / les pieds 3. les yeux 4. les mains 5. les épaules / le dos 6. les jambes / les pieds 7. la bouche / la langue / les dents 8. les bras / les jambes 9. le nez 10. les lèvres

Answer Key. Possible answers: 1. les yeux 2. les pieds 3. le dos / les genoux / le poignet / la cheville 4. le nez 5. les hanches / les genoux / les épaules / les mains, etc. 6. la peau 7. les oreilles 8. la langue

4. Jacqueline Morin est allergologue (les allergies).
5. Kim-Van Ha est rhumatologue (l'arthrite / le rhumatisme).
6. Rafaël Proux est dermatologue.
7. Claude Borine est oto-rhino.
8. Asika Aslan est orthophoniste (la rééducation du langage).

C. Où ont-ils mal? Les personnes suivantes sont très actives, et à cause de leurs occupations, elles ont mal[1]. Dites où elles ont mal exactement. (Quelquefois plus d'une réponse est possible. Choisissez une réponse logique.)

> (🌀) MODÈLE: Abdoula a porté un sac à dos très lourd.
>
> *Il a mal au dos.*

1. Charlotte a joué longtemps du piano.
2. Fatima a participé à un marathon.
3. Lucas a travaillé longtemps à l'ordinateur.
4. Olivier a écouté un concert de rock hier soir.
5. Véronique a fait des abdominaux au centre sportif.
6. Bertrand a joué au tennis pendant trois heures.
7. Béatrice a vu un film hyper-comique cet après-midi.
8. Cyrille a participé à une course à vélo.

Before beginning this activity, remind students of the contraction of à + **le** or **les**. Illustrate using the **modèle**.

Answer Key. Possible answers: 1. les mains / les bras 2. les pieds / les jambes 3. les yeux / la tête 4. les oreilles 5. l'estomac 6. l'épaule / le coude 7. les joues / l'estomac 8. les jambes / les genoux

Structure 1

Les parties du corps et les articles définis et indéfinis

Online Study Center
ACE, Language Skills Practice

In English, there is often a choice between using a possessive adjective or a definite or indefinite article when referring to parts of one's body. For example, it is appropriate to say either of the following:

My hair is blond.	*I have blond hair.*
My nose is small and straight.	*I have a small, straight nose.*

French speakers, however, prefer to use an article, and the possessive adjective is almost never used. Therefore, in French there is only one equivalent for each of the preceding pairs of sentences.

J'ai **les** cheveux blonds.	J'ai **un** petit nez droit.

In many cases, this article is combined with a reflexive verb. The pronoun that accompanies the reflexive verb makes the recipient of the action clear, and therefore a possessive adjective would be redundant. In this instance, it is even more likely that a definite article will be used, rather than a possessive adjective. Compare the following:

*I washed **my** face.*	Je **me** suis lavé **le** visage.
*I brush **my** teeth after dinner.*	Je **me** brosse **les** dents après le dîner.

---

[1]*are in pain*

While there are a few occasions where a possessive adjective is used before a body part (for example, in the proverbial expression **risquer sa tête,** *to place oneself in a dangerous situation*), this is a rare occurrence in French. It is generally best to use an indefinite or definite article: the indefinite if you are talking about a non-specific noun or introducing a noun for the first time, the definite if the noun is specific, is already known to your listener, or is accompanied by a reflexive verb.

Comment sont **les** corps des athlètes?
Ils ont **des** bras et **des** jambes très musclés.

VÉRIFIEZ VOTRE COMPRÉHENSION

Go back to the **Commençons!** text at the beginning of the chapter, and underline all the body parts that you find listed in it. For each one, tell if it is accompanied by a possessive adjective, an indefinite article, or a definite article. Can you explain why?

Pratiquons!

A. Mireille se réveille. Il est sept heures du matin, et Mireille se réveille. En vous servant des verbes suivants, dites ce qu'elle fait, selon les dessins.

Verbes: se brosser, se raser, se maquiller, se laver, se sécher, se doucher, se baigner

Answer Key: 1. Mireille se lave les cheveux. 2. Elle se brosse les dents. 3. Elle se sèche les cheveux. 4. Elle se lave le visage. 5. Elle se rase les jambes. 6. Elle se brosse les cheveux. 7. Elle se maquille les yeux.

1. 2. 3.

4. 5. 6.

7.

Et vous? Écrivez trois phrases pour dire ce que vous faites le matin avant de sortir.

B. Trait caractéristique?
Dites quel est le trait[1] caractéristique de chaque personne ou de chaque animal. S'il y a plus d'une réponse possible, choisissez une réponse logique.

🌀 MODÈLE: Dumbo?

Il a de grandes oreilles.

Remind students that when using a plural adjective before a noun, the indefinite article that accompanies the noun is **de**, as in this example.

1. Une girafe?
2. Cyrano de Bergerac?
3. Shaquille O'Neal?
4. Les Cyclopes?
5. Arnold Schwarzenegger?
6. Un serpent?
7. Sasquatch?
8. Maria Shriver?
9. Les pianistes?
10. Gérard Depardieu?

Answer Key: 1. Elle a un long cou. 2. Il a un long nez. 3. Il a de longues jambes. 4. Ils ont un grand œil. 5. Il a des bras musclés / un corps musclé. 6. Il a une langue très longue / un corps très long et mince. 7. Il a de grands pieds. 8. Elle a de grandes dents / un grand sourire. 9. Ils ont de longs doigts / des mains fines et longues. 10. Il a un nez très grand / un nez très long.

C. Découvrez vos sens!
Trouvez le sens et la partie du corps utilisés dans les expressions suivantes. (Quelquefois plus d'une réponse est possible. Choisissez une réponse logique.)

🌀 MODÈLE: C'est fin!

le toucher—la main

1. C'est mauvais!
2. C'est laid!
3. C'est merveilleux!
4. C'est splendide!
5. C'est atroce!
6. C'est épais!
7. C'est savoureux!
8. Ça pue!
9. C'est mou!
10. Ça sent bon!

Answer Key. Possible answers: 1. le goût—la langue 2. la vue—les yeux 3. l'ouïe—les oreilles / la vue—les yeux 4. l'ouïe—les oreilles / la vue—les yeux 5. le goût—la langue / la bouche; la vue—les yeux; l'ouïe—les oreilles 6. le toucher—la main 7. le goût—la bouche / la langue 8. l'odorat—le nez 9. le toucher—la main 10. l'odorat—le nez

D. Des proverbes.
Pouvez-vous deviner le sens des proverbes et des expressions idiomatiques français suivants? Trouvez l'équivalent en anglais à droite.

1. Je l'ai payé les yeux de la tête.
2. J'ai les yeux plus grands que l'estomac.
3. Mon œil!
4. Je lui ai cassé les oreilles.
5. Je l'ai dévoré des yeux.
6. Je me suis serré les dents.
7. J'ai la gorge serrée par l'émotion.
8. Nous nous sommes serré la main.
9. Je lui ai mis la puce à l'oreille.
10. Je me suis mordu la langue.

a. I'm all choked up.
b. I talked his ear off.
c. We shook hands.
d. I held my tongue.
e. I clenched my teeth.
f. My eyes are bigger than my stomach.
g. I put a bug in his ear (gave him an idea).
h. I eyed him hungrily.
i. My eye! (Yeah, right!)
j. I spent a fortune on it.

Answer Key. 1. j 2. f 3. i 4. b 5. h 6. e 7. a 8. c 9. g 10. d

Explain that the possessive adjective is used in the expression **Mon œil!** because, with no subject or verb, it would be impossible to know whose eye one was talking about without the possessive. Also, time permitting, show the gesture that accompanies this expression: When you do not believe a story that you're hearing, you pull down the lower eyelid of one eye. This gesture may or may not be accompanied by the verbal expression.

Portrait personnel

Choisissez un(e) camarade de classe et décrivez les traits physiques qui le/la caractérisent le mieux. Ensuite, montrez votre paragraphe à votre camarade. Est-il/elle d'accord avec votre description?

---

[1]*feature*

À vous de parler!

A. Interviews. Posez les questions suivantes à au moins trois camarades de classe. Quand vous avez terminé, expliquez les habitudes de votre groupe au reste de la classe.

1. Combien de fois par jour est-ce que tu te brosses les dents?
2. Est-ce que tu te les brosses avant ou après le petit déjeuner?
3. Combien de fois par an est-ce que tu vas chez le dentiste?
4. En général, est-ce que tu te brosses les cheveux, ou est-ce que tu te les peignes[1]?
5. As-tu souvent mal à la tête? Quand tu as mal à la tête, qu'est-ce que tu fais? (Tu prends de l'aspirine, tu dors, tu bois un coca …?)
6. Si quelqu'un faisait une caricature de toi, quel serait[2] le trait distinctif le plus remarquable?
7. Quelle est la partie de ton corps que tu aimes le plus? Et la partie que tu n'aimes pas? Pourquoi?

B. Qui est-ce? Donnez la description d'une personne célèbre. Vos camarades de classe vont essayer de deviner qui c'est. Décrivez tous les traits particuliers pour l'identification de cette personne.

MODÈLE: ÉTUDIANT 1: Cette personne est actrice. Elle a les cheveux roux et bouclés et les yeux verts. Elle est grande et mince, et elle a de longues jambes. Elle danse et chante bien. Elle a approximativement 40 ans. Elle a un accent australien.

ÉTUDIANT 2: C'est Nicole Kidman?

ÉTUDIANT 1: Oui, c'est ça!

Online Study Center
Web Search Activities

Les Français veulent paraître[3] comme ça

Un grand nombre de Français rêvent d'éternelle jeunesse. Les raisons principales pour paraître jeune à 40 ans comme à 60 ans sont la peur de vieillir (et de mourir) et une assurance d'être mieux accepté dans la société. Surtout dans une société qui considère la vieillesse comme synonyme de laideur et d'échec[4] et qui n'accepte que les jeunes. «Place aux jeunes[5]!» est une phrase courante. D'ailleurs, «aujourd'hui, tous les signes extérieurs de vieillesse sont devenus honteux»[6].

Que font les Français pour rester jeunes et pour lutter contre la vieillesse? Les Français sont de plus en plus nombreux à pratiquer la chirurgie esthétique. Les opérations les plus pratiquées sont le lifting et la liposuction. Six pour cent des femmes en France sont passées par la chirurgie esthétique. Un patient sur 10[7] est un homme[8]. Un lifting coûte 4000 euros en moyenne ainsi qu'une opération pour modifier les seins (implantation de prothèses mammaires) et une opération pour modifier le nez[9].

---

[1]*comb* [2]*would be* [3]*look* [4]*failure* [5]*Leave room for the young* [6]Citation tirée de l'hebdomadaire *L'Express* du 3 septembre 2000 dans l'article "La tyrannie du jeunisme" par Marie Huret et Vincent Olivier. [7]*One out of ten* [8]Données tirées de l'article "Ce qui marche, ce qui ne marche pas" paru dans *L'Express* du 11 juin 2003, par Estelle Saget. [9]Ibid.

En général, les Français qui ont succombé à la chirurgie esthétique ne l'annoncent pas. Ni aux amis, ni aux collègues, ni à la famille. Les Français ne sont pas fiers d'avoir eu recours à quelques retouches[1] chirurgicales. La plupart des Français ont horreur de paraître fabriqués synthétiques et superficiels. Ils aiment le naturel et c'est pour cela qu'ils ne révèlent à personne leurs interventions. D'autant plus que[2] pour les personnes qui ne vont pas faire appel[3] à la chirurgie esthétique, «acheter la beauté c'est tricher[4]»[5] car la beauté est un don[6] naturel. Bien sûr les patients sont conscients des risques et des effets secondaires de la chirurgie esthétique. En France, les patients reçoivent des séances[7] informatives obligatoires. Seulement un patient sur vingt regrette d'être passé au bistouri[8] et 5% des interventions donnent des résultats négatifs[9].

Qui désire améliorer son image? Les figures publiques comme les stars, les animatrices et les animateurs de télé, les écrivains, les politiciens, mais aussi les femmes et les hommes d'affaires (pour des raisons professionnelles) et les personnes qui pour des raisons personnelles ont besoin de se remonter le moral ou sont complexées à cause d'un divorce, la perte[10] d'un conjoint, le départ des enfants de la maison familiale, etc. Dans ce cas, le bistouri est un remède psychologique contre la déprime.

En définitive, garder sa jeunesse et prendre soin[11] de son image devient pour beaucoup de Français une obsession. Une fois qu'on a commencé, on ne peut plus s'arrêter et on devient des adeptes du bistouri. Comme le dit le sociologue Gilles Lipovetsky: «Aujourd'hui, il n'y a plus rien de diabolique à vouloir améliorer son image. Au contraire, l'obscène serait plutôt de paraître vieux ou laid[12].»

Réfléchissons

1. Est-ce que les Américains ont recours à la chirurgie esthétique pour les mêmes raisons que les Français (peur de vieillir, être mieux accepté, être moins complexé, etc.)?
2. À votre avis, quelle est l'opération esthétique la plus pratiquée dans votre pays? Pourquoi?
3. Est-ce que les Américains cachent leurs interventions esthétiques ou est-ce qu'ils les annoncent à leurs amis et à leurs familles? Pourquoi?
4. Êtes-vous d'accord avec la phrase «acheter la beauté c'est tricher»? Expliquez votre réponse.
5. Est-ce que les Américains pratiquent le culte de la beauté? Comment?

[1] *touch-ups* [2] *Especially because* [3] *use* [4] *to cheat* [5] Ibid. [6] *gift* [7] *meeting* [8] *scalpel* [9] Ibid. [10] *loss*
[11] *take care* [12] Citation tirée de l'article "La tyrannie du jeunisme".

Continuons!

In this half of the chapter you are going to see a new tense: the conditional tense
(le conditionnel). Before you read further about the uses and the formation of
the conditional in **_Structure 2,_** you need to know that it is used to convey
hypothetical situations that may or may not occur.

Des vacances de rêve ◯

Voici une publicité parue dans le magazine *Partir loin*[1]. Regardez-la et laissez-vous
guider par vos rêves!

Maintenant, vous êtes au bureau face à votre ordinateur et
vous rêvez de vacances entre palmiers et cocotiers. Alors,
imaginez que vos rêves vous
portent à Tahiti! Pourquoi Tahiti?
Parce que vous **pourriez** vous
détendre et vous amuser comme
jamais. Vous **feriez** de la plongée
sous-marine; vous **dormiriez** sur un
hamac au bord de la mer; vous
boiriez des boissons exotiques en
contemplant le coucher de soleil; vous
marcheriez sur le sable fin[2] et tant
d'autres choses de rêves[3]! Vous
passeriez les
meilleures
vacances de
votre vie,
c'est garanti! Vous **seriez aux
anges**[4], c'est promis! Profitez de
notre offre spéciale du 4 octobre au
15 octobre: Paris–Bora Bora une
semaine, transport et hôtel inclus, 3 000 euros.

L'agence de marketing qui travaille pour le magazine *Partir loin* a fait un sondage
pour savoir si les gens[5] peuvent partir en vacances sans prévoir[6] à l'avance. Voici
les questions que l'agence de marketing a posées à six personnes dans plusieurs
villes en France et leurs réponses.

---

[1] *Going far away* [2] *fine sand* [3] *and so many other things you dream of* [4] *you would be in heaven* [5] *people*
[6] *without planning*

Après avoir lu cette publicité, rêvez-vous de sable chaud et de soleil? Si vous pouviez partir à Tahiti tout de suite[1], **partiriez**-vous en vacances en laissant[2] vos obligations derrière vous? Vous **sentiriez**-vous **coupables**[3] ou au contraire **soulagés**[4] de tout quitter?

SYLVIE (LYON): Oui, bien sûr, je **partirais**! Je me **sentirais** très **heureuse** de quitter mon travail et la grisaille[5] de ma ville en hiver. La boîte où je travaille est super cool. Le patron me **donnerait** mes congés sans problème.

FRÉDÉRIC (AIX-EN-PROVENCE): Non, je ne **partirais** pas tout de suite. Je **serais**[6] **angoissé** de partir sans avoir terminé mes cours à l'université.

ZOÉ ET ARNAUD (STRASBOURG): Oh, oui! Nous **partirions** sans hésiter! Nous **serions ravis** de pouvoir passer des vacances tous les deux, en amoureux à Bora Bora. De toute façon, on peut toujours demander à Mamie et Papi de rester avec nos trois enfants.

STÉPHANE ET SANDRINE (BORDEAUX): Euh ... Est-ce que nous **partirions** tout de suite? Non, pas tout de suite. Nous avons deux enfants à la maison qui sont encore petits. Nous **serions** très **préoccupés** et très **nerveux** de les avoir loin de[7] nous. Et puis, nous **serions gênés**[8] de demander des congés à nos patrons sans les prévenir à l'avance.

Et vous, partiriez-vous à Bora Bora tout de suite?

Vous avez bien compris?

Complétez les phrases avec les verbes et/ou les émotions qui manquent.

1. Vous _____ de vacances entre palmiers et cocotiers.
2. À Tahiti, vous pourriez vous _____ et vous _____.
3. Vous _____ sur un hamac au bord de la mer.
4. Vous _____ des boissons exotiques.
5. Vous vous promèneriez _____.
6. Sylvie se sentirait _____ de quitter son travail.
7. Frédéric serait _____.
8. Zoé et Arnaud seraient _____.
9. Stéphane et Sandrine seraient très _____ et très _____ d'avoir les enfants loin.
10. Stéphane et Sandrine seraient _____ de demander des congés.

Answer Key: 1. rêvez 2. détendre / amuser 3. dormiriez 4. boiriez 5. sur le sable fin 6. très heureuse 7. angoissé 8. ravis 9. préoccupés et très nerveux 10. gênés

[1] right away [2] leaving [3] guilty [4] relieved [5] grey weather [6] would be [7] far away from [8] embarrassed

Vocabulaire essentiel

Les émotions

Les sentiments positifs

être aux anges
être calme
être enchanté(e)   *to be happy/pleased*
être heureux (heureuse)   *to be happy*
être soulagé(e)   *to be relieved*

Les sentiments négatifs

être déçu(e)   *to be disappointed*
être désespéré(e)   *to be desperate*
être désolé(e)   *to be sorry*
être horrifié(e)
être jaloux (jalouse)
être malheureux (malheureuse)   *to be unhappy*
être surpris(e)

Point out to students that when the expressions of emotion are followed by a verb, the verb remains in the infinitive and is preceded by the preposition **de**. This occurs only when there is one subject in the sentence, for example: **Je suis heureuse de partir au Maroc. Tu es désolé de rester chez toi.**

Expansion personnelle

Les sentiments positifs

être euphorique
être fier (fière)   *to be proud*
être reconnaissant(e)   *to be grateful*

Les sentiments négatifs

être démoralisé(e)
être dévasté(e)
être effrayé(e)   *to be scared*
être outragé(e)
être soucieux (soucieuse) *to be worried*

Before starting the following activities (A–C), you may want to review the adjectives of emotions that were introduced in previous chapters: **être triste, être content, être stressé, être cool, être patient, être impatient, être optimiste, être pessimiste,** etc.

À vous!

A. Vos sentiments. Dites comment vous vous sentez dans les situations suivantes.

MODÈLE: Quand vous êtes chez le dentiste.

Je suis effrayé(e)!

Answer Key. Possible answers: Je suis … 1. fâché(e) / désespéré(e) 2. énervé(e) / désespéré(e) 3. désolé(e) / déçu(e) / démoralisé(e) 4. euphorique / heureux(se) 5. désespéré(e) / soucieux(se) 6. soucieux(se) / effrayé(e) 7. heureux(se) / content(e) 8. euphorique / ravi(e) / fier(ère) 9. désolé(e) / malheureux(se) / triste 10. ravi(e) / surpris(e) / soulagé(e)

1. Quand vous ne réussissez pas à faire un problème de mathématiques.
2. Quand vous êtes dans un embouteillage pendant une heure.
3. Quand vous n'êtes pas embauché(e) pour le poste que vous désirez.
4. Quand votre petit(e) ami(e) vous demande en mariage.
5. Quand vous attendez un(e) ami(e) qui est en retard.
6. Quand vous êtes dans un avion et il y a des turbulences.
7. Quand votre professeur vous annonce que vous n'avez pas de devoirs.
8. Quand vous recevez votre diplôme universitaire.
9. Quand vos amis ne vous invitent pas à leur fête.
10. Quand votre avion arrive à l'heure.

👥 Maintenant, expliquez à un(e) camarade de classe pourquoi vous ressentez ces sentiments dans les situations précédentes.

◎ MODÈLE: Je suis horrifié(e) quand je suis chez le dentiste parce que je n'aime pas souffrir!

B. Ravi(e) ou désolé(e)? Un(e) camarade de classe vous annonce des nouvelles. Pour chaque nouvelle, exprimez vos sentiments.

◎ MODÈLE: J'ai gagné 10.000 dollars au casino.

Je suis ravi(e)! **or**
Je suis jaloux (jalouse)!

1. Je vais divorcer / Je vais casser avec mon (ma) petit(e) ami(e).
2. Je vais déménager dans un autre état bientôt.
3. Je vais m'acheter une super voiture.
4. Je vais jouer dans une pièce de théâtre / dans un film / dans une bande rock.
5. Je suis allé(e) à un concert de Madonna.
6. Je vais voyager en Europe.
7. Je parle aussi l'espagnol / l'allemand / le japonais.
8. J'ai eu un accident de voiture assez grave (sérieux).

👥 Maintenant, demandez à votre camarade si tout ce qu'il/elle vous a annoncé est vrai. Votre camarade va vous répondre s'il / si elle voudrait que ça soit vrai[1] ou non.

◎ MODÈLE: VOTRE CAMARADE: *J'ai gagné 10.000 dollars au casino.*
VOUS: *C'est vrai?*
VOTRE CAMARADE: *Non, mais je voudrais bien!* **or**
Non, et je ne voudrais pas! **or**
Oui, c'est vrai!

👥👥 **C. Sujets chauds[2]!** Pour chaque sujet proposé, demandez à plusieurs camarades (au moins quatre) quels sont leurs sentiments.

◎ MODÈLE: l'avortement

J'en suis outragé(e). / J'en suis reconnaissant(e).

1. la peine de mort[3]
2. la censure à la télévision
3. le nudisme sur les plages
4. la limitation de vitesse sur les autoroutes
5. la possession d'armes à feu[4]
6. l'interdiction de fumer dans les lieux publics

Ensuite, faites un sondage avec toute la classe et dites quel sujet a provoqué le plus de sentiments positifs et négatifs.

---

[1] *if he/she wishes for it to be true* [2] *Hot topics* [3] *death penalty* [4] *firearms*

Structure 2

Online Study Center
ACE, Language Skills
Practice

Le conditionnel

The **conditionnel** corresponds to the English concepts *would, could* (with **pouvoir**) or *should* (with **devoir**). The conditional has many uses. You already saw one of them in the advertisement that you read at the beginning of the ***Continuons!*** section, page 388. There, the conditional tense was used to express an ideal situation.

- **Formation.** The formation of the **conditionnel** in *regular verbs* is very simple. All verbs use the same endings: **ais, -ais, -ait, -ions, -iez, -aient** (the same endings that are used for the **imparfait.**). The stem is the infinitive. (For **-re** verbs, the final **e** of the infinitive is dropped.) Look at the following examples of **-er, -ir,** and **-re** verbs.

aimer	→	j'aimer**ais**	*I would like*
		tu aimer**ais**	*you would like*
		il/elle/on aimer**ait**	*he/she/one would like*
		nous aimer**ions**	*we would like*
		vous aimer**iez**	*you would like*
		ils/elles aimer**aient**	*they would like*
finir	→	tu finir**ais**	*you would finish*
		ils finir**aient**	*they would finish*
vendre	→	elle vendr**ait**	*she would sell*
		nous vendr**ions**	*we would sell*

Attention! Verbs that have a stem change in the present tense have the same stem change in the conditional, in all persons.

acheter	→	j'ach**è**terais / nous ach**è**terions
appeler	→	j'appe**ll**erais / nous appe**ll**erions

Attention! For *irregular verbs,* the endings are the same; however, the stems are irregular and must be memorized.

aller	**ir-**	→	j'**ir**ais / nous **ir**ions
avoir	**aur-**	→	j'**aur**ais / nous **aur**ions
devoir	**devr-**	→	je **devr**ais / nous devrions
être	**ser-**	→	je **ser**ais / nous **ser**ions
faire	**fer-**	→	je **fer**ais / nous ferions
pouvoir	**pourr-**	→	je **pourr**ais / nous pourrions
venir	**viendr-**	→	je **viendr**ais / nous **viendr**ions
voir	**verr-**	→	je **verr**ais / nous **verr**ions
vouloir	**voudr-**	→	je vou**dr**ais / nous vou**dr**ions

- **Uses**

  1. To express a situation that is ideal (a situation that one dreams about), and that has not happened yet the way we envision it, but may happen that way—or may not!

     À Tahiti, je ne travaillerais pas et je m'amuserais.
     In Tahiti, I would not work and I would have fun.

     Dans ma vie idéale, je serais toujours célibataire!
     In my ideal life, I would always be single!

2. To give advice to someone in a nice way (the verb **devoir** is used).

Tu devrais arrêter de fumer.	*You should stop smoking.*
Vous devriez faire plus de sport.	*You should exercise more.*

3. When a situation or an action is dependent on something else occurring first, it is a hypothetical situation. If a certain condition is met, then the hypothetical situation may occur. To express hypothetical situations, the construction **si + imparfait + conditionnel** is used.

Si j'avais des enfants, je les élèverais de façon très stricte.	*If I had children (but I don't), I would bring them up in a very strict way.*
Si vous gagniez beaucoup d'argent, est-ce que vous le placeriez en bourse?	*If you earned lots of money, would you invest it in the stock market?*

4. As you learned in previous chapters, the conditional is used in order to be polite.

Je voudrais un kilo de crevettes, s'il vous plaît.	*I would like a kilo of shrimp, please.*
Pourriez-vous me donner une baguette bien cuite?	*Could you give me a well-baked baguette?*

VÉRIFIEZ VOTRE COMPRÉHENSION

1. Go back to the advertisement at the beginning of the **Continuons!** section (p. 388) and locate the different uses of the conditional (ideal situation, hypothetical situation, politeness, etc.).

2. When the conditional is used in a sentence with an *if* **(si)** clause that expresses a hypothetical situation, what is the condition that must be met in order for the action expressed by the conditional clause to occur?

Pratiquons!

A. Le moi idéal. Si vous pouviez vous changer, que changeriez-vous? Complétez les dix phrases selon les changements que vous désireriez obtenir. Conjuguez les verbes au conditionnel et choisissez vos changements.

Answer Key: 1. serais 2. aurais 3. dirais 4. ferais 5. écouterais 6. perdrais 7. Je comprendrais / Mes amis me comprendraient

1. Je _____ (être) plus optimiste / moins optimiste.
2. J'_____ (avoir) plus d'humour / moins d'humour.
3. Je _____ (dire) / Je ne _____ (dire) pas toujours ce que je pense.
4. Je _____ (faire) attention de ne pas offenser mes amis. / Je _____ (faire) attention que mes amis ne m'offensent pas.
5. J'_____ (écouter) plus / moins les conseils[1] de mes parents.
6. Je _____ (perdre) du poids[2]. / Je ne _____ (perdre) pas de poids.
7. Je _____ (comprendre) mieux mes amis. / Mes amis me _____ (comprendre) mieux.

---

[1]*advice* [2]*lose weight*

8. Pour être plus zen, je _____ (pratiquer) de la méditation / du yoga.
9. Je me _____ (regarder) plus / moins dans la glace[1].
10. Je m' _____ (accepter) comme je suis. / Les autres m' _____ (accepter) comme je suis.

🗣 **B. Et si ...** À tour de rôle, demandez à un(e) camarade de classe d'indiquer ce qu'il/elle ferait ou comment il/elle se sentirait face à différentes situations.

🌀 MODÈLE: Si ton chien mourrait ... (être malheureux / acheter un autre chien / ne jamais acheter un autre animal domestique)

E1: *Si ton chien mourrait, est-ce que tu serais malheureux(euse)? Est-ce que tu achèterais un autre chien?*

E2: *Je serais malheureux(euse) si mon chien mourrait. J'achèterais tout de suite un autre chien.* **ou** *Je n'achèterais jamais un autre animal domestique de ma vie.*

1. Si ta voiture tombait en panne en plein milieu du désert ... (rester calme et attendre que quelqu'un passe / être désespéré[e] parce que ... penser que personne ne viendra)
2. Si un voleur rentrait dans ta maison pendant que tu étais à l'intérieur ... (être effrayé[e] et sortir par la porte ou par la fenêtre la plus proche / confronter le voleur et téléphoner à la police)
3. Si tu surprenais ton (ta) petit(e) ami(e) dans les bras d'un(e) autre ... (être ravi[e] parce que ça être une bonne excuse pour quitter mon [ma] petit[e] ami[e] / être outragé[e] et ... faire la même chose!)
4. Si tu n'avais pas assez d'argent pour payer l'addition au restaurant ... (être gêné[e] et payer en lavant les assiettes! / partir sans payer!)
5. Si les producteurs de *Survivor* te choisissaient comme un des protagonistes ... (être euphorique et aller au centre commercial m'acheter des vêtements / être très heureux [heureuse] et voir des endroits exotiques)
6. Si tes rêves se réalisaient ... (être surpris[e] mais pouvoir enfin vivre aux Caraïbes / être aux anges parce que ... ne travailler plus de ma vie)

🗣🗣 **C. Le ferais-tu?** Demandez à plusieurs camarades de classe s'ils feraient les choses suivantes. Ensuite, commentez les réponses de vos camarades à la classe.

1. Le premier Starbucks en France a ouvert ses portes à Paris en 2003. Boirais-tu un café ou un thé à Starbucks à Paris? Pourquoi?
2. Les Français ont des chaînes de fast-food comme Quick ou Buffalo Grill, mais ils ont aussi des chaînes américaines comme McDo et Pizza Hut. Iriez-vous manger dans un fast-food si vous étiez en vacances en France? Auquel[2] iriez-vous, dans un fast-food français ou américain? Pourquoi?
3. Saviez-vous[3] qu'au McDo dans toute l'Europe francophone on peut boire de la bière ou du vin? Prendriez-vous un pot au McDo si vous étiez en France, en Suisse ou en Belgique en visite? Pourquoi?
4. En France, vous pouvez loger dans les motels Formule 1 qui sont bon marché et qui sont self-service. C'est-à-dire que quand vous arrivez, avec

---

[1]*mirror* [2]*to which one* [3]*Did you know*

votre carte de crédit vous accédez à la chambre. Votre carte de crédit est à la fois votre clé et votre moyen de paiement. Passeriez-vous une nuit dans un hôtel de ce genre, sans surveillance et sans réception? Pourquoi?

5. En France, les toilettes publiques dans les magasins sont payantes. Utiliseriez-vous quand même les toilettes? Pourquoi?

6. Comme vous le savez déjà, en Europe francophone, sur la plupart des plages il est courant de faire du topless. Le feriez-vous? Pourquoi? (Si vous êtes un homme, feriez-vous du nudisme? Pourquoi?)

Portrait personnel

Demandez à votre camarade de classe de vous décrire son «moi idéal». (Vous pouvez vous inspirer de l'activité A, *Le moi idéal.*) Comment est-ce que votre camarade voudrait être? Écrivez un paragraphe sur le «moi idéal» de votre camarade de classe.

À vous de parler!

A. Si j'étais à ta place[1] **…** Vous êtes au Bistro avec des amis. Vous échangez vos problèmes personnels entre vous. Vous demandez à vos amis de vous donner des conseils afin de résoudre vos problèmes. En groupe de quatre, composez un dialogue en tenant compte des problèmes suivants. Commencez en exprimant les sentiments que vous ressentez: «Je suis désolé(e) …»; «Je suis préoccupé(e) …». Ensuite, continuez avec la phrase «Si j'étais à ta place …».

1. Étudiant 1: Je suis kleptomane. Chaque fois que je vais dans un magasin, je vole quelque chose.
2. Étudiant 2: Moi, je suis gaspilleur (gaspilleuse): je ne peux pas arriver à la fin du mois avec assez d'argent pour payer mon loyer.
3. Étudiant 3: Eh bien moi, je transpire toujours, même quand je reste assis[e] et malgré les douches. J'ai peur d'incommoder mon entourage.[2]
4. Étudiant 4: Alors moi, je perds tout: mes clés, mon sac, mes lunettes, etc. En plus, je ne sais jamais où sont mes affaires. Je suis très désordonné(e)[3]!

B. Les époux modèles. Vous travaillez dans une clinique spécialisée en thérapie de couple. Vous êtes chargés d'élaborer une brochure où vous indiquez les conditions que doivent avoir le compagnon et la compagne idéale pour assurer une bonne entente dans le couple. Ensuite, présentez votre brochure à la classe. Décidez quel est le groupe qui a élaboré la meilleure brochure.

MODÈLE: Le compagnon idéal devrait écouter sa femme et ne jamais lui dire de mensonges …

You may want to review with students vocabulary pertaining to **les relations sentimentales** such as **s'entendre bien/mal, se disputer, se parler, se quitter,** etc.

---

[1]*If I were in your shoes* [2]*I'm afraid I'll make people uncomfortable [with my body odor].* [3]*disorganized*

Les publicités sont comme ça en France

En France, les publicités (ou spots, ou pubs) à la télé durent de 15 à 30 secondes maximum. Les films ne sont pratiquement pas interrompus (une fois ou deux fois tout au plus, selon les chaînes) et il n'y a pas de publicité pendant la diffusion des journaux télévisés. De plus, il est interdit de passer de la pub entre les programmes pour enfants. D'ailleurs, en vue de l'augmentation de l'obésité infantile, les publicités pour la jeunesse ne peuvent plus montrer[1] d'enfants sédentaires qui mangent des sucreries ou qui grignotent constamment. On a même suggéré que les spots alimentaires soient[2] éliminés pendant les émissions pour les enfants, mais cette proposition a été refusée.

À la télé, on annonce l'arrivée de la pub avant sa diffusion. Ainsi on peut voir sur les écrans «Publicité» avant la transmission du premier spot publicitaire. Comme ça, on sait toujours[3] que ce qu'on[4] regarde est bien de la pub et non la continuation du film!

Dans les magazines féminins, à la télévision et sur les panneaux publicitaires, les publicités alimentaires ou gastronomiques sont nombreuses et savoureuses. Elles reflètent l'art culinaire français ainsi que l'importance de la présentation des aliments sur la table et sur les plats. Elles font appel à tous les sens: la vue, mais aussi l'odorat et le goût.

En France, quand vous ouvrez un magazine, vous regardez la télé ou vous vous promenez dans les rues des villes, vous allez peut-être être surpris par la nudité souvent présente dans les publicités. En effet, dans les publicités françaises, le corps (féminin et masculin) est exposé sans tabous. En général, il est plus fréquent de voir une femme nue, qu'un homme nu. Ceci bien sûr est cause de mécontentement et de protestations de la part des groupes féminins politiques ou sociaux pour la défense de la femme qui sont contre les images sexistes parce qu'elles ne respectent pas la dignité des femmes. Ces mêmes groupes affirment que ce n'est pas la nudité qui pose un problème, mais la vulgarité et la violence que l'on voit dans les spots publicitaires. En résumé, la publicité en France s'inspire de la culture française: elle se veut intelligente et perspicace, sensuelle et sexuelle, humoristique et provocante, attrayante et parfois choquante. En effet, en général, les Français apprécient énormément l'intelligence, la finesse et la subtilité. Sans oublier leur passion pour les jeux de mots (une rhétorique qui suggère au lieu de dévoiler à la fois qu'elle fait sourire), la gastronomie, le corps et l'esprit[5].

Discuss the meaning of the slogan in the olive oil ad: «**Entrez dans le cercle des vrais amateurs d'Huile d'Olive; Oli, l'Huile d'Olive avec un grand O**». In the ad, a woman is walking near olive trees on a summer day. The ad evokes warmth, the smell of flowers, bright light, the softness of grass on bare feet.

In the second ad we see two gold watches on a golden pedestal. The background is black to make the gold stand out. The slogan, «**Les très or du temps**», is a play on words (**Les** *trésors* **du temps**).

Réfléchissons

1. Dans votre pays, y a-t-il de la nudité dans la publicité comme en France? Expliquez votre réponse.
2. Donnez votre opinion sur la nudité dans la publicité. D'après vous, est-ce une bonne chose ou une mauvaise chose? Pourquoi?
3. En quoi est-ce que la publicité télévisée française est différente de la publicité télévisée américaine? Donnez des exemples.
4. Y a-t-il des publicités gastronomiques aux États-Unis? Comment sont-elles? À qui sont-elles dirigées?
5. Est-ce que la publicité américaine est aussi un reflet de la culture comme en France? Donnez des exemples. It conveys the concepts of time (**temps**), the purity of the gold (**très or**), and the fact that these watches are a treasured piece of jewelry that captures time (**les très or—trèsors—du temps**).

[1] *show* [2] *be* [3] *one always knows* [4] *what one* [5] *body and mind*

À vous d'écrire!

As a follow-up or supplementary activity to page 396, ask students to compare the ads in a French magazine and in an American magazine (quantity, viewpoint, images, etc). Or you may bring to class some advertisements from both countries and have students comment on them.

Vos rêves deviennent réalité! Imaginez qu'un génie pourrait réaliser tous vos rêves (il est capable de tout faire!), mais que vous ne pouvez demander que trois choses. Qu'est-ce que vous demanderiez? Comment est-ce que votre vie changerait? Qu'est-ce que vous feriez de votre vie? Comment seriez-vous physiquement? Que changeriez-vous de votre corps? Faites les activités suivantes pour répondre à cette question.

A. Stratégies. You have probably noticed that it is difficult, at your current level of proficiency, to make your writing in French sound as sophisticated as your writing in English. In this chapter, you have learned two different sentence types that you can use to add some sophistication to your writing. The first type contains an *if* clause with a verb in the imperfect followed by a clause with the verb in the conditional (**Si j'avais beaucoup d'argent, j'achèterais une voiture de sport.**); the second type contains a conditional statement of emotion, followed by an infinitive (**Je serais heureux de travailler en France**). Using these two sentence types as models, write at least three sentences that you can incorporate into your composition.

B. Organisons-nous! Décidez quelles seraient les trois choses que vous demanderiez au génie, et écrivez-les ici.

1. _____
2. _____
3. _____

Maintenant, imaginez comment votre vie changerait grâce à[1] ces trois choses. Décrivez votre vie idéale et/ou votre corps idéal, avec des verbes au *conditionnel*.

C. Pensons-y! Maintenant, commencez à organiser votre rédaction. Expliquez bien ce que vous demanderiez au génie, en détail, et les changements que cela provoquerait dans votre vie. Écrivez un paragraphe pour chaque chose / chaque changement, et un paragraphe comme conclusion.

D. Révisons! Demandez à un(e) camarade de classe de lire votre rédaction. Il/Elle utilisera[2] les critères suivants pour commenter votre travail.

- Est-ce qu'il y a des parties de la composition que vous ne comprenez pas? Lesquelles[3]? Soulignez-les, et expliquez à votre camarade de classe ce que vous ne comprenez pas.
- Quelle est la meilleure partie de la composition? Et la partie la plus faible? Pourquoi? Qu'est-ce que votre camarade pourrait faire pour améliorer[4] sa composition?
- Est-ce que vous avez trouvé des erreurs d'orthographe ou de grammaire dans la composition? Signalez-les.

E. Écrivons! Récrivez votre composition, suivant les suggestions de votre camarade de classe. Une fois terminée, rendez-la à votre professeur.

Have students use these questions to do a peer review of a classmate's composition. Give students a minimum of 10 minutes to read their partners' compositions, and 20 minutes to consult with one another as they answer the questions. When they have finished, have each student rewrite his/her composition as specified in activity E.

After you are finished grading the compositions, share with the class the most common wishes that students asked to be granted by the **génie**. Have a little discussion about which wishes they believe are realistic and which ones are not.

---

[1]*thanks to* [2]*will use* [3]*Which ones* [4]*to improve*

Lexique 🎧

Vocabulaire essentiel

Les parties externes du corps *parts of the body* (external)

la bouche *mouth*
le bras *arm*
le corps *body*
le cou *neck*
les dents *(f.)* *teeth*
le doigt *finger*
le dos *back*
l'estomac *(m.)* *stomach*

la jambe *leg*
la langue *tongue*
les lèvres *(f.)* *lips*
la main *hand*
le nez *nose*
l'œil / les yeux *(m.)* *eye / eyes*
les oreilles *(f.)* *ears*
les orteils *(m.)* *toes*

la peau *skin*
le pied *foot*
le poignet *wrist*
la poitrine *chest*
la tête *head*
le visage *face*

Les sens *the senses*

le goût *taste*
l'odorat *(m.)* *smell*
l'ouïe *(f.)* *hearing*

le toucher *touch*
la vue *sight*

Other expressions that are used with the senses

Ça pue! *It stinks!*
Ça sent bon! *It smells good!*
Ça sent les fleurs! *It smells like flowers!*
Ça sent mauvais! *It smells bad!*
Ça sent le parfum! *It smells like perfume!*
C'est atroce! *It's atrocious!*

C'est beau! *It's beautiful!*
C'est dégoûtant! *It's disgusting!*
C'est délicieux! *It's delicious!*
C'est doux! *It's soft!*
C'est dur! *It's hard!*
C'est épais! *It's thick!*
C'est fin! *It's fine / thin!*
C'est hideux! *It's hideous!*

C'est magnifique! *It's magnificent!*
C'est mou! *It's fluffy / soft!*
C'est répugnant! *It's repulsive!*
C'est savoureux! *It's tasty!*
C'est splendide! *It's splendid!*
C'est succulent! *It's succulent!*
C'est superbe! *It's superb!*

Les sentiments positifs *positive feelings*

être aux anges *to be in seventh heaven*
être calme *to be calm*
être enchanté(e) *to be happy/ pleased*

être heureux (heureuse) *to be happy*
être soulagé(e) *to be relieved*

Les sentiments négatifs *negative feelings*

être déçu(e) *to be disappointed*
être désespéré(e) *to be desperate*
être désolé(e) *to be sorry*

être horrifié(e) *to be horrified*
être jaloux (jalouse) *to be jealous*

être malheureux (malheureuse) *to be unhappy*
être surpris(e) *to be surprised*

Expansion personnelle

le coude *elbow*
la cheville *ankle*
les épaules *(f.)* *shoulders*

le front *forehead*
le genou *knee*
la hanche *hip*

la joue *cheek*
le menton *chin*
le pouce *thumb*

Les sentiments positifs

être euphorique *to be euphoric*
être fier (fière) *to be proud*
être reconnaissant(e) *to be grateful*

Les sentiments négatifs

être démoralisé(e) *to be demoralized*
être dévasté(e) *to be devastated*
être effrayé(e) *to be scared*

être outragé(e) *to be outraged*
être soucieux (soucieuse) *to be worried*

MISE EN PRATIQUE

À vous de découvrir!

Pour faire les activités suivantes, allez au *Online Study Center* et choisissez **Mise en pratique.** Vous y trouverez des sites Internet correspondant aux mots et phrases en caractères gras dans chaque activité.

La Tunisie

Aujourd'hui, vous allez visiter la **Tunisie.** Pour ceci vous allez entreprendre un voyage virtuel avec plusieurs camarades de classe. Mettez-vous en groupes de quatre pour faire une visite guidée des villes les plus importantes et des endroits les plus pittoresques. Suivez les indications suivantes pour découvrir la Tunisie, ses gens et sa culture.

A. Infos géos[1]. Écrivez tous les renseignements géographiques que vous trouverez sur la Tunisie et comparez vos notes avec vos camarades de classe afin de répondre aux questions suivantes.

1. Où est située la Tunisie? Dans quel continent? Au nord ou au sud?
2. Quelle est la mer qui baigne les plages de la Tunisie?
3. Quelles sont les langues officielles?

---

[1]Informations géographiques

4. Quelle est la monnaie qui est utilisée en Tunisie?
5. Quelle religion pratiquent les Tunisiens?
6. Quelle est la population de la Tunisie? Et sa superficie? À quel état américain peut-on comparer sa superficie?
7. Quel est le climat de la Tunisie? À quel climat peut-on le comparer aux États-Unis?

B. Un peu d'histoire.

Avant de commencer notre visite guidée, vous allez faire quelques recherches pour mieux comprendre la culture tunisienne. D'abord nous allons nous renseigner sur **l'histoire de la Tunisie.**

1. Qu'arrive-t-il en 1881? Et en 1956?
2. Quand est-ce que la République tunisienne est formée?
3. Comment s'appelle le premier président de cette République?
4. Comment s'appelle son successeur?
5. Qui est le président actuel?

C. Tunis, la capitale.

Vous allez découvrir **Tunis,** une «médina» (ville) à la fois moderne et ancienne (en 2002 il y avait plus de 2 millions d'habitants). Répondez aux questions après avoir visité le site.

1. Comment est la ville neuve?
2. Comment s'appelle la grande mosquée de Tunis? Pourquoi est-elle si importante?
3. Que sont les souks?
4. Que sont les dars?

Maintenant, visitez **le Musée Bardo** à Tunis.

5. Que peut-on voir au Musée Bardo? Qu'est-ce que vous préférez? Les mosaïques? Les bijoux? Les masques?

Maintenant, initiez votre **voyage virtuel de Tunis.**

6. Décrivez les villes et les plages. Comment sont-elles?
7. D'après ce que vous voyez sur le site web, qu'est-ce qui vous intéresse le plus? Pourquoi?

D. Sousse.

Sousse est une des villes touristiques et économiques les plus importantes de Tunisie. Renseignez-vous sur **Sousse** pour répondre aux questions suivantes.

1. Sousse est la capitale de quelle région?
2. Qu'est-ce que la Kasbah et Le Ribat?
3. Que peuvent faire les touristes à Sousse?
4. Que pensez-vous de Sousse? Avez-vous envie de la visiter? Pourquoi?
5. Quelles sont les couleurs qui prédominent sur les photos?

E. L'île de Djerba: le paradis!

Notre voyage virtuel se termine avec la visite de **Djerba,** un endroit paradisiaque!

1. Pourquoi est-ce que Djerba est célèbre dans l'Antiquité?
2. Que peut-on faire à Djerba?

Answer Key: 1. Parce qu'Ulysse (de Homère) s'arrête à Djerba lors de son voyage. 2. On peut visiter les souks, bien sûr. On peut aussi visiter des musées d'art, Le Borj El Kébir (une forteresse), des monuments (comme les mosquées), la Ghriba (un temple juif) ou tout simplement on peut aller à la plage.

À vous de déguster!

A. Spécialités gastronomiques tunisiennes. Connaissez-vous des spécialités gastronomiques tunisiennes? Si oui, lesquelles? Si votre réponse est négative, testez vos connaissances[1] en indiquant si les affirmations suivantes vous semblent[2] vraies ou fausses.

1. Les Tunisiens mangent des amandes[3] grillées et salées comme hors-d'œuvre.
   _____ vrai   _____ faux
2. De nombreuses pâtisseries et plats principaux sont faits avec du miel[4].
   _____ vrai   _____ faux
3. En Tunisie, on ne mange pas d'olives. On utilise seulement de l'huile d'olive.
   _____ vrai   _____ faux
4. Les ragoûts tunisiens sont faits le plus souvent avec du poulet.
   _____ vrai   _____ faux
5. La boisson préférée des Tunisiens est le café.
   _____ vrai   _____ faux

Online Study Center
Language Skills Practice

B. Les tajines (ou ragoûts). Le tajine le plus traditionnel est le tajine d'agneau[5]. Les tajines mijotent[6] pendant des heures et des heures avant d'être servis avec du couscous le plus souvent. Nous vous proposons de préparer un tajine d'agneau (vous pouvez remplacer l'agneau par du poulet si vous voulez) pour quatre personnes. La recette est très facile à préparer et encore plus facile à manger!

Bon appétit!

Tajine d'agneau

1½ kg de viande d'agneau pour ragoût coupé en morceaux[7]
Un gros oignon coupé menu[8]
1 cuillère à soupe de gingembre[9] râpé ou en poudre[10]
2 cuillères à café de safran[11]
1 bouillon d'agneau (ou de poulet)

Mettez tous les ingrédients dans une casserole sur feu vif[12] jusqu'à ébullition. Baissez le feu et laissez mijoter de 30 à 40 minutes. Après 30 minutes, ajoutez[13] 200 grammes de pruneaux[14], 100 grammes de raisins secs et deux poignées[15] d'amandes sans peau. Ajoutez également 1 cuillère à soupe de miel délayée dans le jus d'un citron. Laissez mijoter 15 minutes. Et voilà, votre tajine est prêt! Servez-le avec du couscous si vous en avez.

---

[1]knowledge [2]seem [3]almonds [4]honey [5]lamb [6]simmer [7]pieces [8]= en petits morceaux [9]ginger [10]grated or powdered [11]saffron [12]high heat [13]add [14]prunes [15]handfuls

Ⓐ vous d'analyser

A. Première lecture. Vous allez lire un article sur l'immobilier[1] à Tunis écrit par Leïla Ladjimi Sebaï, une écrivaine contemporaine tunisienne très réputée pour ses écrits littéraires. Lisez d'abord le texte une première fois pour obtenir les idées centrales. (Rappelez-vous: il est normal de ne pas tout comprendre la première fois!)

Vivre ailleurs—Tunis, la vie en bord de mer

Un trois pièces-salon pour 400 $ mensuels

Leïla Ladjimi Sebaï

C'est tous les jours, et même deux fois par jour, tôt le matin et assez tard le soir, que Sabrine emprunte[2] la rue Jamaa Zitouna, principale voie de la Médina, puis l'avenue de France, enfin l'avenue Bourguiba, pour se rendre[3] à la gare ferroviaire. Après une journée de labeur[4], elle a hâte[5] de prendre enfin ce que tout le monde appelle le TGM (pour Tunis-Goulette-Marsa), le sympathique petit train qui la conduira chez elle, dans la toute proche banlieue nord de Tunis. Là est sa maison. Sabrine a 27 ans. [...] Sabrine y réside depuis près de trois ans.

Inaccessible centre

Inutile de songer[6] à habiter ce qu'on appelle le centre-ville, dans l'un de ces beaux immeubles de style néoclassique européen, vieillots et désuets[7], presque tous entièrement reconvertis en bureaux, commerces, salles de spectacles et cafés pimpants[8]. [...] On pourra dépenser jusqu'à 1500 D[9] par mois pour un grand appartement dans un immeuble rénové; ces sommes excessives ne sont pas à la portée[10] du Tunisien moyen.

   Dans le train, Sabrine réfléchit[11]; elle n'aurait jamais pu affronter seule la location de 400 D mensuels pour le trois pièces-salon de cette petite villa[12] [...] de La Goulette. Mais Sabrine a eu beaucoup de chance de pouvoir s'y installer avec deux amies et de partager les frais[13]. [...]

   Sabrine est cadre moyen dans une grande banque de la place; travailleuse et déterminée, elle compte bien gravir[14] les échelons[15] et caresse secrètement l'ambition d'occuper un poste plus important—et surtout mieux rémunéré car, en totalisant les mois supplémentaires et les primes[16] de rendement[17], la banque lui octroie[18] royalement une prestation mensuelle nette de 650 D. En Tunisie, il s'agit d'un assez bon salaire. De plus, travailler dans une banque offre des avantages dont Sabrine espère pouvoir bénéficier. Comme la plupart de ses collègues, elle a droit à un prêt qui lui permettra d'acquérir son propre logement[19].

---

[1]*real estate* [2]*prend* [3]*aller* [4]*travail* [5]*est impatiente* [6]*penser, rêver* [7]*obsolète* [8]*élégants* [9]*dinars [un dinar équivaut approximativement à 76 cents américains (juin 2006)]* [10]*à la disposition* [11]*pense* [12]*maison* [13]*dépenses* [14]*monter* [15]*niveaux (levels)* [16]*salaire supplémentaire* [17]*productivité* [18]*donne* [19]*maison ou appartement*

Devenir enfin propriétaire! Un rêve qui s'est transformé en réalité pour les trois quarts des familles tunisiennes, toutes catégories sociales confondues. Bien sûr, tout dépendra de l'emplacement convoité[1] et de la superficie occupée, mais pour 90 000 dinars environ, Sabrine sait qu'elle pourra acquérir, dans un de ces nouveaux quartiers périphériques, un coquet appartement de quatre pièces, muni de tout le confort. [...]

Fins de mois

Sabrine sait calculer. À Tunis, tout le monde calcule et tout le monde se débrouille[2]. Sans cela, la vie ne serait pas possible. Pour arrondir ses fins de mois, elle donne des cours de mathématiques à de jeunes élèves. Cette activité supplémentaire, non déclarée et non imposable, lui permet de doubler pratiquement son salaire.

De plus, elle sait pouvoir compter sur sa famille. De sa campagne natale, elle reçoit toutes les denrées de base nécessaires à son quotidien: huile, beurre, fromage, céréales, œufs, fruits de saison, salaisons[3] et conserves amoureusement mitonnées[4] par sa mère lui permettent de faire de sérieuses économies. Car à Tunis la vie est chère et les tentations multiples. Elle sait aussi pouvoir compter sur son père; il lui avancera la mise de fonds[5] nécessaire: avec 30 000 dinars d'apport personnel, elle est assurée d'obtenir son prêt bancaire. Certes[6], elle s'endettera pour 20 ans au moins et devra assurer un remboursement de 400 D par mois environ, mais elle est jeune, optimiste et dynamique; s'engager ne lui fait pas peur.

B. Deuxième lecture. Lisez le texte une seconde fois et répondez aux questions en groupes de trois ou quatre étudiants.

Premier paragraphe

1. Où va Sabrine une ou deux fois par jour?
2. Pourquoi prend-elle le TGM?
3. Où est la maison de Sabrine? Est-elle au centre-ville?

Inaccessible centre

4. Expliquez les raisons pour lesquelles le Tunisien moyen ne peut pas habiter au centre-ville de Tunis.
5. Est-ce que Sabrine habite seule? Pourquoi?
6. Où travaille Sabrine?
7. Pourquoi est-ce que Sabrine veut obtenir un jour un poste plus important?
8. Quel est l'avantage de travailler dans une banque quand on cherche un logement?
9. Où est-ce que Sabrine pourra s'acheter un logement?

Fins de mois

10. Comment est-ce que Sabrine obtient plus d'argent tous les mois? Pourquoi?
11. Est-ce que Sabrine économise? Comment?
12. Comment est-ce que Sabrine va obtenir son prêt bancaire pour acheter un logement?
13. Pourquoi est-ce que Sabrine n'est pas préoccupée de s'endetter pour 20 ans?

---

[1]désiré [2]manages [3]charcuteries [4]préparées [5]down payment [6]Sûrement; Évidemment

C. Questions de réflexion. Avec votre groupe, répondez aux questions sur le sujet du texte.

1. Vous avez vu que Sabrine utilise le train comme moyen de transport pour se déplacer[1] de son logement à son travail et vice-versa. Quel est le moyen de transport le plus commun qui s'utilise dans votre ville pour les déplacements? Est-ce un bon moyen de transport? Expliquez votre réponse.

2. En général, dans votre pays, est-ce que les jeunes professionnels comme Sabrine—qui a 27 ans—habitent avec des colocataires? Pourquoi? Normalement, qui a des colocataires?

3. Comme vous avez lu dans le texte, habiter au centre-ville à Tunis coûte très cher. Est-ce que c'est la même chose dans votre pays? Est-ce que les gens préfèrent habiter au centre-ville ou en banlieue? Pourquoi?

4. Est-ce que vous avez été surpris(e) de lire que les parents de Sabrine lui envoient de la nourriture et même de l'argent pour qu'elle obtienne un prêt? Pourquoi pensez-vous que les parents tunisiens sont si présents dans la vie de leurs enfants adultes? Est-ce la même chose dans votre pays? Expliquez vos réponses.

À vous de créer!

A. La Société PAPYRUS à Sousse. Vous avez été licencié(e) le mois dernier parce que l'entreprise où vous travailliez à Atlanta a fermé. Vous avez une formation en affaires et commerce[2]. Vous voulez partir en Tunisie parce que vous trouvez que c'est un pays exotique et que vous parlez très bien le français. Arrivé(e) en Tunisie, vous cherchez du travail. La société PAPYRUS à Sousse offre un poste qui serait parfait pour vous. Lisez l'offre attentivement:

La Société
PAPYRUS

à Sousse recherche un responsable commercial chargé de créer et de structurer les ventes
—aux distributeurs ou ventes directes—
et d'améliorer la commercialisation des produits qui existent déjà[3] en Tunisie et à l'export (Maroc, États-Unis, France, etc.).

Formation demandée: BAC + 4[4] en affaires et commerce.
Expérience dans la commercialisation de produits ménagers.
Maîtrise de l'anglais et du français.

Envoyez votre CV et votre lettre de candidature à M. Ahmed Hamna, Directeur Commercial, BP 400-4000, Sousse, Tunisie.

---

[1]*aller* [2]*business* [3]*already* [4]*4 years of college (bachelor's degree)*

1. Avant de postuler pour ce poste, familiarisez-vous avec la compagnie en visitant leur site web.
2. Regardez tous les produits que fabrique PAPYRUS pour mieux les connaître[1].
3. Pensez à la commercialisation interne et à l'exportation des produits.
4. Maintenant, répondez à l'annonce.

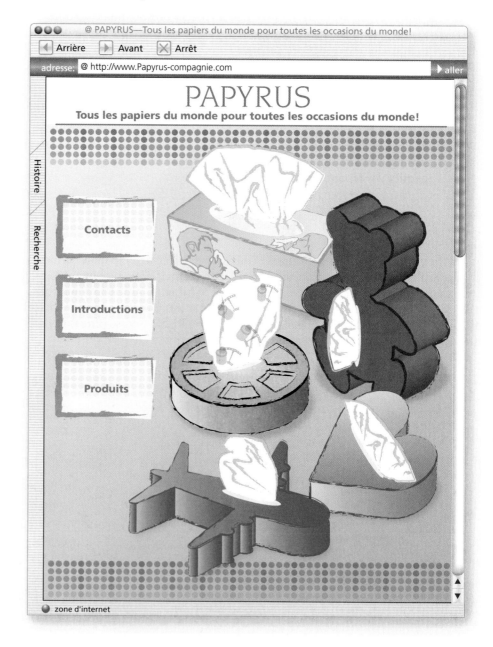

[1] *to know them better*

Monsieur le Directeur,

En réponse à votre annonce, parue dans le journal *Le Quotidien* du
(1) _____, j'ai l'honneur de poser ma candidature au poste de
responsable commercial dans votre société. Je pense que mon expérience
(2) _____ et ma formation en
(3) _____ me qualifient pour cet emploi.

Vous trouverez (4) _____ *(enclosed)* mon curriculum vitae. Je
me tiens à votre entière disposition pour un (5) _____ *(interview)*.

Dans l'espoir d'une réponse favorable, je (6) _____ *(appropriate
polite greeting)*, Monsieur le Directeur, (7) _____.

_____ *(Signature)*

B. Le jour de l'entretien. Vous êtes M. Ahmed Hamna (Directeur
Commercial) ou Mme Leïla Saha (Directrice de Marketing) et vous interviewez
le/la candidat(e). Pour compléter l'entretien suivant, mettez les verbes entre
parenthèses au passé composé ou à l'imparfait.

M. Hamna: Bonjour, Monsieur / Mademoiselle / Madame
(1) _____. Asseyez-vous, s'il vous plaît.

Le/La candidat(e): Bonjour. Merci beaucoup de bien vouloir me recevoir.

Mme Saha: Mais, c'est avec plaisir. Nous voudrions savoir avec un peu plus
de précision ce que vous (2) _____ (faire) dans votre poste
antérieur à Atlanta.

Le/La candidat(e): J(e) (3) _____ (être) le/la responsable du
marketing pour les produits de nettoyage Le Plus Propre et Frotte-Frotte[1]. J(e)
(4) _____ (lancer[2]) la campagne publicitaire Frotte-Frotte
avec Le Plus Propre.

M. Hamna: Oui, en effet, nous connaissons bien cette publicité. On la
passe souvent à la télévision tunisienne. Quel produit (5) _____
(rapporter) le plus de bénéfices à la compagnie?

Le/La candidat(e): Sans doute, Le Plus Propre. Les ventes *(f.)*
(6) _____ (se multiplier) après ma campagne publicitaire.

Mme Saha: Ce n'est pas étonnant! Dans votre poste antérieur, quelle *(f.)*
(7) _____ (être) la situation la plus stressante pour vous?

Le/La candidat(e): Mmm … Voyons … La plus stressante c'est quand on
(8) _____ (commencer) à licencier tous mes collègues.
Je les (9) _____ (voir) partir un à un et la compagnie
(10) _____ (perdre) d'excellents professionnels.

M. Hamna: Comment est-ce que vous (11) _____ (réagir[3])?

Le/La candidat(e): J(e) (12) _____ (continuer) à travailler
et j(e) (13) _____ (attendre) mon tour.

M. Hamna: Nous vous remercions d'être venu(e). Nous vous contacterons
très bientôt.

Le/La candidat(e): Au revoir et merci à vous.

---

[1] *The Cleanest and Scrub-Scrub* [2] *to launch* [3] *to react*

C. Si vous étiez en Tunisie … Complétez les phrases suivantes en utilisant le conditionnel pour indiquer ce que votre camarade et vous feriez si vous étiez en Tunisie.

1. Si nous étions en Tunisie, nous (aller) _____ … .
2. À Djerba, il/elle (faire) _____ … et moi je (faire) _____ … .
3. À Tunis, nous (voir) _____ … .
4. À Sousse, il/elle (manger) _____ … et moi je (boire) _____ … .
5. Nous (se reposer) _____ à … et nous (s'amuser) _____ à … .
6. Nous (acheter) _____ … aux souks.

À vous de décider

Le français pour quoi faire?

Meet Jonathan Fernández. Jonathan is an engineer for an international software company. He is going to share with you how knowing French has made his job easier.

Q: How many languages do you speak?

A: Three. In addition to English, I speak Spanish and French.

Q: What is your job at the company?

A: I work in research and development.

Q: Does your company have offices or sites in countries where French is spoken?

A: We have sales offices in 160 countries. We have a manufacturing and R&D site in France. We also have customer support centers in Europe, Asia, Africa, and Canada that must be able to help customers in their native language. We also have suppliers from all over the world: The engineer who sits right beside me has worked with a tooling company in Switzerland for three years.

Q: How have languages helped you in your work?

A: I work frequently with people from many different parts of the world. Even though English is required in order to work at any of our offices and everyone speaks it very well, it does not mean they feel comfortable with it. Being able to communicate with others in their language makes them more comfortable and helps me make a better connection with them—even if I do not speak it as well as they speak English. They really appreciate the effort and treat you much better—it transforms you from being just another client into being their partner. My co-worker in Mexico speaks very good English, but if you want to connect you need to use Spanish. The French really appreciate that you speak to them in their native language as a sign of appreciation of their culture, which is very important. Some older people from Southeast Asia have a very hard time with English and prefer French because of their cultural legacy. Despite the technical nature of my job, I feel that languages are what make me successful, and my job easier.

Q: What was the most unexpected situation when you used French?

A: It was when I was working with an Italian company. One of their senior engineers had a hard time communicating in English. When I learned that he had worked in France for several years, I switched to French and he became more relaxed. The rest of the day was a lot more fun because he could really express his opinions and I did not have to guess constantly what he meant. Plus he had a great sense of humor that he would not have conveyed as well in English.

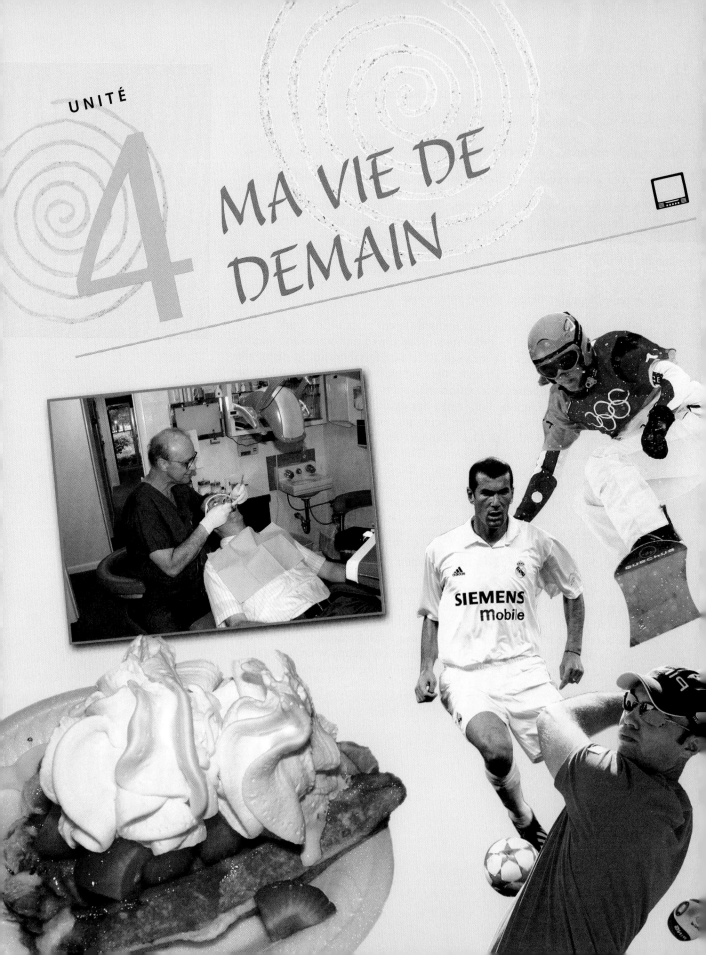

UNITÉ

4 MA VIE DE DEMAIN

Ma vie branchée!

In this chapter, you will learn ways to describe **une vie branchée**—a "connected" life. In French, this concept includes being connected to the latest technology as well as extreme sports and other popular activities, and the phrase is used to speak of someone or something trendy. You will learn how to talk about activities you are familiar with or know how to do, and activities you plan to do in the future. You will also see how various Francophone cultures are **branchées.**

The vocabulary that you will learn includes

Computers, the Internet, and other technology
Extreme sports and other hobbies

The structures that you will learn include

The verbs **connaître** and **savoir**
The future tense

The culture that you will learn includes

The Minitel—the precursor of the Internet
How the Internet is being used in Africa

Commençons!

La technologie de tous les jours

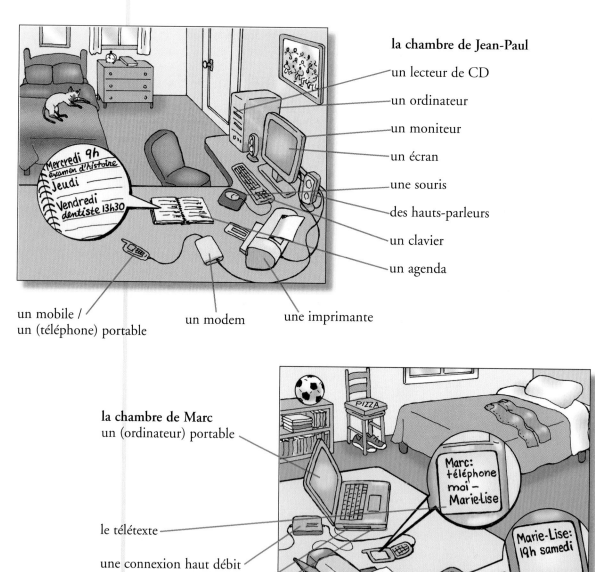

la chambre de Jean-Paul

un lecteur de CD

un ordinateur

un moniteur

un écran

une souris

des hauts-parleurs

un clavier

un agenda

un mobile /
un (téléphone) portable

un modem

une imprimante

la chambre de Marc
un (ordinateur) portable

le télétexte

une connexion haut débit

un lecteur / graveur de CD

un lecteur de DVD

une imprimante couleur

un assistant personnel

Marc est un étudiant très intelligent, qui aime beaucoup la technologie. Pour cette raison, il décide de se spécialiser en informatique. Il est en première année à l'université. Sa chambre est équipée des derniers gadgets technologiques. Faisons le contraste entre la chambre de Marc et la chambre de son ami Jean-Paul:

Dans les chambres de Marc et de Jean-Paul, il y a un lit, une chaise et un bureau, bien sûr. Mais les similarités s'arrêtent là! Jean-Paul a un ordinateur sur son bureau, avec un lecteur de CD. Marc a aussi un ordinateur, mais c'est un portable, qui pèse moins de deux kilos. Il a un lecteur de CD, bien sûr, mais lui, il peut aussi graver un CD. Il sait surfer sur Internet, télécharger de la musique et la sauvegarder sur un CD pour l'écouter plus tard.

Jean-Paul aime surfer sur Internet aussi. Il utilise un modem pour le faire. Marc n'a pas besoin de modem, il a une connexion haut débit, donc il a accès à l'Internet plus rapidement que Jean-Paul, et il peut télécharger de plus gros documents, comme par exemple, des photos ou de la musique. Il a aussi une imprimante couleur, donc il peut imprimer des photos. Jean-Paul lui dit qu'il va avoir des problèmes avec la justice s'il n'arrête pas de télécharger de la musique!

Sur son bureau, Jean-Paul a un agenda où il marque ses cours et ses rendez-vous importants. De temps en temps, pourtant, il manque un rendez-vous parce qu'il oublie de regarder son agenda. Marc a un assistant personnel. Il utilise son ordinateur comme calendrier, et puis il transfère ces informations sur son assistant personnel. Lui, il ne rate jamais ses rendez-vous!

Jean-Paul vient d'acheter un mobile. Il croit qu'il est très branché maintenant! Mais quand il le montre à Marc, Marc n'a pas l'air très impressionné. Jean-Paul veut savoir pourquoi. Alors Marc lui montre son mobile: il peut téléphoner, bien sûr, mais son mobile marche aussi comme télétexte—il peut même recevoir des courriels de ses amis! Jean-Paul aime beaucoup Marc. Ils se connaissent depuis dix ans, et ils sont de bons amis. Mais quand même, Jean-Paul trouve que Marc commence à être un peu snob avec toute sa technologie! Vous ne le trouvez pas aussi?

Vous avez bien compris?

Répondez aux questions suivantes, selon le texte.

1. Quelles sont les différences entre l'ordinateur de Jean-Paul et celui de Marc?
2. Pourquoi est-ce que Jean-Paul pense que Marc va avoir des problèmes avec la justice?
3. Pourquoi est-ce que Marc ne rate jamais de rendez-vous?
4. Pour quelles fonctions est-ce que Jean-Paul peut utiliser son téléphone portable?
5. Et Marc?
6. Pensez-vous que Marc est snob, ou que Jean-Paul est jaloux? Expliquez votre réponse.

Answer Key: 1. Marc a un ordinateur portable. Il peut graver un CD. 2. Parce qu'il télécharge de la musique. 3. Parce qu'il a un assistant personnel. 4. Il peut téléphoner. 5. Il peut téléphoner et aussi envoyer et recevoir des courriels. 6. *Answers will vary.*

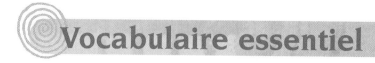

Vocabulaire essentiel

La technologie d'aujourd'hui

le Web = la Toile / le Net
surfer sur Internet / être sur Internet
naviguer sur le Web / naviguer sur la Toile / naviguer sur le Net
une adresse électronique
cliquer
utiliser un moteur de recherche (Google.fr, Wanadoo.fr, etc.)
avoir un mot de passe
envoyer un courriel / un e-mail
envoyer une pièce ci-jointe
recevoir un courriel / un e-mail
utiliser un traitement de texte *(word processor)*
un appareil photo numérique *(digital camera)*
un baladeur numérique *(digital audio player)*
un lecteur de DVD
un graveur de DVD
un scanner
le home cinéma

À vous!

A. La technologie envahit nos vies! À gauche sont les moyens de communication que nos parents et nos grands-parents utilisaient. À droite sont nos moyens actuels. Savez-vous quelles nouvelles technologies à droite correspondent aux anciennes technologies à gauche?

1. une machine à écrire
2. une encyclopédie
3. le code Morse
4. une lettre
5. un disque (45 rpm)
6. un appareil photo 35mm
7. un agenda / un calendrier
8. un magnétophone
9. un magnétoscope

a. le téléphone
b. un appareil photo numérique
c. un compact disque (un CD)
d. un graveur de CD
e. l'Internet
f. un courriel
g. un lecteur / graveur de DVD
h. un ordinateur
i. un assistant personnel

B. Chez vous. Posez les questions suivantes à un(e) partenaire.

1. Est-ce que vous avez un ordinateur? Si oui, est-ce que vous avez un lecteur de CD / DVD? Un graveur de CD / DVD? Si non, où allez-vous quand vous avez besoin d'un ordinateur?
2. Pour quelles fonctions est-ce que vous utilisez votre ordinateur? (comme traitement de texte, pour surfer sur Internet, etc.)
3. À qui est-ce que vous envoyez des courriels le plus souvent? Pourquoi?
4. Vous avez un mobile? De quoi est-il équipé? (téléphone seulement, télétexte) Quand l'utilisez-vous? (dans la voiture, en classe, etc.)
5. Est-ce que vous y parlez souvent ou rarement? À qui est-ce que vous téléphonez?

6. Si vous n'avez pas de mobile, que faites-vous quand vous avez besoin de téléphoner à quelqu'un?
7. Que pensez-vous des personnes qui parlent toujours au téléphone dans des endroits publics (le bus, le restaurant, etc.)?
8. Est-ce que vous pensez que c'est un crime de télécharger de la musique ou des films de l'Internet? Pourquoi ou pourquoi pas? Est-ce que vous le faites?
9. Est-ce que vous connaissez un «snob» de la technologie? Qui?

Portrait personnel

Quand vous avez fini l'activité B, faites un résumé de la technologie que votre partenaire utilise. Ensuite, comparez-le avec le reste de la classe. Est-ce que votre partenaire est plutôt technophile ou plutôt technophobe?

C. La technologie idéale. Dites à un(e) partenaire quelle(s) technologie(s) vous avez chez vous, et laquelle vous voudriez avoir / vous ne voudriez pas avoir. Quand vous avez fini, comparez vos réponses, et commentez vos similarités et vos différences à la classe.

1. J'ai déjà un / une / des … Je l'utilise (les utilise) pour …
2. Je voudrais bien avoir un / une / des … parce que …
3. Je ne voudrais pas avoir de … parce que …
4. Tout le monde devrait avoir un / une / des … parce que …
5. Personne n'a besoin d'un(e) … parce que …
6. Je vais bientôt acheter un / une / des … parce que …

Structure 1

Connaître vs. savoir

Online Study Center
ACE, Language Skills
Practice

In French, there are two verbs that are routinely translated into English as *to know*. These verbs are not interchangeable, however, as they imply two quite different ways of "knowing." Both verbs are irregular.

connaître		savoir	
je connais	nous connaissons	je sais	nous savons
tu connais	vous connaissez	tu sais	vous savez
il / elle / on connaît	ils / elles connaissent	il / elle / on sait	ils / elles savent
passé composé: (avoir) connu		(avoir) su	

- **Connaître** means *to know* in the sense of *to be familiar with* or *acquainted with*. It is always followed by a noun.

Tu connais Paris?	*Do you know / Are you familiar with Paris?*
Oui, j'y ai voyagé l'été dernier.	*Yes, I traveled there last summer.*
Vous connaissez la sœur de Marie?	*Do you know / Are you acquainted with Marie's sister?*
Oui, je l'ai rencontrée il y a deux mois.	*Yes, I met her two months ago.*

- **Savoir** means *to know (a fact)* or *to know how (to do something)*. It can be followed by a noun, an infinitive, or a clause.

Vous savez le numéro de téléphone de Lucas?	*Do you know Lucas's telephone number?*
Oui, c'est le 91.14.03.	*Yes, it's 91.14.03.*
Tu sais envoyer un courriel?	*Do you know how to send an e-mail?*
Ben oui, c'est facile!	*Of course! It's easy!*
Je sais que tu aimes la cuisine chinoise. Veux-tu aller manger avec moi?	*I know that you like Chinese food. Do you want to go eat with me?*
Volontiers!	*Gladly!*

- In a few cases, either **connaître** or **savoir** could be used, depending on the intended meaning and the context.

Je sais quelle est la capitale du Sénégal. C'est Dakar.	*I know the capital of Senegal. It's Dakar. (This is a fact that I know.)*
Je connais la capitale du Sénégal. Je l'ai visitée.	*I know the capital of Senegal. I've visited it. (This is a place that I'm familiar with.)*

- **In the *passé composé* and the imperfect:** The past participle of **savoir** is **su;** the past participle of **connaître** is **connu.** Both are conjugated with **avoir** in the *passé composé:* **j'ai su / j'ai connu.** Notice the very specific meanings of each verb.

J'ai connu ma meilleure amie à l'âge de cinq ans.	*I **met** my best friend at the age of 5.*
J'ai su hier que tu as été malade.	*I **found out** yesterday that you were sick.*

Because they are conjugated with **avoir,** the past participle agrees only with a preceding direct object (see Ch.11 to review this structure).

J'ai connu ma meilleure amie à l'âge de 5 ans. → Je l'ai connue à l'âge de 5 ans.

The two verbs are regular in the imperfect. (Reminder: to form the imperfect, drop the **-ons** ending from the **nous** form in the present indicative, and add the imperfect endings.)

Elle connaissait son ami depuis longtemps.	*She had known her friend for a long time.*
Elle ne savait pas qu'il était malade.	*She didn't know that he was sick.*

Connaître and **savoir** have very different meanings when used in the **passé composé** and the imperfect. Remember that the **passé composé** always implies the completion of an action. In the **passé composé,** therefore, **connaître** means *to meet* or *to make the acquaintance of,* and **savoir** means *to find out.* In the imperfect, on the other hand, no such completion is implied. These verbs in this tense simply mean *to know,* with no implication as to when the knowledge was acquired. Look at the preceding examples in this section and note the differences in meaning between the **passé composé** and the imperfect.

- **In the conditional:** Note that in the conditional, **connaître** maintains the circumflex accent of the infinitive throughout the conjugation. **Savoir** has an irregular stem, which you saw in Chapter 12: **saur-**.

Si j'étais riche, je **connaîtrais** beaucoup de célébrités.
If I were rich, I would know a lot of celebrities.

Si j'avais un ordinateur, je **saurais** envoyer un courriel.
If I had a computer, I would know how to send e-mail.

VÉRIFIEZ VOTRE COMPRÉHENSION

1. Consider the conjugations of **connaître** and **savoir**. In what ways are these verbs irregular? Despite being classified as irregular verbs, what regularities do they have?

2. Go back to the **Commençons!** text at the beginning of the chapter (p.413). Underline all uses of **savoir** and **connaître** that you find. Explain the choice of each verb in the context in which it is used.

3. Explain, in your own words, the differences between **connaître** and **savoir** in the **passé composé** and the imperfect.

À l'écoute!

Écoutez les phrases suivantes et identifiez le temps des verbes **savoir** et **connaître**.

1. ____ présent ____ passé composé ____ imparfait ____ conditionnel
2. ____ présent ____ passé composé ____ imparfait ____ conditionnel
3. ____ présent ____ passé composé ____ imparfait ____ conditionnel
4. ____ présent ____ passé composé ____ imparfait ____ conditionnel
5. ____ présent ____ passé composé ____ imparfait ____ conditionnel
6. ____ présent ____ passé composé ____ imparfait ____ conditionnel
7. ____ présent ____ passé composé ____ imparfait ____ conditionnel
8. ____ présent ____ passé composé ____ imparfait ____ conditionnel

Pratiquons!

A. Connaissances. Répondez aux questions suivantes avec une phrase complète. Quand vous avez fini, comparez vos réponses avec les réponses d'un(e) camarade de classe.

1. Nommez une ville que vous connaissez bien. (Je connais bien …)
2. Nommez un état aux États-Unis que vous ne connaissez pas du tout. Voulez-vous le connaître? Pourquoi ou pourquoi pas?
3. Nommez une célébrité que vous voudriez connaître. Pourquoi?
4. Nommez une célébrité que vous ne voudriez pas connaître. Pourquoi?
5. Nommez quelque chose de surprenant que vous savez bien faire.
6. Nommez une chose que vous ne savez pas du tout faire.
7. Nommez une chose que votre professeur sait probablement faire, et une chose qu'il/elle ne sait probablement pas faire.
8. Nommez une chose que vos parents ne savent pas de vous.

Audioscript: 1. Il a su hier que sa mère était malade. 2. Nous connaissions ce restaurant depuis longtemps. 3. Je connais un très bon avocat. 4. Mon père saurait quoi faire, mais je ne lui ai pas demandé son avis. 5. J'ai connu mon mari il y a trois ans. 6. Est-ce que tu sais la réponse au numéro trois? 7. Il savait faire du ski, mais il ne voulait pas le faire. 8. Demande à ton prof; elle connaît certainement un bon hôtel à Paris.

You may wish to do this as a pair activity. If so, have students compare their responses, and expand on them.

Answer Key. Possible answers: 1. Je connais bien Paris. 2. Je ne connais pas du tout l'Alaska. Oui, je voudrais le connaître, parce que c'est très différent de mon état. 3. Je voudrais connaître Oprah Winfrey, parce que je l'admire beaucoup. 4. Je ne voudrais pas connaître Jack Nicholson parce qu'il a l'air méchant. 5. Je sais jouer de la guitare. 6. Je ne sais pas du tout jouer du piano. 7. Mon professeur sait probablement utiliser le métro à Paris; il/elle ne sait pas utiliser le métro à Tokyo. 8. Mes parents ne savent pas que je fume.

B. Colocataires.

Christine et Sophie sont colocataires. Dites ce que chacune sait / connaît. Attention au choix des verbes!

1. Sophie achète beaucoup de disques compacts. Elle ne _____ pas télécharger de la musique de l'Internet.
2. Christine n'écoute pas souvent le hit parade. Elle _____ mieux la musique classique.
3. Christine et Sophie _____ toutes les deux les amis de l'autre, mais elles ne sortent pas souvent ensemble.
4. Christine _____ le copain de Sophie, mais elle ne _____ pas son nom de famille. Elle _____ son numéro de téléphone, parce qu'elle lui téléphone assez souvent pour parler à Sophie!
5. Sophie _____ l'adresse électronique et le mot de passe de Christine. Quand Christine rentre chez ses parents, Sophie lit ses messages, parce que les parents de Christine n'ont pas d'ordinateur! Christine _____ que Sophie lui téléphonera[1] s'il y a quelque chose d'important.
6. Et vous: est-ce que vous _____ le mot de passe de quelqu'un? Quand est-ce que vous l'utilisez?
7. Est-ce que vous avez un colocataire? Vous _____ sa famille?

C. Questions et réponses.

Utilisez les éléments suivants et le verbe **savoir** ou **connaître** pour créer des questions que vous pourrez poser à vos camarades de classe.

MODÈLE: une célébrité

Tu connais une célébrité?

1. envoyer un courriel
2. les heures de bureau du prof
3. faire des pages Web
4. quelqu'un qui n'a pas d'ordinateur
5. qui a inventé le téléphone
6. qui a découvert[2] la pénicilline
7. un pays francophone (Si oui, lequel?)
8. wanadoo.fr

Maintenant, circulez dans la classe, posez les questions et rapportez les réponses à toute la classe.

D. Dialogue.

Posez les questions suivantes à un camarade de classe. Comparez ses réponses avec les réponses du reste de la classe à la fin.

1. À quel âge est-ce que tu as connu ton/ta meilleur(e) ami(e)? Où et comment l'as-tu connu(e)? Tu connais aussi sa famille?
2. Quand est-ce que tu as su surfer sur Internet? Qui t'a appris?
3. Tu sais utiliser un traitement de texte? Pourquoi est-ce que tu l'utilises?
4. Tu sais envoyer un courriel avec une pièce ci-jointe? À qui est-ce que tu en envoies? Pour quelles raisons? Quand as-tu su le faire?
5. Tu connais le président de ton université? Quand et où l'as-tu connu?
6. Tu sais l'adresse électronique du président de l'université? Vas-tu lui envoyer un courriel un jour? Pourquoi ou pourquoi pas?

---

[1] *will call* [2] *discovered*

À vous de parler!

A. La technologie et moi. Comparez l'usage que vous faites des ordinateurs avec celui d'un(e) partenaire. À la fin, expliquez vos similarités et vos différences au reste de la classe. Suggestion: Utilisez le vocabulaire qui a été présenté dans *Commençons!* Par exemple, traitement de texte, courriel, graveur de DVD, jeux, etc.

> **MODÈLE:** Partenaire A: *J'utilise l'Internet tous les jours pour chercher des informations. Et toi?*
>
> Partenaire B: *Moi non. Je préfère lire les journaux. Mais j'envoie au moins dix courriels par jour. Et toi?*

B. Jeu de vitesse. Par équipes de deux ou trois personnes, dressez une liste de ce qu'il faut connaître ou savoir dans chacune des situations suivantes. Essayez d'avoir une liste plus longue et plus créative que celle des autres groupes de la classe.

> **MODÈLE:** pour réussir à l'université
>
> *Il faut: savoir où se trouve la bibliothèque; connaître tous vos profs; savoir faire les devoirs; savoir choisir de bons cours; connaître les meilleurs profs …*

1. pour utiliser l'Internet intelligemment
2. pour avoir un bon travail
3. pour être un bon mari ou une bonne épouse
4. pour devenir président(e) des États-Unis

Have students play this as a competitive game. Read the directions and model together, then give them two minutes for #1. Award points to the team with the longest list, the team with the most unique responses, etc. Move on to #2, and total points at the end.

Les Français sont branchés[1] comme ça

Online Study Center
Web Search Activities

Les Français ont montré leur esprit innovateur quand ils ont conçu[2] le Minitel en 1981. Le Minitel est comparable à l'Internet dans la mesure où il fournit les mêmes services. Jusqu'au milieu des années 90 la majorité des Français préféraient utiliser le Minitel au lieu de[3] l'Internet car son utilisation est très facile et sa connexion est très sûre[4] et extrêmement rapide. Aujourd'hui, les jeunes Français de 14 à 35 ans préfèrent l'Internet, mais les générations un peu plus âgées continuent d'utiliser le Minitel. Les internautes[5] français restent en moyenne 9 heures par semaine sur l'Internet. 54% des internautes français ont moins de 34 ans. Pour utiliser le Minitel, il suffit de composer un numéro, le 3615, suivi du service désiré. Par exemple, pour voir la programmation de la chaîne ARTE, il faut composer le 3615 Arte. Ce service coûte 0,21 € la minute. Chaque service a un coût différent.

La différence entre le Minitel et l'Internet réside dans le fait que les connexions du Minitel se font exclusivement dans l'Hexagone[6]. Le

---

[1]The word **branché** means *in* or *hip* or, as in this context, *plugged in, wired, technologically up-to-date.* [2]*created* [3]*instead of* [4]*secure* [5]*Internet users* [6]L'Hexagone est un autre nom que l'on utilise pour parler de la France parce que quand on regarde une carte géographique de la France, on voit qu'elle a la forme d'un hexagone!

Minitel fournit[1] un service local, régional, communautaire et non global comme l'Internet. En quelque sorte, on peut dire que le Minitel est le précurseur de l'Internet.

En France en 2004, il y a plus de 6 millions de Minitels dans les foyers[2]. Avant même que l'Internet ne soit aussi répandu[3] dans le monde entier, les Français pouvaient déjà dès le début des années 80 réserver une table au restaurant, une entrée au cinéma, un vol à Air France ou un voyage en train à la SNCF. Les jeunes Français pouvaient aussi s'inscrire[4] à la Fac (l'université), regarder la grille des programmes télévisés ou faire des achats en ligne par Minitel.

Le Minitel a beaucoup évolué depuis ses débuts en 1981. Par exemple, en 2000, le i-Minitel est né. Le i-Minitel est un logiciel[5] qui permet d'accéder aux services du Minitel avec un PC, un MAC ou un téléphone mobile. Aussi, les Français qui désirent accéder au Minitel depuis un site web peuvent le faire grâce au MinitelWeb.

Du fait que le Minitel est employé par de nombreux usagers, la France a un léger retard[6] par rapport aux autres pays européens en ce qui concerne le nombre de foyers qui ont un ordinateur. Comparez les chiffres suivants:

Pourcentage de foyers équipés d'un ordinateur en 2003	
En France	40,2%
En Allemagne[7]	52%
En Belgique	45%
Au Pays-Bas[8]	67%
En Angleterre[9]	45%

Les Français branchés en chiffres	
Pourcentage de PC portables par foyer	8,8%
Nombre d'appareils photos numériques par foyer	15,1%
Nombre de Français qui n'ont jamais surfé	53%
Nombre de Français qui ont utilisé le chat[10]	35%
Nombre de foyers qui font des achats en ligne avec un ordinateur	28%

Réfléchissons

1. Pourquoi dit-on dans le texte que le Minitel est le précurseur de l'Internet?
2. Qui utilise le Minitel en France? Et l'Internet?
3. Vingt-huit pour cent des Français font leurs achats en ligne. Ce pourcentage est relativement petit comparé à cinquante pour cent aux États-Unis. Faites-vous vos achats en ligne? Dans quel secteur: maison, vêtements, livres, produits de beauté, alimentation, voyages?
4. Combien d'heures par semaine est-ce que les internautes français passent sur Internet? Et les Américains, restent-ils plus longtemps sur Internet? Et vous?

---

[1]*provides* [2]*households* [3]*spread* [4]*register* [5]*software* [6]*a slight delay* [7]*Germany* [8]*Netherlands* [9]*England*
[10]On utilise en français aussi le verbe **chatter** de l'anglais *to chat*. L'expression française équivalente c'est la messagerie instantanée.

Continuons!

Les sports extrêmes

Arielle Carnus est journaliste pour l'émission *Vie publique, Vie privée*. Le sujet du magazine cette semaine c'est «Sports et hobbies extrêmes: Quand les pratiquerez-vous et où?» Arielle a interviewé des personnes dans les rues de quelques grandes villes françaises. Écoutez les réponses des personnes qui pratiquent des sports ou des hobbies pas comme les autres.

Online Study Center
Language Skills Practice

This section contains verbs in the future tense. You may want to make students aware of this new tense (the stems are the same as those of the conditional, which they learned in the previous chapter). The future tense is presented in detail in *Structure 2*.

UN PASSANT: Moi, je ferai du saut à l'élastique l'été prochain. Je sauterai du viaduc de L'Isle-Jourdain qui se trouve au nord de Bordeaux. Je veux sentir la sensation de vide[1] sous moi.

UN AUTRE PASSANT: Le week-end prochain j'irai faire du parapente avec ma copine sur la montagne du Salève près de Genève. Nous descendrons chacun avec un moniteur[2] en parachute et nous volerons! Super, non?

UN GROUPE D'AMIS: Pendant nos vacances à Toulouse, nous ferons du deltaplane. Le vol libre nous aidera à nous sentir vraiment libres!

---

[1] *emptiness* [2] *instructor*

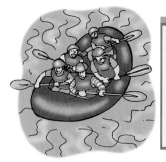

UNE FAMILLE: Bientôt—dans 10 jours exactement—toute la famille prendra un avion pour aller à Montréal où nous ferons du rafting dans les rapides de Lachine sur le fleuve Saint-Laurent. Les rivières du Québec sont les meilleures pour pratiquer ce sport. Dans la famille, nous aimons tous les émotions fortes!

DEUX COPAINS: Demain nous volerons sur l'eau à l'aide d'un bateau en parachute ascensionnel. Nous volerons sur la Méditerranée depuis la baie de Cannes à Mandelieu-La Napoule. Nous aurons chacun notre parachute et nous pourrons admirer les plages depuis une position privilégiée.

UNE PASSANTE: Comme tous les week-ends, samedi prochain je ferai du VTT—vélo tout terrain—avec mes amis. C'est un sport stimulant[1] mais qui me permet de décompresser après une semaine chargée de travail.

Vous avez bien compris?

Définitions. Devinez de quel sport il s'agit d'après les indications données.

1. le rafting
2. le VTT
3. le saut à l'élastique
4. le parachute ascensionnel
5. le deltaplane
6. le parapente

a. On a besoin d'une force qui fait monter haut pour pratiquer ce sport.
b. Ce sport est parfait pour faire des randonnées à bicyclette.
c. On a besoin d'un bateau à moteur assez puissant[2].
d. Dans ce sport on a besoin de bateaux pneumatiques.
e. C'est un sport où le parachute a la forme d'un triangle.
f. Dans ce sport on rebondit quand on se jette dans le vide.

---

[1]*challenging* [2]*powerful*

Vocabulaire essentiel

Les sports d'hiver et d'autres sports

Online Study Center
Flashcards, ACE, Language
Skills Practice

la luge

le ski alpin

le ski de fond

le surf des neiges
(ou le snowboard)

Les sports nautiques

Point out to students that the
vocabulary presented in the
Continuons! section is also
Vocabulaire essentiel.

le jet ski

le ski nautique

la pêche

D'autres sports

la varappe

l'alpinisme *(m.)*

Expansion personnelle

l'escalade *(f.)* sur glace

l'héliski *(m.)*

le traîneau à chiens

la pêche au gros
(requin, thon, etc.)

À vous!

A. Identifications. Regardez les dessins et identifiez les sports.

1. 2. 3. 4.

5. 6. 7. 8.

Maintenant, dites à la classe quel sport de ceux qui sont mentionnés dans l'activité vous pratiquez en ce moment. Quel est le sport le plus pratiqué dans la classe?

B. Quel est leur sport? Décidez quels sont les sports qui vont le mieux aux personnes suivantes.

1. Charlotte adore faire du bateau.
2. Michel aime les randonnées en montagne. Il veut sortir en hiver.
3. Ali a le vertige. Il a peur des hauteurs.
4. Dorothée aime la vitesse.
5. Leila aime les sports d'hiver.
6. Adrien préfère garder les pieds sur terre[1].
7. Margot adore être en contact avec la nature.
8. Aurélien a beaucoup d'équilibre et beaucoup de force dans les bras et les jambes.

C. Quel est ton sport? Posez les questions suivantes à un(e) camarade de classe pour savoir quel genre de sport il/elle préfère.

1. Préfères-tu les sports d'hiver ou les sports nautiques? Pourquoi?
2. As-tu déjà fait du parachute ascensionnel? Voudrais-tu essayer en faire? Pourquoi?
3. As-tu fait du ski? Si oui, préfères-tu le ski de fond ou le ski alpin? Pourquoi?
4. Si c'était permis, ferais-tu du saut à l'élastique du Golden Gate Bridge à San Francisco? Pourquoi?
5. Quelle activité sportive est-ce que tu n'oserais[2] jamais faire? Pourquoi?
6. Quel sport extrême as-tu envie d'essayer? Pourquoi?
7. De quoi as-tu peur? Quel sport t'aiderait à vaincre[3] cette peur?

En fonction des réponses que votre camarade vous a données, déterminez quel genre de personne il/elle est. Choisissez la réponse qui convient le mieux.

a. Tu es une personne audacieuse et courageuse.
b. Tu es une personne qui n'aime ni le danger ni le risque.
c. Tu es une personne qui n'aime pas les défis[4].
d. Tu es une personne qui cherche toujours des sensations fortes.

Qui est l'étudiant(e) le/la plus aventureux(euse)[5] de la classe?

Structure 2

Le futur

Online Study Center
ACE, Language Skills Practice

Uses: As its name implies, the future tense (**le futur**) can be used to express an action that will occur in the future. It may refer to an event in the near future (perhaps tomorrow) or at a later date.

Demain, je paierai les factures.
L'année prochaine, nous partirons pour le Maroc.

Tomorrow I will pay the bills.
Next year, we will leave for Morocco.

---

[1]*ground* [2]*would not dare* [3]*to overcome* [4]*challenge* [5]*daring*

The future tense can also be used in a sentence that has an *if* clause when it is
certain that the event will occur if the event in the *if* clause occurs. In such cases,
the pattern is: **si** + present tense + main clause in the future tense.

S'il pleut demain, nous n'irons pas faire du ski nautique.	*If it rains tomorrow, we will not go water-skiing.*
Si vous arrivez en retard, l'avion partira sans vous.	*If you arrive late, the plane will leave without you.*
Si tu ne m'appelles pas, je ne te parlerai plus.	*If you don't call me, I won't talk to you ever again.*

Formation. For both regular and irregular verbs, the future shares the same stems
as the conditional. However, the endings are different: **-ai, -as, -a, -ons, -ez, -ont.**
To help you remember these endings, think of the verb **avoir** in the present tense:
j'*ai*, tu *as*, il *a*, etc.

Regular verbs		
parler	**partir**	**prendre**
je parler**ai**	je partir**ai**	je prendr**ai**
tu parler**as**	tu partir**as**	tu prendr**as**
il / elle / on parler**a**	il / elle / on partir**a**	il / elle / on prendr**a**
nous parler**ons**	nous partir**ons**	nous prendr**ons**
vous parler**ez**	vous partir**ez**	vous prendr**ez**
ils / elles parler**ont**	ils / elles partir**ont**	ils / elles prendr**ont**

The same verbs that are irregular in the conditional are also irregular in the future,
as they use the same stems.

Irregular verbs	
aller ➡ j'**ir**ai	payer ➡ je **paier**ai
avoir ➡ j'**aur**ai	devoir ➡ je **devr**ai
être ➡ je **ser**ai	vouloir ➡ je **voudr**ai
faire ➡ je **fer**ai	envoyer ➡ j'**enverr**ai
venir ➡ je **viendr**ai	savoir ➡ je **saur**ai
recevoir ➡ je **recevr**ai	acheter ➡ j'**achèter**ai
voir ➡ je **verr**ai	appeler ➡ j'**appeller**ai
pouvoir ➡ je **pourr**ai	

La semaine prochaine, ils ir**ont** faire du rafting.	*Next week, they will go rafting.*
Dans un mois, vous verr**ez** votre famille.	*In a month, you will see your family.*

1. Go back to the **Continuons!** section (pp. 421–422) and identify the verbs in the future tense. Look at the form and think about the subject. For example, in the sentence **Le vol libre nous aidera à nous sentir vraiment libres,** is the subject of the verb in the future tense **nous** or **le vol libre?**

2. Once you have identified all the verbs in the future tense, give the infinitive for each one. Is it an irregular or a regular verb?

À l'écoute! 🎧

Conditionnel ou futur? Écoutez les phrases suivantes au conditionnel et au futur. Indiquez le temps que vous entendez.

1. _____ conditionnel   _____ futur
2. _____ conditionnel   _____ futur
3. _____ conditionnel   _____ futur
4. _____ conditionnel   _____ futur
5. _____ conditionnel   _____ futur
6. _____ conditionnel   _____ futur
7. _____ conditionnel   _____ futur
8. _____ conditionnel   _____ futur
9. _____ conditionnel   _____ futur

Audioscript: 1. Mes parents viendront chez moi. 2. Nous verrons un film. 3. Aurais-tu des enfants? 4. Prendras-tu ta voiture pour aller au ciné? 5. Voudriez-vous du café? 6. Est-ce que Marie sera contente en France? 7. Il pourrait gagner au loto cette fois-ci! 8. Vous ferez du ski alpin en Suisse? 9. Nous devrions partir. Il est tard.

Pratiquons!

A. Que feront-ils demain? Regardez les dessins suivants et dites ce que les personnes feront demain. (Pensez au verbe à l'infinitif d'abord et ensuite, mettez-le au futur.)

1. Clothilde

2. Je

3. Vous

4. Tu

5. Nous

6. Brigitte et Clémentine

Answer Key: 1. Clothilde parlera au téléphone / téléphonera. 2. Je dormirai. 3. Vous nagerez. 4. Tu liras. 5. Nous travaillerons sur l'ordinateur / enverrons des courriels / écrirons des messages par ordinateur. 6. Brigitte et Clémentine boiront un café.

B. Une brochure du Club Vacances. Vous travaillez au Club Vacances et votre patron vous a chargé(e) de terminer une brochure qui annonce les activités qui sont possibles au Club Vacances dans différents pays. Complétez la brochure en mettant les verbes entre parenthèses au futur.

Si vous venez au Club Vacances, vous (1) _____ (être) toujours les bienvenus et vous (2) _____ (s'amuser) comme des **fous! Garanti!**

Au Club Vacances de Fort-de-France en Martinique, les GO (les Gentils Organisateurs) vous (3) _____ (prendre) en charge et ils vous (4) _____ (proposer) de faire de la plongée sous-marine[1]. Après quoi, vous (5) _____ (pouvoir) prendre un bain de soleil sur le sable chaud de la magnifique plage des Salines.

Au Club Vacances d'Agadir au Maroc, vous (6) _____ (pratiquer) tous les sports nautiques de votre choix. Depuis Agadir, on vous (7) _____ (conduire) à Marrakech pour assister à des fêtes locales, comme la Fantasia[2]. Vous (8) _____ (se promener) dans la palmeraie, vous (9) _____ (voir) des objets d'artisanat dans le souk[3] ou vous (10) _____ (faire) des promenades dans les petites rues étroites de la ville.

Au Club Vacances de Chamonix dans les Alpes françaises, les GO vous (11) _____ (guider) sur les pistes[4] de ski où vous (12) _____ (descendre) en ski entre les sapins[5] jusqu'au village.

Pour les moins jeunes, on vous (13) _____ (recommander) le ski de fond.

Chaque soir après le dîner, vous (14) _____ (avoir) toutes sortes de divertissements: danse, bingo et cinéma.

Club Vacances

C. Décidez! D'après la brochure du Club Vacances de l'activité B, choisissez un pays et décidez quelles activités vous pratiquerez pendant vos vacances. D'abord, dites au futur vos projets à un(e) camarade de classe.

> MODÈLE: Pendant les vacances, j'irai au Maroc. Comme sport nautique je ferai du parachutisme ascensionnel et du ski nautique. J'irai à Marrakech et je me promènerai dans les rues de la ville.

Ensuite, racontez à la classe les projets de vacances de votre camarade.

> MODÈLE: Melissa ira au Maroc pendant les vacances. Comme sport nautique elle fera du parachutisme ascensionnel, etc.

---

[1]*deep-sea diving* [2]La Fantasia est une coutume ancestrale, des cavaliers simulent une charge à cheval en tirant des coups de fusil *(shooting)* en l'air. [3]*market* [4]*slopes* [5]*fir-trees*

D. Le week-end prochain. Trouvez cinq camarades de classe qui vont pratiquer les activités et les sports suivants pendant le week-end. Écrivez leurs noms à côté de chaque réponse affirmative. Ensuite, dites à la classe ce que trois étudiants vont faire le week-end prochain. Qui va avoir un super week-end? Et un week-end horrible?

MODÈLE: faire du rafting (où?)

—*Est-ce que tu feras du rafting le week-end prochain?*

—*Oui, j'en ferai. (Oui, je ferai du rafting.)*

—*Où est-ce que tu en feras? (Où feras-tu du rafting?)*

—*J'en ferai au Colorado.*

1. être sur Internet (pourquoi?)
2. envoyer des courriels (à qui?)
3. acheter des vêtements (où?)
4. faire de l'héliski (où?)
5. faire les devoirs (lesquels[1]?)
6. voir un film au cinéma (quel film?)
7. venir à l'université (pourquoi?)
8. faire du saut à l'élastique (où?)
9. se lever très tard (à quelle heure?)
10. recevoir des amis à la maison (pourquoi?)

Portrait personnel

Écrivez un paragraphe où vous comparez trois de vos camarades de classe. Quelles activités aiment-ils? Quel sport est-ce qu'ils ne font jamais? Qui est le plus aventureux (aventureuse)?

À vous de parler!

A. À l'agence des sports et des loisirs[2]. Vous et votre meilleur(e) ami(e) voulez expérimenter des vacances différentes des autres. Pour cela, vous vous rendez dans une agence spécialisée en sports et loisirs extrêmes. Décrivez à l'agent votre personnalité et vos goûts personnels afin qu'il/elle vous trouve des vacances sur mesure[3].

Voici quelques options proposées par l'agence à ses clients:

Sports de glisse[4] dans des snowparks à Avoriaz dans les Alpes

surf des neiges	ski alpin
ski de fond	héliski

Sports nautiques dans l'océan Pacifique à Tahiti

canoë	aquagym[5]	parachutisme ascensionnel
kayak	sandboard	

MODÈLE: CLIENT(E): Bonjour, Monsieur / Madame. Je voudrais partir en vacances dans un endroit où je pourrai expérimenter des émotions fortes. J'adore me trouver[6] face au danger et au risque! Que me proposez-vous?

AGENT: Aimez-vous les sports nautiques ou préférez-vous les sports de glisse? ...

---

[1] *which ones* [2] *leisure activities* [3] *custom made* [4] *snow sports* [5] *water aerobics* [6] *to find myself*

B. Des vacances sur mesure! Vous et votre meilleur(e) ami(e) sortez de l'agence des sports et des loisirs très content(e)s car l'agent vous a proposé des vacances parfaites. Vous retrouvez vos amis au bistro du coin et vous leur racontez tout ce que vous ferez pendant vos vacances. Vos amis vont être très jaloux! Ils vous posent beaucoup de questions pour en savoir plus! Vont-ils vous copier?

MODÈLE: ÉTUDIANT(E) 1: *Alors, raconte, qu'est-ce que l'agent de voyages a suggéré?*

ÉTUDIANT(E) 2: *Il nous a dit que nous pourrons aller à une plage au Maroc et faire du sandboard.*

ÉTUDIANT(E) 3: *Oui, et il nous a aussi dit que nous pourrons faire du kayak dans la mer Méditerranée! Tu imagines?! …*

Online Study Center
Web Search Activities

Les Africains sont branchés comme ça

Malgré un retard considérable en Afrique (1 internaute pour 150 habitants, alors que la moyenne mondiale est de 1 pour 15), le nombre d'Africains qui utilisent l'Internet et d'autres services technologiques de l'information et de la communication commence a augmenter petit à petit. Les 54 pays africains ont tous un accès à l'Internet. Bien sûr la vitesse des connexions n'est pas la même dans tous les pays car elle dépend de la qualité des télécommunications. Par exemple, la vitesse d'accès au Togo et au Niger est de 500 kilobits, au Sénégal de 100 mégabits, au Maroc de 300 mébagits et en Afrique du Sud de 400 mégabits.

Il y a une grande disparité entre le nombre d'Africains francophones qui utilisent l'Internet suivant le pays où ils habitent. En Afrique du Nord, la Tunisie compte 350.000 internautes (pour 9,6 millions d'habitants), le Maroc 500.000 (pour 28,7 millions d'habitants) et l'Algérie 180.000 (pour 30 millions d'habitants).

Dans les grandes villes il existe de nombreux cybercentres et cybercafés. Le premier cybercafé, le Métissacana, est arrivé au Sénégal en 1996. Africa Online, qui est le plus important pourvoyeur[1] d'accès à l'Internet dans le continent africain, a créé beaucoup de cybercentres appelés e-touch. L'ordinateur en Afrique n'est pas individuel et personnel. En effet, son usage est collectif et «social» car il est partagé entre plusieurs personnes dans les cybercafés et les cybercentres.

Cependant, l'utilisation des technologies de télécommunication ne se limite pas à l'usage de l'Internet. À Dakar, par exemple, les paysans et les pêcheurs peuvent avec leurs téléphones portables regarder et comparer les prix des fruits, des légumes et des poissons dans tous les marchés du pays.

Un progrès important en matière de télécommunication a été l'installation à Dakar le 28 mai 2002 du premier cable numérique sous-marin qui connecte le sud au nord. Ce cable, le SAT3, est d'une longueur de 28.000 kilomètres (17.500 milles) et a une capacité de 120 gigabits.

Il reste encore beaucoup à faire pour diminuer le retard technologique en Afrique. Cependant, le regard qui se porte vers le futur se concentre sur l'alphabétisation (plus les gens pourront lire et écrire plus ils profiteront des nouvelles technologies) et l'introduction de l'informatique dans les écoles comme une matière obligatoire. De cette façon, les tout petits se familiariseront avec l'utilisation des ordinateurs et peut-être que demain, ils deviendront les premiers programmateurs et créateurs de logiciels africains.

---

[1] *provider*

Réfléchissons

1. Vous venez de lire qu'en Afrique il existe de nombreux cybercentres et cybercafés. Pourquoi? Est-ce surprenant?
2. Y a-t-il beaucoup de cybercentres dans votre ville? Pourquoi? Aimez-vous aller aux cybercafés? Quand y allez-vous?
3. À quel âge avez-vous appris à utiliser un ordinateur? L'avez-vous appris à l'école? Chez vous?
4. Pourquoi est-ce que le texte prédit[1] qu'il y aura beaucoup plus de programmateurs et de créateurs de logiciels africains dans l'avenir que maintenant?

Answer Key: 1. Non, ce n'est pas surprenant, parce que beaucoup d'Africains n'ont pas leur propre ordinateur. En Afrique l'ordinateur n'est pas individuel, mais collectif/social. 2–3. *Answers will vary.* 4. Parce que l'éducation se concentre maintenant sur l'alphabétisation et l'informatique; donc il y aura plus de personnes qui sauront lire et utiliser un ordinateur.

À vous de lire!

Online Study Center
Language Skills Practice

A. Stratégies. Skimming and Scanning. Earlier, you learned that skimming a text to get a general impression of what it is about is an important strategy when reading, as it helps us to make predictions about the text and thus aids the reading process. An equally important strategy, with a different focus, is that of scanning. When you scan a text, you are trying to determine if the text contains certain information that is of interest to you. If you find the information you are looking for, you may decide to read the text more carefully. If not, you may choose to pass on to another text. We often use scanning (as well as skimming) while reading newspapers and other expository prose: we look for key words and phrases to signal the presence of the information we seek.

Scan the text of *Innovations technologiques: Le tunnel sous la Manche* and determine if it would be a good source of the following information.

1. the history of the Channel Tunnel between France and England
2. prices for taking the tunnel train
3. the speed of the tunnel train, and the amount of time it takes to go from Paris to London
4. alternative means of traveling between Paris and London
5. the types of cabins offered on the tunnel train

Answer Key: 1. oui 2. non 3. oui 4. non 5. non

B. Avant de lire

Considérons le sujet: Le passage suivant concerne le tunnel qui relie la Grande-Bretagne à l'Europe. Avant de lire le passage, faites une liste des informations que vous vous attendez[2] à voir dans un passage de cette sorte. Quelles informations techniques, historiques ou culturelles est-ce que vous pensez que les auteurs vous donneront?

Considérons le vocabulaire: Étant donné le sujet de ce passage, essayez de deviner ce que les mots et expressions suivants veulent dire, et écrivez une définition ou traduction.

1. une traversée en mer

   _____

2. avoir le pied marin

   _____

3. faire preuve d'imagination

   _____

If you have a group of students who express themselves well in French, ask them to write a definition for each term in French, without translating into English. They may find this easier to do in pairs. Alternately, you may ask them to write a translation.

Answer Key: 1. un voyage en mer / *a sea crossing* 2. être habitué à naviguer / *to get your sea legs* 3. avoir beaucoup d'imagination / *to show lots of imagination*

---

[1]*predicts* [2]*expect*

4. bateau sous-marin

5. pont ferroviaire

6. à vive allure

7. foré sous la mer

8. un havre de sécurité

C. Lisons! Lisez le passage maintenant et puis répondez aux questions qui le suivent.

Innovations technologiques: Le tunnel sous la Manche

Il y a quelques 10.000 ans, une parcelle de terre reliait l'Angleterre à la France. Peu à peu, la mer a pris ses droits et la Manche[1] a fait de la Grande-Bretagne une île.

Depuis plus de deux siècles, une grande question technique et politique se posait: comment relier à nouveau les deux pays sans les inconvénients d'une traversée en mer. Même la Reine Victoria qui n'avait pas le pied marin encourageait les projets: «en mon nom et celui de toutes les ladies d'Angleterre».

Les idées ne manquaient pas et des ingénieurs ont fait preuve d'imagination, à la manière parfois des écrivains de science-fiction. Parmi les propositions, on retrouve la construction d':

- un bateau sous-marin sur rail (1869)
- un pont ferroviaire posé sur des piliers à 90 mètres au-dessus de la mer pour laisser passer les navires (1882)

Autant de projets tombés à l'eau en attendant le tunnel sous la Manche que nous connaissons. Commencé en 1988, il a été inauguré le 6 mai 1994 par la Reine d'Angleterre et François Mitterrand, le Président de la République française d'alors.

Grâce à cette fantastique œuvre humaine, l'Europe se tient ... par la Manche. La Grande-Bretagne est devenue une presqu'île: il faut compter 20 minutes de traversée à 40 mètres sous le fond de la mer. Londres (Waterloo Station) se trouve à 3 heures de Paris (Gare du Nord) par Eurostar: le train qui peut accueillir 774 voyageurs. Ce TGV «transmanche» atteint une vitesse de pointe de 300 kilomètres/heure. Le «shuttle», drôle de train-navette, permet aux voitures, bus, camions de se ranger sur de gros wagons pour traverser la Manche à vive allure aussi.

Le tunnel sous la Manche a une longueur de 50 kilomètres; les 39 kilomètres forés sous la Manche en font le plus long tunnel sous-marin au monde. Le système de transport Eurotunnel est formé de trois tunnels: deux tunnels, réservés à la circulation ferroviaire (navettes et trains), reliés à un

---

[1] *English Channel*

troisième tunnel de service central. Le tunnel de service, unique au monde, joue le rôle d'un havre de sécurité; il est en effet maintenu en état de surpression d'air, restant ainsi à l'abri des fumées en cas d'incendie.

57 millions de personnes, ce qui équivaut à la population totale de la Grande-Bretagne, ont emprunté le tunnel sous la Manche par des navettes Eurotunnel, entre 1994 et 2000.

1. Quand est-ce qu'on a commencé à penser à relier l'Europe et la Grande-Bretagne?
2. Est-ce qu'on a pensé tout de suite à faire un tunnel? Si non, quelles ont été les autres suggestions données?
3. Les auteurs comparent ces suggestions à quoi?
4. Quand est-ce qu'on a commencé à creuser le tunnel? Quand est-ce qu'on l'a terminé? Est-ce que cela vous paraît longtemps ou peu de temps? Expliquez votre réponse en citant quelques données technologiques concernant le tunnel.
5. Qu'est-ce qu'il y a d'unique concernant ce tunnel? Pourquoi est-ce que c'est important?
6. Est-ce que le tunnel sous la Manche est bien ou peu utilisé, selon vous? Expliquez votre réponse.

D. Après la lecture. Imaginez que vous allez voyager de Paris à Londres (ou vice versa) par le train. Que ferez-vous? Que verrez-vous? Avec qui est-ce que vous voyagerez? Écrivez un paragraphe où vous décrivez votre journée, en employant le futur.

MODÈLE: Je me lèverai tôt le matin, et j'irai à la gare avec mon amie Gisèle. Nous prendrons le tunnel sous la Manche pour aller à Londres. Le voyage sera court! À Londres, nous visiterons …

Lexique ⌒

Vocabulaire essentiel

La technologie d'aujourd'hui

Les ordinateurs *computers*

un clavier *keyboard*
une connexion haut débit *high-speed connection*
un écran *screen*
un graveur de CD *CD burner*
un haut-parleur *speaker*

une imprimante *printer*
une imprimante couleur *color printer*
un lecteur de CD *CD player*
un lecteur de DVD *DVD player*
un modem *modem*

un moniteur *monitor*
un (ordinateur) portable *laptop computer*
une souris *mouse*

D'autres gadgets technologiques

une adresse électronique *e-mail address*
un agenda *calendar*
un appareil photo numérique *digital camera*
un assistant personnel *PDA*
un baladeur numérique *digital portable audio player*

un graveur de DVD *DVD burner*
le home cinéma *home theater*
l'Internet (m.) / le Net *Internet*
un mobile *cell phone*
un scanner *scanner*
un (téléphone) portable *cell phone*

le télétexte *text message*
le Web / la Toile *World Wide Web*

Des activités technologiques

avoir un mot de passe *to have a password*
cliquer *to click*
envoyer un courriel / un e-mail *to send an e-mail*
envoyer une pièce ci-jointe *to send an attachment*

graver un CD *to burn a CD*
naviguer sur le Web / sur la Toile *to navigate the Web*
recevoir un courriel / un e-mail *to receive an e-mail*
surfer sur Internet / être sur Internet *to surf the Internet*

utiliser un moteur de recherche *to use a search engine*
utiliser un traitement de texte *to use a word processor*

Les sports vol libre ou chute libre *free-fly or free-fall sports*

le deltaplane *hang-gliding*
le parachute ascensionnel *parasailing*

le parapente *paragliding*
le saut à l'élastique *bungee jumping*

Les sports d'hiver *winter sports*

la luge *sledding*
le ski alpin *downhill skiing*
le ski de fond *cross-country skiing*

le surf des neiges (ou le snowboard) *snowboarding*

Les sports nautiques *water sports*

le jet ski *Jet Ski™*
la pêche *fishing*

le rafting *rafting*
le ski nautique *waterskiing*

D'autres sports

l'alpinisme *(m.) mountain
 climbing*

la varappe *rock-climbing*
le VTT *cross-country biking*

Expansion personnelle

l'escalade *(f.) sur glace ice-
 covered mountain climbing*
l'héliski *(m.) heli-skiing*

la pêche au gros (requin, thon,
 etc.) *deep-sea fishing (shark,
 tuna, etc.)*

le traîneau à chiens *dogsledding*

Je suis en forme!

In this chapter, you will learn how to tell what you do to get in shape or stay in shape. You will learn to talk about the activities people can do at a fitness center. You will be able to give advice to a friend or to your family so that they can be in the best shape ever! Finally, you will express your own opinions regarding health issues.

The vocabulary that you will learn includes

Fitness center activities
Staying in shape
Impersonal expressions to express your opinion

The structures that you will learn include

The present subjunctive (regular and irregular verbs)
Usage of the subjunctive vs. an infinitive
Disjunctive pronouns

The culture that you will study includes

How the French pamper themselves to attain well-being
The French and soccer

Commençons!

Au centre de fitness 🎧

Online Study Center
Language Skills Practice

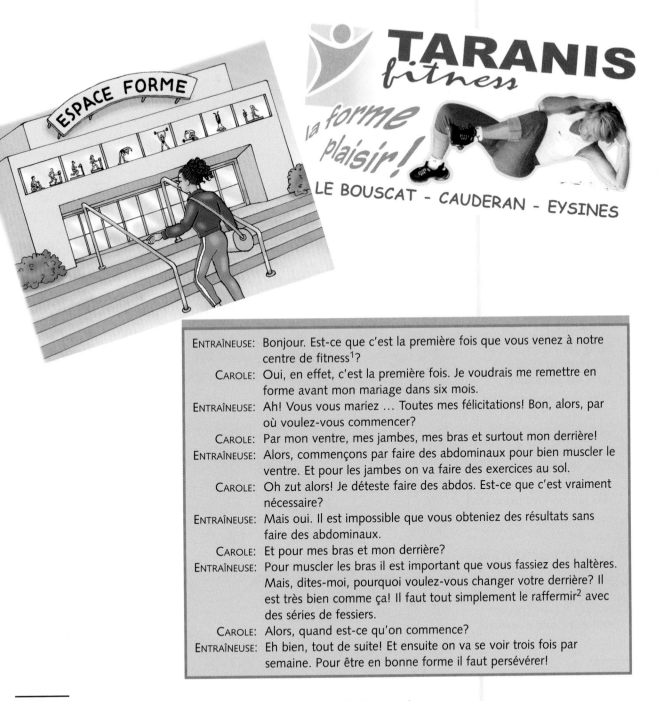

TARANIS *fitness*

la forme plaisir!

LE BOUSCAT - CAUDERAN - EYSINES

ESPACE FORME

ENTRAÎNEUSE: Bonjour. Est-ce que c'est la première fois que vous venez à notre centre de fitness[1]?

CAROLE: Oui, en effet, c'est la première fois. Je voudrais me remettre en forme avant mon mariage dans six mois.

ENTRAÎNEUSE: Ah! Vous vous mariez … Toutes mes félicitations! Bon, alors, par où voulez-vous commencer?

CAROLE: Par mon ventre, mes jambes, mes bras et surtout mon derrière!

ENTRAÎNEUSE: Alors, commençons par faire des abdominaux pour bien muscler le ventre. Et pour les jambes on va faire des exercices au sol.

CAROLE: Oh zut alors! Je déteste faire des abdos. Est-ce que c'est vraiment nécessaire?

ENTRAÎNEUSE: Mais oui. Il est impossible que vous obteniez des résultats sans faire des abdominaux.

CAROLE: Et pour mes bras et mon derrière?

ENTRAÎNEUSE: Pour muscler les bras il est important que vous fassiez des haltères. Mais, dites-moi, pourquoi voulez-vous changer votre derrière? Il est très bien comme ça! Il faut tout simplement le raffermir[2] avec des séries de fessiers.

CAROLE: Alors, quand est-ce qu'on commence?

ENTRAÎNEUSE: Eh bien, tout de suite! Et ensuite on va se voir trois fois par semaine. Pour être en bonne forme il faut persévérer!

---

[1]A fitness center can also be called **un club de gym, un club de fitness,** or **une salle de sports.** [2]*to tone*

Vous avez bien compris?

Quels sont les conseils que l'entraîneuse donne à Carole pour muscler son corps?

1. Pour le ventre il faut …
2. Pour les bras il faut …
3. Pour les jambes il faut …
4. Pour le derrière elle doit …
5. Avant son mariage il faut …
6. Pour être en forme il faut …

a. se remettre en forme.
b. faire des abdominaux.
c. faire des exercices au sol.
d. être discipliné.
e. faire des haltères.
f. faire des fessiers.

The illustration for **s'entraîner** shows a swim team doing laps. You may want to give another example so that students do not think **s'entraîner** means **nager**, e.g., Pour s'entraîner à un triathlon, on peut courir, nager, ramer, pédaler ou faire de la muscu. Et pour se préparer à un marathon, comment s'entraîne-t-on?

Online Study Center
Flashcards, ACE, Language
Skills Practice

Vocabulaire essentiel

Au centre de fitness

1. faire du sport /
   pratiquer un sport
2. faire des abdominaux
   (faire des abdos)
3. **faire des fessiers** *(m.)*
4. faire des haltères *(m.)*
5. faire des exercices *(m.)* au sol
6. **faire des exercices
   d'échauffement
   (s'échauffer)**
7. **faire des exercices
   d'étirement (s'étirer) /
   faire du stretching**
8. **faire des pompes** *(f.)*
9. pédaler
10. **ramer**
11. faire de la musculation
    (faire de la muscu)
12. **se raffermir
    (les jambes, les bras, etc.)**
13. courir[1]
14. marcher
15. nager (faire de la natation)
16. s'entraîner
17. **sauter à la corde**
18. **se faire masser (par un
    masseur / une masseuse)**

[1]La conjugaison de *courir* est irrégulière:
*je cours, tu cours, il court, nous courons,
vous courez, ils courent.*

Expansion personnelle

The vocabulary words that are in boldface in the preceding section are *Expansion personnelle.*

Once students have answered all the questions, you may want to say what is happening in each illustration and have the students act it out (TPR).

À vous!

A. Au club de fitness. Regardez les dessins et décrivez les activités que font les personnes suivantes.

Answer Key: 1. Il fait des haltères. 2. Elle nage. 3. Elles font du stretching / s'étirent. 4. Elle se fait masser. 5. Il fait du jogging. 6. Ils rament. 7. Elle saute à la corde. 8. Ils pédalent.

1. 2. 3. 4.

5. 6. 7. 8.

B. Que fait-on? Indiquez les activités que vous pouvez faire dans chaque cas.

> 🔲 MODÈLE: avant de faire du sport
>
> *On s'étire ou on s'échauffe.*

1. pour être musclé
2. sur une bicyclette
3. sur un bateau
4. avant un marathon
5. dans un gymnase
6. pour ne pas être sédentaire
7. à la piscine
8. avec des haltères
9. avec une corde

Answer Key. Possible answers: 1. On fait des haltères / des pompes / des exercices au sol. 2. On pédale / fait du vélo / fait de la bicyclette. 3. On rame / bronze. 4. On s'étire / s'échauffe / persévère / s'entraîne. 5. On fait du sport / de l'exercice. 6. On fait du sport. 7. On nage / bronze. 8. On fait de la muscu / se muscle (les bras, les jambes, etc.). 9. On saute / s'échauffe.

👥C. Es-tu sportif/sportive? Avec un(e) partenaire, comparez vos routines sportives. Posez-vous les questions suivantes à tour de rôle. Choisissez l'expression qui vous convient ou inventez votre réponse.

1. Je vais au club de gym (une fois par semaine / tous les jours / le week-end / quand j'ai le temps / avec mes amis / quand je mange trop / …).
2. Je ne vais (jamais / pas / plus) au centre de fitness parce que (c'est trop cher / je déteste faire de l'exercice / mon corps est parfait / il n'y a pas de centre de fitness où j'habite / …).
3. Il faut que je fasse du sport pour (être bien dans ma peau[1] / impressionner mon/ma petit(e) ami(e) / avoir une vie équilibrée / avoir un corps bien musclé / …).

---

[1]*to feel good about myself*

4. Pour être en forme je (fais de la muscu tous les jours / cours 3 kilomètres le samedi / …).
5. Avant de faire du sport il est nécessaire que je fasse (…).
6. Quand je vais au club de fitness je fais mes séries d'exercices (avec un[e] entraîneur [entraîneuse] / avec un[e] ami[e] / tout[e] seul[e] / …).

Portrait personnel

Après avoir complété l'activité C, tracez la routine sportive de votre camarade en donnant le plus de détails possible.

Structure 1

Online Study Center
ACE, Language Skills
Practice

Le présent du subjonctif

L'emploi du subjonctif. In previous chapters, you saw various uses of the *indicative mood.* The indicative is used to indicate fact, and it is used in past, present, and future time frames. From the speaker's point of view, the indicative denotes *objectivity:* the activities and states mentioned are virtually certain to occur, or have already occurred. Furthermore, there is little emotional involvement on the part of the speaker; he or she is simply stating fact.

The *subjunctive mood,* in contrast, denotes *subjectivity* on the part of the speaker, who is relating an event as he or she views it, and who acknowledges that this view may not be the same for other speakers. The subjunctive is therefore used following expressions of necessity, emotion, volition, doubt, and possibility. To a native speaker of French, usage of the subjunctive mood implies that other interpretations of the necessity, desirability, or possibility of an activity or state are conceivable. Read the following statements.

Chaque soir, avant de se coucher, Marie **boit** un verre d'eau.
Hier, après avoir fait du jogging, Marie **a bu** un verre d'eau.
Avant de se coucher ce soir, Marie **boira** un verre d'eau.

These three statements indicate simply what Marie does normally, did recently, or will do in the future. Because they indicate fact, they use a form of the indicative. Compare these sentences with the following statement.

Si Marie veut maigrir, il faut qu'elle **boive** huit verres d'eau chaque jour.

This sentence indicates what Marie *needs to do* in order to accomplish some goal. Exactly what is presumed necessary can vary, however, depending on the speaker; this statement is therefore expressed using the subjunctive, to indicate that it is the speaker's point of view that is being expressed.

One of the most common uses of the subjunctive in French is to express necessity. There are several verbal expressions that allow you to do this.

Pour être en bonne santé[1] et bien équilibré(e) …

il faut que tu manges beaucoup de fruits et de légumes.
il est nécessaire que tu dormes huit heures par nuit.
il est essentiel que tu aimes ton travail.
il est indispensable que tu ne te stresses pas trop.
il vaut mieux que[2] tu choisisses un style de vie équilibré.

---

[1]*to be healthy* [2]*it is better that*

La formation du subjonctif des verbes réguliers. The subjunctive mood exists in present and past tense forms only. In *À vous!* you will use only the present subjunctive. The present subjunctive is formed by adding a set of regular endings to a verb stem. These endings, for all verbs except **être** and **avoir,** are as follows.

(je)	**-e**	(nous)	**-ions**
(tu)	**-es**	(vous)	**-iez**
(il / elle / on)	**-e**	(ils / elles)	**-ent**

For regular **-er, -ir,** and **-re** verbs, the subjunctive stem is found by taking the third person plural of the present indicative and dropping the **-ent** ending.

manger – ils mang~~ent~~	finir – ils finiss~~ent~~	vendre – ils vend~~ent~~
Il faut …		
que je **mange**	que je **finisse**	que je **vende**
que tu **manges**	que tu **finisses**	que tu **vendes**
qu'il / elle / on **mange**	qu'il / elle / on **finisse**	qu'il / elle / on **vende**
que nous **mangions**	que nous **finissions**	que nous **vendions**
que vous **mangiez**	que vous **finissiez**	que vous **vendiez**
qu'ils / elles **mangent**	qu'ils / elles **finissent**	qu'ils / elles **vendent**

Notice that the pronunciation and spelling of **-er** verbs differ from the present indicative only for the **nous** and **vous** forms (**vous mangez / que vous mangiez**); however, for **-ir** and **-re** verbs the two moods are different in all persons: **Je finis mes devoirs / Il faut que je finisse mes devoirs. Tu vends ta voiture / Il faut que tu vendes ta voiture.**

 VÉRIFIEZ VOTRE COMPRÉHENSION

1. Look back at the example sentences in **Structure 1: L'usage du subjonctif.** What subjunctive verbs can you find? Underline them and give their infinitive. Do the same with the dialogue on page 437.

2. Why is the subjunctive used instead of the indicative in these sentences?

Pratiquons!

A. Pour bien faire. Refaites chaque phrase avec les pronoms donnés et la forme appropriée du verbe au subjonctif.

1. Avant de courir, il faut que *tu t'étires.* (nous / on / je / vous)
2. Pour être en forme, il faut que *j'écoute* mon entraîneur. (tu / mes amis / nous / on / vous)
3. Pour participer à un triathlon, il est essentiel que *nous nous entraînions* de plusieurs façons: il faut que *nous pédalions,* que *nous ramions* et que *nous courions.* (je / vous / mon frère / tu)
4. Pour pratiquer un sport avec assiduité, il est indispensable que *tu choisisses* un centre de fitness moderne. (nous / mes amis / vous)

Stress the pronunciation differences between the present indicative and the present subjunctive in the **nous** and **vous** forms: Il est indispensable que vous parliez français en classe. / Quels jours est-ce que vous parlez français en classe?; Comment est-ce que vous vous entraînez pour le marathon? / Il vaut mieux que vous vous entraîniez bien pour le marathon.; Il faut que nous utilisions un tapis de course quand il pleut. / Nous utilisons un tapis de course quand il pleut.; Nous regardons le Tour de France en direct. / Il vaut mieux que nous regardions le Tour de France à la télé.

Answer Key: 1. nous nous étirions; on s'étire; je m'étire; vous vous étiriez 2. tu écoutes; mes amis écoutent; nous écoutions; on écoute; vous écoutiez 3. je m'entraîne; je pédale; je rame; je coure / vous vous entraîniez; vous pédaliez; vous ramiez; vous couriez / mon frère s'entraîne; il pédale; il rame; il coure / tu t'entraînes; tu pédales; tu rames; tu coures 4. nous choisissions; mes amis choisissent; vous choisissiez

B. Avec ou sans effort? Choisissez les affirmations qui vous décrivent le mieux. Complétez les phrases qui s'appliquent à votre cas. Discutez vos choix avec vos camarades. Est-ce que vous réussissez à faire les choses dans la vie sans effort ou, au contraire, avec beaucoup d'effort?

1. a. Il faut que j'_____ (étudier) beaucoup pour réussir à mes cours.
   b. Il ne faut pas que j'_____ (étudier) beaucoup pour réussir à mes cours.

2. a. Il est nécessaire que je _____ (travailler) à plein temps pour me payer mes études.
   b. Il n'est pas nécessaire que je _____ (travailler) à plein temps pour me payer mes études.

3. a. Il faut que je _____ (rendre) à mes parents l'argent qu'ils me prêtent.
   b. Il ne faut pas que je _____ (rendre) à mes parents l'argent qu'ils me prêtent.

4. a. Il est indispensable que je _____ (choisir) bien les aliments que je mange pour être en bonne santé.
   b. Il n'est pas indispensable que je _____ (choisir) bien les aliments que je mange pour être en bonne santé.

5. a. Il est nécessaire que je _____ (dormir) huit heures tous les soirs.
   b. Il n'est pas nécessaire que je _____ (dormir) huit heures tous les soirs.

Structure 2

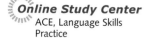

Online Study Center
ACE, Language Skills Practice

La formation du subjonctif des verbes irréguliers

Many irregular verbs in French form the subjunctive in the same way as the regular verbs: by dropping the ending of the third person plural indicative, and adding the subjunctive endings, for example: **connaître: ils connaissent.**

Il est nécessaire …	
que je connaisse	que nous connaissions
que tu connaisses	que vous connaissiez
qu'il / elle / on connaisse	qu'ils / elles connaissent

Three verbs, however, have an irregular stem. These stems must be memorized separately.

faire	fass-	Il faut que je fasse …
pouvoir	puiss-	Il faut que nous puissions …
savoir	sach-	Il faut que tu saches …

Only **avoir** and **être** are completely irregular in the subjunctive; they have both an irregular stem and irregular endings.

être		avoir	
que je **sois**	que nous **soyons**	que j'**aie**	que nous **ayons**
que tu **sois**	que vous **soyez**	que tu **aies**	que vous **ayez**
qu'il / elle / on **soit**	qu'ils / elles **soient**	qu'il / elle / on **ait**	qu'ils / elles **aient**

Stem-changing verbs

You have already seen several verbs in French that have two stems in the indicative. These verbs have the same two stems, for the same persons, in the subjunctive. Consider **boire** in the indicative: **Je *bois* du lait. Nous *buvons* du lait.** Now look at the conjugation of this verb in the subjunctive.

Il faut …
que je **boive** du lait
que tu **boives** du lait
qu'il / elle / on **boive** du lait
que nous **buvions** du lait
que vous **buviez** du lait
qu'ils / elles **boivent** du lait

In the subjunctive just as in the indicative, the **nous** and **vous** forms of **boire** have one stem, while the other four persons have a different stem. This is the case for all stem-changing verbs that you have learned to this point.

aller	que j'**aille**	que nous **allions**
prendre	que je **prenne**	que nous **prenions**
vouloir	que je **veuille**	que nous **voulions**
croire	que je **croie**	que nous **croyions**
devoir	que je **doive**	que vous **devions**
venir	que je **vienne**	que nous **venions**

VÉRIFIEZ VOTRE COMPRÉHENSION

1. Go back to the dialogue at the beginning of the chapter (p. 437), and find the verbs in the subjunctive. What are their infinitives?

2. Do these verbs have regular or irregular stems in the subjunctive? Are the endings regular or irregular?

À l'écoute!

Answer Key: 1. subjonctif 2. indicatif 3. indicatif 4. subjonctif 5. subjonctif 6. indicatif 7. subjonctif 8. subjonctif

Indicatif ou subjonctif? Écoutez les phrases suivantes attentivement. Ensuite, indiquez le mode verbal que vous entendez.

1. _____ subjonctif _____ indicatif 5. _____ subjonctif _____ indicatif
2. _____ subjonctif _____ indicatif 6. _____ subjonctif _____ indicatif
3. _____ subjonctif _____ indicatif 7. _____ subjonctif _____ indicatif
4. _____ subjonctif _____ indicatif 8. _____ subjonctif _____ indicatif

Audioscript: 1. Il faut que tu boives après avoir fait du sport. 2. Il buvait de l'eau pendant le match de foot. 3. Ils viennent voir les Jeux olympiques. 4. Il est nécessaire qu'ils viennent aux Jeux olympiques. 5. Il est indispensable que nous voulions gagner. 6. Nous voulions gagner, mais nous avons perdu. 7. Il vaut mieux qu'il croie en ton équipe. 8. Il est important qu'il croie en ton équipe.

Pratiquons!

A. Une bonne discipline. Récrivez chaque phrase avec les sujets indiqués. Faites bien attention aux formes des verbes (subjonctif et indicatif) dans chaque phrase.

1. Avant de courir, il est nécessaire que *l'on fasse* des exercices d'échauffement. (je / vous / ils / mes sœurs)
2. Si *je veux* être de bonne humeur le matin, il est indispensable que *je dorme* huit heures. (mon prof / nous / mes frères / tu)
3. Si *tu vas* t'entraîner avec un entraîneur, il faut que *tu sois* bien discipliné(e)! (on / vous / ils)
4. Le week-end, il est absolument nécessaire que *nous allions* au cinéma. Il faut aussi que *nous nous amusions* de temps en temps! (je / tu / vous / mes amis)

B. Un entraîneur exigeant. Complétez les phrases suivantes avec la forme nécessaire des verbes entre paranthèses, pour exprimer ce que l'entraîneur demande à ses clients.

1. L'entraîneur dit: «Il est nécessaire que mes clients _____ (arriver) toujours à l'heure.»
2. «Il faut que l'on _____ (vouloir) vraiment changer ses mauvaises habitudes.»
3. «Il vaut mieux que vous _____ (ne ... plus manger) au fast-food.»
4. «Il est indispensable que mes clients _____ (faire) de leur mieux.»
5. «Il vaut mieux que vous _____ (boire) assez d'eau, et que vous _____ (prendre) des vitamines tous les jours.»
6. «Il est important que mes clients _____ (venir) au club de fitness quatre fois par semaine.»
7. «Il est nécessaire que vous _____ (se reposer) deux jours par semaine—il ne faut pas que vous _____ (se faire) mal!»

C. Vous êtes l'entraîneur: que faut-il faire d'autre? Continuez l'activité B, en ajoutant au moins trois phrases. Ensuite, comparez vos idées à celles d'un(e) partenaire.

1. _____
2. _____
3. _____

D. Que faut-il faire pour être en forme? Choisissez la réponse la plus logique pour terminer les phrases suivantes. Comparez vos réponses avec celles d'un(e) partenaire. Êtes-vous d'accord?

1. Pour muscler les bras, il faut que l'on ...
2. Pour raffermir le ventre, il faut que tu ...
3. Avant de commencer une série d'exercices, il est indispensable que tu ...
4. Pour l'entraînement cardio-vasculaire, il est nécessaire que l'on ...
5. Pour muscler les jambes et les bras en même temps, il vaut mieux que l'on ...

À vous de parler!

A. Interview. Posez les questions suivantes à un(e) partenaire. Que faut-il qu'il/elle fasse pour réussir à l'université?

1. Faut-il que tu dormes beaucoup ou peu pendant la semaine? Combien d'heures par nuit est-ce qu'il faut que tu dormes?
2. Est-ce qu'il est nécessaire que tu ailles toujours en classe? Pourquoi ou pourquoi pas?
3. Avant les examens, qu'est-ce qu'il est nécessaire que tu fasses?
4. Est-il indispensable que l'on connaisse bien les professeurs? Pourquoi?
5. Est-ce qu'il faut que tu finisses toujours tes devoirs? Pourquoi ou pourquoi pas?
6. Quelle est la chose la plus importante pour réussir à nos cours universitaires?
7. Qu'est-ce qu'il ne faut pas faire si l'on veut réussir?
8. Pendant l'année académique, est-ce qu'il est nécessaire que tu travailles? Pourquoi ou pourquoi pas?

Maintenant, dites trois choses qu'il faut faire pour ne pas réussir aux cours. (Ne répétez pas les phrases précédentes.) Comparez vos phrases avec vos camarades et décidez qui a trouvé les meilleures choses à faire ou à ne pas faire pour ne pas réussir aux cours.

B. Es-tu sportif (sportive)? Discutez avec votre partenaire vos habitudes sportives. Ensuite, regardez l'enquête faite en France sur les préférences sportives des Français. Comparez vos habitudes avec celles des Français.

1. Quel est ton club de gym préféré?
2. Combien est-ce que tu paies par mois?
3. À quelle heure est-ce que tu aimes aller au club de gym / faire de l'exercice? Pourquoi?
4. Combien d'heures est-ce que tu restes au club de gym / fais du sport?
5. Quels sont tes exercices préférés?
6. Qu'est-ce que tu fais avant de faire du sport? Et après?
7. Est-ce que tu pratiques un sport à l'air libre[1]? Lequel[2]? Où?
8. Est-ce que tu préfères les sports individuels ou en équipes? Pourquoi?
9. Pourquoi est-ce que tu fais du sport / ne fais pas de sport?

Maintenant, regardez le sondage[3] sur les pratiques sportives des Français pour comparer vos habitudes sportives avec celles des Français.

Les pratiques sportives en France

- 32% des Français pratiquent un sport au moins une fois par semaine.
- 63% des Français font du sport pour se détendre et arriver à un bien-être[4] personnel.
- 20% des Français vont faire du sport dans un centre de fitness.
- Le sport en France est associé à des périodes de vacances ou de loisir[5].
- L'été est la saison préférée des Français pour faire du sport.
- Les femmes françaises pratiquent le sport de façon plus régulière que les hommes.
- Les femmes françaises pratiquent des sports moins brutaux que les hommes.
- 50% des Français préfèrent pratiquer des sports individuels.
- Plus de 50% des Français qui pratiquent un sport le font de façon non compétitive.

---

[1] outdoors [2] Which one [3] poll [4] well-being [5] leisure time

Finalement, après avoir comparé vos habitudes sportives avec celles des Français, écrivez en groupes un rapport sur les pratiques sportives des Américains. Répondez aux questions suivantes.

1. Est-ce que les Américains pratiquent un sport pour améliorer leur bien-être personnel ou est-ce qu'ils le font d'une façon compétitive? Est-ce que les Américains préfèrent faire du sport dans un centre de fitness ou à l'air libre? Préfèrent-ils pratiquer des sports individuels ou en équipes?
2. Est-ce que les femmes américaines font du sport plus régulièrement que les hommes? Est-ce que les sports qu'elles pratiquent sont moins brutaux?

Online Study Center
Web Search Activities

Le bien-être s'obtient comme ça en France

Les Français consacrent beaucoup de temps et d'argent à leur bien-être—pas seulement le bien-être physique mais le mental aussi pour arriver à une harmonie entre corps et esprit. Déjà au dix-huitième siècle, Voltaire parlait de l'importance de cultiver son «jardin intérieur», sans oublier le «jardin extérieur», bien sûr. Les Français ont plusieurs choix pour arriver à un bien-être parfait entre le corps et l'esprit.

- **Le thermalisme ou les cures thermales.** Comme le nom l'indique, la méthode qui s'utilise dans les cures thermales est à base de chaleur et de froid pour obtenir différents résultats. Les personnes qui restent pendant plusieurs jours dans une cure thermale reçoivent des bains d'eau chaude, de vase tiède[1] ou d'algues marines froides pour se détendre (l'esprit) et se sentir mieux physiquement (le corps). Les personnes qui se rendent dans les cures thermales ont souvent des problèmes de rhumatisme, de digestion, de peau[2], de respiration ou de circulation. Les cures thermales se trouvent dans des endroits privilégiés (la mer, la montagne) en contact de la nature. La durée d'une cure thermale est de deux à trois semaines. Pour garantir la prise en charge par la sécurité sociale, il faut que le médécin traitant prescrive la cure et choisisse la station thermale où le patient va séjourner.
- **La thalassothérapie (ou la thalasso).** Les soins[3] ou les cures en thalasso sont multiples. La cure la plus populaire est la remise en forme. Mais il y a également la cure antistress, la cure postnatale ou prénatale, les cures antitabac, minceur/diététique (soins anticellulite, aquagym, drainage lymphatique, régime alimentaire, musculation en salle de gym), ménopause, jambes lourdes, la spéciale dos[4] (avec des hydromassages ou des bains de boues) ou la spéciale homme. Le but[5] de la thalasso est de procurer un bon équilibre biologique. On va en thalassothérapie pour améliorer sa forme plutôt que pour se soigner. Avant d'initier une cure en thalasso, il faut que le patient passe un examen médical. Toutes les cures sont supervisées par des professionnels de la santé: des médecins et des kinésithérapeutes[6] ou des nutritionnistes. Quelques-unes des cures sont prises en charge par la sécurité sociale, par exemple les cures spéciales dos, mais la majorité des cures sont à la charge du client.

---

[1]*warm clay* [2]*skin* [3]*treatments* [4]*back* [5]*goal* [6]*physical therapists*

- **Les instituts de beauté ou les centres de bien-être.** Ce sont des centres esthétiques. Généralement dans ces centres il y a un salon de coiffure, un espace sauna, un espace manicure et pédicure et des esthéticiennes spécialistes en maquillage permanent, en drainage lymphatique ou en épilations laser ou à la cire[1].
- **L'homéopathie (ou la médecine douce).** L'homéopathie soigne[2] avec le pouvoir des plantes. Bon nombre de Français préfèrent traiter les symptômes d'une maladie comme le rhume[3], les migraines ou le stress à l'aide de l'homéopathie plutôt[4] qu'avec les remèdes qu'offre la médecine traditionnelle. L'homéopathie est différente de la médecine traditionnelle car elle s'occupe aussi bien de la psychologie du patient que des symptômes physiques (migraines, insomnies, mal au dos). Les traitements homéopathiques sont couverts par la sécurité sociale.
- **La sophrologie[5].** C'est une méthode assez pratiquée en France. Cette méthode combine le yoga, les techniques de relaxation et les techniques orientales de méditation. Elle permet d'affiner l'état de conscience, de vaincre la peur et d'optimiser ses possibilités. On se relaxe physiquement avec la respiration et la visualisation de chaque partie du corps, avec l'aide du son de la voix[6] du sophrologue. Après 10 ou 20 minutes, il faut que le patient arrive à sa conscience par des exercices de visualisation et de concentration, différents selon la pathologie de chaque personne. Une heure de sophrologie coûte 45 €.

Réfléchissons

1. Est-ce que les Américains sont aussi préoccupés que les Français par leur bien-être? Pourquoi? Expliquez votre réponse.
2. Est-ce que dans votre pays[7] il y a autant de centres dédiés à l'obtention du bien-être? Y a-t-il des centres similaires aux centres français? Lesquels[8]?
3. Où vont les Américains pour atteindre une harmonie entre corps et esprit? Que font les Américains pour réduire le stress, par exemple? Pour combattre les migraines?
4. Avez-vous été étonnés de la prise en charge par la sécurité sociale des soins homéopathiques, en cure thermale et en thalasso? Pourquoi? Pensez-vous qu'il est nécessaire que ces soins soient remboursés par la sécurité sociale? Justifiez votre réponse.

---

[1] wax [2] heals [3] the flu [4] rather [5] La sophrologie est l'étude de la conscience, par exemple, par l'hypnose.
[6] sound of the voice [7] country [8] Which ones

Continuons!

Il faut être en forme! ◯

Carole et ses amies Delphine et Annette se retrouvent au café.

DELPHINE: Dis, Carole, ton entraîneuse, qu'est-ce qu'elle t'a dit de faire pour les bras?

CAROLE: C'est simple, il faut faire des haltères. J'en ai fait trois séries l'autre jour.

ANNETTE: C'est beaucoup. Tu n'as pas mal aux bras?

CAROLE: Non, je n'ai pas mal aux bras, mais alors aux jambes, je déguste[1].

ANNETTE: Oh, ma pauvre! Qu'est-ce que tu as fait pour avoir si mal?

CAROLE: J'ai passé vingt minutes à faire des exercices au sol.

DELPHINE: Ce n'est pas beaucoup ça, tu es douillette[2]! Moi, j'en fais une demi-heure par jour.

ANNETTE: Oui, mais toi, Delphine, ça fait un an que tu vas au club de gym tous les jours. Bon alors, Carole, continue. Qu'est-ce qu'elle t'a dit, l'entraîneuse, pour muscler le ventre?

CAROLE: L'entraîneuse m'a dit qu'il est important de faire des abdos. Et moi, je déteste les abdos—c'est encore plus horrible que les exercices au sol!

DELPHINE: Avec cette attitude, Carole, tu ne vas pas durer longtemps au club de gym. N'oublie pas qu'il faut que tu rentres[3] dans ta robe de mariée dans six mois!

Vous avez bien compris?

Dites si les phrases suivantes sont vraies ou fausses. Corrigez les affirmations qui sont fausses.

1. Carole a très mal aux jambes. _____ vrai _____ faux

2. Carole a mal au bras. _____ vrai _____ faux

3. Carole a mal aux jambes parce qu'elle a fait des haltères. _____ vrai _____ faux

4. Delphine a fait plus d'exercices au sol que Carole. _____ vrai _____ faux

5. Annette est douillette. _____ vrai _____ faux

6. Delphine fait du sport régulièrement. _____ vrai _____ faux

7. Carole adore faire du sport. _____ vrai _____ faux

8. Carole va pouvoir porter sa robe de mariée si elle ne fait pas de sport. _____ vrai _____ faux

---

[1]**Déguster** normally means *to savor*, but in this context it is used ironically and means *to feel every pain.*
[2]*wimp* [3]*fit*

Vocabulaire essentiel

Activités et sports

Online Study Center
Flashcards, ACE, Language Skills Practice

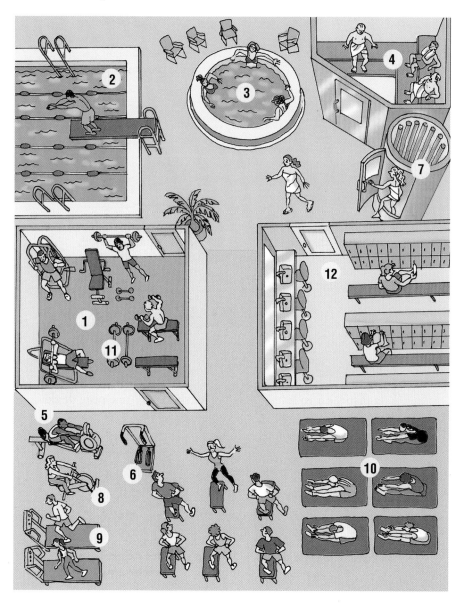

1. la salle de musculation (la salle de muscu)
2. la piscine
3. le Jacuzzi
4. le sauna
5. le vélo-rameur
6. les steps *(m.)*
7. **les cabines** *(f.)* **de bronzage**
8. le vélo statique
9. le tapis de course
10. **les matelas** *(m.)*
11. **des poids** *(m.)*
12. le vestiaire

la raquette / les courts
(f.) de tennis

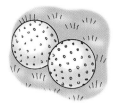

les balles *(f.)* de golf

les clubs *(m.)* de golf / le terrain
(le parcours) de golf

le ballon de foot / le terrain de foot

le ballon de basket / le
terrain de basket

les patins *(m.)* **à glace / la
patinoire**

les rollers *(m.)*

la planche à voile

les skis *(m.)* / une piste de ski

les bottes *(f.)* de ski

les bâtons *(m.)* de ski

**le surf des neiges (avec une
planche à neige)**

la tenue de sport

Expansion personnelle

The vocabulary words that are in boldface in the preceding section are *Expansion personnelle.*

À vous!

A. Où va-t-on? Indiquez où on va ou ce qu'on fait pour les actions suivantes.

 MODÈLE: patiner

> *On va à la patinoire.*

1. nager
2. bronzer
3. pédaler
4. faire de la muscu
5. transpirer[1]
6. faire des abdos
7. courir
8. se relaxer

B. Que manque-t-il? *(What is missing?)* Regardez les dessins et indiquez ce que les personnes ont oublié à la maison pour pratiquer les sports.

MODÈLE:

Elle a oublié son ballon de basket!

---

[1] *to sweat*

C. C'est comment? Répondez avec une des expressions suivantes ou une expression de votre choix. Justifiez vos réponses.

Expressions suggérées: c'est simple, c'est dur, c'est douloureux, c'est pénible, c'est difficile, ce n'est pas nécessaire, c'est horrible, c'est génial, c'est super, c'est ennuyeux

MODÈLE: les fessiers

C'est douloureux! Parce que les crampes aux fesses pendant et après les fessiers sont douloureuses.

1. les exercices au sol
2. le tapis de course
3. sauter à la corde

4. faire des haltères
5. les abdos

D. Célébrités sportives. Regardez les photos des célébrités sportives et devinez quel sport ils pratiquent. Ensuite décrivez leur tenue de sport. Finalement, indiquez quel est votre célébrité sportive préférée et dites pourquoi. Comparez vos réponses avec vos camarades.

1. Zinedine Zidane

2. Sebastian Grosjean

3. Marina Anissina et Gwendal Peizerat

4. Karine Ruby

5. Gregory Havret

Portrait personnel

Décrivez la célébrité sportive préférée de votre camarade et dites pourquoi il/elle admire cette personne.

Structure 3

Le subjonctif vs. l'infinitif

Online Study Center
ACE, Language Skills
Practice

You have probably noticed in the dialogue between Carole, Annette, and Delphine (***Continuons!,*** page 448) that expressions of necessity are not always followed by a verb in the subjunctive in French; sometimes they are quite simply followed by an infinitive. This is possible when the situation refers to people in general, rather than to a specific person or group of people. The difference between these two usages is not only one of grammar, but also one of meaning. Compare the following examples:

> Pour être en bonne santé, il ne faut pas fumer.
> Si tu veux être en bonne santé, il faut que tu ne fumes pas.

The first sentence represents a statement that is true for the population at large, and therefore an infinitive is used after **il ne faut pas.** In the second sentence, however, the action of the verb **fumer** is personalized—it is made specific to the subject pronoun **tu.** With the change of subject from the expression of necessity (impersonal **il**) to the doer of the action **(tu),** the subjunctive becomes necessary. The implication in this sentence is that the person mentioned participates in the action (in this case, smoking), and, according to someone else, must stop that activity in order to remain in good health. This statement is directed at one specific smoker.

VÉRIFIEZ VOTRE COMPRÉHENSION

1. Go back to the dialogue on page 448, and find all the expressions of necessity that are followed by an infinitive. Why is an infinitive used and not a clause with a subjunctive?

2. What would these same sentences look like with a verb in the subjunctive?

Pratiquons!

A. Que faut-il? Dites ce qu'il faut utiliser pour pratiquer les sports suivants.

> MODÈLE: pour jouer au tennis
>
> *Pour jouer au tennis, il faut utiliser une raquette.*

1. pour jouer au golf
2. pour faire de la planche à voile
3. pour jouer au basket
4. pour faire de la muscu
5. pour faire du ski
6. pour faire des exercices au sol
7. pour ramer dans un centre de fitness

Answer Key: 1. ... il faut utiliser des clubs de golf. 2. ... une planche à voile. 3. ... un ballon de basket. 4. ... des poids. 5. ... des skis. 6. ... un matelas. 7. ... un rameur.

B. Différences irréconciliables! Christelle va vous parler des différences entre Armelle, sa camarade de chambre, et elle. Complétez le paragraphe avec le subjonctif ou l'infinitif, selon le cas.

Armelle et moi sommes des personnes très différentes! Elle pense qu'il faut (étudier) (1) _____ pendant des heures chaque soir; moi, je trouve qu'il est nécessaire[1] de (se préparer) (2) _____ seulement un peu avant les examens. Elle n'aime pas cette idée—elle dit que je n'étudie pas assez. D'après[2] Armelle, il est essentiel que j(e) (aller) (3) _____ plus fréquemment à la bibliothèque. Elle dit que c'est là que l'on étudie le mieux. Elle répète souvent qu'il faut (être) (4) _____ sérieux, si l'on veut réussir. Mais moi, je trouve qu'il est important de (connaître) (5) _____ les autres camarades de classe aussi et qu'il est nécessaire de (sortir) (6) _____ avec eux[3]. Mes camarades de classe et moi, nous nous rencontrons souvent au café, et nous discutons de nos cours en prenant une tasse de café. Je pense qu'il est indispensable que les étudiants (être) (7) _____ sociables pour avoir beaucoup d'amis et pour mieux comprendre les cours! Armelle est plutôt solitaire. Il faut qu'elle (sortir) (8) _____ un peu plus au lieu de[4] rester toujours enfermée à la maison. Armelle ne comprend pas cela—elle dit que nous ne pouvons pas vraiment travailler dans un café. Il faut qu'elle (avoir) (9) _____ du silence pour travailler sérieusement. Et vous, êtes-vous d'accord avec elle ou avec moi?

Maintenant, répondez à la question de Christelle.

🗣**C. Jeu de rôles.** Avec un(e) partenaire, jouez les jeux de rôles suivants. (La personne qui est le professeur dans le premier jeu de rôles sera le/la client[e] dans le deuxième.)

🌀 MODÈLE: LE PROF: *Il faut compléter les activités dans le cahier d'exercices.*

L'ÉTUDIANT(E): *Est-ce qu'il faut que je fasse les activités orales dans le cahier aussi?*

LE PROF: *Oui, bien sûr! Il faut que tu les fasses aussi.*

1. Vous êtes professeur et étudiant(e). Le professeur va expliquer à l'étudiant(e) ce qu'il faut faire (de façon générale) pour préparer l'examen. Ensuite, l'étudiant(e) va poser des questions personnelles.
2. Vous êtes entraîneur (entraîneuse) et client(e). L'entraîneur (entraîneuse) va dire au client (à la cliente) ce qu'il faut faire (de façon générale) pour rester en bonne santé. Ensuite, le/la client(e) va poser des questions particulières à son cas.

Portrait personnel

D'après la réponse de votre camarade de classe, dites s'il/si elle est un(e) étudiant(e) comme Christelle ou comme Armelle. Élaborez votre réponse.

🌀 MODÈLE: *Robert est comme Armelle parce qu'il pense qu'il faut ... et qu'il est important de ...*

---

[1]The impersonal expressions *il est nécessaire, il est important, il est essentiel*, etc., are followed by **de** when they are used with an infinitive: *Il est important **de** faire du sport tous les jours.* Exceptions: *il vaut mieux* and *il faut: il vaut mieux faire du sport/il faut faire du sport.* [2]*According to* [3]*them* [4]*instead of*

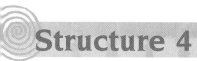

Structure 4

Les pronoms disjoints

Online Study Center
Language Skills Practice

In Chapters 1 and 2 you learned the subject pronouns, which accompany verbs. You have undoubtedly noticed, however, that these pronouns sometimes change form, as in the expression **Je vais bien, et *toi?*** Whenever the subject pronouns fall in a position where they must be stressed, they are changed to a **disjunctive,** or **stress, pronoun.**

These pronouns are as follows:

moi	nous
toi	vous
lui / elle	eux / elles

This happens in various situations in French, for example:

• In one-word responses to questions:

—Qui va au cinéma?
—**Moi.**

• In questions with no verbs:

Je m'appelle Sylvie, et **toi?**

• In sentences that combine a noun and a pronoun:

Ma famille et **moi,** nous partons en vacances.
Julien et **lui,** ils suivent un cours de chimie.

• To emphasize a subject pronoun:

Elles? Elles ne savent pas la réponse!
Et **toi,** qu'est-ce que tu en penses?

• Following a preposition:

Je ne sors plus avec **lui.**
Il s'entend bien avec ses parents. Il dîne toujours chez **eux.**

• After an introductory phrase such as **il y a, c'est,** or **ce sont:**

Dans ma famille, il y a **moi,** mon père et ma sœur. C'est tout!
—C'est ton frère? / Ce sont tes frères?
—Oui, c'est **lui.** / Oui, ce sont **eux.**

VÉRIFIEZ VOTRE COMPRÉHENSION

Go back to activity B, **Différences irréconciliables,** on page 454 and underline all the disjunctive pronouns that you find. (Be careful not to confuse them with the direct and indirect object pronouns, or with subject pronouns, which sometimes look the same!) For each disjunctive pronoun that you find, explain why the stressed form has been used, referring to the categories above.

Pratiquons!

A. C'est qui? Spécifiez la personne dont il s'agit en utilisant des pronoms disjoints dans les phrases suivantes.

> **MODÈLE:** Tu aimes ça?
>
> *Tu aimes ça, toi? / Toi, tu aimes ça?*

1. Il va en France cette année.
2. Nous pensons qu'il faut conserver l'essence, et ne pas voyager.
3. Ils ont besoin de vacances.
4. Elle n'écoute jamais les conseils des autres.
5. Qu'est-ce que vous en pensez?
6. Je déteste les abdos!

B. C'est qui ça? Vous regardez des photos avec un(e) ami(e). Répondez à ses questions, avec un pronom disjoint.

> **MODÈLE:** Sur cette photo, c'est qui ça? C'est ton frère?
>
> *Oui, c'est lui.*

1. C'est ta sœur?
2. Ce sont tes parents?
3. Ce sont tes amis et toi?
4. C'est moi?
5. Ce sont tes actrices préférées?
6. Ce sont mes sœurs et moi quand nous étions petits?

C. Réponses non-répétitives. Avec un(e) partenaire, posez et répondez aux questions suivantes. Utilisez un pronom disjoint dans la réponse, pour ne pas être répétitif.

> **MODÈLE:** dîner / avec tes parents
>
> Question: *Est-ce que tu dînes souvent avec tes parents?*
>
> Réponse: *Oui, je dîne souvent avec eux. / Non, je ne dîne pas souvent avec eux.*

1. habiter toujours / chez tes parents
2. travailler bien / pour ton patron
3. s'entendre bien / avec moi
4. dîner / chez ton/ta prof
5. se disputer souvent / avec ton/ta petit(e) ami(e)
6. se rappeler / de ton instituteur/institutrice quand tu avais 5 ans
7. penser souvent / à tes amis du lycée
8. vouloir sortir / avec mes amis et moi

À vous de parler!

En groupes de trois ou quatre, préparez les situations suivantes. Ensuite, présentez-les à la classe.

A. En montagne. Vous préparez un voyage pour aller aux Alpes. Discutez comment vous allez vous préparer physiquement avant de partir, ce que vous allez apporter (vêtements, tenue de sport, etc.), les activités que vous allez faire ou que vous n'allez pas faire.

B. La Salle Fitness Club à Nice. Vous êtes en France, à Nice, et vous voulez vous inscrire dans une salle de fitness. Vous rentrez dans La Salle Fitness Club à Nice. Posez des questions à l'entraîneur (l'entraîneuse) qui se trouve à l'accueil. Qu'est-ce que vous devez apporter? Où pouvez-vous laisser vos affaires personnelles? Renseignez-vous aussi sur la tenue que vous devez porter, les heures d'ouverture et de fermeture, le coût de l'abonnement, les types d'abonnement, les règles d'usage des appareils et les règles de conduite dans les salles de gym et de muscu. Demandez à l'entraîneur (l'entraîneuse) de vous faire visiter le gymnase. Finalement, regardez le planning hebdomadaire des cours offerts par La Salle Fitness Club et avec votre entraîneur (entraîneuse) décidez quels cours vous conviennent le mieux selon vos besoins[1].

Tell students to go back to the *Commençons!* dialogue at the beginning of the chapter and to use it as a model if they wish.

Note: In 2005, the average fee of a personal trainer was 50 € for one hour. Average fitness center fees were 440 € for one year, 285 € for 6 months, and 175 € for 3 months. The average enrollment fee was 45 €.

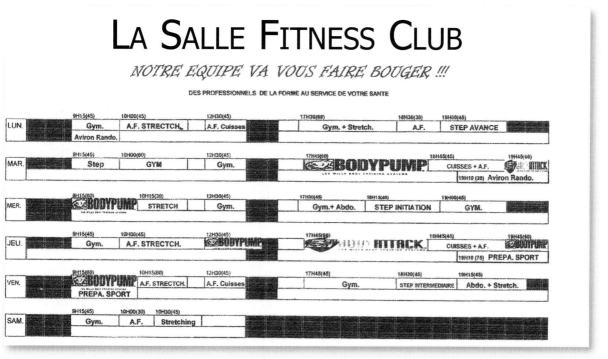

Les Français et le foot sont comme ça

Le football c'est le sport national français! En effet, c'est le sport que les Français préfèrent, avant le basket et le rugby. La télévision diffuse les matchs de foot les plus importants—le Mondial, la Coupe d'Europe, la Coupe de France et la CAN (la Coupe d'Afrique des Nations[2])—et une grande majorité des Français sont collés à leur écran de télévision! Il y a même une chaîne de télé dédiée aux sports exclusivement où le foot est le sport le plus diffusé et le plus regardé. Les Français qui peuvent vont aux stades—par exemple, au stade Parc des Princes ou au Stade de France à Paris—pour voir les matchs en direct et sur le vif. Les supporters sont nombreux et beaucoup suivent leur équipe préférée de ville en ville et de

Online Study Center
Web Search Activities

---

[1]*depending on your needs* [2]La CAN est une compétition entre les pays du continent africain. Elle a lieu tous les deux ans et réunit 16 équipes de différents pays. C'est un événement très important pour l'Afrique et pour les Africains, qui adorent le foot autant que les Français. La Tunisie et le Sénégal sont les pays qui ont remporté le plus de victoires à la CAN.

pays en pays. On appelle «les maillots bleus» ou «les bleus» les joueurs qui sont dans l'équipe française de foot parce qu'ils portent des tee-shirts—les maillots—de couleur bleue. Leur tenue de sport est tricolore—bleu, blanc, rouge—comme le drapeau français. Parfois, il y a des bagarres[1] sur le terrain de foot entre les supporters de différentes équipes et la police doit intervenir. À la différence des matchs américains, en France il n'y a pas de *cheerleaders* pour animer le public. Quand «les bleus» gagnent un match, les fans vont dans les rues de Paris en chantant, en buvant et en célébrant la victoire jusqu'à très tard le soir. La vie intime des joueurs de foot est révélée dans la presse people et elle intéresse beaucoup les supporters. Le rêve de beaucoup de jeunes français est de rentrer dans l'équipe de France de foot car c'est un sport très bien payé et qui a beaucoup de succès. C'est facile de devenir une star et d'apparaître dans les journaux et la télévision quand on est dans l'équipe de France!

Possible answer for #3: There are not as many pauses during a soccer game as there are during a football game. The public may watch a replay of the best moments of the game on one of several big screens in the stadium. Supporters may also drink and talk together. You may want to talk about the fights that sometimes happen during soccer games between supporters of the opposing teams.

Réfléchissons

1. Vous venez de lire que le foot c'est le sport préféré des Français. Quel est le sport préféré aux États-Unis?
2. Y a-t-il des bagarres pendant les matchs de football américain où la police doit intervenir? Est-ce que le public réagit de la même façon quand son équipe gagne?
3. Comme il n'y a pas de *cheerleaders* dans les matchs français, comment croyez-vous que le public s'amuse pendant les pauses?
4. Comment sont les joueurs de football américains en comparaison avec les joueurs français? Deviennent-ils aussi des célébrités?

Online Study Center
Language Skills Practice

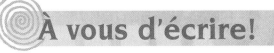

À vous d'écrire!

A. Stratégies. Vous êtes journalistes et chargés(es) d'écrire un article sur les excès ou les addictions de la société actuelle. Nous vous avons fourni[2] un exemple d'article—«Droguées au sport»—qui parle d'une addiction aux sports.

- Lisez l'article une première fois pour en comprendre le sens général.

Droguées au sport

Si vous êtes du genre à nager, courir, ramer, suer[3] quelle que soit[4] l'heure ou l'humeur, vous êtes peut-être devenue […] une «sport addict». Comme souvent en matière d'excès, c'est aux États-Unis que le phénomène «dépendance du sportif» a été pour la première fois observé. En 1976, dans le cadre d'une étude de coureurs de fond, le docteur William Glasser a constaté que certains joggeurs ne peuvent plus se passer de[5] leur sport quotidien, malgré la fatigue et parfois les blessures. La faute aux endorphines (neuromédiateurs du système nerveux central), capables, grâce à leurs propriétés calmantes et euphorisantes, de provoquer, au bout d'une demi-heure d'effort cardio-vasculaire intense (course à pied, natation, vélo, cardio-training), une sensation de bien-être et d'apaisement proche de la béatitude. Une décharge d'endorphines qui se traduit, dans le cerveau, par une activité biochimique similaire à celle provoquée par la morphine ou l'héroïne.

Pratiquer une activité physique de manière intense et répétitive est donc un moyen pour un sportif accro[6] de recréer ces sensations fortes. En sachant que douze

---

[1]*fights* [2]*given* [3]*transpirer* [4]*whatever* [5]*abandonner, arrêter* [6]*accroché (dépendant)*

minutes de crawl ou vingt de stretching suffisent rarement à atteindre le nirvana …
Cependant, les sportifs en herbe[1] sont aussi concernés, puisque, selon une étude
réalisée dans les grandes salles de sport parisiennes, plus de 10% des personnes inscrites
s'entraînent quotidiennement. À commencer par certaines femmes qui n'hésitent pas à
venir transpirer quatre heures par jour, obnubilées[2] par le sacro-saint culte du corps.

Fractures, usure des cartilages, chute de la libido, absence de règles[3], stérilité …
en cas d'abus, l'addiction peut vite devenir salée[4]. Chez les femmes le surentraîne-
ment (quatre-vingt-dix minutes par jour) fait chuter la production d'hormones,
provoquant du même coup une fragilisation des os et un risque accru[5]
d'ostéoporose. Sans oublier la fameuse «mort subite», responsable chaque année en
France du décès de 1 500 personnes. On l'aura compris: dans le sport il n'y a pas
que le dopage qui ruine la santé.

- Maintenant, répondez aux questions suivantes pour centrer votre attention sur
  les points du texte les plus importants.

  1. Que faut-il faire pour devenir un «sport addict»?
  2. Pourquoi est-ce que certains joggeurs ne peuvent plus s'arrêter de courir?
  3. Quels sont les effets biochimiques que provoque une pratique cardio-
     vasculaire intense régulière?
  4. Est-ce que les professionnels sportifs sont les seuls à être affectés? Qui
     d'autre est affecté?
  5. Quelles sont les conséquences d'une pratique sportive poussée à l'extrême?

B. Organisons-nous! Lisez l'article une seconde fois et regardez comment sont
donnés les exemples (avec chiffres à l'appui[6]), les explications (ou le développement du sujet[7]) et la conclusion. Par exemple, la conclusion est tracée avec une
phrase courte mais qui synthétise bien le problème: «On l'aura compris: dans le
sport il n'y a pas que le dopage qui ruine la santé.»

C. Pensons-y!

- Avec un(e) partenaire, pensez aux activités que les membres de la société dans
  laquelle[8] vous vivez font en excès, au point d'être dépendants de ces activités.
  Faites une liste des «addictions» les plus courantes.
- Comparez votre liste avec la classe. Quelles activités avez-vous trouvées en
  commun?

D. Écrivons! Choisissez une activité qui est pratiquée en excès par la société
et composez un paragraphe en vous inspirant de[9] l'article «Droguées aux sports».
Justifiez vos affirmations et vos arguments avec des exemples précis et/ou des
chiffres. N'oubliez pas d'écrire votre conclusion!

E. Révisons! Lisez l'article de votre partenaire et posez-vous les questions
suivantes.

  1. Est-ce que le sujet choisi traite un excès? Lequel?
  2. Est-ce que les arguments sont clairs et bien présentés? Sont-ils justifiés?
     Comment?
  3. Pouvez-vous ajouter[10] d'autres arguments?
  4. Comment est la conclusion? Est-elle bien trouvée[11]? Pouvez-vous l'améliorer[12]?

Ex. C: If students cannot think of activities that are practiced in excess, have them talk about the term *workaholic*. When was it invented? (In the '60s.) What addiction does it refer to? Other addictions you may want to talk about: plastic surgery, types of food, shopping, suntanning.

Ex. E: If you wish to expand on the topic covered in the article "Droguées aux sports," here are some additional questions you can ask: 1. Au commencement du texte on dit que c'est aux États-Unis que les excès de tout genre sont le plus pratiqués. Pensez-vous que cette affirmation soit vraie? Pourquoi? Discutez les autres excès qui existent aux États-Unis. 2. Le texte se centre sur les femmes qui sont «accros» aux sports. Est-ce que les hommes aussi sont accros aux sports? Si oui, est-ce que les hommes et les femmes pratiquent les mêmes sports pour les mêmes raisons? (Tell students that there are also many men who exercise excessively to obtain a perfect body. The sports men and women practice may be different [women tend to do more cardiovascular activities whereas men tend to do more strength training]. In addition, some men take steroids to build more muscle, a practice that has been shown to have negative side effects.) 3. Dans le texte on dit que les Français donnent beaucoup d'importance au «sacro-saint culte du corps». Est-ce que ce culte existe aussi aux États-Unis (ou dans votre pays)? Est-ce qu'il se manifeste de la même façon? Comment est-ce que les Américains (ou les gens de votre pays) expriment le culte de leur corps?

---

[1] *les non-professionnels* [2] *obsédées* [3] *menstruation* [4] *considérable* [5] *plus grand* [6] *supported with numbers (dates,
etc.)* [7] *topic* [8] *in which* [9] *taking your inspiration from* [10] *add* [11] *well chosen* [12] *improve it*

Lexique ☊

Vocabulaire essentiel

Au centre de fitness

avoir mal *to be in pain, to be sore*
courir *to run*
s'entraîner *to train*
un entraîneur / une entraîneuse *trainer*
être douillet / douillette *to be a wimp*
être en forme *to be in shape*
faire des abdominaux *(m.)* (faire des abdos) *to do sit-ups*

faire des exercices *(m.)* au sol *to do floor exercises*
faire de la musculation (faire de la muscu) *to do muscle-building exercises*
faire de la natation *to swim*
faire des haltères *(m.)* *to lift weights*
faire des séries *(f.)* d'exercices *to do exercise repetitions*

faire du sport *to do a sport*
marcher *to walk*
se mettre en forme / se remettre en forme *to get in shape*
nager *to swim*
pédaler *to pedal*
pratiquer un sport *to do a sport*

Expressions de nécessité

il est essentiel que *it is essential that*
il est indispensable que *it is essential that*

il est nécessaire que *it is necessary that*
il faut que *one must; it is necessary that*

il vaut mieux que *it is better that*

Activités et sports

la planche à voile *windsurfing*
la piscine *swimming pool*
un court de tennis *tennis court*
la raquette *racket*
la salle de musculation (la salle de muscu) *weight room*
le ballon de basket *basketball*
le ballon de foot *soccer ball*
le Jacuzzi *Jacuzzi*

le vélo-rameur *pedaling and rowing machine*
une piste de ski *ski slope*
le sauna *sauna*
le terrain de basket *basketball court*
le terrain de foot *soccer field*
le tapis de course *treadmill*
le vélo statique *stationary bike*

le vestiaire *changing room*
les balles *(f.)* de golf *golf balls*
les bâtons *(m.)* de ski *ski poles*
les bottes *(f.)* de ski *ski boots*
les clubs *(m.)* de golf (le terrain / le parcours de golf) *golf clubs, golf course*
les steps *(m.)* *step machine*
les skis *(m.)* *skis*

Expansion personnelle

les cabines *(f.)* de bronzage *tanning booths*
s'échauffer *to warm up*
s'étirer *to stretch*
faire des exercices d'échauffement *to warm up*
faire des exercices d'étirement *to stretch*
faire des fessiers *(m.)* *to do buttock exercises*

faire des pompes *(f.)* *to do push-ups*
faire du stretching *to stretch*
se faire masser *to get a massage*
un masseur / une masseuse *masseur / masseuse*
les matelas *(m.)* *mats*
la patinoire *ice rink*
les patins *(m.)* à glace *ice skates*
des poids *(m.)* *weights*

se raffermir *to tone*
ramer *to row*
les rollers *(m.)* *roller blades*
sauter à la corde *to jump rope*
le surf des neiges *snowboarding*
la tenue de sport *sporting gear*

Ma santé

Are you generally healthy or unhealthy? Do you take good care of yourself? What are some of the most common illnesses that you suffer from? In this chapter, you will learn how to talk about your health and about what you do to stay healthy, and you will have a chance to compare your habits to those of French speakers. You will expand your ability to express your opinions, and you will continue your study of the subjunctive mood.

 The vocabulary that you will learn includes

Health, including common illnesses and remedies
Emotions
Volition, doubt, and certainty

The structures that you will learn include

The subjunctive with expressions of emotion and volition
The subjunctive with expressions of doubt

The culture that you will learn includes

How health care works in France
What the French mean by a **crise de foie**

Commençons!

Chez le docteur

Bernard va chez le docteur.

BERNARD: Docteur, je suis malade depuis plusieurs jours. J'ai très très mal à la tête, j'ai extrêmement mal à la gorge, et j'ai la nausée.

DOCTEUR: Cela a l'air grave. Est-ce que vous avez de la fièvre?

BERNARD: Non, je ne crois pas. Mais je n'ai pas de thermomètre. Il faut que j'en achète un.

DOCTEUR: Oui, il est absolument essentiel d'avoir un thermomètre à la maison. Quand vous avez mal à la tête, est-ce que la douleur est localisée sur le crâne ou derrière les yeux?

BERNARD: Plutôt derrière les yeux. J'ai aussi le nez qui coule et j'ai mal aux dents.

DOCTEUR: Vous avez tous les symptômes d'une sinusite. Je vais vous prescrire de l'antihistaminique. Je voudrais également que vous fassiez trois inhalations par jour. Et si vous avez toujours mal à la gorge, prenez des pastilles à la menthe.

BERNARD: Je suis content que vous puissiez m'aider.

DOCTEUR: Et moi aussi je suis heureux de pouvoir vous aider. J'aimerais bien que vous veniez me voir dans une semaine si vous ne vous sentez pas mieux.

Vous avez bien compris?

Dites si les phrases suivantes sont vraies ou fausses.

1. Bernard a une migraine.
2. Bernard ne sait pas s'il a de la fièvre.
3. Bernard n'a pas envie de vomir.
4. Le docteur conseille à Bernard de prendre de l'aspirine.
5. Pour le mal de gorge, Bernard doit prendre du sirop trois fois par jour.
6. Le docteur est heureux d'avoir trouvé le bon diagnostic.

Answer Key: 1. faux 2. vrai 3. faux 4. faux 5. faux 6. vrai

Vocabulaire essentiel

Les parties internes du corps

Notez bien: Tous les mots en noir sont du vocabulaire esentiel; les mots en **caractères gras** sont de l'expansion personnelle.

Online Study Center
Flashcards, ACE, Language Skills Practice

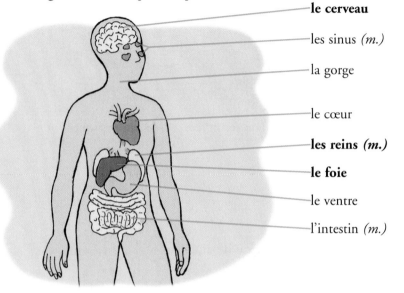

le cerveau

les sinus *(m.)*

la gorge

le cœur

les reins *(m.)*

le foie

le ventre

l'intestin *(m.)*

Les médicaments et les remèdes

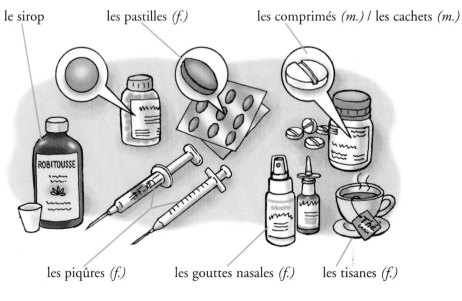

le sirop

les pastilles *(f.)*

les comprimés *(m.)* / les cachets *(m.)*

les piqûres *(f.)*

les gouttes nasales *(f.)*

les tisanes *(f.)*

un calmant   la pommade   un somnifère   les suppositoires *(m.)*

Mots apparentés

les antibiotiques *(m.)*
les antihistaminiques *(m.)*
l'aspirine *(f.)*
les médicaments *(m.)*
les remèdes *(m.)* homéopathiques (ou naturels)
un thermomètre
les vitamines *(f.)*

Les maladies les plus communes

avoir mal à la tête
avoir une migraine
avoir le nez bouché
avoir le nez qui coule
avoir mal à la gorge
avoir de la fièvre
avoir mal au dos
avoir la nausée = avoir mal au cœur
avoir la tête qui tourne = avoir le vertige
avoir une rage de dents *(to have a toothache)*
avoir un rhume / être enrhumé(e) *(to have a cold)*
tousser *(to cough)*

Expansion personnelle

avoir la diarrhée
avoir une crise de foie *(to have digestive problems)*
avoir une crise cardiaque
être constipé(e)
vomir

Dans le Chapitre 12, vous avez vu **les parties externes du corps.** Révisez ce vocabulaire avant de faire les activités suivantes.

Pantomime some of these expressions (e.g., **avoir mal à la tête** or **avoir mal au dos**) to clarify meaning for students. As an extension, you might ask students to explain where they hurt. Remind them of the contraction of **à** and the definite article.

Explain **avoir le nez bouché** by speaking as if you were congested, and **avoir le nez qui coule** by blowing your nose.

You may want to tell students that **tomber dans les pommes** is a common expression meaning *to faint.*

These expressions are included because they are sometimes very important—for example, when traveling!

À vous!

A. Les remèdes. Indiquez quand on prend les remèdes suivants.

1. le sirop
2. les gouttes nasales
3. l'aspirine
4. les antibiotiques
5. les tisanes
6. un antihistaminique
7. un somnifère

B. Cause et effet. Lisez les affirmations suivantes et choisissez une réponse pour chacune. Si plus d'une réponse est possible, choisissez une réponse logique.

> 🌀 MODÈLE: J'ai une crise de foie.
>
> *Vous avez mangé beaucoup de chocolat?*

1. J'ai mal au ventre.
2. Je tousse.
3. J'ai la nausée.
4. J'ai mal au dos.
5. J'ai mal à la tête.
6. J'ai de la fièvre.
7. J'ai une rage de dent.
8. J'ai le nez bouché.

   a. Vous attendez un enfant?
   b. Vous mangez trop de choses sucrées?
   c. Vous avez transporté des objets lourds?
   d. Vous avez trop mangé?
   e. Vous fumez beaucoup de cigarettes?
   f. Vous avez bu trop de vin?
   g. Vous avez des allergies?
   h. Vous avez une infection?

👥 C. Mes petits remèdes. Avec un(e) partenaire, dites quels symptômes vous avez quand vous êtes malades, quels remèdes vous prenez et ce que vous faites pour vous sentir mieux.

> 🌀 MODÈLE: avoir mal au dos
>
> *Qu'est-ce que tu fais quand tu as mal au dos?*
>
> *Je me couche. / Je prends de l'aspirine. / Je m'étire.*

1. être enrhumé(e)
2. avoir une rage de dents
3. être constipé(e)
4. avoir mal à la tête
5. avoir mal à la gorge
6. avoir le nez qui coule[1]
7. avoir la nausée

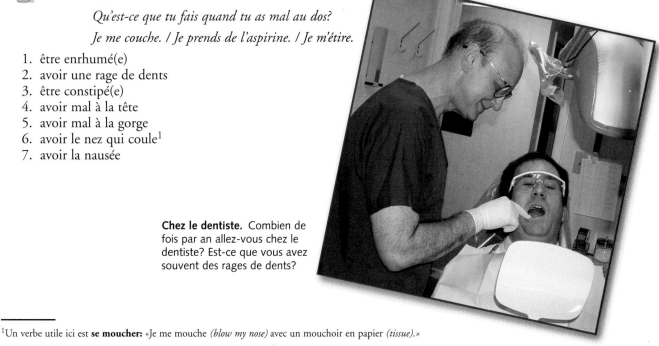

Chez le dentiste. Combien de fois par an allez-vous chez le dentiste? Est-ce que vous avez souvent des rages de dents?

---

[1] Un verbe utile ici est **se moucher:** «Je me mouche *(blow my nose)* avec un mouchoir en papier *(tissue)*.»

Structure 1

Online Study Center
ACE, Language Skills
Practice

Le subjonctif avec les expressions d'émotion et de volonté

In Chapter 14, you used the subjunctive with expressions of necessity. Another common use of the subjunctive in French is with expressions of emotion and desire. These are also subjective, because they represent the speaker's point of view rather than general fact. The use of the subjunctive mood tells the listener that s/he is hearing an opinion: how the speaker feels, or what s/he wants or doesn't want. Compare these sentences:

Marc vient nous voir chaque soir.
Je suis content que Marc vienne nous voir chaque soir.
Je veux que Marc vienne nous voir chaque soir.

The first sentence states general fact, without showing any emotional involvement on the part of the speaker. The second sentence, on the other hand, shows how the speaker feels about Marc's activity; therefore, it uses the subjunctive. The third sentence also involves emotional participation on the part of the speaker: it shows what s/he wants (for Marc to visit), and therefore contains a subjunctive. Note that English uses an infinitive following such expressions of volition.

I **want to go** to the movies.
I **want** you **to go** to the movies with me.

This use of an infinitive is possible in French only when there is no change of subject.

Je **veux aller** au cinéma.   I **want to go** to the movies.

However, when the speaker is referring to the actions of another person, the subjunctive is required.

Je **veux** que tu **ailles**   I **want** you **to go** to
   au cinéma avec moi.   the movies with me.

Following are common expressions of emotion and volition in French.

Les expressions d'émotion

être heureux (heureuse), être content(e)	*to be happy / glad*
être ravi(e)	*to be delighted*
être désolé(e)	*to be sorry*
être furieux (furieuse)	*to be furious*
être déçu(e)	*to be disappointed*
être triste	*to be sad*
être étonné(e)	*to be surprised / shocked*
être surpris(e)	*to be surprised*
être soulagé(e)	*to be relieved*
avoir honte	*to be ashamed*
avoir peur	*to be afraid*
regretter	*to regret, to be sorry*
cela (ça) m'agace	*it bothers me*

Les expressions de volonté

vouloir / ne … pas vouloir
insister pour
recommander
demander
exiger (= insister)

VÉRIFIEZ VOTRE COMPRÉHENSION

1. Now look back at the dialogue at the beginning of the chapter (p. 462).
   Underline all the uses of the subjunctive and all the infinitives that you find.
   With which types of expressions do these verb forms occur?

2. Can you explain why some expressions use the subjunctive, while others use the infinitive?

Pratiquons!

A. Réactions et recommandations. Imaginez que vous êtes le prof et que
vos étudiants vous disent les choses suivantes. Donnez des réactions possibles, en
utilisant les expressions d'émotion ou de volonté suggérées, et le *subjonctif.*

MODÈLE: Je n'ai pas passé l'examen hier, parce que j'étais malade.

> *Je suis content* que vous ne *soyez* plus malade. **ou**

> *J'exige* que vous **passiez** l'examen demain.

1. Je ne peux pas parler en classe, parce que j'ai très mal à la gorge.
   Je suis désolé(e) / Je ne veux pas
2. Je ne suis pas préparé(e); j'avais d'autres choses à faire hier!
   J'insiste pour que / Je voudrais
3. Je ne veux pas lire le texte—j'ai une migraine.
   Je regrette / Je recommande
4. Si je m'endors en classe, c'est parce que je suis enrhumé(e)!
   Je suis furieux (furieuse) / Je suis désolé(e)
5. J'aime bien les voyelles nasales aujourd'hui—j'ai le nez bouché!
   Je suis ravi(e) / Je recommande

B. Une réaction compréhensible. Vous êtes à l'université depuis deux
semaines. Votre mère vous téléphone pour vous donner des nouvelles de la famille.
Réagissez à ce qu'elle vous dit.

MODÈLE: «Papa va en Chine, pour travailler.»

> *Je suis étonné(e) que Papa aille en Chine.*

1. «Mami est à l'hôpital.»
2. «Ta sœur dort maintenant dans ta chambre.»
3. «Ton petit frère ne réussit pas à ses cours ce semestre.»
4. «Papi commence à boire.»
5. «J'arrête de fumer.»
6. «Tonton Michel veut être président des États-Unis.»
7. «Je vais faire la fête avec les voisins ce week-end.»
8. «Ta sœur et moi, nous venons te voir la semaine prochaine!»

Publish these paragraphs on your class web site or in your class newspaper. As a follow-up, have students choose any two and write solutions to them, using the expressions of necessity that they learned in Chapter 14.

C. Votre réaction personnelle. Refaites l'activité B avec un(e) partenaire, mais cette fois-ci, parlez des événements qui ont lieu[1] en ce moment. Pour commencer, écrivez cinq phrases.

MODÈLE: Il y a des guerres dans le monde.

Ensuite, dites ce que vous avez écrit à votre partenaire. Il/Elle va exprimer ses réactions pour chaque situation.

MODÈLE: Je suis déçu(e) qu'il y ait des guerres.

Portrait personnel

Après avoir fait l'activité C, écrivez un paragraphe où vous décrivez ce dont vous avez parlé avec votre partenaire, et ses réactions.

MODÈLE: Sarah est étonnée qu'il y ait beaucoup de pauvres aux États-Unis. Elle est triste que le gouvernement américain ne fasse rien pour résoudre le problème. …

D. Des conversations entre amis. Vous parlez de la vie universitaire avec des amis, qui donnent leurs opinions sur les phrases et les questions suivantes. Indiquez votre point de vue, en utilisant des expressions telles que: **je veux / voudrais, je ne veux pas / je ne voudrais pas, j'insiste pour, je recommande, j'aimerais, j'exige,** etc.

MODÈLE: On devrait aller en classe le samedi.

Oui, je recommande qu'on aille en classe le samedi. **ou**

Mais non, je ne veux pas aller en classe le samedi!

1. Le professeur devrait nous donner plus de devoirs écrits.
2. Les étudiants devraient passer moins de temps à s'amuser.
3. Les bibliothèques devraient vendre des boissons.
4. On devrait avoir des vacances d'hiver plus longues.
5. Qu'est-ce que tu recommandes pour le problème du parking sur le campus?
6. Qu'est-ce qu'il faut faire pour résoudre le problème des étudiants qui trichent[2]?
7. Comment peut-on améliorer les restaurants universitaires?

À vous de parler!

Possible problems: overcrowded classes, high tuition (**les frais de scolarité sont trop élevés**), uncomfortable classrooms, high cost of health insurance, expensive textbooks.

Remind students to use the health-related vocabulary from the beginning of the chapter. Place students in groups ranging from 2 to 4, to allow a variety of conversation types (patient with doctor, several patients talking to one another, etc.). For fun, have students perform their dialogues in front of the whole class and decide who is the "best" hypochondriac.

A. Solutions. Continuez le modèle établi dans l'activité D de *Pratiquons!* Avec deux ou trois camarades de classe, faites une liste des problèmes sur votre campus. Discutez ces problèmes en donnant vos réactions (utilisez des expressions d'émotion) et ensuite proposez des solutions (avec des expressions de volonté ou de nécessité).

B. Chez le docteur. Vous êtes hypocondriaque et vous allez chez le médecin très fréquemment. Imaginez: a.) vos conversations dans la salle d'attente avec d'autres patients aussi hypocondriaques que vous ou b.) votre conversation avec votre docteur dans la salle de consultation.

---

[1]*occur* [2]*cheat*

Les Français se soignent comme ça: les assurances médicales

Online Study Center
Web Search Activities

Pour les Américains, la question de se faire traiter pour une maladie est toujours compliquée. Est-ce que l'on a une assurance médicale? Si la réponse est négative, comment va-t-on payer les frais médicaux? Si oui, est-ce que le traitement est remboursable? Aux États-Unis actuellement, seulement 84% de la population est assurée. Cela laisse 44 millions de personnes qui doivent payer tous leurs frais médicaux sans aucune aide.

En France, la situation est bien différente. Le gouvernement assure les soins médicaux pour tout citoyen, et avec beaucoup de liberté personnelle. Les Français ont le droit de choisir sans contraintes leurs médecins et peuvent les voir aussi souvent qu'ils le veulent, ils peuvent aussi consulter des spécialistes à leur gré[1], soliciter une deuxième (et une troisième!) opinion et se faire admettre dans un hôpital s'ils le jugent nécessaire. Le traitement dans un hôpital public est gratuit; dans un hôpital privé c'est remboursable à 70%. Les visites chez le docteur et les ordonnances sont également remboursées à 70%.

La philosophie concernant la médecine et les traitements médicaux est aussi assez différente en France et aux États-Unis. Les Français connaissent tous le proverbe «Mieux vaut prévenir que guérir»; ils dépensent donc beaucoup d'argent en médecine préventive. Tous ces traitements sont, naturellement, remboursés par l'État.

C'est le système de Sécurité sociale qui assure l'accès universel aux docteurs et aux médicaments. Ce système coûte cher: la France dépense environ 10% de son revenu national, l'équivalent de 92 milliards de dollars, à financer l'assurance médicale de ses citoyens. (En comparaison, par contre, les États-Unis dépensent environ 14% de leur revenu national.) En plus, les contributions obligatoires des employeurs et des employés représentent environ 25% du salaire d'une personne—un montant énorme. Qu'en pensent alors les Français? Ils reconnaissent que le système coûte cher, mais ne veulent rien y changer—il marche bien, après tout. Si bien, qu'en l'an 2000, la France était première dans le monde en traitement médical, selon l'Organisation mondiale de la santé!

Réfléchissons

1. Êtes-vous assuré(e)? Connaissez-vous des personnes qui ne le sont pas? Comment est-ce que les personnes sans assurances peuvent obtenir les soins médicaux nécessaires?
2. Pensez-vous que les États-Unis devraient adopter un système universel comme celui de la France? Pourquoi ou pourquoi pas? Quels avantages et/ou désavantages voyez-vous dans ce système? Et dans le système américain?

---

[1] *at will*

Continuons!

Online Study Center
Language Skills Practice

Quel est votre mode de vie?

Faites le test suivant sur vos habitudes alimentaires et votre style de vie. Quand vous aurez terminé, comptez vos points et déterminez si le régime alimentaire que vous suivez est optimal ou non.

1. **Prenez-vous le petit déjeuner tous les matins?**
   a. Oui, toujours. (1 point)
   b. Non, jamais. (3 points)
   c. De temps en temps. (2 points)

2. **Quand vous prenez votre petit déjeuner, vous mangez ...**
   a. des céréales avec du lait écrémé[1]. (1 point)
   b. des tartines avec du beurre et de la confiture. (2 points)
   c. des œufs avec du bacon. (3 points)

3. **Que buvez-vous le matin?**
   a. Du chocolat chaud avec du lait entier[2]. (3 points)
   b. Un à deux cafés-crème. (2 points)
   c. Un jus de fruit. (1 point)

4. **Pour le déjeuner, vous mangez ...**
   a. aux fast-foods. (3 points)
   b. un repas léger[3] . . . une salade, un yaourt, des fruits, etc. (1 point)
   c. rien du tout. (3 points)

5. **Pour vous déplacer ...**
   a. vous allez à pied. (1 point)
   b. vous prenez votre bicyclette. (1 point)
   c. vous prenez votre voiture ou un moyen de transport public. (3 points)

6. **En général, vous pratiquez un sport ou vous faites de l'exercice ...**
   a. jamais. (3 points)
   b. tous les jours. (1 point)
   c. deux à trois fois par semaine. (2 points)

7. **Pour le dîner, vous préparez votre repas avec ...**
   a. des aliments biologiques et maigres. (1 point)
   b. des légumes et des aliments surgelés. (2 points)
   c. des aliments gras—des frites, du bœuf, du poulet frit. (3 points)

8. **Est-ce que vous mangez beaucoup de fruits et de légumes chaque jour?**
   a. Non, je suis carnivore, je ne mange que de la viande et des hydrates de carbone. (3 points)

---

[1] *skim milk* [2] *whole milk* [3] *light*

b. Oui, je suis végétarien(ne); la base de mon alimentation, ce sont les fruits et les légumes. (1 point)

c. Oui, j'essaie de manger équilibré, c'est-à-dire, un peu de tout. (1 point)

9. Consommez-vous des boissons alcooliques?

a. Rarement ou jamais. (1 point)

b. En abondance. (3 points)

c. Avec modération. (2 points)

10. Après le dîner le soir ...

a. vous restez vautré[1] sur le fauteuil, la télécommande à la main. (3 points)

b. vous faites du sport ou une activité physique. (1 point)

c. vous allez chercher le courrier ou vous sortez le chien. (2 points)

Résultats

De 10 à 15 points: Vous menez une vie bien équilibrée. Nous recommandons que vous ne changiez rien. Vous savez qu'il est important d'être attentif à votre poids[2] et à votre santé.

De 16 à 22 points: Vous pourriez améliorer votre style de vie. Il est préférable que vous fassiez quelques changements dans votre régime alimentaire et dans vos activités de tous les jours.

De 23 à 30 points: Il est dangereux de vivre comme vous le faites. Il faut que vous fassiez des changements immédiats, sinon vous allez le regretter.

---

[1]*spread out* [2]*weight*

Vous avez bien compris?

Répondez aux questions suivantes, selon le texte.

1. Si vous avez un score de 28, est-ce qu'il faut changer quelque chose dans votre style de vie? Pourquoi ou pourquoi pas? Comment pourriez-vous avoir un score moins élevé?
2. Selon le test, est-ce que c'est bien de ne pas prendre le déjeuner? Est-ce que c'est mieux de manger aux fast-foods? Pourquoi?
3. Selon le test, combien de fois par semaine faut-il prendre le petit déjeuner? Que faut-il prendre pour avoir une vie plus saine?
4. Est-ce que c'est mieux d'être végétarien(ne) que de manger équilibré, selon le test? Pourquoi pensez-vous que les auteurs disent cela?
5. Si vous avez un score de 12, qu'est-ce que les auteurs du test recommandent?

Vocabulaire essentiel

Les émotions

être déprimé(e), être malheureux(euse), être insatisfait(e)

être comblé(e), être aux anges, être satisfait(e)

être navré(e), être gêné(e)

être épaté(e), être choqué(e)

être fâché(e), être en colère, être en rage

Le régime alimentaire

des aliments *(m.)* riches en matières grasses

des aliments maigres
  (sans matières grasses)
des produits (m.) allégés
des produits de régime

des produits bio
  (biologiques)

des produits surgelés

Quelques expressions verbales utiles

être costaud
être fort(e)
être gros(se)
être mince = être maigre
être au régime = vouloir perdre du poids[2]
grossir = prendre du poids
maigrir = perdre du poids
garder sa ligne = ne pas prendre de poids
manger sain

---

[1]**Yahourt** is an alternate spelling of **yaourt**. [2]*weight*

À vous!

A. Rappelons-nous. Au début de cette section (p. 472) vous avez vu les expressions d'émotion suivantes. Placez ces émotions sous les photos qui correspondent le mieux. Ensuite, donnez un synonyme pour autant d'expressions que possible.

_____   _____   _____   _____   _____

1. être heureux (heureuse)
2. être étonné(e)
3. être furieux (furieuse)
4. être soulagé(e)
5. être triste
6. avoir honte
7. être content(e)
8. être ravi(e)
9. être navré(e)
10. être surpris(e)
11. être déçu(e)

B. Le contraire. Trouvez une expression qui exprime *le contraire* des expressions suivantes.

1. Je suis au régime.
2. Je suis déprimé(e).
3. Elle perd du poids.
4. Elle est aux anges.
5. Je garde ma ligne.
6. Je suis satisfait.
7. Il maigrit.
8. Il est heureux.
9. Nous mangeons des aliments maigres.
10. Nous sommes minces.

C. Comment se sentent-ils? Avec un(e) partenaire, nommez des personnages de romans ou de films qui sentent les émotions suivantes. Ensuite comparez votre liste avec celles de vos camarades.

1. malheureux
2. déprimé
3. épaté
4. fâché
5. comblé
6. déçu
7. navré

Structure 2

Le subjonctif pour exprimer le jugement et le doute

Online Study Center
ACE, Language Skills Practice

The subjunctive mood is also used with two other types of constructions that show the speaker's point of view: expressions of judgment and of doubt. The rule concerning expressions of judgment is clear-cut: whenever a speaker gives a personal judgment about another person, the verb is in the subjunctive mood.

> Il est juste que le Président ait un avion à sa disposition, mais il est dommage qu'il ne puisse pas voyager par train. Il est agréable de voyager par train!

Note that in the first two clauses, the speaker is expressing a judgment concerning the actions of someone other than him/herself. This judgment is not necessarily shared by others, however. For this reason, the subjunctive is used, pointing out to listeners that this is not fact, but simply one person's perspective. In the final sentence, the speaker continues to express his/her opinion, but because there is no change of subject, this judgment is followed by an infinitive.

Les expressions de jugement

il est bon	il est triste	il est stupide
il est juste	il est dommage	il est agaçant
il est normal	il est regrettable	il est surprenant
il est préférable	il est inacceptable	il est étonnant
il est injuste	il est bizarre	il est agréable

Expressions of doubt are a little less clear-cut in French than expressions of judgment. Speakers of French normally make a distinction between doubt, which requires a subjunctive, and certainty, which requires a verb in the indicative mood.

> Marie doute que son mari la comprenne vraiment. Elle est sûre qu'il fait de son mieux, mais il est peu probable qu'il sache vraiment ce qu'elle veut dans la vie. Et son mari? Il est certain que sa femme ne le comprend pas du tout!

For French speakers there is a continuum, which runs from total doubt on one end to total certainty on the other. Expressions that are closer to expressing doubt **(il est possible)** take the subjunctive, whereas those that are closer to expressing certainty **(il est probable)** take the indicative. The following expressions of doubt take the subjunctive, whereas the expressions of certainty take the indicative.

Les expressions de doute

il est douteux
il est possible / il se peut que
il est impossible / improbable
il est peu possible / peu probable
il n'est pas possible / pas probable
il n'est pas clair
il n'est pas certain
il n'est pas vrai / il est faux
douter: je doute, elle doute, etc.

Go over each expression to make sure students know the meaning, demonstrating **il est dommage** if necessary. Remind students of related expressions that they have already seen: **cela m'agace / il est agaçant, je suis étonné(e) / il est étonnant …**

Les expressions de certitude

il est clair	il est sûr
il est certain	il est probable
il est évident	il n'est pas douteux
il est vrai	ne … pas douter

Les verbes *penser* et *croire*. These two verbs represent one last complication in the question of doubt versus certainty. Used in the affirmative, these verbs generally represent a relative lack of doubt, and therefore take the indicative.

Je pense que le Président est peu rémunéré.
Je crois que nous devrions lui donner un meilleur salaire.

Used in the negative or the interrogative, on the other hand, these verbs generally represent more doubt than certainty, and are followed by the subjunctive.

Pensez-vous que le Président soit peu rémunéré?
Je ne crois pas que nous devions lui donner un meilleur salaire.

VÉRIFIEZ VOTRE COMPRÉHENSION

1. Reread the test in **Continuons!,** and underline all the expressions of judgment, doubt, and certainty that you find in it. Explain which moods are used with these forms, and why.

2. Did you find any expressions of judgment or doubt that are followed by an infinitive? Why is the infinitive appropriate in these sentences?

À l'écoute!

Écoutez les phrases suivantes, et dites si le deuxième verbe est au subjonctif ou à l'indicatif.

1. _____ subjonctif _____ indicatif
2. _____ subjonctif _____ indicatif
3. _____ subjonctif _____ indicatif
4. _____ subjonctif _____ indicatif
5. _____ subjonctif _____ indicatif
6. _____ subjonctif _____ indicatif
7. _____ subjonctif _____ indicatif
8. _____ subjonctif _____ indicatif

Pratiquons!

A. Vos opinions. Donnez vos jugements concernant les phrases suivantes.

MODÈLE: Les étudiants américains doivent payer leurs études.

*Il est injuste (**ou** normal) que les étudiants doivent payer leurs études.*

1. On doit étudier une langue étrangère à l'université.
2. On peut terminer un diplôme en quatre ans.
3. Beaucoup d'étudiants mangent au fast-food tous les jours.
4. Il y a des étudiants qui trichent.
5. Les étudiants connaissent bien leurs professeurs.
6. Les manuels de classe coûtent cher.
7. Il y a beaucoup d'étudiants dans les classes.

Maintenant, exprimez trois opinions personnelles concernant la vie universitaire.

You may want to point out that it is not unusual to find these same forms followed by an indicative, especially in spoken French. There is a nuance of difference between these example sentences with the subjunctive, and the same sentences with the indicative; the difference lies in the degree of the speaker's uncertainty. Regardless of the form that they might use in spoken language, however, most speakers of French consider the subjunctive the more appropriate mood to use when negation or interrogation is combined with these verbs.

Audioscript: 1. Je suis certain(e) que Bernard suivra les conseils du docteur. 2. Il est possible qu'il aille au cinéma avec nous. 3. Mais il est plus probable qu'il se couchera tôt ce soir. 4. Je ne doute pas du tout qu'il prendra des antihistaminiques. 5. Il est peu probable qu'il fasse les inhalations—il déteste les inhalations! 6. Il se peut qu'il retourne chez le docteur dans deux semaines. 7. Il est clair qu'il retournera s'il ne se sent pas mieux. 8. Je pense que le docteur a raison—Bernard a une sinusite.

Answer Key. Possible answers: 1. Il est normal que l'on doive étudier une langue étrangère à l'université. 2. Il est bon que l'on puisse terminer un diplôme en quatre ans. 3. Il n'est pas bon que beaucoup d'étudiants mangent au fast-food tous les jours. 4. Il est inacceptable qu'il y ait des étudiants qui trichent. 5. Il est étonnant que les étudiants connaissent bien leurs professeurs. 6. Il est dommage que les manuels de classe coûtent cher. 7. Il est regrettable qu'il y ait beaucoup d'étudiants dans les classes.

B. Jugements et doutes. Récrivez les phrases suivantes, avec les expressions données, en faisant attention à l'usage du subjonctif ou de l'indicatif.

1. *Il est clair que* nous allons souvent au gymnase. (il est peu probable / il n'est pas vrai / il est évident / elle doute)
2. *Je doute qu'*il fasse du sport tous les jours! (il est certain / il se peut / il est probable / pensez-vous … ?)
3. *Il est impossible que* tu maigrisses avec ce régime. (il est bien probable / je crois / il est douteux / il est possible)

🗣️**C. Transformations.** Posez les questions suivantes à un(e) camarade de classe, pour savoir les changements qui lui arriveront dans l'avenir. Cette personne va répondre avec des expressions de doute ou de certitude.

◎ MODÈLE: Dans dix ans, est-ce que tu habiteras toujours ici?

Il est peu probable que j'habite ici dans dix ans.

1. Dans dix ans, est-ce que tu seras marié(e)?
2. Auras-tu des enfants? Si oui, est-ce que tu garderas ta ligne?
3. Est-ce que tu mangeras mieux? Est-ce que tu achèteras exclusivement des produits allégés ou biologiques?
4. Est-ce que tu feras un régime? Pourquoi?
5. Seras-tu content(e) de ta vie? Pourquoi ou pourquoi pas?
6. Quand tu obtiendras ton premier poste, est-ce que tu seras stressé(e)? Pourquoi ou pourquoi pas?
7. Est-ce que tu seras en bonne santé?

Portrait personnel

Écrivez un paragraphe dans lequel vous comparerez les opinions de votre partenaire avec vos propres opinions. Est-ce que vous serez plutôt semblables ou plutôt différents dans dix ans?

À vous de parler!

👥**A. Quoi manger?** Donnez des exemples pour les aliments et les produits suivants. Ensuite, dites à votre partenaire quels sont les produits que vous consommez le plus souvent. Finalement, faites une enquête dans la classe pour savoir quels sont les produits que vos camarades consomment.

◎ MODÈLE: des produits surgelés

des pizzas, des plats préparés

1. des aliments riches en matières grasses
2. des produits bio
3. des aliments maigres
4. des produits allégés
5. des produits de régime

Dans l'ensemble, quelles sont les habitudes alimentaires des étudiants de la classe? Qui mange mieux et plus équilibré? Pourquoi?

B. Mes sentiments. Avec un(e) partenaire, discutez de ce qu'il faut faire pour éviter le stress et rester en bonne santé.

1. Quand vous avez trop de travail (devoirs, examens, responsabilités familiales, etc.), qu'est-ce qu'il est important de faire pour réduire le stress?
2. Est-il prioritaire que vous mangiez de façon équilibrée? Que vous mangiez des produits biologiques? Est-ce que vous le faites?
3. À votre avis, est-il important que vous vous fassiez vacciner régulièrement? Pourquoi ou pourquoi pas?
4. Est-il essentiel de faire une activité physique tous les jours? Quelle activité est-ce que vous faites de façon régulière?
5. Combien d'heures faut-il que vous dormiez chaque nuit? Est-ce que vous le faites?
6. Est-il important que vous limitiez votre consommation d'alcool et de tabac?

Maintenant, regardez l'enquête sur les Français et comparez vos réponses avec les leurs. Dites à la classe si vous êtes comme les Français, ou plutôt différents.

Question 1: Pour rester en bonne santé ou maintenir votre état de santé, dans votre vie quotidienne, est-il selon vous tout à fait prioritaire, important mais sans plus ou secondaire de …

En pourcentage de personnes qui ont répondu «Tout à fait prioritaire»

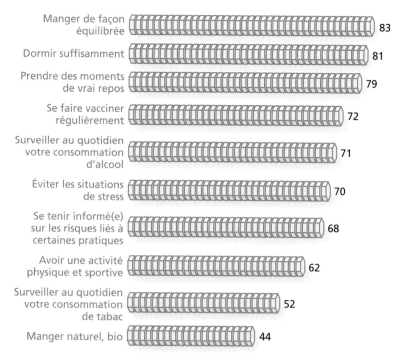

Manger de façon équilibrée	83
Dormir suffisamment	81
Prendre des moments de vrai repos	79
Se faire vacciner régulièrement	72
Surveiller au quotidien votre consommation d'alcool	71
Éviter les situations de stress	70
Se tenir informé(e) sur les risques liés à certaines pratiques	68
Avoir une activité physique et sportive	62
Surveiller au quotidien votre consommation de tabac	52
Manger naturel, bio	44

Question 2: Et personnellement, le faites-vous ou pas?

En pourcentage des réponses «oui»

	Ensemble des Français	Professionnels de la santé
Dormir suffisamment	56	49
Manger de façon équilibrée	55	61
Se faire vacciner régulièrement	53	58
Prendre des moments de vrai repos	49	52
Éviter les situations de stress	43	41
Surveiller au quotidien votre consommation d'alcool	43	69
Surveiller au quotidien votre consommation de tabac	42	76
Avoir une activité physique et sportive	39	45
Se tenir informé(e) sur les risques liés à certaines pratiques	34	42
Manger naturel, bio	20	10

C. Conseils. Votre meilleur(e) ami(e) est très stressé(e) par la vie qu'il/elle mène: il/elle est déprimé(e), travaille trop, boit trop, fume trop, tousse toujours, ne dort pas assez, mange comme quatre, etc. Vous et vos amis vous allez vous occuper un peu de lui/elle. Vous organisez pour lui/elle un plan de beauté et de santé en lui donnant des conseils de nutrition et de mode de vie.

Une crise de foie, c'est comme ça!

Online Study Center
Web Search Activities

Avez-vous jamais été malade après avoir mangé un repas très gras? Quand cela arrive chez les Français, ils disent qu'ils souffrent d'une «crise de foie». Mais qu'est-ce que c'est, exactement, une crise de foie? Pour les Français, c'est la nausée, les vomissements, la diarrhée, les migraines et/ou l'indigestion générale, qui suivent souvent un repas avec beaucoup de matières grasses (la crème, les plats frits, la viande, le chocolat, etc.), et qui ne peuvent pas être expliqués par un autre diagnostic. Quand ils tombent malades sans aucune[1] raison visible, les Français ont tendance à blâmer leur foie, bien que[2] les médecins leur disent que ce n'est pas la faute du foie, mais de tout le système digestif. C'est une explication qui dure depuis des siècles[3], et que l'on entend fréquemment en France de nos jours.

---

[1] *with no* [2] *even though* [3] *centuries*

Même au vingt et unième siècle, quand la médecine moderne a bien démontré que le foie n'est pas responsable, cette expression reste très populaire en France (mais pas dans les autres pays francophones!). Comment expliquer la popularité de cette expression? Selon le professeur Dhumeaux, chef de service à l'hôpital Henri-Mondor de Créteil, c'est dû à «une symbolique mythologique du foie, [...] siège[1] de l'âme[2] humaine, de la colère, de la peur et de la mélancolie, mais aussi outil de la punition (divine) pour avoir péché[3] par excès de plaisirs (de table)».

Réfléchissons

1. Comment est-ce qu'on explique une maladie générale dans votre culture? Est-ce qu'il y a un organe que l'on tient[4] responsable pour les maladies inexplicables?
2. Que pensez-vous de la tendance des Français à blâmer le foie quand ils tombent malades? Est-ce logique? Est-ce amusant? Expliquez votre réponse.
3. Selon le professeur Dhumeaux, le foie est le siège des émotions et de l'âme humaine chez les Français. Est-ce que c'est la même chose dans votre culture? Si non, où se trouvent les émotions et l'âme chez vous?

Dans un parc à Nice. Que font ces hommes pour rester en forme et garder la ligne? Que faites-vous? Est-ce que vous pratiquez un sport régulièrement? Lequel?

---

[1]*seat* [2]*soul* [3]*having sinned* [4]*holds*

A. Stratégies. Scientific texts often use many cognates and jargon terms. When reading these texts, try to identify words that you can understand based on their similarity to English words (but be on the lookout for possible **"faux amis"!**), and avoid the urge to look these terms up in the dictionary. Look for repeated root forms as well, as these often appear in jargon words: you may see a root in a noun, and then the same root in an adjective or a verb. Figuring out the meaning of the root, along with the part of speech of each individual word, will often help you to determine the general meaning of these terms without needing to look them up.

B. Avant de lire

I. Pensons au sujet! Répondez aux questions suivantes avant de lire le texte.

1. Que savez-vous à propos de la médecine alternative? Pour vous, qu'est-ce que ce terme suggère? Quels traitements vous viennent à l'esprit quand vous entendez ces deux mots?
2. Avez-vous jamais essayé la médecine alternative, ou connaissez-vous quelqu'un qui l'utilise? Est-ce que vous avez eu ou est-ce qu'il/elle a eu de bons résultats?
3. Est-ce que vous essaieriez un traitement alternatif si vous étiez malade et que la médecine traditionnelle ne vous aidait pas?

II. Vocabulaire. Le texte contient des termes médicaux et techniques. Essayez d'en comprendre le sens d'après les explications dans la lecture. Expliquez le sens de ces mots (en **caractères gras**) en anglais, d'après le contexte donné.

1. «Le **thermalisme** [= cures thermales] concerne l'utilisation des eaux minérales à des fins thérapeutiques.»
2. «Les cures thermales s'adressent aux **maladies chroniques** que les traitements classiques ne **soulagent** pas …»
3. «Thérapeutique médicale basée sur les bienfaits de l'eau de mer, des algues et du climat marin et leurs **vertus revitalisantes.**»
4. «La thalassothérapie n'est pas **prise en charge** par la Sécurité sociale.»
5. «**L'essentiel des soins** de la thalassothérapie est **à la charge** de la personne.»
6. «La **cure** est assez courte: en règle générale, six à huit jours à raison de quatre **soins** par jour.»
7. «Le médecin **s'engage à prescrire** la station la plus proche du domicile de **l'assuré,** correspondant aux orientations thérapeutiques souhaitées.»

C. Lisons! Lisez le texte à la page 482, et répondez aux questions qui suivent.

Les cures thermales et la thalassothérapie: où vont les Français pour rester en bonne santé?

- ## Cures thermales: qu'est-ce que c'est?

Le thermalisme (crénothérapie) concerne l'utilisation des eaux minérales (telles qu'elles sortent de la source) à des fins thérapeutiques.

Les cures thermales s'adressent aux maladies chroniques que les traitements classiques ne soulagent pas suffisamment et interviennent en complément des traitements habituels.

Fréquentation: On dénombre plus de 500 000 cures par an en France. 80% des cures sont prescrites en orientation rhumatologie et ORL[1]. La France détient 20% du capital thermal européen.

Durée d'une cure: 18 jours de soins effectifs, parfois répartis sur 21 jours de séjour.

- ## Qu'est-ce que la thalassothérapie?

Thérapeutique médicale basée sur les bienfaits de l'eau de mer, des algues et du climat marin et leurs vertus revitalisantes.

La thalassothérapie est indiquée surtout comme cure de remise en forme et de confort; elle n'est donc pas prise en charge par la Sécurité sociale. Dans quelques cas de rééducation fonctionnelle, on peut y bénéficier de soins de kinésithérapie partiellement pris en charge par la Sécurité sociale, mais l'essentiel des soins est à la charge de la personne.

Durée d'une cure: La cure est assez courte: en règle générale, six à huit jours à raison de quatre soins par jour. Un médecin, vu à l'arrivée, établit et propose les soins en fonction des particularités de chacun.

Cures thermales et thalassothérapie: est-ce que c'est la même chose?
La cure thermale est basée sur les vertus thérapeutiques des eaux minérales. Elle est prescrite par le médecin, reconnue et prise en charge par la sécurité sociale en France.

- ## Le séjour

Choix de la station

Le médecin s'engage à prescrire la station la plus proche du domicile de l'assuré, correspondant aux orientations thérapeutiques souhaitées. Le médecin dispose de documentations sur les différentes stations thermales françaises, leurs indications, la composition des eaux, l'agrément. Il est conseillé de se renseigner directement auprès de l'établissement thermal pour la réservation et auprès de l'office du tourisme pour connaître les différentes modalités du séjour (acheminement, hébergement).

Sur place

Le curiste rencontre un médecin thermaliste (libre choix sur une liste fournie par l'établissement) qui seul pourra prescrire, en fonction de la pathologie et de l'état de santé du patient, les soins de cure appropriés.

---

[1] *oto-rhino-laryngologie*

Questions de compréhension

1. Expliquez la différence entre «cure thermale» et «thalassothérapie».
2. Quelles maladies est-ce qu'on peut soigner avec les cures thermales?
3. Combien de jours durent les soins? Expliquez votre réponse.
4. Que fait la thalassothérapie?
5. Est-ce que les cures thermales sont remboursées par la sécurité sociale? Et la thalassothérapie?
6. Combien de jours dure la cure en thalassothérapie?
7. Quel est le rôle du médecin qui prescrit les cures thermales?
8. Quel est le rôle du médecin thermaliste?

Questions d'expansion

1. En général, qui choisit de faire une cure thermale? Expliquez votre réponse.
2. Dans le texte, il est suggéré de consulter l'office de tourisme dans la région où se trouve l'établissement thermal. Pourquoi?
3. Comment est-ce que les médecins choisissent la meilleure station thermale pour leurs patients? Qu'est-ce qu'ils considèrent, spécifiquement? Pensez-vous que ces critères soient raisonnables? Expliquez votre réponse.

D. Après la lecture. Pensez aux questions suivantes et répondez-y.

1. Vous venez de voir dans le texte comment les Français se soignent avec des traitements fondés sur les bienfaits de l'eau. Dans votre pays est-ce qu'il y a des centres naturels similaires? Quels sont les traitements que l'on y applique? Quels sont les coûts[1] de ces traitements? Qui va dans ces centres? Y êtes-vous allés(e)? Quelle a été votre réaction?

2. Que pensez-vous du fait que les soins dans les cures thermales en France sont remboursés par la Sécurité sociale? Croyez-vous que ce soit une bonne idée? Pourquoi? Quels soins sont remboursés dans votre pays par les assurances médicales?

Chez le docteur. Qui sont les personnes sur cette photo? À votre avis, pourquoi est-ce que la femme est venue voir le docteur? Qu'est-ce que le docteur va lui dire de prendre comme médicament?

---

[1]prices

Lexique 🎧

Vocabulaire essentiel

Les parties internes du corps *internal organs*

le cœur *heart*
le foie *liver*
la gorge *throat*
l'intestin *(m.) intestines*
les sinus *(m.) sinuses*
le ventre *stomach*

Les médicaments et les remèdes *medications and remedies*

les antihistaminiques *(m.)* antihistamines
les antiobiotiques *(m.) antibiotics*
l'aspirine *(f.) aspirin*
les cachets *(m.) tablets*
les comprimés *(m.) tablets*

les gouttes *(f.)* nasales *nasal sprays*
les médicaments *(m.) medications*
les pastilles *(f.) lozenges*
les piqûres *(f.) shots*

le sirop *cough syrup*
un thermomètre *thermometer*
les tisanes *(f.) herbal teas*
les vitamines *(f.) vitamins*

Les maladies les plus communes *common illnesses*

avoir de la fièvre *to have a fever*
avoir mal au cœur *to be nauseous*
avoir mal au dos *to have a backache*
avoir mal à la gorge *to have a sore throat*
avoir mal à la tête *to have a headache*

avoir une migraine *to have a migraine*
avoir la nausée *to be nauseous*
avoir le nez bouché *to have a stuffy nose*
avoir le nez qui coule *to have a runny nose*

avoir une rage de dents *to have a toothache*
avoir un rhume *to have a cold*
avoir la tête qui tourne *to be dizzy*
avoir le vertige *to be dizzy*
être enrhumé(e) *to have a cold*
tousser *to cough*

Le régime alimentaire *daily diet*

des aliments *(m.)* riches en matières grasses *rich foods*
des aliments maigres (sans matières grasses) *fat-free foods*
des produits *(m.)* bio (biologiques) *organic foods*
des produits allégés *diet foods*
des produits de régime *diet aids*
des produits surgelés *frozen foods*

Quelques expressions verbales utiles

être costaud(e) *to be stocky*
être fort(e) *to be heavy*
être gros(se) *to be overweight*
être maigre *to be thin, skinny*
être mince *to be slim*

être au régime *to be on a diet*
garder sa ligne *to maintain one's weight*
grossir *to gain weight*
maigrir *to lose weight*

manger sain *to eat healthy foods*
perdre du poids *to lose weight*
prendre du poids *to gain weight*

Les expressions d'émotion

avoir honte *to be ashamed*
avoir peur *to be afraid*
cela (ça) m'agace *it bothers me*
être aux anges *to be on cloud nine*
être choqué(e) *to be shocked*
être en colère *to be angry*
être comblé(e) *to be very happy*
être content(e) *to be happy / glad*
être déçu(e) *to be disappointed*
être déprimé(e) *to be depressed*

être désolé(e) *to be sorry*
être épaté(e) *to be dumbfounded*
être étonné(e) *to be surprised / shocked*
être fâché(e) *to be angry*
être furieux (furieuse) *to be furious*
être gêné(e) *to be sorry / embarrassed*
être heureux (heureuse) *to be happy*

être insatisfait(e) *to be dissatisfied*
être navré(e) *to be sorry*
être malheureux (malheureuse) *to be unhappy*
être en rage *to be enraged*
être ravi(e) *to be delighted*
être satisfait(e) *to be satisfied*
être soulagé(e) *to be relieved*
être surpris(e) *to be surprised*
être triste *to be sad*
regretter *to regret / to be sorry*

Les expressions de volonté

demander *to ask / to require*
exiger *to insist*
insister (pour) *to insist (on)*

recommander *to recommend*
vouloir *to want*

Les expressions de jugement

il est agaçant *it's bothersome*
il est agréable *it's enjoyable / agreeable*
il est bizarre *it's bizarre*
il est bon *it's good*
il est dommage *it's a pity*

il est étonnant *it's stunning*
il est inacceptable *it's unacceptable*
il est injuste *it's unfair*
il est juste *it's right / fair*
il est normal *it's normal*

il est préférable *it's preferable*
il est regrettable *it's regrettable / unfortunate*
il est stupide *it's dumb / stupid*
il est surprenant *it's surprising*
il est triste *it's sad*

Les expressions de doute

douter *to doubt*
il est douteux *it's doubtful*
il est faux *it's false*
il est impossible *it's impossible*
il est improbable *it's improbable*
il est peu possible *it's not very likely*
il est peu probable *it's not very probable*
il est possible *it's possible*
il n'est pas certain *it's not certain*
il n'est pas clair *it's not clear / obvious*
il n'est pas possible *it's not possible*
il n'est pas probable *it's not probable*
il n'est pas vrai *it's not true*
il se peut que *it's possible*

Les expressions de certitude

il est certain *it's certain*

il est clair *it's obvious / clear*

il est évident *it's evident*

il est probable *it's probable*

il est sûr *it's certain / sure*

il est vrai *it's true*

il n'est pas douteux *it's not doubtful*

ne ... pas douter *not to doubt*

Expansion personnelle

Les parties internes du corps *internal organs*

le cerveau *brain*

les reins *kidneys*

Les médicaments et les remèdes *medications and remedies*

un calmant *tranquilizer*

la pommade *ointment*

un somnifère *sleep aid*

les suppositoires *(m.)* *suppositories*

Les maladies les plus communes *common illnesses*

avoir une crise cardiaque *to have a heart attack*

avoir une crise de foie *to have digestive problems*

avoir la diarrhée *to have diarrhea*

être constipé(e) *to be constipated*

vomir *to vomit*

Mes voyages et mes souvenirs

In this chapter, you will learn useful expressions for traveling by plane or train. You will visit Belgium and learn about its specialties, and you will share memories of past trips with your classmates.

Point out to students that the word **souvenir** has several uses in French: as a noun meaning *a memory;* as a verb **(se souvenir de)** meaning *to remember;* and finally, as a noun used in the same sense as *souvenir* in English: *a keepsake.* In the title of this chapter, **souvenirs** is intended to imply all these possibilities.

The vocabulary that you will learn includes

Traveling by plane or train
Visiting a country or a city
Activities to do when visiting a country or a city
Making hotel, plane, and train reservations

The structures that you will learn include

Prepositions used with the names of continents, countries, and cities
The verbs **se souvenir de** and **se rappeler**
Relative pronouns

The culture that you will study includes

How the French buy, drink, and serve wine
The cultural and historical significance of the expression **"Je me souviens"** in Québec

Commençons!

Un voyage en avion

Luc et Léa sont à l'aéroport de Paris-Orly. Ils partent en voyage en Guadeloupe, à Pointe-à-Pitre, pour leur lune de miel[1]. Nous allons les accompagner pour leur souhaiter un bon voyage!

À l'enregistrement au comptoir d'Air France

Luc et Léa ont deux valises et deux bagages à main. Luc place les deux valises sur le tapis roulant pour les enregistrer. L'hôtesse au sol leur pose quelques questions.

L'HÔTESSE: Vous voulez enregistrer deux valises?

LUC: Oui, c'est bien ça.

L'HÔTESSE: Combien de bagages à main avez-vous?

LÉA: Nous en avons deux.

L'HÔTESSE: Très bien. Veuillez me montrer vos billets d'avion et une pièce d'identité, s'il vous plaît. Avez-vous une carte Fréquence Plus[2]?

LÉA: Voici nos passeports et nos billets. Et voici notre carte Fréquence Plus d'Air France.

L'HÔTESSE: Voyons … Vous avez les sièges 15B et 15C. Madame, votre siège est près du couloir. Préférez-vous la fenêtre?

LÉA: Oh, non! J'aime être près du couloir, comme ça je peux aller aux toilettes plus facilement!

L'HÔTESSE: Votre vol à destination de Pointe-à-Pitre est direct—sans escale. Votre embarquement[3] s'effectuera à 15 heures 30 au terminal T, porte 10.

---

[1] *honeymoon* [2] *frequent flyer* [3] *boarding*

Au contrôle sûreté

LE CONTRÔLEUR: Placez vos bagages à main sur le tapis roulant, merci.

LÉA: Luc, tu veux passer le premier par le détecteur de métaux? N'oublie pas de vider[1] tes poches.

LUC: Oui, je vais passer d'abord. Voilà mes clés et mon mobile.

LE CONTRÔLEUR: Merci. C'est bon. Au suivant[2]!

À la douane

LE DOUANIER: Bonjour. Vos pièces d'identité et vos billets d'avion, s'il vous plaît.

LUC ET LÉA: Bonjour, Monsieur. Les voilà.

LE DOUANIER: Vous partez en Guadeloupe?

LUC: Oui, nous allons passer notre lune de miel en Guadeloupe. Nous allons visiter la Guadeloupe et après, nous irons à Fort-de-France en Martinique.

LE DOUANIER: Vous avez de la chance! J'ai souvent visité la Guadeloupe et j'adore Pointe-à-Pitre. Bon, je vois que tout est en règle! Bon voyage!

Au terminal

LE HAUT-PARLEUR: *Embarquement immédiat porte 10 pour les passagers à destination de Pointe-à-Pitre sur le vol AF 1777.*

LÉA: Vite, Luc, dépêche-toi. Nous allons manquer[3] notre vol!

LUC: J'arrive, Léa. On voit que tu ne portes pas les bagages. Ils sont lourds[4], tu sais!

---

[1]*to empty* [2]*Next* [3]*to miss* [4]*heavy*

À bord du vol AF 1777

L'HÔTESSE DE L'AIR: Messieurs les passagers, bonjour! Le capitaine Yvan Cendrard et tout l'équipage à bord du vol Air France 1777 à destination de Pointe-à-Pitre vous souhaitent la bienvenue. Nous vous demandons de bien vouloir placer vos bagages à main dans les compartiments ou sous le siège devant vous. Nous vous prions également d'éviter[1] de circuler en cabine pendant le vol. Le décollage aura lieu dans quelques instants. Veuillez attacher vos ceintures de sécurité, merci.

LÉA: Super! On est assis à côté de la sortie de secours! Comme ça, on a plus d'espace!

LUC: Ou comme ça, on peut sortir les premiers si l'avion s'écrase[2]!

Vous avez bien compris?

Identifiez les dessins avec les mots suivants.

1. le décollage
2. l'enregistrement
3. l'hôtesse de l'air
4. le siège
5. le billet
6. la valise
7. une pièce d'identité
8. la ceinture de sécurité
9. l'embarquement

a. _____ b. _____ c. _____

d. _____ e. _____ f. _____

———————
[1] to avoid [2] crashes

g. _____   h. _____   i. _____

Vocabulaire essentiel

Les trains

1. le wagon-lit / le train à couchettes
2. le wagon-restaurant
3. la voie
4. le quai
5. l'horaire *(m.)* des trains
6. un billet non-fumeur
7. le guichet
8. composter un billet

À l'aéroport et dans l'avion

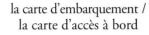

la carte d'embarquement /
la carte d'accès à bord

la remise des bagages

l'étiquette *(f.)* de la valise

l'avion *(m.)* atterrit /
l'atterrissage *(m.)*

l'avion décolle / le
décollage *(m.)*

la piste de décollage / la
piste d'atterrissage

le magasin hors taxe

le steward *(m.)* / l'hôtesse de l'air *(f.)*

l'agent *(m.)* / l'hôtesse au sol

le pilote

les turbulences *(f.)*

la douane

Avez-vous quelque chose à déclarer? Non, je n'ai rien à déclarer.

À vous!

A. L'interprète. Vous êtes interprète-traducteur pour l'aéroport de Paris-Orly. Vous aidez les passagers qui désirent recevoir un service ou obtenir un renseignement en traduisant pour eux. Pour chacune des situations suivantes, choisissez la réponse correcte.

1. Un voyageur voudrait savoir l'heure de départ de son TGV (train à grande vitesse). Il part pour Nantes. Quelle question doit-il poser?

   a. «À quelle heure arrive le TGV en provenance de Nantes?»
   b. «À quelle heure part le TGV depuis Nantes?»
   c. «À quelle heure part le TGV à destination de Nantes?»

2. Des voyageurs à Lyon souhaitent aller à Bruxelles. Ils ne veulent pas revenir à Lyon après. Que disent-ils pour faire leur réservation?

   a. «Nous voudrions un billet simple.»
   b. «Nous voudrions un billet aller-retour.»
   c. «Nous voudrions réserver une place en première classe.»

3. Un passager voudrait voyager de nuit et dormir dans le train à destination de Strasbourg. Comment va-t-il faire sa réservation?

   a. «Je voudrais acheter un billet wagon-lit pour le train en provenance de Strasbourg.»
   b. «Je voudrais acheter un billet wagon-lit pour le train à destination de Strasbourg.»
   c. «Je voudrais acheter un billet au wagon-restaurant en provenance de Strasbourg.»

4. Un passager a quatre valises. Il veut monter dans l'avion sans ses quatre valises. Que dit-il à l'hôtesse au sol?

   a. «Je voudrais mettre mes quatre valises dans le compartiment.»
   b. «Je voudrais enregistrer mes quatre valises.»
   c. «Je voudrais chercher mes quatre valises à la remise des bagages.»

5. Un voyageur voudrait savoir à quelle heure il faut monter dans l'avion. Comment pose-t-il cette question à l'agent au sol?

   a. «À quelle heure est l'atterrissage?»
   b. «À quelle heure est le décollage?»
   c. «À quelle heure est l'embarquement?»

6. Une dame veut être assise à côté de la fenêtre dans l'avion parce qu'elle est malade si elle ne peut pas regarder à l'extérieur. Que dit-elle à l'hôtesse au sol?

   a. «Je voudrais un siège près de la sortie de secours.»
   b. «Je voudrais un siège près du couloir.»
   c. «Je voudrais un siège près de la fenêtre.»

B. La bonne réponse. En petits groupes, trouvez la bonne réponse aux questions suivantes. Essayez de faire cette activité sans regarder le *Vocabulaire essentiel!*

1. Avez-vous quelque chose à déclarer?
2. Quel type de billet achète-t-on quand on ne fume pas?
3. Qui sont les personnes qui s'occupent des passagers dans l'avion?
4. À l'aéroport, comment s'appelle l'endroit où les passagers font des achats qui leur coûtent moins cher?
5. Où va-t-on chercher les bagages?
6. Que fait-on pour valider un billet à la gare?
7. Que fait un avion qui arrive à sa destination finale?
8. Comment s'appelle le papier qui sert à identifier les bagages?
9. Où est-ce que les passagers attendent leurs trains?
10. Où décollent les avions?

C. Quel genre de voyageur (voyageuse) êtes-vous? Est-ce que vous êtes un(e) bon(ne) ou un(e) mauvais(e) voyageur (voyageuse)? Posez les questions suivantes à vos camarades de classe pour en découvrir la réponse.

1. Quand tu rentres aux États-Unis après un voyage à l'étranger, est-ce que tu rapportes des produits qui sont interdits dans ton pays (par exemple, du fromage frais, de la viande, des cigares, des fruits)?
2. Tu es dans l'avion et tu as un siège près des toilettes. Une femme enceinte rentre dans l'avion en se plaignant[1] car son siège est loin des toilettes. Est-ce que tu lui proposes ta place?
3. Un vieux monsieur ne peut pas mettre ses bagages dans le train. Vas-tu l'aider?
4. Derrière toi dans l'avion, il y a un enfant qui pleure constamment. Est-ce que tu te retournes et dis à sa mère de le faire taire[2]?
5. Quand tu voyages en avion, est-ce que tu dois absolument avoir un siège près du couloir ou près de la fenêtre? Ou ça n'a pas d'importance[3]?
6. Es-tu malade en avion? Dois-tu prendre des médicaments?
7. Est-ce que tu essaies de passer plus d'un bagage à main dans l'avion?
8. Dans l'avion, est-ce que tu occupes toute la place dans le compartiment avec tes bagages et tes affaires personnelles?
9. Est-ce que tu as déjà manqué un vol? En général arrives-tu en retard ou à l'heure à l'aéroport?
10. Est-ce que tu restes assis(e) sur ton siège avec la ceinture de sécurité attachée ou est-ce que tu circules dans la cabine pendant le vol?

Maintenant, vous pouvez répondre à la question initiale. D'après vous, est-ce que vos camarades sont de bons voyageurs ou de mauvais voyageurs? Pourquoi?

Portrait personnel

Avec les renseignements que vous avez obtenus dans l'activité C, décrivez quel genre de voyageur (voyageuse) est votre camarade de classe.

---

[1]*complaining* [2]*to keep the child quiet* [3]*it doesn't matter*

Structure 1

Les expressions géographiques

Online Study Center
ACE, Language Skills
Practice

- **Cities** *(les villes)*. When talking about going *to* a city, living *in* a city, or being *in* a city, use the preposition **à.**

  Je vais **à** Bordeaux.
  J'habite **à** Bordeaux.
  Je suis **à** Bordeaux maintenant.

  When talking about visiting a city or liking/disliking a city, do not include the preposition **à.**

  Je visite Montréal tous les ans.
  J'adore Berlin!

  When talking about the city you come *from* or the city you are departing *from,* use the preposition **de.**

  Béatrice vient **de** Paris.
  Mes parents sont **de** Lyon.
  Le train part **de** Rome.

- **Countries** *(les pays)* **and continents** *(les continents)*. Countries and continents in French are either feminine or masculine. Feminine countries end in **-e,** with one exception: **le Mexique.** Look at the following maps. The feminine countries and continents are in red and the masculine ones are in green.

Students are not responsible for knowing all countries on the map. They are presented for recognition only.

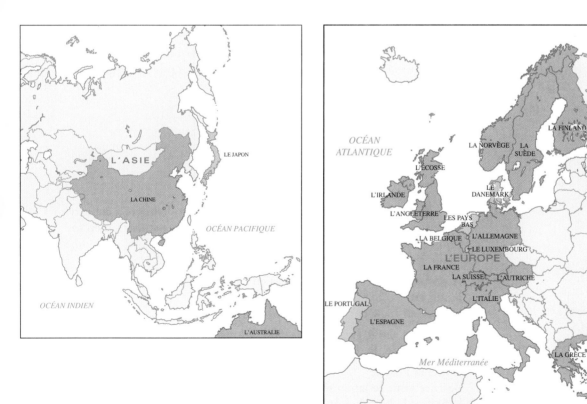

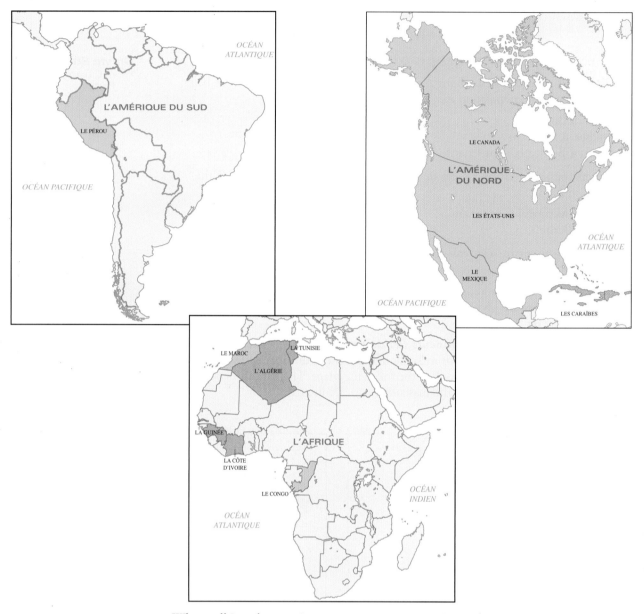

When talking about going *to* a country or a continent, living *in* a country or a continent, or being *in* a country or a continent, use the preposition **en** for feminine nouns and **au** for masculine nouns. Use **aux** for plural masculine and feminine nouns.

Je vais **au** Maroc, mais ma sœur va **en** Angleterre.
Je suis **au** Canada depuis une semaine.
J'habite **en** Italie et mes parents habitent **aux** États-Unis.

When talking about visiting or liking/disliking a country or a continent, use the definite article **le, la, l',** or **les.**

J'aime **la** France.
Béatrice visite **le** Japon souvent.
Je préfère **la** Norvège, et toi?

When you want to indicate which country (or continent) someone comes *from*, use **de** (or **d'** before a vowel or mute **h**) for feminine nouns, **du** for masculine nouns, and **des** for plural nouns.

> Je suis **de** Belgique *(f.)*. / Je suis **d'**Argentine *(f.)*.
> Pierre est **du** Portugal *(m.)*.
> Nous sommes **des** États-Unis *(pl.)*.

The same rule applies to all verbs that take **de,** such as **venir de** *(to come from)*, **entrer de** *(to come/to enter from)*, **rentrer de** *(to come back from)*, **partir de** *(to leave from)*, etc.

> Mes parents viennent **d'**Afrique *(f.)*.   *My parents come from Africa.*
> Tu rentres **des** Caraïbes.   *You come back from the Caribbean.*
> Martine part **du** Canada pour aller   *Martine leaves from Canada to go*
>   **en** Europe.   *to Europe.*

VÉRIFIEZ VOTRE COMPRÉHENSION

Go back to the dialogues at the beginning of the chapter (pp. 488–490). Find the sentences in which geographical expressions are used, and explain each use. For example, why does the **douanier** say **"J'ai visité la Guadeloupe"** and **"J'adore la Guadeloupe"**? Why is **Guadeloupe** feminine? Why does he say **la** rather than **en**?

Pratiquons!

A. Un long voyage! Sylvie a fait un long voyage pendant les vacances d'été. Elle va vous le raconter. Écrivez les prépositions ou les articles corrects.

Bonjour, mes amis! Je suis de retour à Paris. Je suis rentrée (1) _____ Maroc où j'ai passé un super séjour (2) _____ Afrique du Nord. D'abord, j'ai visité (3) _____ Algérie. Je suis restée (4) _____ Alger, la capitale, pendant trois jours. Après, je suis allée (5) _____ Tunisie. J'ai passé une semaine (6) _____ Tunis, la capitale. J'adore (7) _____ Tunisie! J'ai fait des promenades en chameau[1] dans le désert et j'ai goûté à tous les méchouis[2]. Ils étaient tous délicieux. Finalement, je suis partie (8) _____ Tunisie en avion pour aller visiter (9) _____ Maroc. Bien sûr, je suis restée (10) _____ Casablanca. J'ai préféré (11) _____ Maroc à (12) _____ Algérie. Je pense qu'il faisait trop chaud (13) _____ Alger, c'est pour ça[3]. Je suis partie (14) _____ Casablanca pour rentrer à Paris. J'étais très triste de quitter les dunes au sable chaud et de retrouver la circulation et la grisaille[4] parisiennes.

This activity can be done as a game. Divide the class into groups of 3 or 4 students. The group that knows all the answers wins!

Answer Key: 1. du 2. en 3. l' 4. à 5. en 6. à 7. la 8. de 9. le 10. à 11. le 12. l' 13. à 14. de

B. Vous connaissez votre géographie? En groupes de trois ou quatre, dites dans quels pays se trouvent les villes suivantes. L'équipe qui a trouvé le plus grand nombre de pays a gagné!

🌀 MODÈLE: New York

> *New York se trouve aux États-Unis.*

1. Tijuana	6. Larissa	11. Helsinki
2. Malaga	7. Berne	12. Oslo
3. Édimbourg	8. Tanger	13. Shanghai
4. Lisbonne	9. Oran	14. Lima
5. Turin	10. Laval	15. Kyoto

Answer Key: 1. au Mexique 2. en Espagne 3. en Écosse 4. au Portugal 5. en Italie 6. en Grèce 7. en Suisse 8. au Maroc 9. en Algérie 10. au Canada 11. en Finlande 12. en Norvège 13. en Chine 14. au Pérou 15. au Japon

[1]*camel* [2]*stews* [3]*that's why* [4]*gray skies*

C. Tes voyages. Posez les questions suivantes à un(e) camarade de classe à propos de ses voyages.

1. Quels pays as-tu visités? (Ou quelles villes américaines as-tu visitées?)
2. Quels pays et quelles villes voudrais-tu visiter? Pourquoi?
3. Quelle est la ville américaine que tu aimes le plus? Et le moins? Pourquoi?
4. Quelle ville étrangère connais-tu bien? Qu'y a-t-il à voir d'intéressant? (Des musées, des monuments, des sites historiques, etc.)
5. Dans quelle ville, pays ou état ne veux-tu jamais aller? Pourquoi?
6. Aimes-tu prendre l'avion ou préfères-tu la voiture ou le train? Pourquoi?
7. Dans quelle ville ou pays as-tu passé tes dernières vacances?
8. Où irais-tu si tu avais beaucoup d'argent et beaucoup de temps libre? Pourquoi?

À vous de parler!

A. Un voyage difficile! Vous et votre ami(e) êtes à l'aéroport dans un pays francophone. Vous voulez partir en voyage (choisissez votre destination), mais vous avez beaucoup de problèmes. Par exemple, vous êtes au comptoir de la compagnie aérienne et vous voulez enregistrer vos bagages. L'hôtesse (ou l'agent) au sol n'est pas très sympathique et vous pose des problèmes: votre siège n'est pas réservé, votre valise pèse trop lourd, etc. Ensuite, au contrôle sûreté et à la douane les problèmes continuent. À la porte d'embarquement vous avez aussi des problèmes. Même dans l'avion! En groupes de quatre, inventez un voyage difficile et présentez-le à la classe. Jouez les rôles de l'agent ou l'hôtesse au sol, du douanier, du contrôleur, de l'hôtesse de l'air ou du steward, d'autres passagers, etc.

B. Un exposé oral. Vous travaillez pour l'office de tourisme. En groupes de quatre, choisissez un pays francophone et préparez une présentation orale dans le but de faire découvrir à vos touristes potentiels (vos camarades) les beautés et les spécialités du pays et des villes que vous avez choisis. Une fois que tous les groupes ont présenté, dites quel(s) pays vous voudriez découvrir.

Encourage students to make their presentations as appealing as possible, pretending that they are selling the country to potential tourists. Students may choose to do PowerPoint presentations, for example, including information and pictures from the Internet.

Online Study Center
Web Search Activities

Les Français achètent et consomment leur vin comme ça

L'importance du vin. Le vin fait partie de la culture française. Boire du vin lors d'un repas est une tradition, une habitude alimentaire. Le vin accompagne un repas convivial entre amis, une célébration, une fête, ou tout simplement un repas en famille. La gastronomie française est très liée au vin. Un bon vin aide à apprécier encore mieux la bonne cuisine. Le vin fait tellement partie de la culture et de l'identité française qu'à la question posée lors d'un sondage[1] «Être français, c'est selon vous d'abord[2]...», la troisième réponse a été «Aimer le bon vin», juste après «Parler français» et «Être né en France».

[1] *poll* [2] Cette question a été posée pour un sondage *(poll)* sur "Les Français et leur histoire" pour le numéro 100 du mensuel *l'Histoire*.

Comment choisir le vin. Pour accompagner un bon repas, il faut trouver un bon vin. Trouver un bon vin c'est facile si on sait comment le chercher. Les critères les plus importants pour choisir un bon vin se trouvent sur l'étiquette de la bouteille de vin.

- **La région de production**
- **Le millésime** (l'année de production)
- **Les appellations d'origine contrôlée (AOC, ou appellations contrôlées)** (Bordeaux, Margaux, Médoc, Pauillac)
- **L'endroit de mise en bouteille** (au château ou à la coopérative)
- **Les cépages** (la variété de vigne: Sauvignon, Cabernet, Riesling, Merlot, Pinot Gris, etc.)
- **Nom de l'exploitation viticole** (Château Margaux, Domaine du Cigalou, ou marque commerciale)
- **Les médailles ou les prix**
- **L'indication de la teneur en alcool** (12% vol.)
- **Volume du vin contenu dans la bouteille** (75 cl)
- **Pays d'origine pour l'exportation** («Product of France»)

1978

75 cl

CHÂTEAU DE BUBAS
Bordeaux
APPELLATION BORDEAUX CONTROLEE
mis en bouteille au château
par B. Portal propriétaire à Langon (Gironde)
PRODUCE OF FRANCE

Où est-ce que les Français achètent le vin? La majorité des Français achètent généralement leur vin dans les grandes surfaces: supermarchés ou hypermarchés. En effet, les grandes surfaces offrent un choix important de vins. Il y a souvent plusieurs rayons destinés au vin. On peut y trouver des vins excellents, comme un Château Margaux de l'année 2000 à 513,90 euros la bouteille pour une célébration spéciale, ou des vins de table beaucoup moins chers à consommer tous les jours, comme un Mâcon-Village ou un Beaujolais entre 10 et 15 euros la bouteille.

Une minorité de Français achètent leurs vins directement chez le producteur (aux châteaux), dans des salons[1] ou dans des magasins spécialisés en liqueurs et en vins. Souvent, les châteaux organisent des dégustations de vins[2] et des tours guidés dans les caves[3].

Comment consommer le vin. 21% des Français consomment du vin tous les jours (surtout ceux qui sont âgés de plus de 30 ans). Plus de 80% des Français en consomment pour fêter une occasion spéciale. En France, il n'y a pas de limite d'âge pour consommer de l'alcool, et par conséquent un adolescent de 14 ans peut boire du vin à table avec l'autorisation de ses parents.

Le vin rouge se sert avec les viandes rouges et le vin blanc sec[4] avec les poissons et les fruits de mer. Le vin blanc doux[5], comme le Sauternes (une

---

[1]*wine expos* [2]*wine tastings* [3]*wine cellars* [4]*dry* [5]*sweet*

AOC de Bordeaux) se sert avec le foie gras et les desserts. Le vin se boit dans des coupes ou dans des verres à vin. Les coupes où l'on boit le vin rouge sont plus grandes que celles où l'on boit le vin blanc. Le champagne se boit dans une flûte à champagne.

Quelques vins exceptionnels. Nous avons choisi des vins de la région de Bordeaux parce que c'est là où se trouve le plus vaste vignoble[1] du monde, avec plus de 150.000 hectares et cinquante-trois (53) appellations contrôlées. La région de Bordeaux a plus de 3.000 châteaux. Deux cents de ces 3.000 châteaux sont très célèbres. Voici une sélection des meilleurs vins français:

Pétros

Château Cheval Blanc

Château Mouton Rothschild

Château Margaux

Château Latour

Château Lafite Rothschild

Quelques mots utiles

Quand on boit trop de vin:

être ivre *(formal)*; l'ivresse[2]

être saoul

être beurré *(slang)*

être un ivrogne[3]

Quand on boit du vin avec modération:

être sobre

Quand on fête une occasion spéciale:

On lève le verre et on trinque[4].

Quelques proverbes:

La jeunesse est une ivresse sans vin et la vieillesse est un vin sans ivresse.

L'eau fait pleurer, le vin chanter.

Les parents boivent, les enfants trinquent.

Réfléchissons

1. Pourquoi est-ce que le vin occupe une place si importante en France? Occupe-t-il une place aussi importante dans votre pays?
2. Est-ce que les gens dans votre pays donnent autant d'importance à la sélection du vin? Comment est-ce que les personnes dans votre pays choisissent leur vin?
3. La majorité des Français achètent leur vin au supermarché. Où est-ce que les personnes dans votre pays / ville achètent leur vin? Y a-t-il des magasins spécialisés?
4. Quelles boissons (alcoolisées ou non) consomme-t-on dans votre pays pour accompagner les repas de tous les jours? Et les repas spéciaux?
5. Connaissez-vous les meilleurs vins de votre pays? Et les plus grands vignobles?
6. En anglais, y a-t-il des proverbes ou des chansons sur le vin?

---

[1]*vineyard* [2]*intoxication* [3]*to be a lush* [4]*makes a toast*

Continuons!

Une visite à Bruxelles 🎧

Online Study Center
Language Skills Practice

Bienvenue à Bruxelles, capitale de la Belgique et de l'Europe!

Cette ville bilingue (français et flamand) accueille[1] des visiteurs du monde entier et offre de quoi plaire[2] à tout le monde. Votre séjour parmi nous est garanti d'être un des plus agréables. Nous proposons des activités intéressantes pour tout le monde: pour les personnes qui voyagent seules, en couple ou en famille.

la Grand-Place

Si vous vous intéressez à l'histoire, il faut surtout voir le palais royal (où le roi habite toujours!) et la Grand-Place, un endroit absolument magique entouré de bâtiments construits au quinzième et au seizième siècles. Leurs sculptures ciselées à la main démontrent le talent artistique des anciens; leurs façades dorées luisent[3] au soleil, rendant cette place vraiment très grande. Le week-end, le marché aux fleurs, qui couvre le centre de la Grand-Place, rajoute de la couleur à cette place déjà si belle.

Pas très loin de la Grand-Place, dans une petite rue à côté, se trouve le garçon le plus aimé de toute la ville: le Manneken Pis[4].

le Manneken Pis

Cette statue représente tout ce qui est non conventionnel dans l'art. Il est tellement aimé qu'il possède des costumes différents (presque 650 en tout!) qui lui ont été donnés; il fête donc la diversité du pays en même temps que les gestes les plus naturels du monde. Il y a toute une mythologie qui entoure cette statue et que nous vous laissons découvrir pendant votre visite!

l'Union européenne

Si c'est la politique qui vous intéresse, une visite au centre de l'Union européenne est conseillée.

Ici, vous pourrez apprendre toute l'histoire de l'Union européenne, depuis ses débuts jusqu'à sa configuration actuelle. Vous verrez les drapeaux des nations membres, vous ferez le tour du musée, et vous pourrez même assister à une séance publique de la commission des nations membres, si cela vous intéresse.

Une fois en Belgique il faut goûter nos spécialités! Les gourmands et les gourmets vont se régaler à Bruxelles.

Nos spécialités régionales vont vous tenter: vous pourrez commencer avec nos plats principaux—moules-frites, par exemple—et passer ensuite aux desserts. Il faut absolument goûter le chocolat belge (le meilleur au monde!), manger une gaufre bien moelleuse et sucrée avec de la crème chantilly[5], et boire une de nos 400 bières, toutes très différentes les unes des autres. En plus, chacune[6] sera servie dans un verre spécial, réservé uniquement à cette bière pour en accentuer ses saveurs.

Les musées à Bruxelles sont parmi les plus reconnus du monde; une Carte Visite vous donne libre entrée à trente musées pendant trois jours pour un montant minime de 30€. À ne pas manquer: les musées royaux des Beaux-Arts, qui possèdent l'une des collections les plus réputées en art flamand (Breughel, Rubens, Van Dyck, etc.). Le musée de la bière est aussi une visite importante pendant votre séjour. On y retrace l'histoire de la bière belge et on vous offre des dégustations. Finalement, vous ne pouvez pas manquer une visite au musée du chocolat, où vous apprendrez l'histoire fascinante de ce mets[7] adoré de tous. Vous vous rappellerez longtemps cette visite mémorable!

Été comme hiver, Bruxelles vous attend et vous tend les bras! Riche dans sa diversité historique, linguistique et artistique, cette ville vous séduira tous. Venez connaître une ville et une culture dont vous vous souviendrez toujours!

Vous avez bien compris?

Répondez aux six questions suivantes, selon le texte.

1. Si vous vous intéressez à l'histoire, qu'est-ce qu'il faut visiter à Bruxelles? Qu'est-ce qu'il y a de spécial à ces endroits-là?
2. Où faut-il aller pour voir le Manneken Pis? Qu'est-ce que vous pensez, personnellement, de cette statue? (C'est marrant? C'est mignon? C'est offensant? C'est dérangeant?) Expliquez votre réponse.

Answer Key. Possible answers: 1. Il faut visiter des musées, des monuments très anciens comme le Palais Royal et la Grand-Place et le Manneken Pis. 2. Il faut aller à côté de la Grand-Place.

---

[1]*welcomes* [2]*please* [3]*shine* [4]The Manneken Pis often appears nude, in his original form, as in the photo provided here, but it is not uncommon to see him dressed in one of his costumes! [5]*whipped cream* [6]*each one* [7]*delicacy*

3. Qu'est ce que vous pouvez faire au siège central de l'Union européenne? Quelles personnes est-ce que cela intéresserait, en général, et pourquoi?
4. Quelles spécialités est-ce que vous pouvez manger et boire pendant votre visite? Lesquelles vous intéressent personnellement? Lesquelles ne vous intéressent pas? Pourquoi?
5. Pourquoi est-ce que chaque bière a son propre verre en Belgique?
6. Si vous aimez les musées, quelles sortes de choses est-ce que vous pouvez voir à Bruxelles? Est-ce que vous diriez que les musées sont très similaires ou très différents les uns des autres dans cette ville?

Vocabulaire essentiel

Le voyage

Pendant le séjour

réserver une chambre d'hôtel
avec salle de bains / sans salle de bains
avec WC / sans toilettes
avec douche
avec un lit double
avec deux lits
qui donne sur la terrasse[1]
avec balcon
réserver une table au restaurant
pour deux / trois / quatre personnes
à l'intérieur / à l'extérieur

Comme activités touristiques

aller aux musées
regarder / admirer les tableaux *(m.)*
regarder / admirer les sculptures *(f.)*
apprendre l'histoire *(f.)*
visiter les monuments *(m.)*
  les statues *(f.)*
  les bâtiments *(m.)*
  les places publiques *(f.)*
  les parcs nationaux *(m.)*
regarder les gens dans une place publique
  les familles *(f.)*
  les couples *(m.)*
  les mimes *(m.)*
  un spectacle public
se reposer dans un parc
  sur un banc
  couché sous un arbre
  à côté d'un lac

[1] *that overlooks the terrace*

goûter les spécialités régionales
  les entrées *(f.)*
  les plats principaux *(m.)*
  le fromage
  les pâtisseries *(f.)* / les desserts *(m.)*
  les gourmandises *(f.)* / le chocolat
  les vins *(m.)* / les bières *(f.)*
acheter des souvenirs *(m.)*
  des cartes postales *(f.)*
  des diapositives *(f.)* *(slides)*
  des sweat-shirts *(m.)*
  des tee-shirts *(m.)*
  des statuettes *(f.)*
  des livres *(m.)*
prendre des photos *(f.)*
  en couleur
  en noir et blanc
  numériques

À vous!

A. En visite chez moi! Imaginez que vous allez recevoir des invités dans votre ville. Répondez aux questions suivantes pour préparer leur visite.

1. Dans votre ville, quels monuments ou musées faut-il absolument voir?
2. Quelles sont les spécialités régionales qu'il faut goûter (plats principaux, pâtisseries, etc.)?
3. Est-ce qu'il y a des restaurants ou des hôtels dans votre ville que vous recommanderiez? Pourquoi?
4. Si quelqu'un veut prendre des photos qui représentent bien la culture de votre ville (nature, musée, infrastructure, etc.), où devrait-il/elle aller?
5. Si quelqu'un veut acheter un souvenir qui représente bien votre ville, qu'est-ce que vous suggéreriez qu'il/elle achète?
6. Est-ce qu'il y a des saisons dans votre région ou dans votre ville où il faut absolument venir, et d'autres où il ne faut pas venir? Pourquoi?
7. Qu'est-ce que les familles peuvent faire le week-end chez vous? Et les couples?

B. Des souvenirs pour toute la famille. Imaginez que vous êtes en voyage—à vous de choisir où!—et que vous cherchez des souvenirs pour votre famille. Donnez une brève description de quatre membres de votre famille, et décidez quel souvenir vous pourriez offrir à chacun, selon cette description.

> MODÈLE: (Je voyage au Sénégal.) Ma mère adore la nature; elle aime faire de longues promenades dans les parcs et les forêts. Je vais lui offrir un livre avec des photos des forêts nationales de Sénégal.

C. Je cherche un compagnon de voyage! Imaginez que vous allez bientôt voyager en Europe et que vous cherchez un compagnon de voyage. Posez les questions suivantes à un(e) partenaire, et notez ses réponses. À la fin, décidez si vous pourriez voyager ensemble ou non, et dites pourquoi.

1. Quand tu voyages, comment est-ce que tu préfères voyager? (En train, en voiture, en avion, etc.)

Time permitting, ask students to bring in photos of the family members they have chosen and to present their descriptions either in small groups or before the whole class. These presentations could be extended over several days and used as a warm-up or a cool-down activity.

2. Quand tu voyages en avion ou en train, quelle classe est-ce que tu préfères?
3. Est-ce que tu aimes explorer de nouvelles villes?
4. Quels types de monuments et de musées est-ce que tu aimes voir? Qu'est-ce que tu n'aimes pas du tout?
5. Au restaurant, est-ce que tu prends généralement une table à l'intérieur ou à l'extérieur?
6. Est-ce que tu aimes goûter de nouveaux aliments?
7. À l'hôtel, quel type de chambre est-ce que tu prends?
8. Est-ce que tu te couches tôt ou tard? À quelle heure est-ce que tu te lèves quand tu voyages?

Structure 2

Online Study Center
ACE, Language Skills
Practice

Les verbes *se souvenir (de)* et *se rappeler*

There are two verbs in French that mean *to remember;* both are irregular and reflexive. The first is **se souvenir (de),** which is conjugated like the verb **venir.**

se souvenir	
je me souv**iens**	nous nous souv**enons**
tu te souv**iens**	vous vous souv**enez**
il / elle / on se souv**ient**	ils / elles se souv**iennent**

The past participle of this verb is **souvenu;** because the verb is reflexive, it is conjugated with **être** in the **passé composé: je me suis souvenu(e).** The irregular stem for the future and conditional is **souviendr-;** as for all verbs, the regular future and conditional endings are added to this stem: **je me souviendrai** (future); **je me souviendrais** (conditional).

The second verb that means *to remember* is **se rappeler.** It undergoes the same spelling changes as the verb **appeler.**

se rappeler	
je me rapp**elle**	nous nous rapp**elons**
tu te rapp**elles**	vous vous rapp**elez**
il / elle / on se rapp**elle**	ils / elles se rapp**ellent**

The past participle is regular: **rappelé—je me suis rappelé(e).** In both the future and the conditional, the spelling change in the stem carries throughout all forms: **je me rappellerai / vous vous rappellerez** (future); **tu te rappellerais / nous nous rappellerions** (conditional).

Notice that the verb **se souvenir** is followed by **de** if there is a direct object or an infinitive in the sentence.

Je me souviens **de** ce jour.   *I remember that day.*
Je ne me suis pas souvenu **de** m'arrêter   *I didn't remember to stop at the bank!*
    à la banque!

When the direct object is not named, the pronoun **en** takes the place of **de** + *noun*.

Tu te souviens de ta visite au Québec?   *Do you remember your trip to Quebec?*
Oh oui, je m'**en** souviens bien!   *Of course, I remember it well!*

Point out to your students that **se rappeler** is followed by a direct object, and thus uses a direct object pronoun in a similar sentence: *Je me rappelle ce jour: je me le rappelle.* Before an infinitive, however, **de** is inserted, as with **se souvenir**: *Je ne me suis pas rappelé de m'arrêter à la banque!* The preposition **de** is also inserted in front of a personal pronoun (or a **pronom disjoint** such as **toi, voux, eux**): *Je me rappelle de toi parfaitement.*

VÉRIFIEZ VOTRE COMPRÉHENSION

1. Pouvez-vous trouver des exemples de ces deux verbes dans la brochure de Bruxelles? À quel(s) temps se trouvent ces verbes? Pourquoi?

2. Pouvez-vous donner l'*imparfait* de ces verbes?

3. Notez bien que le *passé composé* de ces verbes est formé avec **être**. Pouvez-vous expliquer pourquoi?

Pratiquons!

A. Il faut s'en souvenir! Martine et André voyagent en Europe. Dites de quoi ils se souviennent / se rappellent.

MODÈLE: Martine / les billets

        Martine se souvient des billets. **ou** *Martine se rappelle les billets.*

Le jour avant …

1. André / faire le linge
2. Martine et André / la date du vol
3. Martine / aller à l'agence de voyage

Le jour même …

4. Martine / les passeports
5. André et Martine / les valises
6. Martine / l'heure du vol
7. André / les lunettes de soleil
8. Martine et André / prendre de l'argent au distributeur

Answer Key: 1. André se souvient / se rappelle de faire le linge. 2. Ils se souviennent de la date du vol / se rappellent la date du vol. 3. Martine se souvient / se rappelle d'aller à l'agence de voyage. 4. Elle se souvient des passeports / se rappelle les passeports. 5. Ils se souviennent des valises / se rappellent les valises. 6. Elle se souvient de l'heure du vol / se rappelle l'heure du vol. 7. Il se souvient des lunettes / se rappelle les lunettes de soleil. 8. Ils se souviennent / se rappellent de prendre de l'argent au distributeur.

Et vous—quand vous voyagez, de quoi est-ce que vous vous souvenez? Écrivez deux phrases.

B. Tu t'en souviens? Avec un(e) partenaire, répondez aux neuf questions suivantes.

MODÈLE: Tu te souviens du numéro de téléphone de ton meilleur ami?

        Oui, je m'en souviens. C'est le 03-18-72. **ou**
        Non, je ne m'en souviens pas.

1. Tu te souviens du courriel de ton prof de français?
2. Tu te rappelles la date de l'examen final?

3. Tu te rappelles ta première journée à l'université? Comment c'était?
4. Tu te souviens du nom de ton prof de français du semestre passé?
5. Tu te souviens de la date de l'anniversaire de ta mère? Qu'est-ce que tu lui offres normalement comme cadeau?
6. En général, est-ce que tes parents se rappellent ton anniversaire? Qu'est-ce qu'ils t'offrent?
7. Tes amis se souviennent-ils de te téléphoner de temps en temps? Souvent ou rarement?
8. Est-ce que ton/ta meilleur(e) ami(e) se rappelle le moment où vous vous êtes rencontré(e)s? Et toi, est-ce que tu t'en souviens?
9. De quoi est-ce que tu ne te souviens pas, en général?

Structure 3

Online Study Center
ACE, Language Skills
Practice

Les pronoms relatifs *qui* et *que*

Like other pronouns, relative pronouns replace a noun in a sentence, therefore helping us to avoid repeating the noun. Relative pronouns have a special function, however, and that is to link two independent clauses (sentences that can stand alone) to form one sentence. When this happens, one of the clauses becomes subordinate to the other and can no longer exist separately. In English, the relative pronouns are *who, that, which,* and *whom.* These are generally chosen depending on whether the noun being replaced is a person or a thing.

In French, however, the main concern when choosing a relative pronoun is the role that that pronoun will play in the subordinate (or relative) clause. French distinguishes between relative pronouns that are the *subject* of the following clause, those that are the *direct object* of the following clause, or those that are the *object of the preposition* **de.** There is also a relative pronoun that is used to refer to specific *times, dates,* and *places.*

- **Qui** is used to refer to either persons or things that are the *subject* of the relative clause. In the following examples, pay close attention to the role of the relative pronoun in the *second* clause.

  J'ai acheté **une carte postale. La carte postale** montre une vue de Paris de la tour Eiffel.
  J'ai acheté une carte postale **qui** montre une vue de Paris de la tour Eiffel.

  Rashid est un homme d'affaires belge. **Rashid** voyage beaucoup.
  Rashid est un homme d'affaires belge **qui** voyage beaucoup.

  Because it is the subject of the second clause, **qui** is always followed by a verb. It never elides before a vowel or a mute **h.**

  Voilà un professeur **qui** aime beaucoup parler avec ses étudiants.
  La Belgique est un pays **qui** est très riche en diversité.

- **Que** is used to refer to either persons or things that are the *direct object* of the relative clause. In the following sentences, note the role of **que** in the *second* clause.

> J'ai acheté **une carte postale.** Je vais envoyer **cette carte postale** à ma mère.
> J'ai acheté une carte postale **que** je vais envoyer à ma mère.

> **Rashid** est un homme d'affaires belge. J'ai rencontré **Rashid** la semaine dernière.
> Rashid est un homme d'affaires belge **que** j'ai rencontré la semaine dernière.

Because it is a direct object, **que** is followed by a subject and a verb. It elides (becomes **qu'**) before a vowel or a mute **h.** In addition, because it is a direct object, if it precedes a verb in the **passé composé,** the past participle of the verb agrees in number and gender with the noun that **que** replaces.

> Charlotte a acheté **des T-shirts.** Elle a donné **ces T-shirts** à ses petits frères.
> Charlotte a acheté des T-shirts **qu'**elle a donné**s** à ses petits frères.

Que is never omitted in French, although it may be omitted in English.

> Rashid est un homme d'affaires belge **que** j'ai rencontré la semaine dernière.
>
> *Rashid is a Belgian businessman (who/whom) I met last week.*

VÉRIFIEZ VOTRE COMPRÉHENSION

Les phrases suivantes viennent de la brochure du début du chapitre. Trouvez le(s) pronom(s) relatif(s) dans chacune, et expliquez ce que chaque pronom remplace et son rôle dans la proposition relative.

1. Le week-end, le marché aux fleurs, qui couvre le centre de la Grand-Place, ajoute encore de la couleur à cet endroit enchanté.

2. Il y a toute une mythologie qui entoure cette statue et que nous vous laissons découvrir pendant votre visite!

3. Si c'est la politique qui vous intéresse, une visite au centre de l'Union européenne est obligatoire.

4. À ne pas manquer: les musées royaux des Beaux-Arts, qui possèdent l'une des collections les plus réputées en art flamand (Breughel, Rubens, Van Dyck, etc.).

À l'écoute!

Dites si le pronom relatif dans les phrases suivantes joue le rôle du *sujet* ou de l'*objet* de la phrase.

	sujet	*objet*
1.	_____	_____
2.	_____	_____
3.	_____	_____
4.	_____	_____
5.	_____	_____

For reinforcement, you could ask students to break down this complex sentence into two simple sentences without relative pronouns.

Audioscript: 1. Paris est une ville que je visite souvent. 2. Amadou est l'homme qu'elle a rencontré à Dakar. 3. Je veux trouver un livre qui explique l'histoire de Paris. 4. Il a envoyé une lettre qu'il a écrite hier soir. 5. Brigitte aime les musées qui ont beaucoup de sculptures.

Answer Key: 1. objet 2. objet 3. sujet 4. objet 5. sujet

Pratiquons!

A. Une visite à Paris. Liez les deux phrases avec un pronom relatif pour créer une seule phrase. Attention à l'accord du participe passé, quand besoin est.

MODÈLE: La dernière fois que j'ai visité Paris, je suis resté dans un hôtel. L'hôtel se trouvait près de la Sainte-Chapelle.

> *La dernière fois que j'ai visité Paris, je suis resté dans un hôtel **qui** se trouvait près de la Sainte-Chapelle.*

1. C'était un vieil hôtel. Il avait beaucoup de charme.
2. J'ai loué une chambre. La chambre donnait sur la terrasse.
3. Le soir, j'ai écrit des cartes postales. J'ai envoyé ces cartes postales à tous mes amis.
4. Pendant la journée, j'ai visité des musées. Ces musées étaient très différents les uns des autres.
5. Un jour, je suis allé au musée d'Orsay. Ce musée se spécialise en art impressionniste.
6. Là, j'ai vu beaucoup de très belles peintures. J'ai beaucoup aimé ces peintures.
7. J'étais très triste de quitter cette ville. J'adore la ville de Paris!

B. Dans la boutique des souvenirs. Remplissez les blancs avec **qui** ou **que (qu')**, selon le cas.

Hier, je suis entrée dans une boutique de souvenirs à Québec (1) _____ avait des choses très intéressantes. Pour mon neveu Daniel, (2) _____ a 10 ans, j'ai choisi un drapeau canadien, avec la feuille d'érable[1], (3) _____ il va beaucoup aimer. Il peut le mettre dans sa chambre, (4) _____ il partage avec son frère Patrice. Pour Patrice, (5) _____ adore le hockey sur glace, c'était facile. J'ai choisi une crosse[2] de hockey (6) _____ est imprimée avec le logo des Canadiens. Mais pour ma nièce Émilie, c'était beaucoup plus difficile. Elle a déjà beaucoup de jouets (7) _____ elle n'aime pas, des vidéos (8) _____ elle ne regarde jamais, et des T-shirts (9) _____ ne sont pas «beaux» et (10) _____ elle ne veut plus porter! Pour elle, j'ai enfin choisi des sucreries faites avec du sirop d'érable. Ce n'est pas quelque chose de durable, mais elle va certainement les aimer!

Structure 4

Les pronoms relatifs *dont* et *où*

As we noted in ***Structure 3,*** there is a relative pronoun in French that replaces an object of the preposition **de** and one that refers to specific dates, times, and places.

- **Dont** is used to refer to either persons or things that are the *object of the preposition* **de** in the relative clause.

   J'ai **deux frères.** Je suis très fière **de mes frères.**
   J'ai deux frères **dont** je suis très fière.

   Il a **un chien.** Les enfants ont peur **de ce chien.**
   Il a un chien **dont** les enfants ont peur.

---

[1]*maple leaf* [2]*stick*

In French, **dont** is frequently used to show possession, and translates into English as *whose*.

Cette femme habite à Paris. Je connais
  la fille **de cette femme.**
Cette femme, **dont** je connais la fille,   *That woman, **whose** daughter I know,*
  habite à Paris.   *lives in Paris.*

L'homme a été très reconnaissant.
Elle a trouvé le passeport **de cet homme.**
L'homme **dont** elle a trouvé le   *The man **whose** passport she*
  passeport a été très reconnaissant.   *found was very grateful.*

- **Où** is used to replace a specific place, date, or time. It may translate into English as either *where* or *when*.

Voici **le café.** J'ai rencontré mon
  mari **dans ce café.**
Voici le café **où** j'ai rencontré mon mari.   *That's the café **where** I met my husband.*

C'était un **jour** mémorable. J'ai
  rencontré mon mari **ce jour-là.**
C'était le jour **où** j'ai rencontré   *It was the day (**when**) I met my*
  mon mari.   *husband.*

Vérifiez votre compréhension

Les phrases suivantes s'inspirent de la brochure de Bruxelles (p. 501). Trouvez le(s) pronom(s) relatif(s) dans chacune, et expliquez ce que chaque pronom remplace et son rôle dans la proposition relative.

1. Ici, on trace l'histoire de cette spécialité belge, dont on vous offre des dégustations.

2. On ne peut pas manquer le musée du chocolat, où vous apprendrez l'histoire fascinante de ce mets adoré de tous!

3. Venez connaître une ville et une culture dont vous vous souviendrez toujours!

Pratiquons!

A. Près de la Sorbonne. Liez les deux phrases avec le pronom relatif **dont** ou **où,** pour créer une seule phrase.

1. Près de la Sorbonne, il y a beaucoup de petits restaurants. Les étudiants peuvent bien manger dans ces restaurants et pour pas trop cher.
2. Il y a des distributeurs automatiques. On peut retirer de l'argent de ces distributeurs.
3. Près de la Sorbonne, il y a pas mal de bars. On peut sortir avec ses amis dans ces bars.
4. Sur le campus, il y a une grande bibliothèque. Je travaille souvent dans cette bibliothèque.
5. Près de la Sorbonne, il y a un fleuriste. Je me souviens bien de ce fleuriste—j'y ai acheté beaucoup de fleurs.

Answer Key: 1. ... petits restaurants **où** les étudiants ... 2. ... distributeurs automatiques **dont** on peut ... 3. ... bars **où** on peut ... 4. ... bibliothèque **où** je travaille ... 5. ... un fleuriste **dont** je me souviens ...

B. Tous ensemble! Terminez les phrases suivantes avec le pronom relatif approprié **(qui, que, où** ou **dont)** et une deuxième proposition logique. Pour vous aidez, les numéros 1 et 2 sont un choix multiple. Après, c'est à vous de créer une proposition relative logique.

1. Paris est une ville …
   - où ＿＿＿
   - qui ＿＿＿
   - qu(e) ＿＿＿
   - dont ＿＿＿

   a. on parle souvent.
   b. j'aime beaucoup.
   c. les touristes dépensent beaucoup d'argent.
   d. ne dort jamais.

2. Le Canada est un pays …
   - qui ＿＿＿
   - qu(e) ＿＿＿
   - où ＿＿＿
   - dont ＿＿＿

   a. on parle joual[1].
   b. est officiellement bilingue.
   c. il ne connaît pas très bien.
   d. j'ai quelques cartes postales.

3. Bruxelles est une ville …
   - qui ＿＿＿＿＿＿＿
   - que ＿＿＿＿＿＿＿
   - où ＿＿＿＿＿＿＿

4. (votre ville) est un endroit …
   - où ＿＿＿＿＿＿＿
   - dont ＿＿＿＿＿＿＿
   - qui ＿＿＿＿＿＿＿

C. Interactions. Posez les questions suivantes à un(e) camarade de classe. À la fin, dites ses réponses aux autres, en utilisant une phrase avec une proposition relative.

1. Est-ce qu'il y a un professeur de lycée dont tu te souviens bien? Pourquoi?
2. Est-ce qu'il y a une chose que tu regrettes de ta vie universitaire?
3. Y a-t-il un pays que tu voudrais bien visiter? Lequel? Que tu ne voudrais pas visiter? Pourquoi?
4. Est-ce qu'il y a une carrière qui t'intéresse beaucoup? Laquelle et pourquoi?
5. Y a-t-il un restaurant où tu manges beaucoup? C'est quel type de cuisine?

Portrait personnel

En vous basant sur les réponses de votre camarade de classe que vous avez obtenues dans l'activité C, écrivez un paragraphe pour décrire les goûts de votre camarade de classe.

- Quel(s) pays a-t-il/elle visité(s)? Pourquoi les a-t-il/elle aimés ou pas aimés?
- Quel(s) pays ne veut-il/elle pas visiter et pourquoi?
- Quelle carrière professionnelle l'intéresse et pourquoi?
- Quelle est la cuisine qu'il/elle préfère?

---

[1]**Joual** is a dialect spoken in the province of Quebec.

À vous de parler!

A. Au restaurant. Téléphonez à un restaurant pour réserver une table. N'oubliez pas de dire quel jour et à quelle heure vous arrivez, pour combien de personnes il vous faut la table, si vous voulez une table à l'intérieur ou sur la terrasse, etc. Si vous terminez avant les autres, changez de rôles et refaites la conversation.

> **MODÈLE:** RESTAURATEUR: Allô … ?
> VOUS: Allô, bonjour. Est-ce que c'est Chez Levantin?
> RESTAURATEUR: Oui, Monsieur / Madame.
> VOUS: Je voudrais réserver une table pour demain soir pour trois personnes.
> RESTAURATEUR: Très bien. Pour quelle heure? …

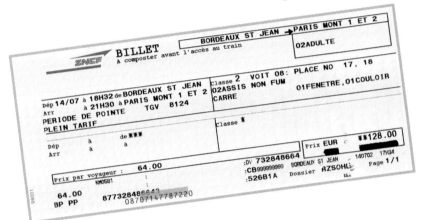

Voici un billet de train. Quel est le train dans lequel le passager va voyager? Est-ce que le passager a un siège fumeur ou non-fumeur? Quelle est la ville de départ? Et la destination?

B. À l'hôtel. Imaginez que vous êtes en voyage et que vous n'avez pas réservé de chambre d'hôtel. Vous entrez dans un hôtel pour demander s'ils ont des chambres et pour en louer une. Avec un(e) partenaire, jouez les rôles du (de la) réceptionniste et du (de la) cliente. Continuez votre conversation jusqu'à ce que vous ayez exactement la chambre que vous voulez. N'oubliez pas de demander le prix!

> **MODÈLE:** RÉCEPTIONNISTE: Bonjour, Monsieur / Madame!
> VOUS: Bonjour. Est-ce que vous avez des chambres de libres?
> RÉCEPTIONNISTE: Oui, Monsieur / Madame. Que voulez-vous comme chambre?
> VOUS: J'aimerais bien avoir une chambre avec salle de bains …

C. Une pub! En groupes de trois ou quatre personnes, créez une publicité télévisée pour votre ville. Dites ce qu'il faut voir et faire pendant une visite de votre ville. Soyez très imaginatifs et créatifs—vous voulez attirer des touristes chez vous! Quand vous aurez fini, présentez votre pub au reste de la classe.

To make this activity more realistic, have students sit with their backs to one another so that they cannot use body language. If they wish, they might also hold their cell phones up to their ears. Point out that it is considered polite in France to inquire first if you have reached the right number (**Est-ce que c'est Chez Levantin?**) before proceeding with the call.

Le train dans lequel va voyager le passager est un TGV. Le passager a un siège non-fumeur. Le train sort de Bordeaux à destination de Paris.

For a challenging role-play, divide students into pairs (receptionist and client) and then into groups of 8–10. Each receptionist has only one type of room available, and each client has specific preferences. (Place this information on an index card—in English—so that each knows what s/he has to offer or is looking for.) Students circulate in their groups until they find the hotel that can meet their needs.

To use this as a final project, have students videotape their ads or create a PowerPoint presentation using still photos or drawings, and present them to the whole class. Then vote on which ad is most creative, which portrays your town most accurately, most amusingly, most positively, which has the best photos or video, etc.

Les Québécois se souviennent comme ça!

Si vous avez déjà voyagé au Québec, vous avez probablement vu que les plaques d'immatriculation de toute la province disent «Je me souviens». En fait, c'est la devise[1] officielle de la province. Mais de quoi, exactement, est-ce que les Québécois se souviennent? Cette question est au centre d'un mystère qui règne au Québec depuis presque un siècle. Demandez à n'importe quel[2] Québécois, et il vous donnera une réponse, mais il est fort probable que la réponse sera différente chaque fois! Pour beaucoup de personnes, cette devise fait référence aux difficultés éprouvées par les Canadiens francophones en général, et surtout à leur lutte[3] continuelle pour protéger leur langue et leur culture contre les anglophones. Pour d'autres, la référence est même plus spécifique—ils pensent que cette phrase fait référence à la conquête du Canada par les Britanniques (et donc à un seul jour spécifique dans l'histoire de ce pays), et à la déportation des Canadiens francophones vers des autres pays (la France et les États-Unis surtout). La phrase «Je me souviens» est donc devenue un cri de ralliement[4] pour les séparatistes, qui veulent une séparation politique entre le Québec et le reste du Canada.

À vrai dire, on ne sait pas exactement ce à quoi cette phrase fait référence. Ce que l'on sait, c'est qu'en 1883, Eugène-Étienne Taché, architecte responsable de la construction du bâtiment législatif du Québec (ce qui est maintenant l'Assemblée nationale), a décidé de faire graver au-dessus de la porte centrale de ce bâtiment les armoiries[5] du Québec et ces trois mots très simples: «Je me souviens». Taché n'a jamais expliqué à personne ce qu'il voulait dire par cette phrase, mais on sait qu'il a dédié le bâtiment à toute l'histoire du Québec. La façade extérieure de ce bâtiment contient des sculptures en bronze des peuples amérindiens, des explorateurs, des missionnaires et des soldats, entre autres. Plusieurs historiens pensent donc qu'il faisait référence à cette histoire en général, plutôt qu'à un seul événement. L'interprétation reste cependant ouverte, à chaque génération de la comprendre comme elle veut.

Réfléchissons

1. Pensez-vous qu'il soit nécessaire de savoir exactement ce à quoi la phrase «Je me souviens» fait référence? Quels sont les avantages de le savoir? et de ne pas le savoir?

2. Pourquoi est-ce qu'il est important pour un groupe culturel d'avoir une devise? Qu'est-ce qu'une devise représente, en général?

---

[1] *motto* [2] *any* [3] *struggle* [4] *rallying cry* [5] *coat of arms*

3. Est-ce qu'il y a une devise dans votre ville, votre état ou votre pays? Que représente-t-elle? Quelle est la controverse qu'elle provoque de temps en temps?
4. Si vous deviez créer une devise pour votre université, que dirait-elle? Et pour votre ville? Pour votre pays?

À vous d'écrire!

Online Study Center
Language Skills Practice

Une publicité et un communiqué publicitaire. Vous travaillez pour une agence de publicité et votre patron vous a demandé de créer une publicité et un communiqué publicitaire[1] pour vendre à l'étranger un produit typique ou une spécialité de votre pays ou de votre région.

A. Stratégies. Une publicité est plus courte qu'un communiqué publicitaire. Le message de la publicité est transmis par un slogan ou une phrase courte et par une image ou une photo. Le message d'un communiqué publicitaire est plus long (un paragraphe) et il informe le consommateur en détail sur un produit. Comparez la publicité et le communiqué publicitaire suivants.

---

[1] *information bulletin*

Le slogan est: «Gardez-en pour demain si vous pouvez». Le slogan est court. Il est assez réussi parce que le message est clair et même humoristique. C'est une publicité de la mayonnaise Amora. L'ustensile à servir la glace indique que cette mayonnaise est aussi bonne qu'une glace!

Oui, il y a un slogan: «Vive la cuisine inventive». C'est un bon slogan qui est court et qu'on se rappelle facilement, grâce à l'allitération. La marque est le fromage Boursin. Comme un communiqué est plus long qu'une publicité, il faut regarder et lire plus attentivement pour savoir de quoi ça parle. En principe, la marque qu'un communiqué annonce est placée en haut de la page et le slogan juste après, en grosses lettres. En gros, le communiqué parle des différentes recettes qui peuvent se préparer avec le fromage Boursin, ce qui le rend plus pratique et plus attrayant aux consommateurs.

Trouvez le slogan dans la publicité. Comment est le slogan? Court? Long? Évident? Pas clair? Est-ce un bon slogan? Mauvais? Pourquoi? C'est une publicité de quoi? Qu'indique l'ustensile à servir la glace?

Maintenant, regardez le communiqué. Y a-t-il un slogan? Lequel? Quelle est la marque qui est l'objet de la publicité? Est-ce clair? En gros[1], de quoi parle le communiqué?

B. Organisons-nous! Décidez quels produits ou quelles spécialités vous allez promouvoir[2] dans votre publicité et dans votre communiqué.

1. Dans la publicité: produit/spécialité régionale: _____
2. Dans le communiqué: produit/spécialité régionale: _____

Donnez trois raisons pour expliquer pourquoi vous avez choisi les produits/specialités dans votre publicité et dans votre communiqué.

1. Dans la publicité. 3 raisons de mon choix:

   a. _____
   b. _____
   c. _____

2. Dans le communiqué. 3 raisons de mon choix:

   a. _____
   b. _____
   c. _____

Regardez la carte de France avec les produits régionaux pour chaque région. Quels produits avez-vous goûtés? Dites si vous avez aimé ou pas.

---

[1] *In a nutshell* [2] *to promote*

C. Pensons-y!

- Maintenant, commencez à penser au slogan pour votre publicité. Quelle caractéristique voulez-vous souligner[1]? Pensez aussi à la photo ou au dessin qui va accompagner le slogan pour mieux l'illustrer.
- Ensuite, pensez à votre communiqué. Comment va être l'introduction où vous allez présenter aux consommateurs le produit / la spécialité? Dans le texte principal, comment allez-vous mettre en valeur[2] le produit / la spécialité? Qu'est-ce que vous allez mettre en valeur? Comment va être votre conclusion pour persuader le consommateur d'acheter votre produit / spécialité?
- Écrivez un premier brouillon[3] de votre publicité et de votre communiqué.

D. Révisons! Demandez à un(e) camarade de classe de regarder vos publicités. Votre camarade de classe va commenter vos publicités selon les critères suivants.

1. Comment est le slogan de la publicité? Est-il clair? Concis? Vise-t-il[4] le bon public? Comment est-ce que votre camarade pourrait améliorer son slogan?
2. Comment est la photo ou le dessin? Est-ce qu'il/elle illustre bien le slogan ou le produit / la spécialité? Pouvez-vous suggérer à votre camarade une meilleure photo ou un meilleur dessin?
3. Comment est l'introduction du communiqué? Est-elle trop longue? Trop courte? Annonce-t-elle bien le produit ou la spécialité dont va parler le texte?
4. Comment est le texte principal? Informatif? Pas assez d'informations?
5. Est-ce que le texte peut être amélioré pour mieux informer le consommateur et l'attirer[5] à acheter? Comment?
6. Comment est la conclusion? Est-elle assez persuasive? Convaincante[6]? Comment est-ce que votre camarade pourrait l'améliorer?
7. Comment sont les photos / les dessins? Informatifs? Utiles ou inutiles?
8. Avez-vous trouvé des erreurs grammaticales ou d'orthographe? Signalez-les à votre camarade.

E. Écrivons!
Écrivez vos deux publicités en suivant les suggestions de votre camarade de classe. Ensuite, rendez votre travail à votre professeur.

Have students use this section to do a peer review of a classmate's advertisements. Give them a minimum of 10 minutes to read their partner's ads, and 20 minutes to consult with one another as they answer the questions. When they have finished, have each student rewrite his/her ads, as specified in activity E.

Have students vote on the best ad and discuss why they voted for that ad (the language, the humor, the product, etc.).

---

[1] *to emphasize* [2] *to highlight/emphasize* [3] *draft* [4] *Does it target* [5] *to attract* [6] *Convincing*

Lexique 🎧

Vocabulaire essentiel

À l'aéroport *at the airport*

l'agent *(m.)* au sol / l'hôtesse *(f.)* au sol *ground personnel*
un bagage à main *carry-on luggage*
un billet d'avion *plane ticket*
la carte d'embarquement / la carte d'accès à bord *boarding pass*
le contrôle sûreté *security gate*
le détecteur de métaux *metal detector*
la douane *customs*

l'embarquement *(m.)* *boarding*
enregistrer / l'enregistrement *(m.)* *to check in / the check-in*
le haut-parleur *loudspeaker*
le magasin hors taxe *duty-free shop*
manquer le vol *to miss a flight*
le passager (la passagère) *passenger*
le passeport *passport*
une pièce d'identité *proof of identity*

la porte *gate*
la remise des bagages *baggage claim*
le tapis roulant *conveyor belt*
le terminal *terminal*
une valise *suitcase*
le vol *flight*
le vol à destination de *the flight to*
le vol en provenance de *the flight from*

Dans l'avion *on the plane*

à bord *on board*
l'atterrissage *(m.)* *landing*
l'avion *(m.)* atterrit *the plane is landing*
l'avion décolle *the plane is taking off*
la cabine *plane cabin*
les ceintures *(f.)* de sécurité *seat belts*

les compartiments *(m.)* *overhead compartments*
le décollage *take-off*
l'équipage *(m.)* *crew*
l'étiquette *(f.)* de la valise *baggage tag*
l'hôtesse *(f.)* de l'air / le steward *flight attendant*
le pilote *pilot*

la piste de décollage / la piste d'atterrissage *runway*
le siège *seat*
la sortie de secours *emergency exit*
les turbulences *(f.)* *turbulence*

À la gare *at the train station*

le billet fumeur / non-fumeur *smoking / non-smoking ticket*
composter un billet *to validate a ticket*

le guichet *ticket counter*
l'horaire *(m.)* des trains *train schedule*
le quai *platform*

la voie *railroad track*
le wagon-lit *sleeper train*
le wagon-restaurant *restaurant car*

Pendant le séjour *during a trip*

réserver une chambre d'hôtel *to reserve a hotel room*
  avec balcon *with a balcony*
  avec douche *with a shower*
  avec un lit double *with a double bed*
  avec deux lits *with two beds*
  avec salle de bains / sans salle de bains *with / without a bathroom*

avec WC / sans toilettes *with / without a half-bath*
qui donne sur la terrasse *that overlooks the terrace*
réserver une table au restaurant *to reserve a table in a restaurant*

à l'extérieur / sur la terrasse *outside / on the terrace*
à l'intérieur *inside*
pour deux / trois / quatre personnes *for 2 / 3 / 4 people*

Comme activités touristiques *tourist activities*

acheter des souvenirs *(m.)* *to buy souvenirs*
  des cartes postales *(f.)* *postcards*
  des diapositives *(f.)* *slides*
  des livres *(m.)* *books*
  des statuettes *(f.)* *knickknacks*
  des sweat-shirts *(m.)* *sweatshirts*
  des tee-shirts *(m.)* *tee-shirts*
aller aux musées *(m.)* *to go to museums*
  apprendre l'histoire *(f.)* *to learn history*
  regarder / admirer les tableaux *(m.)* *to look at / admire paintings*
  regarder les sculptures *(f.)* *to look at sculptures*
goûter les spécialités régionales *(f.)* *to taste regional specialties*

les entrées *(f.)* *appetizers*
le fromage *cheese*
les gourmandises *(f.)* / le chocolat *sweets / chocolate*
les pâtisseries *(f.)* / les desserts *(m.)* *pastries / desserts*
les plats principaux *(m.)* *main dishes, entrees*
les vins / les bières *(f.)* *wines / beers*
prendre des photos *(f.)* *to take photos*
  en couleur *in color*
  en noir et blanc *in black and white*
  numériques *digital*
regarder les gens dans une place publique *to people-watch in a public square*
  les couples *(m.)* *couples*
  les familles *(f.)* *families*

les mimes *(m.)* *mimes*
un spectacle public *a public performance*
se reposer dans un parc *to relax in a park*
  à côté d'un lac *beside a lake*
  couché sous un arbre *lying down under a tree*
  sur un banc *on a bench*
visiter les monuments *(m.)* *to visit the monuments*
  les bâtiments *(m.)* *buildings*
  les parcs nationaux *(m.)* *national parks*
  les places publiques *(f.)* *public squares*
  les statues *(f.)* *statues*

UNITÉ 4

MISE EN PRATIQUE

Ⓐ vous de découvrir!

Online Study Center

Pour faire les activités suivantes, allez au *Online Study Center* et choisissez **Mise en pratique.** Vous y trouverez des sites web correspondants aux mots ou phrases en caractères gras dans chaque activité.

Le Québec

Aujourd'hui, vous allez visiter le Québec à l'aide des sites web suivants. Répondez aux questions avec votre partenaire; à la fin, vous présenterez ce que vous avez vu à la classe.

Montréal, ville ancienne–ville moderne

A. La géographie. Allez au **site touristique officiel du gouvernement de Québec** et cliquez sur **Informations Utiles,** puis sur **Géographie.**

1. Où se trouve cette région?
2. Est-ce une grande province (vis-à-vis des autres au Canada), ou une petite?
3. Faites une comparaison avec votre état ou pays et cette province. Lequel est plus grand?
4. Pouvez-vous nommer quelques-unes des villes principales?

B. Découvrez la région et ses activités. Pour répondre aux questions suivantes, retournez au **site touristique officiel du gouvernement de Québec.**

1. Quels sites touristiques peut-on visiter?
2. Identifiez les activités ou les sports les plus typiques. Quelle activité vous intéresse le plus? Pourquoi? Quel sport voudriez-vous pratiquer? Pourquoi?
3. Au Canada, on emploie le terme le magasinage au lieu de faire du shopping, faire les magasins ou faire du lèche-vitrines[1]. Si vous voulez faire les magasins au Québec, quelles sont vos possibilités? Est-ce que cela vous paraît intéressant? Pourquoi ou pourquoi pas?
4. Trouvez des renseignements sur les traîneaux à chiens. Dites à la classe ce que vous avez trouvé: qu'est-ce que les traîneaux à chiens, qui utilise les traîneaux à chiens, etc.
5. Est-ce que vous aimeriez monter sur un traîneau à chiens? Pourquoi ou pourquoi pas?
6. La vie animale est très respectée au Québec. Quels animaux peut-on observer?

Québec, ville européenne

Maintenant, faites un résumé de vos impressions générales de cette région, de sa géographie et des différentes activités que l'on peut y faire. Voudriez-vous y aller? Expliquez votre réponse. See p. 523 for possible answers.

Le Château Frontenac, Québec: hôtel de luxe

---

[1]*window shopping*

Point out to students the difference between *le Québec* (the province) and **Québec** (the city). Have them note the diversity of the cities in this region—the large city of Montréal, with its combination of old-world charm and new-world flavor, and cities like Quebec, which have maintained much of the look and lifestyle of Europe. Point out that the Château Frontenac was built originally to serve as a hotel, but one that evoked the châteaux of the Loire Valley, hence its name.

C. Découvrez de futures vacances au Québec. Retournez au **site touristique officiel du gouvernement de Québec** et répondez aux questions suivantes.

1. Quand on parle du Québec on dit souvent que c'est «Le Royaume des extrêmes» à cause des températures extrêmes. Cherchez les températures minimales du Québec en hiver. Pouvez-vous convertir ces températures en Fahrenheit? Sont-elles vraiment extrêmes ou est-ce une exagération?

2. Combien de neige est-ce qu'il y a au Québec en moyenne? Vous aimez la neige? Pourquoi ou pourquoi pas? Pensez-vous que les Québécois aiment la neige? Qu'est-ce qui vous fait penser cela? Voudriez-vous visiter le Québec en hiver? Expliquez votre réponse.

3. Trouvez les activités que l'on peut faire pendant d'autres saisons (en été, automne et printemps). Dites à la classe les activités que vous préférez faire et expliquez pourquoi.

À vous de déguster!

A. Spécialités gastronomiques canadiennes. Dans cette section, nous allons découvrir la gastronomie du Québec. Est-ce que vous la connaissez déjà un peu? Testez vos connaissances.

1. Ce fruit est rond et petit. Il pousse dans les forêts. On l'utilise souvent pour faire de la confiture. En France, on l'appelle *myrtille,* mais il a un nom différent au Canada.

   a. la framboise   b. le bleuet   c. le raisin

2. C'est un sirop très sucré qui est fait avec la sève[1] de l'arbre national du Canada.

   a. le sirop de maïs   b. le sirop de betterave   c. le sirop d'érable

3. Cette boisson légèrement alcoolisée est à base de pommes, et se boit au dîner, comme le vin ou la bière.

   a. le cognac   b. le rhum   c. le cidre

4. On le trouve dans les régions du Bas-Saint-Laurent et de la Gaspésie.

   a. le poisson   b. le bœuf   c. le veau

5. Ce produit laitier se mange dans des sandwichs et s'utilise dans la préparation de beaucoup de plats différents. En 2002, il a gagné un prix mondial d'alimentation.

   a. le yaourt   b. le cheddar   c. le lait

B. Découvrez les spécialités gastronomiques du Québec. Retournez au **site touristique officiel du gouvernement de Québec** et cherchez quelles sont les spécialités gastronomiques du Québec.

Choisissez-en deux et décrivez-les à la classe. (Comment sont-elles préparées, de quoi sont-elles faites, où les fait-on, etc.)

Answers will vary. You might consider bringing some real maple syrup into class for students to taste. While there are maple syrup producers in the U.S., much of the maple syrup sold here is produced in Canada. Real maple syrup is thinner and sweeter than the pancake syrups that are typically sold here (which have molasses or corn syrup as a base), so you have to be certain to buy the pure product. It can, of course, be eaten on pancakes and waffles, but is also delicious over ice cream. In areas where maple syrup is produced, it is also sometimes eaten over new-fallen snow—a favorite among children!

---
[1]*sap*

Answer Key: 1. Il s'agit d'extrêmes climatiques: de température et de précipitation. Les températures au Québec varient entre –30°C et 30°C (–20F à 90F). 2. L'accumulation de neige varie en moyenne entre 2 mètres par an au sud de Montréal jusqu'à 5 mètres par an dans la partie nord de la région (dans les Laurentides). 3. *Possible answers:* En été, on peut observer des phoques ou faire du VTT; on peut aussi faire du rafting ou jouer au golf. En automne on peut admirer le changement de couleur des arbres; on peut faire des randonnées, du vélo ou monter à cheval. On peut également récolter des pommes. Au printemps, on peut manger des desserts au sirop d'érable; on peut faire du ski, du rafting, pêcher ou faire un pique-nique.

Answer Key: 1. b 2. c 3. c 4. a 5. b

You might wish to share with students the following information taken from www.bonjourquebec.com: The 3-year-old cheddar cheese "Britannia" from the cheese maker *Agropur* won first place at the World Championship Cheese Contest for the category "best aged cheddar in the world." Another Québécois cheddar finished in second place.

C. Faites un milk-shake aux bleuets. Aimez-vous les bleuets? Si oui, nous avons une recette délicieuse (et très facile à préparer) pour vous. Elle est aussi très bonne pour la santé!

Un milk-shake aux bleuets

1 banane
¾ de tasse de bleuets
¼ de tasse de yaourt à la vanille
¾ de tasse de lait écrémé
½ tasse de glaçons pilés

Mettez tous les ingrédients
dans un mixeur.
Couvrez et mélangez bien.
À déguster tout de suite!

À vous d'analyser

Vous allez lire un extrait d'un roman très célèbre au Canada, *Les Fous de Bassan*, écrit par Anne Hébert en 1982. Après une dispute avec son père, Stevens Brown, âgé de 15 ans, quitte le Canada pour les États-Unis. Cinq ans plus tard, il retourne à son pays natal, où il essaie de se réinventer. Pour le faire, il doit quand même confronter ses souvenirs, ses émotions et même sa famille.

Answer Key: la joie, la tristesse, la peur, la jalousie

A. Souvenirs et émotions. En lisant le passage suivant, où Stevens décrit sa mère et la naissance de ses sœurs jumelles, cochez les émotions qu'il ressent. Soulignez la (les) phrase(s) qui indique(nt) cette émotion.

_____ la joie	_____ la peur	_____ la surprise
_____ la mélancolie	_____ la jalousie	_____ la tristesse

Être quelqu'un d'autre, quelle idée est-ce là qui me poursuit toujours. Organiser les souvenirs, disposer les images, me dédoubler franchement, tout en restant moi-même. Pouvoir témoigner de ma vie passée, sans danger, sans être obligé d'y rentrer à nouveau et dire: Voilà c'est moi, Stevens Brown, fils de John Brown et de Béatrice Jones. Une sorte de jeu dont on peut se retirer à volonté.

Inutile de me leurrer. La mémoire résonne dans tout mon corps, rumeur vivante en ondes sonores, vibre jusqu'au bout de mes ongles. Ce soir, une sensation de froid me pénètre peu à peu, à mesure que je surveille la nuit entre les fentes de la grange et la grande ombre double au-delà des ténèbres. La nuit fraîche n'explique rien du tout. Ce froid vient d'ailleurs, des profondeurs confuses de la naissance, du premier attouchement des mains glacées de ma mère sur mon corps d'enfant.

Cette femme a une très mauvaise circulation, dit le Dr. Hopkins. Elle dégage du froid comme d'autres de la chaleur. C'est encore étonnant qu'elle puisse mettre au monde des enfants vivants, sortis d'un ventre aussi polaire, on aurait pu croire que seuls des cadavres d'enfants … Ces deux-là sont bien vivantes. Deux d'un coup c'est trop, dit-elle. Elle pleure et affirme qu'elle ne veut pas de ces deux enfants. Elle répète «mes jumelles», une dans chaque bras. Un frisson lui parcourt l'échine. Elle secoue la tête.

—Je peux pas, je peux pas, je peux pas.

Je ferme les yeux. Qu'est-ce qu'on va faire des jumelles, les noyer comme des petits chats, les donner aux cochons, peut-être, ou les perdre dans les bois? Je quitte la chambre en courant. Quand je reviens, sur la pointe des pieds, je constate que rien n'a encore été fait. Les deux jumelles sont toujours là, accrochées, à tour de rôle, au sein de ma mère, blafarde et effarée, regorgeante de lait, pareille à une fontaine glacée. Toute la chambre s'en ressent de cette source de froid, installée sur le grand lit, avec deux nouveaux-nés qui s'égosillent. Et moi, dans mon coin, je prends en glace, comme un bonhomme de neige. J'entends ma propre voix, petit filon encore liquide, à l'intérieur de la glace. Et moi et moi et moi … C'est pas le lait tout cru qu'elle m'a donné, Béatrice ma mère, c'est la faim et la soif. Le désir.

B. Relations familiales. Après avoir lu le texte, décrivez les relations probables entre Stevens et sa mère. Comment est sa mère? La froideur dont il parle, est-ce que c'est une condition médicale, ou est-ce que c'est autre chose? Quelles seront probablement ses relations avec ses sœurs?

C. Comparaisons. Faites une comparaison entre vos relations familiales et celles de Stevens Brown. Comment sont les membres de votre famille? Êtes-vous très proche de votre mère? Et de votre père? Sont-ils affectueux? Est-ce qu'ils vous comprennent ou est-ce qu'ils vous jugent? Vous vous disputez souvent? Quelles émotions ressentez-vous quand vous vous disputez avec vos parents? Comment réagissez-vous quand vous n'êtes pas d'accord avec eux? Et quand vous êtes d'accord?

D. Réinventons nos vies. Si vous pouviez réinventer votre vie, comment est-ce que vous la changeriez? Est-ce que vous vous changeriez personnellement? Est-ce que vous changeriez vos relations avec vos proches? Votre travail / vos études? Votre passé? Écrivez un paragraphe où vous racontez votre nouvelle vie.

À vous de créer!

A. Ce que je sais / ce que je connais. Remplissez le paragraphe suivant. Dans le premier tiret, mettez le verbe **savoir** ou **connaître,** comme nécessaire. Dans le deuxième tiret, mettez le bon pronom relatif **(qui, que, dont, où),** selon le cas.

1. Je ne _____ pas le restaurant _____ tu m'as recommandé, mais je vais y aller. Est-ce que c'est facile d'y avoir une table?

2. Je ne _____ pas sauter en parachute; c'est un sport _____ me fait peur.

C'est une femme froide. Elle est triste au point d'être presque morte. Elle n'est pas capable d'aimer ses enfants—et ils ressentent cette froideur. Ils deviennent froids eux-mêmes à cause de cela. Stevens a de la peine pour les jumelles. Peut-être qu'il jouera le rôle du grand frère et il les protégera.

Answer Key: 1. connais; que 2. sais; qui

3. Et vous, est-ce que vous _____ quelqu'un _____ a sauté en parachute?

4. Mes amis _____ la ville _____ j'ai grandi. Ce n'est pas très loin de notre université.

5. Nous _____ utiliser un ordinateur pour chercher des informations sur Internet. C'est une capacité _____ est essentielle de nos jours!

6. Est-ce que vous _____ que vous pouvez sortir en hiver quand vous avez les cheveux mouillés[1]? J'ai un frère _____ la femme est médecin et elle m'a dit que les cheveux mouillés ne causent pas de rhumes!

B. Un voyage inoubliable. Asha et sa sœur Nadja ont fait un voyage inoubliable récemment. Utilisez les mots suivants pour compléter leur histoire.

alpin	l'Internet
à	héliski
aller-retour	l'escalade sur glace
la cheville	valises
en	en avion
deltaplane	des

Il y a deux mois, nous avons décidé de voyager (1) _____ Europe. Nous avons voyagé (2) _____. Il est très facile de préparer un voyage aujourd'hui. D'abord, nous avons acheté deux billets (3) _____ sur (4) _____. Le jour de notre voyage, nous sommes parties pour l'aéroport avec nos deux (5) _____—elles étaient très lourdes! Nous sommes parties (6) _____ États-Unis avec 250 autres personnes dans un très grand avion (mon premier voyage intercontinental!), et nous sommes arrivées (7) _____ Genève le lendemain matin. Nous sommes toutes les deux fanatiques des sports d'hiver, donc nous avons beaucoup aimé la Suisse. Le premier jour, nous avons fait du ski (8) _____ sur les plus hautes montagnes en Europe. Pour y arriver, il fallait faire de (9) _____ (avec un guide/entraîneur, bien sûr!). Pendant le trajet, nous portions nos skis sur le dos et nous allions lentement. Quand nous sommes arrivées au sommet, nous avons mis nos skis, et nous sommes descendues. C'était très impressionnant! Le deuxième jour, Nadja voulait faire de l'(10) _____, mais moi, j'avais un peu peur. Je n'ai jamais volé[2] dans un hélicoptère! Donc, nous avons décidé de faire du (11) _____. Quand on vole comme ça, on a l'impression d'être aussi libre qu'un oiseau! Le troisième jour nous sommes restées en ville. Tout en marchant sur le trottoir, Nadja est tombée, et elle s'est tordu (12) _____.

C'est toujours comme ça—on peut faire des sports extrêmes sans se blesser, mais pendant les activités de tous les jours, on a un accident! Le reste de notre voyage était donc beaucoup plus calme, mais toujours très intéressant. La Suisse est un pays magnifique!

---

[1]*wet* [2]*have never flown*

C. Ma vie dans dix ans. Remplissez les tirets avec le futur, le présent du subjonctif ou l'infinitif du verbe indiqué, selon le contexte.

Dans dix ans, il est absolument certain que je (1) _____ (ne ... plus habiter) dans la ville où j'habite maintenant. Après avoir terminé mes études, je veux (2) _____ (trouver) un poste dans une grande ville comme New York ou Chicago. Il est même possible que j(e) (3) _____ (aller) à Paris ou à Londres! Il (4) _____ (être) important que j(e) (5) _____ (déménager) dans une de ces villes, parce que j(e) (6) _____ (avoir) plus de possibilités de trouver le poste que je désire.

Mais dans dix ans j(e) (7) _____ (être) probablement marié. Il faut que ma femme (8) _____ (vouloir) habiter une grande ville aussi; si non, nous (9) _____ (trouver) un compromis— peut-être une ville de taille moyenne. Il est sans doute plus facile de (10) _____ (conduire) dans des petites villes, mais il y a moins de bus, et moins de choses à faire. Je suis toujours content d(e) (11) _____ (aller) aux concerts et aux musées, et il faut que je (12) _____ (pouvoir) voir un film étranger au cinéma de temps en temps!

À vous de décider

Le français pour quoi faire?

Why have you chosen to study French? Perhaps for you, your French course fulfills a language requirement that is part of your degree program. Perhaps you are convinced that knowledge of a foreign language will benefit you in your chosen career or in your graduate studies. But perhaps you are also one of the thousands of world citizens who are interested in the humanitarian efforts of organizations such as the Peace Corps, the International Red Cross/Red Crescent, or Médecins Sans Frontières (Doctors Without Borders), to name only a few. The need for speakers of fluent French within such organizations is critical. In the past two decades alone, these organizations and others like them have dispatched volunteers to parts of Asia and Africa that were especially hard-hit by natural disasters, medical crises, famine, and wars, or that were simply in need of community-building and development of infrastructure. As the world's population grows, so do the needs of developing countries, and volunteer organizations are often leading the way. Because French is used so frequently as an administrative and/or official language in developing countries throughout the world, being fluent helps a volunteer to get to know the people with whom s/he will be working, and, in some cases, opens doors that might otherwise be difficult to penetrate. Although most volunteer aid organizations can provide language training to their volunteers if necessary, those who are already fluent in a language are able to be placed much more quickly, thus accomplishing more rapidly the purpose of joining such an organization in the first place—working in the field with those most in need of help.

REFERENCE SECTION

Appendice A

Dans la classe de français

À vous de parler au prof | Your turn to talk to the instructor

À vous de parler au prof	Your turn to talk to the instructor
Que veut dire «plage»?	*What does* plage *mean?*
Comment écrit-on «plage»?	*How does one write* plage*?*
Comment épelle-t-on «plage»?	*How does one spell* plage*?*
Comment dit-on «*beach*» en français?	*How does one say "beach" in French?*
C'est à quelle page?	*What page is it on?*
C'est quelle activité?	*Which activity is it?*
Pouvez-vous répéter?	*Could you repeat?*
Quels sont les devoirs?	*What is the homework assignment?*
C'est pour quel jour les devoirs?	*What day is the homework due?*
Je ne comprends pas.	*I don't understand.*
Je ne sais pas.	*I don't know.*
Désolé(e).	*Sorry.*
S'il vous plaît.	*Please.*
Merci.	*Thank you.*
D'accord!	*All right!*

Le prof vous parle | The instructor talks to you

Le prof vous parle	The instructor talks to you
Ouvrez le livre à la page 4.	*Open the book to page 4.*
Fermez le livre.	*Close the book.*
Écoutez.	*Listen.*
Ne répétez pas.	*Do not repeat.*
Répétez.	*Repeat.*
Silence, ne parlez pas!	*Silence, don't speak!*
Prenez une feuille de papier.	*Take a sheet of paper.*
Regardez le tableau/l'écran.	*Look at the board/screen.*
Ne regardez pas le livre.	*Don't look at the book.*
Levez-vous!	*Stand up!*
Asseyez-vous!	*Sit down!*
Circulez dans la classe.	*Walk around the classroom.*
Faites l'activité B à la page 4.	*Do activity B on page 4.*
Faites l'activité B avec un partenaire.	*Do activity B with a partner.*
Écrivez l'activité B.	*Write activity B.*
Faites l'activité B oralement.	*Do activity B orally.*
N'écrivez pas l'activité B.	*Don't write activity B.*
Cherchez un partenaire.	*Look for a partner.*
Travaillez avec un partenaire.	*Work with a partner.*
Formez des groupes de trois.	*Form groups of three.*
Je cherche un volontaire pour corriger l'activité B.	*I'm looking for a volunteer to go over activity B.*
Lisez la lecture.	*Do the reading.*
Répondez aux questions.	*Answer the questions.*
Répondez avec des phrases complètes.	*Answer in complete sentences.*
Très bien!	*Very good!*

Excellent!
Parfait!
Non ... qui peut l'aider?
Les devoirs sont à faire pour mardi.
Les devoirs sont à rendre mardi.

Excellent!
Perfect!
No . . . who can help him/her?
The homework is to be done for Tuesday.
The homework is to be turned in on Tuesday.

À vous de parler aux étudiants

Veux-tu travailler avec moi?
Veux-tu être dans mon groupe?
Tu sais faire l'activité B?
Je peux travailler avec toi?
C'est moi qui donne la réponse?
C'est à moi?
C'est à toi.
Qu'est-ce qu'il a dit, le prof?
Qu'est-ce que le prof a dit?
Tu comprends le prof?
À demain!
À plus!

Your turn to speak to your fellow students

Do you want to work with me?
Do you want to be in my group?
Do you know how to do activity B?
Can I work with you?
Is it up to me to give the answer?
Is it my turn?
It's your turn.
What did the instructor say?
What did the instructor say? (more formal)
Do you understand the instructor?
See you tomorrow!
See you (later)!

Appendice B

Les États-Unis et le Canada

Les États-Unis

ÉTAT	in or to	ÉTAT	in or to
l'Alabama (m.)	dans l'Alabama / en Alabama	le Maine	dans le Maine
l'Alaska (m.)	dans l'Alaska / en Alaska	le Maryland	dans le Maryland
l'Arizona (m.)	dans l'Arizona / en Arizona	le Massachusetts	dans le Massachusetts
		le Michigan	dans le Michigan
l'Arkansas (m.)	dans l'Arkansas / en Arkansas	le Minnesota	dans le Minnesota
la Californie	en Californie	le Mississippi	dans le Mississippi
la Caroline du Nord	en Caroline du Nord	le Missouri	dans le Missouri
la Caroline du Sud	en Caroline du Sud	le Montana	dans le Montana
le Colorado	dans le Colorado / au Colorado	le Nebraska	dans le Nebraska
		le Nevada	dans le Nevada
le Connecticut	dans le Connecticut	le New Hampshire	dans le New Hampshire
le Dakota du Nord	dans le Dakota du Nord	le New Jersey	dans le New Jersey
le Dakota du Sud	dans le Dakota du Sud	l'état de New York	dans l'état de New York
le Delaware	dans le Delaware	le Nouveau-Mexique	au Nouveau-Mexique
la Floride	en Floride	l'Ohio (m.)	dans l'Ohio
la Géorgie	en Géorgie	l'Oklahoma (m.)	dans l'Oklahoma
Hawaii (m.)	à Hawaii / aux îles Hawaii	l'Oregon (m.)	dans l'Oregon
		la Pennsylvanie	en Pennsylvanie
l'Idaho (m.)	dans l'Idaho	le Rhode Island	dans le Rhode Island dans le
l'Illinois (m.)	dans l'Illinois / en Illinois	le Tennessee	Tennessee
l'Indiana (m.)	dans l'Indiana	le Texas	au Texas
l'Iowa (m.)	dans l'Iowa	l'Utah (m.)	dans l'Utah
le Kansas	dans le Kansas	le Vermont	dans le Vermont
le Kentucky	dans le Kentucky	la Virginie	en Virginie
la Louisiane	en Louisiane	la Virginie-Occidentale	en Virginie-Occidentale
		l'état de Washington	dans l'état de Washington
		le Wisconsin	dans le Wisconsin
		le Wyoming	dans le Wyoming

Le Canada

PROVINCE	in or to	TERRITOIRE	in or to
l'Alberta	dans l'Alberta	le Nunavut	au Nunavut
la Colombie-Britannique	en Colombie-Britannique	les Territoires du Nord-Ouest	dans les Territoires du Nord-Ouest
l'île du Prince-Édouard	dans l'île du Prince-Édouard	le Yukon	au Yukon
le Manitoba	au Manitoba		
le Nouveau-Brunswick	au Nouveau-Brunswick		
la Nouvelle-Écosse	en Nouvelle-Écosse		
l'Ontario	dans l'Ontario		
le Québec	au Québec		
le Saskatchewan	au Saskatchewan		
Terre-Neuve	à Terre-Neuve		

Appendice C

L'alphabet phonétique international (API)

Consonants

/ p /	*P*ierre
/ t /	*t*u
/ k/	*c*omme
/ b /	*b*onjour
/ d /	*d*e
/ g /	*g*arçon
/ f /	*f*ille
/ s /	mer*c*i, profe*ss*eur
/ ʃ /	*ch*ez

/ v /	*v*ous
/ z /	bi*s*e
/ ʒ /	bon*j*our
/ l /	*l*a
/ ʀ /	ga*r*çon
/ m /	*m*ain
/ n /	A*nn*e
/ ɲ /	poi*gn*ée
/ ŋ /	park*ing*

Vowels

/ i /	b*i*se
/ e /	caf*é*
/ ɛ /	app*e*lle
/ a /	v*a*
/ ɔ /	c*o*mme
/ o /	*au*
/ u /	v*ou*s

/ y /	*u*ne
/ ø /	d*e*, p*eu*
/ œ /	h*eu*re
/ ɛ̃ /	bi*en*, *un*, m*ain*
/ ɑ̃ /	connaiss*an*ce
/ ɔ̃ /	fais*ons*

Semivowels

/ j /	P*i*erre
/ w /	*ou*i
/ ɥ /	n*u*it

Mute e

/ ə /	*je*, *fe*rai

Appendice D

Conjugaison des verbes

Les verbes réguliers

A. Conjugaison régulière

| Infinitif | Indicatif | | |
	Présent	Passé composé	Imparfait
Verbes en **-er** **parler**	je parle tu parles il/elle/on parle nous parlons vous parlez ils/elles parlent	j'**ai** parlé tu **as** parlé il **a** parlé nous **avons** parlé vous **avez** parlé ils **ont** parlé	je parlais tu parlais il parlait nous parlions vous parliez ils parlaient
Verbes en **-ir** **finir**	je finis tu finis il/elle/on finit nous finissons vous finissez ils/elles finissent	j'**ai** fini tu **as** fini il **a** fini nous **avons** fini vous **avez** fini ils **ont** fini	je finissais tu finissais il finissait nous finissions vous finissiez ils finissaient
Verbes en **-re** **répondre**	je réponds tu réponds il/elle/on répond nous répondons vous répondez ils/elles répondent	j'**ai** répondu tu **as** répondu il **a** répondu nous **avons** répondu vous **avez** répondu ils **ont** répondu	je répondais tu répondais il répondait nous répondions vous répondiez ils répondaient
Verbes pronominaux **se laver**	je me lave tu te laves il/on se lave elle se lave nous nous lavons vous vous lavez ils se lavent elles se lavent	je me **suis** lavé(e) tu t'**es** lavé(e) il s'**est** lavé elle s'**est** lavée nous nous **sommes** lavé(e)s vous vous **êtes** lavé(e)(s) ils se **sont** lavés elles se **sont** lavées	je me lavais tu te lavais il se lavait elle se lavait nous nous lavions vous vous laviez ils se lavaient elles se lavaient

Futur	Conditionnel Présent	Subjonctif Présent	Impératif
je parler**ai** tu parler**as** il parler**a** nous parler**ons** vous parler**ez** ils parler**ont**	je parler**ais** tu parler**ais** il parler**ait** nous parler**ions** vous parler**iez** ils parler**aient**	que je parl**e** que tu parl**es** qu'il/elle/on parl**e** que nous parl**ions** que vous parl**iez** qu'ils/elles parl**ent**	parl**e** parl**ons** parl**ez**
je finir**ai** tu finir**as** il finir**a** nous finir**ons** vous finir**ez** ils finir**ont**	je finir**ais** tu finir**ais** il finir**ait** nous finir**ions** vous finir**iez** ils finir**aient**	que je fini**sse** que tu fini**sses** qu'il/elle/on fini**sse** que nous fini**ssions** que vous fini**ssiez** qu'ils/elles fini**ssent**	fini**s** fin**issons** fin**issez**
je répondr**ai** tu répondr**as** il répondr**a** nous répondr**ons** vous répondr**ez** ils répondr**ont**	je répondr**ais** tu répondr**ais** il répondr**ait** nous répondr**ions** vous répondr**iez** ils répondr**aient**	que je répond**e** que tu répond**es** qu'il/elle/on répond**e** que nous répond**ions** que vous répond**iez** qu'ils/elles répond**ent**	répond**s** répond**ons** répond**ez**
je me laverai tu te laveras il se lavera elle se lavera nous nous laverons vous vous laverez ils se laveront elles se laveront	je me laverais tu te laverais il se laverait elle se laverait nous nous laverions vous vous laveriez ils se laveraient elles se laveraient	que je me lave que tu te laves qu'il/on se lave qu'elle se lave que nous nous lavions que vous vous laviez qu'ils se lavent qu'elles se lavent	lave-toi lavons-nous lavez-vous

B. Verbes à modification orthographique

Infinitif	Indicatif		
	Présent	Passé composé	Imparfait
acheter	j'achète tu achètes il/elle/on achète nous achetons vous achetez ils/elles achètent	j'ai acheté	j'achetais
préférer	je préfère tu préfères il/elle/on préfère nous préférons vous préférez ils/elles préfèrent	j'ai préféré	je préférais
payer	je paie tu paies il/elle/on paie nous payons vous payez ils/elles paient	j'ai payé	je payais
appeler	j'appelle tu appelles il/elle/on appelle nous appelons vous appelez ils/elles appellent	j'ai appelé	j'appelais
commencer	je commence tu commences il/elle/on commence nous commençons vous commencez ils/elles commencent	j'ai commencé	je commençais tu commençais il/elle/on commençait nous commencions vous commenciez ils/elles commençaient
manger	je mange tu manges il/elle/on mange nous mangeons vous mangez ils/elles mangent	j'ai mangé	je mangeais tu mangeais il/elle/on mangeait nous mangions vous mangiez ils/elles mangeaient

| | Conditionnel | Subjonctif | Impératif |
Futur	Présent	Présent	
j'achèterai	j'achèterais	que j'achète que tu achètes qu'il/elle/on achète que nous achetions que vous achetiez qu'ils/elles achètent	achète achetons achetez
je préférerai	je préférerais	que je préfère que tu préfères qu'il/elle/on préfère que nous préférions que vous préfériez qu'ils/elles préfèrent	préfère préférons préférez
je paierai	je paierais	que je paie que tu paies qu'il/elle/on paie que nous payions que vous payiez qu'ils/elles paient	paie payons payez
j'appellerai	j'appellerais	que j'appelle que tu appelles qu'il/elle/on appelle que nous appelions que vous appeliez qu'ils/elles appellent	appelle appelons appelez
je commencerai	je commencerais	que je commence que tu commences qu'il/elle/on commence que nous commencions que vous commenciez qu'ils/elles commencent	commence commençons commencez
je mangerai	je mangerais	que je mange que tu manges qu'il/elle/on mange que nous mangions que vous mangiez qu'ils/elles mangent	mange mangeons mangez

Les verbes auxiliaires

Infinitif	Indicatif		
	Présent	Passé composé	Imparfait
avoir	j'ai tu as il/elle/on a nous avons vous avez ils/elles ont	j'ai eu	j'avais
être	je suis tu es il/elle/on est nous sommes vous êtes ils/elles sont	j'ai été	j'étais

Les verbes irréguliers

Infinitif	Indicatif		Passé composé	Imparfait
	Présent			
aller	je vais tu vas il/elle/on va	nous allons vous allez ils/elles vont	je suis allé(e)	j'allais
s'asseoir	je m'assieds tu t'assieds il/elle/on s'assied	nous nous asseyons vous vous asseyez ils/elles s'asseyent	je me suis assis(e)	je m'asseyais
boire	je bois tu bois il/elle/on boit	nous buvons vous buvez ils/elles boivent	j'ai bu	je buvais
conduire	je conduis tu conduis il/elle/on conduit	nous conduisons vous conduisez ils/elles conduisent	j'ai conduit	je conduisais

Futur	Conditionnel Présent	Subjonctif Présent	Impératif
j'aurai	j'aurais	que j'aie que tu aies qu'il/elle/on ait que nous ayons que vous ayez qu'ils/elles aient	aie ayons ayez
je serai	je serais	que je sois que tu sois qu'il/elle/on soit que nous soyons que vous soyez qu'ils/elles soient	sois soyons soyez

Futur	Conditionnel Présent	Subjonctif Présent	Autres verbes ayant une conjugaison semblable
j'irai	j'irais	que j'aille que nous allions	
je m'assiérai	je m'assiérais	que je m'asseye que nous nous asseyions	
je boirai	je boirais	que je boive que nous buvions	
je conduirai	je conduirais	que je conduise que nous conduisions	

Infinitif	Indicatif		Passé composé	Imparfait
	Présent			
connaître	je connais tu connais il/elle/on connaît	nous connaissons vous connaissez ils/elles connaissent	j'ai connu	je connaissais
courir	je cours tu cours il/elle/on court	nous courons vous courez ils/elles courent	j'ai couru	je courais
croire	je crois tu crois il/elle/on croit	nous croyons vous croyez ils/elles croient	j'ai cru	je croyais
devoir	je dois tu dois il/elle/on doit	nous devons vous devez ils/elles doivent	j'ai dû	je devais
dire	je dis tu dis il/elle/on dit	nous disons vous dites ils/elles disent	j'ai dit	je disais
écrire	j'écris tu écris il/elle/on écrit	nous écrivons vous écrivez ils/elles écrivent	j'ai écrit	j'écrivais
envoyer	j'envoie tu envoies il/elle/on envoie	nous envoyons vous envoyez ils/elles envoient	j'ai envoyé	j'envoyais
faire	je fais tu fais il/elle/on fait	nous faisons vous faites ils/elles font	j'ai fait	je faisais
falloir	il faut		il a fallu	il fallait
lire	je lis tu lis il/elle/on lit	nous lisons vous lisez ils/elles lisent	j'ai lu	je lisais

Futur	Conditionnel Présent	Subjonctif Présent	Autres verbes ayant une conjugaison semblable
je connaîtrai	je connaîtrais	que je connaisse que nous connaissions	
je courrai	je courrais	que je coure que nous courions	
je croirai	je croirais	que je croie que nous croyions	
je devrai	je devrais	que je doive que nous devions	
je dirai	je dirais	que je dise que nous disions	prédire (vous prédisez)
j'écrirai	j'écrirais	que j'écrive que nous écrivions	décrire récrire
j'enverrai	j'enverrais	que j'envoie que nous envoyions	renvoyer
je ferai	je ferais	que je fasse que nous fassions	
il faudra	il faudrait	qu'il faille	
je lirai	je lirais	que je lise que nous lisions	relire

Infinitif	Indicatif		Passé composé	Imparfait
	Présent			
mettre	je mets tu mets il/elle/on met	nous mettons vous mettez ils/elles mettent	j'ai mis	je mettais
ouvrir	j'ouvre tu ouvres il/elle/on ouvre	nous ouvrons vous ouvrez ils/elles ouvrent	j'ai ouvert	j'ouvrais
partir	je pars tu pars il/elle/on part	nous partons vous partez ils/elles partent	je suis parti(e)	je partais
pleuvoir	il pleut		il a plu	il pleuvait
pouvoir	je peux tu peux il/elle/on peut	nous pouvons vous pouvez ils/elles peuvent	j'ai pu	je pouvais
prendre	je prends tu prends il/elle/on prend	nous prenons vous prenez ils/elles prennent	j'ai pris	je prenais
recevoir	je reçois tu reçois il/elle/on reçoit	nous recevons vous recevez ils/elles reçoivent	j'ai reçu	je recevais
savoir	je sais tu sais il/elle/on sait	nous savons vous savez ils/elles savent	j'ai su	je savais

	Conditionnel	Subjonctif	Autres verbes ayant une conjugaison semblable
Futur	Présent	Présent	
je mettrai	je mettrais	que je mette que nous mettions	admettre permettre promettre
j'ouvrirai	j'ouvrirais	que j'ouvre que nous ouvrions	rouvrir
je partirai	je partirais	que je parte que nous partions	dormir (j'ai dormi) s'endormir (je me suis endormi) sentir (j'ai senti) servir (j'ai servi) sortir (je suis sorti)
il pleuvra	il pleuvrait	qu'il pleuve	
je pourrai	je pourrais	que je puisse que nous puissions	
je prendrai	je prendrais	que je prenne que nous prenions	apprendre comprendre
je recevrai	je recevrais	que je reçoive que nous recevions	
je saurai	je saurais	que je sache que nous sachions	

Infinitif	Indicatif		Passé composé	Imparfait
	Présent			
venir	je viens tu viens il/elle/on vient	nous venons vous venez ils/elles viennent	je suis venu(e)	je venais
vivre	je vis tu vis il/elle/on vit	nous vivons vous vivez ils/elles vivent	j'ai vécu	je vivais
voir	je vois tu vois il/elle/on voit	nous voyons vous voyez ils/elles voient	j'ai vu	je voyais
vouloir	je veux tu veux il/elle/on veut	nous voulons vous voulez ils/elles veulent	j'ai voulu	je voulais

Futur	Conditionnel Présent	Subjonctif Présent	Autres verbes ayant une conjugaison semblable
je viendrai	je viendrais	que je vienne que nous venions	devenir (je suis devenu) revenir (je suis revenu) se souvenir (je me suis souvenu)
je vivrai	je vivrais	que je vive que nous vivions	
je verrai	je verrais	que je voie que nous voyions	prévoir (je prévoirai)
je voudrai	je voudrais	que je veuille que nous voulions	

French-English Vocabulary

The French-English vocabulary list contains all productive and receptive vocabulary that appears in the student text. Productive vocabulary includes words and expressions that appear in the **Commençons!, Continuons!,** and **Vocabulaire essentiel** sections, and in charts and word lists that are part of the grammar explanations. Receptive vocabulary consists of words and phrases that were introduced in the **Expansion personnelle** lists in the text as well as those that are given an English gloss in textual material throughout the book: readings, photo captions, exercises, activities, and authentic documents. Productive vocabulary entries are followed by the number of the chapter in which they are first introduced.

The following abbreviations are used:

adj.	adjective	*fam.*	familiar	*n.*	noun
adv.	adverb	*form.*	formal	*pl.*	plural
conj.	conjunction	*inv.*	invariable	*pron.*	pronoun
f.	feminine	*m.*	masculine	*sing.*	singular
f. pl.	feminine plural	*m. pl.*	masculine plural	*v.*	verb

A

à to; in; at, 16
~ **bientôt** see you soon, 1
~ **bord** on board, 16
~ **côté** next to, 4; beside, 16
~ **coup sûr** for sure
~ **demain** see you tomorrow, 1
~ **droite** to the right, 4
~ **gauche** to the left, 4
~ **l'air libre** outdoors
~ **la mode** hip, fashionable, 9
~ **laquelle** to which (*f. sing.*)
~ **la radio** *f.* on the radio
~ **la télé** *f.* on TV, 7
~ **la une** on the front page (of the newspaper)
~ **mi-temps** part-time, 10
~ **plein temps** full-time, 10
~ **plus (tard)** see you later, 1
~ **proximité** nearby
~ **qui le tour?** Whose turn is it?, 5
~ **son gré** at will
~ **table!** Dinner/Lunch is ready!, 6
~ **temps complet** full-time, 10
~ **temps partiel** part-time, 10
~ **tout ~ l'heure** see you in a while, 1
abdominal *m.* (*pl.* **abdominaux**) sit-up

abdos *m. pl.* abdominal muscles
abonné(e) *n.* subscriber, 7
abonnement *m.* magazine/ newspaper subscription, 7
absolu(e) absolute
absolument absolutely
accélérateur *m.* gas pedal, accelerator 8
accélérer to accelerate, 8
accepter to accept
s'~ to accept oneself, 9
accident *m.* accident, 7
accouchement *m.* labor, 9
accoucher to give birth, 9
accueillant(e) cozy
accueillir to welcome
achat *m.* purchase, 5
acheter to buy, 3
activité *f.* activity, 16
actualités *f. pl.* news, 7
adolescence *f.* adolescence, 9
adolescent(e) (**ado** *fam.*) adolescent, 9
adopté(e) adopted, 3
adresse *f.* address
~ **électronique** e-mail address, 13
adverbe *m.* adverb, 6
aéroport *m.* airport, 5
affirmer to assert, 9
agaçant(e) bothersome

agacer to bother, 15
agenda *m.* desk calendar, 13
~ **électronique** electronic planner
agent *m.* agent
~ **au sol** ground personnel, 16
~ **de police** police officer
~ **de voyage** travel agent, 3
agréable enjoyable, agreeable, 15
agréer to accept
Ah bon? Oh, really?
aider to help, 5
ail *m.* garlic
ailleurs elsewhere
~ **que** other than
d'~ moreover
aimer to like, to love
~ **à la folie** to love madly, 8
s'~ to love each other, 8
ainsi that way
~ **que** as well as
ajouter to add
alcoolisme *m.* alcoholism, 9
aller to go, 4
~ **à pied** to walk
billet *m.* ~**-retour** round-trip ticket, 5
billet *m.* ~ **simple** one-way ticket, 5
Je vais bien, et toi? I'm doing well, and you?; I'm good, and you?, 1

Je vais bien, merci I'm doing well, thank you, 1
   s'en ~ to leave
alors so; then
   ~ que while
   et ~! so what!
alpinisme *m.* mountain climbing, 13
amant *m.* lover
âme *f.* soul
améliorer to improve
amener to bring; to lead
amer (amère) bitter
amour *m.* love, 8
   grand ~ soulmate, 8
   mon ~ my love, 8
amoureux (amoureuse) in love, 3
amoureux *n. m. pl.* lovebirds, lovers, 8
amusant(e) amusing, funny, 2
amuser to amuse
   s'~ to have fun, 8
analphabétisation *f.* illiteracy
ange *m.* angel, 9
   être aux ~s to be in seventh heaven, 12; to be on cloud nine, 15
animal *m.* (*pl.* **animaux**) animal
   ~ domestique pet, 3
animateur (animatrice) DJ, host (hostess), 7
animer to announce, to host (a show), 7
année *f.* year, 3
anniversaire *m.* birthday, 3
antibiotique *m.* antibiotic, 15
antihistaminique *m.* antihistamine, 15
antipathique unfriendly, 2
août *m.* August, 3
appareil photo *m.* **numérique** digital camera, 13
appartement *m.* apartment, 4
appauvrissement *m.* impoverishment
appeler to call, 3
   s'~ to be named, 3
apporter to bring
apprendre to learn, 5
appuyer to push, 8
après-midi *f.* afternoon

aquagym *f.* water aerobics
arachide *f.* peanut
arbre *m.* tree, 16
arc-en-ciel *m.* rainbow
architecte *m./f.* architect, 3
arête *f.* fishbone
argent *m.* money; silver
arithméthique *f.* math
arme *f.* **à feu** firearm
armoire *f.* armoire, 4
armoirie *f.* coat of arms
arrêt *m.* stop
   ~ de bus bus stop, 5
   ~ de métro subway stop, 5
arrêter to stop
   s'~ to stop, 8
arrière: siège ~ back seat, 8
arriver to arrive
article *m.* article, 7
ascenseur *m.* elevator, 4
asperge *f.* asparagus, 6
aspirateur *m.* vacuum cleaner, 4
aspirine *f.* aspirin, 11
s'asseoir to sit (down)
assez quite; rather, 6
   ~ de enough of, 5
assiette *f.* plate, 6
   ~ à dessert dessert plate, 6
   ~ à soupe soup bowl, 6
assis(e) seated
assistant *m.* **personnel** PDA, 13
assister à to attend
assurance *f.* **médicale** medical insurance, 10
athlétisme *m.* athletics, 2
atroce atrocious, 12
attelage *m.* **de chiens** dogsled
attendre to wait, 5
   ~ son tour to wait one's turn
   ~ un enfant to be pregnant, 9
   s'~ à to expect
atterrir to land, 16
atterrissage *m.* landing, 16
attirer to attract
au (= à + le)
   ~ centre in the center, 5
   ~ coin in the corner, 5; on time-out, 9
   ~ fait by the way
   ~ fond at the end

   ~ four baked, 6
   ~ lieu de instead of
   ~ moins at least
   ~ plus tard at the latest
   ~ régime on a diet, 15
   ~ revoir goodbye, 1
   ~ secours! Help!
   ~ suivant! Next!
au-dessus (de) above, over, 4
aujourd'hui today, 1
auquel (= à + lequel) to which
aussi also
autobus *m.* city bus, 5
autocar *m.* motorcoach, 5
automne *m.* autumn, 4
autour around
auxquel(le)s (= à + lesquel[le]s) to which
avant before; front, 8
   ~ de partir before leaving
   siège ~ front seat
avant-hier the day before yesterday
avantages *m. pl.* benefits, 10
avec with
aventure *f.* adventure, 2; love affair
avion *m.* airplane, 5
avoir to have
   ~ besoin (de) to need, 6
   ~ chaud to be hot, 6
   ~ de la chance to be lucky, 6
   ~ des crampes to be sore, 14
   ~ du mal to have a hard time
   ~ envie (de) to want/to feel like, 6
   ~ faim to be hungry, 6
   ~ froid to be cold, 6
   ~ honte to be ashamed, 15
   ~ l'air to seem, 6
   ~ la priorité to have the right of way
   ~ la tête qui tourne to be dizzy, 15
   ~ le vertige to be dizzy, 15
   ~ lieu to occur, to take place
   ~ mal to have pain, to be in pain, 14
   ~ peur to be afraid, 6
   ~ raison to be right, 6
   ~ soif to be thirsty, 6

~ **sommeil** to be sleepy, 6
~ **tort** to be wrong, 6
avouer to admit
avril *m.* April, 3

B

bac *m.* **à sable** sandbox
bâcler to botch
bagage *m.* **à main** carry-on
luggage, 16
bagarre *f.* fight
baguette *f.* loaf of French bread
~ **bien cuite** well-baked loaf, 5
~ **pas trop cuite** not too dark
loaf, 5
baie *f.* **vitrée** bay window, 4
baignoire *f.* bathtub, 4
baladeur *m.* **numérique** digital
portable audio player, 13
balcon *m.* balcony, 4
balle *f.* **de golf** golf ball, 14
banane *f.* banana, 6
banc *m.* bench
bande *f.* **sonore** soundtrack
banlieue *f.* suburb
banquier *m.* personal banker, 11
barbant(e) boring
bas *m. pl.* sheer stockings, 5
base-ball *m.* baseball, 2
basket *m.* basketball, 2
ballon *m.* **de** ~ basketball, 2
terrain *m.* **de** ~ basketball
court, 14
bâtiment *m.* building, 16
bâtir to build, 4
bâton *m.* **de ski** ski pole, 14
bavard(e) talkative, 2
~ **comme une pie** as talkative
as a magpie
beau (belle) beautiful, handsome,
2
~ **comme un dieu** as
handsome as a god
~ **comme un astre!** as beautiful
as a star
beaucoup (de) a lot (of), 5
beau-frère *m.* brother-in-law
beau-père *m.* stepfather,
father-in-law, 3
beige beige, 4
belle *f.* beautiful, 2

Belle au Bois Dormant Sleeping
Beauty
belle-mère *f.* stepmother,
mother-in law, 3
belle-sœur *f.* sister-in-law, 3
besoin *m.* need
bête silly
Ne sois pas ~**!** Don't be silly!
bicyclette *f.* bicycle, 5
bidet *m.* bidet, 4
bien well, 6
~ **que** although
bien-être *m.* well-being
bienvenue welcome
Bienvenue chez moi! Welcome
to my place!
bière *f.* beer, 5
bijou *m. (pl.* **bijoux**) jewel, 5
bijouterie *f.* jewelry store, 5
bikini *m.* two-piece bathing suit,
bikini, 5
billet *m.* ticket, 5; bill, 11
~ **aller-retour** round-trip ticket, 5
~ **aller simple** one-way ticket, 5
~ **d'avion** plane ticket
~ **fumeur/non-fumeur**
smoking/non-smoking ticket,
16
bistouri *m.* scalpel
bizarre bizarre, 15
blanc(he) white, 4
bled *m. (slang)* the boonies
bleu(e) blue, 2
blond(e) blond, 2
bœuf *m.* beef, 5
boire to drink
~ **un pot** to have a drink
boisson *f.* beverage, 6
boîte *f. (slang)* workplace; box, 5
~ **aux lettres** mailbox, 4
~ **de nuit** nightclub, 9
~ **de conserve** can (of food), 11
bol *m.* bowl, 6
bon(ne) good
Bon! Well!
bon *m.* **d'abonnement**
subscription form, 7
bon marché *inv.* cheap,
affordable, 5
C'est bon. It is good., 6
bonbon *m.* candy, 5

bondé(e) full
bonheur *m.* happiness
bonhomme *m.* **de neige**
snowman
bonjour hello, 1
botte *f.* boot, 5
~ **de ski** ski boot, 14
bouche *f.* mouth, 12
boucherie *f.* butcher shop, 5
boucherie-charcuterie *f.* butcher
shop and deli, 4
boulangerie *f.* bakery, 5
boulangerie-pâtisserie bakery
and pastry shop, 4
boulette *f.* **de viande** meatball, 6
boulot *m. (slang)* job, 10
boum *f.* party, 9
bouquet *m.* bouquet, 6
bourse *f.* scholarship, 11
bouteille *f.* bottle, 5
boutique *f.* shop, store, 5
branché(e) *(slang)* hip, tech-savvy,
13
brasserie *f.* brewery, 4
bricolage *m.* repair work, 4
briquet *m.* cigarette lighter
brosser to brush
se ~ **les dents** to brush one's
teeth, 8
brouillon *m.* draft
brûler to burn, 6
brun(e) brown, 2
buffet *m.* dresser, 4
bulletin *m.* **d'abonnement**
subscription form, 7
bureau *m.* desk; office, 4
~ **d'échange** currency exchange
office, 11
~ **de tabac** tobacco shop, 5
bus *m.* city bus, 5

C

ça it; that, 1
~ **n'a pas d'importance** it
doesn't matter
~ **peut aller** it could be better, 1
~ **te dit?** What do you say
about it?
~ **va.** It's going okay/well., 1
~ **va?** How's it going?, 1
~ **va bien.** It's going well., 1

~ va pas mal. It's going all right., 1

cabine *f.* cabin; plane cabin, 16
- **~ de bronzage** tanning booth, 14
- **~ d'essayages** fitting room, 5

cabinet *m.* office
- **~ de toilettes** toilets, 4

cachet *m.* tablet, 15

cachette *f.*: **en ~** in secret, in hiding

café *m.* coffee
- **~ au lait** coffee with milk, 6
- **~ crème** coffee with cream, 6
- **~ noir** black coffee, 6

cafetière *f.* coffee maker, 4

caisse *f.* teller window, cash drawer, 11

caissier (caissière) cashier, 5; bank teller, 11

caleçon *m.* man's underwear, 5

calmant *m.* tranquilizer, 15

calme calm, 12

calmer to calm
- **se ~** to calm down, 8

cambriolage *m.* burglary, break-in, 7

camion *m.* truck

campagne *f.* country

canapé *m.* couch, 4

canard *m.* duck, 6

candidat(e) candidate, 10

cantine *f.* cafeteria, 9

car *conj.* because

car *m.* motorcoach, 5

carafe *f.* **d'eau** jug of tap water

carnet *m.* group of tickets, 11
- **~ de chèques** checkbook, 11

carotte *f.* carrot, 6

carte *f.* menu, 6
- **~ d'accès à bord/ d'embarquement** boarding pass, 16
- **~ de crédit** credit card, 11
- **~ postale** postcard

Carte Bleue debit/credit card, 11

Carte Intégrale monthly or yearly métro pass, 5

Carte Orange weekly or monthly métro pass, 5

casquette *f.* cap, 5

cauchemar *m.* nightmare

causer to cause, 7

cave *f.* wine cellar

CD *m. inv.* CD

ce *pron.* this; it, 1 (see also **c'est**)
- **~ que** what

ce (cette) *adj.* this, that, 1

ceinture *f.* **de sécurité** seat belt, 8

céleri *m.* celery, 6

célibataire single, 3

celle(s) *f.* the one(s)

celui *m.* the one

centre *m.* **de fitness** fitness center

cerise *f.* cherry

certain(e) certain, 15

cerveau *m.* brain, 15

ces these, those, 1
- **~ derniers temps** lately

c'est it's; this is, 1
- **~ bon** it's good, 6
- **~ dommage** what a pity; it's a pity, 15
- **~ pour cela/ça** that is why
- **~ tout** that is all, 5

cette *f. adj.* this, 1

ceux *m.* the ones

chacun(e) each one

chaîne *f.* channel
- **~ stéréo** stereo, 4
- **changer de ~** to change channels, 7

chaise *f.* chair, 4

chambre *f.* room; bedroom, 4
- **~ d'hôtel** hotel room, 16

chameau *m.* camel

champignon *m.* mushroom, 6

chance *f.* luck

changer to change
- **~ de fréquence** to change the radio station, 7

chanter to sing, 3

chapeau *m.* hat, 5

charcuterie *f.* delicatessen; pork butcher shop, 11

chariot *m.* **à provisions** shopping cart, 5

chasser to hunt

chat(te) cat, 3

châtain *inv.* light brown, 2

chaton *m.* kitten
- **mon petit ~** my kitten, 8

chaud(e) hot, 6

chaussette *f.* sock, 5

chaussure *f.* shoe, 5
- **~ de sport** sneaker, 5

chef *m.* **d'entreprise** head of a company, 10

cheminée *f.* fireplace, 4

chemise *f.* man's shirt, 5

chemisier *m.* woman's shirt, blouse, 5

chèque *m.* check, 11
- **~ de voyage** traveler's check, 11
- **~ sans provisions** check with no funds, 11

chéquier *m.* checkbook, 11

cher (chère) expensive

chercher to look for, 3

chéri(e) darling
- **mon/ma ~** my darling, 8

cheveu *m.* (*pl.* **cheveux**) hair, 2

cheville *f.* ankle, 12

chewing-gum *m.* chewing gum, 11

chez elle/lui/vous at her/his/ your place
- **~ le traiteur** at the caterer's, 6

chien(ne) dog, 3

chiffre *m.* number, 3
- **~s à l'appui** supporting numbers

chocolat *m.* chocolate, 5

chocolaterie *f.* chocolate shop, 5

chœur *m.* choir, 7

choisir to choose, 4

chômage *m.* unemployment, 10
- **être au ~** to be unemployed, 10

chômeur (chômeuse) unemployed person, 10

chou *m.* cabbage
- **mon ~** my dear (*lit:* my cabbage), 8

chouette cool, nice

chou-fleur *m.* cauliflower, 6

Chut! Shh!, Hush!

chute *f.* **libre** free fall, 13

ciao see you, 1

ci-dessus above

cigare *m.* cigar, 5, 11
cigarette *f.* cigarette, 5
ci-joint(e) enclosed
cire *f.* wax
citron *m.* lemon, 6
clair(e) clear, obvious, 15
classement *m.* **des tubes** music hit parade, 7
classique classic, 2
clavier *m.* keyboard, 13
clé *f.* key
client(e) customer; client, 10
clientèle *f.* clientele, 10
cliquer to click, 13
club *m.* **de fitness** fitness center
Coca *m.* Coke, 6
cochon *m.* **d'Inde** guinea pig, 3
cœur *m.* heart, 15
coffre-fort *m.* safe, 11
coin *m.* corner, 4
colère *f.* anger
  en ~ angry, 15
collège *m.* middle school, junior high school, 9
colocataire *m./f.* roommate, 4
combien (de) how many, how much, 5
  C'est ~? How much is it?
  ~ de temps? how long?
comblé(e) very happy, 15
comédie *f.* comedy, 2
  ~ musicale musical comedy, 2
  ~ romantique romantic comedy, 2
comique comic
commander to order
comme like; as
  ~ avant as before
  ~ ci, ~ ça so-so, 1
commencer to begin, 3
comment how
  ~ allez-vous/vas-tu? How are you?, 1
  ~ ça va? How is it going?, 1
  ~ dit-on ... ? How do you say...?
  ~ tu t'appelles? What's your name *(fam.)*?, 1
  ~ vous appelez-vous? What is your name *(form.)*?, 1
commerçant *m.* shop, 5

commerce *m.* business, 10
commettre un crime to commit a crime, 7
commode *f.* chest of drawers, 4
commun(e) common, 15
communiqué *m.* **publicitaire** information bulletin
compagne *f.* partner (female), 8
compagnie *f.* company, 10
compagnon *m.* partner (male), 8
compartiment *m.* overhead compartment, 16
complexé(e): être ~ to have a complex, 9
comporter: se ~ to behave
composter to validate, 16
comprendre to understand, 5
comprimé *m.* tablet, 15
comptabilité *f.* accounting, 10
compte *m.* account
  ~ courant checking account, 11
  ~ en banque bank account, 11
  ~ épargne savings account, 11
concevoir to create
condiment *m.* seasoning, 6
conduire to drive, 8
confiserie *f.* candy shop, 5
confiture *f.* **de fraises** strawberry jam, 6
congés payés *m. pl.* paid holidays, 10
connaître to know
connexion *f.* **haut-débit** high-speed connection, 13
conseil *m.* advice
conserve *f.* canned food
consoler to comfort, 9
constamment constantly
constant(e) constant
constipé(e) constipated, 15
conte *m.* tale
content(e) happy, 2
continent *m.* continent
continuer to continue, 5
contravention *f.* ticket
contrôle *m.* **sûreté** security gate, 16
convaincant(e) convincing
coquille *f.* **Saint-Jacques** scallop, 6
corde *f.* rope, 14
corps *m.* body
costaud stocky, 15

costume *m.* man's suit, 5
Côte d'Ivoire *f.* Ivory Coast
côtelette *f.* **d'agneau** *m.* lamb chop, 6
cou *m.* neck, 12
se coucher to go to bed, 8; to lie down, 16
coucou! hey!, hi!, peek-a-boo!
coude *m.* elbow, 12
couleur *f.* color, 4
coup *m.* blow
  ~ de foudre love at first sight, 8
  ~ de fusil a shot (from a gun)
coupable guilty
coupe *f.* cut
couper to cut
couple *m.* couple, 16
courageux (courageuse) courageous, brave, 2
courir to run
couronner to crown
courriel *m.* e-mail, 13
course *f.* race
  faire les courses to do the food shopping, 4
court(e) short, 2
cousin(e) cousin, 3
coût *m.* price
couteau *m.* knife, 6
couturier *m.* designer
couturière *f.* seamstress
couverts *m. pl.* cutlery, 6
couvre-lit *m.* bedspread, comforter
cravate *f.* tie, 5
crème *f.* cream, 4
  ~ brûlée crème brûlée, 6
  ~ chantilly whipped cream
crémerie *f.* dairy, 5
crêpe *f.* crepe, 6
creuser to dig
crevé(e) flat, 8
crevette *f.* shrimp, 5
cri *m.* **de ralliement** rallying cry
crier to scream, shout, 9
crise *f.* **cardiaque** heart attack, 15
crise *f.* **de foie** stomach/digestive problems, 15
croire to believe, to think
croissance *f.* growth
cuillère *f.* spoon

~ à café teaspoon, 6
~ à soupe tablespoon, 6
cuisine *f.* cooking; kitchen, 4
cuisinier (cuisinière) cook
cuisinière *f.* stove, 4
culotte *f.* woman's underwear (briefs), 5
culturel(le) cultural, 7

D

d'accord all right
　être ~ to agree
dame *f.* lady
dans in, 4
　~ quelques années in a few years
danser to dance, 3
d'après according to
　~ vous in your opinion
d'autant plus que furthermore
de *art.* any, some, 5; *prep.* from, of
　~ rien you're welcome, 5
décembre *m.* December, 3
déception *f.* **amoureuse** heartbreak, 8
déclarer to declare, 16
Avez-vous quelque chose à ~? Do you have anything to declare?
décollage *m.* take-off, 16
décoller to take off, 16
décompresser to relax, to decompress
déçu(e) disappointed, 12
défi *m.* challenge
défilé *m.* parade
　~ de mode fashion show
dégâts *m. pl.* damage
dégoûtant(e) disgusting, 12
dégueulasse *(slang)* disgusting, 6
dégustation *f.* **de vins** wine tasting
déjà already
déjeuner *m.* lunch, 6
délicieux (délicieuse) delicious, 6
délinquance *f.* juvenile crime, 9
délit *m.* misdemeanor
deltaplane *m.* hang-gliding, 13
demander to ask, to require, 15
　~ des renseignements to ask directions, 5
　~ un prêt to ask for a loan, 11

demandeur (demandeuse) d'emploi job applicant, 10
se démaquiller to remove one's makeup, 8
démarches *f. pl.* steps
démarrer to start the engine, 8
demi *m.* glass of draft beer
demi-frère *m.* half-brother, stepbrother, 3
demi-sœur *f.* half-sister, stepsister, 3
démon *m.* devil, 9
démoralisé(e) demoralized, 12
dent *f.* tooth, 12
dentifrice *m.* toothpaste, 11
dentiste *m.* dentist, 3
dénuder to uncover
se dépêcher to hurry (up), 8
dépenser to spend, 11
dépenses *f. pl.* spending
dépensier (dépensière) spendthrift, 11
déprimé(e) depressed, 15
depuis since; for
　~ combien de temps? for how long?
　~ deux ans for two years
dernier (dernière) last
dernièrement lately
derrière behind, in back of, 4
dès que as soon as
descendre to get down, to go down, 5
désespéré(e) desperate, 12
se déshabiller to remove one's clothes, 8
désirer to like, 5
désobéir to disobey, 9
désolé(e) sorry, 12
dessert *m.* dessert, 6
dessin *m.* drawing
　~ animé cartoon, 7
détecteur *m.* **de métaux** metal detector, 16
se détendre to relax
détester to hate
　se ~ to hate each other, 8
dette *f.* debt, 11
devant in front of, 4
dévasté(e) devastated, 12
deviner to guess

devise *f.* motto
devoir to be supposed to; to have to, must
devoirs *m. pl.* homework
diapositive *f.* slide, 16
diarrhée *f.* diarrhea, 15
difficulté *f.* difficulty, 9
diffuser to broadcast, 7
dimanche *m.* Sunday, 3
dîner *m.* dinner, 6
dire to say, 7
　se ~ to tell each other, 8
direction *f.* direction, 5
discothèque *f.* discotheque, 9
diseur (diseuse) de bonne aventure fortune-teller
se disputer to argue (with each other), 8
divertissements *m. pl.* TV games, 7
divorcé(e) divorced, 3
divorcer to get a divorce, 8
documentaire *m.* documentary, 7
doigt *m.* finger, 12
don *m.* gift
données *f. pl.* data
donner to give, 5
　~ des coups de pied to kick
　~ la fessée to spank, 9
　~ le biberon to bottle-feed
　~ sur to overlook, 16
　~ un baiser to kiss (on the lips), 8
　~ un concert to perform a concert, 7
　~ une conférence to present a paper, 7
dormir to sleep
dos *m.* back, 12
dot *f.* dowry
douane *f.* customs, 16
double double, 16
douche *f.* shower, 4
doudou *m.* sweetie, 8
douillet(te): être ~ to be a wimp
douter to doubt, 15
douteux (douteuse) doubtful, 15
doux (douce) sweet, soft, 12
douzaine *f.* dozen, 5
dragée *f.* lozenge, 11
draguer to flirt

drap *m.* linen
drapeau *m.* flag
se droguer to use drugs, 9
droit *m.* right
~ **à rien** right to anything
droite *f.* right
à ~ on the right
dur(e) hard

E

eau *f.* water
~ **gazeuse** carbonated water, 6
~ **plate** mineral water, 6
échange *m.* exchange
s'échauffer to warm up, 14
échec *m.* failure
école *f.* **primaire** elementary school, 9
économe thrifty, 11
économiser to save, 11
écouter to listen to, 3
~ **une conférence** to listen to a conference, 7
écran *m.* screen, 7
s'écraser to crash
écrire to write, 7
écrivain(e) writer
éditeur *m.* editor, 7
effrayé(e) scared, 12
égoïsme *m.* selfishness
élégant(e) elegant, 2
élève *m./f.* student (elementary/middle school), 9
élever to raise, 9
elle she, it, 2; her
elles they; them
elle-mêmes themselves
éloigné(e) way off
e-mail *m.* e-mail
embarquement *m.* boarding, 16
embauché(e) hired
embaucher to hire
embêter to annoy
embouteillage *m.* traffic jam
embrasser to kiss
s' ~ to kiss (each other), 8
émission *f.* program, 7
s'empêcher to keep oneself (from doing something)
emploi *m.* job, 10
employé(e) employee, 10

empressé(e) devoted
emprunt *m.* **hypothécaire** mortgage loan, 11
emprunter (à) to borrow (from), 11
en in
~ **bonne santé** healthy
~ **chair et** ~ **os** live
~ **cours de route** in transit
~ **direct** live, 7
~ **face** in front, 4; across, 5
~ **gros** in a nutshell
~ **haut** upstairs
~ **moyenne** average
~ **plein jour** in broad daylight
~ **rage** enraged, 15
~ **solde** on sale, 5
~ **train de** in the process of
enceinte pregnant, 9
enchanté(e) happy, pleased, 12
Enchanté(e). It's nice to meet you., 1
endetté(e) in debt, 11
s'endormir to fall asleep, 8
s'énerver to get nervous, 8
enfance *f.* childhood, 9
enfant *m./f.* child, 3
~ **gâté(e) pourri(e)** spoiled rotten child
~ **bien élevé(e)** well-behaved child
~ **mal élevé(e)** badly behaved child, 9
enfant-roi *m./f.* child-king
enjeu *m.* stake
ennemi(e) enemy, 3
s'ennuyer to be bored, 8
ennuyeux (ennuyeuse) boring, 2
enquête *f.* survey
enregistrement *m.* check-in, 16
enregistrer to check in, 16
enrhumé(e): être ~ to have a cold, 15
ensemble together, 8
ensuite next
entendre to hear, 5
s' ~ **bien** to get along well, 8
s' ~ **mal** not to get along, 8
entier (entière) whole
entraîneur (entraîneuse) trainer, 14
entre between, 4

entrée *f.* appetizer, 16
entreprise *f.* company, 10
entrer (dans) to come (into); to enter
entretien *m.* interview
avoir un ~ to have an interview
passer un ~ to have an interview
enveloppe *f.* envelope, 5
envoyer to send, 13
épais(se) thick, 12
épanoui(e) fulfilled
épargner to save, 11
épaté(e) dumbfounded, 15
épaule *f.* shoulder
épeler to spell
Comment ça s'épelle? How do you spell it?
épicé(e) spicy, 6
épicerie *f.* convenience store, 4; grocery, 11
s'épiler to use an epilator, 8
épinards *m. pl.* spinach, 6
s'époumoner to shout oneself hoarse
épousseter to dust, 4
épouvante *f.* horror, 2
époux (épouse) spouse, 8
équipage *m.* crew, 16
équipe *f.* team
érable *m.* maple
escalade *f.* **sur glace** ice-covered mountain climbing, 13
escalier *m.* stairs, 4
espoir *m.* hope
esprit *m.* mind
essayer to try on, 5
essence *f.* gas
essentiel(le) essential, 14
essuie-glace *m.* windshield wiper, 8
essuyer to wipe
estomac *m.* stomach, 12
et and
~ **avec ceci?** Anything else?, 5
~ **voilà ...** and here is…, 1
étage *m.* floor, 4
États-Unis *m. pl.* United States
été *m.* summer, 4
étendre le linge to hang clothes to dry, 4
étiquette *f.* ID tag, 16
s'étirer to stretch, 14

étonnant(e) stunning, 15
étonné(e) surprised/shocked, 15
être to be
  ~ à la mode to be hip, fashionable, 9
  ~ à la recherche de to seek, 9
  ~ à la retraite to be retired, 10
  ~ au chômage to be unemployed, 10
  ~ aux anges to be in seventh heaven, 12; to be on cloud nine, 15
  ~ bien dans sa peau to feel good
  ~ cambriolé(e) to be burglarized, 7
  ~ complexé(e) to have a complex, 9
  ~ douillet(te) to be a wimp
  ~ en rage to be enraged, 15
  ~ enrhumé(e) to have a cold, 15
  ~ gourmand(e) to have a sweet tooth
  ~ pénible to be a pain
  ~ utile to help
  ~ volé(e) to be robbed, 7
étudiant(e) student, 1
étudier to study, 3
euphorique euphoric, 12
eux them
eux-mêmes themselves
événement *m.* event
évident(e) evident, 15
évier *m.* kitchen sink, 4
éviter to avoid
examen *m.* test
Excusez-moi! Excuse me!, 1
exercices *m. pl.* **au sol** floor exercises, 14
exiger to insist, 15
express *m.* espresso, 6
exquis(e) exquisite, 6
extérieur outside, 16
  à l'~ outside, 16
externe external, 12

F

fabrication *f.* production, 10
fâché(e) angry, 15
se fâcher to get mad, 8

facteur (factrice) postal worker
faire to do, to make
  ~ de la natation to swim, 14
  ~ des câlins to cuddle, 9
  ~ des caprices to throw a tantrum, 9
  ~ des chatouilles to tickle
  ~ des exercices d'échauffement to warm up, 14
  ~ du stretching/des exercices d'étirement to stretch, 14
  ~ du zapping to channel surf, 7
  ~ la cuisine to cook, 4
  ~ la lessive to do the laundry, 4
  ~ la queue to wait in line
  ~ la vaisselle to do the dishes, 4
  ~ l'école buissonnière to skip school, 9
  ~ le linge to do the laundry, 4
  ~ le mur to sneak out, 9
  ~ le plein to fill up, 8
  ~ les courses to do the food shopping, 4
  ~ les magasins to go shopping, 5
  ~ les valises to pack suitcases, 4
  ~ mal to hurt
  ~ taire to keep someone else quiet
  ~ un emprunt to give a loan, 11
  ~ une fugue to run away, 9
  ~ un voyage to take a trip, 4
  se ~ la bise to kiss (on the cheeks), 8
  se ~ mal to hurt oneself, 9
faire-part *m.* birth announcement
falloir to be necessary
famille *f.* family, 3
faussement falsely
fauteuil *m.* armchair, 4
faux (fausse) false
féculent *m.* starchy food, 6
fée *f.* fairy
femme *f.* woman; wife, 3
  ~ au foyer housewife
  ~ d'affaires *f.* businesswoman, 3
  ~ de sa vie one's true love (female), 8
fenêtre *f.* window, 4
fermer un compte to close an account, 11

fermier (fermière) farm-raised, 5
fessiers *m. pl.* buttock exercises, 14
fêter to celebrate
feu *m.* fire
feuille *f.* leaf
feuilleton *m.* **romantique** soap opera, 7
février *m.* February, 3
fiançailles *f. pl.* engagement
fiancé(e) engaged, 3; *m./f.* fiancé(e), 8
se fiancer to get engaged, 8
fidèle faithful, 8
fier (fière) proud, 12
fièvre *f.* fever, 15
se figurer to imagine
filer to weave
fille *f.* girl; daughter, 3
  ~ unique only child (female)
film *m.* movie
  ~ dramatique drama, 2
  ~ policier detective film, 2
fils *m.* son, 3
  ~ unique only child (male)
fin(e) fine, thin, 12
finir to finish, 4
flacon *m.* bottle
fleur *f.* flower, 11
fleuriste *m./f.* florist, 11
foi *f.* faith
foie *m.* liver, 15
  ~ gras goose liver pâté, 6
folie *f.* crazy thing
foot *m.* soccer, 2
  ballon de ~ soccer ball, 14
  terrain de ~ soccer field, 14
football *m.* soccer, 2
  ~ américain football, 2
formation *f.* **littéraire** specialization in the humanities, 10
formation *f.* **scientifique** specialization in the sciences, 10
forme *f.* shape
  être en ~ to be in shape
  se mettre en ~ to get in shape, 14
  se remettre en ~ to get back in shape, 14
fort(e) strong, 2; heavy, 15
  ~ comme un taureau as strong as a bull

forum *m.* **de discussion** chat room
fou (folle) crazy
foulard *m.* scarf, 5
four *m.* oven, 4
⁓ **à micro-ondes** microwave, 4
fourchette *f.* fork, 6
fournir to give
foyer *m.* household
frais *m. pl.* **de scolarité** tuition fee
fraise *f.* strawberry, 6
frein *m.* brake, brake pedal, 8
freiner to brake, 8
Fréquence Plus frequent flyer program
frère *m.* brother, 3
⁓ **jumeau** twin brother, 3
frisé(e) curly, 2
frites *f. pl.* French fries, 6
froid(e) cold, 6
fromage *m.* cheese, 16
fromagerie *f.* cheese store, 11
front *m.* forehead, 12
fruit *m.* fruit, 6
⁓**s de mer** seafood, 5
fruité(e) flavored with fruit
fumer to smoke, 3
furieux (furieuse) furious, 15
futon *m.* futon, 4
futur *m.* future

G

gagner to earn; to win
garage *m.* garage, 4
garçon *m.* boy
garder sa ligne to maintain one's weight, 15
gare *f.* train station
⁓ **routière** bus station, 5
garer to park
gaspiller to waste, 11
gâté(e) spoiled, 3
gâteau *m.* cake, 4
gâter to spoil, 9
gauche *f.* left
à ⁓ on the left
gendarme *m./f.* police officer
gendarmerie *f.* police station
gêné(e) sorry, embarrassed, 15

genou *m.* knee, 12
genre *m.* kind
gens *m. pl.* people
gentil(le) nice, 2
gérant(e) manager, 10
gérer to manage
gestion *f.* management, 10
gilet *m.* cardigan sweater, 5
glace *f.* ice cream, 6
golf *m.* golf, 2
club de ⁓ golf club, 14
terrain/parcours de ⁓ golf course, 14
gonfler to put air in, 8
gorge *f.* throat, 15
gourmand(e): être ⁓ to have a sweet tooth
gourmandises *f. pl.* sweets, 16
gousse *f.* clove (of garlic)
goût *m.* taste, 12
goûter *m.* afternoon snack, 6; *v.* to taste, 16
gouttes *f. pl.* **nasales** nasal sprays, 15
grâce à thanks to
gramme *m.* gram, 5
grand(e) big, tall, 2
⁓**e surface** *f.* supermarket, 5
le (la) plus ⁓ the tallest
grand-mère *f.* grandmother, 3
grand-père *m.* grandfather, 3
graver un CD to burn a CD, 13
graveur *m.* **de CD** CD burner, 13
grenier *m.* attic, 4
grève *f.* strike, 10
grille-pain *m.* toaster, 4
gris(e) gray, 2
grisaille *f.* gray weather
gros(se) big, fat, 2; overweight, 15
grossir to gain weight, 15
groupe *m.* group; band, 7
guerre *f.* war, 2
guichet *m.* ticket counter
⁓ **automatique** ATM
⁓ **de caisse** teller window, 11
guide *m.* guide
⁓ **des programmes télévisés** television guide
⁓ **télé** TV guide, 7
gymnase *m.* gymnasium, 9

H

habiller to dress
s'⁓ to get dressed, 8
habiter to live, 3
haltère *f.* weight, dumbbell, 14
hamster *m.* hamster, 3
hanche *f.* hip, 12
haricot *m.* red bean, 6
⁓**s verts** green beans, 6
haut-parleur *m.* speaker, 13; loudspeaker, 16
hebdomadaire *m.* weekly magazine, 7
héliski *m.* heli-skiing, 13
henné *m.* henna
heure *f.* **de pointe** rush hour
heureux (heureuse) happy, 12
heurter to run into
hideux (hideuse) hideous, 12
hier yesterday
avant-⁓ the day before yesterday
⁓ **après-midi** yesterday afternoon
⁓ **matin** yesterday morning
⁓ **soir** last night
histoire *f.* history, 16
historique historical, 2
hit parade *m.* top music hits, 7
hiver *m.* winter, 4
HLM (habitation à loyer modéré) *f.* subsidized housing
home cinéma *m.* home theater, 13
homéopathique homeopathic, 15
homme *m.* man
⁓ **d'affaires** businessman, 3
⁓ **de sa vie** one's true love (male), 8
horaire *m.* schedule, 16
horrifié(e) horrified, 12
hors-d'œuvre *m. inv.* appetizers, 6
hôtesse *f.* **au sol** ground personnel, 16
hôtesse *f.* **de l'air** flight attendant, 16
huile *f.* oil
⁓ **d'olive** olive oil, 6
huître *f.* oyster

I

identité *f.* identity, 9
il he; it, 2
⁓ **est dommage** it's a pity, 15

~ fait beau it's nice out, 4
~ fait chaud it's warm out, 4
~ fait du soleil it's sunny, 4
~ fait du vent it's windy, 4
~ fait frais it's cool out, 4
~ fait froid it's cold out, 4
~ faut (que) one must/it is necessary (that), 14
~ se peut (que) it's possible (that), 15
~ vaut mieux que it is better that, 14
~ y a there is, there are; ago
ils they, 2
immeuble *m.* building, 4
imperméable *m.* raincoat, 5
impossible impossible, 15
imprimante *f.* **(couleur)** (color) printer, 13
improbable improbable, 15
imprudemment carelessly, 8
inacceptable unacceptable, 15
indispensable essential, 14
individualité *f.* individuality, 9
infirmière *f.* nurse, 3
informations (les infos) *f. pl.* newscast, 7
~ routières traffic report, 7
informatique *f.* computing
informer to inform
s'~ to get information
ingénieur *m.* engineer, 3
injuste unfair, 15
inoubliable unforgettable
insatisfait(e) dissatisfied, 15
inscrire to register
s'~ to register
insister (pour) to insist (on), 15
inspirer to inspire
s'~ to inspire oneself
instituteur (institutrice) elementary school teacher
intelligemment intelligently
intelligent(e) intelligent, 2
intérieur inside
à l'~ inside, 16
interminable endless
internaute *m./f.* Internet user
Internet *m.* Internet, 13
intestin *m.* intestines, 15
investir to invest, 11

inviter to invite
ivrogne *m./f.* drunkard

J

jacuzzi *m.* Jacuzzi, 14
jaloux (jalouse) jealous, 12
jamais never
jambe *f.* leg, 12
jambon *m.* ham, 11
janvier *m.* January, 3
jardinage *m.* gardening, 4
jaune yellow, 4
jazz *m.* jazz, 2
je I, 1
~ vous en prie. You're welcome., 5
jean(s) *m.* jeans, 5
jet ski *m.* Jet Ski, 13
jeu *m.* (*pl.* **jeux**) TV games, 7
jeudi *m.* Thursday, 3
jeune young, 2
jeunesse *f.* youth
job *m.* job, 10
joue *f.* cheek, 12
jouer to play, 9
~ à to play (a sport), 3
jour *m.* day, 3
journal *m.* (*pl.* **journaux**) newspaper, 5
~ télévisé (le JT) television news, 7
journaliste *m./f.* journalist, 7
judo *m.* judo, 2
juillet *m.* July, 3
juin *m.* June, 3
jumeau *m.* (*pl.* **jumeaux**) twin (brother), 3
jumelle *f.* twin (sister)
jupe *f.* skirt, 5
jusqu'à as far as; until, 5
juste right, fair, 15

K

karaté *m.* karate, 2
kilo *m.* kilo, 5
kinésithérapeute *m./f.* physical therapist, chiropractor
kiosque *m.* **(à journaux)** newsstand, 11
kitchenette *f.* kitchenette, 4

L

la (see **le/la/l'/les**)
là-bas over there
lac *m.* lake, 16
lâcher to fail
laid(e) ugly, 2
laisser to leave
lait *m.* milk
~ écrémé skim milk
~ entier whole milk
lampe *f.* lamp, 4
lancer to launch
langouste *f.* lobster, 6
langue *f.* tongue, 12
lapin *m.* rabbit, 6
mon ~ my dear (*lit:* my rabbit), 8
lasagnes *f. pl.* lasagna, 6
lavabo *m.* bathroom sink, 4
lavage *m.* **à sec** dry-cleaning, 11
laver to wash
se ~ to wash, 8
lave-vaisselle *m.* dishwasher, 4
le/la/l'/les *art.* the, 2; *pron.* him, her, it, them, 11
lèche-vitrine *m.* window shopping, 5
lecteur (lectrice) reader, 7
lecteur de CD CD player, 13
lecteur de DVD DVD player, 4
léger (légère) slight; light
légume *m.* vegetable, 6
lent(e) slow
lentement slowly
lentille *f.* lentil, 6
lequel/laquelle/lesquel(le)s which one(s)
les (see **le/la/l'/les**)
lettre *f.* letter, 7
se lever to get up, 8
lèvre *f.* lip, 12
librairie *f.* bookstore, 5
libre free, 1
licencié(e) fired, 10
lieu *m.* place
limonade *f.* lemon-lime soda, 6
lire to read, 7
lisse straight, 2
liste *f.* list, 5
lit *m.* bed, 4

litre *m.* liter, 5
livre *m.* book, 5
livrer to deliver
livreur (livreuse) delivery person
locataire *m./f.* tenant, 4
logement *m.* housing, 4
loger to live
logiciel *m.* software
loin (de) far (from), 4
loisir *m.* leisure activity
long(ue) long, 2
lourd(e) heavy
loyer *m.* rent, 4
luge *f.* sledding, 13
lui he; him; (to) him, her, 11
luire to shine
lumineux (lumineuse) sunny
lundi *m.* Monday, 3
lune *f.* moon
~ de miel honeymoon
lunettes *f. pl.* glasses, 5
~ de soleil sunglasses, 5
lutte *f.* struggle
lycée *m.* high school, 9
lycéen(ne) high school student, 9

M

machine *f.* à laver washing
machine, 4
magasin *m.* store, 4
~ hors taxe duty-free shop, 16
magazine *m.* magazine, 5; exposé, 7
magnéto(scope) *m.* video player, 4
magnifique magnificent, 12
mai *m.* May, 3
maigre slim; fat-free, 15
maigrir to lose weight, 15
maillot *m.* de bain one-piece
bathing suit, 5
main *f.* hand, 12
les ~s pleines handfuls
~ dans la ~ hand in hand
maintenant now
maison *f.* house, 4
~ de la presse magazine and
newspaper store, 5
maître *m.* d'hôtel head waiter
maîtresse *f.* female lover
mal poorly, badly, 6
avoir ~ à la gorge to have a
sore throat, 15

avoir ~ *m.* à la tête to have a
headache, 15
avoir ~ *m.* au dos to have a
backache, 15
avoir ~ au cœur to be
nauseous, 15
maladie *f.* illness, 15
malgré cela in spite of this
malheureux (malheureuse)
unhappy, 12
maman *f.* mother
manger to eat, 3
~ sain to eat healthy foods, 15
manquer to miss, 16
manteau *m.* coat, 5
maquillage *m.* makeup, 11
se maquiller to put makeup on, 8
marchand(e) vendor, 11
~ de journaux newsstand, 7
marche *f.* walking
marcher to walk; to work
mardi *m.* Tuesday, 3
mari *m.* husband, 3
marié(e) married, 3
marier to marry
se ~ to get married, 8
marmaille *f.* gang of brats
Maroc *m.* Morocco
marraine *f.* godmother
marron *inv.* chestnut brown, 2
mars *m.* March, 3
masser to massage
se faire ~ to get a massage, 14
masseur (masseuse) masseuse, 14
match *m.* de foot soccer game, 7
matelas *m.* mat, 14
matin *m.* morning, 1
tous les ~ every morning
mauvais(e) bad, 6
mayonnaise *f.* mayonnaise, 6
méchant(e) mean, 2
méchoui *m.* stew
médecin *m.* doctor, 3
médicament *m.* medicine, 5;
medication, 15
meilleur(e) better, 6
le (la/les) meilleur(e)(s) the best, 6
~ ami(e) best friend
melon *m.* cantaloupe, 6
même(s) same
ménage *m.* housecleaning, 4

mensuel *m.* monthly magazine, 7
menton *m.* chin, 12
mer *f.* sea
merci thank you, 5
mercredi *m.* Wednesday, 3
mère *f.* mother, 3
météo *f.* weather report, 7
métro *m.* subway, 5
mets *m.* delicacy, 16
metteur *m./f.* en scène movie
director, 1
mettre to put; to put on, 5; to
place, 9
~ en valeur to highlight, to
emphasize
~ la table to set the table, 6
~ les essuie-glaces to start the
windshield wipers, 8
~ les freins to put on the
brakes, 8
meubler to furnish
miel *m.* honey
mignon(ne) cute, 2
migraine *f.* migraine, 15
mi-long shoulder-length, 2
mime *m.* mime, 16
mince thin, 2; slim, 15
miroir *m.* mirror, 4
mis(e) à la porte fired, kicked
out, 10
mi-temps: à ~ part-time, 10
modem *m.* modem, 13
moderne modern, 2
mœurs *f. pl.* social habits, customs
moi me
~ aussi! me too!
~ c'est ... my name is . . .; me,
I'm . . ., 1
moins less, 5
mois *m.* month, 3
monde *m.* world
le ~ entier all over the world
moniteur *m.* monitor, 13
moniteur (monitrice) instructor
montant *m.* amount
montrer to show
monument *m.* monument, 16
se moquer (de) to make fun (of)
morceau *m.* piece, 5
mordre to bite, 5
mort *f.* death

mot *m.* word
  ~ de passe password, 11
  ~s tendres pet names
moteur *m.* **de recherche** search engine, 13
moto(cyclette) *f.* motorcycle, 4
mou (molle) fluffy, soft, 12
se moucher to blow one's nose
mouchoir *m.* **en papier** tissue
moule *f.* mussel, 5
mouvementé(e) busy
moyen *m.* means, 5
moyenne *f.* average
multinational(e) international
mur *m.* wall
muscu(lation) *f.* weight-lifting, 2; muscle-building, 14
musée *m.* museum, 16
musical(e) musical, 7
musique *f.* music, 2

N

nager to swim, 14
naissance *f.* birth, 9
nappe *f.* tablecloth, 6
natation *f.* swimming, 2
  faire de la ~ to swim, 14
national(e) national, 16
nausée *f.* nausea, 15
navré(e) sorry, 15
ne (n') not, 2
  ~ ... jamais never, 8
  ~ ... pas not, 2
  ~ ... personne nobody, not anyone, 8
  ~ ... plus no longer, 8
  ~ ... que only
  ~ ... rien nothing, not anything, 8
  n'importe quel(le) any whatsoever
né(e) born
néanmoins nevertheless
nécessaire necessary, 14
négatif (négative) negative, 12
neige *f.* snow
neiger to snow, 4
nettoyage *m.* **à sec** dry cleaning
nettoyer to clean
neveu *m.* nephew, 3
nez *m.* nose, 12

~ bouché stuffy nose, 15
~ qui coule runny nose, 15
nid *m.* nest
nièce *f.* niece, 3
noir(e) dark, 2; black, 4
non plus neither
normal(e) normal, 15
note *f.* grade
nous we, 2; (to) us, 11
nouveau-né *m.* newborn
novembre *m.* November, 3
numérique digital, 16

O

obéir (à) to obey, 4
octobre *m.* October, 3
odorat *m.* smell, 12
œil *m.* (*pl.* **yeux**) eye, 2
oignon *m.* onion, 6
oiseau *m.* bird, 3
omelette *f.* omelet, 6
on people; one; we
  ~ y va? shall we go?
oncle *m.* uncle, 3
opéra *m.* opera, 2
optimiste optimistic, 2
orange *f.* orange, 6
orange *adj. inv.* orange, 4
orchestre *m.* orchestra, 7
ordinateur *m.* computer, 4
  ~ portable laptop computer, 13
oreille *f.* ear, 12
organiser to organize
orphelin(e) orphan, 3
orteil *m.* toe, 12
osé(e) daring
oser to dare
ou or
  ~ plus or more
où where
  ~ se trouve ... ? where is . . . located?, 5
ouais yeah
oublier to forget
ouïe *f.* hearing, 12
outragé(e) outraged, 12

P

pain *m.* bread, 5
pantalon *m.* pants, 5
paparazzi *m./f.* paparazzi, 7

papeterie *f.* stationery store, 5
papier *m.* paper, 5
paquet *m.* pack, 5
par via
  ~ contre however
parachute *m.* **ascensionnel** parasailing, 13
  ~ nautique parasailing on a boat, 13
parapente *m.* paragliding, 13
parc *m.* park, 16
parce que because
pardon excuse me, 1
pardonnez-moi pardon me, 1
pare-brise *m.* windshield, 8
parfois occasionally, sometimes, 6
parfum *m.* perfume, 5
parfumerie *f.* perfume store, 5
parler to speak, 3
participer to participate
  ~ à un défilé (parade) to march/participate in a parade
  ~ à un match to play in a match/game
  ~ à une manifestation to take part in a demonstration, 7
partie *f.* part, 12
  ~s (internes) du corps internal organs, 15
partir to leave (for an undetermined period of time), 8
  ~ de to leave from
pas not
  ne ~ not, 2
  ~ mal not bad, 1
passager (passagère) passenger, 16
passant(e) pedestrian
passeport *m.* passport, 16
  passer to run, 4; to broadcast, 7
  se ~ to happen
  ~ les vitesses to switch gears, 8
passe-temps *m.* hobby
pastèque *f.* watermelon, 6
pastille *f.* lozenge, 15
pâté *m.* **de campagne** pâté, 6
pâtes *f. pl.* pasta, 6
patin *m.* **à glace** ice skate, 14
patinoire *f.* skating rink, 9
pâtisserie *f.* pastry shop, bakery, 5; pastry, 16
patron(ne) boss, 10

pauvre poor, 2
pays *m.* country
PDG (président directeur
	général) *m.* CEO, 10
peau *f.* skin, 12
pêche *f.* peach, 6; fishing, 13
	~ au gros deep-sea fishing, 13
pêcher to fish; to sin
pédalage *m.* pedaling, 14
pédaler to pedal, 14
peigner to comb
	se ~ les cheveux to comb one's
	hair, 8
peindre to paint
peine *f.* penalty
pendant during, 16
	~ que while
pénible: être ~ to be a pain
penser (à) to think (about)
pension *f.* boarding school, 9
pensionnaire *m./f.* boarding
	school student, 9
perdre to lose, 5
	~ du poids to lose weight, 15
	~ un match to lose a match/
	game, 7
perdu(e) lost
père *m.* father, 3
période *f.* time
personnalité *f.* personality, 9
personne *f.* person
	ne ... ~ no one, nobody, not
	anyone, 8
	~ ne no one, nobody, 8
personnel(le) personal
perte *f.* loss
peser to weigh
pessimiste pessimistic, 2
petit(e) small, 2
petit ami *m.* boyfriend, 3
petit déjeuner *m.* breakfast, 6
petite amie *f.* girlfriend, 3
petit-fille *f.* granddaughter
petit-fils *m.* grandson
peu not very, 15
	~ de little, few, 5
peut-être maybe, 6
pharmacie *f.* pharmacy, 4
photo photo, 16
	~ noir et blanc black-and-
	white photo, 16

photographe *m./f.* photographer, 7
pichet *m.* pitcher, 6
pièce *f.* play, 2; room, 4
	~ ci-jointe attachment, 13
	~ de monnaie coin, 11
	~ d'identité proof of identity,
	16
	~ dramatique drama, 2
	~ musicale musical play, 2
pied *m.* foot, 12
pilote *m./f.* pilot, 3
pipe *f.* pipe, 11
piqûre *f.* shot, injection, 15
piscine *f.* swimming pool, 14
piste *f.* slope
	~ de décollage/
	d'atterrissage runway, 16
	~ de ski ski slope
	~ de tennis tennis court, 14
placard *m.* closet, 4
place *f.* square, 16
	~ aux jeunes! leave room for
	the young!
placer to invest, 11
plage *f.* beach
se plaindre to complain
plaire to please
planche *f.* à voile windsurfing, 14
plante *f.* plant, 11
plat *m.* dish, 16
	~ principal entrée, main dish, 6
pleurer to cry, 9
pleuvoir to rain, 4
plongée *f.* sous-marine diving, 13
plus more, 5
	~ bas below
plusieurs several
plutôt instead; rather
	~ que rather than
pneu *m.* tire, 8
poème *m.* poem, 7
poids *m.* weight, 14
poignet *m.* wrist, 12
poilu(e) hairy, 2
poire *f.* pear, 6
poisson *m.* fish
	~ rouge goldfish, 3
poissonnerie *f.* fish market, 4
poitrine *f.* chest, 12
poivre *m.* pepper
poivron *m.* rouge red pepper, 6

pommade *f.* ointment, 15
pomme *f.* apple, 6
	~ de terre potato, 6
pompes *f. pl.* push-ups, 14
pompier *m.* firefighter
porc *m.* pork, 6
portail *m.* main entrance, 4
porte *f.* door; gate, 16
porter to wear, 5
portion *f.* part
se poser des questions to ask
	oneself questions
	positif (positive) positive, 12
posséder to possess
possible possible, 15
poste *f.* post office, 4
poste *m.* position, 10
postulant(e) candidate, 10
postuler to apply, 10
potins *m. pl.* gossip items
pouce *m.* thumb, 12
poulet *m.* chicken, 11
pour for, 16
pourboire *m.* tip
pourquoi why
pourri(e) rotten, 6
pourtant however
pourvoir to provide
pourvoyeur (pourvoyeuse)
	provider
pouvoir to be able to, can, 5
pratiquer to practice, to
	participate in, 3
	~ un sport to do (a sport), 14
précoce early, 9
prédire to predict
préférable preferable, 15
prendre to take, 5
	~ des photos to take photos,
	16
	~ du poids to gain weight, 15
	~ soin to take care
préparer to prepare, 3
près (de) close (to), near, 4
présentateur (présentatrice) de
	télévision television anchor, 1
présenter to introduce; to present, 7
	Je te/vous présente ...
	This is.... 1
presse *f.* du cœur entertainment
	magazines, 7

pressé(e) in a hurry
se presser to hurry (up), 8
pression *f.* draft beer, 6
prêt *m.* **hypothécaire** mortgage loan, 11
prétendre to claim
prêter to lend, 11
prévoir to plan
prévu(e) planned
prime *f.* bonus
printemps *m.* spring, 4
priorité *f.* right of way, 8
prise *f.* outlet
privé(e) private, 10
prix *m.* prize, 7
   ~ Goncourt Goncourt Prize, 7
   ~ Nobel Nobel Prize, 7
   ~ Pulitzer Pulitzer Prize, 7
probable probable, 15
prochain(e) next
proche near
proches *m. pl.* loved ones
produit *m.* product
   ~ bio(logique) organic food
   ~ de régime diet aid
   ~ laitier dairy product, 5
   ~ allégé / light diet food
   ~ surgelé frozen food, 15
professeur *m.* professor, 3; high school or college teacher, 9
profession *f.* profession, 3
profil *m.* experience
profond(e) deep
programme *m.* program, 7
se promener to go for a walk, 8
promouvoir to promote
provisions *f. pl.* food supplies, 5; funds, 11
provocateur (provocatrice) provocative, 2
prudemment carefully, 8
prudent(e) careful
pruneau *m.* prune
psy *m. (slang)* "shrink" (psychiatrist)
public (publique) public, 4
publicité *f.* advertisement, 7
publier to publish, 7
puce *f.* flea
   ma ~/mon puçon *f./m.* my dear, 8

puer to stink, 12
pull(-over) *m.* pullover, sweater, 5
punir to punish, 4
pyjama *m.* pajamas, 5

Q

quai *m.* platform, 16
quand when
quartier *m.* neighborhood, 4
que what; that
quel(le) what, which
   Quel canon! *(slang)* What a beautiful woman!
   Quel est ton/votre numéro de téléphone? What's your phone number?, 1
   Quel temps fait-il? What's the weather like?, 4
quelque chose something
quelque part somewhere
quelquefois sometimes
quelqu'un someone
qu'est-ce que what
qui who
   ~ est-ce? who is it?
   ~ es-tu? / ~ êtes-vous? who are you?, 1
quiche *f.* quiche, 6
quitter to leave, 8
   se ~ to leave each other, 8
quotidien *m.* daily newspaper, 7

R

raconter to tell
   se ~ tout to tell each other everything, 8
raffermir to tone, 14
rafting *m.* rafting, 13
rage *f.* **de dent** toothache, 15
raisins *m. pl.* grapes, 6
ramer to row, 14
ranger to arrange
rap *m.* rap, 2
râpé(e) grated, 6
rappeler to remind, 1
   se rappeler (de) to remember, 16
raquette *f.* racket, 14
rarement rarely
raser to shave, 8
   se ~ to shave, 8
ravi(e) delighted, 15

rayon *m.* department, 5
   ~ boucherie meat department, 5
   ~ crémerie dairy department, 5
   ~ poissonnerie seafood department, 5
se rebeller to rebel, 9
recevoir to receive; to earn, 10
réchauffer to warm up
recherché(e) sought after
récipient *m.* serving dish
réciproque reciprocal
recommander to recommend, 15
se réconcilier to reconcile, 8
reconnaissant(e) grateful, 12
récré(ation) *f.* recess, 9
réfléchi(e) reflexive
réfrigérateur *m.* refrigerator, 4
regarder to look at, 16
   ~ le monde to people-watch, 16
   se ~ to look at each other, 8
régime *m.* **alimentaire** daily diet, 15
régional(e) regional, 16
regrettable regrettable, unfortunate, 15
regretter to regret, to be sorry, 15
rein *m.* kidney, 15
relations *f. pl.* **sexuelles** sexual relations, 9
relevé *m.* statement
   ~ de compte *m.* bank statement, 11
rembourser to pay back, 11
remèdes *m. pl.* remedies, 15
remise *f.* **des bagages** baggage claim, 16
remplir un chèque to write a check, 11
rencontre *f.* meeting
se rencontrer to meet (each other), 8
rendre to pay; to return, to give back, 5
rentrer to come home, to go back
   ~ dans to fit into (clothing)
   ~ de to come back from
répandre to spread
repas *m.* meal, 6
repassage *m.* ironing, 4
répondeur *m.* **automatique** answering machine, 4
répondre to respond, to answer, 5

réponse *f.* answer, response
reportage *m.* report, 7
se reposer to rest, to relax, 8
répugnant(e) repulsive, 12
réserver to reserve, 16
résidence *f.* boarding school residence, dormitory, 9
restaurant *m.* restaurant, 16
restes *m. pl.* leftovers
retard *m.* delay
retouche *f.* fix
retraite *f.* retirement, 10
   être à la ~ to be retired
   toucher la ~ to receive a pension, 10
retraité(e) retiree, 10
rétroviseur *m.* rearview mirror, 8
réussir (à) to succeed (in), 4
rêve *m.* dream
se réveiller to wake up, 8
revenir to get back, 8
revue *f.* magazine
   ~ critique de cinéma movie review magazine
   ~ cuisine cooking magazine, 7
   ~ de cuisine cooking magazine, 7
   ~ de mode fashion magazine, 7
   ~ de sport sports magazine, 7
   ~ du cœur entertainment magazine, 7
rhume *m.* cold, 15
riche rich, 2
   ~ en matières grasses rich, fatty, 15
rideau *m.* curtain, 4
rien nothing
   de ~ you're welcome, 5
   ne ... ~ nothing, not anything, 8
rigoler to laugh
riz *m.* rice, 6
robe *f.* dress, 5
rocade *f.* bypass highway
rock *m.* rock, 2
rollers *m. pl.* rollerblades, 14
rompu(e) broken
ronger to bite
   se ~ les ongles to bite one's nails, 8
rose pink, 4
rouge red, 4

rouler to drive, 8
roux (rousse) red, 2
rue *f.* street
   ~ piétonne pedestrian street, 5
rugby *m.* rugby, 2
rupture *f.* breakup

S

sable *m.* sand
sac *m.* bag, 5
sage well-behaved, 9
saison *f.* season, 4
salade *f.* salad, 6
salaire *m.* salary, 10
sale dirty
salé(e) salty, 6
salir to dirty, 4
salle *f.* room
   ~ à manger dining room, 4
   ~ de bains bathroom, 4
   ~ de muscu(lation) weight room, 14
   ~ de séjour family room, 4
   ~ de sports fitness center
salon *m.* living room, 4; wine expo, 16
   ~ de coiffure hairdresser, 5
salut *(inf.)* hi, bye, 1
samedi *m.* Saturday, 3
sandales *f. pl.* sandals, 5
sandwich *m.* sandwich, 6
sans without
   ~ aucun(e) with no
santé *f.* health, 7
sapin *m.* fir tree
sardine *f.* sardine, 6
satisfait(e) satisfied, 15
saucisse *f.* sausage, 11
saucisson *m.* salami, summer sausage, 11
saumon fumé *m.* smoked salmon, 6
sauna *m.* sauna, 14
saut *m.* **à l'élastique** bungee jumping, 13
sauter to jump, 14
sauver to save
   ~ la vie à quelqu'un to save someone's life, 7
savoir to know, 1
savoureux (savoureuse) tasty, 12

scanner *m.* scanner, 13
science-fiction *f.* science fiction, 2
sculpture *f.* sculpture, 16
se himself, herself, itself, themselves, 8
sec (sèche) dry
sécher to dry
   se ~ les cheveux to dry one's hair, 8
secrétaire *m./f.* secretary, 3
seins *m. pl.* chest
séjour *m.* trip, 16
sel *m.* salt
selon according to, depending on
semaine *f.* week, 3
sens *m.* sense, 12
sentir to smell
   ~ bon to smell good, 12
   ~ mauvais to smell bad, 12
   se ~ bien/mal to feel well/bad, 8
séparé(e) separated, 3
se séparer to be apart, to separate, 8
septembre *m.* September, 3
série *f.* **(télévisée)** TV series, 7
série *f.* **d'exercices** exercise repetition, 14
serveur (serveuse) waiter (waitress)
serviette *f.* napkin, 6
servir to serve
seulement only
shampooing *m.* shampoo, 5
short *m.* shorts, 5
si as, so; if; yes
   ~ besoin est if need be
sida *m.* AIDS
siècle *m.* century
siège *m.* seat, 16
sieste *f.* nap, 9
signer to sign
silencieusement silently
silencieux (silencieuse) silent
s'il vous plaît please, 5
sinon if not
sinus *m.* sinus, 15
sirop *m.* syrup, 11
ski *m.* ski, 14
   ~ alpin downhill skiing
   ~ de fond cross-country skiing
   ~ nautique waterskiing, 13
SMIC *m.* minimum wage, 10

smicard(e) minimum wage earner, 10
société *f.* corporation, 10
sœur *f.* sister, 3
sofa *m.* sofa, 4
soigner to heal
soin *m.* treatment
soir *m.* night; evening, 1
soldé(e) on sale, 5
soldes *f. pl.* sales, 5
sommeil *m.* sleep
sommelier *m.* wine waiter
somnifère *m.* sleep aid, 15
son *m.* sound
sondage *m.* poll, survey
sort *m.* spell
sortie *f.* **de secours** emergency exit, 16
sortir to go out; to get out of, to leave (for a short time), 8
 ~ avec to go out with
soucieux (soucieuse) worried, 12
souk (Tunisia) *m.* market
soulagé(e) relieved, 12
se soûler to get drunk, 9
souligner to underline
soupe *f.* soup, 6
sourire to smile
souris *f.* mouse, 4
sous under, 4
soutien-gorge *m.* (*pl.* **soutiens-gorge**) bra, 5
souvenir *m.* memory; souvenir, 16
 se ~ de to remember, 16
souvent often, 6
spécialité *f.* specialty, 16
spectacle *m.* performance, 16
splendide splendid, 12
sport *m.* sport, 7
 ~ de glisse snow sport, 13
 ~ d'hiver winter sport/snow sport, 13
 ~ nautique water sport, 13
sportif (sportive) athletic, 2
stade *m.* stadium, 9
stage *m.* internship, 10
stagiaire *m./f.* trainee
statue *f.* statue, 16
statuette *f.* knickknack, 16
steps *m. pl.* step machine, 14
steward *m.* flight attendant, 16

stupide dumb, stupid, 2
succulent(e) succulent, 12
sucre *m.* sugar
sucré(e) sweet, 6
suis (see **être**) (**I**) am, 1
suivant following
sujet *m.* topic
super super, 2
superbe superb, 12
supervision *f.* supervision, 10
suppositoire *m.* suppository, 15
sur on top of, 4; on, 16
 ~ les ondes on the airwaves
 ~ mesure custom made
sûr(e) certain, sure, 15
surf *m.* surfing, 2
 ~ des neiges snowboarding, 13
surprenant(e) surprising, 15
surpris(e) surprised, 12
survêtement *m.* jogging suit, sweatsuit, 5
sweat-shirt *m.* sweatshirt, 16
sympathique friendly, 2

T

tabac *m.* tobacco; tobacco shop, 11
tabagisme *m.* smoking addiction, 9
table *f.* table, 4
 ~ de nuit nightstand, 4
tableau *m.* painting, 4
taffe *f.* drag (on a cigarette)
tailleur *m.* woman's suit, 5
talk-show *m.* talk show, 7
tant de so many
tante *f.* aunt, 3
tapis *m.* area rug, 4
 ~ de course treadmill, 4
 ~ de fitness treadmill, 4
 ~ roulant conveyor belt, 16
tarte *f.* **salée** quiche, 6
tartelette *f.* mini tart, 6
tasse *f.* **à café** coffee cup, 6
taux *m.* rate
taxi *m.* taxi, cab, 5
tchatcher to chat, to yack
tee-shirt *m.* T-shirt, 5
teinturerie *f.* dry cleaner, 11
télécommande *f.* remote control
téléfilm *m.* TV movie, 7

téléphone *m.* phone, 4
 ~ portable cell phone, 13
 ~ sans fil cordless phone, 4
téléphoner (à) to telephone, 3
 se ~ to call each other, 8
télé-réalité *f.* reality shows, 7
télévision *f.* television, 4
témoin *m.* witness
temps *m.* time; weather, 4
 à plein ~ full-time, 10
 à ~ complet full-time, 10
 à ~ partiel part-time, 10
 Quel ~ fait-il? What's the weather like?, 4
tenir to hold
tennis *m.* tennis, 2; *f. pl.* tennis shoes, 5
tenue *f.* **de sport** sporting gear, 14
terminal *m.* terminal, 16
terminer to finish, 3
terrasse *f.* terrace, 16
terre *f.* ground
tête *f.* head, 12
thé *m.* tea
 ~ au citron tea with lemon, 6
 ~ nature plain tea, 6
théâtre *m.* theater, 2
thermomètre *m.* thermometer, 15
thon *m.* **grillé** grilled tuna, 6
thriller *m.* thriller, 2
ticket *m.* **de bus** bus ticket, 11
timbre *m.* stamp
timide timid, shy, 2
tire-bouchon *m.* cork opener, 6
tisane *f.* herbal tea, 15
Toile *f.* World Wide Web, 13
toilettes *f. pl.* half-bath, 16
tomate *f.* tomato
 ~s provençales stuffed baked tomatoes, 6
tombe *f.* grave
tomber to fall
 ~ amoureux (amoureuse) to fall in love, 8
 ~ dans les pommes (*slang*) to faint
 ~ raide mort(e) to fall over dead
toucher *m.* touch, 12
toucher to receive, 10
 ~ un chèque to cash a check, 11
toujours always

tour *m.* turn, 5
tournage *m.* filming
tourner to turn, 5
tousser to cough, 15
tout *adv.:* **du ~** at all
~ **de suite** right away
~ **droit** straight through, 5
~ **le temps** all the time
tout *pron.* everything; very
~**(e) petit(e)** little one, 8
tout/toute/tous/toutes all, every, each; the whole
tous les deux both
toux *f.* cough
toxicomanie *f.* drug addiction, 9
trahison *f.* betrayal
train *m.* train, 5
traîneau *m.* **à chiens** dogsled, 13
trait *m.* feature
traitement *m.* **de texte** word processor, 13
traiteur *m.* caterer, 11
trajet *m.* commute; voyage, trip, 5
tranche *f.* slice, 5
transport *m.* transportation, 5
travail *m.* job, work 10
travailler to work, 3
~ **à son compte** to be self-employed
travaux *m. pl.* **ménagers** household chores, 4
traverser to cross, 5
très very, 6
tricher to cheat
trinquer to make a toast
triste sad, 2
tromper (quelqu'un) to cheat (on someone), 8
trop too, too much, 5
troubles *m. pl.* problems
~ **alimentaires** eating disorders, 9
~ **familiaux** family problems, 9
trouver to find, 3
se ~ to be located
truite *f.* trout, 6
tu *(fam.)* you, 1
turbulences *f. pl.* turbulence, 16
tuyau *m.* hint
typique typical

U

un sur ... one out of . . .
utile useful
être ~ to help
utiliser to use

V

vache *f.* cow, 12
vaisselle *f.* dishes, 6
valise *f.* suitcase, 16
vanille *f.* vanilla, 6
varappe *f.* rock-climbing, 13
vase tiède *f.* warm clay
vautré(e) spread out
veau *m.* veal, 6
vélo *m.* bicycle, 5
~**-rameur** *m.* pedaling and rowing machine, 14
~ **statique** stationary bike, 14
vendeur (vendeuse) sales clerk
vendre to sell, 5
vendredi *m.* Friday, 3
venir to come
~ **de** to come from
vente *f.* sale, 10
ventre *m.* belly, stomach, 15
verbe *m.* verb, 4
verre *m.* glass
~ **à eau** water glass, 6
~ **à vin** wine glass, 6
vert(e) green, 2
veste *f.* jacket, 5
vestiaire *m.* changing room, 14
vêtement *m.* garment, article of clothing
se vêtir to dress
veuf (veuve) widower (widow), 3
viande *f.* meat, 5
victime victim, 7
vide empty; *m.* emptiness
vider to empty
vie *f.* life
viennoiserie *f.* pastry, 5
vieux (vieille) old, 2
vignoble *m.* vineyard
vilain(e) bad, naughty, 9
vin *m.* wine, 4
~ **rouge/blanc/rosé** red/white/blush wine, 6
vinaigre *m.* vinegar

violet(te) purple, 4
virgule *f.* comma
visage *m.* face, 12
viser to target
visiter to visit, 16
vitamine *f.* vitamin, 15
vite rapidly, quickly, 6
vitesse *f.* speed; gear, 8
vitre *f.* window, 4
vivre to live
vœu *m.* wish
voie *f.* railroad track, 16
voir to see
voiture *f.* car, 4
voix *f.* voice
vol *m.* flight, 5; robbery, theft, 7
~ **libre** free fall, 13
~ **à destination de** flight to
~ **en provenance de** flight from, 16
volaille *f.* poultry, 5
volant *m.* steering wheel, 8
volé(e) robbed
volet *m.* shutter, 4
voleur (voleuse) thief
volley *m.* volleyball, 2
vomir to vomit, 15
vouloir to want, 15
~ **dire** to mean
vous you, 2; (to) you, 11
voyage *m.* trip, 5
voyager to travel, 3
vrai(e) real, true, 2
vraiment really
VTT *m.* cross-country biking, 13
vue *f.* sight, 12

W

wagon-lit *m.* sleeper train
wagon-restaurant *m.* restaurant car, 16
WC *m.* half-bath, 16
Web *m.* World Wide Web, 13
week-end *m.* weekend, 1
western *m.* western, 2

Y

y it, there, to there
il ~ a there is, there are; ago
yaourt *m.* yogurt
yoga *m.* yoga, 2

English-French Vocabulary

The English-French vocabulary list contains all productive and receptive vocabulary that appears in the student text. Productive vocabulary includes words and expressions that appear in the *Commençons!, Continuons!,* and *Vocabulaire essentiel* sections, and in charts and word lists that are part of the grammar explanations. Receptive vocabulary consists of words and phrases that were introduced in the *Expansion personnelle* lists in the text as well as those that are given an English gloss in textual material throughout the book: readings, photo captions, exercises, activities, and authentic documents.

The following abbreviations are used:

adj.	adjective	*inf.*	informal	*n.*	noun
adv.	adverb	*interj.*	interjection	*pl.*	plural
conj.	conjunction	*inv.*	invariable	*pron.*	pronoun
f.	feminine	*m.*	masculine	*sing.*	singular
f. pl.	feminine plural	*m. pl.*	masculine plural	*v.*	verb

A

a un(e), 1
   ~ lot beaucoup
abdominal muscles abdos *m. pl.*
above au-dessus, ci-dessus
absolute absolu(e)
absolutely absolument
accelerate accélérer
accelerator accélérateur *m.*
accept agréer
   ~ oneself s'accepter
accident accident *m.*
according to d'après, selon
account compte *m.*
accounting comptabilité *f.*
across (from) en face (de)
activity activité *f.*
add ajouter
address adresse *f.*
admit avouer
adolescence adolescence *f.*
adolescent ado, adolescent(e)
adopted adopté(e)
adverb adverbe *m.*
advertisement publicité *f.*
advice conseil *m.*
affair aventure *f.*
affordable bon marché
afternoon après-midi *f.*
   ~ snack goûter *m.*
agree être d'accord
agreeable agréable

AIDS sida *m.*
airplane avion *m.*
airport aéroport *m.*
alcoholism alcoolisme *m.*
all tout(e)(s), tous
   ~ over the world le monde entier
   ~ right d'accord
   ~ the time tout le temps
already déjà
also aussi
although bien que
always toujours
am suis (see **être**)
   I ~ doing well, and you? Je vais bien, et toi?
amount montant *m.*
amusing amusant(e)
and et
   ~ here is . . . et voilà . . .
angel ange *m.*
anger colère *f.*
angry fâché(e)
ankle cheville *f.*
announce animer
annoy embêter
answer réponse *n.*; répondre *v.*
answering machine répondeur *m.* automatique
antibiotic antiobiotique *m.*
antihistamine antihistaminique *m.*
any whatsoever n'importe quel(le)
anything else? et avec ceci?
apartment appartement *m.*

appetizer entrée *f.*; hors-d'œuvre *m.*
apple pomme *f.*
apply postuler
April avril *m.*
architect architecte *m./f.*
area rug tapis *m.*
argue (with each other) se disputer
armchair fauteuil *m.*
armoire armoire *f.*
around autour (de)
arrange ranger
arrive arriver
article article *m.*
as aussi, si; comme
   ~ before comme avant
   ~ far ~ jusqu'à
   ~ handsome as a god beau comme un dieu
   ~ soon ~ dès que
   ~ well ~ ainsi que
ask demander
   ~ oneself a question se poser une question
asparagus asperge *f.*
aspirin aspirine *f.*
assert affirmer
at à; dans; en
   ~ all du tout
   ~ her/his/your place chez elle/lui/toi/vous
   ~ least au moins

~ **the end** au fond
~ **the latest** au plus tard
~ **will** à son gré
athletic sportif (sportive)
athletics athlétisme *m.*
ATM guichet *m.* automatique
atrocious atroce
attend assister à
attic grenier *m.*
attract attirer
August août *m.*
aunt tante *f.*
autumn automne *m.*
average moyenne *f.*; en moyenne
avoid éviter

B

back dos *m.*
~ **seat** siège *m.* arrière
backache mal *m.* au dos
bad mauvais(e); vilain(e)
badly mal
~ **behaved child** enfant *m./f.* mal élevé(e)
bag sac *m.*
baggage claim remise *f.* des bagages
baked au four
bakery boulangerie *f.*, viennoiserie *f.*
~ **and pastry shop** boulangerie-pâtisserie *f.*
balcony balcon *m.*
banana banane *f.*
band groupe *m.*
bank banque *f.*
~ **account** compte *m.* en banque
~ **statement** relevé *m.* de compte
~ **teller** caissier (caissière)
baseball base-ball *m.*
basketball basket *m.*; ballon *m.* de basket
~ **court** terrain de basket *m.*
bathroom salle *f.* de bains
~ **sink** lavabo *m.*
bathtub baignoire *f.*
bay window baie *f.* vitrée
be être
~ **a pain** être pénible

~ **a spendthrift** être dépensier (dépensière)
~ **a wimp** être douillet(te)
~ **able to** pouvoir
~ **afraid** avoir peur
~ **apart** se séparer
~ **ashamed** avoir honte
~ **bored** s'ennuyer
~ **burglarized** être cambriolé(e)
~ **cold** avoir froid
~ **dizzy** avoir la tête qui tourne, avoir le vertige
~ **enraged** être en rage
~ **fashionable** être à la mode
~ **hip** être à la mode
~ **hot** avoir chaud
~ **hungry** avoir faim
~ **in debt** être endetté(e)
~ **in pain** avoir mal
~ **in seventh heaven** être aux anges
~ **in shape** être en forme
~ **located** se trouver
~ **lucky** avoir de la chance
~ **named** s'appeler
~ **necessary** être nécessaire
~ **on cloud nine** être aux anges
~ **on strike** faire la grève
~ **pregnant** attendre un enfant
~ **retired** être à la retraite
~ **right** avoir raison
~ **robbed** être volé(e)
~ **sleepy** avoir sommeil
~ **self-employed** travailler à son compte
~ **sore** avoir des crampes
~ **sorry** regretter
~ **supposed to** devoir
~ **thirsty** avoir soif
~ **unemployed** être au chômage
~ **wrong** avoir tort
beach plage *f.*
beautiful beau (belle)
because parce que, car
bed lit *m.*
bedroom chambre *f.*
bedspread couvre-lit *m.*
beef bœuf *m.*
beer bière *f.*
draft ~ pression *f.*

glass of draft ~ demi *m.*
before avant
begin commencer
behave se comporter
behind derrière
beige beige
believe croire
belly ventre *m.*
below plus bas
bench banc *m.*
benefits avantages *m. pl.*
beside à côté
best *adj.* le/la/les meilleur(e)(s); *adv.* le mieux
~ **friend** meilleur(e) ami(e)
betrayal trahison *f.*
better *adj.* meilleur(e)(s); *adv.* mieux
between entre
beverage boisson *f.*
bicycle bicyclette *f.*, vélo *m.*
bidet bidet *m.*
big grand(e); *(overweight)* gros(se)
bikini bikini *m.*
bill *(banknote)* billet *m.*
bird oiseau *m.*
birth naissance *f.*
~ **announcement** faire-part *m.*
birthday anniversaire *m.*
bite mordre; ronger
~ **one's nails** se ronger les ongles
bitter amer (amère)
bizarre bizarre
black noir(e)
blond blond(e)
blouse chemisier *m.*
blow one's nose se moucher
blue bleu(e)
boarding embarquement *m.*
boarding: ~ **pass** carte *f.* d'accès à bord, carte d'embarquement
~ **school** pension *f.*
~ **school residence** résidence *f.*
~ **school student** pensionnaire *m./f.*
body corps *m.*
bonus prime *f.*
book livre *m.*
bookstore librairie *f.*
boonies bled *m.*

boot botte *f.*

boring ennuyeux (ennuyeuse), barbant(e)

born né(e)

borrow emprunter

boss patron(ne)

botch bâcler

bother agacer

bothersome agaçant(e)

bottle bouteille *f.*, flacon *m.*
~ **feed** donner le biberon à

bouquet bouquet *m.*

bowl bol *m.*

box boîte *f.*

boy garçon *m.*

boyfriend petit ami *m.*

bra soutien-gorge *m.* (*pl.* soutiens-gorge)

brain cerveau *m.*

brake freiner, mettre les freins
~ **pedal** frein *m.*

brave courageux (courageuse)

bread pain *m.*

break-in cambriolage *m.*

breakup rupture *f.*

breakfast petit déjeuner *m.*

brewery brasserie *f.*

bring amener, apporter

broadcast diffuser

broken rompu(e)

brother frère *m.*

brother-in-law beau-frère *m.*

brown brun(e); *(light brown)* châtain *inv.*

brush brosser
~ **one's teeth** se brosser les dents

build bâtir

building bâtiment *m.*, immeuble *m.*

bungee jumping saut *m.* à l'élastique

burglary cambriolage *m.*

burn brûler
~ **a CD** graver un CD

bus bus *m.*, autobus *m.*
~ **station** gare *f.* routière
~ **stop** arrêt *m.* de bus
~ **ticket** ticket *m.* de bus

business commerce *m.*

businessman homme *m.* d'affaires

businesswoman femme *f.* d'affaires

busy mouvementé(e)

butcher shop boucherie *f.*, charcuterie *f.*
~ **and deli** boucherie-charcuterie *f.*

buttock exercises fessiers *m. pl.*

buy acheter

by par, en
~ **the way** au fait

bye salut

bypass highway rocade *f.*

C

cab taxi *m.*

cabbage chou *m.*

cafeteria cantine *f.*

cake gâteau *m.*

call appeler
~ **each other** se téléphoner

calm calme
~ **(oneself) down** se calmer

camel chameau *m.*

can *(to be able to)* pouvoir

can (of food) boîte *f.* de conserve

candidate candidat(e) *m./f.*, postulant(e) *m./f.*

candy bonbon *m.*
~ **shop** confiserie *f.*

canned food conserve *f.*

cantaloupe melon *m.*

cap casquette *f.*

car voiture *f.*

cardigan gilet *m.*

careful prudent(e)

carefully prudemment

carelessly imprudemment

carrot carotte *f.*

carry-on luggage bagage *m.* à main

cartoon dessin *m.* animé

cash: ~ **a check** toucher un chèque
~ **drawer** caisse *f.*

cashier caissier (caissière) *m./f.*

cat chat(te) *m./f.*

caterer traiteur *m.*

cauliflower chou-fleur *m.*

cause *v.* causer

CD CD *m. inv.*
~ **burner** graveur *m.* de CD

~ **player** lecteur *m.* de CD

celebrate fêter

celery céleri *m.*

cell phone téléphone *m.* portable

century siècle *m.*

CEO PDG (président directeur général) *m.*

certain certain(e)

chair chaise *f.*

challenge défi *m.*

change changer
~ **gears** passer les vitesses
~ **the radio station** changer de fréquence

changing room vestiaire *m.*

channel chaîne *f.*
~ **surf** faire du zapping

chat room forum de discussion *m.*

cheap bon marché

cheat (on someone) tromper (quelqu'un)

check chèque *m.*
~ **book** chéquier *m.*, carnet *m.* de chèques
~ **in** enregistrer
~ **with no funds** chèque *m.* sans provisions

check-in enregistrement *m.*

checking account compte *m.* courant

cheek joue *f.*

cheese fromage *m.*
~ **store** fromagerie *f.*

cherry cerise *f.*

chest poitrine *f.*; seins *m. pl.*
~ **of drawers** commode *f.*

chestnut brown marron *inv.*

chewing gum chewing-gum *m.*

chicken poulet *m.*

child enfant *m./f.*

child-king enfant-roi *m./f.*

childhood enfance *f.*

chin menton *m.*

chiropractor kinésithérapeute *m./f.*

chocolate chocolat *m.*
~ **cake** gâteau au chocolat *m.*
~ **shop** chocolaterie *f.*

choose choisir

cigar cigare *m.*

cigarette cigarette *f.*
  ~ lighter briquet *m.*
claim *v.* prétendre
classic *adj.* classique
classical classique
clean nettoyer
clear clair(e)
clerk vendeur (vendeuse)
click cliquer
client client(e)
clientele clientèle *f.*
close *adj.* près (de)
close an account fermer un compte
closet placard *m.*
clothing (article of) vêtement *m.*
  ~ store boutique *f.* de vêtements
clove (of garlic) gousse *f.*
coat manteau *m.*
  ~ of arms armoirie *f.*
coffee café *m.*
  black ~ café noir
  ~ cup tasse *f.* à café
  ~ maker cafetière *f.*
  ~ with milk café au lait
  ~ with cream café crème
coin pièce *f.* de monnaie
Coke Coca *m.*
cold *adj.* froid(e)
  it's ~ (out) il fait froid
  to be ~ avoir froid
cold *n.* rhume *m.*
  to have a ~ être enrhumé(e)
color couleur *f.*
comb peigner
  ~ one's hair se peigner les cheveux
come venir
  ~ back from rentrer de
  ~ from venir de, entrer de
  ~ in entrer
comedy comédie *f.*
comfort consoler
comforter couvre-lit *m.*
comic comique
comma virgule *f.*
commit a crime commettre un crime
common commun(e)
commute trajet *m.*
company société *f.*; compagnie *f.*; entreprise *f.*

complain se plaindre
computer ordinateur *m.*
  laptop ~ ordinateur *m.* portable
computing informatique *f.*
constant constant(e)
constantly constamment
constipated constipé(e)
continent continent *m.*
continue continuer
conveyor belt tapis *m.* roulant
convincing convaincant(e)
cook *n.* cuisinier (cuisinière); *v.* faire la cuisine
cooking cuisine *f.*
cool frais (fraîche); chouette *(slang)*
it's cool (out) il fait frais
corkscrew tire-bouchon *m.*
corner coin *m.*
corporation société *f.*
couch canapé *m.*
cough *n.* toux *f.*; *v.* tousser
country pays *m.*; campagne *f.*
couple couple *m.*
courageous courageux (courageuse)
cousin cousin(e)
cow vache *f.*
cozy accueillant(e)
crash *v.* s'écraser
crazy fou (folle)
  ~ thing folie *f.*
cream crème *f.*
create concevoir
credit card carte *f.* de crédit; Carte Bleue *f.*
crew équipage *m.*
cross traverser
cross-country biking VTT *m.*
cross-country skiing ski *m.* de fond
crown couronner
cry pleurer
cuddle faire des câlins
curly frisé(e)
currency exchange office bureau *m.* d'échange
curtain rideau *m.*
custom made sur mesure
customer client(e)
customs douane *f.*
cut *n.* coupe *f.*; *v.* couper

cute mignon(ne)
cutlery couverts *m. pl.*

D

daily: ~ diet régime *m.* alimentaire
  ~ newspaper quotidien *m.*
dairy crémerie *f.*
  ~ product produit *m.* laitier
  ~ department rayon *m.* crémerie
damage dégâts *m. pl.*
dance danser
dare oser
daring osé(e)
dark noir(e)
darling chéri(e)
data données *f. pl.*
daughter fille *f.*
day jour *m.*
death mort *f.*
debit card Carte Bleue *f.*
debt dette *f.*
December décembre *m.*
declare déclarer
decline baisse *f.*
deep profond(e)
deep-sea fishing pêche *f.* au gros
delay retard *m.*
delicacy mets *m.*
delicatessen charcuterie *f.*
delicious délicieux (délicieuse)
delighted ravi(e)
deliver livrer
delivery person livreur (livreuse)
demoralized démoralisé(e)
dentist dentiste *m./f.*
department rayon *m.*
depending on selon, d'après
depressed déprimé(e)
designer couturier *m.*
desk bureau *m.*
  ~ calendar agenda *m.*
desperate désespéré(e)
dessert dessert *m.*
detective film film *m.* policier
devastated dévasté(e)
devil démon *m.*
devoted empressé(e)
diarrhea diarrhée *f.*
diet: ~ aid produit *m.* de régime
  ~ food produit *m.* allégé / light

difficulty difficulté *f.*
dig creuser
digital numérique
  ~ **camera** appareil photo *m.* numérique
  ~ **portable audio player** baladeur *m.* numérique
dining room salle *f.* à manger
dinner dîner *m.*
  ~ **is ready!** à table!
direction direction *f.*
dirty *adj.* sale
dirty *v.* salir
disappointed déçu(e)
discotheque discothèque *f.*
disgusting dégoûtant(e), dégueulasse
dish plat *m.*
  main ~ plat *m.* principal
  serving ~ récipient *m.*
dishes vaisselle *f.*
dishwasher lave-vaisselle *m.*
disobey désobéir
dissatisfied insatisfait(e)
diving plongée *f.* sous-marine
divorced divorcé(e)
DJ animateur (animatrice)
do faire
  ~ **a sport** pratiquer un sport
  ~ **homework** faire les devoirs
  ~ **the dishes** faire la vaisselle
  ~ **the food shopping** faire les courses
  ~ **the housecleaning** faire le ménage
  ~ **the laundry** faire la lessive
doctor médecin *m.*
documentary documentaire *m.*
dog chien(ne)
dogsled attelage *m.* de chiens, traîneau *m.* à chiens
door porte *f.*
dormitory résidence *f.*
double double
doubt douter
doubtful douteux (douteuse)
downhill skiing ski *m.* alpin
dowry dot *f.*
dozen douzaine *f.*
draft brouillon *m.*
  ~ **beer** pression *f.*

drag (on a cigarette) taffe *f.*
drama film *m.* dramatique; pièce *f.* dramatique
drawing dessin *m.*
dream rêve *m.*
dress *n.* robe *f.*; *v.* se vêtir, s'habiller
dresser buffet *m.*
dressing room vestiaire *m.*
drink boire
drive conduire, rouler
drug addiction toxicomanie *f.*
drunkard ivrogne *m./f.*
dry sec (sèche)
  ~ **cleaner** teinturerie *f.*
  ~ **cleaning** nettoyage *m.* à sec, lavage *m.* à sec
dry one's hair se sécher les cheveux
duck canard *m.*
dumb stupide
dumbfounded épaté(e)
during pendant
dust épousseter
duty-free shop magasin *m.* hors taxe
DVD player lecteur *m.* de DVD

E

each chaque; tout(e)(s), tous
  ~ **one** chacun(e)
ear oreille *f.*
earn toucher; recevoir
earn gagner
eat manger
  ~ **healthy foods** manger sain
eating disorders troubles *m. pl.* alimentaires
editor éditeur *m.*
eight huit
eighteen dix-huit
eighty quatre-vingts
elbow coude *m.*
electronic planner agenda *m.* électronique
elegant élégant(e)
elementary school école *f.* primaire
  ~ **teacher** instituteur (institutrice)
elevator ascenseur *m.*
eleven onze
elsewhere ailleurs
e-mail e-mail *m.*, courriel *m.*

  ~ **address** adresse *f.* électronique
embarrassed gêné(e)
emergency exit sortie *f.* de secours
emphasize mettre en valeur
employee employé(e)
emptiness vide *m.*
empty *adj.* vide; *v.* vider
enclosed ci-joint(e)
endless interminable
enemy *adj., n.* ennemi(e)
engaged fiancé(e)
engagement fiançailles *f. pl.*
engineer ingénieur *m.*
enjoyable agréable
enough (of) assez (de)
enter entrer (dans)
entrance portail *m.*
entrée plat *m.* principal
envelope enveloppe *f.*
essential essentiel(le); indispensable
espresso express *m.*
euphoric euphorique
evening soir *m.*
event événement *m.*
every tout(e)(s), tous
  ~ **morning** tous les matins
everything tout
evident évident(e)
exchange échange *m.*
excuse me excusez-moi, pardon
exercise exercice *m.*
  ~ **repetitions** série *f.* d'exercices
expect s'attendre à
expensive cher (chère)
experience profil *m.*
exquisite exquis(e)
external externe
eye œil *m.* (*pl.* yeux)

F

face visage *m.*
fail lâcher
failure échec *m.*
faint *v.* tomber dans les pommes (*slang*)
fair *adj.* juste
fairy fée *f.*
faith foi *f.*
faithful (to someone) fidèle (à quelqu'un)

fall tomber
- **~ asleep** s'endormir
- **~ in love** tomber amoureux (amoureuse)
- **~ over dead** tomber raide mort(e)

false faux (fausse)
falsely faussement
family famille *f.*
- **~ problems** troubles *m. pl.* familiaux
- **~ room** salle *f.* de séjour

far (from) loin (de)
farm-raised fermier (fermière)
fashion show défilé *m.* de mode
fashionable à la mode
fat gros(se)
father père *m.*
father-in-law beau-père *m.*
feature trait *m.*
February février *m.*
feel se sentir
- **~ good in one's skin** être bien dans sa peau
- **~ like (doing something)** avoir envie de
- **~ well/bad** se sentir bien/mal

fever fièvre *f.*
few peu (de)
fiancé(e) fiancé(e)
fifteen quinze
fifty cinquante
fight bagarre *f.*
fill up faire le plein
filming tournage *m.*
find trouver
fine fin(e)
finger doigt *m.*
finish finir, terminer
fir (tree) sapin *m.*
fire feu *m.*
firearm arme *f.* à feu
fired licencié(e)
firefighter pompier *m.*
fireplace cheminée *f.*
fish *n.* poisson *m.*
- **~ bone** arête *f.*
- **~ market** poissonnerie *f.*

fish *v.* pêcher
fishing pêche *f.*
fit into (clothing) rentrer dans

fitness center centre *m.* de fitness, club *m.* de gym/fitness, salle *f.* de sports
fitting room cabine *f.* d'essayages
five cinq
fix *(alteration)* retouche *f.*
flag drapeau *m.*
flat crevé(e)
flea puce *f.*
flight vol *m.*
- **~ attendant** steward *m.*, hôtesse *f.* de l'air
- **~ from** vol en provenance de
- **~ to** vol à destination de

flirt draguer
floor étage *m.*
- **~ exercises** exercices *m. pl.* au sol

florist fleuriste *m./f.*
flower fleur *f.*
fluffy mou (molle)
following *adj.* suivant(e)
food aliment *m.*
- **~ supplies** provisions *f. pl.*
- **frozen ~** produit *m.* surgelé
- **organic ~** produit *m.* bio(logique)
- **starchy ~** féculent *m.*
- **to do the ~ shopping** faire les courses

foot pied *m.*
football football *m.* américain
for pour
- **~ how long?** depuis combien de temps?
- **~ sure** à coup sûr
- **~ two years** depuis deux ans

forty quarante
forehead front *m.*
forget oublier
fork fourchette *f.*
fortune-teller diseur (diseuse) de bonne aventure
four quatre
fourteen quatorze
free libre
- **~ fall** chute *f.* libre
- **~ fly** vol *m.* libre

French fries frites *f. pl.*
frequent flyer program Fréquence Plus
Friday vendredi *m.*

friendly sympathique
from de
front seat siège *m.* avant
fruit fruit *m.*
fruit-flavored fruité(e)
fulfilled épanoui(e)
full bondé(e)
full-time *adv.* à plein temps, à temps complet
funny amusant(e)
furious furieux (furieuse)
furnish meubler
furthermore d'autant plus que
futon futon *m.*

G

gain weight grossir, prendre du poids
gang *(of brats)* marmaille *f.*
garage garage *m.*
gardening jardinage *m.*
garlic ail *m.*
gas essence *f.*
- **~ pedal** accélérateur *m.*

gate porte *f.*
gear vitesse *f.*
get: ~ a divorce divorcer
- **~ along well** s'entendre bien
- **~ a massage** se faire masser
- **~ back** revenir, rentrer
- **~ dressed** s'habiller
- **~ drunk** se soûler
- **~ engaged** se fiancer
- **~ in shape** se mettre en forme
- **~ information** s'informer
- **~ mad** se fâcher
- **~ married** se marier
- **~ nervous** s'énerver
- **~ up** se lever
- **not to ~ along** s'entendre mal

gift don *m.*
girl fille *f.*
girlfriend petite amie *f.*
give donner, fournir
- **~ back** rendre
- **~ birth** accoucher

glass verre *m.*
glasses lunettes *f. pl.*
go aller
- **~ down** descendre
- **~ for a walk** se promener

~ **out with** sortir avec

~ **shopping** faire les magasins

~ **to bed** se coucher

godmother marraine *f.*

goldfish poisson *m.* rouge

golf golf *m.*

~ **ball** balle *f.* de golf

~ **club** club *m.* de golf

~ **course** terrain *m.*/parcours *m.* de golf

good bon(ne)

it's ~ c'est bon

to smell ~ sentir bon

goodbye au revoir

gossip items potins *m. pl.*

grade note *f.*

gram gramme *m.*

granddaughter petite-fille *f.*

grandfather grand-père *m.*

grandmother grand-mère *f.*

grandson petit-fils *m.*

grapes raisins *m. pl.*

grateful reconnaissant(e)

grave tombe *f.*

gray gris(e)

~ **weather** grisaille *f.*

green vert(e)

~ **beans** haricots *m. pl.* verts

grilled tuna thon *m.* grillé

grocery épicerie *f.*

ground terre *f.*

~ **personnel** agent *m.*/hôtesse *f.* au sol

group groupe *m.*

~ **of tickets** carnet *m.*

growth croissance *f.*

guess deviner

guilty coupable

guinea pig cochon *m.* d'Inde

gymnasium gymnase *m.*

H

hair cheveux *m. pl.*

hairdresser salon *m.* de coiffure

hairy poilu(e)

half: ~ **bath** WC *m.*, toilettes *f. pl.*

half-brother demi-frère *m.*

half-sister demi-sœur *f.*

ham jambon *m.*

hamster hamster *m.*

hand main *f.*

~ **in** ~ main dans la main

~**fuls** les mains pleines

handsome beau (belle)

hang clothes to dry étendre le linge

hang-gliding deltaplane *m.*

happen se passer

happiness bonheur *m.*

happy content(e), heureux (heureuse)

hard dur(e)

hat chapeau *m.*

hate détester

~ **each other** se détester

have avoir

~ **a cold** être enrhumé(e)

~ **a complex** être complexé(e)

~ **a drink** boire un pot

~ **a hard time** avoir du mal

~ **a sweet tooth** être gourmand(e)

~ **fun** s'amuser

~ **pain** avoir mal

~ **the right of way** avoir la priorité

~ **to** devoir

head tête *f.*

~ **of a company** chef *m.* d'entreprise

~ **waiter** maître d'hôtel *m.*

headache: to have a ~ avoir mal à la tête

heal soigner

health santé *f.*

healthy en bonne santé

hear entendre

hearing ouïe *f.*

heart cœur *m.*

~ **attack** crise *f.* cardiaque

heartbreak déception *f.* amoureuse

heavy lourd(e); fort(e)

heli-skiing héliski *m.*

hello bonjour

help aider, être utile

help! au secours!

henna henné *m.*

herbal tea tisane *f.*

hey! coucou!

hi salut; coucou

hideous hideux (hideuse)

high school lycée *m.*

~ **student** lycéen(ne)

highlight mettre en valeur

high-speed Internet connection connexion *f.* haut-débit

himself se

hint tuyau *m.*

hip *adj.* branché(e) *(slang)*

hip *n.* hanche *f.*

hire embaucher

history histoire *f.*

hobby passe-temps *m.*

hold tenir

home theater home cinéma *m.*

homeopathic homéopathique

homework devoirs *m. pl.*

honey miel *m.*

honeymoon lune *f.* de miel

hope espoir *m.*

horrified horrifié(e)

host *v.* animer; *n.* animateur (animatrice)

hot chaud(e)

it's ~ **(out)** il fait chaud

to be ~ avoir chaud

house maison *f.*

household foyer *m.*

~ **chores** travaux *m. pl.* ménagers

housewife femme *f.* au foyer

housing logement *m.*

how comment

~ **are you? / ~'s it going?** Comment vas-tu/allez-vous?, Ça va?

~ **do you say . . . ?** Comment dit-on … ?

~ **do you spell it?** Comment ça s'épelle?

~ **long . . . ?** combien de temps … ?

~ **many** *(+ noun)*? combien de … ?

~ **much** combien de … ?

~ **much is it?** c'est combien?

however par contre, pourtant

hundred cent

hunt chasser

hurry se dépêcher, se presser

hurt oneself se faire mal

husband mari *m.*
hush! chut!

I

I je
 ~ **am doing well, thank you.** Je vais bien, merci.
ice: ~ **cream** glace *f.*
 ~ **skate** patin *m.* à glace
ID tag étiquette *f.*
if si
 ~ **need be** si besoin est
 ~ **not** sinon
illiteracy analphabétisation *f.*
illness maladie *f.*
imagine se figurer
impossible impossible
impoverishment appauvrissement *m.*
improbable improbable
improve améliorer
in à; dans; en
 ~ **a few years** dans quelques années
 ~ **a hurry** pressé(e)
 ~ **a nutshell** en gros
 ~ **back of** derrière
 ~ **broad daylight** en plein jour
 ~ **front of** en face de, devant
 ~ **love** amoureux (amoureuse)
 ~ **spite of this** malgré cela
 ~ **the center** au centre
 ~ **the process of** en train de
 ~ **transit** en cours de route
 ~ **your opinion** d'après vous
individuality individualité *f.*
information: ~ **bulletin** communiqué *m.* publicitaire
 get ~ s'informer
inside à l'intérieur
insist exiger
insist (on) insister (pour)
inspire oneself s'inspirer
instead plutôt
 ~ **of** au lieu de
instructor moniteur (monitrice)
intelligent intelligent(e)
intelligently intelligemment
internal organs parties *f. pl.* internes du corps
Internet Internet *m.*
 ~ **user** internaute *m./f.*

internship stage *m.*
interview entretien *m.*
 to have an ~ avoir/passer un entretien
intestines intestin *m.*
introduce présenter
invest investir
 ~ **money** placer de l'argent
investment investissement *m.*
invite inviter
ironing repassage *m.*
it il, elle; ça, cela
 ~ **could be better** ça peut aller
 ~ **does not matter** ça n'a pas d'importance
 ~ **is better that** il vaut mieux que
 ~ **is delicious** c'est délicieux
 ~ **is necessary (that)** il faut (que)
 ~'**s** c'est
 ~'**s a pity** il est dommage, c'est dommage
 ~'**s going okay/well/all right** ça va/ça va bien/ça va pas mal
 ~'**s nice out** il fait beau
 ~'**s nice to meet you.** Enchanté(e).
 ~'**s possible (that)** il se peut (que)
 ~'**s raining** il pleut
 ~'**s snowing** il neige
 ~'**s warm out** il fait chaud
Ivory Coast Côte d'Ivoire *f.*

J

jacket veste *f.*
Jacuzzi jacuzzi *m.*
January janvier *m.*
jazz jazz *m.*
jealous jaloux (jalouse)
jeans jean(s) *m.*
Jet Ski jet ski *m.*
jewelry bijoux *m. pl.*
 ~ **store** bijouterie *f.*
job emploi *m.*, job *m.*, travail *m.*, boulot *m. (slang)*
 ~ **applicant** demandeur (demandeuse) d'emploi
jogging suit survêtement *m.*
journalist journaliste *m./f.*

judo judo *m.*
July juillet *m.*
jump sauter
June juin *m.*
junior high school collège *m.*

K

karate karaté *m.*
keep: ~ **oneself (from)** s'empêcher (de)
 ~ **(someone else) quiet** faire taire
key clé *f.*
keyboard clavier *m.*
kick donner des coups de pied
kicked out mis(e) à la porte
kidney rein *m.*
kilo kilo *m.*
kind genre *m.*
kiss embrasser
 ~ **each other** s'embrasser
 ~ **on the cheeks** se faire la bise
 ~ **on the lips** donner un baiser
kitchen cuisine *f.*
 ~ **sink** évier *m.*
kitchenette kitchenette *f.*
kitten chaton *m.*
knee genou *m.*
knickknack statuette *f.*
knife couteau *m.*
know connaître, savoir

L

labor *(pregnancy)* accouchement *m.*
lady dame *f.*
lake lac *m.*
lamb chop côtelette *f.* d'agneau
lamp lampe *f.*
land atterrir
landing atterrissage *m.*
laptop computer ordinateur *m.* portable
lasagna lasagnes *f. pl.*
last dernier (dernière)
lately dernièrement, ces derniers temps
laugh rigoler
launch lancer
lead amener
leaf feuille *f.*
learn apprendre

leave laisser; *(someone or something)* quitter; *(for an undetermined period of time)* partir, s'en aller; *(for a short time)* sortir
   ~ **each other** se quitter
   ~ **room for the young!** place aux jeunes!
left gauche *f.*
   on the ~ à gauche
leftovers restes *m. pl.*
leg jambe *f.*
leisure activity loisir *m.*
lemon citron *m.*
lemon-lime soda limonade
lend prêter (à)
lentil lentille *f.*
less moins (de)
letter lettre *f.*
lie down se coucher
life vie *f.*
light léger (légère)
like aimer
linen drap *m.*
lip lèvre *f.*
list liste *f.*
listen écouter
liter litre *m.*
little petit(e)
   a ~ un peu (de)
live *adj.* en direct *(broadcasting)*; en chair et en os
live *v.* habiter; vivre; loger
liver foie *m.*
   ~ **pâté** foie gras *m.*
living room salon *m.*
loaf of French bread baguette *f.*
lobster langouste *f.*
long long(ue)
look (at) regarder
   ~ **at each other** se regarder
   ~ **for** chercher
lose perdre
   ~ **weight** maigrir, perdre du poids
loss perte *f.*
loudspeaker haut-parleur *m.*
love *n.* amour *m.*
   ~ **at first sight** coup *m.* de foudre
love *v.* aimer
   ~ **each other** s'aimer
   ~ **madly** aimer à la folie

lovebirds amoureux *m. pl.*
loved ones proches *m. pl.*
lover amant *m.*; maîtresse *f.*
   ~**s** amoureux *m. pl.*
lozenge dragée *f.*, pastille *f.*
luck chance *f.*
lunch déjeuner *m.*

M

magazine revue *f.*, magazine *m.*
   cooking ~ revue de cuisine
   entertainment ~ presse *f.* people
   entertainment ~**s** presse du cœur
   fashion ~ revue de mode
   ~ **and newspaper store** maison *f.* de la presse
   ~ **subscription** abonnement *m.*
   monthly ~ mensuel *m.*
   sports ~ revue de sport
   weekly ~ hebdomadaire *m.*
magnificent magnifique
magpie pie *f.*
mailbox boîte *f.* aux lettres
mail carrier facteur (factrice)
maintain one's weight garder sa ligne
make faire
   ~ **a toast** trinquer
   ~ **fun (of)** se moquer (de)
   ~ **funny faces** faire le clown
makeup maquillage *m.*
man homme *m.*
manage gérer
management gestion *f.*
manager gérant(e)
maple érable *m.*
March mars *m.*
march in a parade participer à un défilé
market marché *m.*, souk *m. (Tunisia)*
married marié(e)
massage masser
mat matelas *m.*
math maths *m. pl.*
math test examen *m.* d'arithmétique
May mai *m.*
maybe peut-être
mayonnaise mayonnaise *f.*

me moi
   ~, **my name is . . .** Moi, c'est ...
   ~ **too!** moi aussi!
meal repas *m.*
mean *adj.* méchant(e); *n.* moyen *m.*; *v.* vouloir dire
meat viande *f.*
   ~ **department** rayon *m.* boucherie
meatball boulette *f.* de viande
medical insurance assurance *f.* médicale
medication médicament *m.*
meet (each other) se rencontrer
meeting rencontre *f.*
memory souvenir *m.*
menu carte *f.*
metal detector détecteur *m.* de métaux
microwave four *m.* à micro-ondes
middle school collège *m.*
migraine migraine *f.*
milk lait *m.*
mime mime *m.*
mind esprit *m.*
minimum wage SMIC *m.*
   ~ **earner** smicard(e)
mirror miroir *m.*
misdemeanor délit *m.*
miss manquer
modem modem *m.*
modern moderne
Monday lundi *m.*
money argent *m.*
monitor moniteur *m.*
month mois *m.*
monument monument *m.*
moon lune *f.*
more plus
moreover d'ailleurs
morning matin *m.*
Morocco Maroc *m.*
mortgage prêt *m.* hypothécaire, emprunt *m.* hypothécaire
most (the most) le/la/les plus ...
mother mère *f.*, maman *f.*
mother-in law belle-mère *f.*
motorcoach autocar *m.*, car *m.*
motorcycle motocyclette *f.*, moto *f.*
motto devise *f.*

mountain climbing alpinisme *m.*
  ice ~ escalade *f.* sur glace
mouse souris *f.*
mouth bouche *f.*
movie film *m.*
  adventure ~ film d'aventure
  historical ~ film historique
  horror ~ film d'épouvante
  ~ director metteur *m.* en scène
  romantic comedy comédie *f.* romantique
  science-fiction ~ film de science-fiction
  TV ~ téléfilm *m.*
  war ~ film de guerre
museum musée *m.*
mushroom champignon *m.*
music musique *f.*
  ~ hits classement *m.* des tubes
musical musical(e)
  ~ comedy comédie *f.* musicale
  ~ play pièce *f.* musicale
  ~ program émission *f.* musicale
mussel moule *f.*
must devoir; il faut

N

napkin serviette *f.*
nasal spray gouttes *f. pl.* nasales
national national(e)
naughty vilain
nausea mal *m.* au cœur, nausée *f.*
near à proximité, près (de)
  ~ future futur *m.* proche
necessary nécessaire
neck cou *m.*
need *n.* besoin *m.*; *v.* avoir besoin
negative négatif (négative)
neighborhood quartier *m.*
nephew neveu *m.*
nest nid *m.*
never jamais
nevertheless néanmoins
newborn nouveau-né *m.*
news actualités *f. pl.*
newscast informations (infos) *f. pl.*
newspaper journal *m.* (*pl.* journaux)
  ~ vendor marchand(e) de journaux

newsstand kiosque *m.* (à journaux)
next ensuite; prochain(e)
next! au suivant!
  ~ to à côté de
nice gentil(le)
niece nièce *f.*
night nuit *f.*; soir *m.*
nightclub boîte *f.* de nuit
nightstand table *f.* de nuit
nightmare cauchemar *m.*
nine neuf
nineteen dix-neuf
ninety quatre-vingt-dix
nobody personne, personne ne, ne ... personne
normal normal(e)
nose nez *m.*
not pas
  ~ bad pas mal
  ~ very peu
November novembre *m.*
now maintenant
number chiffre *m.*
nurse infirmière *f.*

O

obey obéir (à)
obvious clair(e)
occasionally parfois
October octobre *m.*
office bureau *m.*; cabinet *m.*
often souvent
oh, really? ah bon?
oil huile *f.*
  olive ~ huile d'olive *f.*
ointment pommade *f.*
old vieux (vieille)
omelet omelette *f.*
on sur
  ~ a diet au régime
  ~ board à bord
  ~ sale soldé(e), en solde
  ~ the corner au coin
  ~ the front page à la une
  ~ the left à gauche
  ~ the radio à la radio, sur les ondes
  ~ the right à droite
  ~ time out au coin
  ~ top of sur
  ~ TV à la télé

one *adj.; number* un(e)
  ~ out of ... un sur ...
  ~-piece bathing suit maillot *m.* de bain
  ~-way aller-simple *m.*
one *pron.* on
onion oignon *m.*
only seulement
  ~ child fils *m.*/fille *f.* unique
opera opéra *m.*
optimistic optimiste
or ou
  ~ more ou plus
orange *adj.* orange *inv.*
orange *n.* orange *f.*
orchestra orchestre *m.*
order *v.* commander
organic bio(logique)
organize organiser
orphan orphelin(e)
other autre
  ~ than ailleurs que
outdoors à l'air libre
outlet prise *f.*
outraged outragé(e)
outside à l'extérieur
oven four *m.*
over there là-bas
overhead compartment compartiment *m.*
overlook donner sur
overweight gros(se)
oyster huître *f.*

P

pack paquet *m.*; **to pack suitcases** faire les valises
paid holidays congés payés *m. pl.*
pain: to be a ~ être pénible
paint peindre
painting tableau *m.*
pajamas pyjama *m.*
pants pantalon *m.*
paparazzi paparazzi *m./f.*
paper papier *m.*
parade défilé *m.*
paragliding parapente *m.*
parasailing parachute *m.* ascensionnel (nautique)
park *n.* parc *m.*; *v.* garer
part partie *f.*; portion *f.*

participate (in) participer (à)
partner compagnon (compagne)
part-time à mi-temps, à temps partiel
party boum *f.*
passenger passager (passagère)
passport passeport *m.*
password mot *m.* de passe
pasta pâtes *f. pl.*
pastry pâtisserie *f.*
~ **shop** pâtisserie *f.*
pâté pâté de campagne *m.*; *(goose liver)* foie gras *m.*
pay rendre
~ **back** rembourser
PDA assistant *m.* personnel
peach pêche *f.*
peanut arachide *f.*
pear poire *f.*
pedal pédaler
pedaling pédalage *m.*
~ **and rowing machine** vélo-rameur *m.*
pedestrian passant(e)
~ **street** rue *f.* piétonne
penalty peine *f.*
people gens *m. pl.*
people on *pron.*
pepper poivre *m.*; poivron *m.*
perform a concert donner un concert
performance spectacle *m.*
perfume parfum *m.*
~ **store** parfumerie *f.*
person personne *f.*
personal personnel(le)
~ **banker** banquier *m.*
personality personnalité *f.*
pessimistic pessimiste
pet animal *m.* (*pl.* animaux) domestique(s)
~ **names** mots tendres *m. pl.*
pharmacy pharmacie *f.*
photo photo *f.*
photographer photographe *m./f.*
physical therapist kinésithérapeute *m./f.*
piece morceau *m.*
pilot pilote *m./f.*
pink rose
pipe pipe *f.*

pitcher pichet *m.*
place *n.* lieu *m.*; *v.* mettre
plan prévoir
plane avion *m.*
~ **cabin** cabine *f.*
~ **ticket** billet *m.* d'avion
planned prévu(e)
plant plante *f.*
plate assiette *f.*; (plates) vaisselle *f.*
platform quai *m.*
play *n.* pièce *f.*; *v.* jouer; *(a sport)* jouer à ... ; *(in a match/game)* participer à un match/un jeu
please *interj.* s'il vous plaît, s'il te plaît
please *v.* plaire
pleased enchanté(e)
poem poème *m.*
police station gendarmerie *f.*
police officer agent *m.* de police, gendarme *m.*
poll sondage *m.*
poor pauvre
poorly mal
pork porc *m.*
position poste *m.*
positive positif (positive)
possess posséder
possible possible
possibly peut-être
post office poste *f.*
postcard carte *f.* postale
potato pomme *f.* de terre
poultry volaille *f.*
practice pratiquer
predict prédire
preferable préférable
pregnant enceinte
prepare préparer
present présenter
~ **a paper** donner une conférence
price coût *m.*
printer imprimante *f.*
private privé(e)
prize prix *m.*
probable probable
problem problème *m.*
family ~**s** troubles *m. pl.* familiaux
product produit *m.*
production fabrication *f.*

profession profession *f.*
professor professeur *m.*
program émission *f.*; programme *m.*
promote promouvoir
proof of identity pièce *f.* d'identité
proud fier (fière)
provide pourvoir
provider pourvoyeur (pourvoyeuse)
provocative provocateur (provocatrice)
public public (publique)
publish publier
pullover pullover (*also* pull) *m.*
punish punir
purchase achat *m.*
purple violet(te)
push appuyer
push-ups pompes *f. pl.*
put mettre
~ **air in** gonfler
~ **makeup on** se maquiller
~ **on** *(clothing)* mettre
~ **on the brakes** mettre les freins

Q

quiche quiche *f.*, tarte *f.* salée
quickly vite
quite assez

R

rabbit lapin *m.*
race course *f.*
racket raquette *f.*
rafting rafting *m.*
railroad track voie *f.*
rain pleuvoir
it's ~**ing** il pleut
rainbow arc-en-ciel *m.*
raincoat imperméable *m.*
raise élever
rallying cry cri *m.* de ralliement
rap rap *m.*
rapidly vite
rarely rarement
rate taux *m.*
rather assez; plutôt
~ **than** plutôt que
read lire
reader lecteur (lectrice)

real vrai(e)
really vraiment
rearview mirror rétroviseur *m.*
rebel *v.* se rebeller
receive recevoir; toucher
recess récréation (*also* récré) *f.*
reciprocal réciproque
recommend recommander
reconcile se réconcilier
red rouge; *(hair)* roux (rousse)
  ~ bean haricot *m.*
  ~ pepper poivron *m.* rouge
reflexive réfléchi(e)
refrigerator réfrigérateur *m.*
regional régional(e)
register (s')inscrire
regret regretter
regrettable regrettable
relax se détendre, se reposer,
  décompresser
relieved soulagé(e)
remedies remèdes *m. pl.*
remember se souvenir (de); se
  rappeler (de)
remind rappeler
remote control télécommande *f.*
remove: ~ one's clothes se
  déshabiller
  ~ one's makeup se démaquiller
return *(an item)* rendre; *(go back)*
  revenir, rentrer
rent loyer *m.*
repair work bricolage *m.*
report reportage *m.*
repulsive répugnant(e)
require demander
reserve réserver
respond répondre
rest se reposer
restaurant restaurant *m.*
  ~ car wagon-restaurant *m.*
retiree retraité(e)
retirement retraite *f.*
rice riz *m.*
rich riche; *(fatty)* riche en
  matières grasses
right *(entitlement)* droit *m.*;
  (direction) droite *f.*; juste *adj.*
  ~ away tout de suite
  ~ of way priorité *f.*
  on the ~ à droite

robbery vol *m.*
rock rock *m.*
rock-climbing varappe *f.*
roller blades rollers *m. pl.*
room salle *f.*, pièce *f.*, chambre *f.*
  hotel ~ chambre *f.* d'hôtel
roommate colocataire *m./f.*
rope corde *f.*
rotten pourri(e)
round-trip ticket billet
  aller-retour *m.*
row ramer
rugby rugby *m.*
run courir; *(broadcast)* passer
  ~ away faire une fugue
  ~ into heurter
runny nose nez *m.* qui coule
runway piste *f.* de décollage/
  d'atterrissage
rush hour heure *f.* de pointe

S

sad triste
safe *n.* coffre-fort *m.*
salad salade *f.*
salami saucisson *m.*
salary salaire *m.*
sale soldes *f. pl.*; vente *f.*
salt sel *m.*
salty salé(e)
sand sable *m.*
sandbox bac *m.* à sable
sandals sandales *f. pl.*
sandwich sandwich *m.*
sardine sardine *f.*
satisfied satisfait(e)
Saturday samedi *m.*
sauna sauna *m.*
sausage saucisse *f.*
save économiser; épargner; sauver
  ~ someone's life sauver la vie à
  quelqu'un
savings account compte *m.* épargne
say dire
scallop coquille *f.* Saint-Jacques
scalpel bistouri *m.*
scanner scanner *m.*
scared effrayé(e)
scarf foulard *m.*
schedule horaire *m.*
scholarship bourse *f.*

school école *f.*
scream *v.* crier
screen écran *m.*
sculpture sculpture *f.*
sea mer *f.*
seafood fruits *m. pl.* de mer
  ~ department rayon *m.*
  poissonnerie
seamstress couturière *f.*
search engine moteur *m.* de
  recherche
season saison *f.*
seasoning condiment *m.*
seat siège *m.*
  ~ belt ceinture *f.* de sécurité
secretary secrétaire *m./f.*
security gate contrôle *m.* sûreté
see voir
  ~ you ciao
  ~ you in a while à tout à l'heure
  ~ you later à plus (tard)
  ~ you soon à bientôt
  ~ you tomorrow à demain
seek one's own identity être à la
  recherche de son identité
seem avoir l'air
selfishness égoïsme *m.*
seller marchand(e)
send envoyer
  ~ an attachment envoyer une
  pièce ci-jointe
  ~ an e-mail envoyer un
  courriel/un email
sense sens *m.*
separate se séparer
separated séparé(e)
September septembre *m.*
serve servir
set the table mettre la table
seven sept
seventeen dix-sept
seventy soixante-dix
several plusieurs
sexual relations relations *f. pl.*
  sexuelles
shall we go? on y va?
shampoo shampooing *m.*
shape forme *f.*
shave se raser
shh! chut!
shine luire

shirt *(man's)* chemise *f.*; *(woman's)* chemisier *m.*

shocked surpris(e), étonné(e)

shoe chaussure *f.*

shoot (a gun) coup *m.* de fusil

shop boutique *f.*; commerçant *m.*

shopping cart chariot *m.* à provisions

short court(e)

shorts short *m.*

shot piqûre *f.*

shoulder épaule *f.*

shoulder-length hair cheveux mi-longs

shout crier

~ **oneself hoarse** s'époumoner

show *n.:* **reality** ~ télé-réalité *f.*

show *v.* montrer

shower douche *f.*

shrimp crevette *f.*

shutter volet *m.*

shy timide

sight vue *f.*

sign *v.* signer

silent silencieux (silencieuse)

silently silencieusement

silly bête

silver argent *m.*

sin pêcher

sing chanter

single célibataire

sinus sinus *m.*

sister sœur *f.*

sister-in-law belle-sœur *f.*

sit (down) s'asseoir

situp abdominal *m.* *(pl.* abdominaux)

six six

sixteen seize

sixty soixante

skating rink patinoire *f.*

ski ski *m.*

~ **boot** botte *f.* de ski

~ **pole** bâton *m.* de ski

~ **slope** piste *f.* de ski

skiing: cross-country ~ ski *m.* de fond

downhill ~ ski *m.* alpin

skim écrémé(e)

skin peau *f.*

skip school faire l'école buissonnière

skirt jupe *f.*

skydiving parapente *m.*

sledding luge *f.*

sleep dormir *v.*; sommeil *m.*

~ **aid** somnifère *m.*

sleeper train wagon-lit *m.*

Sleeping Beauty Belle *f.* au Bois Dormant

slice tranche *f.*

slide diapositive *f.*

slight léger (légère)

slim maigre; mince

slow lent(e)

slowly lentement

small petit(e)

smell *n.* odorat *m.*; *v.* sentir

~ **bad** sentir mauvais

~ **good** sentir bon

smile sourire

smoke fumer

smoked salmon saumon *m.* fumé

smoking addiction tabagisme *m.*

sneak out faire le mur *(slang)*

sneaker chaussure *f.* de sport

snow *n.* neige *f.*

~ **sport** sport *m.* de glisse

snow *v.* neiger

snowboarding surf *m.* des neiges/ snowboard *m.*

snowman bonhomme *m.* de neige

so alors, si

~ **many** tant

~ **what!** et alors!

soap opera feuilleton *m.* romantique

soccer football *(also* foot*) m.*

~ **ball** ballon *m.* de foot

~ **game** match *m.* de foot

social habits mœurs *f. pl.*

sock chaussette *f.*

sofa sofa *m.*

soft doux (douce); mou (molle)

software logiciel *m.*

some de

someone quelqu'un

something quelque chose

sometimes quelquefois, parfois

somewhere quelque part

son fils *m.*

sore throat mal *m.* à la gorge

sorry désolé(e), navré(e)

so-so comme ci, comme ça

sought after recherché(e)

soul âme *f.*

sound son *m.*

soundtrack bande *f.* sonore

soup soupe *f.*

souvenir souvenir *m.*

spank donner la fessée (à)

speak parler

speaker haut-parleur *m.*

specialization: ~ **in the humanities** formation *f.* littéraire

~ **in the sciences** formation *f.* scientifique

specializing spécialisé(e)

specialty spécialité *f.*

speed vitesse *f.*

spell épeler; sort *m.*

spend dépenser

spending dépenses *f. pl.*

spicy épicé(e)

spinach épinards *m. pl.*

splendid splendide

spoil gâter

spoiled gâté(e)

~ **rotten child** enfant *m.* gâté pourri

sport sport *m.*

sporting gear tenue *f.* de sport

spouse époux (épouse)

spread *v.* répandre

spread out *adj.* vautré(e)

spring *(season)* printemps *m.*

square place *f.*

stadium stade *m.*

stairs escalier *m.*

stake enjeu *m.*

stamp timbre *m.*

start: ~ **the engine** démarrer

~ **the windshield wipers** mettre les essuie-glaces

statement relevé *m.*

stationary bike vélo *m.* statique

stationery store papeterie *f.*

statue statue *f.*

steering wheel volant *m.*

step: ~ **machine** steps *m. pl.*

~**s** démarches *f. pl.*

stepbrother beau-frère *m.*

stepfather beau-père *m.*

stepmother belle-mère *f.*

stepsister belle-sœur *f.*
stereo chaîne *f.* stéréo
stew méchoui *m.*
stink puer
stockings bas *m. pl.*
stocky costaud
stomach estomac *m.*, ventre *m.*
  ~ **problems** crise *f.* de foie
stop *n.* arrêt *m.; v.* (s')arrêter
store magasin *m.*
stove cuisinière *f.*
straight lisse
  ~ **through** tout droit
strawberry fraise *f.*
  ~ **jam** confiture *f.* de fraises
street rue *f.*
stretch s'étirer, faire des exercices
    d'étirement
strike grève *f.*
strong fort(e)
struggle lutte *f.*
student *(high school and college)*
    étudiant(e); *(elementary and*
    middle school) élève *m./f.*
study étudier
stuffy nose nez *m.* bouché
stunning étonnant(e)
stupid stupide
subscriber abonné(e)
subscription form bon *m.*/
    bulletin *m.* d'abonnement
subsidized housing HLM
    (Habitation à Loyer Modéré) *f.*
suburb banlieue *f.*
subway métro *m.*
  ~ **stop** arrêt *m.* de métro
succeed (in) réussir (à)
succulent succulent(e)
sugar sucre *m.*
suit *(man's)* costume *m.; (woman's)*
    tailleur *m.*
suitcase valise *f.*
summer été *m.*
Sunday dimanche *m.*
sunglasses lunettes *f. pl.* de soleil
sunny lumineux (lumineuse)
  it's ~ il fait du soleil
super super
superb superbe
supermarket grande surface *f.*
supervision supervision *f.*

suppository suppositoire *m.*
sure sûr(e)
surf surf *m.*
surprised surpris(e), étonné(e)
surprising surprenant(e)
survey enquête *f.*, sondage *m.*
sweater pull(over) *m.*
sweatshirt sweat-shirt *m.*
sweatsuit survêtement *m.*
sweet doux (douce); sucré(e)
sweetie doudou *m.*
sweets gourmandises *f. pl.*
swim nager, faire de la natation
swimming natation *f.*
  ~ **pool** piscine *f.*
switch channels changer de chaîne
syrup sirop *m.*

T

table table *f.*
tablecloth nappe *f.*
tablespoon cuillère *f.* à soupe
tablet cachet *m.*, comprimé *m.*
take prendre
  ~ **a nap** faire une sieste
  ~ **a trip** faire un voyage
  ~ **care** prendre soin
  ~ **part (in)** participer (à)
  ~ **photos** prendre des photos
  ~ **place** avoir lieu
take off *v.* décoller; **take-off** *n.*
    décollage *m.*
tale conte *m.*
talk parler
  ~ **show** talk-show *m.*
talkative bavard(e)
tall grand(e)
tanning booth cabine *f.* de bronzage
target viser
taste *n.* goût *m.; v.* goûter
tasty savoureux (savoureuse)
taxi taxi *m.*
tea thé *m.*
  herbal ~ tisane *f.*
  plain ~ thé nature
  ~ **with lemon** thé au citron
team équipe *f.*
teaspoon cuillère *f.* à café
tech-savvy branché(e)
telephone téléphoner à *v.;*
    téléphone *m.*

cordless ~ téléphone sans fil
television télévision *f.*
  ~ **anchor** présentateur
    (présentatrice) de télévision
  ~ **guide** guide *m.* des
    programmes télévisés
  ~ **news** journal *m.* télévisé (le JT)
tell raconter
  ~ **each other** se dire
  ~ **each other everything** tout se
    raconter
teller caissier (caissière)
teller window guichet *m.* de
    caisse; caisse *f.*
ten dix
tenant locataire *m./f.*
tennis tennis *m.*
  ~ **court** piste *f.* de tennis
  ~ **shoes** tennis *m. pl.*
terminal terminal *m.*
terrace terrasse *f.*
thank you merci
thankful reconnaissant(e)
thanks to grâce à
that *adj.* ce (cette)
  ~ **way** ainsi
that *pron.* ça, ce
  ~ **is all, thank you.** C'est tout,
    merci.
  ~ **is why** c'est pour cela/ça
that *relative pron.* que
the le, la, l', les
  ~ **day before yesterday**
    avant-hier
  ~ **one** celui/celle
  ~ **ones** ceux/celles
  ~ **same** le/la/les même(s)
  ~ **tallest** le (la) plus grand(e)
  ~ **whole** le/la tout(e)
theater théâtre *m.*
theft vol *m.*
them les, leur; eux, elles
themselves eux-mêmes
    (elles-mêmes)
then alors
there là; là-bas; y
thermometer thermomètre *m.*
these *adj.* ces
thick épais(se)
thief voleur (voleuse)
thin mince

think croire
think penser (à)
thirteen treize
thirty trente
this *adj.* ce, cet, cette
   ~ is c'est
those *adj.* ces
thousand mille *inv.*
three trois
thrifty économe
thriller thriller *m.*
throat gorge *f.*
throw jeter
   ~ a tantrum faire des caprices
thumb pouce *m.*
Thursday jeudi *m.*
ticket billet *m.*; contravention *f.*
   smoking/non-smoking ~ billet fumeur/non-fumeur
   ~ counter guichet *m.*
tickle faire des chatouilles
tie cravate *f.*
time période *f.*; temps *m.*
timid timide
tip pourboire *m.*
tire pneu *m.*
tissue mouchoir *m.* en papier
to à, en, dans
   ~ her lui
   ~ him lui
   ~ the left à gauche
   ~ the right à droite
   ~ them leur
   ~ which auquel/à laquelle/auxquels/auxquelles
toaster grille-pain *m.*
tobacco tabac *m.*
   ~ shop tabac *m.*, bureau *m.* de tabac
today aujourd'hui
toe orteil *m.*
together ensemble
toilets toilettes *f. pl.*, cabinet *m.* de toilettes
tomato tomate *f.*
tone *v.* raffermir
tongue langue *f.*
too trop
tooth dent *f.*
toothache rage *f.* de dent
toothpaste dentifrice *m.*

topic sujet *m.*
touch *v.* toucher *m.*
traffic jam embouteillage *m.*
traffic report informations *f. pl.* routières
train train *m.*
   ~ station gare *f.*
trainee stagiaire *m./f.*
trainer entraîneur (entraineuse)
tranquilizer calmant *m.*
transportation transport *m.*
travel voyager
   ~ agent agent *m.* de voyage
traveler's check chèque *m.* de voyage
treadmill tapis *m.* de course/de fitness
treatment soin *m.*
tree arbre *m.*
trip séjour *m.*, voyage *m.*, trajet *m.*
trout truite *f.*
truck camion *m.*
true vrai(e)
try on essayer
T-shirt tee-shirt *m.*
Tuesday mardi *m.*
tuition fee frais *m. pl.* de scolarité
turbulence turbulences *f. pl.*
turn *n.* tour *m.*; *v.* tourner
TV télé *f.*
   ~ games divertissements *m. pl.* jeux *m. pl.*
   ~ guide guide *m.* télé
   ~ movie téléfilm
   ~ series série *f.* (télévisée)
twelve douze
twenty vingt
twin jumeau (jumelle)
   ~ brother frère *m.* jumeau
   ~ sister sœur *f.* jumelle
two deux
two-piece bathing suit bikini *m.*
typical typique

U

ugly laid(e)
unacceptable inacceptable
uncle oncle *m.*
uncover dénuder
under sous
underline souligner

understand comprendre
underwear *(man's)* caleçon *m.*; *(woman's)* culotte *f.*
unemployed person chômeur (chômeuse)
unemployment chômage *m.*
unfair injuste
unforgettable inoubliable
unfortunate regrettable
unfriendly antipathique
unhappy malheureux (malheureuse)
United States États-Unis *m. pl.*
upstairs en haut
use utiliser
   ~ an epilator s'épiler
   ~ drugs se droguer

V

vacuum cleaner aspirateur *m.*
validate (a ticket) composter (un billet)
vanilla vanille *f.*
veal veau *m.*
vegetable légume *m.*
vendor marchand(e)
verb verbe *m.*
very très
   ~ good/well très bien
   ~ happy comblé(e)
via par
videocassette player magnéto(scope) *m.*
vinegar vinaigre *m.*
vineyard vignoble *m.*
visit visiter
vitamin vitamine *f.*
voice voix *f.*
volleyball volley *m.*
vomit vomir
voyage trajet *m.*

W

wait attendre
   ~ in line faire la queue
   ~ one's turn attendre son tour
waiter serveur *m.*
waitress serveuse *f.*
wake up se réveiller
walk aller à pied, marcher
walking marche *f.*
wall mur *m.*

want vouloir; avoir envie (de)
warm up se réchauffer; faire des exercices d'échauffement, s'échauffer
wash se laver
  ~ the windows faire les vitres
washing machine machine *f.* à laver
waste gaspiller
watch regarder
water eau *f.*
  carbonated ~ eau gazeuse
  mineral ~ eau plate
  ~ aerobics aquagym *f.*
  ~ sport sport *m.* nautique
watermelon pastèque *f.*
water-skiing ski *m.* nautique
wax cire *f.*
way off éloigné(e)
wear porter
weather temps *m.*
  ~ report météo *f.*
weave filer
Wednesday mercredi *m.*
week semaine *f.*
weekend week-end *m.*
weekly hebdomadaire *adj.*
weigh peser
weight poids *m.*; haltère *f.*
  ~ room salle *f.* de muscu(lation)
weightlifting muscu(lation) *f.*
welcome accueillir
  ~ to my place! bienvenue chez moi!
well bien
  ~ -behaved sage; bien élevé(e)
  ~! bon!
well-being bien-être *m.*
western western *m.*
what que; quel/quelle/quels/quelles; ce que
  ~ is it? Qu'est-ce que c'est?

  ~ are you like? Comment tu es?
  ~'s your name? Comment vous appelez-vous?/Comment tu t'appelles?
  ~'s the weather like? Quel temps fait-il?
when quand
where où
  ~ is ... located? Où se trouve ... ?
which quel (quelle)
  ~ one(s)? lequel/laquelle/lesquels/lesquelles?
while alors que, pendant que
whipped cream crème *f.* chantilly
white blanc(he)
who qui
  ~ are you? Qui es-tu?/Qui êtes-vous?
  ~ is it? Qui est-ce?
whole entier (entière)
Whose turn is it? À qui le tour?
why pourquoi
widow veuve *f.*
widower veuf *m.*
wife femme *f.*
wimp: to be a ~ être douillet(te)
win gagner
window fenêtre *f.*
  ~ shopping lèche-vitrine *m.*
windshield pare-brise *m.*
  ~ wiper essuie-glace *m.*
windsurfing planche *f.* à voile
windy: it's ~ il fait du vent
wine vin *m.*
  red/white/blush ~ vin rouge/blanc/rosé
  ~ cellar cave *f.*
  ~ tasting dégustation *f.* de vins
  ~ waiter sommelier *m.*

winter hiver *m.*
  ~ sport sport *m.* d'hiver
wipe essuyer
wish vœu *m.*
with avec
  ~ no . . . sans aucun(e) ...
without sans
witness témoin *m.*
woman femme *f.*
word processor traitement de texte *m.*
work *n.* emploi *m.*; job *m.*; travail *m.*; boulot *m. (slang)*
work *v.* travailler; marcher
workplace boîte *f. (slang)*
world monde *m.*
World Wide Web Web *m.*, Toile *f.*
worried soucieux (soucieuse)
wrist poignet *m.*
write écrire
  ~ a check remplir un chèque
writer écrivain(e)

Y

yack tchatcher
yeah ouais
year an *m.*; année *f.*
yellow jaune
yesterday hier
  ~ afternoon hier après-midi
  ~ morning hier matin
  ~ night hier soir
yoga yoga *m.*
yogurt yaourt (*also* yahourt)
you vous; tu; te; toi
  ~'re welcome je vous (t')en prie, de rien
young jeune
youth jeunesse *f.*

Index

Index

Index

cinq cent soixante-dix-neuf **579**

Credits

Chapitre 9
p. 319: © LABAT/TF1/SIPA

Mise en pratique 3
p. 400 *(top):* © Alexander Hubrich/zefa/Corbis; p. 400 *(bottom):* © Inge Yspeert/CORBIS

Chapitre 13
p. 419: © Goodshoot/Alamy

Chapitre 14
p. 452 *(top left):* © Getty Images; p. 452 *(top center):* © Eric Gaillard/Reuters/Corbis; p. 452 *(top right):* © Reuters/CORBIS; p. 452 *(bottom left):* © John G. Mabanglo/epa/Corbis; p. 452 *(bottom right):* © Getty Images

Realia

Chapitre 7
p. 218 *(top):* www.nrj.fr; p. 218 *(bottom):* TF1; p. 226: *(top left):* Courtesy *Paris Match* and photo © Frederic Stevens/Sipa; p. 226 *(top right):* Courtesy *Le Nouvel Observateur*; p. 226 *(middle):* Courtesy *Marie-Claire*; p. 226 *(bottom left):* Courtesy L'EXPRESS; p. 226 *(bottom right):* Le Figaro; p. 227 *(top left):* Courtesy *Le Monde*; p. 227 *(top right):* Télé; p. 227 *(bottom left):* Top santé; p. 227 *(bottom right):* Courtesy *Maxi Cuisine*; p. 227 *(bottom center):* Les Cahiers du cinéma; p. 228 *(top):* © LE SOLEIL, page une, 30 mai 2003; p. 228 *(bottom):* © Manon Boyer exclusively for Châtelaine magazine; p. 229 *(top):* Courtesy Groupe *Marie-Claire*; p. 229 *(bottom):* Courtesy *Prima* and Prisma Presse

Mise en pratique 2
p. 289 *(left):* Alibi Théâtre; p. 289 *(top center):* Le Capitole; p. 289 *(bottom center):* Théâtre le Petit Louvre; p. 289 *(bottom right):* Le Paris; p. 289 *(top right):* Acte 5-Strasbourg

Chapitre 11
p. 361: Courtesy BNP Paribas; p. 367: © Neutrogena Corp., USA

Chapitre 12
p. 396 *(top):* Olï and agency: Dassas; p. 396 *(bottom):* Courtesy Festina

Chapitre 14
pp. 437 & 457: Taranis Fitness

Chapitre 15
p. 479: *Doctissimo*

Chapitre 16
p. 513 *(left):* Amora Unilever France; p. 513 *(right):* Courtesy *Maxi Cuisine* and photo © Yves Bagros

Illustrations

All illustrations by Anna Veltfort except page 514 by Leslie Evans.

Maps

All maps by Patti Isaacs/Parrot Graphics.

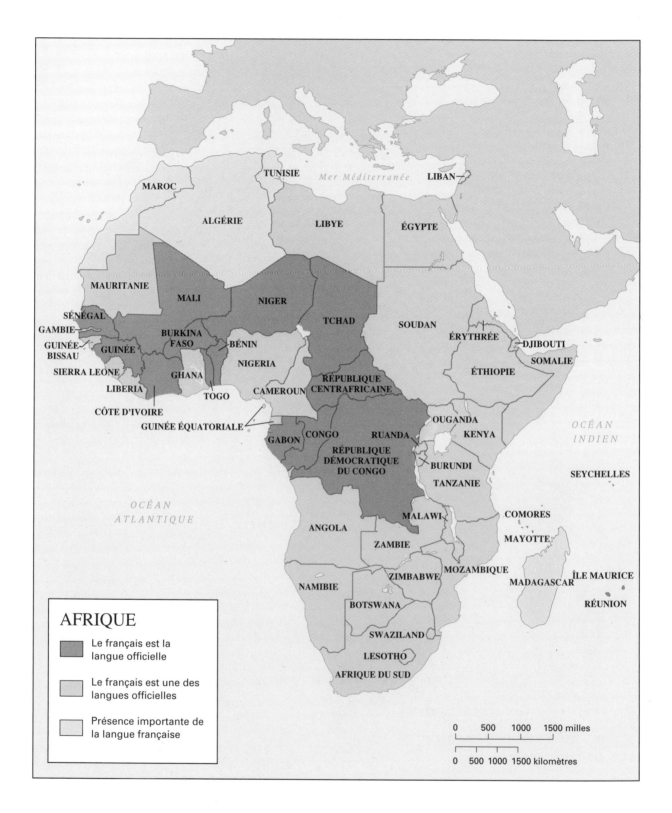

AFRIQUE

MAROC

TUNISIE

Mer Méditerranée

LIBAN

ALGÉRIE

LIBYE

ÉGYPTE

MAURITANIE

MALI

NIGER

TCHAD

SOUDAN

ÉRYTHRÉE

DJIBOUTI

SÉNÉGAL

GAMBIE

GUINÉE-
BISSAU

GUINÉE

BURKINA
FASO

BÉNIN

SOMALIE

ÉTHIOPIE

SIERRA LEONE

GHANA

NIGERIA

LIBERIA

TOGO

CÔTE D'IVOIRE

GUINÉE ÉQUATORIALE

CAMEROUN

RÉPUBLIQUE
CENTRAFRICAINE

GABON

CONGO

RUANDA

RÉPUBLIQUE
DÉMOCRATIQUE
DU CONGO

OUGANDA

KENYA

BURUNDI

TANZANIE

SEYCHELLES

MALAWI

COMORES

ANGOLA

ZAMBIE

MAYOTTE

MOZAMBIQUE

MADAGASCAR

ÎLE MAURICE

NAMIBIE

ZIMBABWE

RÉUNION

*OCÉAN
INDIEN*

*OCÉAN
ATLANTIQUE*

BOTSWANA

SWAZILAND

LESOTHO

AFRIQUE DU SUD

AFRIQUE

■ Le français est la
langue officielle

■ Le français est une des
langues officielles

□ Présence importante de
la langue française

0   500   1000   1500 milles

0   500 1000 1500 kilomètres